# Global Perspectives in Forensic Psychiatry



*Global Perspectives in Forensic Psychiatry: International Approaches to Practice, Policies, and the Law* is an essential guide to understanding the international landscape of forensic mental health systems.

This book presents global perspectives in forensic psychiatry and research, highlighting how national contexts and legal frameworks shape mental healthcare systems across multiple continents. Contributors from over 25 countries describe national approaches to the assessment, treatment, and management of justice-involved individuals with mental disorders. In doing so, the contributors encourage policymakers to draw from both well-established and developing forensic psychiatric systems to inform international discourse, interpret research, and enhance the ongoing evolution of best practice approaches. Key topics include historical and cultural principles, training and quality assurance, and contemporary policies and procedures.

This volume is an essential resource for forensic mental health professionals, clinicians, and researchers. It will inform training, service delivery, and future research on justice-involved individuals with mental disorders.

**Gary Chaimowitz** is a professor in the Department of Psychiatry and Behavioural Neurosciences at McMaster University and Head of Service for the Forensic Psychiatry Program at St. Joseph's Healthcare Hamilton, Hamilton, Canada. He holds the Forensic Psychiatry Founder designation with the Royal College of Physicians and Surgeons of Canada, an MBA, and is a certified physician executive.

**Mini Mamak** is an associate professor in the Department of Psychiatry and Behavioural Neurosciences at McMaster University and a senior psychologist in the Forensic Psychiatry Program at St. Joseph's Healthcare Hamilton, Hamilton, Canada. She is a co-developer of the electronic Hamilton Anatomy of Risk Management (eHARM) and the Aggressive Incidents Scale (AIS), two innovative methods of assessing and documenting risk.

**Heather Moulden** is an associate professor in the Department of Psychiatry and Behavioural Neurosciences at McMaster University, where she is also an associate member in the Neuroscience Graduate Program and the Department of Psychology. She is a psychologist in the Forensic Psychiatry Program at St. Joseph's Healthcare Hamilton, Hamilton, Canada.

**Drew Kingston** is the executive clinical director and director of research of the HOPE program, a statewide agency in California, United States, that provides services to individuals who have committed a sexual offence. He is licensed as a psychologist in California, United States, and in Ontario, Canada. Dr. Kingston is a senior scientist at the Royal Ottawa Hospital's Institute of Mental Health Research, Ottawa, Canada, and an adjunct clinical professor in the Department of Psychiatry and Behavioural Neurosciences at McMaster University, Hamilton, Canada.

"Forensic psychiatry thrives on connection across jurisdictions. This volume reflects that spirit by bringing together diverse perspectives and highlighting the structural, legal, and ethical complexities that shape forensic mental health systems worldwide. It will be a valuable resource for those working to build services that are responsive, equitable, and evidence-informed."

**Prof. Sandy Simpson,** *Research Chair in Forensic Psychiatry and Senior Scientist at Centre for Addictions and Mental Health (CAMH), Canada*

"*Global Perspectives in Forensic Psychiatry* offers a rare opportunity to reflect on how forensic psychiatry is shaped in different countries, through policy decisions, clinical demands, and shifting ideas of risk and responsibility. With a strong focus on systems and context, it will be useful to those working in research, service delivery, and program development."

**Dr. Nathan J. Kolla,** *Professor of Forensic Psychiatry, Centre for Forensic Behavioural Science, Swinburne University of Technology, Australia*

"This book reflects the kind of international exchange we need more of in forensic psychiatry. By exploring how different jurisdictions address complex clinical and legal issues, it offers practical insight for those leading and reforming services worldwide."

**Dr. Carlos Hugo Isaac Serna,** *Secretary of the Forensic Psychiatry Section, World Psychiatric Association*

**International Perspectives on Forensic Mental Health**
*A Routledge Book Series*
Edited by Patricia Zapf
*Palo Alto University*

The goal of this series is to improve the quality of health care services in forensic and correctional settings by providing a forum for discussing issues and disseminating resources related to policy, administration, clinical practice, and research. The series addresses topics such as mental health law; the organization and administration of forensic and/or correctional services for persons with mental disorders; the development, implementation and evaluation of treatment programs and interventions for individuals in civil and criminal justice settings; the assessment and management of violence risk, including risk for sexual violence and family violence; and staff selection, training, and development in forensic and/or correctional systems.

**Published Titles**

**Safeguarding the Quality of Forensic Assessment in Sentencing**
A Review Across Western Nations
*Edited by Michiel van der Wolf*

**Globalization, Displacement, and Psychiatry**
Global Histories of Trauma
*Edited by Sanaullah Khan and Elliott Schwebach*

**Approaches to Offender Rehabilitation in Asian Jurisdictions**
*Edited by Chi Meng Chu and Michael Daffern*

**Innovative Treatment Approaches in Forensic and Correctional Settings**
*Edited by Michael Siglag*

**Global Perspectives in Forensic Psychiatry**
International Approaches to Practice, Policies, and the Law
*Edited by Gary Chaimowitz, Mini Mamak, Heather Moulden, and Drew Kingston*

For more information about this series, please visit: www.routledge.com/International-Perspectives-on-Forensic-Mental-Health/book-series/IPFMF

# Global Perspectives in Forensic Psychiatry

## International Approaches to Practice, Policies, and the Law

**Edited by Gary Chaimowitz, Mini Mamak, Heather Moulden, and Drew Kingston**

Routledge
Taylor & Francis Group
NEW YORK AND LONDON

Designed cover image: stellalevi © Getty Images

First published 2026
by Routledge
605 Third Avenue, New York, NY 10158

and by Routledge
4 Park Square, Milton Park, Abingdon, Oxon, OX14 4RN

*Routledge is an imprint of the Taylor & Francis Group, an informa business*



ISBN: 978-1-032-45277-7 (hbk)
ISBN: 978-1-032-45275-3 (pbk)
ISBN: 978-1-003-37624-8 (ebk)

DOI: 10.4324/9781003376248

Typeset in Times New Roman
by Apex CoVantage, LLC

# Contents

# About the Editors and Authors

## Editors

**Gary Chaimowitz** is a professor in the Department of Psychiatry and Behavioural Neurosciences at McMaster University and Head of Service for the Forensic Psychiatry Program at St. Joseph's Healthcare Hamilton, Hamilton, Canada.

**Drew Kingston** is the executive clinical director and director of research of the HOPE Program, California, United States, and an adjunct clinical professor in the Department of Psychiatry and Behavioural Neurosciences at McMaster University, Hamilton, Canada.

**Mini Mamak** is an associate professor in the Department of Psychiatry and Behavioural Neurosciences at McMaster University and a senior psychologist in the Forensic Psychiatry Program at St. Joseph's Healthcare Hamilton, Hamilton, Canada.

**Heather Moulden** is an associate professor in the Department of Psychiatry and Behavioural Neurosciences at McMaster University and a psychologist in the Forensic Psychiatry Program at St. Joseph's Healthcare Hamilton, Hamilton, Canada.

## Authors

### *Foreword*

**Joel Watts** is a forensic psychiatrist and chair of the Forensic Psychiatry Specialty Committee, Royal College of Physicians and Surgeons of Canada, Ottawa, Canada.

### *Canada*

**Hy Bloom** is a forensic psychiatrist in private practice and at the Centre for Addictions and Mental Health (CAMH), Toronto, an assistant professor in the Department of Psychiatry at the University of Toronto, Toronto, Canada, and an assistant clinical professor in the Department of Psychiatry and Behavioural Neurosciences at McMaster University, Hamilton, Canada.

**John Bradford** is a full professor in the Department of Psychiatry and Behavioural Neuroscience at McMaster University, Hamilton, Canada, an emeritus professor at the University of Ottawa, and a senior scientist at the Royal Ottawa Hospital's Institute of Mental Health Research, Ottawa, Canada.

**Mathieu Dufour** is a forensic psychiatrist, Head of the Department of Psychiatry at the Institut national de psychiatrie légale Philippe-Pinel, and an associate clinical professor in the Department of Psychiatry and Addictions, Faculty of Medicine, University of Montreal, Montréal, Canada.

**Richard D. Schneider** is a justice of the Ontario Court of Justice, a deputy judge of the Territorial Courts of the Yukon and Northwest Territories, and an adjunct professor of psychiatry and forensic science at the University of Toronto, Toronto, Canada.

***The United States of America***

**Dr. Susan Hatters Friedman** is the Phillip Resnick professor of Forensic Psychiatry at Case Western Reserve University in Cleveland, Ohio, and a past president of the American Academy of Psychiatry and the Law.

**Dr. Monika Pietrzak** is a forensic psychiatrist and an assistant professor of Psychiatry at the University of Massachusetts T.H. Chan Medical School in Worcester, Massachusetts, United States.

***Argentina***

**Jorge Oscar Folino** is a professor of psychiatry at the National University of La Plata in La Plata, Argentina.

**María José Lescano** has a doctorate in penal law and is a judge and professor in Buenos Aires, Argentina.

***Brazil***

**Elias Abdalla-Filho** is a co-chair of the Forensic Psychiatry Section of the World Psychiatric Association, former coordinator of the Forensic Psychiatry Department of the Brazilian Psychiatric Association, and former coordinator of the Forensic Psychiatry Sector of the Institute of Legal Medicine of Brasília, Brazil.

**Lisieux E. de Borba Telles** is an assistant professor in the Department of Psychiatry and Legal Medicine, Federal University of Rio Grande do Sul, Porto Alegre, Brazil.

### *Chile*

**Claudio Filippi** is a forensic psychiatrist with the Public Criminal Defense Office in Chile.

### *England and Wales*

**Megan Georgiou** is a group head of quality improvement at Elysium Healthcare, Borehamwood, England, and a postgraduate researcher at the University of Surrey.

**Quazi Haque** is a co-founder and chief medical officer of Elysium Healthcare.

**Phil Huckle** is a regional operations director for Wales at Elysium Healthcare.

**Patrick Neville** is a strategic development director at Elysium Healthcare.

**Piyal Sen** is the medical director at Elysium Healthcare.

### *France*

**Estébanine Moulia-Pelat** is a staff psychiatrist at the Centre intégré de santé et des services sociaux de l'Outaouais in Gatineau, Québec, and an assistant clinical professor at McGill University, Montréal, Québec, Canada.

**Sébastien Prat** is an associate professor and staff psychiatrist at McMaster University and St. Joseph's Healthcare Hamilton, Ontario, Canada.

### *Germany*

**Birgit Völlm** is a professor in Forensic Psychiatry and the medical director of the Forensic Hospital at the University of Rostock, Germany.

### *Ireland*

**Harry G. Kennedy** is an adjunct professor of Forensic Psychiatry, Trinity College Dublin (The University of Dublin); Honorary Skou Professor of Forensic Psychiatry, Aarhus University, Denmark; and visiting professor of forensic psychiatry, University of Bari Aldo Moro, Italy.

### *Lithuania*

**Arūnas Germanavičius** is a professor in the Clinic of Psychiatry, Institute of Clinical Medicine, Vilnius University, and director of the Republican Vilnius Psychiatric Hospital in Lithuania.

**Ilona Laurinaitytė** is a professor of forensic psychology at the Institute of Psychology, Faculty of Philosophy, Vilnius University, Lithuania.

**Vaiva Martinkienė** is a psychiatrist, a certified forensic psychiatry expert, and the chief of the Republican Department of the Lithuanian National Forensic Psychiatry Service.

*The Netherlands*

**Vivienne de Vogel** is a psychologist and professor of Forensic Mental Health Care at Maastricht University and at the University of Applied Sciences Utrecht in the Netherlands. She is also a researcher at the Van der Hoeven Kliniek De Forensische Zorgspecialisten, a forensic psychiatric centre in Utrecht, and a scientific adviser on the Dutch Advisory Board on Review of Leave.

**Michiel van der Wolf** is a psychologist and legal scholar, professor of forensic psychiatry at the Institute for Criminal Law and Criminology at Leiden University, and associate professor of criminal law at the University of Groningen in the Netherlands. He is a deputy judge at the Criminal Court in Amsterdam and the Court of Appeal in Leeuwarden.

*Norway*

**Terje Tørrissen** is a specialist in psychiatry and a forensic psychiatrist in private forensic practice in Ottestad, Norway.

*Poland*

**Inga Markiewicz** is with the Forensic Psychiatry Clinic, Institute of Psychiatry and Neurology, Warsaw, Poland.

*Portugal*

**Ricardo Barroso** is a forensic psychologist, associate professor at the University of Trás-os-Montes and Alto Douro, and senior researcher at the Centre of Psychology of the University of Porto, Portugal.

**Márcia Mota** is a forensic psychiatrist at Psychiatry Service of Unidade Local de Saúde de São João, Porto, Portugal.

**Maria João Peixoto** is a forensic psychiatrist at Psychiatry Service of Unidade Local de Saúde de São João, Porto, Portugal.

*Scotland*

**Caroline Kelly** is Manager of the Forensic Mental Health Managed Care Network in Scotland.

**Lindsay Thomson** is a director of the Forensic Mental Health Managed Care Network and medical director of The State Hospitals Board for Scotland.

***Spain***

**Carles Martín-Fumadó** is a forensic doctor and professor of Forensic and Legal Medicine at the Faculty of Medicine and Health Sciences, UIC Barcelona—Universitat Internacional de Catalunya, Spain.

**Vicenç Tort-Herrando** is a Penitentiary Psychiatrist at Parc Sanitari Sant Joan de Déu in Barcelona, Spain. He holds a master's degree in Legal Psychiatry from the Complutense University of Madrid. He is a lecturer in the Master's Program in Forensic and Legal Psychopathology at UIC Barcelona—Universitat Internacional de Catalunya, Spain.

***Israel***

**Naama Barkai** is a research assistant in Lev-Hasharon Mental Health Center in Tsur Moshe, Israel.

**Shmuel Hess** is a ward director in Lev-Hasharon Mental Health Center in Tsur Moshe, Israel, and a clinical lecturer by special appointment in Tel Aviv University Faculty of Medical and Health Sciences.

**Nathan Kaspi** is the head of the forensic unit in Lev-Hasharon Mental Health Center in Tsur Moshe, Israel.

**Michal Shayit** is a clinical psychologist in the forensic unit of Lev-Hasharon Mental Health Center in Tsur Moshe, Israel.

**Assaf Shelef** is a deputy hospital director of the Lev-Hasharon Mental Health Center in Tsur Moshe, Israel, and a senior lecturer in Tel Aviv University Faculty of Medical and Health Sciences.

***Kuwait***

**Abdulmohsen Al-Humoud** is a consultant forensic psychiatrist. He is the head of the Forensic Mental Health Services (FMHS) at the Kuwait Centre for Mental Health (KCMH), Kuwait City, Kuwait. He was previously an assistant professor in the Department of Psychiatry at Queen's University in Kingston, Ontario, Canada. He served as the Kuwait Psychiatric Association (KPA) president between 2018 and 2022. Dr. Al-Humoud was the leading psychiatrist behind Kuwait Mental Health Law, 2019.

***Oman***

**Badar Al Habsi** is a forensic psychiatry consultant associated with the Ministry of Health, Oman. He currently serves as a director of Al Masarra Hospital, a major psychiatric facility.

**Lara Al Harthi** is a psychologist and research assistant in the Department of Behavioural Medicine at Sultan Qaboos University, Muscat, Oman. She holds a BSc in Psychology (Mazoon College, Oman) and an MSc in Forensic Psychology & Mental Health (University of Manchester, UK).

***Türkiye***

**Yasin Hasan Balcıoğlu and Fatih Öncü** are with the Forensic Psychiatry Unit, Bakırköy Prof. Mazhar Osman Training and Research Hospital for Psychiatry, Neurology and Neurosurgery, Istanbul, Türkiye.

***China***

**Xiaoping Wang** is a psychiatrist with the Department of Psychiatry & Mental Health Institute of the Second Xiangya Hospital, Central South University, Changsha City, Hunan Province, China.

***India***

**Rakesh K. Chadda** is a professor and the head, Department of Psychiatry, Amrita Institute of Medical Sciences and Research Centre, Faridabad; former professor and head, Department of Psychiatry; and Chief, National Drug Dependence Treatment Centre, All India Institute of Medical Sciences, New Delhi. He has served as a professor of Psychiatry at the Institute of Human Behaviour and Allied Sciences, Delhi; Head, Department of Psychiatry at University College of Medical Sciences & GTB Hospital, Delhi; and consultant psychiatrist in the National Health Service of the United Kingdom.

**Sanjiv Gulati** is Associate Chief, Integrated Forensic Program, the Royal Mental Health Centre, Brockville, Ontario, and Assistant Professor at the University of Ottawa, Ottawa, Ontario, Canada.

***Japan***

**Chiyo Fujii** is with the Department of Community Mental Health and Law, National Institute of Mental Health, National Center of Neurology and Psychiatry, Kodaira, Japan.

**Miki Hirano** is with Faculty of Law, Kagawa University, Takamatsu, Japan.

**Akiko Kikuchi** is with the Faculty of Human Sciences, Musashino University, Ariake, Japan, and the Department of Community Mental Health and Law,

National Institute of Mental Health, National Center of Neurology and Psychiatry, Kodaira, Japan.

**Junko Koike** is with the Department of Community Mental Health and Law, National Institute of Mental Health, National Center of Neurology and Psychiatry, Kodaira, Japan.

***Pakistan***

**Dr. Tariq Hassan** is a past associate professor and Division Chair (Forensic Psychiatry), Department of Psychiatry, Queen's University, Kingston, Ontario, Canada.

***South Africa***

**Nyameka Dyakalashe** is the head of Clinical Unit, Forensics Mental Health Services, Western Cape, South Africa.

***Tanzania***

**Enock Eteregho Changarawe** is a psychiatrist at Mirembe National Mental Health Hospital in Dodoma region, Tanzania. He trained as a medical doctor and completed a masters of medicine in Psychiatry and Mental Health at Muhimbili University of Health and Allied Sciences (MUHAS) in Dar es Salaam, Tanzania. He has worked in the Isanga Institution, part of Mirembe National Mental Health Hospital, since 2013.

***Uganda***

**Mark Mohan Kaggwa** is a clinical fellow in the Department of Psychiatry and Behavioural Neurosciences, McMaster University, Hamilton, Canada.

**Julius Muron** is a psychiatrist with the World Health Organization.

**Irene Apio Wengi** is with the Forensic Psychiatry Unit of the Butabika National Referral Hospital, Kampala, Uganda.

***Aotearoa New Zealand***

**Jennifer Falce** is a locum consultant forensic psychiatrist at the Central Regional Forensic Mental Health Service, Te Whatu Ora/Health New Zealand, Wellington, New Zealand.

**Jacqueline Short** is a clinical director and director of Area Mental Health Services at the Central Regional Forensic Mental Health Service, Te Whatu Ora/Health New Zealand, Wellington, New Zealand.

***Analysis***

**Mary Davoren** is a clinical senior lecturer in Forensic Psychiatry, Trinity College Dublin (The University of Dublin), Ireland.

**Harry G. Kennedy** is an adjunct professor of Forensic Psychiatry, Trinity College Dublin (The University of Dublin); Honorary Skou professor of Forensic Psychiatry, Aarhus University, Denmark; and visiting professor of forensic psychiatry, University of Bari Aldo Moro, Italy.

# Foreword

Millennia of societal evolution and centuries of legal precedent have refined how humanity grapples with the complexity of mental health and its interaction with the rule of law. No matter how complex and seemingly sophisticated the field of forensic psychiatry has become, it is worthwhile to take a step back and consider the historical and current global landscape of forensic psychiatry. Indeed, it is a humbling experience and serves to remind us how young modern forensic psychiatry is and just how much we have yet to learn and develop.

This review of the history, frameworks, and practices in forensic psychiatry around the world, edited by Drs. Chaimowitz, Moulden, Mamak, and Kingston, is an eye-opening read and will certainly provoke thoughtful reflection and cross-jurisdictional research in ways that can help us grow and improve forensic mental health care overall. Their stated goal is to promote international research and encourage development of forensic mental health care.

Forensic mental health systems vary from country to country, and failure to understand this has historically been a barrier to international forensic mental health research. As a practitioner keenly interested and involved in education, I am very excited about the educational value of this important book. It widens our field of view and understanding and will broaden the quality of forensic psychiatry training in Canada and around the world.

This book is certain to interest a wide array of forensic mental health practitioners and jurists. The layout of each chapter is thoughtful and helpful for those who want to use it as a quick reference as well as those who seek more in-depth understanding. The country-by-country reviews of each country's legal history, mental health frameworks, and forensic psychiatry-specific laws are fascinating and will be most appreciated by experts working in jurisdictions where legal precedent is an expected and important part of their work. Learning the structure and function and knowing who the important decision makers are in each system are vital to understanding the inner workings of each country's forensic mental health system. This book carefully summarizes all these important factors. Practitioners who work in the trenches of forensic mental health will also appreciate the authors' views on the strengths and weaknesses of their system.

Many countries also experience broad and local challenges, especially those with larger populations, vast geography, and multiple linguistic and cultural diversities. It is helpful to learn about specific provision of care issues that are influenced by these factors. Readers will certainly broaden their understanding and may be inspired or reassured to see similarities and possible solutions to those they may be experiencing themselves. The discussion of the training and role of the forensic psychiatrist in each country is also certain to spark curiosity and deeper reflection. I hope this book also inspires us to reflect on our wider humanity and ethics within the forensic mental health field.

Dr. Chaimowitz and his co-editors should be commended for their broad and inclusive approach. It would have been easy to simply include English-dominant, Commonwealth, or common-law jurisdictions that already dominate forensic mental health literature. Instead, they have included diverse countries and cultures that differ widely and greatly from these traditions. The result is a truly impressive collection. This book is likely the most comprehensive international review of forensic psychiatry practice landscape ever attempted—and it is a fascinating and compelling read.

The educational value of this book is great, but its potential to promote understanding, collaboration, communication, research, and improvement in expertise around the world is even greater. I expect it will become essential reading for practitioners, educators, and learners alike and will most certainly serve as an oft-consulted source of information and inspiration for years to come.

Joel Watts, MD, FRCPC
Forensic Psychiatrist and Chair, Forensic Psychiatry Specialty Committee, Royal College of Physicians and Surgeons of Canada

# Acknowledgments

We would like to thank the many people whose dedication and collaboration were instrumental in making this book possible.

Kyle Vaughn Roerick, as managing copy editor, played a central role in shaping the manuscript and overseeing the editing process. He worked closely with contributors to refine structure, improve clarity, and bring together a cohesive collection that reflects the depth and diversity of expertise in forensic psychiatry represented in this volume. His judgment and steady guidance were essential throughout this project.

Arianna Davids played an important role in the early stages, providing editorial input and coordinating foundational work that helped establish the direction of the book.

Carolyn Brown provided project management and editorial support during the final stages of manuscript preparation. Her leadership and attention to detail helped ensure a smooth progression from early drafts to final submission.

We also want to thank the research assistants who contributed at various stages.

This publication was made possible with the support of the Forensic Psychiatry Program at St. Joseph's Healthcare Hamilton, Canada.

# Preface

## Understanding the Global Landscape of Forensic Psychiatry

Forensic psychiatry occupies a unique position within both the medical and legal fields. It serves as a bridge between the understanding of mental health and the practice of law, ensuring that mental illness is considered in legal proceedings. Whether it's determining a defendant's fitness to stand trial, assessing criminal responsibility, or deciding the appropriate course of treatment for individuals with mental illness, forensic psychiatrists play a pivotal role (Arboleda-Flórez, 2006). Yet, despite its importance, forensic psychiatry is a field where the practice, training, and legal context can vary dramatically from one country to another.

In recent decades, the global nature of research and practice in forensic psychiatry has become increasingly important and clear, driven by advances in communication, international collaborations, and the recognition that forensic mental health transcends borders. However, one of the most pressing challenges in forensic psychiatry is comparing systems, practices, and outcomes across countries. The diversity of legal frameworks, cultural values, health systems, and economic conditions presents significant barriers to international forensic psychiatric training, research collaboration, and clinical practice (Arboleda-Flórez, 2006). Often, forensic psychiatry systems in one country cannot be directly compared to those in another, even when the same legal or clinical questions are at the forefront.

The crux of the challenge lies in the fact that each country's forensic psychiatry system is shaped by its laws, regulations, economic resources, and culture. These factors determine how forensic psychiatry is practised, the scope of its involvement in the legal system, and even the nature of the individuals assessed by forensic psychiatrists (Gunn & Taylor, 2014). How do we conduct international research or make valid comparisons among practices when the very definitions of what constitutes a patient in forensic psychiatry can differ so drastically?

In the United States, for example, the legal concept of *insanity* has profound implications for criminal justice, with courts determining whether a defendant's mental state absolves them of criminal responsibility, termed 'not guilty by reasons of insanity' or the 'insanity defence' (Morse, 2019). The United States also has a relatively adversarial legal system, which impacts how forensic evaluations are conducted and how psychiatrists are often tasked with providing testimony (Morse, 2019).

In contrast, in many European countries, the relationship between psychiatry and the law is more integrated into the healthcare system, where the focus is often on rehabilitation rather than deterrence and punishment, and forensic psychiatrists may be seen more as clinicians than as legal experts. The issue of diminished responsibility and even the definition of mental illness (including personality disorders) continues to be debated in forensic psychiatry and legal circles. The U.S. system is adversarial, whereas many European systems are inquisitorial, lessening the tensions (Völlm et al., 2018). Moreover, countries in the Global South, particularly in regions with fewer resources, may have forensic systems that are still in their nascent stages or are shaped by entirely different priorities—such as addressing overcrowded prisons or managing the intersection of mental health and extreme poverty (Balcıoğlu, 2024).

Understanding the global variations in forensic psychiatry is essential if we are to conduct meaningful research, promote international collaboration, or formulate policies that can be applied across borders. What is, in fact, a patient in forensic psychiatry in the countries being compared? Without a clear understanding of how forensic psychiatry systems differ, any research attempting to draw international conclusions is at risk of comparing apples to oranges. We cannot assess the effectiveness of forensic interventions globally unless we first understand what 'forensic psychiatry' looks like in each unique context.

Take, for instance, the concept of patients in forensic psychiatry. In some countries, these patients may be individuals incarcerated for crimes, with the primary goal of treatment being rehabilitation or management of psychiatric symptoms (Howner et al., 2020). In others, these patients may be defined primarily by their legal status—whether they are awaiting trial or have been deemed not criminally responsible due to mental illness. The criteria for determining who qualifies as a forensic patient can vary, and so too can the types of interventions and treatments offered (Howner et al., 2020). In high-income countries, there may be sophisticated rehabilitation programs, with access to psychiatric care and therapeutic interventions. In low- or middle-income countries, however, mental health resources may be limited, leading to different, sometimes more punitive, approaches to handling individuals with mental health issues in the criminal justice system (Balcıoğlu, 2024).

Furthermore, forensic psychiatry training is shaped by local educational and legal systems (Wasser et al., 2022). Forensic psychiatrists in one country may undergo years of postgraduate training, gaining in-depth knowledge of the forensic psychiatric and criminal justice system, while, in another, their focus might be almost exclusively on psychiatric diagnosis and treatment, with little exposure to the law (Wasser et al., 2022). The role and responsibilities of a forensic psychiatrist in one country may be vastly different from those in another, depending on the legal framework they operate under and the degree to which psychiatry and law intersect in their national context. The way forensic psychiatry is taught, the skills emphasized, and the professional scope all vary significantly across borders, influenced by cultural expectations, resource availability, and societal attitudes toward mental health and crime. This book helps to identify differences in the health and legal frameworks, and emerging practice leaders in the field, highlights critical gaps in training and service delivery, and raises important research questions aimed at advancing forensic psychiatry globally. By addressing these areas, the book contributes to the development of more standardized, effective training models and facilitates cross-border collaborations to enhance the field's global impact. This includes the awareness of mental health issues in offenders, both in specific countries and in international forums such as the United Nations.

## Why This Book Matters

The purpose of this book is to shed light on these critical differences in forensic psychiatry systems around the world and to begin a conversation about how we can understand and, where possible, reconcile these discrepancies. By exploring the ways in which various countries approach forensic psychiatry—from training to practice to policy—we aim to provide a clearer picture of what forensic psychiatry looks like on a global scale. This work will help expose the gaps in knowledge that hinder international collaboration and research. It will also highlight the systemic challenges that forensic psychiatrists face in different parts of the world. We present our understanding of the forensic psychiatry systems in a large array of countries. But our scope has limitations. It is but a first step. The list of countries is not exhaustive. Some of what we described may have changed between when a chapter was written and when it is published. In some countries, we may not have captured all the relevant information. Yet this is an important start to an important issue for forensic psychiatry globally.

This book is not only an exploration of the current state of forensic psychiatry around the globe but also a call to action. If we are to improve the way we conduct research, the way we train future forensic psychiatrists, and the way we shape forensic policies, we need a deeper understanding of how forensic psychiatry operates in different cultural, legal, and economic contexts. This book provides the first step toward an international dialogue on these issues. By comparing and contrasting forensic psychiatry systems, we can start to ask the hard questions: What does it mean to be a patient in forensic psychiatry in different parts of the world? How do cultural values, legal definitions, and economic conditions shape the treatment and management of offenders with mental illness? How can we learn from each other's successes and challenges? It is also an opportunity to seek out system improvements by being able to see what other countries or jurisdictions do.

## The Path Forward

Forensic psychiatry is inherently tied to the legal system. Because legal systems are culturally specific, forensic psychiatry will always be shaped by the broader societal context in which it is practised. This book will not offer a simple or singular solution to the challenges of international forensic psychiatry, but it will offer a framework for understanding the complex relationship between law, psychiatry, and society. By gathering insights from forensic psychiatrists, researchers, and policymakers around the world, we hope to lay the groundwork for future research and collaboration.

The path forward is clear: before we can compare systems, before we can conduct truly international research, we must first come to a deeper understanding of how forensic psychiatry systems are structured, practised, and experienced around the globe. A patient in forensic psychiatry is not the same in each country; in fact, the similarities may be few in many countries. This book is the first step in what we hope will be a longer journey toward more informed, more globally relevant research and better, more compassionate care for individuals at the intersection of mental health and the criminal justice system.

This exploration is the beginning of a much-needed global conversation about the future of forensic psychiatry.

Gary Chaimowitz, MB ChB, FRCPC, MBA

## References

Arboleda-Flórez, J. (2006). Forensic psychiatry: Contemporary scope, challenges and controversies. *World Psychiatry*, *5*(2), 87–91.

Balcıoğlu, Y. H. (2024). Promoting academic forensic psychiatry in low-income and middle-income countries. *Lancet Psychiatry*, *11*(11), 872–874. https://doi.org/10.1016/S2215-0366(24)00175-5

Gunn, J., & Taylor, P. (Eds.) (2014). *Forensic psychiatry: Clinical, legal, and ethical issues* (2nd ed.). CRC Press.

Howner, K., Hofvander, B., & Tapp, J. (2020). Editorial: What works for forensic psychiatric patients: From treatment evaluations to short and long-term outcomes. *Frontiers in Psychiatry*, *11*, 615473. https://doi.org/10.3389/fpsyt.2020.615473

Morse, S. J. (2019). The insanity defense. In H. LaFollette et al. (Eds.), *International encyclopedia of ethics* (2nd ed.). Wiley-Blackwell.

Völlm, B. A., Clarke, M., Herrando, V. T., Seppänen, A. O., Gosek, P., Heitzman, J., & Bulten, E. (2018). European Psychiatric Association (EPA) guidance on forensic psychiatry: Evidence based assessment and treatment of mentally disordered offenders. *European Psychiatry*, *51*, 58–73. https://doi.org/10.1016/j.eurpsy.2017.12.007

Wasser, T., Chandra, S., Chaffkin, J., & Michaelsen, K. (2022). A multi-site survey of general psychiatry residents' forensic training. *Journal of the American Academy of Psychiatry and the Law*, *50*(2), 231–239. Retrieved from https://jaapl.org/content/50/2/231

# Part I

# North America

# 1 Canada

*Mathieu Dufour and John Bradford*

## Brief Description

| | |
|---|---|
| **Location** | Canada is located in North America. |
| **Size** | 9.98 million $km^2$ |
| **Population** | 40,100,000 |
| **Languages** | English and French are the two official languages. As a result of Canada's high level of cultural diversity, approximately 12.7% of Canadians predominantly speak a language other than English or French at home. A small proportion of Canadian citizens, approximately 0.6% of the population, speak Indigenous languages. |
| **Political system** | Canada is a constitutional monarchy and a parliamentary democracy. Canada functions as a federation, where lawmaking responsibilities are divided between the central (federal) government, 10 provinces, and three territories. |

## Legal System

Canada has two legal traditions: common law, which applies in most provinces and territories, and civil law, which is used in the province of Québec for civil matters. Like other common-law countries, the Canadian criminal court system operates under an adversarial system, in which the prosecution (Crown) and defence are represented separately. The federal government legislates criminal laws for the entire country, as codified in the *Criminal Code of Canada* (1985). In turn, provinces and territories apply the Criminal Code through different levels of provincial courts. Each province has three levels: provincial and territorial, or lower courts; superior courts; and appeal courts. The Nunavut Court of Justice is the only exception, as this territory has a single-level trial court (a single court manages the cases of both the lower and the superior court). After a trial goes to the Court of Appeal, the verdict can later be appealed to the Supreme Court of Canada, the highest court in Canada.

DOI: 10.4324/9781003376248-2

***Mental Health Laws***

The evolution of the legal system in Canada related to offenders with mental illness was influenced by developments in Britain: the trial of James Hadfield in 1800 for the attempted assassination of King George III, the resulting *Criminal Lunatics Act*, the adoption of the M'Naghten rules in 1843, and the English draft *Criminal Code,* introduced in 1880 but never adopted in Britain.

Following the founding of Canada (Confederation) in 1867, in 1892, the Canadian Parliament introduced the *Criminal Code of Canada*, which contained provisions for the automatic detention of individuals found not guilty by reason of insanity (NGRI) under a warrant of the Lieutenant-Governor, the representative of the Crown in each province (Glancy & Regehr, 2020). Detention was in a provincial asylum or mental hospital and indefinite—the legal term was 'at the pleasure of the Lieutenant-Governor.'

The law related to offenders with mental illness was looked at in 1969, when an amendment to the *Criminal Code* empowered the Lieutenant-Governor to appoint an advisory board to review cases of those kept in custody. This was a significant innovation as, for the first time, a multidisciplinary panel put in motion an annual review. The board consisted of a chair who was a retired superior court judge, a lawyer, a member of the lay public, and psychiatrists. Before this, review of any cases was a legal matter and was referred to the Lieutenant-Governor. This referral was sent to the provincial cabinet, which looked at it as only a legal referral and did not review any clinical aspects of progress that the detainee may have achieved. This was followed, in 1976, by a report by the Law Reform Commission to Parliament on mental disorder in the criminal process (Law Reform Commission, 1976), which made wide-sweeping recommendations to make the system more humane, to update archaic wording and to abolish Lieutenant-Governor's warrants for NGRI accused.

In 1982, the *Charter of Rights and Freedoms* was enacted as part of the *Constitution Act, 1982*, which patriated Canada's Constitution from the United Kingdom. The same year, the federal Department of Justice launched the Mental Disorder Project, which published its report in 1985. This report recommended modernizing the sections of the *Criminal Code* that applied to what were termed at the time 'mentally abnormal offenders.' Although legislation was introduced in Parliament to do so, it was not passed before an election was called.

In 1991, the case of *R v. Swain* involved a constitutional challenge to the legislation governing mentally abnormal offenders. The constitutional test was for a violation of Charter rights, specifically rights under Section 7 to life, liberty and security of the person and the right not to be deprived thereof except in accordance with the principles of fundamental justice, Section 9 providing a right not to be arbitrarily detained, and Section 15 guaranteeing equal protection and benefit of the law to all individuals, mentioning discrimination based on 'mental disability.' The Supreme Court of Canada ruled that the sections of the Criminal Code that dealt with insanity were unconstitutional and in breach of the *Charter of Rights and Freedoms* (*R. v. Swain*, 1991). Three issues were specifically analyzed: (1) the constitutionality of the Crown raising the 'insanity defence' over the wishes of the accused, (2) whether the relevant section of the *Criminal Code* is within the jurisdiction of Parliament, and (3) whether 'automatic detention' violates the Charter.

The Supreme Court struck down the existing legislation and gave Parliament six months to create a new mental disorder legislation for the *Criminal Code of Canada*. This resulted in Bill C-30 in 1992, which forms the most part of Part XX.1 of the *Criminal Code* and introduced major changes on issues related to mental disorders. Section 16, referring to the insanity defence, change from a finding of 'not guilty by reason of insanity' (NGRI) to 'not criminally responsible by reason of a mental disorder' (NCR-MD). The patient was identified as the 'accused.' The Lieutenant-Governor's role over the advisory board was removed, and review boards with decision-making authority were established for every province and territory, with adjudicative rather than advisory powers. And these boards gave a disposition for the accused. The amendment also provided that an appeal from a review board went directly to the Court of Appeal of the particular province where the disposition was issued. The automatic 'strict custody' requirement after a person was found NCR-MD was removed. The accused can be 'absolutely discharged' from the Review Board if deemed not 'a significant threat to the safety of the public.' The presiding court could make a disposition immediately following a verdict.

### *Fitness to Stand Trial and Criminal Responsibility*

In Canada, two laws apply to legally involved persons with a mental disorder under the *Criminal Code of Canada*: unfit to stand trial (UST) and not criminally responsible on account of a mental disorder (NCR-MD).

#### *Unfit to Stand Trial*

The Criminal Code of Canada contains laws regarding the fitness of the accused to stand trial. If a mental disorder prevents them from understanding the nature or purpose of the proceedings, the consequences, or communicating with their counsel, they may be found unfit to stand trial. The accused is presumed fit to stand trial unless the court is satisfied, on the balance of probabilities, that the accused is unfit.

In Canada, the threshold for being deemed unfit is relatively low, due in part to the restricted range of cognitive-capacity tests that offenders must undergo during fitness assessments. In this test, offenders with mental illnesses are not required to demonstrate analytical capacity or prove that they acted in their best interest to be deemed unfit. Rather, they must establish a 'limited cognitive capacity' to communicate with their counsel and demonstrate a comprehensive understanding of judicial proceedings (*R v Taylor*, 1992; *R v Whittle*, 1994). If it is determined that a treatment will likely make the accused fit within 60 days, a treatment order is issued. However, if such a treatment is deemed unlikely, the accused is transferred to the jurisdiction of a provincial or territorial review board, which will determine the appropriate placement and treatment, based on factors such as security level, and whether the patient should receive inpatient or outpatient care.

#### *Criminal Responsibility*

The *Criminal Code of Canada* includes the law regarding criminal responsibility. If an individual's mental disorder (defined in the Code) renders them incapable of appreciating the nature and quality of their actions or comprehending the wrongfulness of those actions, they may be found not NCR-MD. Individuals deemed NCR-MD are placed under the supervision of a provincial or territorial review board that assesses their placement and conditions. Section 16 (1) of the *Criminal Code* states:

> No person is criminally responsible for an act committed or an omission made while suffering from a mental disorder that rendered the person incapable of appreciating the nature and quality of the act or omission or of knowing that it was wrong.

Significant case law affects the interpretation of Section 16 (1) of the *Criminal Code of Canada*, which will not be reviewed here.

### ***Decision Makers in Forensic Psychiatry***

When a person is accused of committing a criminal offence, the governing police service arrests them. The accused person is charged with an offence by the Crown Attorney and appears before a judge in a provincial or territorial court. Forensic psychiatrists and other experts may be summoned to provide testimony during the trial to assist the judge or jury in reaching a decision. A judge or a jury renders a verdict and is, therefore, the decision maker for forensic psychiatry-related issues. Governments have a broader role in legislating laws that are later applied by the courts.

## Forensic Psychiatry System

### ***Structure and Function of the Forensic Psychiatry System***

Individuals who are determined to be NCR-MD or found to be unfit to stand trial, even after receiving treatment, are transferred to a provincial or territorial review board. After a court decision, accused individuals are typically relocated to a forensic facility. The review board conducts an initial hearing, usually between 45 and 90 days after an individual is found NCR-MD, during which the placement (including security levels and inpatient versus outpatient options) and other conditions are determined. The board conducts an annual review of the disposition, or sooner if a change in disposition is necessary.

The forensic systems and facilities vary significantly across provinces. Several provinces, including British Columbia and Nova Scotia, have a centralized system where the majority of forensic assessments and care provision are focused on one main facility. Other provinces, like Québec, have a decentralized forensic system, and more than 40 different centres provide forensic psychiatric assessments and care. In Ontario, Canada's most populous province, 10 forensic programmes form the forensic system, with a high level of standardization between programmes. Most provinces have a specialized, high-secure forensic hospital (or unit) for their higher risk forensic patients.

### *Role of Forensic Psychiatry*

Forensic psychiatry refers to the intersection of psychiatry and law. Its primary clinical focus is on criminal cases, including evaluations for trial readiness, assessments of criminal responsibility, and care for patients under provincial and territorial review boards. In Canada, forensic psychiatrists, and occasionally general psychiatrists in certain jurisdictions, provide the primary expert opinions used by courts to determine criminal responsibility and fitness to stand trial. Other fields in which forensic psychiatrists work include correctional psychiatry, risk assessment, sexual offending behaviours, civil psychiatry, and youth forensic psychiatry. Forensic psychiatrists may also participate in teaching and providing training to medical students and residents (in both general and forensic psychiatry), where they receive specialized medical training.

### *Forensic Psychiatry Profession*

#### *Qualifications or Specialized Training*

In Canada, forensic psychiatry is a subspeciality of general psychiatry (Bloom & Schneider, 2017). Forensic psychiatrists are overseen by the Royal College of Physicians and Surgeons of Canada. They must undergo and complete a five-year residency in general psychiatry, and after their residency, an extra year of training in their specialty (forensic psychiatry). A formal and written examination is required to obtain certification in forensic psychiatry (Booth et al., 2021). Forensic psychology is also a specialized field in Canada.

In Canada, there are currently 4,770 psychiatrists practising in general psychiatry (Canadian Psychiatric Association, n.d.), while over 217 practise forensic psychiatry (Royal College of Physicians and Surgeons of Canada, n.d.).

However, there is no database in the country that tracks the number of forensic psychologists, making it unclear and inaccurate to determine the exact number of these mental health practitioners.

*National Networks and Collaborations*

The Canadian Academy of Psychiatry and the Law (CAPL) is the national body representing Canadian psychiatrists interested in forensic psychiatry. With more than 150 members representing all Canadian provinces, CAPL is an active organization that generates practice guidelines regarding forensic psychiatry and offers academic opportunities through its annual conference and other initiatives.

## Forensic Psychiatric Service (Provision of Care)

### *Forensic Patient Characteristics*

In Canada, 'forensic patients' are those assessed for their fitness to stand trial or their criminal responsibility, and those found unfit to stand trial or NCR-MD, with a disposition under a provincial or territorial review board. A large-scale national study, called the National Trajectory Project (NTP), is one of the most inclusive and comprehensive studies on Canadian forensic patients to date (Crocker, Nicholls et al., 2015). This study investigated the psychosocial and criminological characteristics of forensic patients admitted to psychiatric hospitals from 2000 to 2005 across three provinces: British Columbia, Ontario, and Québec. It revealed important interprovincial differences in the trajectories and characteristics of NCR-MD forensic patients. Results indicated that the most common clinical profile found among Canadian forensic patients declared NCR-MD was a primary diagnosis of a psychotic disorder with comorbid substance abuse, in approximately one-third of the cases (Crocker, Nicholls et al., 2015; Penney et al., 2018). More specifically, the researchers found that 71% of forensic patients found NCR-MD were diagnosed with a psychotic disorder, and 31% had a substance use disorder (Crocker, Nicholls et al., 2015). On average, 84% of the forensic patients found NCR-MD were men around 36 years old, and men were more likely to be diagnosed with a psychotic disorder or substance use disorder (Crocker, Nicholls et al., 2015; Nicholls et al., 2015). In addition to these findings, women who were found NCR-MD were generally older when they entered the forensic system, had fewer charges, and were more likely to be diagnosed with a mood or personality disorder (Crocker, Nicholls et al., 2015; Penney et al., 2018). The study also revealed that the majority of index offences among the accused were threats (27%), assault (27%), and property offences (17%). Only a tiny subset of offenders with mental illnesses committed severe violent crimes (9%) (Crocker, Nicholls et al., 2015). Interestingly, the study revealed that forensic patients declared NCR-MD in Ontario were held under a detention order longer than in other Canadian provinces. This study has revealed a lower recidivism rate for forensic patients compared to a general offender population (Charette et al., 2015; Crocker, Charette et al., 2015).

### *Exiting the System and Length of Stay*

When patients exit the forensic system is decided by the provincial review boards, which assess and monitor patients' dispositions until they are no longer considered a significant risk to public safety. The patient is deemed not a threat unless one of the parties (such as the hospital treating them, or the defence) can prove otherwise under a balance of probabilities. If this threshold is no longer met, the review board must grant an absolute discharge, meaning the individual is free of any legal conditions and officially exits the forensic system.

Length of stay varies greatly between provinces. The NTP confirmed these differences in its study: after five years, 19% of patients declared NCR-MD continued to be under a review board in Québec, 31% in British Columbia, and 58% in Ontario (Charette et al., 2015).

### *Assessment, Treatment, and Rehabilitative Programmes*

Provincial forensic systems use different frameworks concerning treatment. However, most forensic facilities endorse the rehabilitation and recovery models, where an individual's psychiatric symptoms, as well as their psychological, social, academic, and occupational needs, are addressed. The recovery model recognizes that each individual has a unique journey, and the principles of the model include hope, dignity, self-determination, and responsibility (Mental Health Commission of Canada, n.d.).

Some forensic settings use the Risk-Needs-Responsivity (RNR) model, emphasizing the importance of addressing criminogenic risk factors related to the patients' index offences (Ward et al., 2007). The RNR model references the *risk* principle (offenders at higher risk for reoffending will benefit most from higher levels of intervention), the *need* principle (only those factors associated with reductions in recidivism should be targeted in intervention), and the *responsivity* principle (programmes should be matched to offender characteristics). More recently, various forensic centres have implemented the DUNDRUM tools, where different treatment pillars are monitored and matched to specialized programmes in addictions, physical health, family and intimate relationships, etc. The norm in Canada's forensic programmes consists of an interdisciplinary approach where multiple mental health professionals administer treatment.

## Strengths and Weaknesses

The diversity of forensic systems in Canada is a strength, as each province or territory can inspire others by sharing best practices in their frameworks and methods. The small but innovative group of forensic psychiatrists is well connected throughout the country, making the profession appealing to younger recruits. The formal recognition of forensic psychiatry as a subspecialty with a certification process has catalyzed a greater standardization of practice across Canada.

The heterogeneity of Canada's forensic systems can also be viewed as a weakness, since the experiences of forensic patients can vary, depending on the province where they live. In addition, the small number of forensic psychiatrists and the extra training required for a formal certification prevent the profession from being responsive when demands increase and more specialists are needed.

## References

Bloom, H., & Schneider, R. D. (2017). *Mental disorder and the law: A primer for legal and mental health professionals*. Toronto, Canada: Irwin Law.

Booth, B. D., Chatterjee, S., Watts, J., & Glancy, G. (2021). Toward a new model of training in Canadian forensic psychiatry. *Journal of the American Academy of Psychiatry and the Law*, *49*(3), 381–395. https://doi.org/10.29158/JAAPL.200112-20

Canadian Psychiatric Association. (n.d.). *Frequently asked questions* [webpage]. Retrieved from https://www.cpa-apc.org/faqs/

Charette, Y., Crocker, A. G., Seto, M. C., Salem, L., Nicholls, T. L., & Caulet, M. (2015). The national trajectory project of individuals found not criminally responsible on account of mental disorder in Canada. Part 4: criminal recidivism. *Canadian Journal of Psychiatry*, *60*(3), 127–134. https://doi.org/10.1177/070674371506000307

*Criminal Code of Canada, R.S.C.* 1985, c. C-46.

Crocker, A. G., Charette, Y., Seto, M. C., Nicholls, T. L., Côté, G., & Caulet, M. (2015). The national trajectory project of individuals found not criminally responsible on account of mental disorder in Canada. Part 3: trajectories and outcomes through the forensic system. *Canadian Journal of Psychiatry*, *60*(3), 117–126. https://doi.org/10.1177/070674371506000306

Crocker, A. G., Nicholls, T. L., Seto, M. C., Charette, Y., Côté, G., & Caulet, M. (2015). The national trajectory project of individuals found not criminally responsible on account of mental disorder in Canada. Part 2: the people behind the label. *Canadian Journal of Psychiatry*, *60*(3), 106–116. https://doi.org/10.1177/070674371506000305

Glancy, G., & Regehr, C. (2020). *Canadian landmark cases in forensic mental health*. Toronto, Canada: University of Toronto Press.

Law Reform Commission of Canada. (1976). *A report to parliament on mental disorder in the criminal process*. Ottawa, Canada: Information Canada. Retrieved from https://publications.gc.ca/collections/collection_2022/jus/J31-18-1976-eng.pdf

Mental Health Commission of Canada. (n.d.). *Recovery* [webpage]. Retrieved from https://mentalhealthcommission.ca/recovery/

Nicholls, T. L., Crocker, A. G., Seto, M. C., Wilson, C. M., Charette, Y., & Côté, G. (2015). The national trajectory project of individuals found not criminally responsible on account of mental disorder. Part 5: how essential are gender-specific forensic psychiatric services? *Canadian Journal of Psychiatry*, *60*(3), 135–145. https://doi.org/10.1177/070674371506000308

Penney, S. R., Prosser, A., & Simpson, A. I. F. (2018). Age onset of offending and serious mental illness among forensic psychiatric patients: A latent profile analysis. *Criminal Behaviour and Mental Health*, *28*(4), 335–349. https://doi.org/10.1002/cbm.2069

Royal College of Physicians and Surgeons of Canada. (n.d.). *Royal college directory* [webpage]. Retrieved from https://rclogin.royalcollege.ca/webcenter/portal/rcdirectory_en/RCDirectorySearch

*R v Swain*, [1991], 1 SCR 933.
*R v Taylor*, [1992].
*R v Whittle*, [1994], 2 SCR 914.
Ward, T., Melser, J., & Yates, P. M. (2007). Reconstructing the risk-need-responsivity model: A theoretical elaboration and evaluation. *Aggression and Violent Behavior*, *12*(2), 208–228. https://doi.org/10.1016/j.avb.2006.07.001

# 2 Canada

## Legal Aspects of Forensic Psychiatry

*Richard D. Schneider and Hy Bloom*

*Editors' note: This book's editors work in forensic health care in Canada, and the detailed aspects of law affecting decision making and practice in Canada may be of interest to both our Canadian and global colleagues. We have therefore asked two leading experts to delve more deeply into these aspects.*

### Introduction: Canada's Legal System

The criminal law of Canada was, in broad form, inherited from the British, as Canada was once a British colony. Although Britain remains without a *Criminal Code*, Canada seized upon and adopted a British draft from 1892. The *Criminal Code of Canada* has evolved, with many legislative amendments, additions, and deletions over time (*Criminal Code of Canada*, 1985, Chap. C-46). As in Britain, criminal offences are comprised of two essential components: a guilty act (*actus reus*) and a guilty mind (*mens rea*). All accused (the term used in the *Criminal Code of Canada*) are presumed to be innocent until both components are proven beyond a reasonable doubt. No defence is required until the Crown has presented a *prima facie* case—a case to meet. Under Canada's federal system, the *Criminal Code* is legislated at the federal level, and provincial and territorial Ministries of the Attorney General prosecute all criminal matters on behalf of the Crown. By far, most trials are heard by a judge sitting alone. However, for indictable (more serious) matters, the accused may elect to be tried by a judge and jury. Trials are party-driven, adversarial events, unlike the more inquisitorial nature of the European criminal court system.

Trial courts interpret the *Criminal Code* and produce a body of common law that is 'persuasive' with respect to parallel courts and 'binding' upon lower courts. From the two levels of the criminal trial court, appeals may be taken to provincial or territorial Courts of Appeal and, from there, to the Supreme Court of Canada.

### Law on Accused With a Mental Disorder

The law pertaining to accused persons with a mental disorder ('forensic patients') is contained in Part XX.1 of the *Criminal Code of Canada,* unlike some

DOI: 10.4324/9781003376248-3

jurisdictions where this population is managed pursuant to civil legislation. By contrast, civil mental health legislation and service delivery is a matter of provincial or territorial competence and therefore varies across Canada. Certain provincial and territorial statutes dealing with, for example, civil commitment, treatment competence, and substitute decision making apply to forensic patients. However, oversight and management is, for the most part, provided pursuant to the *Criminal Code of Canada*.

All federal, provincial, and territorial legislations, and the Criminal Code in particular, are subject to the overriding jurisdiction of the *Canadian Charter of Rights and Freedoms* (*Charter*, 1982) which, among other things, guarantees all persons subject to prosecution, detention, or potential curtailment of rights, the right to 'life, liberty, and the security of the person' (s.7), and the presumption of all innocence (s.11(d)).

The two principal psycholegal issues for the trial courts are unfitness to stand trial and criminal responsibility. Both verdicts are founded upon the necessary but not sufficient finding of an underlying 'mental disorder.' Mental disorder is defined as "any illness, disorder or abnormal condition which impairs the human mind" (*R v Cooper*, 1980). Assessment orders to determine the issue of fitness to stand trial would far outnumber those made to inform the issue of criminal responsibility.

### *Fitness to Stand Trial*

The test for whether an accused is unfit to stand trial is set out in Section 2 of the *Criminal Code of Canada* as follows:

> Unfit to stand trial means unable on account of mental disorder to conduct a defence at any stage of the proceedings before a verdict is rendered or to instruct counsel to do so, and, in particular, unable on account of mental disorder to
>
> a) understand the nature or object of the proceedings,
> b) understand the possible consequences of the proceedings, or
> c) communicate with counsel.

The fundamental question is whether the accused will receive a fair trial (Schneider & Bloom, 2018). The requirement that an accused be 'fit to stand trial' stems from the ancient notion that an accused must be present to respond to accusations of the state. The rules originally developed at common law were codified in 1992 and are contained in Section 2 of the *Criminal Code of Canada.* A historical review of the fitness rules makes clear that an accused must be able to participate in the judicial process in a 'meaningful way' or instruct counsel 'rationally.' A person may not be tried if they are unable to understand the purpose and meaning of the trial or if they are unable to rationally participate because of some mental disability. At common law, an accused who was unable to act rationally in his own defence or to understand the nature and object of the proceedings against him could not be tried.

The issue of fitness may be raised by the prosecutor, the defence, or the court, despite the objections of either party. While fitness is presumed, the fitness of an accused may be brought into question more than once at trial and again on appeal, and the party alleging unfitness must prove it on a balance of probabilities. Fitness is determined by the trier of fact, whether that is a judge sitting alone, or by the jury, in a trial by jury. The presiding judge or magistrate decides whether an inquiry into the accused's fitness is warranted. Where an accused is found unfit, the trial on the merits is delayed and does not resume until the accused is declared fit.

The test for unfitness is based upon 'inabilities' due to mental disorder, not upon ignorance. Mental disorder is a necessary but not sufficient condition for unfitness. The statutory definition for unfitness includes the timeline only up to the point of a verdict, although courts and most commentators are of the view that an accused must be 'fit' in order to be sentenced (Schneider, 1998; *R v GB*, 2003). Based on case law, an accused must be capable of communicating 'rationally' with counsel or the court in order to be fit. This includes an inquiry into whether an accused can understand relevant information, apply that information in the context of their decision making, and communicate intelligibly.

The touchstones of the fitness inquiry are whether the accused can be meaningfully present and participate at their trial. These questions, answered from the perspective of *this accused*, facing *these charges,* will inform a purposive interpretation and application of the fitness test.

With respect to an accused's ability to 'communicate with counsel,' they must have at least a rudimentary factual understanding of their legal predicament (*R v Taylor*, 1992). Various courts and commentators have subsequently found that an accused must be able to participate in a 'meaningful way' and have a 'rational understanding' of their legal predicament. Courts have consistently been of the view that an accused need not be able to act in their own best interests (*R v Taylor*, 1992; *R v Bharwani*, 2023). In this regard, Canadian courts may not fully appreciate that mental illness can infiltrate an individual's mental processes to a degree that they are incapable of acting in their own best interests; it is not a matter of everyday poor decisions such as those that individuals without mental illness may make (Bloom & Schneider, 2013; Schneider & Bloom, 2018, note 11; Bloom, 2023). If the accused's decision making is impacted by mental disorder, they are, arguably, unfit notwithstanding the objective 'rightness' or 'wrongness' of their decision.

Arguably, 'fitness' may be a function of the timelines within which the accused must be 'fit,' the complexity of the legal proceedings, and whether the accused has counsel to assist in the defence. An inherent aspect of the test in

Section 2 is a degree of congruence between the accused's capacities and the complexity of the legal proceedings for which a defence is required and is, therefore, not absolutely static. A contextual assessment of fitness is critical.

Various courts and commentators are of the view that an accused person with a mental disorder may be able to conduct a defence with the assistance of counsel and are, on that basis, 'fit.'

The issue of fitness can arise at any point in the proceedings but it is tested only after a *prima facie* case is presented and after the Crown has made its election. An accused must be fit to plead (guilty or not guilty) and, in our view, to be sentenced.

A bail hearing is not part of the prosecution *per se*. Therefore, an accused does not need to be 'fit' in order to have a bail hearing or to be released on bail. Mental disorders may nevertheless be relevant in considering the primary (will the accused, if released, return to court?) or secondary (will the accused, if released, reoffend?) grounds. There are no provisions in the *Criminal Code* for the Court to order an assessment to assist with bail. Provincial or territorial mental health legislation may provide options to accomplish this.

Accused are most often found to be unfit to stand trial due to psychosis, with the most common diagnostic category being schizophrenia. Intellectual deficit or organic disorders may also give rise to unfitness. Suffering post-stroke expressive and receptive aphasia can so compromise meaningful communication and participation such that an accused can be rendered unfit due to this condition (*R v Witol*, 2023).

An inability to remember the events leading to the charge before the court (amnesia) does not, by itself, lead to a finding of unfitness (*R v Morrissey*, 2007), nor does being deaf and unable to speak (*R v Isaac*, 2009). From a fairness perspective, it is central that an accused's capacity to judge and choose has not been compromised by a mental disorder. The ability to rationally communicate with counsel has been seen by some courts to be an essential ability. Meaningful participation in the trial process requires a modicum of rationality (*R v Adam*, 2013).

Courts must make Assessment Orders upon 'reasonable grounds.' Applications for Orders may come from any party or may be made by the court upon its own motion. Assessments are presumptively (assumed to be) done on an out-of-custody (outpatient) basis.

Numerous Canadian publications have set out detailed protocols for the psychiatric assessment of fitness to stand trial. There are many fitness tools, including specific tools to assess psychopathology and intellectual limitation, to assist in the determination of fitness to stand trial (Bloom, 2023; Bloom & Schneider, 2013, 2017; Schneider & Bloom, 2018).

A trial of the issue of fitness to stand trial requires reasonable grounds to believe that the accused may be unfit. Where the accused's fitness to stand trial is an issue, counsel must be assigned; *amicus curiae* is not a substitute. Barring exceptional circumstances, the accused must be present at a trial of the issue.

Fitness to stand trial pertains to a specific charge(s) on a specific information or indictment. Assessors should not assume that an accused who is fit or unfit to stand trial on one of multiple charges is fit or unfit for the others as ability to conduct a defence or instruct counsel to do so must be considered on a sliding scale of gravity or complexity.

Upon a verdict of unfit to stand trial, the Crown may apply for a Treatment Order that would permit the involuntary treatment of the accused (including any necessary monitoring) for up to 60 days for the limited purpose of rendering the accused 'fit.' If the accused remains unfit to stand trial following treatment, they become subject to the jurisdiction of the provincial or territorial Review Board, which assesses the accused at least annually. Within every two years following the verdict, the Crown must demonstrate that it remains able to prove a *prima facie* case.

In all but the rarest of cases, the hospital's consent is required before making a Treatment Order. It is within the Court's discretion, however, to override the hospital's decision not to admit an accused for treatment (most commonly because of bed shortage) where delay would violate the accused's s.7 *Charter* rights; in this instance, an order for immediate treatment is an appropriate remedy for such violation (*R. v. Conception*, 2014).

In addition to Treatment Orders, the court may make 'Keep Fit Orders' if there is a verdict of 'fit' but the accused would likely become unfit if not detained in hospital.

Accused are subject to the jurisdiction of the court and the Review Board only as long as they remain unfit to stand trial. The Review Board offers its opinion to the court that the accused may now be fit, which triggers a retrial of the issue. Only the court may reverse the verdict of 'unfit to stand trial.' When an accused returns to court to have their fitness retried, any previously made disposition remains in effect until the court reverses the verdict on a balance of probabilities.

However, an accused's status as 'unfit' might not carry on 'in perpetuity.' Upon application, a court may order a stay of proceedings if it is satisfied, on the basis of clear information, that the accused (1) remains unfit, (2) is unlikely to ever become fit, and (3) does not pose a significant threat to the safety of the public. The court must also be satisfied that a stay is in the interests of the proper administration of justice. To assist, a Review Board may order an Assessment if evidence about the accused's mental condition is necessary to determine the matters set out in s.672.851 of the *Criminal Code*. Principles set out in the *Winko* case—a significant threat means a real risk of physical or psychological harm to the public through acts that are criminal in nature and beyond annoying or trivial—are applicable to determine whether an accused who is permanently unfit poses a significant threat to the safety of the public (*Winko v British Columbia (Forensic Psychiatric Institute)*, 1999). In assessing the provisions of s.672.851, a clinician therefore has to assess not only the issue of 'significant threat' but also the likelihood that the accused will remain unfit to stand trial. In assessing likelihood, the clinician reviews the accused's history with respect to unfitness and the extent to which educational attempts have been made. More often, these provisions are applicable to accused suffering from intractable conditions.

### *Not Criminally Responsible on Account of Mental Disorder*

In 1992, Parliament replaced the 'insanity defence' with the defence of 'not criminally responsible on account of mental disorder' (NCR-MD). The statutory changes consist largely of modernizing the wording used. Section 16 of the *Criminal Code of Canada* articulates the principle. The test to be met is strictly legal, not medical. The relevant *Criminal Code* provision is as follows:

> 16.(1) No person is criminally responsible for an act committed or an omission made while suffering from a mental disorder that rendered the person incapable of appreciating the nature and quality of the act or omission or of knowing that it was wrong.
>
> (2) Every person is presumed not to suffer from a mental disorder so as to be exempt from criminal responsibility by virtue of subsection (1), until the contrary is proved on the balance of probabilities.
>
> (3) The burden of proof that an accused was suffering from a mental disorder so as to be exempt from criminal responsibility is on the party that raises the issue.

The issue may arise at several points. As with any defence, the accused may assert the defence of NCR-MD at the outset of the trial or may raise it at the conclusion of the Crown's case if, and only if, there is a case to meet calling for a defence. It may be raised as late as upon a finding of guilt but before conviction. The fundamental rights of the accused include the right to make a full answer and defence, including the right to control one's own defence. However, the right to control one's own defence is not absolute (*R v Bouvier*, 2011; *R v Kobzar*, 2012; *R v Vassell*, 2013; *R v Dickson*, 2013).

When an accused does not want to rely on a Section 16 defence of NCR-MD, the Crown may raise the issue independently but must meet the ordinary burden of proof before raising the issue (*R v Eli*, 2014; *R v Hosack*, 2013; *R v McBride*, 2012). The Crown must prove *actus reus* and *mens rea* beyond a reasonable doubt. As a result of the Supreme Court of Canada decision in *R v Swain* (1991), the Crown may raise the defence over the accused's objection at one of two junctures: (1) during the accused's own defence, when the accused puts mental capacity in issue or (2) after the trier of fact (judge or jury) has concluded that the accused is otherwise guilty.

This common law rule provides procedurally for a 'bifurcated trial.' If the issue is not raised by the accused at the outset of the trial, the issue may be raised by either party—but only after the accused is proven otherwise guilty. The accused may call evidence at the first phase of the bifurcated trial and may raise other issues or defences such as identification or alibi, while reserving the right to respond with the defence of NCR-MD only if the trier of fact finds them guilty (*R v Swain*, 1991).

Another question is whether the court should raise the defence on its own accord. In *R v Piette* (2005), the court on its own motion ordered an assessment to determine the accused's criminal responsibility despite an argument against such an order by the accused *and* the Crown. The trial judge, after obtaining an assessment that suggested that the accused was significantly impaired, including with respect to his ability to 'appreciate,' then found that the accused's condition brought him within the ambit of Section 16 without first finding the requisite mental element. The Crown and the defence were content that the accused's mental disorder simply negated the requisite *mens rea*.

At appeal, the court observed that the new provisions contained in Part XX.1 of the *Criminal Code* no longer result in an acquittal upon a finding of NCR-MD, but rather a hybrid verdict (i.e., the accused is found to have committed the act but is not responsible for it on account of mental disorder) that is neither an acquittal nor a conviction, nor something 'in-between.' The hybrid verdict may, on a case-by-case basis, prove to be more onerous than a conviction would have been. The appeal court found that the issue of criminal responsibility must be raised by either the accused or the Crown at the appropriate juncture, and, further, that for the court to pursue the defence on its own motion deprived the accused of his constitutional right to control the conduct of his defence at trial.

The condition that qualifies an accused for an NCR-MD defence must be a recognized condition. Ultimately, it is not so much the diagnosis that is important, but the condition's effect on the brain functions that mediate the various capacities touched on in Section 16 of the *Criminal Code*.

'Appreciate' means more than mere knowledge of the physical quality of the act, but also conveys its implications in a wider sense (*R v Simpson*, 1977), whereas 'nature and quality' refers to the physical consequences of the act (*R v Landry*, 1991).

In regard to the accused's capacity to understand the wrongfulness of the act committed, the analysis must not merely focus on a general capacity to distinguish right from wrong, or lack thereof. Rather, the focus must be on the deficiency of the defendant's capacity to know that the particular act is wrong, having regard to the everyday standards of the reasonable person (*R v Gavrilovic*, 2010; *R v Morine*, 2011) and ordinary moral standards of society (*R v Minassian*, 2021). Of concern is the defendant's degree of deficiency regarding their capacity for rational perception and rational choice about the rightness or wrongness of their specific actions (*R v Oommen*, 1994).

The basis of incapacities—regarding the accused's appreciation of the nature and quality of their acts or knowing their wrongfulness—can manifest itself in a number of ways, depending upon the accused's claims (*R v J.R.V.*, 2011).

The defence should not apply in certain situations:

- if an accused is capable of knowing that his specified actions are contrary to the law and that he ought not to do an act that is contrary to the law (*R v Schoenborn*, 2010).
- if an accused is incapable of knowing that their actions are contrary to the law but is capable of knowing that the act is generally condemned by people (*R v Gavrilovic*, 2010).

However, the defence should apply:

- if an accused is incapable of knowing that his actions are contrary to the law and that the specified act is generally condemned by the public (*R v Schoenborn*, 2010; *R v Dobson*, 2018).
- if an accused is "aware that it is ordinarily wrong to commit a crime but, by reason of mental illness believes that it would be right according to the ordinary moral standard of his society to commit the crime in a particular context" (*R v Klinard*, 2011).

An accused's claim of mental incapacity can give rise to the denial of *actus reus* or *mens rea*. An accused can claim—by reason of mental illness—that he was not acting consciously, denying the essential element of voluntary *actus reus* on the basis of an internal cause (*R v Stone*, 1999). In Canadian jurisprudence, involuntary acts (i.e., automatisms) are presumed to be secondary to mental disorder. *R v Stone* and subsequent decisions that follow the so-called 'Stone analysis,' set out a protocol to assist courts (and clinicians) in determining how to understand involuntariness, whether it was caused by an internal or external cause, and whether an accused is a continuing or recurrent danger to the public.

A claim to mental incapacity can also be manifested as a "defence in the nature of an excuse or justification based on the fact that the accused's mental condition rendered him incapable of knowing that the act was wrong" (*R v J.R.V.*, 2011), while consciously and voluntarily committing an intentional act. For example, an accused—by reason of mental disorder—"believed that the victim was evil incarnate and would destroy the earth if the accused did not kill him" (*R v J.R.V.*, 2011).

## Forensic Patients

In these various arenas, we speak of 'forensic patients' as if that term is, clinically speaking, a relatively homogenous pool from jurisdiction to jurisdiction.

However, the definition can vary from one jurisdiction to another. Broadly speaking, 'forensic patient' refers to a patient with mental health issue(s) relevant to a legal issue(s), and the patient has become involved with the criminal justice system.

Individuals come to be known as 'forensic patients' as a result of entering the 'forensic system' through one of a number of legal portals. The portals result from certain legal thresholds being met, certain legal questions being asked, verdicts being obtained, or particular treatments ordered. So, definitions of 'fitness to stand trial,' 'criminal responsibility,' 'mental disorder'; provisions for court-ordered assessments; and treatment, frequency, methods of review, and thresholds for discharge all shape the forensic patient's clinical profile. These variables may create considerable heterogeneity both within and across jurisdictions and make international comparisons of 'forensic patients' difficult, if not misleading.

The legal system creates the architecture for these various portals and the pathways into the forensic system. And it is the legal system that shapes the forensic population, the forensic system, the services provided, and the practitioners brought in to support that population. To the extent that legal systems differ, so do the clinical demographics of the patient population, the infrastructure created, and the practitioners engaged both within and across jurisdictions (Edworthy et al., 2016).

In Canada, the term 'forensic patient' means those ordered by either a Court or a provincial or territorial Review Board to a forensic facility to be assessed, treated, housed, or supervised. Review boards are quasi-judicial administrative tribunals that oversee all individuals who have obtained verdicts of either unfit to stand trial or not criminally responsible on account of mental disorder. Forensic facilities are hospitals designated by the provincial or territorial Minister of Health for this purpose. 'Forensic patients' may also include individuals who have been incarcerated and placed in a hospital or a quasi-hospital part of a correctional facility due to the presence of a mental disorder, whether or not it affected the verdict.

Also, depending upon where in the prosecutorial stream an individual enters the forensic system, their clinical profile and the services engaged will generally differ. For example, individuals for whom Assessment Orders have been made to determine fitness to stand trial are likely to be in a relatively decompensated state, given the legal thresholds in Canada. Fitness to stand trial is an issue that is often (but not always) canvassed at the beginning of the prosecutorial process, and therefore soon after the offence, when the individual is likely to be in a more decompensated state. On the other hand, individuals found by the courts to be NCR-MD have likely been supervised and treated for some time, either in or out of custody. Many or most would have had psychopharmacological treatment and would generally be much more stable. At a minimum, they would, of necessity, have been fit to stand trial, which requires that they could be meaningfully present and meaningful participants in the trial process (*R v Bharwani*, 2023).

In each case, the individual enters the forensic system as a result of a hearing that is subject to review by an appellate court. In each case as well, the forensic patient's status is indefinite and determined through legal proceedings. And, unlike psychiatric patients in other arenas, assessment and treatment of the forensic patient are typically involuntary and for the benefit of the individual as well as the protection or safety of the public.

It is said that the system often tilts towards the protection of the public and away from the patient's interests or objectives (Carroll et al., 2004; Boyd-Caine, 2012). This imbalance is fueled by media hype. Furthermore, the 'forensic patient' is almost invariably *not* the assessor's 'client.' The 'client' is the court that ordered the assessment or counsel who retained the expert to provide an opinion. Therefore, patients' expectations with respect to confidentiality must be addressed at the outset of any assessment. It is essential that the accused/assessee understands the nature of their relationship with the assessor and the purpose of the assessment. The issue of bias and the assessor's non-partisan stance, lack of confidentiality, and the critical importance of clarity, openness, and honesty are also addressed before substantive subjects are gone into.

## Oversight of Unfit to Stand Trial and NCR-MD

Jurisdiction of individuals who have received verdicts of either unfit to stand trial or NCR-MD from the criminal trial courts is assumed by the provincial or territorial Review Board, under Part XX.1 of the *Criminal Code of Canada*. These quasi-judicial administrative tribunals maintain jurisdiction of accused who are unfit to stand trial as long as they remain unfit, and of accused who are NCR-MD as long as they constitute a 'significant threat to the safety of the public' (Section 672.52 of the *Criminal Code of Canada*). All accused are reviewed by the Review Board of the province or territory at least every 12 months from the date of the verdict by a five-member panel made up of two legal practitioners, two psychiatrists (or a psychiatrist and a psychologist), and a lay person. At the conclusion of each hearing, a disposition and written reasons are provided to the parties. The disposition imposed must be the 'least onerous and restrictive' available, taking into account the safety of the public (the paramount consideration), the mental condition of the accused, the reintegration of the accused into society, and the other needs of the accused.

## Exiting the System

When an accused who is NCR-MD is not found to be a significant threat to the safety of the public, they are discharged absolutely; otherwise, the accused is either detained in the custody of a designated facility or required to report to a designated facility. While obviously interrelated, an absolute discharge is a legal decision based upon 'threat of harm' rather than upon 'recovery' *per se*. Where an accused found unfit to stand trial is reviewed and assessed as fit to stand trial, the matter is returned to the trial court for the issue to be retried. The disposition rendered by the Review Board binds all parties, namely, the Crown, the designated forensic facility, and the accused. With respect to either verdict, an accused's oversight by the Review Board is indeterminate and is generally longer than a typical sentence if the accused had been convicted of the same offence (Crocker et al., 2015).

While most provinces in Canada have their own designated forensic facilities, the three territories in the north of Canada do not. These jurisdictions maintain contractual relationships with neighbouring provinces to the south for the provision of these services. Dispositions of the Review Boards are appealable to the provincial or territorial Courts of Appeal and, from there, to the Supreme Court of Canada.

## Forensic Patient Characteristics

A study of the psychosocial and criminological characteristics of 1,800 accused who were NCR-MD from three of Canada's most populous provinces provides a profile of this population (Crocker et al., 2015). Most accused with verdicts of either unfit to stand trial or NCR-MD are male (85%). The most common diagnoses were within the psychotic spectrum of disorders. The average age of accused found NCR-MD was 36 years. Approximately one-third of the NCR-MD population had a severe mental illness and a concomitant substance use disorder. Most (72.4%) had at least one prior hospitalization for mental health issues. The most common victims were family members, as well as police and mental healthcare workers. The most common index offences were assaults and threats of bodily harm. With respect to the accused found unfit to stand trial, cognitive disorders and intellectual deficits were common. Rarely do the accused present with a single diagnosis. Substance use disorders are very common in conjunction with mental illnesses. Most accused have index offences of at least moderate seriousness. Accused with relatively minor offences may be amenable to 'diversion'—an option solely available at the Crown's (prosecution's) discretion. The net effect, if the individual meets criteria (i.e., the offence is non-violent and the accused agrees to participate in a rehabilitation programme) for diversion, is a pathway out of the criminal justice system and back to the civil mental healthcare system. In such instances, the Crown will stay or withdraw the charge.

As mentioned at the outset, the issues that must be addressed by the forensic mental health practitioner, the treatment provided, the level and sort of supervision required, the assessments, and reports prepared will inevitably differ greatly, depending on how and why the forensic patient entered the system.

## Trends in Forensic Populations

Canada underwent a comprehensive reworking of its legislation at the interface of mental disorder and criminal law in 1992, in the wake of a decision of the Supreme Court of Canada in *R v Swain* (1991). Suffice it to say that the new provisions are far less draconian than previous provisions and have made the verdicts of either unfit to stand trial or NCR-MD more attractive. The range of discretion given to the review boards, the requirement that dispositions be the 'least onerous and least restrictive,' and the onus being most often born by the state, create a less harsh array of consequences that may be considerably better than had the accused been convicted and sent to jail. Before the new legislation was proclaimed, approximately 90% of the forensic population had committed homicides or other very serious offences. With the change in legislation, the numbers have essentially reversed. Now, only 10% of the population has committed offences at the most serious end of the spectrum. This trend signals that the accused who had previously avoided these verdicts are now availing themselves of the verdicts with less hesitation.

## Forensic Psychiatry Profession

### *Qualifications and Specialized Training*

There are no specific professional credentials required for a clinician to provide an expert opinion in court in Canada, provided the psychiatrist or other mental health professional holds a medical or other relevant licence and a higher qualification in the speciality of psychiatry or psychology (Gold & Bloom, 2013).

Expertise in specific areas, such as domestic violence or sexual offending, in which there is no formal qualification, are assessed by the court in a *voir dire* focused on the proposed expert's expertise unique to the specific subject matter being considered by the court.

In 2013, the Royal College of Physicians and Surgeons of Canada (RCPSC) implemented a Canadian subspecialty designation in forensic psychiatry. The RCPSC website (www.royalcollege.ca) provides a detailed list of criteria that need to be met before the candidate is eligible for subspeciality certification, including training experiences in key areas of criminal and civil forensic psychiatry, and familiarity with landmark Canadian jurisprudence in the field. Generally, the candidate must already be credentialed by the RCPSC as a psychiatrist or be eligible for the psychiatry exam.

There is a written examination in short answer questions (SAQ) style, for which the required pass score is 70%. The areas that the examination covers and their weighting are also set out on the site.

Most, if not all, forensic psychiatric training programmes offer didactic lectures in the various subjects generally falling under the heading of psychiatry and the law, and provide clinical opportunities to assess evaluees, either those under court order or referred by agencies or lawyers, and to write court reports and testify, observed by and with the critical input of a supervisor.

The educational and experiential pathway to becoming a forensic psychiatrist has become increasingly structured over the last two decades, with a variety of university-based fellowship programmes in forensic psychiatry now available across Canada.

### *Role of Forensic Psychiatry*

In Canada, the range of psycholegal tasks amenable to forensic psychiatric expertise has expanded over time (Table 2.1), as has the literature on numerous aspects of psychiatry and the law, particularly sexual offending, dangerousness and risk assessment, the relationship between mental disorder and violence, and psychopathy, to name just a few.

The scope of this chapter does not allow for a review of the various psycholegal issues forensic clinicians may be called upon to address in the course of a criminal prosecution.

While the nature of, and scenarios for, forensic psychiatric practice differ from one province or territory to another and one community to another, there is opportunity within the field to assume wide and varied roles, including practice within a forensic psychiatric hospital, consulting to correctional facilities, tribunal work, private practice, or a combination.

As an expert retained by a party (i.e., defence, prosecution, plaintiff, defendant, management, union), the expert's forefront duty is to serve as consultant to that party, by assessing a litigant, reviewing documents, critically appraising the reports of other experts, etc. Although the expert's involvement and role are driven by their consulting (contractual) relationship, professional and ethical

*Table 2.1* Psycholegal assessments in a criminal prosecution (Bloom & Schneider, 2013)

- Suitability for bail
- Suitability for diversion
- Capacity to make a confession/voluntariness of a statement
- Fitness to stand trial
- Criminal responsibility and automatism
- Diminished responsibility (capacity to form intent)
- Duress, self-defence, and provocation
- Sentencing
    - Risk and recidivism
    - Dangerousness, dangerous offender, and long-term offender proceedings
    - Rehabilitation potential
    - Treatability of sex offender
    - Psychological factors/motivations underpinning offence
    - Review Board-risk (significant threat) assessment for derestriction or release

obligations, particularly self-monitoring for bias, are moment-to-moment considerations. Most Canadian provinces and territories have laws requiring experts to attest to their impartiality, based on conclusions by law commissions on the use of expert evidence in the justice system and jurisprudence in this area.

### *Forensic Facilities*

Designated forensic facilities provide assessments, care, oversight, treatment, and reports to both courts and Review Boards. These facilities are staffed by teams of professionals, which include nurses, social workers, occupational therapists, recreational therapists, psychologists, and psychiatrists, all of whom contribute to the assessments and reports.

As noted earlier, the three northern (and relatively sparsely populated) territories do not have their own forensic facilities and rely on southern provincial hospitals to meet their forensic psychiatric needs. Most of the provinces have a number of forensic psychiatric hospitals of varying levels of security, with the exception of some of the provinces with less population—Prince Edward Island, Newfoundland, Nova Scotia, and New Brunswick—which each have one forensic facility. British Columbia is unique in that it has a central authority—the Forensic Psychiatric Services Commission—with a number of satellite facilities and clinics around the province. Québec is also unique in that it has designated more than 50 general and psychiatric hospitals as facilities that can assess and treat forensic patients, in addition to having several specific (tertiary-level) forensic psychiatric hospitals.

## Violence Risk Assessment

Canadian scholarship has held a vanguard position on the world stage in the research, creation, and clinical implementation of various specific-to-purpose risk assessment tools (Bloom et al., 2005), beginning with the Violence Prediction Scheme (VPS; Webster et al., 1994), a tool that focused on static risk factors, in the late 1980s. Other well-known schemes developed over the years include the Historical, Clinical, Risk Management (HCR-20), now in its third version (Douglas et al., 2013). The list of notable Canadian contributions to the field is long, including the following:

- Violence Risk Appraisal Guide (VRAG-R) (3rd ed.) (Harris et al., 2015)
- Hare Psychopathy Checklist-Revised (PCL-R) (2nd ed.) (Hare, 2003), PCL:Screening Version (PCL:SV) (Hart et al., 1995), and PCL:Youth Version (PCL:YV) (Kosson et al., 2013)
- Sexual Violence Risk-20, Version 2 (SVR-20V2) (Boer et al., 2017)
- Risk for Sexual Violence Protocol (RSVP) (Hart & Boer, 2011)
- Sexual Offender Risk Assessment Guide (SORAG) (Quinsey et al., 1995)

- Structured Assessment of Violence Risk in Youth (SAVRY) (Borum et al., 2020)
- STATIC 99 (Harris et al., 2003)
- Spousal Assault Risk Assessment Guide—Version 2 (SARA-V2) (Kropp & Hart, 2015)
- Level of Service Inventory—Revised (LSI-R) (Andrews & Bonta, 2000)
- Ontario Domestic Assault Risk Assessment (ODARA) (Rice et al., 2011)
- Brief Spousal Assault Form for the Evaluation of Risk—Second Edition (B-SAFER-2) (Kropp et al., 2005)
- Early Assessment Risk Lists for Boys (EARL-20B) (Augimeri et al., 2001)
- Early Risk Assessment List for Girls (EARL-21G) (Levene et al., 2001)

The Risk-Need-Responsivity (RNR) model (Andrews & Bonta, 2010), first published in the late 1980s and used in many parts of the world, is yet another significant Canadian contribution to the field of risk assessment and management. The approach aims at matching offender risk with interventions to help allocate precious resources based on the risk posed by offenders.

## Future Challenges

Challenges persist with respect to resources and the timely turnaround of assessments and reports to the courts and Review Boards, especially in the northern regions of the country. The transfer of accused both within and between facilities is often too slow. Too often, the accused are in forensic facilities (hospitals) because there is no appropriate placement, for example, community housing with various degrees of supervision and group homes, in the community. Of course, the cost of creating appropriate supervised housing in the community would be much less than the cumulative cost of having a patient occupy a hospital bed.

A significant proportion of new forensic patients coming into the system have previously had contact with, or received care in, the civil mental health system. It is often said that a forensic patient is a 'failed' civil patient, a misnomer as the failure lies in the civil mental health system. There is little doubt that money spent to expand the capacity and efficacy of the civil mental health system would greatly reduce the demand for resources in the forensic mental health system.

## References

Andrews, D. A., & Bonta, J. (2000). *The level of service inventory-revised*. Toronto, Canada: Multi-Health Systems.

Andrews, D. A., & Bonta, J. (2010). *The psychology of criminal conduct* (5th ed.). New Providence, NJ, US: Matthew Bender & Company, Inc.

Augimeri, L. K., Koegl, C. J., Webster, C. D., & Levene, K. S. (2001). *Early assessment risk list for boys: EARL-20B, Version 2*. Toronto, Canada: Earlscourt Child and Family Centre.

Bloom, H. (2023). *Fitness to start trial*, Forensic Psychiatry Rapid Reference Series, no. 3. Toronto, Canada: Tapestry Press and workplace.calm inc.
Bloom, H., & Schneider, R. D. (2013). *Law and mental disorder: A comprehensive and practical approach*. Toronto, Canada: Irwin Law.
Bloom, H., & Schneider, R. D. (2017). *Mental disorder and the law: A primer for legal and mental health professionals* (2nd ed.). Toronto, Canada: Irwin Law.
Bloom, H., Webster, C., Hucker, S., & De Freitas, K. (2005). The Canadian contribution to violence risk assessment: History and implications for current psychiatric practice. *Canadian Journal of Psychiatry*, *50*(1), 3–11.
Boer, D. P., Hart, S. D., Kropp, P. R., & Webster, C. D. (2017). *Manual for the sexual violence risk—20, version 2: Professional guidelines for assessing risk of sexual violence*. Vancouver, Canada: Protect International Risk and Safety Services Inc.
Borum, R., Lodewijks, H. P. B., Bartel, P. A., & Forth, A. E. (2020). The structured assessment of violence risk in youth (SAVRY). In K. S. Douglas, & R. K. Otto (Eds.), *Handbook of violence risk assessment* (2nd ed., pp. 438–461). Routledge.
Boyd-Caine, T. (2012). *Protecting the public? Detention and release of mentally disordered offenders*. Routledge.
*Canadian Charter of Rights and Freedoms, s.15, Part I of the Constitution Act,* 1982, being Schedule B to the Canada Act, 1982 (UK) 1982, C11.
Carroll, A., Lyall, M., & Forrester, A. (2004). Clinical hopes and fears in forensic mental health. *Journal of Forensic Psychiatry and Psychology*, *15*(3), 407–425. https://doi.org/10.1080/14789940410001703282
*Criminal Code of Canada, R.S.C,* [1985], c. C-46
Crocker, A. G., Nicholls, T. L., Seto, M. C., Charette, Y., Côté, G., & Caulet, M. (2015). The national trajectory project of individuals found not criminally responsible on account of mental disorder in Canada. Part 2: the people behind the label. *Canadian Journal of Psychiatry*, *60*(3), 106–116. https://doi.org/10.1177/070674371506000305
Douglas, K. S., Hart, S. D., Webster, C. D., & Belfrage, H. (2013). *HCR-20 V3: Assessing risk for violence*. Burnaby, BC: Mental Health, Law, and Policy Institute, Simon Fraser University.
Edworthy, R., Sampson, S., & Völlm, B. (2016). Inpatient forensic-psychiatric care: Legal frameworks and service provision in three European countries. *International Journal of Law and Psychiatry*, *47*, 18–27.
Gold, A., & Bloom, H. (2013). Giving evidence as an expert witness. In H. Bloom, & R. Schneider (Eds.), *Law and mental disorder: A comprehensive and practical approach*. Toronto: Irwin Law.
Hare, R. D. (2003). *Manual for the revised psychopathy checklist* (2nd ed.). Toronto, Canada: Multi-Health Systems.
Harris, A., Phenix, A., Hanson, R. K., & Thornton, D. (2003). *Static 99: Coding rules revised 2003*. Ottawa, Canada: Solicitor General Canada.
Harris, G. T., Rice, M. E., Quinsey, V. L., & Cormier, C. A. (2015). *Violent offenders: Appraising and managing risk* (3rd ed.). American Psychological Association.
Hart, S. D., & Boer, D. P. (2011). Structured professional judgment guidelines for sexual violence risk assessment: Sexual Violence Risk-20 (SVR-20) and Risk for Sexual Violence Protocol (RSVP). In R. K. Otto, & K. S. Douglas (Eds.), *Handbook of violence risk assessment* (1st ed., pp. 279–304). Routledge.
Hart, S. D., Cox, D. N., & Hare, R. D. (1995). *Hare psychopathy checklist: Screening version (PCL:SV)*. Toronto, Canada: Multi-Heath Systems.
Kosson, D. S., Neumann, C. S., Forth, A. E., Salekin, R. T., Hare, R. D., Krischer, M. K., & Sevecke, K. (2013). Factor structure of the Hare Psychopathy Checklist: Youth Version (PCL: YV) in adolescent females. *Psychological Assessment*, *25*(1), 71–83.

Kropp, P. R., & Hart, S. D. (2015). *The spousal assault risk assessment guide version 3 (SARA-V3)*. ProActive Resolutions Inc.

Kropp, P. R., Hart, S. D., & Belfrage, H. (2005). *Brief spousal assault form for the evaluation of risk (B-SAFER) manual* (2nd ed.). Vancouver, Canada: Protect International Risk and Safety Services Inc.

Levene, K. S., Augimeri, L. K., Pepler, D. J., Walsh, M. M., Webster, C. D., & Koegl, C. J. (2001). *Early assessment risk list for girls: EARL-21G, Version 1, consultation edition*. Toronto, Canada: Earlscourt Child and Family Centre.

Quinsey, V. L., Rice, M. E., & Harris, G. T. (1995). Actuarial prediction of sexual recidivism. *Journal of Interpersonal Violence*, *10*(1), 85–105.

Rice, M. E., Harris, G. T., & Hilton, N. Z. (2011). The violence risk appraisal guide and sex offender risk appraisal guide for violence risk assessment and the Ontario domestic assault risk assessment and domestic violence risk appraisal guide for wife assault risk assessment. In R. K. Otto, & K. S. Douglas (Eds.), *Handbook of violence risk assessment* (1st ed., pp. 99–119). Routledge.

*R v Adam,* [2013] OJ No222 (SCJ).

*R v Bharwani, [*2023] ONCA.

*R v Bouvier*, [2011] SJ 463.

*R. v. Conception*, [2014], SCC.

*R v Cooper,* [1980] 1 SCR 1149.

*R v Dickson*, [2013] OJ 6418.

*R v Dobson*, [2018].

*R v Eli*, [2014] BCJ 2766.

*R v Gavrilovic*, [2010] OJ 960.

*R v GB*, [2003] OJ No 784 (SCJ).

*R v Hosack*, [2013] BCJ 2975.

*R v Isaac,* [2009] OJ No 5804.

*R v J.R.V.*, [2011] BCJ 223.

*R v Klinard*, [2011] OJ 2536 at 14.

*R v Kobzar*, [2012] OJ 2179.

*R v Landry*, [1991] ISCR 99 (SCC).

*R v McBride*, [2012] OJ 6506.

*R v Minassian, [*2021] ONSC 1258.

*R v Morine*, [2011] NSJ 61.

*R v Morrissey*, [2007].

*R v Oommen*, [1994] 2 SCR502 (SCC).

*R v Piette,* [2005] BCSC 1724.

*R v Schoenborn,* [2010] BCJ 291.

*R v Simpson*, [1977] 35 CCC (2d) (Ont. CA).

*R v Stone,* [1999] 2 SCR 290c.

*R v Swain*, [1991] 1 SCR 933.

*R v Taylor*, [1992].

*R v Vassell*, [2013] OJ 2848.

*R v Witol*, [2023] OCJ.

Schneider, R. D. (1998). Fitness to be sentenced. *Criminal Law Quarterly*, *41*, 261–272.

Schneider, R. D., & Bloom, H. (2018). *Fitness to stand trial: Fairness first & foremost*. Toronto: Irwin Law.

Webster, C. D., Harris, G. T., Rice, M. E., Cormier, C., & Quinsey, V. L. (1994). *The violence prediction scheme: Assessing dangerousness in high-risk men*. Toronto, Canada: University of Toronto Centre of Criminology.

*Winko v British Columbia (Forensic Psychiatric Institute),* [1999] 2 SCR 625.

# 3 The United States of America

*Monika Pietrzak and Susan Hatters Friedman*

## Basic Description

| | |
|---|---|
| **Location** | The United States of America is primarily located in North America, south of Canada, with the state of Alaska situated to the northwest of Canada and Hawai'i in the Pacific Ocean. |
| **Size** | 9,833,520 km$^2$ |
| **Population** | 341,218,756 |
| **Languages** | English is the most common language, but there is no official language. |
| **Political system** | The United States of America is a federal republic with a government comprised of three branches: the executive (President), the legislative (Congress: Senate and House of Representatives), and the judicial (Supreme Court and lower courts). The country comprises 50 states and the District of Columbia, each with its own government that operates under the political framework set by the United States Constitution. |

## Legal System

### *Legal Context*

The United States has a constitution-based federal government that operates within a framework of parallel federal and state systems (United States Courts, n.d.). At the federal level, federal authority is limited to explicitly 'enumerated powers,' including levying taxes, regulating commerce, establishing immigration laws, managing the postal system, establishing federal courts below the Supreme Court, punishing piracy and international crimes, maintaining a military, declaring war, and creating laws for District of Columbia (Steenken & Brooks, n.d.). Conversely, state governments retain residual powers not delegated federally, such as police powers to protect public safety, health, and welfare. Each state has its unique legal system based on its specific legal sources and court system, which allows states to autonomously address regional issues and serve as laboratories for policy experimentation. Both federal and state governments share concurrent powers within

DOI: 10.4324/9781003376248-4

a particular jurisdiction, creating a decentralized, multifaceted network of legal sources (constitution, statutes, rules, regulations, and case law) (Erler, 1986/1992). Federal laws take precedence over conflicting state laws when conflicts arise between legal sources. The hierarchy of legal sources within a particular jurisdiction typically identifies the following, in order of decreasing authority: (1) constitutions, (2) statutes, (3) court opinions, and (4) administrative regulations.

The United States judicial system is adversarial and based on common law. It provides a forum for opposing parties, represented by lawyers, to argue their cases before an impartial decision maker (judge or jury) (Freedman, 1998). Procedural rules and traditions serve as the bedrock of the adversarial process and embody constitutional principles of equal protection and due process. A core tenet of common law is *stare decisis* ('let the decision stand'), which indicates that judges should follow precedent from prior cases (American Bar Association, 2022).

Much like the dual division of legal sources, the judicial system is structured into two parallel systems of federal and state courts, each further subdivided into several levels. The types of cases that each level will hear of courts will depend on jurisdiction, which establishes the power of a court to exercise judicial authority over a particular matter. The court hierarchy shapes which court decisions will have a binding effect on another court. The United States Constitution establishes federal courts and have jurisdiction to hear cases involving federal laws, treaties, or the United States Constitution (Congressional Research Service, 2023). They also have diverse jurisdiction over disputes between citizens of different states or foreign countries if the amount in controversy exceeds a certain monetary threshold. The federal court system is composed of three main levels: (1) the 94 district courts serve as trial-level courts; (2) the 13 Courts of Appeals represent intermediate appellate courts, which are split into 12 regional circuits and a Federal Circuit with nationwide jurisdiction to hear appeals in specialized cases; and (3) the United States Supreme Court is the highest court in the country and the final arbiter of federal constitutional questions (United States Courts, n.d.). There additionally exist specialized federal courts and tribunals that have limited jurisdiction in specialized matters. States have their own state court systems whose structures vary widely across different jurisdictions. Still, every state generally has a trial-level court, at least one intermediate appellate court, and a state supreme court (Congressional Research Service, 2023). There are one or more courts in each state that have general jurisdiction to hear any case involving either state or federal law, subject to limited exceptions where federal statutes expressly or implicitly provide for exclusive federal court jurisdiction. Some states may also have specialized courts like probate, family, juvenile, and small claims courts.

### *Mental Health Laws*

#### *Incompetence to Stand Trial*

In the United States, all criminal defendants have a fundamental constitutional right to be competent during court proceedings. Adjudicative competence safeguards a defendant's due process right to a fair trial and is regarded as a cornerstone of the adversarial justice system. Defendants must be able to understand and retain information relevant to the decision in question, apply that understanding to their specific circumstances in the context of their individual values, and reason among options available to them.

The modern legal standards for competence to stand trial have been established by case law. In 1960, in its landmark opinion in *Dusky v. United States*, the United States Supreme Court concluded that it was not enough for a defendant to merely be oriented to time and place and to have some recollection of events. Instead, the opinion articulated a two-prong test as the minimum constitutional standard for adjudicative competency. Commonly known as the Dusky standard, the Supreme Court held that competence to stand trial hinges on "whether [a defendant] has sufficient present ability to consult with his lawyer with a reasonable degree of rational understanding—and whether he has a rational as well as factual understanding of the proceedings against him" (*Dusky v. United States*, 1960). Legally, all criminal defendants are presumed competent to stand trial, which is rebuttable by a preponderance of the evidence.

In *Drope v. Missouri*, building upon its earlier decision in *Dusky,* the Supreme Court clarified that the issue of competency may be raised at any point in the adjudication process by either party or the court, *sua sponte* (*Drope v. Missouri*, 1975). Although the Supreme Court did not designate specific criteria that would invariably trigger bona fide concerns about a defendant's competence to stand trial, it supported a low constitutional threshold for raising the need for a competency hearing. Generally, once the issue of competency is raised, the trial court will order the defendant to undergo a forensic evaluation by a mental health professional. While trial court judges are tasked with the ultimate decision regarding a defendant's competence to stand trial, they commonly adopt the opinions of the forensic evaluators (Roesch et al., n.d.).

There are an estimated 160,000 annual evaluations for competency to stand trial. Of the 8%–15% of defendants whose attorneys have concerns about trial competency, it is estimated that 20%–30% are initially found incompetent (Wall & Lee, 2020). For defendants found incompetent to stand trial, the legal proceedings are suspended while they undergo a process of restoration to competency. Pursuant to the 1972 Supreme Court landmark decision of *Jackson v. Indiana*, criminal defendants who are incompetent to stand trial cannot be confined "for more than the reasonable period of time necessary to determine whether there is a substantial probability that they will attain that capacity in the foreseeable future" (*Jackson v. Indiana*, 1972).

Within these constitutional contours, each state has its own competence to stand trial statutes that set forth the specific state procedures for competency evaluation and restoration of competency. For instance, some states have specific time limits for restoring a defendant's competency to stand trial, while others set forth the maximum allowed time for competency restoration as a proportion of the defendant's potential criminal sentence. The American Academy of

Psychiatry and the Law Practice Guideline for the Evaluation of Competence to Stand Trial provides a table outlining each state's legal provisions for competence to stand trial, including the definition of incompetence and the test for competency restoration, the types of mental health professionals who may perform a forensic competency evaluation of the defendant, the settings where a defendant may undergo restoration to competency, and the maximum time period for restoration (Mossman et al., 2007).

*Not Guilty by Reason of Insanity*

An individual's criminal liability stems from the presence of two essential elements: (1) *actus reus*, which is defined as the prohibited act and (2) *mens rea,* which is defined as the guilty state of mind. To convict a defendant of a crime, the government must prove, beyond a reasonable doubt, each element of the charged criminal offense. Under the United States Constitution, states have the discretion to enact their own statutory provisions that define a defendant's criminal responsibility for each offense and to determine whether legal insanity can be raised as an affirmative defense to excuse the defendant's criminal conduct.

The insanity defense is rooted in the long-standing legal principle that certain defendants should not be punished for the criminal offenses they committed while they were mentally unwell. This principle has evolved into a variety of historical formulations of the insanity defense, including the following: (a) the strict "wild beast" standard that required a defendant to be "totally deprived of his understanding and memory, so as to not know what he is doing, no more than an infant, a brute or a wild beast," (b) the "irresistible impulse" standard that required a defendant's mental illness to be "the acting power within [the defendant's conduct] which he could not resist," and (c) the 1843 M'Naghten rule from England that required an insane defendant to not know either the nature and quality or the wrongfulness of the offense due to severe mental illness or intellectual disability (West & Noffsinger, 2006). Against this historical backdrop, modern American jurisprudence comprises a legal patchwork of several different state and federal insanity standards.

While the United States Constitution does not require the government to establish an insanity defense as a matter of fundamental fairness, most U.S. jurisdictions have adopted specific criteria for evaluating a defendant's criminal responsibility. In approximately 35 of the 50 states, a modern version of the M'Naghten standard is used. An additional 10 states added an 'irresistible impulse' component, which was considered an additional part of the insanity test by the American Legal Institute (ALI) 1955 Model Penal Code. In states with ALI language, a defendant may either meet the M'Naghten standard or the 'irresistible impulse' standard—meaning that either the defendant, because of mental illness or intellectual disability, did not know the wrongfulness of their acts or was unable to comport their behavior to the requirements of the law. New Hampshire uses a so-called 'product test.' This is the broadest test, which considers whether the behavior was a product of mental illness (separate from knowledge of wrongfulness). Notwithstanding the same, four states (Idaho, Kansas, Montana, and Utah) have no provision for a finding of not guilty by reason of insanity (NGRI). The American Academy of Psychiatry and the Law Practice Guideline for Forensic Psychiatric Evaluation of Defendants Raising the Insanity Defense provides tables compiling the state and federal legal standards for criminal responsibility, including whether each provided insanity defense originated from the M'Naghten or ALI historical standard, the legal terminology used to describe insanity, and any explicitly identified exclusions (Janofsky et al., 2014).

Notably, as an alternative to the insanity defense, various states recognize a special verdict of 'guilty but mentally ill' (Lyons, 2019) for defendants who are found to have a mental illness that does not meet the standard for legal insanity. Generally, they are sentenced in the same manner as other guilty defendants but may be eligible to receive psychiatric treatment in a forensic hospital while serving their sentence.

## Forensic Psychiatry System

### *Structure and Function of the United States' Forensic Psychiatry System*

The United States' forensic psychiatry system serves as a bridge between the behavioral health and judicial systems, delivering necessary mental health services for court-involved people with psychiatric illnesses. The system is highly decentralized and multilayered, as each state has its own framework of laws and regulations governing the organization and operation of forensic mental health programs. In addition, courts exercise significant control over the psychiatric evaluation and treatment process for forensic patients.

In the United States, forensic mental health hospitals are part of the state systems and are often former state hospitals. More than 80% of forensic patients are treated in maximum- and medium-security public (state and county) psychiatric hospitals run by state departments of mental health (Lutterman, 2022). As of 2020, there were 177 state-operated psychiatric hospitals across the United States (National Association of State Mental Health Program Directors Research Institute [NASMHPD], 2021a). The number of public hospitals in each state ranged from a low of only one hospital in 14 states (Alaska, Arizona, Arkansas, Hawai'i, Montana, New Hampshire, New Mexico, North Dakota, Rhode Island, South Dakota, Oregon, Utah, Vermont, and Wyoming) and the District of Columbia, to a high of 23 hospitals in the state of New York, with the median state operating two separate hospitals (NASMHPD Research Institute, 2021a). There are significant state-to-state differences in the structure of state psychiatric hospitals and the types of mental health services they deliver. States vary in how they allocate their hospital beds to serve civil and forensic populations, who are usually treated in different hospital wards or specialized facilities, given that they require distinct services and programming.

State psychiatric hospital beds have dramatically declined over the past 65 years. They reached a historic low of 36,150 total beds in 2023, with 18,848 (52%) allocated to manage forensic populations (Silver & Hancq, 2024). As the demand for inpatient forensic services increased, largely driven by the explosion of pre-trial defendants in need of competence evaluation or restoration, an increasing majority of states experienced shortages of inpatient psychiatric beds (NASMHPD Research Institute, 2021a). The median forensic bed occupancy rate in 2023 was 96% (Silver & Hancq, 2024). Most states maintained wait-lists for state inpatient psychiatric beds; the average wait time varied substantially from state to state, with many individuals spending time in jail for a forensic bed to open. In 2023, more than 5,500 court-involved individuals in jails were waiting for a forensic hospital bed (Silver & Hancq, 2024). States with the longest wait times included Texas, Mississippi, Wyoming, and Louisiana, and a growing number of states have been sued over their forensic bed waiting times (Fuller et al., 2016).

In recent years, some states have built specialized psychiatric units within correctional facilities run by their Department of Corrections to care for incarcerated people with mental illness (Bloom et al., 2008). Three states (Kentucky, New Hampshire, and South Dakota) exclusively utilize prison forensic units to provide forensic mental health services to incarcerated individuals (Bloom et al., 2008). In addition, as of 2016, nine states (Arizona, California, Colorado, Florida, Georgia, Louisiana, Tennessee, Texas, and Virginia) have developed alternative jail-based competency restoration programs (Wik, 2016). The Federal Bureau of Justice Statistics indicates that it is planning to include the identification of such resources in future surveys of jails and prisons. Still, no comprehensive data about the treatment capacity of these units is currently available (Lutterman, 2022).

The most common hospital-based forensic services involve treatment for restoration to competency to stand trial (CST) and of those found legally insane. Still, states are embracing less restrictive, community-based alternatives for select court-involved individuals. Most CST evaluations are conducted on an outpatient basis in court clinics and jails (NASMHPD Research Institute, 2021b). Courts can also mandate that CST evaluations be completed in forensic hospitals, but this is infrequent. Around 30% of evaluated defendants are subsequently found to be incompetent to stand trial (IST) and then frequently involuntarily committed to a forensic psychiatric hospital for CST restoration.

Additionally, formal outpatient competency restoration programs have been developed in 15 states (Arkansas, California, Colorado, Connecticut, Florida, Georgia, Hawai'i, Louisiana, Nevada, Ohio, Oregon, Tennessee, Texas, Virginia, and Wisconsin) and the District of Columbia for court-involved individuals charged with low-level misdemeanor or nonviolent felony charges (Wik, 2018). As of 2021, almost 3,000 IST defendants received outpatient competency restoration services per year (NASMHPD Research Institute, 2021c). Overall, IST defendants who received forensic services as inpatients had the highest likelihood of regaining CST, usually within six months (Danzer et al., 2019).

States differ considerably in how they define a reasonable time frame for competency restoration, and 27 states do not have a specific statutory time limit (NASMHPD Research Institute, 2021c). IST defendants unable to be restored to competency are adjudicated as incompetent to stand trial and unrestorable (ISTU) and have their criminal charges dismissed, typically without prejudice (Bloom & Kirkorsky, 2020). In most states, ISTU defendants are either released to the community or psychiatrically hospitalized under regular civil commitment procedures. A handful of states have expanded their civil commitment statutes, adding special procedures to pursue long-term commitment of defendants adjudicated as ISTU and dangerous to others.

Individuals found not guilty by reason of insanity (NGRI) are relieved of criminal responsibility. However, NGRI acquittees are most commonly committed to the hospital based on evidence of a current mental illness and dangerousness (Hailey-Dunsheath & Price, 2022) The purpose of the commitment is twofold: (1) to provide mental health treatment and (2) to protect society and the NGRI acquittee from their potential dangerousness. Forensic psychiatrists may perform evaluations after the finding of NGRI to consider this need for treatment and risk. NGRI acquittees typically remain hospitalized in forensic mental health units for extended periods that range from months to years, and it is possible for the commitment to exceed the maximum penal sentence for the charged offense (Wendzel, 2020). In the United States, the average length of stay after a finding of NGRI was over four years (1,592 days), which ranged from a low of almost two years (640 days) in Tennessee to a high of almost nine years (3,175 days) in Colorado (Fuller et al., 2016). In 2023, NGRI acquittees occupied around 30% of forensic psychiatric beds (Silver & Hancq, 2024).

Since the 1990s, more than 20 states and the federal government have enacted legislation allowing for civil commitment of certain people who have committed sex offenses, classified as sexually violent persons/predators, usually for several years following the completion of their criminal sentence. As of 2018, over 6,300 individuals were detained under these statutes (Hoppe et al., 2020).

### *Exiting the System*

State laws and the courts control hospital admission and discharge decisions for involuntarily committed forensic patients. To exit the forensic system, an application to the court may include forensic psychiatric reports and testimony regarding risk. Further, some states utilize separate boards to make formal discharge recommendations to the court. The length of stay varies depending on the severity of the patient's criminal and mental health status.

IST defendants who are court-ordered for CST restoration will exit the forensic system once they are restored to competency in up to 90% of cases (West &

Noffsinger, 2006), usually within six months (Danzer et al., 2019). State psychiatric hospitals have the highest rates of being restored to competency, around 80% to 90%, while the restoration rates in outpatient community-based settings were around 54% to 70%, and in jail-based restoration settings, around 55% to 86% (Danzer et al., 2019).

Under the Due Process Clause of the Fourteenth Amendment of the United States Constitution, an NGRI acquittee may be detained in a forensic state hospital "as long as he is both mentally ill and dangerous, but no longer" (*Foucha v. Louisiana*, 1992). Most states have established conditional release (CR) programs to facilitate the discharge of NGRI acquittees from the hospital to the community. Often, individuals may be granted CR after an initial period of hospital-based treatment. The CR procedures vary widely in different states. Courts generally consider whether the NGRI acquittee would present an undue risk to the community due to a mental disease or defect if released under supervision. NGRI acquittees have the burden of proof that they are entitled to CR (Wendzel, 2020). Individuals who are granted CR are required to adhere to mandated outpatient conditions, such as residing in approved housing, continuing psychiatric treatment, maintaining sobriety from drugs and alcohol, and following prohibitions on possessing weapons. Failure to do so can lead to CR revocation. Only a few states place a specific time limit on how long an NGRI acquittee may remain on CR (Finch, 2014).

There has been an increasing push for the implementation of evidence-based programs to intercept and divert people with serious mental illness from the criminal justice system to mental health treatment. Such programs tend to use the therapeutic jurisprudence (West et al., 2012) model and include community diversion centers, specialty mental health court dockets, and reentry programs linking incarcerated individuals to community mental health services upon their release.

### *Decision Makers in Forensic Psychiatry*

Many individuals are responsible for making decisions at various stages in the admission process. The final decision maker might be a judicial officer, an administrative law judge, or a panel of administrative and treating psychiatrists. Police seldom make final decisions, and experts provide advice, but they also seldom make final decisions. Decision makers about funding tend to be governmental. However, programs may be championed by judicial leaders, for example.

## Forensic Psychiatry Service (Provision of Care)

### *Forensic Patient Characteristics*

Individuals are considered forensic patients if they have been found IST or NGRI. If someone has been committed after a finding of unrestorability to CST, they may also be considered a forensic patient.

In the United States, serious mental illness has become so prevalent in jails and prisons that correctional facilities have been commonly labeled the 'new asylums.' In 44 states and the District of Columbia, a correctional facility currently holds more people with serious mental illness than the largest remaining state psychiatric hospital (Fuller et al., 2016). At least half of individuals incarcerated in correctional settings have a substance use disorder (Office of Forensic Mental Health Services, 2019). Furthermore, it is estimated that at least 20% of individuals incarcerated in jails and 15% of individuals incarcerated in state prisons have a serious mental illness (Treatment Advocacy Center, 2016). These diagnoses include psychotic disorders such as schizophrenia; affective disorders, including both major depressive disorder and bipolar disorder; personality disorders, especially antisocial personality disorder; trauma-related disorders; and intellectual and developmental disability. Among older inmates (above 50 years), it is estimated that 33.5% of those in jail and 20% of those in prison have a cognitive disability (Sabatino et al., 2022). There is also concern for possible malingering for the purpose of evading criminal prosecution.

### *Role of Forensic Psychiatrists*

Forensic psychiatrists are responsible for completing civil and criminal psychiatric evaluations in the United States. Forensic psychiatrists can work for the court or be hired by the prosecution or defense or plaintiff. Forensic psychiatrists may work for forensic hospitals, provide treatment, or work in correctional facilities to provide treatment. Forensic psychiatrists may also work in state, private, or academic settings to provide advice on civil competency, suicide risk, and danger to others. Forensic psychiatrists conduct research in many areas and provide expertise on public policy to local, state, and federal governments.

There are currently 1,952 board-certified forensic psychiatrists in the United States, per the American Board of Psychiatry and Neurology, Inc. Of these, 1,310 had their primary certification awarded in 1987 or later. However, in the United States, a psychiatrist is not required to have a forensic board certification to practice forensic psychiatry.

#### *Qualifications and Specialized Training*

Becoming a forensic psychiatrist begins with completing four years of university. Following this, an individual must complete four years of medical school and then four years of psychiatry residency. Then, there is a one-year fellowship in forensic psychiatry (Friedman, 2021). This fellowship involves didactic teaching, learning about landmark cases in the United States, completing evaluations, court reports, testimony, and correctional psychiatry experience.

*National Networks and Collaborations*

Founded in 1969, the national forensic psychiatry body in the United States is the American Academy of Psychiatry and the Law (AAPL). It is a professional organization dedicated to excellence in forensic psychiatry practice, teaching, and research. Annual meetings are held each October with scientific sessions and continuing education activities. During the Covid-19 pandemic, educational virtual sessions were added monthly. AAPL also publishes a peer-reviewed journal (*Journal of the American Academy of Psychiatry and the Law*) and a newsletter (*Newsletter of the American Academy of Psychiatry and the Law*) with legal and scientific articles.

The American Board of Psychiatry and Neurology, Inc. first recognized the subspecialty of forensic psychiatry in 1992 and established the Committee on Certification of Qualifications in Forensic Psychiatry. It sets certification standards for forensic psychiatrists and administers examinations to provide a means of identifying qualified forensic psychiatrists.

The National Association of State Mental Health Program Directors is an organization that represents state mental health commissioners/directors and their agencies, whose forensic division was established in 1982. It aims to provide a mechanism for gathering data about state forensic systems and promote the development of forensic psychiatry standards and best practices in forensic administration.

***Approaches to Assessment and Treatment***

In a forensic setting, all individuals are court-ordered to be admitted for psychiatric assessment and treatment. The treatment is focused on psychiatric symptoms. There is also special concern for possible malingering to evade criminal prosecution. The rehabilitation programs vary by location and funding.

Violence risk assessments are commonly utilized within forensic settings for a variety of purposes. These purposes include determining forensic hospital placement or security-level decisions, preparing forensic reports for the courts regarding eligibility for involuntary commitment or release from state psychiatric hospitals, and planning services or conditions for patients transitioning to less restrictive settings. Evaluating an individual's risk of violence is complex. Erroneous risk assessments can have significant consequences in forensic settings, potentially leading to either undue risk to public safety (due to underestimating violence risk) or unjustified restrictions on forensic patients' liberty (due to overestimating violence risk) (Beltrani, n.d.). To address this, most state forensic hospitals utilize standardized violence risk assessment instruments. These instruments assist mental health professionals in determining psychiatric treatment needs, determining hospital privilege levels, and evaluating the need for civil commitment of NGRI acquittees and ISTU individuals and suitability for conditional release plans (NASMHPD Research Institute, 2021d). The most frequently used standardized measure is the Historical Clinical Risk Management-20 (HCR-20), Version 3, a structured professional judgment instrument that provides a structured approach for evaluating violence risk factors while considering professional judgment within the decision-making process.

Standardized psychometric tests may also be utilized within forensic settings to aid in detecting malingering. They can be helpful in forensic psychiatric evaluations of CST or sanity at the time of the act. A common screening instrument is the Miller Forensic Assessment of Symptoms Test (M-FAST), most commonly completed by psychologists. The M-FAST consists of a 25-item structured interview and is used with other methods of detecting malingering, such as supporting clinical evidence or more comprehensive malingering testing. The Structured Interview of Reported Symptoms, 2nd Edition (SIRS-2) is a frequently used 172-item structured interview tool that was designed to assess for malingered symptoms.

A significant proportion of forensic patients in state psychiatric hospitals are individuals who were found to be IST and court-ordered to receive competency restoration services. This includes educational interventions aimed at helping IST defendants regain their ability to understand the court process and assist their attorneys in their defense and usually treatment with psychiatric medications (Wik et al., 2020). Although a vast majority of forensic psychiatric hospitals surveyed psychiatric medication as the most prevalent intervention for restoration, almost 90% also indicated that they employed didactic or psychoeducational group interventions that were commonly facilitated by specially trained staff (Pinals, 2005). In *Sell v. United States,* the Supreme Court held that states may involuntarily treat IST detainees with psychotropic medications in order to restore them to competency to stand trial when certain factors were present (such as an important governmental interest being at stake) (*Sell v. United States*, 2003).

## Strengths and Weaknesses

A strength of the forensic psychiatry system in the United States is that the provision of and funding of forensic services is delegated to the constituent states, which allows each state to structure its forensic system based on its local demands and to tailor its resources to the needs of its population. This allows the states to act as laboratories for innovation, enabling them with more efficient methods for delivering forensic services to serve as models for other states dealing with similar challenges. However, these potential benefits of decentralization have not been realized in practice due to the lack of a robust centralized system of data collection from each state. Rather, there is currently a scarcity of easily accessible nationwide data regarding forensic populations, despite a significant proportion of publicly financed institutional resources being devoted to managing this cohort (Bloom & Novosad, 2017).

Another weakness relates to the availability of support and reintegration programming, as well as follow-up for those being released into the community. Studies have shown that the five-year rearrest rate for people with serious mental illness is approximately 40% for those discharged from psychiatric hospitals and 60% for those released from correctional facilities (Torrey et al., 2017). This could be ameliorated in part by adequate available evidence-based support to assist people with serious mental illness as they reenter their communities.

## References

American Bar Association. (2022). *Understanding stare decisis*. Retrieved from https://www.americanbar.org/groups/public_education/publications/preview_home/understand-stare-decisis/

Beltrani, A. (n.d.). *An introduction to violence risk assessments*. Palo Alto University. Retrieved from https://concept.paloaltou.edu/resources/business-of-practice-blog/intro-violence-risk-assessments#:~:text=Violence%20risk%20assessment%20is%20a,health%20care%2C%20and%20higher%20education.

Bloom, J. D., & Kirkorsky, S. E. (2020). Incompetent to stand trial, not restorable, and dangerous. *Journal of the American Academy of Psychiatry and the Law*, *48*(2), 169–177.

Bloom, J. D., Krishnan, B., & Lockey, C. (2008). The majority of inpatient psychiatric beds should not be appropriated by the forensic system. *Journal of the American Academy of Psychiatry and the Law*, *36*, 438–442.

Bloom, J. D., & Novosad, D. (2017). The forensic mental health services census of forensic populations in state facilities. *Journal of the American Academy of Psychiatry and the Law*, *45*(4), 447–451.

Congressional Research Service. (2023). *Federal and state courts: Structure and interaction*. Retrieved from https://crsreports.congress.gov/product/pdf/R/R47641

Danzer, G., Wheeler, E., April, A., & Wasser, T. (2019). Competency restoration for adult defendants in different treatment environments. *Journal of the American Academy of Psychiatry and the Law*, *47*(1). https://doi.org/10.29158/JAAPL.003819-19

*Drope v. Missouri*, 420 U.S. 162 (1975).

*Dusky v. United States*, 362 U.S. 402 (1960).

Erler, E. (1986/1992). *Articles from the encyclopedia of the American Constitution*. Macmillan Publishing Company. Retrieved from https://www.claremont.org/old/js/ckeditor/ckfinder/userfiles/files/Encyclopedia-Amer-Const-Arts.pdf

Finch, W. L. (2014). *White paper: Forensic mental health services in the United States*. National Association of State Mental Health Program Directors.

*Foucha v. Louisiana*, 504 U.S. 71 (1992).

Freedman, M. H. (1998). Our constitutionalized adversary system. *Chapman Law Review*, *1*(57), 57–90.

Friedman, S. H. (2021). *Forensic psychiatry and crime fiction*. Retrieved from https://www.crimefiles.co.uk/author-post/2020/08/06/forensic-psychiatrists-and-crime-fiction-top-ten-myths-corrected-by-susan-hatters-friedman-md/

Fuller, D. A., Sinclair, E., Geller, J., Quanbeck, C., & Snook, J. (2016). *Going, going, gone: Trends and consequences of eliminating state psychiatric beds (updated for Q2 data)*. Treatment Advocacy Center. Retrieved from https://www.treatmentadvocacycenter.org/storage/documents/going-going-gone.pdf

Hailey-Dunsheath, M., & Price, J. (2022). *An appellate defender's guide to the insanity defense and not guilty by reason of insanity commitments*. First District Appellate Project Training Webinar, First District Appellate Project.

Hoppe, T., Meyer, I. H., DeOrio, S., & others. (2020). *Civil commitment of people convicted of sex offenses in the United States*. UCLA School of Law, Williams Institute. Retrieved from https://williamsinstitute.law.ucla.edu/wp-content/uploads/SVP-Civil-Commitments-Oct-2020.pdf

*Jackson v. Indiana*, 406 U.S. 715 (1972).

Janofsky, J. S., Hanson, A., Candilis, P. J., & Myers, W. C. (2014). AAPL practice guideline for forensic psychiatric evaluation of defendants raising the insanity defense. *Journal of the American Academy of Psychiatry and the Law*, *42*(4), S1–S76.

Lutterman, T. (2022). *Trends in psychiatric inpatient capacity, United States and each state, 1970 to 2018*. National Association of State Mental Health Program Directors.

Lyons, C. L. (2019). *The insanity defense*. CQ Researcher. https://doi.org/10.4135/cqresrre20191011

Mossman, D., Noffsinger, S. G., Ash, P., Frierson, R. L., & American Academy of Psychiatry and the Law. (2007). AAPL practice guideline for the forensic psychiatric evaluation of competence to stand trial (2007 supplement). *Journal of the American Academy of Psychiatry and the Law*, *35*(4), S1–S72.

NASMHPD Research Institute. (2021b). *Competency to stand trial: Use of state hospitals, community-based, and jail-based approaches*. NRI's 2020–2021 State Profiles. Retrieved from https://www.nri-inc.org/media/qhadgyzj/nri_2020_profiles_-*competency_to_stand_trial_evaluations*-_use_of_state_hospitals-_community-based-_and_jail-based_approaches-_november_2021.pdf

NASMHPD Research Institute. (2021c). *Competency restoration: Use of state hospitals, community-based, and jail-based approaches*. NRI's 2020–2021 State Profiles. Retrieved from https://www.nri-inc.org/profiles/

NASMHPD Research Institute. (2021d). *Assessing violence risk using standardized measures and their application to legal "dangerousness"*. NRI's 2020–2021 State Profiles. Retrieved from https://www.nri-inc.org/profiles/

National Association of State Mental Health Program Directors (NASMHPD) Research Institute. (2021a). *Use of state psychiatric hospitals: NRI's 2020–2021 state profiles*. Retrieved from https://www.nri-inc.org/profiles/

Office of Forensic Mental Health Services. (2019). *Washington state legal system guide to forensic mental health services*. Washington State Department of Social & Health Services. Retrieved from https://www.dshs.wa.gov/sites/default/files/BHSIA/FMHS/WAStateLegalSystemGuidetoForensicMentalHealth.pdf

Pinals, D. A. (2005). When two roads meet: Restoration of competence to stand trial from a clinical perspective. *Criminal & Civil Confinement*, *31*, 81–108.

Roesch, R., Zapf, P. A., Golding, S. L., & Skeem, J. L. (n.d.). *Defining and assessing competency to stand trial*. Retrieved from https://www.justice.gov/sites/default/files/eoir/legacy/2014/08/15/Defining_and_Assessing_Competency_to_Stand_Trial.pdf

Sabatino, C., et al. (2022). *Persons living with dementia in the criminal legal system*. American Bar Association Commission on Law & Aging. Retrieved from https://www.nri-inc.org/media/0h0fbcju/2022-dementia-crim-just-rpt.pdf

*Sell v. United States*, 539 U.S. 169 (2003).

Silver, S., & Hancq, E. S. (2024). *Prevention over punishment: Finding the right balance of civil and forensic state psychiatric hospital beds*. Treatment Advocacy Center. Retrieved from https://www.treatmentadvocacycenter.org/reports_publications/state-psychiatric-hospital-beds/

Steenken, B., & Brooks, T. M. (n.d.). *Sources of American law: An introduction to legal research.* Retrieved from https://sourcesofamericanlaw.lawbooks.cali.org/chapter/the-united-states-legal-system/

Torrey, E. F., Dailey, L., Lamb, H. R., Sinclair, E., & Snook, J. (2017). *Treat or repeat: A state survey of serious mental illness, major crimes, and community treatment.* Treatment Advocacy Center. https://www.treatmentadvocacycenter.org/treat-or-repeat

Treatment Advocacy Center. (2016). *Serious Mental Illness (SMI) prevalence in jails and prisons.* Treatment Advocacy Center. Retrieved from https://www.treatmentadvocacycenter.org/reports_publications/serious-mental-illness-prevalence-in-jails-and-prisons/

United States Courts. (n.d.). *Comparing federal and state courts.* Retrieved from https://www.uscourts.gov/about-federal-courts/court-role-and-structure/comparing-federal-state-courts#:~:text=As%20the%20supreme%20law%20of,an%20intermediate%20Court%20of%20Appeals

Wall, B., & Lee, R. (2020). Assessing competency to stand trial. *Psychiatric Times, 37*(10), 14–16.

Wendzel, B. (2020). Not guilty, yet continuously confined: Reforming the insanity defense. *American Criminal Law Review, 57*(2), 391–411.

West, S., Friedman, S. H., & Shand, J. P. (2012). Therapeutic jurisprudence. In A. Jamieson, & A. Moenssens (Eds.), *Encyclopedia of forensic sciences* (2nd ed.). John Wiley & Sons.

West, S., & Noffsinger, S. (2006). Is this patient not guilty by reason of insanity? *Current Psychiatry, 5*(8), 54–62.

Wik, A. (2016). *Alternatives to inpatient competency restoration programs: Jail-based competency restoration programs.* National Association of State Mental Health Program Directors Research Institute. Retrieved from https://www.nri-inc.org/media/1500/jbcr_website-format_oct2018.pdf

Wik, A. (2018). *Alternatives to inpatient competency restoration programs: Community-based competency restoration programs.* National Association of State Mental Health Program Directors Research Institute. Retrieved from https://www.nri-inc.org/media/1508/ocr_website-format_oct2018.pdf

Wik, A., Hollen, V., & Fisher, W. H. (2020). Forensic patients in state psychiatric hospitals: 1999–2016. *CNS Spectrums, 25*, 196–206.

# Part II

# South America

# 4 Argentina

*María José Lescano and Jorge Oscar Folino*

## Brief Description

| | |
|---|---|
| **Location** | Argentina is a country in southeastern South America. |
| **Size** | 2,780,400 km$^2$ |
| **Population** | 46,044,703 |
| **Languages** | The official language of Argentina is Spanish. However, the country recognizes and protects Indigenous languages, such as Quechua, Mapudungun, and Guaraní, in certain regions. |
| **Political system** | Argentina is a federal, republican, representative democracy with a presidential system of government. The country has 23 provinces and one autonomous city (Buenos Aires). Each province has its own constitution and government structures, but all must adhere to the National Constitution. The federal government comprises three branches: the executive (president), the legislative (National Congress: Chamber of Deputies and Senate), and the judiciary, with the Supreme Court as the highest court in the land. |

## Legal System

Argentina has two judicial systems: federal and provincial. Although a penal code (Congress of the Argentine Nation [*Congreso de la Nación Argentina*], 1921) is enforced throughout the country, each province has its own procedural code. The Argentine National Constitution (*Constitución de la Nación Argentina*) establishes that Argentina adopts a representative, republican, and federal form of government. Each province has the autonomy to create its own institutional framework and enact its own procedural codes for criminal, civil, and commercial matters. However, all provinces must protect individual rights and guarantees recognized by the Constitution for all citizens.

In 1994, an amendment to the Constitution established that human rights treaties must be considered an inseparable part of the constitutional text, reinforcing previously recognized rights and guarantees. This reflects Argentina's commitment to expanding fundamental rights, and such political decisions have driven a significant legal reform process, including legislation related to mental health.

DOI: 10.4324/9781003376248-6

Argentina has recently implemented new legislation and regulations focusing on the overlap between mental health and the legal system, specifically in forensic psychiatry. The National Mental Health Law No. 26657, enacted in 2010, includes principles and rights derived from various human rights treaties based on the recognition of an individual's dignity as an essential component of any state intervention (Congress of the Argentine Nation [*Congreso de la Nación Argentina*], 2010). This legislation plays a pivotal role in defining the rights and protections of individuals with mental health conditions. However, it should be noted that general mental health laws may not explicitly cover the intersection of forensic psychiatry and criminal proceedings.

As a federal system, each province in Argentina may have laws governing mental health that regulate procedures and identify the institutions responsible for intervening in cases involving individuals with mental illnesses. For example, Law No. 14580, titled 'Right to Mental Health Protection,' was enacted by the Province of Buenos Aires in 2014 and is similar to national regulations (Senate of the Province of Buenos Aires [*Senado de la Provincia de Buenos Aires*], 2014). This regulation aims to ensure that residents of the Province of Buenos Aires have access to services and strives to promote and protect the mental health of all citizens.

### *Mental Health Laws: Fitness to Stand Trial and Criminal Responsibility*

Since 1921, the Argentine Penal Code has specified the 'insanity defense' and preventive measures to be taken in cases involving individuals deemed dangerous. A defendant is found 'inimputable' (equivalent to the U.S. classification of not guilty by reason of insanity) under the provisions of Article 34 of the National Penal Code. Based on Section 1, Article 34 of the National Penal Code, the offender is exempt from punishment if they

> have not been able to understand its criminality, nor to govern their actions at the time of the event, either due to inadequacy of their abilities, morbid alterations of the mind, unconscious state, error, or ignorance which cannot be attributed to their determination.
>
> (Congress of the Argentine Nation [*Congreso de la Nación Argentina*], 1921)

It should be noted that the Argentinian standard includes conditions other than mental disorders.

When a perceived risk exists, also known as 'dangerousness,' as defined in the code, the courts may order the defendant to be confined in a forensic hospital or another health institution for security purposes. Forensic experts assess this risk, a crucial factor in determining the court's decision. Individuals deemed incompetent may be legally overseen by the penal execution court or family courts to manage the case.

Two matters require clarification: evaluating the mental capacity of the accused during the commission of the crime and throughout the legal proceedings. If an individual, while committing a crime, was completely unconscious or had a severe mental disorder that prevented them from understanding the legal implications or controlling their behavior, they cannot be held criminally responsible. If such an individual poses a certain and imminent danger to themselves or others, a security measure may be imposed in a suitable facility to ensure they receive the necessary medical treatment.

In certain cases, a person may be able to comprehend their actions when they commit a crime. However, their mental health may be impacted later on during the investigation. In cases where there is no specific legal proceeding to determine if the defendant is fit to stand trial, procedural codes allow the legal process to be suspended until the individual has recovered or can be declared inimputable. If this happens, the case will be archived, and urgent intervention will be sought from a family court.

The Argentine legal system acknowledges the significance of upholding the rights of individuals with mental health conditions. The National Mental Health Law (Congress of the Argentine Nation [*Congreso de la Nación Argentina*], 2010) and other related regulations emphasize protecting the rights of individuals with mental disorders, including those involved in criminal proceedings. Argentina's new rights-based paradigm addresses mental health issues, ensuring individuals have certainty about their rights. This includes the right to defense, which must be guaranteed in any judicial process. The idea that confining individuals with psychiatric disorders is beneficial from a therapeutic standpoint has been abandoned. The National Mental Health Law has eliminated the old approach of the mental health system, which was based on confinement. The system that used to rely on compulsory psychiatric admission for indefinite periods is now shifting toward practices that are more focused on protecting the rights of the patient.

Today, the law operates on the principle that health should be approached through an interdisciplinary framework, emphasizing inclusive and community-based care. The health system is expected to prioritize the restoration of individual rights through substantial state intervention, while any measures that restrict freedom should be used only as a last resort.

The National Mental Health Law (Congress of the Argentine Nation [*Congreso de la Nación Argentina*], 2010) affirms that mental health is shaped by historical, socioeconomic, cultural, biological, and psychological factors. Promoting and preserving mental health involves a socially constructed dynamic grounded in respect for each individual's human and social rights. As a result, addressing mental health conditions requires coordinated and well-defined legal and institutional interventions to ensure greater freedom and contribute to the individual's recovery in an integrative, community-based context.

These principles have significantly transformed how the criminal justice system intervenes in such cases, moving away from historically rooted concepts of 'dangerousness' influenced by the Positivist School (Ferri, 1933). In this context, it is essential to guarantee the individual the greatest degree of freedom possible. When there is a clear and imminent risk to oneself or others, any restrictive security measure must be applied cautiously and under strict professional supervision.

Penal doctrine and jurisprudence have emphasized the need to eliminate abusive and rights-violating practices associated with compulsory psychiatric hospitalization. These practices have revealed serious flaws in the criminal justice system, in which individuals were rendered invisible and subjected to paternalistic or institutionalized forms of treatment. Even from a criminal justice perspective, respecting human rights requires ensuring the patient's right to health. This implies that the state should promote recovery through alternative measures rather than hospitalization and encourage strong support from the patient's family and community.

### *Decision Makers in Forensic Psychiatry*

In Argentina, experts play an important role in the judicial process. However, judges ultimately have the final say in matters such as involuntary commitment, involuntary treatment, and release in both criminal and civil cases. These decisions are typically based on reports from forensic psychiatrists working for the court or from psychiatrists affiliated with mental health facilities, including those within the penitentiary service. A jurisdiction's legal framework and regulations may influence the criteria used to determine the appropriate facility for individuals found inimputable. Legal authorities may consider factors such as the individual's mental health condition, the nature of the offense, and the recommendations of mental health professionals.

The specific reasons for referral can vary depending on the jurisdiction, the unique circumstances of the case, and the availability of services in the region. Decisions are often made through a collaborative process involving legal, psychiatric, and healthcare professionals. Referral to an institution under the Ministry of Health may require coordination with mental health services and government-provided resources. Public treatment options and infrastructure availability within the healthcare system can significantly influence the outcome.

## Forensic Psychiatry System

### *Structure and Function of the Forensic Psychiatric System in Argentina*

A person found to be inimputable may be subject to involuntary commitment in a forensic hospital, private clinic, or an institution designated by the Ministry of Health, depending on the circumstances related to 'dangerousness.' Most provinces have a formal forensic system, with some operating specialized forensic hospitals and others maintaining smaller forensic units.

When a defendant is found inimputable in Argentina, legal proceedings shift from traditional criminal penalties to the determination of appropriate security measures and mental health treatment. Individuals may receive care in specialized psychiatric institutions within the penitentiary system or through public or private healthcare systems. During the commitment period, psychiatric evaluations are conducted as needed or regularly to guide legal decisions regarding the individual's status. According to the National Mental Health Law, a review board must be established within the institutional framework of the Ministry of Defense. This implementation is in progress, and review boards are expected to be available across all jurisdictions.

### *Role of Forensic Psychiatry*

In Argentina, the primary role of a forensic psychiatrist is to provide expert testimony to the court based on professional assessment and diagnosis. Unlike in other countries—where the scope of forensic psychiatry may include treatment within prisons and forensic hospitals or collaboration with law enforcement—the practice in Argentina remains more limited. Although academic efforts have been made to conceptually expand the field to include these roles, the impact of such efforts remains unclear.

### *Forensic Patient Characteristics, Assessment, and Provision of Care*

There is limited information available in Argentina regarding the demographics and mental health diagnoses of forensic patients. Some early reports on this topic were published in the Province of Buenos Aires (Folino et al., 2000). More recent national-level data provide information on the number of individuals found inimputable and the general prison population (National Directorate of Criminal Policy in Justice and Criminal Legislation [*Dirección Nacional de Política Criminal en Materia de Justicia y Legislación Penal*], 2021). According to the most recent source, between 2007 and 2021, the average national population of individuals found inimputable was 364 (range: 241–590), representing between 0.3% and 1.2% of the total prison population.

The category of 'forensic patient' refers to individuals found inimputable and placed in psychiatric facilities. However, individuals under civil commitment are not classified as forensic patients. Those facing criminal charges while also living with mental health conditions often experience additional vulnerabilities, including economic hardship, social instability, and family-related challenges. These conditions are commonly observed among populations in prisons and forensic hospitals, where rates of substance use disorders are high. Substance use may impair individuals' ability to comply with the law and can further complicate adherence to treatment (Folino & Benitez, 2006a, 2006b; Folino & Urrutia, 2001).

The decision to place individuals found inimputable in a forensic hospital, private clinic, or an institution under the Ministry of Health depends on several factors. These include the required level of security and supervision, the availability of qualified mental health professionals capable of managing violent behaviors, and the proximity to the individual's family. Forensic hospitals typically provide a higher level of security and supervision than private clinics. The choice of referral may also depend on the availability of facilities in a given region.

In provinces with specialized forensic hospitals, individuals are often referred there. In areas lacking such facilities, smaller forensic units or private clinics may be used instead. Forensic hospitals are staffed with professionals and equipped with resources specifically designed to manage individuals with mental health conditions who are involved in the criminal justice system. A person who requires more complex or specialized psychiatric care may be referred to an appropriate facility through the Public Health Service of Argentina.

In addition to provincial-level facilities, the Federal Penitentiary Service and the Argentine Inter-ministerial Mental Health Program—established by the Ministry of Justice and Human Rights and the Ministry of Health of the Nation—also play key roles in the forensic mental health system (Argentine Federal Penitentiary Service [*Servicio Penitenciario Federal Argentino*], 2012). This program aims to address the challenges faced by individuals housed in psychiatric units within the Federal Penitentiary Service, as well as in other detention facilities.

There has been a lack of established specialized treatment programs for individuals with a history of violent or sexual offenses. Some federal programs have been developed to assist specific forensic subpopulations, including individuals who have committed sexual offenses (Argentine Federal Penitentiary Service [*Servicio Penitenciario Federal Argentino*], 2015). However, the effectiveness of these programs has not yet been formally evaluated (National Program on Science and Justice [*Programa Nacional de Ciencia y Justicia*], 2022).

In terms of evaluation, the Province of Buenos Aires implemented a violence risk-assessment program whose methods and findings were gradually shared across Argentina and other Latin American countries (Folino et al., 2016; Folino, Marengo et al., 2004; León-Mayer et al., 2014; Ochoa Balarezo et al., 2016; Ochoa et al., 2017; Singh et al., 2013). The program utilized widely recognized instruments such as the Hare PCL-R (Hare, 2003; Folino et al., 2003; Folino & Castillo, 2006; Folino & Hare, 2005; Folino & Mendicoa, 2006); Historical, Clinical, Risk Management (HCR)-20 (Folino, 2003; Folino, Castillo, et al., 2004; Webster et al., 1997); Violence Risk Appraisal Guide (VRAG) (Folino, 2009, 2015; Harris et al., 2015); and Spousal Assault Risk Assessment Guide (SARA) (Arbach-Lucioni & Folino, 2021; Folino, 2004; Kropp et al., 1995). The reliability and validity of these instruments were tested in multiple studies, including the first Latin American cohort study of forensic patients and parole-released individuals over a 10-year follow-up period (Folino, 2015; Folino, Arado, et al., 2004; Folino et al., 2005).

More recently, a new approach to assessing juvenile competence to stand trial was developed in Argentina. This research contributed to the adaptation of the MacArthur Competence Assessment Tool-Criminal Adjudication (Hoge et al., 1999) for use in juvenile court proceedings. The adapted tool is known as the *Test de competencia para el desempeño en proceso del fuero de responsabilidad penal juvenil MacArthur: Versión Argentina* (MacCAT-CA: VA) (Folino et al., 2014; León-Mayer et al., 2016).

### *Length of Stay and Exiting the System*

To exit the forensic system, an individual must no longer be considered a risk to themselves or others. If the individual is found guilty, the criminal court is responsible for determining an appropriate sentence based on the offense. However, if the person is found inimputable, the case must be transferred to family court. There is no set length of stay for individuals under forensic measures, and, in many cases, a period of supervised release may precede full release. The law does not establish a fixed timeline for granting freedom, as this depends on the absence of risk. However, the Supreme Court has ruled that judges must set a maximum duration for such measures to comply with the principle of proportionality, considering the severity of the offense committed.

## Forensic Psychiatry Training

In Argentina, specialized forensic psychiatrists may receive training through various pathways. One common option is postgraduate specialization in legal medicine, open to psychiatrists and other medical professionals. This program typically lasts around two years and is offered by various universities and medical associations. It covers various medical topics relevant to the legal system, including pathology, injury assessment, capacity evaluations, and risk assessment. In some cases, general physicians with training in legal medicine may also carry out certain aspects of forensic psychiatric work. Besides these established academic approaches, forensic psychiatrists can enhance their knowledge through supervised practical experience or short courses. These short-certified programs do not lead to an academic degree but provide valuable training and a solid foundation for competing for a forensic psychiatry position.

Until 1998, the traditional legal medicine track was the most common route for professionals entering the field. However, a second pathway emerged with the introduction of the Master Course in Forensic Psychiatry at the National University of La Plata and the Master Course in Forensic Mental Health. These programs were developed in response to the recognized need for psychiatrists and other professionals to receive in-depth training specific to the forensic context (Folino & Raverta, 2006). The master's program is a two-year course totaling

1,200 hours and is also available to international students. It can be completed in a blended format, combining online and in-person components.

### *National Networks and Collaborations*

In Argentina, there are two prominent psychiatric organizations related to forensic psychiatry. The first is the Association of Psychiatrists of Argentina (*Asociación de Psiquiatras de Argentina*), which includes a dedicated chapter on forensic psychiatry. The second is the Association of Forensic Doctors of the Argentine Republic (*Asociación de Médicos Forenses de la República Argentina*), which is composed of physicians employed by the courts and the police force, including forensic psychiatrists. This association organizes annual local, national, and international conferences.

## Strengths and Weaknesses

Argentina's forensic psychiatry system offers a notable advantage: the court covers the costs of forensic experts, providing individuals involved in criminal or civil proceedings with access to expert evaluations at no personal expense. However, the system's main limitation is the lack of comprehensive specialized treatment programs and the absence of systematic, community-based follow-up. Although such programs remain limited, Argentina has made significant progress in violence risk assessment and research on recidivism, becoming the first Latin American country to develop and implement these practices. Additionally, Argentina established the first official university-level master's program in forensic psychiatry in the region.

For over two decades, the Province of Buenos Aires risk-assessment program has generated extensive data on recidivism, risk factors, and the effectiveness of assessment tools. This pioneering approach was shared with other Latin American countries. The National University of La Plata School of Medicine launched the first master's program in forensic psychiatry, supporting the training of psychiatrists across Latin America. In 2008, the program evolved into a master's program in forensic mental health, expanding its scope to include psychologists and social workers.

## References

Arbach-Lucioni, K., & Folino, J. O. (2021). La Valoración del Riesgo de Reincidencia en Imputados por Violencia contra la Pareja: un Estudio Longitudinal con la Guía SARA. *Anuario de Psicología Jurídica*, *31*, 35–44. https://doi.org/10.5093/apj2021a4

Argentine Federal Penitentiary Service [Servicio Penitenciario Federal Argentino]. (2012). Programa interministerial de salud mental argentino (PRISMA). In *Boletín Público Normativo N° 484* (Vol. 19). Ministerio de Justicia y Derechos Humanos.

Argentine Federal Penitentiary Service [Servicio Penitenciario Federal Argentino]. (2015). Programa de tratamiento para ofensores sexuales. In *Boletín Público Normativo N° 576* (Vol. 22). Ministerio de Justicia y Derechos Humanos.

Congress of the Argentine Nation [Congreso de la Nación Argentina]. (1921). *Código Penal de la Nación Argentina [Penal Code of Argentina]* (Law 11179). Boletín Nacional del 03-Nov–1921.
Congress of the Argentine Nation [Congreso de la Nación Argentina]. (2010). *Ley N° 26.657. Ley Nacional de Salud Mental*. Boletín Oficial de la Nación Argentina, 2010/12/03.
Ferri, E. (1933). *Principio de derecho criminal*. Editorial Reus.
Folino, J. O. (2003). *Evaluación de Riesgo de Violencia—HCR-20—Versión en español, adaptada y comentada*. Editorial Interfase Forense.
Folino, J. O. (2004). *Guía para la evaluación del riesgo de violencia conyugal—SARA—Versión en español adaptada y comentada*. Editorial Interfase Forense.
Folino, J. O. (2009). Investigación latinoamericana en evaluación de riesgo de violencia y psicopatía [Latin-American research on violence risk assessment and psychopathy]. *Proceedings of the XXXI Congress International Academy of Law and Mental Health*, 444.
Folino, J. O. (2015). Predictive efficacy of violence risk assessment instruments in Latin-America. *European Journal of Psychology Applied to Legal Context*, *7*(2), 51–58.
Folino, J. O., Arado, M. G., Ferrari, L. A., & Marengo, M. (2004). Prevención de recidiva delictual en abusadores de sustancias. *Revista Médica de La Plata*, *38*(3), 20–24.
Folino, J. O., Astorga, C., Sifuentes, M., Ranze, S., & Tenaglia, D. (2003). Confiabilidad de la Hare Psychopathy Checklist-Revised en población psiquiátrico forense argentina. *Alcmeon—Revista Argentina de Clínica Neuropsiquiátrica, Año XIV; V*, 5–11.
Folino, J. O., & Benitez, C. (2006a). Características del abuso de sustancias en la población carcelaria de la Provincia de Buenos Aires, Parte II. *Revista de La Facultad de Ciências Médicas de La Universidad Nacional de La Plata*, *1*(3), 53–58. Retrieved from http://revista.med.unlp.edu.ar/index.php/numeros-anteriores/10-nros-anteriores/29-octubre-2006
Folino, J. O., & Benitez, C. (2006b). Características del abuso de sustancias en población carcelaria de la Provincia de Buenos Aires, Parte I. *Revista de La Facultad de Ciências Médicas de La Universidad Nacional de La Plata*, *1*(3), 47–52. Retrieved from http://revista.med.unlp.edu.ar/index.php/numeros-anteriores/10-nros-anteriores/29-octubre-2006
Folino, J. O., Cáceres, M. S., Campos, M. L., Silveri, M., Ucín, S., & Ascazibar, M. (2005). Evaluación de factores dinámicos de riesgo de violencia. *Vertex, Revista Argentina de Psiquiatría*, *XVI*, 188–195.
Folino, J. O., & Castillo, J. L. (2006). Las facetas de la psicopatía según la Hare Psychopathy Checklist-Revised y su confiabilidad. *Vertex, Revista Argentina de Psiquiatría*, *XVII*, 325–330.
Folino, J. O., Castillo, J. L., Cáceres, M. S., Campos, M. L., Silveri, M., & Ucín, S. (2004). Confiabilidad de la versión argentina de la HCR–20. *Medicina Forense Argentina—Boletín de La Asociación de Médicos Forenses de La República Argentina*, *27*, 2–5.
Folino, J. O., & Hare, R. D. (2005). Listado revisado para verificación de la psicopatía: su estandarización y validación en la Argentina. *Acta Psiquiátrica y Psicológica de América Latina*, *51*, 94–104.
Folino, J. O., León-Mayer, E., Goldstein, N. E. S., Leonardi, M. C., & Lescano, M. J. (2014). *Test de competencia para el desempeño en proceso del fuero de responsabilidad penal juvenil MacArthur: Versión Argentina [MacCAT-CA: VA]*. Unpublished manuscript authorized for research.
Folino, J. O., & Mendicoa, G. (2006). La Psicopatía, el MMPI y la Hare PCL-R. *Alcmeon—Revista Argentina de Clínica Neuropsiquiátrica*, *13*, 43–54.
Folino, J. O., Marengo, C. M., Marchiano, S. E., & Ascazibar, M. (2004). The risk assessment program and the court of penal execution in the province of Buenos Aires,

Argentina. *International Journal of Offender Therapy and Comparative Criminology, 48*, 49–58.

Folino, J. O., & Raverta, M. J. (2006). Forensic psychiatry in Argentina: A training forum for Latin America. *American Academy of Psychiatry and the Law Newsletter, 31*, 28–29.

Folino, J. O., & Urrutia, M. I. (2001). Mental disturbances and criminological characteristics in crime-accused insane as recorded at the Judiciary Office in La Plata, Argentina, for 10 years. *International Journal of Law and Psychiatry, 24*(4–5). https://doi.org/10.1016/S0160-2527(01)00076-0

Folino, J. O., Sarmiento, D. R., & Montero Vazquez, J. (2000). Forensic psychiatric system in the Province of Buenos Aires, Argentina. *International Journal of Law and Psychiatry, 23*(5–6, Sep/Oct–Nov/Dec), 567–578.

Folino, J. O., Villaba, D. K., & Singh, J. P. (2016). Violence risk Assessment in Latin America. In J. P. Singh, S. Bjørkly, & S. Fazel (Eds.), *International perspectives on violence risk assessment* (pp. 181–191). Oxford University Press.

Hare, R. D. (2003). *The hare psychopathy checklist-revised, 2nd edition, technical manual*. Multi-Health Systems, Inc.

Harris, G. T., Rice, M. E., Quinsey, V. L., & Cormier, C. A. (2015). *Violent offenders: Appraising and managing risk* (3rd ed.). American Psychological Association.

Hoge, S. K., Bonnie, R. J., Poythress, N., & Monahan, J. (1999). *The MacArthur competence assessment tool—Criminal adjudication*. Psychological Assessment Resources, Inc.

Kropp, P. R., Hart, S. D., Webster, C. D., & Eaves, D. (1995). *Manual for the spousal assault risk assessment guide* (2nd ed.). Burnaby, British Columbia, Canada: Institute on Family Violence, Simon Fraser University.

León-Mayer, E., Cortés, M. S., & Folino, J. (2014). A multi-dimensional description of Chilean inmates. *Psicoperspectivas, 13*(1). https://doi.org/10.5027/PSICOPERSPECTIVAS-VOL13-ISSUE1-FULLTEXT-243

León-Mayer, E., Iseas, C., Campagnolo, L., Elias, C., Del Castillo, B. R., Delucchi, G., Goldstein, N. E., & Folino, J. (2016). La evaluación de la capacidad juvenil para desempeñarse en proceso judicial. *Vertex (Buenos Aires, Argentina), 27*(125).

National Directorate of Criminal Policy in Justice and Criminal Legislation [Dirección Nacional de Política Criminal en Materia de Justicia y Legislación Penal]. (2021). *Sistema Nacional de Estadística sobre Ejecución de la Pena—Informe Ejecutivo SNEEP 2021*. Retrieved from https://www.argentina.gob.ar/sites/default/files/2022/10/informe_sneep_argentina_2021_0.pdf

National Program on Science and Justice [Programa Nacional de Ciencia y Justicia]. (2022, June 21). *Aportes de la ciencia para el abordaje de ofensores sexuales y agresores de género*. Retrieved from https://www.Conicet.Gov.Ar/Aportes-de-La-Ciencia-Para-El-Abordaje-de-Ofensores-Sexuales-y-Agresores-de-Genero/

Ochoa, J., Guillén, X., Ullauri, D., Narvaez, J., León-Mayer, E., & Folino, J. O. (2017). Sistematización de la evaluación de riesgo de violencia con instrumentos de juicio profesional estructurado en Cuenca, Ecuador. *Maskana, 8*(1), 1–14. https://doi.org/10.18537/mskn.08.01.01

Ochoa Balarezo, J., Guillén, X., Ullauri, D., Narvaez, J., León-Mayer, E., & Folino, J. O. (2016). Relevancia de la evaluación del riesgo de violencia y de la psicopatía en el ámbito forense. *Juris, 1*(16), 113–127.

Senate of the Province of Buenos Aires [Senado de la Provincia de Buenos Aires]. (2014). Ley N° 14580. Ley Nacional de Salud Mental-Salud Pública-Política Sanitaria-Establecimientos Asistenciales Adhesión Provincial. In *Boletín Oficial de la Provincia de Buenos Aires*, 2014/02/06.

Singh, J. P., Condemarín, C., & Folino, J. O. (2013). El uso de instrumentos de evaluación de riesgo de violencia en Argentina y Chile [The use of violence risk assessment instruments in Argentina and Chile]. *Revista Criminalidad, 55*(3), 279–290.

Webster, C. D., Douglas, K. S., Eaves, D., & Hart, S. D. (1997). *HCR-20: Assessing risk for violence version 2*. Burnaby, British Columbia, Canada: Mental Health, Law, and Policy Institute, Simon Fraser University.

# 5 Brazil

*Elias Abdalla-Filho and*
*Lisieux E. de Borba Telles*

## Brief Description

| | |
|---|---|
| **Location** | Brazil is a country located in South America. |
| **Size** | 8,515,767 km$^2$ |
| **Population** | 212.5 million |
| **Language** | The official language of Brazil is Portuguese. |
| **Political system** | Brazil (the Federative Republic of Brazil) is a federal republic with a presidential system of government, which is divided between the executive branch (president), the legislative branch (bicameral National Congress: the Chamber of Deputies and the Federal Senate), and the judicial branch, with the Supreme Federal Court as the highest court in Brazil. Brazil is divided into 26 states and one federal district. Each state has its own constitution and state government. |

## Legal System

Brazil, officially the Federative Republic of Brazil, is a federal republic comprising 26 states and one federal district, where federal laws take precedence over state laws. The country's primary federal laws include the Constitution of the Federative Republic of Brazil (*Constituição da República Federativa do Brasil*), which is the supreme law and defines the legislative powers of the federal government, states, and municipalities (Brasil, 1988). The Penal Code (*Código Penal*) (Decree-Law No. 2848/40; Brasil, 1940), amended by Law No. 7209/84, exempts legally incompetent individuals from punishment for crimes and, in some cases, allows for reduced criminal responsibility (Brasil, 1984a). The Penal Execution Law (*Lei de Execuções Penais*) (Law No. 7210/84) establishes the agencies responsible for enforcing sentences and defines the types of facilities used to incarcerate both ordinary offenders and individuals with mental illnesses who have committed crimes. Furthermore, the law outlines the process for committing individuals with mental disorders to a psychiatric institution within a hospital or, if that is not possible, to a prison facility. It also establishes

DOI: 10.4324/9781003376248-7

the psychiatric evaluation procedures required for both ordinary criminals and those undergoing criminal commitment to serve their sentences (Brasil, 1984b). Finally, the Penal Procedural Code (Decree-Law No. 3689/41) sets out the procedures for expert evaluations to determine whether a defendant has a mental disorder (Brasil, 1941).

In Brazil, the criminal justice system is a complex network of organizations and state institutions responsible for preventing, investigating, and prosecuting crimes, as well as enforcing penalties and sentencing convicted individuals. The Brazilian criminal justice process follows three main phases: investigation, judicial proceedings, and judgment.

The first phase is inquisitorial, during which police authorities conduct a thorough investigation into the alleged crime (Brasil, 1941). The adversarial system is introduced in the judicial proceedings phase, where both the prosecution and defense present their evidence. This stage concludes with the finalization of the criminal sentence (*transit in rem judicatam*), which can result in one of four key outcomes: conviction, conviction with a substitution of punishment by criminal commitment, acquittal based on the defendant's lack of criminal responsibility, or full acquittal.

### *Mental Health Laws*

#### *Fitness to Stand Trial*

In Brazil, there is no specific legislation addressing fitness to stand trial. The country follows the Roman-Germanic legal tradition, in which defendants take a passive role and do not actively participate in their defense during the trial—unlike in Anglo-Saxon legal systems (Abdalla-Filho & Bertolote, 2006).

#### *Criminal Responsibility*

Brazilian law determines criminal responsibility based on an individual's mental state during the crime. A defendant may be found not criminally responsible (*inimputável*) due to a mental disorder and, as a result, be subject to security measures (*medidas de segurança*), which typically include involuntary psychiatric treatment instead of a traditional prison sentence.

The Penal Imputability Exam is the most critical forensic evaluation in such cases. It is regulated by Articles 149 and 154 of the Penal Procedural Code (*Código de Processo Penal*) and is used to determine whether the defendant meets the criteria for lack of criminal responsibility or *inimputabilidade,* as defined in Article 26 of the Penal Code (*Código Penal*).

Article 26 of the Penal Code exempts from punishment any individual who, due to mental illness or incomplete or delayed mental development, was completely incapable at the time of the act or omission of understanding the wrongful nature of their actions or making decisions based on this understanding. Furthermore, it allows for a sentence reduction of one- to two-thirds if the individual, due to a mental disorder or incomplete or delayed mental development, had only a partial ability to comprehend the wrongful nature of their actions or to make decisions accordingly (Brasil, 1984a).

Article 26 of the Brazilian Penal Code is divided into two parts. The first part addresses cases of total unimputability, where individuals are deemed not criminally responsible due to *lato sensu* mental illness. This serves as the legal basis for Brazil's equivalent of not guilty by reason of insanity (NGRI) decisions in Anglo-Saxon law. The second part concerns individuals with diminished criminal responsibility. In these cases, the defendant's culpability is reduced, allowing for a lighter sentence or, depending on the circumstances, hospitalization as a security measure.

## Forensic Psychiatry System

### *Structure and Function of the Forensic Psychiatry System*

The Brazilian forensic psychiatric system is rooted in Roman law, sharing the same origins as other Latin American legal systems. Unlike the Anglo-Saxon model, criminal forensic evaluations in Brazil consider cognitive aspects and volitional factors when assessing criminal responsibility. Therefore, beyond determining whether an individual understands the criminal nature of their actions, it is also necessary to evaluate their ability to act in accordance with that understanding.

During a trial, if there is suspicion that the defendant has a mental disorder, the judge orders a forensic psychiatric evaluation. The forensic psychiatrist must then produce a report determining whether the defendant, at the time of the crime, had a mental disorder that impaired their ability to understand the criminal nature of their actions and/or their capacity to control their behavior. This report is used to assess criminal responsibility and helps the judge determine the most appropriate sentence.

In Brazil, there are four possible legal outcomes: conviction—if the defendant is found to have full or diminished criminal responsibility at the time of the crime; conviction with substitution of punishment by criminal commitment—if the defendant had diminished criminal responsibility; acquittal due to insanity (NGRI equivalent)—if the defendant is found not criminally responsible; and acquittal based on innocence—if there is insufficient evidence or proof of noninvolvement.

In cases of conviction with substitution of punishment by criminal commitment and acquittal due to insanity, the individual is required to undergo psychiatric treatment in a specialized forensic psychiatric hospital known as the Hospital for Custody and Psychiatric Treatment (*Hospital de Custódia e Tratamento*

*Psiquiátrico*). These hospitals are found across the country, with the number of wards and beds varying by location. In Brazil, there is no classification of forensic psychiatric hospitals into high-, medium-, or low-security levels, and there is no predefined duration for treatment. The length of hospitalization depends on the individual's progress, and discharge is only granted after an expert evaluation determines a low probability of reoffending.

The patient is under the care of psychiatrists hired specifically for this purpose and undergoes forensic evaluations approximately once a year. In Brazil, the psychiatrist responsible for treating the patient cannot conduct forensic assessments, as these are separate roles performed by different professionals. There is no set average length of stay, but hospitalization typically lasts no less than three years.

### *Decision Makers in Forensic Psychiatry*

In Brazil, the judge is the primary decision maker in criminal cases, with forensic experts playing an advisory role. The medical report produced by forensic psychiatrists serves as a legal document and can be used as evidence. For instance, the expert evaluation determining the presence or absence of a mental disorder at the time of the crime significantly influences how the accused is perceived and treated by the criminal justice system. If the prosecution's argument is accepted, this assessment becomes crucial in the judge's decision on whether the individual will receive a criminal penalty or be subject to criminal commitment, ultimately determining whether they will be sent to prison or a forensic psychiatric hospital.

### *Role of the Forensic Psychiatrist*

Forensic psychiatrists conduct psychiatric assessments in civil and criminal cases in Brazil. However, healthcare professionals are separately employed to treat patients who have committed a crime but are deemed not criminally responsible. It is considered unethical for a doctor to conduct a forensic evaluation on a patient they have previously treated, ensuring that the roles of treatment and forensic assessment remain distinct.

#### *Qualifications and Specialized Training*

The study of forensic psychiatry initially began with teaching programs designed to provide psychiatry residents with academic training. Today, forensic psychiatry is integrated into all psychiatry residency curricula. After completing general psychiatric training, residents can pursue a specialization in forensic psychiatry, which offers the most immersive learning experience in the field. This intensive program combines theoretical knowledge with hands-on forensic practice, including technical skill assessments. Additionally, trainees refine their interviewing techniques and ethical competencies under the supervision of a senior resident with three years of clinical experience in psychiatry. This supervisory component occurs in the fourth year of residency (Telles & Abdalla-Filho, 2016). However, forensic psychiatry residency programs in Brazil are still in their early stages and are currently available in only five states: Rio Grande do Sul, São Paulo, Rio de Janeiro, Minas Gerais, and Ceará.

## Forensic Psychiatry Service (Provision of Care)

### *Forensic Patient Characteristics*

Although demographic, psychosocial, and criminological data on individuals in the Brazilian forensic system have been documented, the available information is outdated.

### *Approaches to Assessment and Treatment*

The healthcare system in Brazil provides two primary forms of support for forensic patients: hospitalization and outpatient treatment. The choice of treatment depends on the nature of the crime committed and the patient's mental disorder. Unlike some countries, Brazilian forensic hospitals do not classify facilities into high-, medium-, or low-security levels, although specialized forensic treatment is available. Treatment approaches may be adjusted based on the individual's progress. Correctional facilities offer rehabilitation and treatment programs for forensic patients, including psychotherapy and psychopharmacotherapy. However, there is no standardized type of psychotherapy in these treatments or established guidelines to ensure consistency and adherence to evidence-based practices.

Psychiatric treatment is provided to forensic patients in Brazil, including those who have been civilly committed, those found not criminally responsible due to mental illness, and common prisoners who require inpatient care. Forensic institutions offer a range of treatments, including psychopharmacological and psychotherapeutic interventions, as well as educational workshops and vocational training.

In prisons, inmates with mental health disorders receive care through psychiatric evaluations conducted at forensic psychiatric hospitals. These evaluations are carried out by psychiatrists working within the penitentiary system, who also provide psychotherapy and psychopharmacotherapy as needed.

The healthcare system and support for forensic patients vary across different states in Brazil. In some states, forensic mental health teams have implemented progressive discharge programs for patients within the forensic system. Where these programs exist, they have contributed to better social and familial reintegration, improved recovery, and successful discharge outcomes. Forensic patients deemed mentally stable and no longer a threat to public safety may be granted conditional discharge and provided with follow-up treatment at community outpatient clinics.

## Strengths and Weaknesses

In Brazil, there are significant regional disparities in the provision of mental health care for both forensic patients and inmates. These differences partly arise because some aspects of mental health legislation are determined at the federal level. In contrast, others fall under state jurisdiction, leading to legal norms and implementation variations. Additionally, economic disparities among states affect forensic hospital resources and psychiatric care availability. Brazil has 26 forensic hospitals nationwide, with a notable concentration in certain regions—eight specialized hospitals in Rio de Janeiro and two each in São Paulo and Minas Gerais.

Unfortunately, several states in Brazil lack specialized forensic hospitals, leading to the frequent placement of offenders with mental illnesses in regular psychiatric hospitals. This situation creates challenges for both nonspecialized clinical staff and other patients. Another major issue is that forensic patients are often housed in penitentiaries alongside individuals without mental illness, resulting in inadequate psychiatric care that is often limited to medication management. While these individuals interact with those around them, their psychiatric limitations can hinder meaningful social integration. Additionally, there is a significant gap between the public health system and correctional facilities, where prisoner health care remains inadequate. The quality of forensic psychiatric care in Brazil also varies depending on the region or state, further contributing to disparities in treatment and rehabilitation.

A final criticism concerns the public health system in Brazil, which is founded on the principles of universality and forensic mental health assistance. This means every Brazilian citizen has the right to comprehensive health care and free medical services. However, a significant issue arises when these citizens are incarcerated. Health care for inmates with mental illnesses is not covered by the public health system, resulting in inadequate support and treatment. This exclusion from healthcare coverage may be considered unconstitutional discrimination (Taborda et al., 2013).

In recent years, national and international universities have collaborated to enhance prison assistance and psychiatric services for forensic patients, leading to some progress in this area. The proximity of correctional facilities and forensic psychiatric hospitals to university centers has facilitated research in criminal justice, contributing to the professional development and training of staff. However, further efforts are needed in education and training in forensic mental health to ensure that Brazil has a well-qualified workforce capable of providing effective psychiatric treatment, recovery support, and rehabilitation services for offenders reintegrating into the community.

## References

Abdalla-Filho, E., & Bertolote, J. M. (2006). Sistemas de psiquiatria forense no mundo. *Brazilian Journal of Psychiatry*, *28*(supplement II), S56–S61.

Brasil. (1940). Decreto-lei No. 2.484/40 (Código Penal [Penal Code]). Diário Oficial da União, 31/dez/1940.

Brasil. (1941). Decreto-lei No. 3.689/41 (Código de Processo Penal [Penal Procedural Code]). Diário Oficial da União, 24/out/1941.

Brasil. (1984a). Lei No. 7.209/84 (Alteração do Código Penal [amendment to the Penal Code]). Diário Oficial da União, 13/jul/1984.

Brasil. (1984b). Lei No. 7.210/84 (Lei de Execuções Penais [Penal Executions Law]). Diário Oficial da União, 13/jul/1984.

Brasil. (1988). Constituição da República Federativa do Brasil. Diário Oficial da União, 5/out/1988.

Taborda, J. G. V., Telles, L. E. B., & Bins, H. D. C. (2013). Forensic mental health in Brazil. In N. Konrad, B. Völlm, & D. Weisstub (Eds.), *Ethical issues in prison psychiatry* (pp. 153–161). Dordrecht, Netherlands: Springer.

Telles, L. E. B., & Abdalla-Filho, E. (2016). Ensino da Psiquiatria Forense no Brasil. In E. Abdalla-Filho, M. Chalub, & L. E. B. Telles (Eds.), *Psiquiatria Forense de Taborda* (3rd ed., pp. 27–34). Porto Alegre, Brazil: Artmed.

# 6 Chile

*Claudio Filippi*

**Brief Description**

| | |
|---|---|
| **Location** | Chile is a country in the far southwest of South America. |
| **Size** | 756,626 km$^2$ |
| **Population** | 20.2 million |
| **Languages** | The official language of Chile is Spanish. However, Indigenous languages such as Mapudungun, Aymara, and Rapa Nui are spoken in some regions. |
| **Political system** | Chile, officially the Republic of Chile, is a democratic republic with a presidential system. It has a unitary government, meaning political power is centralized at the national level, though regional governments and municipalities operate under the authority of the central government.<br>The government consists of three branches: the executive, led by the president; the legislative, composed of the Chamber of Deputies and the Senate; and the independent judiciary, headed by the Supreme Court. The Constitutional Court also plays a key role in reviewing laws. |

## Legal System

### *Legislative Framework*

Several legal bodies constitute the framework within which forensic psychiatry operates in Chile. The Political Constitution of the Republic of Chile, initially drafted under the military dictatorship of Augusto Pinochet, was enacted in 1980. Pinochet's regime governed Chile from 1973 to 1990 following the military overthrow of democratically elected president Salvador Allende. The Constitution (Ministry of the General Secretariat of the Presidency, 2005) has undergone multiple amendments since the late 1980s, with significant revisions in recent years.

The Constitution establishes key provisions for the country, including a body of constitutional rights outlined in Article 19, which guarantees all

DOI: 10.4324/9781003376248-8

individuals the right to physical and mental integrity. Article 19(2) ensures equality before the law, while Article 19(3) guarantees equal protection under the law in exercising rights. It also establishes the right to legal defense, including free criminal defense for victims and defendants. Furthermore, it mandates that individuals may only be tried by the appropriate Courts of Justice, reinforcing the presumption of innocence until proven guilty in court. Chapter VI (Articles 76–82) defines the constitutional framework for the Judicial Branch, while Chapter VII (Articles 83–91) does the same for the Public Prosecutor's Office.

Beyond the Constitution, several legal instruments govern forensic psychiatry. The Organic Code of Courts regulates the judiciary's structure, organization, and operation (Ministry of Justice, 1999; Oberg & Manso, 2011). The Penal Code classifies offenses as crimes, simple offenses, or misdemeanors and establishes their corresponding penalties (Ministry of Justice, 2001). From a forensic psychiatric perspective, Articles 10 and 11 outline circumstances that exempt or mitigate criminal liability. The Criminal Procedure Code defines procedural rules for criminal proceedings, ensuring due process. The Civil Code regulates civil capacity in Articles 1445 and 1446, while the Civil Procedure Code sets out procedural rules for civil cases.

A specialized legal framework for mental health rights is established by Law No. 21331, which addresses the recognition and protection of a person's rights in mental health care (Ministry of Health, 2021). Additionally, Resolution 8083 Exempt approves the updated technical expert normative guide for mental health in psychiatry, psychology, and forensic social work (Ministry of Justice, 2015).

### *Legal System*

The justice system in Chile follows the continental European model, which differs from the Anglo-Saxon model. The continental European model, or civil law, is based on a combination of Roman, Germanic, ecclesiastical, feudal, commercial, and customary law. The legal systems of Continental Europe, including Spain, originate from this tradition. Following the colonization of the Americas, Spain transmitted its legal principles to much of the continent. Later, during the Napoleonic era, the codification of laws became a defining feature of these legal systems (Carozza et al., 2024).

A key distinction between civil law and the Anglo-Saxon common law system is its reliance on written law based on formally enacted laws and regulations issued by the executive and legislative branches. In this system, jurisprudence does not serve as a source of law creation, nor does custom establish legal rules. According to Sturner (2007), the objective of codification is to formulate legal rules abstractly, ensuring they provide solutions to all conceivable legal questions.

### *Administration of Justice*

The judiciary in Chile is independent and responsible for resolving legal conflicts (Orellana Torres, Tomo I, 2018). It operates through a hierarchical structure, with specialized courts of first instance handling criminal, civil, and family matters. These courts function under the jurisdiction of the Courts of Appeal, of which there are 17 across the country. Two of these courts are located in the Metropolitan Region, in Santiago and San Miguel. Their jurisdiction extends to the first and second instances, ensuring that legal matters are reviewed at multiple levels.

At the top of the judicial hierarchy is the Supreme Court, the highest court in Chile. Its primary function is to ensure the proper application of the law, maintaining legal consistency and oversight across the judicial system. It serves as a collegiate, ordinary, judicial, and permanent institution with directive, corrective, and economic supervision over all other courts, except for the Constitutional Court, the Electoral Qualifying Court, and the Regional Electoral Courts. The Supreme Court, headquartered in Santiago, exercises broad judicial powers, including hearing appeals. It also reviews appeals to overturn final judgments in criminal cases when applicable under procedural law. Additionally, it adjudicates cases related to Amparo, Economic Amparo, and other legal protections.

A unique function of the Supreme Court is its authority to grant the title of Lawyer to individuals who hold a Bachelor of Legal Sciences degree from a university in accordance with the law. This process ensures that legal professionals meet the necessary qualifications to practice law within the country.

Chile also has Military Courts, which hold jurisdiction over both Chileans and foreigners in cases concerning military competence. These courts operate under the provisions of the Code of Military Justice, other legal codes and special laws. They handle offenses committed exclusively by military personnel or jointly by civilians and military personnel, ensuring that national security and military discipline are addressed appropriately (Biblioteca del Congreso Nacional, 2017).

The procedural framework governing judicial processes in Chile is established in the Constitution, procedural law, Concerted Decisions of the Supreme Court, jurisprudence, national and foreign legal doctrine, and procedural practices. These sources ensure that legal procedures are standardized and applied consistently across different cases, reinforcing the stability and predictability of the judicial system.

### *The Criminal Process*

The Chilean criminal process follows an accusatory system in which the roles of investigation, prosecution, and adjudication are distinct. While the investigation and accusation are conducted separately, the responsibility for sentencing rests with the judiciary. This system is oral and public, ensuring transparency and allowing the public to follow the proceedings. It also guarantees the accused the right to a proper defense.

The criminal process consists of several stages, beginning with the investigation and culminating in sentencing after the necessary trial hearings. Each stage is designed to uphold procedural fairness and due process, ensuring that judicial decisions are based on thorough examination and adherence to legal standards (Orellana Torres, Volume V, 2018).

### *Mental Health Laws*

#### *Fitness to Stand Trial*

The capacity to stand trial is defined by León (2010) as "the condition of being legally qualified to perform an act and/or make a decision." He further explains that "it is based on the idea that when someone does not understand the nature and purpose of the criminal or civil proceedings in which he or she is involved, these should not continue." According to the same author, evaluating trial capacity involves assessing a series of skills, including the ability to express a choice, understand the information presented, comprehend the situation in which they find themselves, and rationally process the information provided.

As noted, this evaluation applies in both civil and criminal contexts. In the civil sphere, the Chilean Civil Code addresses legal capacity in Articles 1445 and 1446, stating that "every person is legally capable, except those whom the law declares incapable." The same legal framework categorizes incapable individuals into absolute and relative incapacity.

Absolute incapacity applies to individuals who can only act through a legal representative, such as a guardian or curator. This includes prepubescent children, people considered insane, and people who are deaf or deaf-mute and cannot make themselves clearly understood (Article 1447). Relative incapacity applies to individuals who generally require representation for most legal actions but may act independently under certain conditions, provided they have the necessary authorization. This category includes minors between 12 and 18 years old and individuals who have been judicially interdicted from managing their own property due to excessive spending (Jarufe-Contreras, 2022). In criminal matters, Article 459 of the Criminal Procedure Code establishes that if there is evidence suggesting the accused suffers from mental insanity, their rights will be exercised by a curator ad litem appointed for this purpose.

Determining a person's capacity to stand trial is the responsibility of the Courts of Justice, which base their decisions on clinical evaluations conducted by qualified professionals. This process ensures that people who lack the necessary cognitive or mental competence receive appropriate legal protections and representation.

#### *Criminal Responsibility*

Chilean criminal law defines criminal responsibility (*imputabilidad*) as the ability to understand the illegality of an act and act accordingly. This capacity is the general rule but can be altered in specific cases established by the Penal Code under Article 10, Numbers 1 and 9. Article 10 states that individuals are "exempt from criminal responsibility" under certain conditions. Number 1 provides that "the madman or insane person, unless he has acted in a lucid interval, and the one who, for any cause independent of his will, is deprived of reason" are exempt from liability. Number 9 extends this exemption to individuals "who act under an irresistible force or are driven by an insurmountable fear."

Additionally, Chilean criminal law recognizes the possibility of attenuated or reduced criminal responsibility. Article 11, Number 1, states that this applies to "those mentioned in the previous article (Article 10) when all the requirements to exempt from liability in their respective cases are not met." Determining full, partial, or absent criminal responsibility falls to the Courts of Justice, supported by forensic psychiatrists and psychologists. These professionals assess the presence or absence of mental disorders that could affect an individual's legal capacity.

## Forensic Psychiatry System

### *Structure and Function of the Forensic Mental Health System*

As part of the Mental Health Thematic Network (Ministry of Health, 2018), a series of specialized units has been established, forming what is known as the Sub-network of Forensic Psychiatry. This sub-network began operating in late 1998 with the participation of the Ministries of Justice and Health, the Health Services, the Gendarmerie of Chile, and the Legal Medical Service. It comprises various specialized units designed to provide comprehensive forensic psychiatric services, including assessments, treatments, and expert testimonies, to support the justice system in cases involving people with mental health considerations.

Its creation was driven by the need to address the increasing demands for forensic psychiatric services following the implementation of the Criminal Procedure Reform. This reform replaced the inquisitorial criminal system, in which the judge was responsible for investigating, prosecuting, and sentencing, with an accusatory system, where these functions are separated. The transition to the new system was completed in 2005.

#### *High-Complexity Unit*

The first unit within the Sub-network of Forensic Psychiatry is a high-complexity forensic psychiatry unit located at the Dr. Philippe Pinel Psychiatric Hospital in Putaendo, Valparaíso. Established in 2002, this unit has 20 beds. It serves as the national reference center for the comprehensive psychiatric treatment of patients over 18 years of age who have a mental illness posing a risk to themselves or others.

Patients admitted to this unit require specialized care from a transdisciplinary team with expertise in clinical psychopathology and behavioral risk assessment.

Their hospitalization is mandated by a criminal court-issued security measure due to the severity of their condition. The unit's therapeutic objectives include comprehensive treatment, psychosocial rehabilitation, and social reintegration.

The facility was specifically designed to address the healthcare needs of this population while ensuring that security standards are met. The unit operates with the support of Gendarmerie personnel—the uniformed prison service under the Ministry of Justice and Human Rights, responsible for the custody, rehabilitation, and reintegration of people serving sentences or in pretrial detention.

### *Medium-Complexity Units*

Medium-complexity forensic psychiatry units are administratively linked to a high-complexity or specialty hospital under the Ministry of Health. There are two medium-complexity units at the Dr. Philippe Pinel Psychiatric Hospital in Putaendo, Valparaíso, established in 2000 and 2006, with a combined total of 50 beds. Additionally, a medium-complexity unit at the Dr. José Horwitz Barak Psychiatric Institute in Santiago provides 40 beds. Another medium-complexity unit, established in 2012, operates at the Guillermo Grant Benavente Regional Hospital in Concepción, offering 18 beds.

Medium-complexity units serve as temporary care facilities for people over 18 years of age who have been declared exempt from criminal responsibility by the courts in criminal cases and are subject to an internment security measure. These people, due to their psychopathological condition and behavioral disturbances, require intensive and prolonged interventions to stabilize their mental health, ensure continuity of psychiatric treatment, and support their psychosocial rehabilitation with the goal of eventual discharge and reintegration into the community.

These units accommodate people awaiting compliance with their security measures, reintegration into their families, or placement in a 'forensic residence unit' or community-based facility upon discharge. It ensures a continuum of care, addressing varying levels of psychopathological complexity while aligning with judicial measures and individualized treatment plans.

Both the high-complexity and medium-complexity units serve men and women over 18 years of age, taking into account cultural context and gender considerations. Patients admitted to these units must have a mental illness, be compensated or partially compensated at the time of transfer, and show a reduction in dangerous behaviors toward themselves or others. In criminal cases, those declared exempt from criminal responsibility must have an active internment security measure at the time of transfer and throughout their stay. They may be referred from the high-complexity forensic unit or directly by the criminal courts.

### *Unit for the Evaluation of Accused Persons*

The Unit for the Evaluation of Accused Persons (*Unidad de Evaluación de Personas Imputadas* [UEPI]) is administratively linked to a high-complexity hospital and/or specialty hospital, or to a health service. It is technically overseen by the Ministry of Health. A clinical forensic unit provides closed, transitory hospitalization under a public health network hospital or health service.

The primary purpose of the UEPI is to conduct expert evaluations and, when applicable, stabilization of people with suspected or diagnosed severe mental disorders who have been charged with a criminal offense. These people require an inpatient forensic assessment because an outpatient evaluation is not feasible. The evaluations conducted within this unit are essential for the criminal courts to determine criminal responsibility or lack thereof.

The UEPI serves people over 18 years of age who have been accused of a criminal offense and who either have or are suspected of having a severe and complex mental illness resulting in significant cognitive impairment or behavioral disturbances. These individuals may pose a risk to themselves or others, necessitating inpatient clinical evaluation to produce an expert report for the competent criminal court. The report determines the presence of mental illness and assists in the ruling on criminal responsibility or exemption from responsibility. Admission to a UEPI requires a judicial internment order issued by a criminal court of justice as a precautionary measure while the judicial process is ongoing.

In Chile, there are three UEPIs. The first, located at the Dr. José Horwitz Barak Psychiatric Institute in Santiago, was established in 2007 and has 39 beds. That same year, a second unit was created at the Dr. Philippe Pinel Psychiatric Hospital in Putaendo, Valparaíso, with a capacity of 20 beds. In 2009, a third unit was established at the Dr. Hernán Henríquez Aravena Regional Hospital in Temuco, Araucanía Region, providing 10 beds for forensic evaluations.

*Temporary Forensic Psychiatric Units*

Temporary forensic psychiatric units are administratively linked to a hospital or the directorate of a health service. They function as a closed and outpatient forensic clinic inside prisons, with custody and perimeter protection provided by the Gendarmerie. In Chile, there are three such units. One is attached to the Psychiatric Hospital of El Salvador in the Valparaíso Region, with a capacity of 16 beds. Another operates in the Arica Region, providing 14 beds, while the third is located in Punta Arenas, Magallanes Region, with six beds. These units are situated within the prisons of their respective cities, ensuring on-site forensic psychiatric evaluation and care.

Temporary forensic psychiatric units serve as a critical component of forensic mental health care, ensuring that individuals within the criminal justice system receive proper psychiatric assessment. These units serve people over 18 years of age who either have been charged with a crime and temporarily interned or are convicted people suspected of having a mental illness. The primary function of these units is to conduct psychiatric evaluations to determine the presence or absence of a mental illness and to issue expert psychiatric reports as ordered by a criminal court judge. To undergo evaluation, individuals must be admitted to the unit for provisional hospitalization.

*Forensic Residence Units*

Forensic residence units are administratively linked to a health service, a high- or medium-complexity hospital, or a psychiatric hospital and are technically overseen by the Ministry of Health. They serve as a residential facility for people with mental illness who either are fulfilling a measure of custody and treatment or have completed a period of confinement in a forensic hospital. Admission to these residences is granted to individuals who have shown a reduction in dangerousness and retain the psychological, cognitive, and functional abilities necessary for independent living. Continued hospitalization in a forensic unit would risk further deterioration of their social and occupational skills, making a therapeutic residential environment more appropriate for their reintegration.

Forensic residence units provide a structured environment that balances security and care, facilitating a gradual transition to independent living. These facilities conduct interventions tailored to the mental and criminal health condition of residents, promoting social reintegration and community inclusion.

One residence operates at the Dr. José Horwitz Barak Psychiatric Institute in Santiago, offering 10 beds. It is administratively dependent on the Medium-Complexity Unit of the same hospital. This facility serves as an alternative and temporary residential placement for people with moderate psychiatric illnesses who have committed violent crimes and have been deemed a danger to themselves or society.

As a result, they are subject to a Security Measure of Hospitalization in a hospital facility, as outlined in Articles 455 and 457 of the Criminal Procedure Code. Once these people achieve psychiatric stabilization, authorization is sought from the court to transfer them to a community-based residential facility. This transfer marks the beginning of a structured reintegration process, allowing for family, social, and/or occupational reintegration before the completion of their sentence.

In addition to the forensic residence units, the Detoxification and Treatment Unit for Adolescents with Severe Behavioral Disorders (UDAC) operates at the Dr. José Horwitz Barak Psychiatric Institute in Santiago. Established in 2007, this unit provides specialized care for adolescents experiencing severe behavioral disturbances.

### *Exiting the System and Average Length of Stay*

Patients in forensic residence units are discharged upon completing their court-ordered sentence. According to available data from 2012, the length of stay in forensic residence units varied significantly. Only 1% of patients remained hospitalized for more than 10 years, while 9.2% had stays between 5 and 10 years. A more significant proportion, 30.9%, remained hospitalized for one to four years, whereas the majority, 58.9%, had a stay of less than one year. These figures show no significant variation compared to the data from 2004 (Ministerio de Salud, 2014).

#### *Decision Makers in Forensic Psychiatry*

Decisions regarding the legal status of individuals who are assessed, accused, or convicted in Chile fall exclusively under the jurisdiction of the Courts of Justice. Judges are the sole authorities competent to determine legal responsibility and issue rulings. The role of forensic psychiatrists is to support the judicial process through expert evaluations. This work is defined as the evaluation process conducted by a psychiatrist at the request of a competent institution within the justice system to clarify matters or facts deemed relevant by the court (Ministry of Justice, 2015). The process involves preparing an expert report to guide and inform the requesting authority on medical-legal matters.

### Forensic Psychiatry Service (Provision of Care)

#### *Forensic Patient Characteristics*

Although no studies have been found in the reviewed literature specifically on patients within the Sub-network of Forensic Psychiatry in Chile, Alvarado et al. (2015) conducted a study on a sample of 1,008 individuals who had been charged, prosecuted, or convicted. They were recruited from seven prisons across the northern, central-north, central, central-south, and southern macro-zones, with the sample proportionally representing the prison population in each region. The Composite International Diagnostic Interview, validated in Chile, was applied to assess psychiatric disorders within this group.

The study found that 12.6% of participants had addictive disorders, while 8.3% were diagnosed with anxiety disorders. Affective disorders were present in 8.1% of cases, and intermittent explosive disorder was identified in 5.7% of the sample. Attention deficit disorder in adults affected 2.2%, and non-affective psychosis was observed in 0.8% (Alvarado et al., 2015).

When comparing the prevalence of psychiatric disorders between people who had been incarcerated and the general population, notable differences emerged. Major depressive disorder was more frequent among men who were incarcerated (6.1%) than among men in the general population (3.7%). Illicit drug abuse was also more prevalent among men (3.3%) and women (2.6%) who were incarcerated compared to men (0.6%) and women (0.1%) in the general population. Similarly, illicit drug dependence was significantly higher among men who had been incarcerated (3.4%) than among men in the general population (1.1%) (Alvarado et al., 2015).

Conversely, some psychiatric conditions were more common among the general population than among people who had been incarcerated. Dysthymia, simple phobia, and social phobia were diagnosed at higher rates in women from the general population compared to women who were incarcerated. Likewise, alcohol abuse and dependence were more prevalent among men in the general population than among those who had been incarcerated (Alvarado et al., 2015).

### *Forensic Psychiatry Profession*

#### *Qualifications and Specialized Training*

In Chile, psychiatry is a medical specialty that requires additional training after completing a Medical Surgeon (*Médico Cirujano*) degree, the official title for physicians in the country. This specialization is primarily obtained through academic programs in medical schools, which consist of three years of full-time training. Alternatively, psychiatry can be pursued through a practical training pathway, which involves working in a psychiatric service at a healthcare center or a public health service for a minimum of five years, with a workload of 22 hours per week.

Chile's specialty certification system does not formally recognize psychiatric subspecialties, including forensic psychiatry. However, forensic psychiatry is understood as a subspecialty of psychiatry that applies clinical and scientific expertise to legal contexts, covering areas such as criminal, civil, labor, correctional, regulatory, and legislative matters (Ministry of Health, 2005–2006; Dresdner Cid, 2010).

### *Approaches to Assessment and Treatment*

Psychiatrists and psychologists conduct comprehensive patient assessments, which include clinical evaluation, supplementary psychodiagnosis, and essential laboratory examinations, such as imaging studies and electroencephalographic tests. The treatment approach in Chile varies depending on the type of forensic psychiatric unit where the patient is placed.

The primary objective of high- and medium-complexity units is to stabilize the patient's mental health and develop a comprehensive care plan. Treatment includes medication, psychotherapy, and psychosocial support, with social workers and occupational therapists contributing to patient rehabilitation in high-complexity units. Additionally, patients participate in recreational and training activities as part of their rehabilitation process.

In a forensic residence unit, pharmacological treatment is provided, and the care plan incorporates crisis intervention, coping strategies, problem-solving techniques, and stress management approaches. Treatment providers emphasize community rehabilitation, recreational engagement, and social reintegration activities to prepare patients for independent living.

The UEPI primarily focuses on expert forensic evaluation rather than treatment. The goal is to assess the presence or absence of a mental illness concerning the index offense or crime. The evaluation process involves interviews and applying standardized instruments as part of the forensic assessment. Additionally, with guidance from the hospital facility to which they are attached, the legal aspects of the case are reviewed. When appropriate, treatment may be initiated to stabilize acute psychiatric symptoms, including medication management and crisis intervention.

In a temporary forensic psychiatry unit, treatment is provided to stabilize acute psychiatric conditions when necessary. A psychiatric consultation is conducted upon admission to determine the diagnosis and initiate treatment for patients presenting with an acute or decompensated mental health condition. Treatment typically includes pharmacological intervention and psychotherapy, with a comprehensive treatment plan developed to guide ongoing care.

### *National Collaborations or Networks*

In 2012, Decree 285 established the National Commission of Forensic Psychiatry to advise the Minister of Justice and the Minister of Health on regulatory matters outlined in Titles 7 and 8 of Book Four of the Criminal Procedure Code (Ministry of Justice, 2012). These sections govern the exclusive application of security and precautionary measures for people with mental illness who have committed or are accused of committing a legally defined offense. The Commission provides recommendations and technical guidance to the respective State Secretariats to ensure the proper application of these legal provisions.

The Commission consists of two representatives, each from the Ministry of Health and the Ministry of Justice and Human Rights, along with one representative from each health service that operates a psychiatric care unit for individuals serving sentences or subject to security measures due to mental illness. Additional members include two representatives from the Chilean Gendarmerie and one representative each from the Legal Medical Service, the Public Criminal Defense Office, the judiciary, the Public Prosecutor's Office, the Medical Association, and the Bar Association.

## Strengths and Weaknesses

The Sub-network of Forensic Psychiatry emerged as an intersectoral initiative involving various public institutions linked to the justice system, the protection and safeguarding of minors, drug prevention and control, and the health sector. This interdisciplinary approach is one of its greatest strengths, as it allows for integrating diverse perspectives and experiences. However, this broad participation also highlights the need to clarify the roles and responsibilities of the different institutions involved, particularly concerning key aspects of forensic psychiatric care and legal procedures.

Rather than being a fixed and rigid structure, the Sub-network of Forensic Psychiatry remains highly adaptable to Chile's evolving social and judicial landscape. Recent challenges, such as migration processes and broader societal changes, have already introduced new complexities that the network must address. Participating entities must work toward expanding and further developing the network to meet these growing demands and ensure that forensic psychiatric services are made available across all regions of the country. Given Chile's significant social and geographic diversity, increasing coverage is essential to providing equitable forensic psychiatric care.

Another critical area requiring attention is the development of forensic psychiatry training programs within universities. Formal training opportunities in forensic psychiatry remain scarce, likely due to a historical lack of interest and understanding within the health sector regarding medical-legal issues. Expanding educational programs would strengthen forensic psychiatric services and foster greater research and academic engagement, which remains limited in Chile.

Finally, the relevant regulatory bodies must officially recognize forensic psychiatry as a subspecialty. Establishing formal certification and accreditation would contribute to the professionalization and standardization of forensic psychiatric practice in the country, ensuring that specialists receive adequate training and institutional recognition.

## References

Alvarado, R., Fritsch, R, Mundt, A., & Priebe, S. (2015). Prevalencia de Trastornos Mentales En Cárceles Chilenas. VIII Congreso Nacional de Investigación sobre Violencia y Delincuencia. Santiago de Chile. Fundación Paz Ciudadana.

Biblioteca del Congreso Nacional. (2017). Competencias de los Tribunales Militares. Ley fácil. Retrieved from https://www.bcn.cl/portal/leyfacil/recurso/competencia-de-los-tribunales-militares

Carozza, P., Rheinstein, M., & Glendon, M. A. (2024, November 8). Civil law. *Encyclopedia Britannica.* Retrieved from https://www.britannica.com/topic/civil-law-Romano-Germanic

Dresdner Cid, R. (2010). *Psiquiatría Forense en lo Penal.* Santiago de Chile: Ediciones de la Sociedad de Neurología, Psiquiatría y Neurocirugía de Chile.

Jarufe-Contreras, D. (2022). The capacity of exercise: A critical analysis of the rules of the civil law and the need for a modernization, beyond the interpretation of article 12 of the international convention on the rights of persons with disabilities. *Revista chilena de derecho privado, 38*, 9–61. https://doi.org/10.4067/S0718-80722022000100009

León, J. (2010). Capacidad para enfrentar juicio. In R.Dresdner Cid (Eds.), *Psiquiatría Forense en lo Penal.* Santiago de Chile: Ediciones de la Sociedad de Neurología, Psiquiatría y Neurocirugía de Chile.

Ministerio de Salud. (2014). *Informe nacional de salud mental y psiquiatría forense*. Santiago, Chile: Ministerio de Salud.

Ministry of Health. (2005–2006). *Política Nacional de Psiquiatría Forense*. Working Document. Santiago de Chile: Interinstitutional Working Group on Public Policies on Forensic Psychiatry.
Ministry of Health. (2018). *En Chile, Modelo de Gestión*. Santiago de Chile: Mental Health Thematic Network in the General Health Network.
Ministry of Health. (2021). *Law 21331*. On the recognition and protection of people's rights in mental health care. Retrieved from https://bcn.cl/2p863
Ministry of Justice. (1999). *Law 19640 establishes the constitutional organic law of the public prosecutor's office*. Retrieved from https://bcn.cl/27hn7
Ministry of Justice. (2001). *Law 19718*. Creates the Public Criminal Defense Office. Retrieved from https://bcn.cl/2jm4f
Ministry of Justice. (2012). *Decree 285*. Creates National Forensic Psychiatry Commission. Retrieved form https://bcn.cl/3ltxa
Ministry of Justice. (2015). *Resolution 8083 Exempt*. Approves update of the guide text on expert technical regulations on Mental Health in Psychiatry, Psychology and Legal Medical Social Work. Retrieved from https://bcn.cl/2lwlq
Ministry of the General Secretariat of the Presidency. (2005). *Decree 100*. Establishes the revised, coordinated, and systematized text of the political constitution of the Republica of Chile. Retrieved from https://bcn.cl/2eph2
Oberg, H., & Manso, M. (2011). *Derecho Procesal Orgánico*. Santiago: Legal Publishing Chile.
Orellana Torres, F. (2018). *Manual De Derecho Procesal*. Tercera Edición. Tomo I. Santiago de Chile: Librotecnia.
Orellana Torres, F. (2018). *Manual De Derecho Procesal*. Tercera Edición. Tomo V. Santiago de Chile: Librotecnia.
Sturner, M. (2007). Tendiendo un puente entre el Common Law y el derecho continental. ¿Constituyen las diferentes metodologías de trabajo un obstáculo contra una mayor armonización del derecho privado europeo? *Revista jurídica*, *15*, 177–193. Retrieved from https://revistas.uam.es/revistajuridica/article/download/6112/6575

# Part III

# Europe

# 7 England and Wales

*Megan Georgiou, Quazi Haque, Patrick Neville, Phil Huckle, and Piyal Sen*

## Brief Description

| | |
|---|---|
| **Location** | England and Wales are located in the United Kingdom, in Europe. |
| **Size** | England: 130,279 km$^2$; Wales: 20,761 km$^2$ |
| **Population** | England has an estimated population of 56.3 million. Wales has an estimated population of 3.1 million. |
| **Languages** | The official language of England is English, while the official languages of Wales are Welsh and English. |
| **Political system** | England and Wales follow a single legal system, known as English law. England is directly governed by the Parliament and government of the United Kingdom. Following devolution in 1997, Wales has a degree of self-government, which allows it to pass its own laws. |

## Legal System

Criminal law in England and Wales is designed to bring criminal suspects to justice by fair trial, thereby acquitting the innocent and convicting and punishing the guilty. It also has some obligation to rehabilitate people convicted of criminal acts. Criminal liability is based on actions (*actus reus*) and thoughts (*mens rea*). The standard test of criminal liability is expressed in the Latin phrase *actus reus non facit reum nisi mens sit rea,* which means that an act alone will not give rise to criminal liability unless done with a guilty state of mind. In English criminal law, judgements are made according to the principle 'beyond reasonable doubt'.

The English criminal justice system comprises three agencies (Crown Prosecution Service [CPS], 2017). First, there are the police. There are 43 police forces across England and Wales responsible for investigating crime, collecting evidence, and arresting or detaining suspected offenders. The *Police and Criminal Evidence Act 1984* provides a legislative framework for the powers of police officers in combating crime. Another agency is the Crown Prosecution Service, an independent authority that prosecutes criminal cases investigated

DOI: 10.4324/9781003376248-10

by the police and other investigative organisations in England and Wales. His Majesty's Courts and Tribunals Service are responsible for administering criminal, civil, and family courts and tribunals in England and Wales. Concerning the levels of court, all criminal cases start in the magistrates' court, where cases are presided over by professional or lay judges; there is no jury. Youth courts are special magistrates' courts for young people between 10 (the age of criminal responsibility) and 17 years old. For the remainder of criminal trials, those that are classed as the most serious offences, such as murder and rape, are tried by judge and jury at the Crown Court. It is the jury alone that decides on guilt or innocence. The judge is responsible for directing on the law and sentencing. The court system in England and Wales is predominantly adversarial. In case of new evidence or serious procedural error, appeals are heard by the Court of Appeal. The Supreme Court is the highest appeal court; however, it rarely hears criminal cases. Other agencies pertaining to England's criminal justice system include the Ministry of Justice, which is responsible for the courts, prisons, probation services, and attendance centres; the Home Office, which is the lead government for immigration and passports, drug policy, crime, fire, counterterrorism, and the police; and finally, His Majesty's Prison and Probation Service, whose core purpose is to carry out sentences handed down by the courts.

### *Mental Health Laws*

The *Mental Health Act 1983* sets out the provisions that apply to people with mental health problems who come into contact with the criminal justice system. 'Civil' patients are detained under Part II of the Act. Where there is suspicion of a mental disorder, Section 2 is applied for assessment and treatment for up to 28 days. This can be converted to Section 3 for further treatment. Patients with a known mental disorder are usually admitted directly under Section 3. 'Forensic' patients are detained under Part III of the Act due to their involvement in the criminal justice system via the courts and prisons. The treatment needs of civil patients require greater emphasis on their mental illness, whereas forensic patients have additional offence-related treatment needs. As a result, treatment plans should be person-centred to ensure patients are cared for in the most appropriate setting and at the earliest opportunity (Galappathie et al., 2017).

#### *Fitness to Plead*

Regarding prosecution, the Crown Prosecution Service has published guidance on mental health conditions and disorders regarding fitness to plead (CPS, 2019). Fitness to plead refers to a person's ability to participate in their criminal trial at the time of prosecution. In the Crown Court, the approach is set out in Sections 4 and 4A of the *Criminal Procedure (Insanity) Act 1964*. It is determined as soon as the question of fitness to plead arises, unless there is reason for the court to believe it is in the interests of justice to postpone consideration of fitness to be tried until any time up to the opening of the case for the defence. A judge must determine if the defendant is fit to plead and stand trial, and the decision is determined based on the balance of probabilities.

If the defendant raises or contests the issue, the prosecution must satisfy the court beyond reasonable doubt. Written or oral evidence by two or more registered medical practitioners (at least one of whom is approved by the Home Secretary) is required which states that the defendant is incapable of understanding the charges, deciding whether to plead guilty or not, exercising the right to challenge jurors, instructing solicitors and counsel, following the course of the proceedings, and/or giving evidence (Sections 4 and 4A of the *Criminal Procedure (Insanity) Act 1964* as amended and *R v John M*, 2003, following Pritchard, 1836).

The trial continues if the judge finds the defendant fit to plead. Medical evidence is only required to determine unfitness, and a judge can determine that a defendant is fit to plead without receiving medical evidence. Where the judge finds the defendant unfit to plead, a jury will determine whether the defendant committed the act without considering the defendant's *mens rea*. This hearing is not considered a trial, and upon a finding of unfitness, a trial should 'not proceed or further proceed'. The defendant is acquitted where they are deemed not to meet the criminal standard, and they receive a hospital order (with or without a restriction order), a supervision order, or an order for absolute discharge.

### *Not Guilty by Reason of Insanity*

Section 2 of the *Trial of Lunatics Act 1833* states that when the common law defence of 'insanity' is applied, it must be proved that, at the time of committing the act, the suspect was labouring under a 'defect of reason' from a 'disease of the mind' so as to not to know the nature and quality of the act being done, or that the suspect did not know what was being done was wrong ('wrong' meaning contrary to the law; Johnson, 2007; M'Naghten, 1843).

'Insanity', according to the legal definition, is assessed by a prosecutor and, where appropriate, by the court applying the M'Naghten criteria. The court must reach a special verdict by a jury in the Crown Court pronouncing the special verdict or by a finding of not guilty in the youth court or magistrates' court. Upon the return of the special verdict, the court must order a hospital order (with or without a restriction order), a supervision order, or an order for absolute discharge.

For both fitness to plead and not guilty by reason of insanity, it is important to note that the *Criminal Procedure (Insanity) Act 1964* does not apply in the magistrates' court and youth court. The statutory framework for dealing with issues of fitness to plead in the magistrates' court is set out by a combination of Section 37(3) of the *Mental Health Act 1983* and Section 11(1) of the *Power of Criminal Courts (Sentencing) Act 2000*. A youth court is a magistrates' court per Section 37(3) of the *Mental Health Act 1983*.

### *Decision Makers for Forensic Psychiatry*

#### *Mental Health Tribunals*

Mental health tribunals are for people who have been admitted to hospital under Section 2 or Section 3 of the *Mental Health Act 1983* or are being treated outside hospital under a Community Treatment Order. They take the form of formal hearings where an independent panel, comprising a judge, a tribunal doctor, and a specialist lay member, assesses whether an individual should remain in hospital or a Community Treatment Order (Royal College of Psychiatrists [RCPsych], 2015). In England, the First-tier Tribunal (Mental Health) handles appeals against detention. In Wales, this is managed by the Mental Health Review Tribunal for Wales.

## Forensic Psychiatry System

### *Structure and Function of the Forensic Psychiatry System in England and Wales*

England and Wales have formal forensic psychiatry systems. The forensic psychiatric system consists of pathways moving between secure mental health services, the criminal justice system, and non-secure settings, including the community. An individual's pathway may change depending on their needs and circumstances, and the care must be planned in consultation with the patient.

England and Wales provide secure mental health services. These services typically provide care and treatment for adults aged 18 years and over with complex chronic mental disorders that are linked to offending or seriously harmful behaviour. These include mental illness, personality disorder, and neurodevelopmental disorders, including learning disabilities and autism; people who are culturally deaf (D) or audiologically deaf (deaf); and people with an acquired brain injury. In most cases, patients are detained under the *Mental Health Act 1983*, and it has been deemed that their risk of harm to others and risk of escape from hospital cannot be managed safely within other mental health settings. Individuals may be involved with the criminal justice system and have restrictions imposed by the Ministry of Justice. There are high secure services which provide care and treatment to adults who present a grave and immediate risk to the public and who must not be able to escape from hospital. Medium secure services provide care and treatment to adults who present a serious risk of harm to others and whose escape from hospital must be prevented. Finally, low secure services provide care and treatment to adults who present a significant risk of harm to others and whose escape from hospital must be impeded (National Health Service [NHS] England, 2018a, 2018b). In England, forensic psychiatric service provision consists of three high-secure forensic hospitals (800 beds), approximately 60 medium-secure forensic hospitals (3,000–4,000 beds), approximately 112 low-secure forensic hospitals (3,000–4,000 beds), and prison psychiatric services (7,917 people recorded as receiving treatment for mental health illnesses in prison in England in March 2017; 31,328 people in prison report having mental health or wellbeing issues) (Sampson et al., 2016; RCPsych, 2019; National Audit Office, 2017). Recent research reported an increasing number of patients detained in hospital with restriction orders, from 3,118 patients in 2003 to 4,679 in 2016 (Hill et al., 2019). There was also an increase in patients transferred from prison and those admitted via other means. During this same period, the prison population increased.

### *Role of Forensic Psychiatry*

Forensic psychiatry provides assessment and treatment of people who are subject to legal restrictions and have mental health problems. They most commonly provide treatment in secure hospitals or prisons or deliver specialist community services. Most patients are referred from the criminal justice system. Still, health service referrals can also be received when a patient is perceived as a risk to themselves or others and cannot be safely managed in a less secure environment. Forensic psychiatrists provide specialist advice to the courts, the probation service, the prison service, and other health colleagues. They provide a detailed assessment of the risk of harm to others, risk management, treatment approaches, formulation, and therapeutic use of security. There are specialities within forensic psychiatry, including adolescent forensic psychiatry, forensic learning disability psychiatry, and forensic psychotherapy (NHS, 2021a).

In 2021, the Royal College of Psychiatrists recently conducted a census and captured information about the number of forensic psychiatrists in the United Kingdom (UK). However, these data represent 84% of National Health Service (NHS) organisations and eight independent healthcare providers; therefore, the figures do not accurately represent total posts. The data is separated by sector: NHS England, NHS Wales, and the independent sector. The independent sector represents posts across the United Kingdom. The relevant data from the census can be viewed in Table 7.1.

*Table 7.1* Forensic psychiatry posts

| *Country* | *Forensic psychiatry* | *Total (across all full and part-time posts)* | *Vacant or unfilled* |
|---|---|---|---|
| **NHS England** | Consultants | 371 | 27 |
| | Speciality doctors | 105 | 24 |
| **NHS Wales** | Consultants | 13 | |
| | Speciality doctors | 3 | 2 |
| **Independent** | Consultants | 80 | 1 |
| | Speciality doctors | 12 | 2 |

*Source:* Royal College of Psychiatrists, 2021a.

### *Forensic Psychiatry Profession*

#### *Specialist Training and Qualifications*

Before training as a psychiatrist, a Bachelor of Medicine, Bachelor of Surgery (MBBS, MBChB) degree must be completed. A two-year foundation programme is followed by three years of core training. After completing the first year of foundation training, trainees become eligible for registration as a doctor with the General Medical Council. Foundation training includes undertaking rotations in a range of specialties, including psychiatry.

Psychiatry training comprises two main stages. The first stage, core psychiatry training (CTI-3), lasts three years. It provides experience in the different areas of psychiatric practice through four to six-month training posts. Following core psychiatry training, there is specialised training in psychiatry (ST4–6), which lasts three years. This training leads to membership of the Royal College of Psychiatrists (RCPsych). It comprises three blocks of 12 months each of approved clinical training. An annual portfolio review and assessments of various skills demonstrated during the training in areas relevant to the speciality, such as forensic psychiatry. One needs at least 36 months of full-time experience in psychiatry (not including foundation modules) or 36 months of full-time training in psychiatry posts in a European Union country before being accepted. On completion of training, psychiatrists receive a Certificate of Completion of Training (CCT), which will be entered into the General Medical Council's specialist register. This enables trained psychiatrists to apply for consultant posts. In addition, there are Speciality Doctors and Associate Specialists working in psychiatry who are neither trainees nor consultants but form an important part of the psychiatric team (RCPsych, 2025).

#### *National Collaborations and Networks*

NHS England is responsible for commissioning adult secure mental health services for people detained under the *Mental Health Act 1983*, which it delegated to Provider Collaboratives through lead provider contracts for defined geographic areas of England. NHS Wales commissions directly through the commissioning structures of NHS Wales itself. Service specifications define the standards of care expected by funded providers (NHS England, 2018a, 2018b). Furthermore, The Royal College of Psychiatrists is home to the Faculty of Forensic Psychiatry (RCPsych, 2025). Its purpose is to provide leadership in the field and foster multidisciplinary and inter-agency working.

In addition, the Quality Network for Forensic Mental Health Services and the Quality Network for Prison Mental Health Services, part of the Royal College of Psychiatrists' Centre for Quality Improvement, offer peer-based networks. These initiatives adopt a multidisciplinary approach to improving quality using specialist quality standards. Member services, consisting of providers across the United Kingdom and Ireland, are subject to an annual peer-review process to support service development and access opportunities for sharing and learning best practices and networking. The process engages senior managers, frontline staff, patients, family and friends of patients, and key stakeholders (RCPsych, 2021b).

## Forensic Psychiatry Service (Provision of Care)

### *Forensic Patient Characteristics*

Patients are generally admitted to forensic mental health services from other hospitals, the community, or the criminal justice system. The patient population is characterised by people with psychotic disorders, personality disorders, cognitive disorders, learning disabilities, and substance misuse (associated with other mental disorders).

In England and Wales, female patients are a minority in forensic services. Only 18% of patients are women, which is still the highest in Europe (Tomlin et al., 2021). A typical long-stay forensic patient was born in the United Kingdom and had a mean age of 45 years. Almost 60% were classified as violent offenders, with just over 20% having committed both violent and sexual offences. The proportion of primary sex offenders was less than 6%, but about 20% had convictions for arson. Of those with an index offence, offence against a person was the most common, followed by sexual offence. About 16.5% had no index offence prompting admission (Völlm et al., 2018).

### *Exiting the System*

In England and Wales, patients in secure psychiatric settings typically remain much longer than those in general psychiatric settings. Their stays often exceed the length of time they would have served if imprisoned for the same offence. In the United Kingdom, forensic services consume up to a fifth of the mental health budget while looking after a relatively small proportion of patients. On average, a service user would occupy a high secure bed in the United Kingdom for 70 months and a medium-secure bed for 26 months (Dima et al., 2024; Völlm et al., 2017). Moreover, a 2018 study found that 22% of patients in high security and 18% of patients in medium security met the definition of 'long-stay' (long-stay status was defined as 5 years in medium secure care or 10 years in high secure care, or 15 years in a combination of high- and medium-secure settings). Of these, 20% stayed longer than 20 years (Völlm et al., 2018). The criteria for absolute discharge would be recovery from mental disorder and the resultant reduction of risk to a degree that the person can be managed in the community or a general psychiatric setting, not requiring a secure inpatient psychiatric setting any longer.

***Assessment, Treatment, and Rehabilitation Programmes***

In England and Wales, secure services provide evidence-based care and treatment by appropriately qualified practitioners, including specialist treatment programmes. Interventions are recovery-orientated and outcome-focused. This includes a model for collaborative risk assessment and management. Tools like HCR-20 are commonly used in forensic settings for violence risk assessment, following research which indicates they are better at identifying risk than clinician opinions (Ægisdóttir et al., 2006). Providers must deliver training to service users around risk assessment, but tools to monitor the quality of risk assessment are lacking in clinical practice (Sen et al., 2015). Services aim to support the patient in safely returning to the community, stepping down to a lower level of security or out of secure services, or being transferred to prison or an immigration removal centre.

Locally, models of care vary between providers, service types, and populations. The model of care broadly defines the way health services are delivered across the care pathway and according to best practice. It should interlink with the service's policies and procedures and be designed to deliver effective care and treatment. A recent paper identifies the four key elements of a model of care within forensic mental health services. These include goals, pathways and processes, treatment programmes, and systematic evaluation. Applying a common approach, this framework contributes to a service's shared vision, mission, and values through improved engagement and involvement of all stakeholders (Kennedy, 2021).

Care and treatment focus on a reduction and/or management of risk through programmes addressing offending and risk behaviours. The core to providing effective therapeutic interventions in secure services is the application of physical, procedural, and relational security measures. These are necessary to ensure a safe and recovery-focused environment. The Care Programme Approach provides a framework for multidisciplinary working, evidence-based care, and inter-agency collaboration. This whole care pathway approach supports patients to engage with their care plan and transition to the next point of care in their pathway. Patients are supported to access social, educational, occupational, and vocational opportunities that are meaningful to them and reflect the point of the pathway they have reached. They should be available to them during the day and evening, seven days a week. Physical healthcare needs should also be assessed and managed, with the same access to the full range of primary healthcare interventions in the community, and access to secondary physical healthcare services should be facilitated where required.

A leave of absence may be planned into a patient's pathway to support rehabilitation and recovery. This is task-orientated and should support the development of social, interpersonal, and practical skills and community reintegration. Leave is planned with other appropriate agencies, and care staff may escort patients. Discharge planning should start at the point of assessment, and an estimated discharge date should be agreed upon within the first four weeks of admission.

Women have distinct needs and profiles. They often come into secure services without a criminal conviction and are admitted due to the risk to themselves rather than others (Bartlett et al., 2014). Therefore, women's secure services provide gender-sensitive and specific care. Care should emphasise dignity, empowerment, and relational security to support women to feel safe and engage in treatment.

### *Transforming Care*

In 2016, around 1,300 people with a learning disability and/or autism were recorded in secure forensic inpatient settings in England. As part of the Transforming Care agenda, efforts were made to reduce the number of people from these populations in secure settings and to increase forensic capacity within the community by reducing inappropriate hospital admissions and length of stay (NHS England, 2017).

### *Personality Disorder Services*

When people have a mental illness alongside a personality disorder, and they are at risk of causing harm to others, they may require admission to a secure hospital for treatment. The Offender Personality Disorder Pathway, co-commissioned and managed by NHS England and His Majesty's Prison and Probation Service, supports identifying, assessing, and treating people in prisons, secure hospitals, and the community who have a personality disorder. The pathway supports men and women who present a high risk of harm to others and are likely to have a severe personality disorder linked to their offending behaviour. For adults, personality disorder services are arranged in tiers of increasing intensity of intervention, from local specialist services to high secure hospital placements. To support patients with a personality disorder transition through the criminal justice system, over 200 English prisons and probation facilities have introduced supportive, contained environments known as Psychologically Informed Planned Environments. Concerns remain about the way society treats people who experience difficulties relating to a personality disorder diagnosis (RCPsych, 2020). A recent review recommended that the secure hospital and community forensic pathway should include a network of specialist providers from high, medium, and low secure hospital services to support patients' therapeutic goals. Integration should also occur with the Offender Personality Disorder Programme, and further resources are required for community forensic mental health services to ensure appropriate provision (RCPsych, 2020).

### *NHS-Led Provider Collaboratives*

Within England, a national model was introduced to transform services for people requiring forensic mental health care and treatment. Known as Provider Collaboratives or New Care Models, the aim was to introduce consistent care pathways and protocols and reduce referrals placed out-of-area (NHS England, 2020). The model takes a system-wide approach to ensure patients are supported in the most appropriate setting for their requirements. Greater investment has been promised to community-based services to increase step-down and rehabilitation opportunities further and reduce lengths of stay. Five new forensic pathways were introduced to support this, including women's, acute, assertive rehabilitation, community, and specialist (NHS England, 2018c). Each of these pathways aimed to step down patients whose only previous experience was in traditional inpatient settings, leading to new teams with specialist clinicians in these groups working to look for alternatives to admissions. The specialist pathway includes patients with neurodevelopmental impairments, like intellectual disability or autism. Each pathway includes specialist clinicians working to find the best outcome for the patients. In Wales, the *Mental Health (Wales) Measure 2010* outlines how people with mental health problems are supported. Those who require more specialised care and support have care coordinators and an individualised care and treatment plan.

### *The 'Trieste Model'*

In England, a national pilot is trialling a new initiative to reduce the likelihood of people requiring formal admission or detention to psychiatric services. Known as the 'Trieste Model', community-based 24/7 mental healthcare hubs have been designed to help anyone in distress access crisis services and wider support without a referral. The model was influenced by the Department of Mental Health in Trieste, Italy, which pioneered the prioritisation of social context in supporting people with mental health needs (British Medical Association, 2024). This pilot has the potential to transform the way people access mental health services and reduce the frequency of admissions and lengths of stay in inpatient settings (Parliament UK, 2021).

## Strengths and Weaknesses of the Forensic Systems of England and Wales

Developing secure services over the last four decades has been an incremental policy development that has seen capacity across low- and medium secure care rise as high secure capacity has reduced. The ambition to have locally available low- and medium-secure beds across England and Wales has been a success; each locality now has sufficient capacity to meet the majority of needs. Nationally agreed standards (College Centre for Quality Improvement) and specifications (NHS England and NHS Wales) developed over the last 12 years have improved the consistency of services and the quality of the service environment regarding both safety and the need to commission new or enhanced capacity. This is a success and a strength of the system.

The improved estate and the consistency of specification and standards have improved the provision of care and treatment as a system. Individual experience is wholly subject to personal needs. Still, with the ambition to have service user engagement in service development, the journey to increase service users and carer engagement is a success, but more work is required to make these changes substantial and effective in future service design and provision to make it a strength.

It should be noted that the policy changes around the forensic estate have created pressures as the range and capacity of non-forensic services have reduced across the mental health and social care system. This has led to changes in the effectiveness of care pathways as delay and placement difficulties have reduced the forensic system's efficiency as the length of stay increases. This policy impact outside the forensic system has been a weakness in the integrated ambition of an NHS-led mental health forensic system.

The healthcare systems of England and Wales have also seen resources reduced in real terms. Since austerity measures were introduced by the UK government in 2010, service delivery has been significantly compromised, and mental health services are failing the criminal justice system (Brooker & Coid, 2022; Sen et al., 2022). This is a consequence of both national policy changes and the unique way the NHS funds services in mental health without an effective funding system tailored to the provision of mental health service, but rather using proxy efficiency gain from non-tariff mechanisms. This has led to significant funding reductions in real terms since the financial crisis. This has contributed to the reduction of available non-forensic pathway options across health and social care, exacerbating the care pathway challenges and leading to a significant increase in delayed care, which remains a critical weakness.

The Provider Collaborative model implemented by NHS England supports the integration of local forensic services to improve the quality of the service and pathway. This is welcome, and the allocation of funding to these collaboratives supports better oversight of the effectiveness of the system. These are clinically led models with the care pathway, types of intervention, and planning for population needs led by the local forensic system. It is early in the process, but it is a welcome development to provide specialised services with effective local leadership and should be a strength in future commissioning.

## References

Ægisdóttir, S., White, M. J., Spengler, P. M., Maugherman, A. S., Anderson, L. A., Cook, R. S., Nichols, C. N., Lampropoulos, G. K., Walker, B. S., Cohen, G., & Rush, J. D. (2006). The meta-analysis of clinical judgment project: Fifty-six years of accumulated research on clinical versus statistical prediction. *The Counseling Psychologist*, *34*(3), 340–382. https://doi.org/10.1177/0011000005285875

Bartlett, A., Somers, N., Fiander, M., & Harty, M. A. (2014). Pathways of care of women in secure hospitals: Which women go where and why. *British Journal of Psychiatry*, *205*, 298–306. https://doi.org/10.1192/bjp.bp.113.137547

British Medical Association. (2024). Mental health: No locks, no stigma. Retrieved from https://thedoctor.bma.org.uk/articles/health-society/mental-health-no-locks-no-stigma/

Brooker, C., & Coid, J. (2022). Mental health services are failing the criminal justice system. *BMJ, 376*, e069776. https://doi.org/10.1136/bmj-2021-069776

*Criminal Procedure (Insanity) Act 1964*. Retrieved from https://www.legislation.gov.uk/ukpga/1964/84/contents

Crown Prosecution Service. (2017). *The criminal justice system* [Webpage]. Retrieved from https://www.cps.gov.uk/about-cps/criminal-justice-system

Crown Prosecution Service. (2019). *Mental health conditions and disorders: Draft prosecution guidance*. Retrieved from https://www.cps.gov.uk/publication/mental-health-conditions-and-disorders-draft-prosecution-guidance

Dima, A., Wazir, A., Clark-Castillo, R., Zakopoulos, I., Smith, S., & Gaughran, F. (2024). Factors influencing the length of stay in forensic psychiatric settings: A systematic review. *BMC Health Services Research, 24*(1), 400. https://doi.org/10.1186/s12913-024-10863-x

Galappathie, N., Khan, S., & Hussain, A. (2017). Civil and forensic patients in secure psychiatric settings: A comparison. *BJPsych Bulletin, 41*(3), 156–159. https://doi.org/10.1192/pb.bp.115.052910

Hill, S. A., Riordan-Eva, E., & Hosking, A. (2019). Trends in the number of restricted patients in England and Wales 2003–2016: Implications for forensic psychiatry services. *Medicine, Science and the Law, 59*(1), 42–48. https://doi.org/10.1177/0025802419825596

*Johnson, [2007],* EWCA Crim 1978.

Kennedy, H. (2021). Models of care in forensic psychiatry. *BJPsych Advances, 28*(1), 48–59. https://doi.org/10.1192/bja.2021.34

*M'Naghten's Case,* [1843], 10 Cl & F 200.

*Mental Health Act 1983*. Retrieved from https://www.legislation.gov.uk/ukpga/1983/20/contents

*Mental Health (Wales) Measure 2010*. Retrieved from https://www.legislation.gov.uk/mwa/2010/7/contents

National Audit Office. (2017). *Mental health in prisons*. Retrieved from https://www.nao.org.uk/wp-content/uploads/2017/06/Mental-health-in-prisons.pdf

National Health Service. (2021a). *Forensic psychiatry* [Webpage]. Retrieved from https://www.healthcareers.nhs.uk/explore-roles/doctors/roles-doctors/psychiatry/forensic-psychiatry

National Health Service England. (2017). *Transforming care. Model service specifications: Supporting implementation of the service model*. Retrieved from https://www.england.nhs.uk/wp-content/uploads/2017/02/model-service-spec−2017.pdf

National Health Service England. (2018a). *Service specification: Low secure mental health services (adult)*. Retrieved from https://www.england.nhs.uk/publication/service-specification-low-secure-mental-health-services-adult/

National Health Service England. (2018b). *Service specification: Medium secure mental health services (adult)*. Retrieved from https://www.england.nhs.uk/publication/service-specification-medium-secure-mental-health-services-adult/

National Health Service England. (2018c). *Transforming services for forensic patients* [Blog]. Retrieved from https://www.england.nhs.uk/blog/transforming-services-for-forensic-patients/

National Health Service England. (2020). *NHS-led provider collaboratives: Specialised mental health, learning disability and autism services*. Retrieved from https://www.england.nhs.uk/mental-health/nhs-led-provider-collaboratives/

Parliament UK. (2021). *The treatment of autistic people and people with learning disabilities*. Retrieved from https://publications.parliament.uk/pa/cm5802/cmselect/cmhealth/21/2104.htm

*Police and Criminal Evidence Act 1984*. Retrieved from https://www.legislation.gov.uk/ukpga/1984/60/contents

*Power of Criminal Courts (Sentencing) Act 2000*. Retrieved from https://www.legislation.gov.uk/ukpga/2000/6/contents

*Pritchard*, [1836], EWHC KB 1

*R v John M*, [2003], EWCA Crim 3452

Royal College of Psychiatrists. (2015). *Guide to mental health tribunals* [Webpage]. Retrieved from https://www.rcpsych.ac.uk/mental-health/treatments-and-wellbeing/guide-to-mental-health-tribunals

Royal College of Psychiatrists. (2019). *Quality network for forensic mental health services: Aggregated report LSU cycle 6 2017–2019*. Retrieved from https://www.rcpsych.ac.uk/docs/default-source/improving-care/ccqi/quality-networks/secure-forensic/forensic-annual-reports-qnfmhs/qnfmhs-lsu-aggregated-report-2017–2019.pdf?sfvrsn=10e285e1_2

Royal College of Psychiatrists. (2020). *Services for people diagnosable with personality disorder (PS01/20)*. Retrieved from https://www.rcpsych.ac.uk/docs/default-source/improving-care/better-mh-policy/position-statements/ps01_20.pdf?sfvrsn=85af7fbc_2

Royal College of Psychiatrists. (2021a). *Census 2021: Workforce figures for consultant psychiatrists, specialty doctor psychiatrists and physician associates in mental health*. Retrieved from https://www.rcpsych.ac.uk/docs/default-source/improving-care/workforce/census-2021-completed-draft.pdf?sfvrsn=191319cb_2

Royal College of Psychiatrists. (2021b). *QNFMHS standards for forensic mental health services—Fourth edition*. Retrieved from https://www.rcpsych.ac.uk/improving-care/ccqi/quality-networks-accreditation/forensic-mental-health-services/publications-and-resources

Royal College of Psychiatrists. (2025). *Faculty of forensic psychiatry* [Webpage]. Retrieved from https://www.rcpsych.ac.uk/members/your-faculties/forensic-psychiatry

Sampson, S., Edworthy, R., Völlm, B., & Bulten, E. (2016). Long-term forensic mental health services: An exploratory comparison of 18 European Countries. *International Journal of Forensic Mental Health*, *15*(4), 333–351. https://doi.org/10.1080/14999013.2016.1221484

Sen, P., Forrester, A., Georgiou, M., Haque, Q., Ismail, N., & Neville, P. (2022). Mental health in the criminal justice system: austerity must now be reversed [letter]. *BMJ*, *376*, o727.

Sen, P., Lindsey, S., Chatterjee, N., Rama-Iyer, R., & Picchioni, M. (2015). An audit of the quality of HCR-20 violence risk assessments in a low secure service. *Journal of Psychiatric Intensive Care*, *11*(S1), e3.

Tomlin, J., Lega, I., Braun, P., Kennedy, H. G., Herrando, V. T., Barroso, R., Castelletti, L., Mirabella, F., Scarpa, F., Völlm, B., & the experts of COST Action IS1302. (2021). Forensic mental health in Europe: Some key figures. *Social Psychiatry and Psychiatric Epidemiology*, *56*, 109–117. https://doi.org/10.1007/s00127-020-01909-6

*Trial of Lunatics Act 1883*. Retrieved from https://www.legislation.gov.uk/ukpga/Vict/46-47/38/contents

Völlm, B. A., Edworthy, R., Holley, J., Talbot, E., Majid, S., Duggan, C., Weaver, T., & McDonald, R. (2017). A mixed-methods study exploring the characteristics and needs of long stay patients in high and medium secure settings in England: Implications for service organisation. *Health and Social Care Delivery Research*, *5*(11), 1–234. https://doi.org/10.3310/hsdr05110

Völlm, B. A., Edworthy, R., Huband, N., Talbot, E., Majid, S., Holley, J., Furtado, V., Weaver, T., McDonald, R., & Duggan, C. (2018). Characteristics and pathways of long-stay patients in high and medium secure settings in England: A secondary publication from a large mixed-methods study. *Frontiers in Psychiatry*, *9*, 140. https://doi.org/10.3389%2Ffpsyt.2018.00140

# 8 France

*Sébastien Prat and Estébanine Moulia-Pelat*

## Brief Description

| | |
|---|---|
| **Location** | France is located in Western Europe. |
| **Size** | 551,695 km$^2$ |
| **Population** | 68 million |
| **Language** | The official language of France is French. |
| **Political system** | France is a unitary semi-presidential republic where executive power is shared between the President and the Government, led by the Prime Minister.<br>The President, elected for five years, appoints the Prime Minister, presides over the Council of Ministers, and represents France internationally. The Prime Minister leads the Government, implements laws, and oversees administration.<br>The bicameral Parliament consists of the National Assembly (elected for five years) and the Senate (elected for six years). The National Assembly passes laws and scrutinises the Government, while the Senate reviews and amends legislation.<br>The independent judiciary ensures the rule of law. Ordinary courts handle civil and criminal cases, with the *Cour de cassation* as the highest court. |

## Legal System

### *Legislative Framework*

France operates under both an inquisitorial system and a civil law system. The judicial system is a cornerstone of its democratic society, ensuring justice and the rule of law. The court system is organised hierarchically into three levels. At the base are the courts of first instance (*tribunaux de première instance*, renamed *tribunaux judiciaires* in 2020). These ordinary courts handle civil and criminal cases. For criminal matters, the *tribunaux correctionnels* handle misdemeanours, while the *tribunaux de police* deal with minor offences. The most serious crimes, such as murder, are tried in the *cour d'assises*, which includes a jury of citizens

DOI: 10.4324/9781003376248-11

and a judge. Appeals from these courts are heard in a *cour d'appel*, and the highest level of appeal is the *Cour de cassation*, which functions similarly to the Supreme Court in Canada or the United States.

In French law, offences committed by an individual are categorised into *amendes*, *délits*, and *crimes* based on the severity of the offence and the maximum possible sentence. *Amendes* are minor offences punishable by fines with no possibility of jail time. *Délits* are more serious and can result in imprisonment of up to 10 years, along with possible fines. *Crimes* are the most severe offences punishable by over 10 years of imprisonment. When a *crime* is committed, the trial is held in a specialised court for serious offences called the *cour d'assises*, which is composed of jurors and presided over by judges. The *cour d'assises* convenes only when there is a need to judge the most serious offences, such as those classified as crimes under French law.

### ***Mental Health Laws***

#### *Fitness to Stand Trial and Criminal Responsibility*

The French Criminal Code (*code pénal*) contains no concept of fitness to stand trial. However, it is not uncommon for a judge to order a mental health assessment to be conducted by a psychiatrist or psychologist, in which the question regarding the ability to understand the sentencing will be addressed. Nevertheless, the Criminal Code clearly outlines the laws pertaining to criminal responsibility. In France, there are three designations of criminal responsibility: (i) no criminal responsibility, (ii) diminished criminal responsibility, and (iii) full criminal responsibility. Article 122-1 of the Criminal Code addresses the grounds for no and diminished criminal responsibility in the forensic context. The law states:

> A person who, when the act was committed, was suffering from a psychological or neuropsychological disorder that abolishes his discernment or his ability to control his action, is not criminally liable.
>
> (Loi n°2014-896, Article 122-1-1)

> A person who, at the time he acted, was suffering from a psychological or neuropsychological disorder that reduced his discernment or impeded his ability to control his actions, remains punishable; however, the court shall take this into account when it decides the penalty and determines its regime.
>
> (Loi n°2022-52, Article 122-1-2)

The Criminal Code does not explicitly address 'full responsibility'. It is implied that if the discernment or ability to control actions is not abolished or diminished, the individual has a full ability to understand and control their actions. Hence, they are considered responsible and can be sentenced.

The judge makes the decision regarding criminal responsibility and will rely on the clinical opinion provided by the psychiatric or psychological assessment. The Criminal Code does not explicitly mention any specific mental health disorder. Instead, it refers to a ‘psychological or neurological disorder’, allowing the expert to consider any relevant condition. If an individual is found not criminally responsible, they are not subject to any sentence, as it is deemed that they could not understand the nature of their actions. Consequently, they lacked volitional intent and cannot be punished. This typically applies to people who have psychosis and exhibited active symptoms at the time of the offence.

If an individual is deemed to have diminished responsibility, the judge can adjust the sentencing by reducing prison terms by up to one-third or converting a life sentence to a maximum of 30 years, taking this circumstance into account. However, this reduction in sentence is not mandatory and is at the judge’s discretion. It is considered that the individual had some understanding of their actions. However, due to the nature of their illness, they cannot fully control their behaviour and, therefore, cannot be punished to the full extent. This typically applies to people with a personality disorder involving impulse control issues or depressive symptoms but without significant cognitive impairment. Other sentences, such as fines or community service, can also be reduced. In practice, it has been observed that some legal decisions may, at times, be more severe, as the person is seen as unable to fully control their actions, which may pose a risk of future offences.

Considering the prevalence of substance use in the general population, it is very common for psychiatric and psychological assessments ordered by the court to address the implications of substance use (alcohol, cannabis, or other drugs; cannabis remains illegal in France) in the commission of the offence, particularly regarding the development of the symptoms reported by the accused or observed by others. The concept of substance use disorder and its implications for criminal responsibility has been widely debated in France. Before 2022, the French Criminal Code did not specify anything regarding the origin of this disorder.

As a result, substance-induced psychosis was previously grounds for a finding of not criminally responsible. However, a new law that revised certain aspects of criminal responsibility (Loi n° 2022-52), enacted in January 2022, has altered how judges assess substance use in determinations of criminal responsibility. This change in French law regarding criminal responsibility and substance-induced psychosis was influenced by a high-profile murder case in which the accused, while under the influence of cannabis, argued that it triggered a psychotic episode. In 2021, the accused was found not criminally responsible, and this ruling generated significant controversy, ultimately prompting these legal reforms (Lemoine, 2021).

Introduced with the new law, Article 122-1-2 of the Criminal Code now addresses the use of substances and diminished responsibility (Loi n° 2022-52, Article 122-1-2). It specifies that a reduced sentence cannot be applied when a finding of diminished responsibility is made if the act was committed under the influence of the voluntary consumption of psychoactive substances illegally or excessively. The new law also addresses individuals who committed a crime. At the same time, their discernment or ability to control their actions was impaired—in other words, those who were unaware of what they were doing due to substance use close to the time of the offence. The interpretation of this new article in the code is more complex and has been described by some authors as ineffective (Couturier, 2022). How it is written seems to address people who deliberately use substances to help them manifest criminal behaviour. However, Article 122-1-2 is only applicable if the substance has incapacitated the person to the point of losing control over their actions. There is still ambiguity regarding how these two elements can be reconciled from both behavioural and clinical viewpoints. One might argue that a person with the intention of committing an offence would not willingly consume substances that could hinder their ability to do so.

However, it is likely that this provision will apply only rarely and may not be relevant to people already diagnosed with a severe mental disorder. Future cases will likely help clarify the nuances and practical implications of this new law. What may happen, however, is that defining the role of substances through these new sections could effectively close the theoretical debate on substance-induced psychosis in people who did not intend to commit a crime. This specific aspect is not clearly addressed in the law and may still be considered a legitimate reason to find someone not criminally responsible. Overall, legal decisions related to the impact of substances on behaviour, commonly assessed in forensic mental health evaluations, will require time to be fully understood within the French context.

## Forensic Psychiatry System

### *Structure and Function of the Forensic Psychiatric System*

France does not have a formal forensic system. When an individual is found not criminally responsible in France, their level of dangerousness is also evaluated. If they are determined not to pose a risk to the community, they can be released without any sentencing. In such cases, there may be no requirement for treatment. However, if an individual is deemed not criminally responsible but considered a risk to the community, they are placed in the civil system under involuntary status. The entirety of France's forensic psychiatric system operates within its civil framework.

In France, there are no specialised forensic units for individuals deemed not criminally responsible but considered a risk to community safety. Instead, these individuals can be admitted to any hospital within their local area, where they are treated alongside other patients, both voluntary and involuntary. The units primarily consist of a diverse range of diagnoses and needs. As a result, a forensic patient might share a room with someone who is receiving psychiatric treatment voluntarily. Furthermore, this set-up can lead to clinical teams lacking specific training in conducting risk assessments to determine a patient's privileges.

One specific unit often used for forensic patients is the Unit for Difficult Patients (*unité pour malades difficiles*). These units accommodate patients who have been found not criminally responsible and considered dangerous, as well as those who may not have committed any crimes but are difficult to treat and exhibit violent behaviour. France has 10 such units, functioning as fully equipped care facilities offering intensive care and patient treatment (Bouchard et al., 2022). They are designed with an exterior perimeter that effectively controls the risk of escape, while the interior focuses on providing appropriate care (de Chantérac, 2023).

Involuntary treatment, including in forensic settings, can also be provided on an outpatient basis. In France, the term 'involuntary care' is preferred over 'involuntary admission', as individuals are not required to remain hospitalised for the entire duration of their time in the forensic system. This terminology was updated with the 2012 reform of involuntary status. Instead of remaining in a hospital, patients can transition from inpatient to outpatient care with a community treatment plan while retaining the same involuntary status. This approach ensures a continuum of care without significant changes to the care plan or clinical team, allowing for easier patient readmission if the care plan is not followed or proves inadequate.

### *Role of Forensic Psychiatry*

Forensic psychiatrists primarily perform court-ordered assessments, mainly in criminal cases, which involve evaluating criminal responsibility and conducting a risk assessment. They also conduct assessments within the civil sector, including independent medical examinations. Regarding treatment, forensic psychiatrists are not responsible for caring for forensic patients. Instead, general psychiatrists provide treatment in the hospitals where these patients are located. Some forensic psychiatrists may offer care in detention centres. Due to the limited scope of their work, most forensic psychiatrists engage in clinical practice outside the forensic field.

### *Decision Makers in Forensic Psychiatry*

Identifying decision makers in forensic psychiatry is a complex task, as France does not have a formal forensic system. Consequently, who is considered a decision maker depends on how forensic psychiatry is defined. Several parties are involved in the decision-making process, including forensic psychiatrists, who conduct the initial assessments of criminal responsibility. However, even if an expert provides an opinion, the judge is not obligated to follow it. Therefore, the judge remains a key decision maker for forensic patients in France. If a person is admitted to hospital for treatment, a general psychiatrist will also be involved in care-related decision making. They become the primary figure in the care process and any potential discharge back into the community. They are also responsible for designing an outpatient treatment plan, which allows the clinical team to maintain some level of mandatory care while the individual resides in the community. A practical point to note is that psychiatrists and clinical teams may not have any forensic or formal violent risk-assessment training. As a result, their decisions may not fully consider established literature on risk assessment and risk management in the forensic context.

Unlike other countries, France does not have tribunals that make decisions for forensic patients once they have been admitted for treatment. There may be instances where a panel of professionals will review a case, but this occurs only in particular circumstances, such as when the patient is deemed to present an extreme risk, and the *préfet* (the state-appointed regional representative responsible for public administration and security) requires additional information (Loi n° 2011-803, Article L3213-5-1). This committee consists of three members: the treating psychiatrist, a psychiatrist not involved in treating the patient (but from the same institution), and another member of the patient's treatment team (Loi n° 2011-803, Article L3211-9).

### *Reports by Forensic Experts*

In criminal matters, a forensic psychiatric assessment can be requested at various stages of the judicial process and by several professionals. During the investigation (*instruction*) phase, it is not uncommon for reports to be requested by the police, who operate under the authority of the office of the prosecutor (*juge d'instruction*). These reports help guide the next steps of the process, including the decision to proceed with the prosecution or to recommend a finding of not criminally responsible. Prosecutors can also order psychiatric assessments to be conducted. Responsible for investigating criminal cases before trial, the prosecutor oversees the remainder of the investigation during the preliminary phase. They then prepare recommendations for the court and, more generally, for the judge.

The investigation occurs when further evidence is needed to determine whether one or more individuals should be charged with a crime. The prosecutor has additional powers to collect evidence beyond their initial investigative authority. A key principle of the investigation phase is its impartiality. The prosecutor must avoid any appearance of bias towards one party or individual. In identifying a suspect, they must seek evidence supporting their guilt and evidence that could exonerate them. One of the tools available to the prosecutor is the ability to request a psychiatric or psychological assessment.

In criminal cases, the assessment and subsequent report must determine whether the individual's psychological or neurological disorder directly contributed to the crime or impaired their ability to control their actions. In France, these assessments are typically conducted by a psychiatrist or a psychologist. In some jurisdictions, psychiatrists primarily evaluate offenders, while psychologists assess victims, although no formal rule dictates this division. The French model, in which a single clinician conducts the assessment, contrasts with practices in other countries where cases are often examined collaboratively through discussion among multiple professionals.

In France, psychiatrists or psychologists gather all relevant information themselves—without input from social workers for social history—and conduct assessments following a consult-based model. There is no dedicated funding for inpatient admission to facilitate these evaluations. While some assessors use risk assessment tools, their use is neither mandatory nor widespread. Instead, psychiatrists often rely on their professional judgement rather than employing a structured professional judgment (SPJ) tool, a scientifically developed method designed to assess risk factors while minimising biases. However, this practice is gradually evolving with the increasing dissemination of risk-assessment education and its strong scientific foundation. Forensic expert reports are typically based on a single interview with the accused.

According to Protais and Moreau (2009), prosecutors have eight standard questions they can ask a forensic expert. However, they may also include additional questions at their discretion. The typical questions are as follows:

1. Does the examination reveal any mental or psychological abnormalities? If so, describe the related disorders.
2. Is the offence related to this disorder?
3. Does the person present a danger to themselves or others?
4. Is the person able to understand the penal sanction?
5. Can the person be treated or rehabilitated?
6. Did the person suffer from a mental or neuropsychological disorder that impaired their discernment or ability to control their actions at the time of the offence?
7. Provide information about the appropriateness of a court-ordered treatment.
8. Provide any observation deemed useful for establishing the truth.

Based on this list, it is evident that a single assessment and report cover a broad scope, addressing criminal responsibility, the individual's capacity to understand sentencing, and future risk. While the expert provides their professional opinion, judges are not obligated to follow the recommendations outlined in the assessment report.

Another type of assessment in criminal matters involves adjusting incarceration or probation terms, a process overseen by a specific judge—a *judge d'application des peines*. Their role is to ensure that the sentences are properly carried out while considering the person's rehabilitation and reintegration into society. Sentences can be amended, but only if such adjustments are permitted by the French Criminal Code, which imposes strict guidelines. To determine the next steps—whether during imprisonment or probation—the judge may request a psychiatric assessment to evaluate the person's risk factors and rehabilitation needs.

Forensic psychiatry experts are also called upon to conduct these assessments at the request of another special judge (*juge des libertés et de la détention*), who ensures that the deprivation of freedom follows the legal principles. This judge oversees both detention centres and psychiatric facilities. When an individual is incarcerated in a detention centre for a crime they have committed (before or after sentencing), this judge ensures that the decision to incarcerate is justified, necessary, and appropriate in accordance with legal principles. When the judge intervenes in psychiatric institutions, their role is to ensure that involuntarily admitted patients (whose freedom is restricted by medical decisions) continue to have their rights upheld, including the right to contest the decision.

The judge oversees every decision regarding involuntary care from the 12th day onwards or when the *préfet* opposes a release requested by the psychiatrist. The judge has the final decision in all cases and may either uphold or withdraw the involuntary status. Even if some involuntary psychiatric care is not related to a criminal offence, when there is disagreement regarding the discharge of a patient under involuntary status (either because the *préfet* has opposed the decision or because the judge deems it necessary to gather additional information before making a final decision), the judge may request a psychiatric assessment. This assessment focuses on the risk posed by the patient to themselves or others and the necessity of maintaining or lifting the involuntary status to mitigate that risk.

The French Public Health Code (*code de la santé publique*, Article L3211-12-1) imposes certain circumstances where a forensic psychiatric assessment is mandatory. This specifically applies to individuals admitted involuntarily after committing a crime. In cases where an individual is found not criminally responsible due to a mental disorder, the typical outcome is their release, with no treatment or other restrictions imposed. However, in certain circumstances, a judge who has pronounced a verdict of not criminally responsible may request that the individual be admitted to a psychiatric hospital for treatment and supervision. This occurs when the judge believes there is an ongoing risk to public safety.

The decision is based on a psychiatric assessment indicating the presence of such a risk (*code de procédure pénale* Article 706-135; Loi n° 2011-803, *code de la santé publique*, Article L3213-1). The individual then becomes a patient in a psychiatric hospital within their local area and will be treated under a special designation, similar to 'forensic status'. Any decision to discharge the patient back into the community will be made by the *juge des libertés et de la détention*, after a forensic psychiatric assessment has been conducted by two psychiatrists (Loi n° 2023-1059, *code de la santé publique,* Article L3211-12-1).

### *Forensic Psychiatry Profession*

#### *Qualifications and Specialised Training*

There is a shortage of specialised training in forensic psychiatry in France. Individuals interested in practising forensic psychiatry can pursue an additional degree that provides legal or clinical expertise. Alternatively, individuals may shadow forensic psychiatrists for training, although no formal training programme has been established. As of 2015, over 700 individuals in France were qualified as expert witnesses to address forensic matters, including criminal responsibility (Davidson, 2015). When the court requires an assessment, it must consult this list of designated experts.

Although the court may occasionally choose to involve a practitioner who is not formally designated, it must provide a clear explanation for this decision, often due to the unavailability of a designated expert. Becoming an expert witness involves a formal procedure in which the practitioner swears an oath to the court. After a probation period of three years, the designation becomes valid for five years. It can be renewed every five years, provided the expert continues to demonstrate that their knowledge and experience remain relevant to answering the legal questions related to their expertise, such as mental health (Loi n° 2016-1547, Article 2).

#### *National Network and Collaborations*

In France, the French Association of Biological Psychiatry and Neuropsychopharmacology (AFPBN), the national association of psychiatric experts, hosts a national network of forensic psychiatry. The forensic psychiatry section of the AFPBN seeks to establish best practice standards, develop structured training programmes, promote research, and increase the visibility of the French approach on the international stage.

## Forensic Psychiatry Service (Provision of Care)

### *Forensic Patient Characteristics*

Defining who constitutes a forensic patient in France is challenging due to the absence of a formal forensic system. The term typically refers to individuals who have been civilly committed after being found not criminally responsible. However, those deemed not dangerous and not required to undergo treatment are not considered forensic patients. Patients in Units for Difficult Patients are only classified as forensic if they have also been found not criminally responsible. Furthermore, because forensic and general psychiatric patients are not segregated, obtaining accurate demographic, psychosocial, and criminological data is difficult. Limited research suggests that most forensic patients are men, around 41 years old, and diagnosed with schizophrenia or bipolar disorder (Moulia-Pelat et al., 2022).

### *Exiting the System*

Individuals involuntarily admitted after being found not criminally responsible may be discharged based on the recommendations of their treating psychiatrist. However, approval is required from several authorities, including the *préfet*, the *juge des libertés et de la détention*, and an expert committee that conducts an independent psychiatric assessment (Loi n°2011-803, Article L3213-5-1). While risk assessments may be conducted before release, they are neither mandatory nor routinely performed. The average length of stay for forensic patients in France is unknown.

Additionally, it is important to understand that the decisions made by the *préfet* are administrative. The treating psychiatrist sends a request for release in the form of a certificate containing clinical information. This certificate requests the release of the patient. When the *préfet* decides against the psychiatrist's recommendation, they do so without any direct or indirect contact with the patient. Furthermore, the *préfet*'s decision does not need to be justified. Although they may rely on previous certificates produced to admit the patient, there is no formal process to ensure that a clinical opinion guides the *préfet*'s decision at that stage (Coldefy & Fernandes, 2017).

### *Approaches to Assessment and Treatment*

In France, forensic psychiatrists primarily focus on evaluating criminal responsibility through expert reports, while their involvement in assessing and treating patients is limited. Instead, these processes occur in general psychiatric hospitals, where treating psychiatrists typically lack formal forensic training. It remains uncertain whether assessments, including risk evaluations, are performed regularly, if at all. Treatment typically consists of psychotherapy and pharmacological interventions. However, there is no mandated or standardised treatment approach, and the available treatments vary by hospital—forensic patients receive the same care as those in the civil system. The focus remains on managing psychiatric symptoms rather than addressing criminogenic factors, given the absence of forensic specialisation among treating psychiatrists. Attention is given to social determinants of health, with provisions for vocational activities and supportive housing. Standard therapeutic approaches include cognitive-behavioural therapy, cognitive rehabilitation, and mindfulness, although treatment depends on the resources and programmes available at the admitting hospital.

## Strengths and Weaknesses

The French psychiatric system has both strengths and weaknesses. One notable strength is the flexibility of involuntary care within the civil system, where patients can receive care while living in the community under a community treatment order. This system offers a structured transition from inpatient to outpatient care while maintaining involuntary status.

Weaknesses primarily stem from the absence of a formal forensic system or framework. Without an established forensic system, there is a lack of standardisation, which leads to disparities in assessments across different hospitals. The extent to which risk assessment tools are used remains unclear, and there is no well-defined training pathway for forensic psychiatrists. Additionally, individuals found not criminally responsible but deemed 'not dangerous' are neither sanctioned nor placed under a treatment order, yet the criteria for determining dangerousness remain ambiguous.

## References

Bouchard, J. P., Brulin-Solignac, D., & Le Bihan, P. (2022). Les unités pour malades difficiles. *Soins*, *67*(870–871), 34–36.

Coldefy, M., & Fernandes, S. (2017). Les soins sans consentement en psychiatrie: bilan après quatre années de mise en œuvre de la loi du 5 juillet 2011. *Question d'Economie de la Santé*, *222*, 1–8. Retrieved from https://www.irdes.fr/recherche/questions-d-economie-de-la-sante/222-les-soins-sans-consentement-en-psychiatrie.pdf

Couturier, M. (2022). Irresponsabilité pénale et consommation de produits psychoactifs: une nouvelle loi aux effets limités. *Éditions législatives*. Retrieved from https://www.editions-legislatives.fr/actualite/irresponsabilite-penale-et-consommation-de-produits-psychoactifs-une-nouvelle-loi-aux-effets-limites/

Davidson, C. (2015). France's forensic psychiatry provision—is it up to scratch? *Lancet Psychiatry*, *2*(5), 385–387.

de Chantérac, A. (2023). *The most dangerous patients: Inside France's high-security mental health facility for severe offenders* [documentary]. Retrieved from https://www.youtube.com/watch?v=8HwPqn9lvbo

Lemoine, J. (2021). La réforme de l'irresponsabilité pénale définitivement adoptée par le Parlement. *Le Monde*. Retrieved from https://www.lemonde.fr/societe/article/2021/12/16/la-reforme-de-l-irresponsabilite-penale-definitivement-adoptee-par-le-parlement_6106341_3224.html

Loi n° 2011-803 du 5 juillet 2011 relative aux droits et à la protection des personnes faisant l'objet de soins psychiatriques et aux modalités de leur prise en charge. JORF du 6 juillet 2011, Article L3211–9, Code de la santé publique. *Légifrance*. Retrieved from https://www.legifrance.gouv.fr/codes/article_lc/LEGIARTI000024316472

Loi n° 2011-803 du 5 juillet 2011 relative aux droits et à la protection des personnes faisant l'objet de soins psychiatriques et aux modalités de leur prise en charge. JORF du 6 juillet 2011, Article L3213-5-1, Code de la santé publique. *Légifrance*. Retrieved from https://www.legifrance.gouv.fr/codes/article_lc/LEGIARTI000024314422

Loi n° 2014-896 du 15 août 2014 relative à l'individualisation des peines et renforçant l'efficacité des sanctions pénales. JORF du 1er Octobre 2014. Article 122–1, Code pénal. *Légifrance*. https://www.legifrance.gouv.fr/codes/article_lc/LEGIARTI000045068712

Loi n° 2016-1547 du 18 novembre 2016 de modernisation de la justice du XXIe siècle. JORF n°0269 du 19 novembre 2016, Article 2.

Loi n° 2022-52 du 24 janvier 2022 relative à la responsabilité pénale et à la sécurité intérieure. JORF du 26 janvier 2022. Article 122-1-1, Code pénal. *Légifrance*. Retrieved from https://www.legifrance.gouv.fr/codes/article_lc/LEGIARTI000045068712

Loi n° 2022-52 du 24 janvier 2022 relative à la responsabilité pénale et à la sécurité intérieure. JORF du 26 janvier 2022. Article 122-1-2, Code pénal. *Légifrance*. Retrieved from https://www.legifrance.gouv.fr/codes/article_lc/LEGIARTI000045068714

Loi n° 2023-1059 du 20 novembre 2023 d'orientation et de programmation du ministère de la justice 2023-2027. JORF n°0269 du 21 novembre 2023, Article L3211-12-1.

Moulia-Pelat, E., Pons, R., & Nabhan-Abou, N. (2022). L'article 122–1 et après? Devenir des patients reconnus irresponsables sur le plan pénal, entre 2015 et 2019, dans l'Ouest de la France. *Annales Médico-psychologiques*, *180*(4), 294–300.

Protais, C., & Moreau, D. (2009). L'expertise psychiatrique entre l'évaluation de la responsabilité et de la dangerosité, entre le médical et le judiciaire. Commentaire du texte de Samuel Lézé. *Champ penal*, *6*. https://doi.org/10.4000/champpenal.7557

# 9 Germany

*Birgit Völlm*

**Brief Description**

| | |
|---|---|
| **Location** | Germany is a country in Western Europe. |
| **Size** | 357,021 km$^2$ |
| **Population** | 84.48 million |
| **Language** | German (*Deutsch*) is the official language in Germany. It is spoken by over 95% of the population. |
| **Political system** | Germany is a democratic, federal parliamentary republic composed of 16 constituent states (*Länder*), each with a high degree of autonomy in law and governance. Germany has a bicameral parliament consisting of the *Bundestag* (Federal Diet) and the *Bundesrat* (Federal Council). The Chancellor is the head of government and executive power, while the Federal President is the head of state. Germany is a member state of the European Union. |

## Legal System

The German legal system is based on civil law. The German Constitution, also known as the Basic Law for the Federal Republic of Germany (*Grundgesetz*), outlines and safeguards the fundamental human rights of all people. The court system adjudicates matters of public law (*Öffentliches Recht*), which also comprises criminal law (*Strafrecht*) and private law (*Privatrecht*).

Germany's detailed codified law is implemented through an inquisitorial system in which judges play an active role in investigating the facts and conducting the trial. Germany's court system comprises ordinary (*ordentliche Gerichtsbarkeit*) and specialised (*besondere Gerichtsbarkeit*) courts. Ordinary courts, the most common court in Germany, hear civil and criminal cases. There are four tiers of ordinary courts in Germany. The lowest level comprises the local courts (*Amtsgerichte*), followed by the regional courts (*Landgerichte*), the higher regional courts (*Oberlandesgerichte*), and then the highest ordinary court, which is the Federal Court of Justice (*Bundesgerichtshof*). Criminal cases can be assigned

DOI: 10.4324/9781003376248-12

to any of the first three courts, while civil matters are typically assigned to the first two. Additionally, appeals can be made to the two higher courts.

Specialised courts refer to administrative, finance, labour, and social courts. Additionally, there is the constitutional jurisdiction, which includes the Federal Constitutional Court (*Bundesverfassungsgericht*) and the constitutional courts of each German state (*Landesverfassungsgerichte*). Depending on the court, the tribunal may comprise a single professional judge for minor cases or a panel of professional and lay judges for more severe cases.

The responsibility of mental health laws in Germany falls under the jurisdiction of the 16 German states (*Länder*). However, concerning offenders with mental disorders, federal laws outline the basis for assessing criminal responsibility, admission, and discharge from forensic psychiatric hospitals (Müller-Isberner et al., 2000). However, state law outlines compulsory treatment legislation and varies markedly across states.

### *Mental Health Laws*

#### *Fitness to Stand Trial*

The Code of Criminal Procedure (*Strafprozeßordnung*) governs the regulations for determining the fitness to stand trial. In a case of unfitness to stand trial, the trial is deferred to a later time. If a person's mental fitness does not improve, and it seems likely that a mental health-related decision or treatment (disposition) will be necessary, such a decision can still be made, even for someone considered unfit to stand trial. Interestingly, fitness to stand trial is rarely raised in German courts, possibly due to the role of the judge in investigating the facts from a range of sources.

#### *Criminal Responsibility*

The age of criminal responsibility in Germany is 14 years. Individuals over 14 who have been accused of criminal offences may be found not responsible for their actions or to have a reduced level of responsibility, as outlined in Section 20 or 21 of the Federal Criminal Code (*Strafgesetzbuch*). According to Section 21 of the Criminal Code, an individual is found not guilty by reasons of insanity (NGRI) if they were unable to comprehend the wrongfulness of their actions or act accordingly due to a mental disorder. This can include major mental disorders, such as psychosis, mania, depression, organic brain damage, an extreme disturbance of consciousness due to emotional situations, a mental handicap such as intellectual disability, or any other severe mental abnormality present at the time of the criminal act. Section 21 of the Criminal Code defines diminished responsibility as a situation where an individual's ability to recognise the wrongfulness of their actions or to act in accordance is not entirely absent but significantly diminished. If an individual is found to have diminished responsibility, they may receive a reduced sentence or be admitted to a forensic psychiatric hospital.

During a trial, individuals who are suspected of being NGRI may be held in preliminary detention at a forensic psychiatric hospital for up to six months until expert opinions can be obtained. Individuals who are determined NGRI or to have diminished responsibility may be detained under Section 63 of the Criminal Code in a psychiatric hospital if an evaluation determines that, due to their condition, they pose a danger to the general public and are likely to commit serious unlawful acts in the future because of their condition and past offences.

#### *Decision Makers in Forensic Psychiatry*

In Germany, forensic psychiatrists provide expert testimony and opinions and perform evaluations and treatment as part of the legal process, which the court can consider when adjudicating their final decision. The court is highly involved in forensic psychiatry and has the authority to determine admission and discharge in the forensic mental health system. Even if an individual is still unwell, the court may decide to discharge them from the hospital under the condition that their hospitalisation duration surpasses the sentence length that a criminally responsible person would receive for the same offence. The court is very strict regarding mandatory interventions, such as mechanical restraints and compulsory medication. Court orders are needed for these interventions and often require an external expert opinion.

### Forensic Psychiatry System

#### *Structure and Function of the Forensic Psychiatry System*

Germany has a formal forensic psychiatry system. If the accused is found not criminally responsible or their responsibility is diminished, the court has the authority to order their placement in a psychiatric hospital as per Section 63 of the Federal Criminal Code. Germany has around 80 forensic psychiatric hospitals, with patient counts ranging from 50 to 400. Although these hospitals do not have formal security levels such as 'high', 'medium', or 'low', they may have varying levels of security and offer different functions within the same facility.

In Germany, there are forensic hospitals that also serve as addiction treatment facilities for individuals convicted of committing unlawful acts while under the influence of alcohol or other intoxicating substances due to a tendency towards substance abuse. Under Section 64 of the Criminal Code, an individual can only be sent to an addiction treatment facility if there is a likelihood of successful rehabilitation. The determination of the probability is based on an initial expert opinion and a final decision made by the court. In this substance abuse treatment, reduced criminal responsibility is not an entry criterion. Most individuals detained under Section 64 of the Criminal Code are fully responsible; this is a different strand compared to typical forensic patients (such as those with psychosis who offend). Another difference is that the placement is limited to a maximum of two years plus two-thirds of the length of the parallel prison sentence given to those criminally responsible. Patients can also be moved to prison if treatment is not successful.

### *Psychiatric Hospitals for Patients Found NGRI or of Reduced Criminal Responsibility*

If an individual is found NGRI or of reduced criminal responsibility, they can exit the psychiatric hospital system once they are no longer considered dangerous, as determined by a court relying on the expert opinion of the attending psychiatrist. However, an independent opinion (that is, by an expert not part of the institution where the patient is detained) is required after three and six years of detention and thereafter every two years. On average, individuals spend 8–10 years in this form of detention. However, after six years, proportionality becomes more important, and experts must consider the length of a sentence for individuals found criminally responsible for the same crime. This ensures that the length of the sentence is proportional to the severity of the crime. Furthermore, the potential seriousness of future offences must be significant to justify ongoing detention.

After exiting the system, mandatory follow-up treatment may last up to five years, though follow-up can continue beyond this time. Patients who have been discharged must comply with court-mandated conditions, including attending clinic appointments at varying intervals (usually biweekly and less frequently over time) and undergoing drug tests. The primary goal of this follow-up is surveillance rather than to provide therapy (§68 a and b StGB).

### *Addiction Treatment Facilities*

The duration of placement in an addiction treatment facility cannot usually exceed two years. However, if a prison sentence is also imposed, the maximum time at the facility can be extended by two-thirds of the length of the sentence so that the time spent at the facility is credited against the sentence. Individuals in this stream are reviewed every six months; on average, the length of stay is two to two and a half years. They are subject to the same follow-up arrangements as described earlier.

### *Role of Forensic Psychiatry*

In Germany, forensic psychiatrists act as expert witnesses, providing opinions on criminal responsibility, the level of danger an individual may pose, and the level of supervision or security needed for that individual. In addition, they will provide a prognosis on whether the patient is ready for discharge. Forensic psychiatrists can act as expert witnesses in several types of fitness trials, such as those assessing the patient's fitness to drive, take care of themselves or others, stand trial, or be imprisoned.

Forensic psychiatrists provide expert testimony and perform hospital assessments and treatment. However, no standardised assessments exist for determining fitness or other criteria. The absence of standardised pretrial assessments leads to a significant variation in patients found in forensic psychiatry units.

*Qualifications or Specialised Training Required in Forensic Psychiatry*

In Germany, there are two ways to become a certified forensic psychiatrist. The first is to obtain a certificate from the German Association for Psychiatry, Psychotherapy and Psychosomatics. This requires the individual to have completed specialist training in psychiatry and have worked for at least one year in a forensic psychiatric hospital or prison. For the certificate, 240 hours of theoretical courses and the completion of 70 expert opinions in different areas are required. The certificate is valid for five years, after which individuals must be recertified.

The other way to become certified as a forensic psychiatrist is through the State Chambers of Physicians (*Landesärztekammern*). Generally, after completing higher training in general psychiatry, one spends two years gaining experience as a forensic psychiatrist, writing expert opinions, and fulfilling other duties. These duties differ from state to state, as the Chambers differ in each of the 16 states, and each sets its own requirements. Each of these 16 states would track the number of practising forensic psychiatrists certified via this route. However, this information remains unknown on a federal level.

While these are two ways to become a forensic psychiatrist in Germany, it is unnecessary to specialise in forensic psychiatry to work in the field. Although individuals are preferred to specialise in forensic psychiatry, any general psychiatrist can still perform the duties of a forensic psychiatrist.

*National Collaborations or Networks*

There is no national forensic psychiatry organisation in Germany. A branch of the German Association for Psychiatry, Psychotherapy and Psychosomatics is dedicated to forensics, but no specific forensic network exists.

## Forensic Psychiatry Service (Provision of Care)

### *Forensic Patient Characteristics*

In Germany, no national database collects information on the demographic, psychological, or criminological profiles of forensic patients. According to the

Federal Office of Statistics (Statistisches Bundesamt, 2020), there were 5,926 Section 63 patients in 2019; however, this does not include patients from the states of Brandenburg, Rhineland-Palatinate, Saxony-Anhalt, and Thuringia. In 2021, 3,559 patients were detained under Section 64 (Statistisches Bundesamt, 2022). The numbers have increased for years, particularly for Section 64 patients (Tomlin et al., 2024).

### *Approaches to Forensic Psychiatric Assessment and Treatment*

A court-appointed expert typically conducts assessments pertaining to criminal responsibility, sometimes in provisional accommodation in psychiatric hospitals. The expert's initial evaluation determines whether the legal criteria for a mental disorder were present and whether that disorder led to a diminished or absence of responsibility. The expert will conduct a risk assessment to determine whether the individual's mental illness is likely to result in future offences (Osterheider & Dimmek, 2005). As of 2000, risk assessments in Germany were dominated by unstructured clinical assessment without reliable or valid structural guidelines (Müller-Isberner et al., 2000).

In Germany, the emphasis on treatment is based on rehabilitation rather than criminal punishment. However, the treatment provided to forensic patients can vary, as there is no standardised treatment plan, leading to variability between different psychiatric hospitals. There are no guidelines pertaining to forensic psychiatry. Still, relevant guidance would be used for different disorders, such as schizophrenia (Müller et al., 2017), as required medications are used, as well as psychotherapeutic approaches. Offending-specific approaches, such as the Reasoning and Rehabilitation programme or Dialectical Behavioural Therapy—Forensic (DBT-F), are underused.

Very strict laws regarding compulsory interventions, such as mechanical restraints or medication, require court orders. The use of compulsory medication as a treatment is highly regulated and only allowed in cases where there is a clear danger to oneself or others. This approach has both advantages and disadvantages. Requiring a court order for administering compulsory medication ensures the involvement of an independent expert's opinion, which can be seen as an advantage. While this approach has its benefits, it can result in patients having untreated psychosis for extended periods. Compulsory medication is typically utilised not as a treatment but as a means to restore an individual's capacity to make their own treatment decisions.

## Strengths and Weaknesses

The German forensic system has strengths and weaknesses, with some major strengths centring around the courts. The courts control admission and discharge and ensure that individuals are discharged even if they are still unwell if the sentence is no longer proportionate to the sentence an individual who is criminally responsible would receive for the same crime. From a human rights point of view, this ensures that people with mental disorders are not discriminated against by being detained longer than individuals without such disorders for the same offence. Another strength of the German forensic system is the success rate for rehabilitating patients. Due to Germany's robust data protection laws, individuals typically experience a high success rate when seeking employment after release. Not all employers require criminal record checks, for example, and there is no duty on services to inform employers, except in rare circumstances. In addition, most criminal records expire after certain times and are no longer available during checks. A final strength of the German forensic system is that, after release, there is a compulsory follow-up after treatment, which allows for surveillance as well as support in the process of reintegration.

Germany's forensic system is poorly regulated and decentralised, with each of its 16 states responsible for its own operations. Consequently, there is a lack of uniformity and oversight across the country. While England has the Care Quality Commission overseeing its forensic system, no equivalent body exists in Germany to review the quality of care patients receive. This lack of oversight is not specific to forensics but to all German hospitals. Consequently, the country's standards of treatment and care are not as high as they could be.

Another weakness of the German forensic system is that little data is collected on individuals' demographic, psychological, and criminological profiles due to the lack of a national database. This makes it difficult to analyse trends in the system. The German forensic system is not well funded, which has a negative impact on various areas of the forensic system. For example, it is often not possible to use 1:1 nursing to support patients in distress, thereby leading to continuing distress and potentially restrictive measures such as separation, instead of higher levels of staff interaction to manage risk.

Lastly, Germany faces a shortage of specialists in forensic psychiatry. As a result, individuals without formal certification in forensic psychiatry may be performing the roles typically reserved for certified specialists, such as conducting assessments to determine criminal responsibility. This shortage also leads to variability in the quality of treatment, further exacerbated by the absence of an overseeing regulatory body.

## References

Müller, J. L., Saimeh, N., Briken, P., Eucker, S., Hoffmann, K., Koller, M., Wolf, T., Dudeck, M., Hartl, C., Jakovljevic, A.-K., Klein, V., Knecht, G., Müller-Isberner, R., Muysers, J., Schiltz, K., Seifert, D., Simon, A., Steinböck, H., Stuckmann, W., Weissbeck, W., Wiesemann, C., & Zeidler, R. (2017). Standards für die Behandlung im Maßregelvollzug nach §§63 und 64 StGB. *Forensische Psychiatrie Psychologie, Kriminologie*, *12*, 93–125. https://doi.org/10.1007/s11757-017-0445-0

Müller-Isberner, R., Freese, R., Jöckel, D., & Cabeza, S. G. (2000). Forensic psychiatric assessment and treatment in Germany. *International Journal of Law and Psychiatry, 23*(5–6), 467–480. https://doi.org/10.1016/S0160-2527(00)00056-X

Osterheider, M., & Dimmek, B. (2005). Concepts and procedures in the member states—Germany. In the European Commission, Health & Consumer Protection Directorate, *Involuntary Placement and Involuntary Treatment of Persons with Mental Health Problems*. https://doi.org/10.1163/2210-7975_HRD-9992–0022

Statistisches Bundesamt (Destatis). (2020). *Im psychiatrischen Krankenhaus und in der Entziehungsanstalt aufgrund strafrichterlicher Anordnung Untergebrachte (Maßregelvollzug) im Jahr 2018 und zum Stichtag 31. März 2019.*

Statistisches Bundesamt (Destatis). (2022). *Rechtspflege—Strafverfolgung. Fachserie 10 Reihe 3, Berichtsjahr 2021*. Retrieved from https://www.destatis.de/DE/Themen/Staat/Justiz-Rechtspflege/Publikationen/Downloads-Strafverfolgung-Strafvollzug/strafverfolgung−2100300217004.pdf?blob=publicationFile

Tomlin, J., Meise, E., Wegner, J., & Völlm, B. (2024). Mandatory substance use treatment for justice-involved persons in Germany: A systematic review of reoffending, treatment and the recurrence of substance use outcomes. *Frontiers in Psychiatry, 14*, 1217561. https://doi.org/10.3389/fpsyt.2023.1217561

# 10 Ireland

*Harry G. Kennedy*

## Brief Description

| | |
|---|---|
| **Location** | Ireland (Éire) is a country in Western Europe, occupying most of the island of Ireland. |
| **Size** | 70,273 km$^2$ |
| **Population** | 5.4 million |
| **Languages** | Ireland's first official language is Irish, and English is the second. |
| **Political system** | Ireland is a constitutional republic with a parliamentary system of government. The National Parliament (Oireachtas) consists of two houses: Dáil Éireann (the lower house) and Seanad Éireann (the upper house). The President of Ireland is the head of state, while the Prime Minister is the head of government. |

## Legal System

### *Legislative Framework*

Mental health law, including forensic law, originates in the common law tradition of legal precedent rather than careful legislation (McAuley, 1993). Psychiatric defences in Ireland have been influenced by its sociocultural and economic history, historical alliances, and influences of ideas and laws from many other nations (Prior, 2003, 2008, 2017). Violence often occurred in the context of revolutionary protests and was sometimes exploited for political purposes in the press. One instance of this was the Maamtrasna Murders of 1882, where a clear miscarriage of justice occurred because the Irish-speaking defendants could not understand the proceedings conducted in English (Kelleher, 2018).

### *Mental Health Laws*

The *Mental Treatment Act, 1945*, consisting of 284 sections, was enacted to regulate the detention and treatment of individuals with mental illnesses. The Act permitted involuntary detention based on broad clinical assessments of diagnosis

DOI: 10.4324/9781003376248-13

and need. Once a person was detained, treatment without consent was authorised under a status test, and there was no formal mechanism for regular review of detention.

Many white papers, green papers, and acts passed through Parliament. Still, they did not advance to becoming law until the enactment of the *Mental Health Act, 2001*, which reformed and modernised civil detentions. However, these reforms were not implemented until 2006. The long process leading to this legislation has been described elsewhere (O'Neill, 2005; Casey & Craven, 1999; Casey, 2010). The Act was based on the 2004 'standards' (effectively a model mental health act) and the cumulative recommendations of the Council of Europe (Council of Europe Committee of Ministers, 2004), which codify the rulings of the European Court of Human Rights. These rulings are now being reinterpreted in accordance with the United Nations Convention on the Rights of Persons with Disabilities (European Union Agency for Fundamental Rights, 2012), which is itself based on the European Convention on Human Rights and its inspection body, the Committee for the Prevention of Torture and Inhumane or Degrading Treatment or Punishment (CPT) (Council of Europe, n.d.).

It is worth noting that European mental health legislation is largely based on the 2004 document and CPT standards. Its predecessors and successors, following the European Convention on Human Rights, are binding across all Council of Europe member states. Additionally, its interpretation by the European Court of Human Rights is legally binding, ensuring compliance with the rule of law, fair process, and respect for expert medical evidence. It is widely respected and remains largely unaffected by the fads and trends of postmodernist populism that influence other international conventions.

The *Mental Health Act, 2001* (Law Reform Commission, 2004) defines a mental disorder as mental illness, severe dementia, or significant intellectual disability, with further elaboration on these categories provided later in the Act. The Act also established a Mental Health Commission (MHC) and the Office of the Inspector of Mental Health Services, which reports to the MHC rather than the Minister for Justice. Treatment under the Act is permitted only in approved centres, which must undergo regular inspection by the Inspector and comply with established rules and regulations (Mental Health Commission, 2010; Irish Statute Book, 2006). Additionally, the Act also established Mental Health Tribunals (MHTs) to review cases of detention under its provisions. Each MHT consists of a legal chair with at least seven years of experience of professional practise, an independent consultant psychiatrist, and a layperson.

Opened in 1850, the Central Mental Hospital (CMH) in Dublin is the only secure forensic hospital in Ireland. The CMH is recognised in the *Mental Health Act, 2001* as an approved centre, but with a status distinct from other approved centres. Admission to the CMH is possible under the Act without any criminal process, but it requires approval by a civil MHT for the purpose of obtaining special treatment. Consequently, civilly detained and transferred patients at the

CMH are reviewed by a civil MHT, unlike forensic patients detained under the *Criminal Law (Insanity) Act 2006*. Such civil patients do not have access to early release and supervised reintegration into the community through conditional discharge, as provided under the Act of 2006.

In Ireland, the *Assisted Decision-Making (Capacity) Act 2015* is the relevant legislation concerning capacity matters. The Act was signed into law on December 17, 2022, and came into effect on April 26, 2023 (Law Reform Commission, 2023). It establishes a functional, decision-specific test for capacity, assessing an individual's ability to comprehend information, retain it, adequately problem-solve, and communicate their needs.

The Act introduced a statutory framework for supported and substitute decision making into Irish law through a structured system of decision-support arrangements. This includes decision-making assistants and substitute decision makers. The Act also established the legal basis for an Advance Healthcare Directive (AHD) and enduring power of attorney. It also repealed the previous Ward of Court system, under which individuals lacking the capacity to manage their individual and property were placed under the wardship, with the High Court making decisions regarding their welfare. As a result, since April 2023, no new wardship orders have been legally possible in Ireland.

The Act also established a new regulatory body, the Decision Support Service, to oversee and register decision-support arrangements, maintain a panel of experts to act as decision-making representatives when required and review and investigate any complaints made under the Act. The Decision Support Service operates as part of the MHC. One significant change made by this law was the expansion of professionals authorised to conduct capacity assessments. For the first time, in addition to medical practitioners, other registered allied health professionals—such as occupational therapists, registered nurses, midwives, social workers, and speech and language therapists—were permitted to conduct these assessments. Psychologists were excluded from the group, as they were not yet subject to statutory regulation.

The *Assisted Decision-Making (Capacity) Act 2015* appears primarily directed towards short-term physical health or financial decisions and will likely continue being used mainly in this context. One critique of the Act is that it does not provide legal safeguards or protections for deprivation of liberty. As a result, any vulnerable individual who lacks the capacity to consent to their placement and requires ongoing care now necessitates a High Court order to authorise that placement. Since the introduction of the Act, there has been a significant increase in requests for High Court orders for the placements of vulnerable individuals. Concerns have also been raised regarding the Act's provisions on the AHD, particularly in the context of mental disorders (Law Reform Commission, 2024a). Under the Act, any AHD that is in writing and refers to a specific circumstance must be followed by clinicians once the patient lacks the capacity to make or communicate their decisions. This includes decisions that refuse or request the withdrawal of life-sustaining treatments. The potential implications for individuals experiencing mental health crises, particularly those who present after episodes of self-harm, remain unexplored by the Irish courts. However, it is worth noting that, if an AHD contains any ambiguity, it must be interpreted in favour of preserving life.

***Legislation—Forensic Psychiatry***

Until 2006, Ireland continued to use 19th-century legislation concerning individuals found 'unfit to plead' or 'guilty but insane'. The *Criminal Law (Insanity) Act 2006* was passed in some haste (Law Reform Commission, 2024b)—it has only 26 sections and is, to some extent, dependent on the definitions of the *Mental Health Act, 2001* (Kennedy, 2007). The Act of 2006 applies only in 'designated centres' and established the CMH in Dublin as the first (and, to date, the only) designated centre in Ireland where prisoners can be transferred from prison for treatment that can only be provided in a hospital setting. Under the Act, individuals treated in designated centres are referred to as 'patients' if they are found unfit to stand trial or not guilty by reason of insanity. The distinction between 'prisoners' and 'patients' is significant, as only patients can be granted leave from the hospital, subject to a recommendation from the legal clinical director and approval from the Minister for Justice. Detention, on the other hand, is reviewed by a newly established Mental Health (Criminal Law) Review Board (MHRB), chaired by a lawyer with no less than 10 years of experience in practice or a judge or former judge of a higher court, an independent psychiatrist, and a layperson.

The *Criminal Law (Insanity) Act 2006* defines a mental disorder as including mental illness, mental disability, dementia, or any disease of the mind. However, it does not include intoxication as a mental disorder. These criteria are much broader than the criteria for a mental disorder in the *Mental Health Act, 2001*, yet the Act of 2006 often refers to the definitions in the Act of 2001, which can lead to anomalies.

**Unfit to be tried:** Cannot be prosecuted due to a mental disorder and capacity. A patient found unfit to be tried may regain fitness, return to court for a trial, or be conditionally or absolutely discharged by the MHRB.

**Not guilty by reason of insanity (NGRI):** A special verdict following legal trial. The individual found NGRI is sent to the CMH in Dublin to be assessed to determine whether they meet the criteria for a mental disorder in the Act of 2001. These criteria are significantly much more rigorous than in the Act of 2006. This ought to lead to occasional defendants walking from court and places a de facto pressure on the forensic psychiatrist carrying out this late assessment. Detention under the Act of 2006 is reviewed every six months by the MHRB (Mental Health (Criminal Law) Review Board, 2024). Patients may then have their detention renewed or be conditionally or absolutely discharged.

Remanded or sentenced prisoners can be transferred from prison to a designated centre if medically certified and consenting. If the prisoner is unwilling or unable to voluntarily consent to the transfer, the prisoner may be certified for transfer by two registered medical practitioners and the Governor of the prison. If a voluntarily transferred prisoner refuses to receive care or treatment in the designated centre, two registered medical practitioners may certify the prisoner requires treatment to keep them in the designated centre. While transferred to a designated centre, the prisoner is reviewed by the MHRB with a view to continued detention in the designated centre or transfer back to prison. When the clinical director of the designated centre believes that the prisoner no longer requires inpatient care or treatment, the clinical director, after consultation with the Minister for Justice, directs the transfer of the prisoner back to the prison.

Part 4 of the *Mental Health Act, 2001*, which governs consent to treatment and treatment without consent, is incorporated into the *Criminal Law (Insanity) Act* 2006. However, the sections of the Act of 2001 concerning bodily restraint and seclusion are elaborated in the MHC rules and are not replicated or incorporated into the Act of 2006. Despite this, the designation of the CMH in Dublin as an approved centre has resulted in the application of Part 4 of the Act of 2001 and the MHC rules to all individuals detained there, regardless of whether they are held under this Act or the Act of 2006. Notably, the Act of 2006 does not address essential aspects of therapeutic security, such as prohibited items, searches, surveillance, and controls over communication or visits.

The most valuable part of the Act of 2006 is the power of the MHRB to grant conditional discharge, which was made possible by an amendment to the Act in 2010. Conditions typically are that the patient adheres to medication as prescribed, remains abstinent from all intoxicants, lives in a place agreed with the treating team and any other conditions relevant to preventing the causes of relapse of symptoms, relapse of substance misuse, or violent or other offending behaviour. These are, in practice, based on the model of care for the National Forensic Mental Health Service, in particular, the seven domains of treatment and forensic recovery (Kennedy, O'Flynn, et al., 2019; Kennedy, 2021) as measured by the DUNDRUM Toolkit (Davoren et al., 2013; Abidin et al., 2013; Davoren, Hennessy et al., 2015).

In Ireland, a draft of designated centre safety and security rules for the new secure forensic hospital has not been given time in Parliament. However, such statutory rules exist for forensic hospitals in other jurisdictions (Department of Health and Social Care, 2019). These provide a legal basis for searches, prohibited items of contraband, control over visitors and parcels, and other procedural safety and security measures to prevent access to weapons, drugs, and other contraband.

## Forensic Psychiatry System

### *Prison Rules and Statutory Instruments for Therapeutic Security*

In Ireland, severe mental illness is found in 3%–4% of prisoners when they are first admitted and in cross-sectional samples (Curtin et al., 2009; Duffy et al., 2006; Kennedy et al., 2005; Linehan et al., 2005; Wright et al., 2006; Davoren, FitzPatrick et al., 2015). This prevalence is consistent with international meta-analyses (Fazel & Seewald, 2012; Favril et al., 2024). Although there are provisions for the transfer of prisoners with mental disorders from prison to the CMH, Dublin, most treatment is provided by the National Forensic Mental Health Service through psychiatrist-led multidisciplinary teams in prison in-reach clinics. Forensic psychiatry prison in-reach clinics exist in all the prisons in Ireland. Practising in prison requires knowledge of the legal, ethical, and human rights structures to ensure that prisoners are deprived of their freedom and not any other right. In Ireland, prison rules exist as a statutory instrument (Law Reform Commission, 2024b) and are in keeping with recommended European Prison Rules (Council of Europe, 2020). They set out standards for mental health care in prisons. They also create sociocultural effects on the mental health of prisoners via such rules as permit searches, rights and limitations on access to means of communication, observation and access to funds, and rights and limitations for visits.

### *Model of Care*

Following an inspection report by the Council of Europe CPT in 1998, the CMH, then located in Dundrum, Dublin, was deemed to be a building unfit for purpose. It had been constructed between 1845 and 1850 during the asylum construction era (Quinlan, 2021).

The new hospital was built to high-security standards on the site of a former asylum located on a coastal peninsula in Portrane, North County Dublin. Its design follows the 'village' model used at LVR-Klinik Düren, Rhineland, Germany, and at Forensicare, Melbourne, Victoria, Australia. Within a secure perimeter, there are 130 secure beds for adults in nine spacious villas. The admission and high-dependency building includes a 10-bed high-dependency/intensive care unit, a 15-bed male admission unit, and a 15-bed sub-acute unit. A second villa provides two 15-bed, medium-term, medium-secure units. A 20-bed unit serves as a rehabilitation and pre-discharge unit. There is also a dedicated villa providing 20 beds for women, comprising a 10-bed acute and sub-acute unit, a 6-bed, medium-term unit, and a 4-bed rehabilitation and pre-discharge unit. Another 20-bed unit is designated for those individuals with developmental disorders, divided into two 10-bed units. Adjacent to the secure hospital for adults, there is a separate 10-bed secure forensic child and adolescent mental health service. Additionally, a 30-bed forensic intensive care and rehabilitation unit for adults (two 15-bed wards) provides acute and sub-acute secure hospital care for those not requiring the high- or medium-secure levels of care in the main hospital. This last unit is intended to be the first of four intensive care rehabilitation units, with three more planned for Cork, Galway, and Mullingar (Lynch, 2022). Also included within the model of care but not yet funded are 60 long-term, medium-secure and low-secure beds. The built environment is designed to be uplifting, with vistas visible from all areas, including gardens, natural light, and natural materials (Seppänen et al., 2018).

Pathways and processes in the secure forensic hospital are set out according to the principles of stratified therapeutic security, with formal triage according to the level of therapeutic security required (Flynn et al., 2011; Flynn et al., 2011; Freestone et al., 2015; Williams et al., 2020; Jeandarme et al., 2019; Jones et al., 2019) followed by active management of length of stay based on prior analysis and modelling of length of stay in cross-sectional and prospective studies (Sharma et al., 2015; Davoren, Byrne et al., 2015). The model of care is a working quantitative model. It sets out explicit goals for progress through the stages of the recovery pathway.

The Inter-Departmental High Level Task Force (Lynch, 2022) provided a very useful mathematical model of imminent return to long waiting lists due to the accumulation of new long-stay patients in the absence of planned long-term beds (Devlin, 2022). This is already evident within the time frame projected. The reasons for this accumulation are complex. The natural history of treatment-resistant schizophrenia and schizophrenia with comorbid personality disorder and substance misuse is undoubtedly one factor; risk aversiveness may be another, although the locus of resistance may be in several places (Jewell et al., 2018).

## Forensic Psychiatry Service (Provision of Care)

### *Treatment*

In the admission, sub-acute, and high-dependency units, treatment emphasises the pharmacological rapid titration of anti-psychotic and mood-stabilising medication as indicated (Warburton & Stahl, 2016; Cummings & Stahl, 2021).

By the time patients move to the medium-term units, they should have benefitted from optimised medication and the first phase of the seven pillars of care and treatment. They should have recovered enough concentration and motivation to engage in substantive treatment programmes. This preparedness may be enhanced by cognitive remediation therapy (O'Reilly et al., 2016; O'Reilly, Donohoe et al., 2019) followed by metacognitive therapy (Naughton et al., 2012) regarding mental health, relapse prevention, and working alliance. Substance misuse programmes are abstinence-oriented due to the intrinsic violence risk inherent in this population (Adshead & Marshall, 2024).

The model of care is explicit in providing sufficient specialist staff and skills mix to deliver not only 25 hours of structured activities per week for all patients but, within this, at least 5 hours a week of face-to-face time, whether individually or in small groups, concerning mental health, substance misuse, and offence-related treatment (Davoren et al., 2013; Abidin et al., 2013; Davoren, Hennessy, et al., 2015; O'Dwyer et al., 2011; Davoren et al., 2012; Richter et al., 2018; McCullough et al., 2020; Lam et al., 2022; Wharewera-Mika et al., 2020; Jewell et al., 2023; Parente et al., 2023).

Conditional discharge is structured around negotiation and progressive concordance concerning adherence to the benefits of treatment in relation to all relevant domains of treatment in the model of care and the DUNDRUM-3 and the recovery measures in the DUNDRUM-4 (Davoren, Hennessy, et al., 2015). The assessment of individual outcomes is considered in four domains: symptomatic recovery (Pillay et al., 2008), functional recovery (Abidin et al., 2013), civil recovery (Moynihan et al., 2018; Fernandez et al., 2017; Dornan et al. (2015), and personal recovery (Kennedy, 2021; Davoren et al., 2022).

### *Professionals in Forensic Psychiatry*

Ireland has low rates of violent crime and homicide compared to other Northern European countries, along with a low imprisonment rate and a particularly low number of secure forensic beds per capita (Tomlin et al., 2020; Chow & Priebe, 2016).

The training needs specific to forensic psychiatric practice have been summarised in the curriculum for basic and higher specialist training of the College of Psychiatrists of Ireland (College of Psychiatrists in Ireland, 2024). This includes modules on forensic psychiatry. The use of formal structured professional judgement tools relevant to the key decisions made by specialists is a training aid, bridging the gap between a beginner and an advanced trainee. Training improves inter-rater reliability and should also help to improve deliberative judgement and reduce heuristic bias.

Forensic psychiatrists in Ireland are registered medical practitioners (MB, BCh, BAO) who, on completing a five- or six-year undergraduate degree which includes basic science and clinical practice, undergo a 12-month preregistration year of supervised clinical practice before entry to full registration as a trainee specialist.

A further foundation year is followed by three years of basic specialist training, rotating every six months through a range of psychiatric placements, including general adult psychiatry, child and adolescent psychiatry, intellectual disability, forensic psychiatry, and other specialist areas. Higher specialist training takes at least a further three years. This separates adult psychiatry, child and adolescent psychiatry, and psychiatry of intellectual disability. Most subspecialties, including forensic psychiatry, are included in adult psychiatry. The

Health Service Executive employs consultant forensic psychiatrists who must have completed three years of higher training in forensic psychiatry. The College of Psychiatry in Ireland only recommends specialist registration for those who completed three years of higher training in general adult psychiatry. In Ireland, a forensic psychiatrist typically completes six years of higher specialist training after basic specialist training. The training of 'super-specialists' in forensic child and adolescent and forensic intellectual disability psychiatry is even more difficult. There are various routes to achieve dual training. University lecturer posts have always been the primary route into forensic psychiatry training and experience in Ireland, with an expectation that part of specialist training would be in centres of excellence abroad to ensure breadth and depth of experience, exposure to recent progress, and a diversity of approaches. Overseas training has become more difficult within these structures. The pressures of competency-based training make opportunities for research-based higher degrees in clinical research much less common (the MD degree is a postgraduate research doctorate in Ireland and the United Kingdom, comparable to a PhD). Competency-based training ensures a standard below which training does not fall but is not always sufficient for a subject that is in many ways defined by the role of 'expert' (Kennedy et al., 2019; McLaughlin et al., 2023). The trainees who benefit from high-quality mentorship benefit from research training and overseas experience.

The European Union requires that all professional qualifications be interchangeable across member states. The European Union of Medical Specialists is a European body that harmonises medical qualifications. This has functions including the assessment of European examinations for medical specialists (CESMA), encouraging the highest standards of continuing medical education and continuing professional development (EACCME), and promotion of clinical skills education through accreditation of skills centres (NASCE) (European Union of Medical Specialists (UEMS), 2024). The European Union of Medical Specialists and European Psychiatric Association are engaged in preparing a board certification examination in psychiatry, equivalent to basic specialist training, which will include a forensic section (European Psychiatric Association, 2024; European Union of Medical Specialists (UEMS), 2024).

### *Characteristics of Offenders With Mental Disorders*

Offenders with mental disorders in Ireland have been described in many recent research publications, including prison psychiatric morbidity surveys and hospital studies. There is remarkably little variation between the clinical profiles of forensic patients across Europe, North America, Australia, and New Zealand. In Ireland, individuals may not be detained under mental health legislation on the grounds of personality disorder alone. Social deviation, including sexual offenders, is not included. Substance misuse and addictions are not grounds for detention. Remarkably simple, operationalised criteria for assessing the need for therapeutic security and for assessing progress in treatment and recovery in a forensic context appear to accurately reflect the needs of forensic patients and models of care to meet those needs in a range of countries, both in common law jurisdictions (Davoren, Hennessy et al., 2015; Flynn, O'Neill, & Kennedy, 2011; Flynn, O'Neill, McInerney, et al., 2011; Freestone et al., 2015; Williams et al., 2020; Jones et al., 2019; McCullough et al., 2020; Lam et al., 2022; Wharewera-Mika et al., 2020; Jewell et al., 2023; Lawrence et al., 2018; Adams et al., 2018; McKenna & Sweetman, 2021) and in continental law jurisdictions (Parente et al., 2023; Habets et al., 2019; Jeandarme et al., 2021; Eckert et al., 2017).

## Challenges and Dilemmas in Forensic Psychiatry

### *Short-Term Challenges*

Before the move to the new secure forensic hospital in Portrane, Ireland, had the lowest number of secure beds per capita in Northern Europe (2 per 100,000 population). When fully open, the new secure forensic hospital at Portrane will increase this only marginally, given the recent increase in population. It may be that the relatively low crime rate in Ireland does not require a high allocation of secure forensic beds. Still, the extremely low number of acute adult beds for the general population and the abrupt, unplanned nature of that reduction a decade ago suggest systemic service strain. The waiting list for transfer from prison to the CMH, Dublin, also indicates service strain (O'Reilly, Allison et al., 2019). In light of the new evidence that prolonged duration of untreated psychosis is harmful (O'Keeffe et al., 2022; Zoghbi et al., 2023) and evidence that at-risk mental states are particularly common in younger prisoners (Flynn et al., 2012), this now requires an urgent review of service capacity. The rapid commissioning of all built secure beds, the rapid progression to commissioning additional slow-stream/long-term secure beds, and an increase in conditional discharge are now obvious practical solutions to a medical emergency. However, the governance and management of the Health Service Executive, the national agency for public health services, is managerial, not medical, with a separate government department for finance observed to take precedence (Schulmann et al., 2024).

Recruitment of sufficient nurses will be a challenge for the foreseeable future. As before, it is unlikely that the current Health Service Executive or government governance structures will solve this. Training and retention of the best psychiatrists for this challenging and complex work is also likely difficult. All means of minimising the duration of untreated psychosis in prisoners should be implemented urgently. This is likely to include prison regime reforms for prevention by minimising exposure to drugs and violence in prisons (Lynch, 2022; Devlin, 2022).

### *Medium-Term Challenges*

Disease-modifying treatments are beginning to appear in psychiatry. Metabolic syndrome is common among people living with severe mental illnesses. GLP-1 agonists operate on the causes of metabolic syndrome by modifying central homeostatic mechanisms. Disease-modifying treatments are likely to appear soon for Alzheimer's disease. Although Alzheimer's disease is of little relevance to forensic psychiatry, where most patients have schizophrenia, these treatments may lead to disease-modifying treatments for those in the earliest stages of schizophrenia. Such at-risk mental states are particularly numerous among young offender groups (Flynn et al., 2012).

### *Medium- to Long-Term Challenges*

In the future, psychiatric training will inevitably shift from a psycho-social and ethos-based curriculum to a more conventional medical model, where expertise in epigenetics, immune modulation, and neuroendocrinology will be essential. Forensic psychiatrists will require the clinical and scientific skills to treat the most severely ill, including those who fall through the gaps in preventive and early intervention services. The decline in mind-body dualism will occur last, if ever, in the courts. Forensic psychiatrists will need to be experts in these emerging assessment and treatment methods, as these new scientific paradigms will inevitably be used to explore the limits of free will and responsibility in the courts.

In Ireland, clinical science will be in step with international best practices and, in some fields like genetics, remain at the forefront. The evolution of mental health law and processes will have to reconsider the legal basis for the use of disease-modifying treatments. A move from common law adversarial processes and common law legal culture to continental law inquisitorial processes would be desirable, as it would engage with medical ethical values in a fundamentally different way.

## References

Abidin, Z., Davoren, M., Naughton, L., Gibbons, O., Nulty, A., & Kennedy, H. G. (2013). Susceptibility (risk and protective) factors for in-patient violence and self-harm: Prospective study of structured professional judgement instruments START and SAPROF, DUNDRUM-3 and DUNDRUM-4 in forensic mental health services. *BMC Psychiatry*, *13*, 197. https://doi.org/10.1186/1471-244X-13–197

Adams, J., Thomas, S. D. M., Mackinnon, T., & Eggleton, D. (2018). The risks, needs and stages of recovery of a complete forensic patient cohort in an Australian state. *BMC Psychiatry*, *18*(1), 35. https://doi.org/10.1186/s12888-018-1627-7

Adshead, G., & Marshall, J. (2024). Forensic psychotherapy and psychological therapies in forensic mental health settings. In M. Davoren, & H. G. Kennedy (Eds.), *Seminars in forensic psychiatry* (2nd ed., pp. 343–361). Cambridge University Press.

Casey, P. R. (2010). *Psychiatry and the law*. Blackhall Publishing.

Casey, P. R., & Craven, C. (1999). *Psychiatry and the law*. Oak Tree Press.

Chow, W. S., & Priebe, S. (2016). How has the extent of institutional mental healthcare changed in Western Europe? Analysis of data since 1990. *BMJ Open*, *6*(4), e010188. https://doi.org/10.1136/bmjopen-2015-010188

College of Psychiatrists in Ireland. (2024). *Curriculum and regulations*. Dublin: College of Psychiatrists in Ireland. Retrieved from https://irishpsychiatry.ie/postgraduate-training/curriculum-regulations/

Council of Europe. (2020). *Revised European Prison Rules (July 2020): Recommendation Rec(2006)2-rev of the Committee of Ministers to member States on the European Prison Rules*. Retrieved from https://search.coe.int/cm?i=09000016809ee581

Council of Europe. (n.d.). *European Committee for the Prevention of Torture and Inhuman or Degrading Treatment or Punishment (CPT): Standards*. Retrieved from https://www.coe.int/en/web/cpt/standards

Council of Europe Committee of Ministers. (2004). *Recommendation No. REC(2004)10 of the Committee of Ministers to Member States concerning the protection of the human rights and dignity of individuals with mental disorder* (adopted by the Committee of Ministers on 22 September 2004 at the 896th meeting of the Ministers' Deputies). Retrieved from https://rm.coe.int/rec-2004–10-em-e/168066c7e1

Cummings, M., & Stahl, S. M. (2021). *Management of complex treatment-resistant psychotic disorders*. Cambridge University Press. https://doi.org/10.1017/9781108787983

Curtin, K., Monks, S., Wright, B., Duffy, D., Linehan, S., & Kennedy, H. G. (2009). Psychiatric morbidity in male remanded and sentenced committals to Irish prisons. *Irish Journal of Psychological Medicine*, *26*(4), 169–173. https://doi.org/10.1017/S0790966700001056

Davoren, M., Abidin, Z., Naughton, L., Gibbons, O., Nulty, A., Wright, B., et al. (2013). Prospective study of factors influencing conditional discharge from a forensic hospital: The DUNDRUM-3 programme completion and DUNDRUM-4 recovery structured professional judgement instruments and risk. *BMC Psychiatry*, *13*, 185. https://doi.org/10.1186/1471-244X-13–185

Davoren, M., Byrne, O., O'Connell, P., O'Neill, H., O'Reilly, K., & Kennedy, H. G. (2015). Factors affecting length of stay in forensic hospital settings: Need for therapeutic security and course of admission. *BMC Psychiatry*, *15*, 301.

Davoren, M., Fitzpatrick, M., Caddow, F., Caddow, M., O'Neill, C., O'Neill, H., et al. (2015). Older men and older women remand prisoners: Mental illness, physical illness, offending patterns and needs. *International Psychogeriatrics*, *27*(5), 747–755. https://doi.org/10.1017/S1041610214002635

Davoren, M., Hennessy, S., Conway, C., Marrinan, S., Gill, P., & Kennedy, H. G. (2015). Recovery and concordance in a secure forensic psychiatry hospital—The self-rated DUNDRUM-3 programme completion and DUNDRUM-4 recovery scales. *BMC Psychiatry*, *15*, 61. https://doi.org/10.1186/s12888-015-0440-y

Davoren, M., O'Dwyer, S., Abidin, Z., Naughton, L., Gibbons, O., Doyle, E., et al. (2012). Prospective in-patient cohort study of moves between levels of therapeutic security: The DUNDRUM-1 triage security, DUNDRUM-3 programme completion and DUNDRUM-4 recovery scales and the HCR−20. *BMC Psychiatry*, *12*, 80. https://doi.org/10.1186/1471-244X-12–80

Davoren, M., O'Reilly, K., Mohan, D., & Kennedy, H. G. (2022). Prospective cohort study of the evaluation of patient benefit from the redevelopment of a complete national forensic mental health service: The Dundrum Forensic Redevelopment Evaluation Study (D-FOREST) protocol. *BMJ Open*, *12*(7), e058581. https://doi.org/10.1136/bmjopen-2021-058581

Department of Health and Social Care. (2019). *Guidance on the High Security Psychiatric Services (Arrangement for Safety and Security) Directions 2019*. Gov.UK.

https://assets.publishing.service.gov.uk/media/5d0a06aced915d094666a74f/the-high-security-psychiatric-services-directions–2019.pdf

Devlin, J. (2022). Chapter 4, Subgroup 2, Demand and Capacity. In Department of Health and Department of Justice (Eds.), *High Level Task Force to consider the mental health and addiction challenges of those who come into contact with the criminal justice sector: Final report* (pp. 81–155). Department of Health and Department of Justice. Retrieved from file:///Users/Harry/Downloads/236035_0de04b4d-817a-41cf-9779–771ab57703ac−1.pdf

Dornan, J., Kennedy, M., Garland, J., Rutledge, E., & Kennedy, H. G. (2015). Functional mental capacity, treatment as usual and time: Magnitude of change in secure hospital patients with major mental illness. *BMC Research Notes*, *8*, 566. https://doi.org/10.1186/s13104-015-1551-4

Duffy, D., Linehan, S., & Kennedy, H. G. (2006). Psychiatric morbidity in the male sentenced Irish prisons population. *Irish Journal of Psychological Medicine*, *23*(2), 54–62.

Eckert, M., Schel, S. H., Kennedy, H. G., & Bulten, B. H. (2017). Patient characteristics related to length of stay in Dutch forensic psychiatric care. *Journal of Forensic Psychiatry & Psychology*, *28*(6), 863–880. https://doi.org/10.1080/14789949.2017.1349743

European Psychiatric Association (EPA). (2024). *European Board Examination in Psychiatry*. Retrieved from https://www.europsy.net/european-board-exam/

European Union Agency for Fundamental Rights (FRA). (2012). *Involuntary placement and involuntary treatment of individuals with mental health problems*. Retrieved from https://fra.europa.eu/en/publication/2012/involuntary-placement-and-involuntary-treatment-individuals-mental-health-problems

European Union of Medical Specialists (UEMS). (2024). Retrieved from https://www.uems.eu/

Favril, L., Rich, J. D., Hard, J., & Fazel, S. (2024). Mental and physical health morbidity among people in prisons: An umbrella review. *Lancet Public Health*, *9*(4), e250–e260. https://doi.org/10.1016/S2468-2667(23)00212–3

Fazel, S., & Seewald, K. (2012). Severe mental illness in 33,588 prisoners worldwide: Systematic review and meta-regression analysis. *British Journal of Psychiatry*, *200*(5), 364–373. https://doi.org/10.1192/bjp.bp.111.096370

Fernandez, C., Kennedy, H. G., & Kennedy, M. (2017). The recovery of factors associated with decision-making capacity in individuals with psychosis. *BJPsych Open*, *3*(3), 113–119.

Flynn, D., Smith, D., Quirke, L., Monks, S., & Kennedy, H. G. (2012). Ultra high risk of psychosis on committal to a young offender prison: An unrecognised opportunity for early intervention. *BMC Psychiatry*, *12*, 100. https://doi.org/10.1186/1471-244X-12–100

Flynn, G., O'Neill, C., & Kennedy, H. G. (2011). DUNDRUM-2: Prospective validation of a structured professional judgment instrument assessing priority for admission from the waiting list for a forensic mental health hospital. *BMC Research Notes*, *4*, 230.

Flynn, G., O'Neill, C., McInerney, C., & Kennedy, H. G. (2011). The DUNDRUM-1 structured professional judgment for triage to appropriate levels of therapeutic security: Retrospective-cohort validation study. *BMC Psychiatry*, *11*, 43. https://doi.org/10.1186/1471-244X-11–43

Freestone, M., Bull, D., Brown, R., Boast, N., Blazey, F., & Gilluley, P. (2015). Triage, decision-making and follow-up of patients referred to a UK forensic service: Validation of the DUNDRUM toolkit. *BMC Psychiatry*, *15*, 239. https://doi.org/10.1186/s12888-015-0621-8

Habets, P., Jeandarme, I., & Kennedy, H. G. (2019). Applicability of the DUNDRUM-1 in a forensic Belgium setting. *Journal of Forensic Practice*, *21*(1), 85–94. https://doi.org/10.1108/JFP-05-2019-0016

Irish Statute Book. (2006). *Mental Health Act 2001 (Approved Centres) Regulations 2006*. Government of Ireland. Retrieved from https://www.irishstatutebook.ie/eli/2006/si/551/

Jeandarme, I., Habets, P., & Kennedy, H. (2019). Structured versus unstructured judgment: DUNDRUM-1 compared to court decisions. *International Journal of Law and Psychiatry*, *64*, 205–210. https://doi.org/10.1016/j.ijlp.2019.02.004

Jeandarme, I., Habets, P., O'Reilly, K., & Kennedy, H. G. (2021). Is non-completion of treatment related to security need? *Criminal Behaviour and Mental Health*, *31*(5), 321–330. https://doi.org/10.1002/cbm.2222

Jewell, A., Cocks, C., Cullen, A. E., Fahy, T., & Dean, K. (2018). Predicting time to recall in patients conditionally released from a secure forensic hospital: A survival analysis. *European Psychiatry*, *49*, 1–8. https://doi.org/10.1016/j.eurpsy.2017.12.002

Jewell, M., Pillai, K., Cavney, J., Garrett, N., & McKenna, B. (2023). Examining the need for a high level of therapeutic security at a regional forensic mental health service in Aotearoa New Zealand. *Psychiatry, Psychology and Law*, 1–18. https://doi.org/10.1080/13218719.2023.2170568

Jones, R. M., Patel, K., & Simpson, A. I. F. (2019). Assessment of need for inpatient treatment for mental disorder among female prisoners: A cross-sectional study of provincially detained women in Ontario. *BMC Psychiatry*, *19*(1), 98. https://doi.org/10.1186/s12888-019-2080-3

Kelleher, M. (2018). *The Maamtrasna murders: Language, life, and death in nineteenth-century Ireland*. University College Dublin Press.

Kennedy, H. G. (2007). *The annotated mental health acts*. Blackhall Publishing.

Kennedy, H. G. (2021). Models of care in forensic psychiatry. *BJPsych Advances*, 1–14. https://doi.org/10.1192/bja.2021.1

Kennedy, H. G., Monks, S., Curtin, K., Wright, B., Linehan, S. A., & Duffy, D. M., et al. (2005). *Mental health in Irish prisoners: Psychiatric morbidity in sentenced, remanded and newly committed prisoners*. Dublin: National Forensic Mental Health Service.

Kennedy, H. G., O'Flynn, P., Timmons, D., & O'Malley, D. (2019). *National forensic mental health services model of care* (p. 50). Health Service Executive (HSE). https://www.researchgate.net/publication/381801122_National_Forensic_Mental_Health_Service_Ireland_Model_of_Care_November_2019

Kennedy, H. G., Simpson, A., & Haque, Q. (2019). Perspective on excellence in forensic mental health services: What we can learn from oncology and other medical services. *Frontiers in Psychiatry*, *10*, 733. https://doi.org/10.3389/fpsyt.2019.00733

Lam, A. A., Penney, S. R., & Simpson, A. I. F. (2022). Construct validity and concordance of clinician-and patient-rated DUNDRUM programme completion and recovery scales. *International Journal of Forensic Mental Health*, *22*(3), 252–261. https://doi.org/10.1080/14999013.2022.2151671

Law Reform Commission. (2004). *Mental Health Act 2001: Revised updated to 26 April 2023*. Law Reform Commission. Retrieved from https://revisedacts.lawreform.ie/eli/2001/act/25/front/revised/en/html

Law Reform Commission. (2023). *Assisted Decision-Making (Capacity) Act 2015: Revised*. Government of Ireland. Retrieved from https://revisedacts.lawreform.ie/eli/2015/act/64/revised/en/html

Law Reform Commission. (2024a). *Criminal Law (Insanity) Act 2006: Revised, updated to 1 November 2023*. Government of Ireland. Retrieved from https://revisedacts.lawreform.ie/eli/2006/act/11/front/revised/en/html

Law Reform Commission. (2024b). *Making of advance directives (Section 84) Assisted Decision-Making (Capacity) Act 2015*. Retrieved from https://revisedacts.lawreform.ie/eli/2015/act/64/section/84/revised/en/html

Law Reform Commission. (2024c). *S.I. No. 252 of 2007 Prison Rules 2007 Revised.* Government of Ireland. Retrieved from https://revisedacts.lawreform.ie/eli/2007/si/252/revised/en/pdf?annotations=true

Lawrence, D., Davies, T.-L., Bagshaw, R., Hewlett, P., Taylor, P., & Watt, A. (2018). External validity and anchoring heuristics: Application of DUNDRUM-1 to secure service gatekeeping in South Wales. *BJPsych Bulletin*, *42*(1), 10–18.

Linehan, S. A., Duffy, D. M., Wright, B., Curtin, K., Monks, S., & Kennedy, H. G. (2005). Psychiatric morbidity in a cross-sectional sample of male remanded prisoners? *Irish Journal of Psychological Medicine*, *22*(4), 128–132.

Lynch, K. (2022). *Final report of the High Level Task Force to consider the mental health and addiction challenges of those who come into contact with the Criminal Justice Sector*. Department of Health and Department of Justice.

McAuley, F. (1993). *Insanity, psychiatry, and criminal responsibility*. Round Hall Press.

McCullough, S., Stanley, C., Smith, H., Scott, M., Karia, M., Ndubuisi, B., et al. (2020). Outcome measures of risk and recovery in Broadmoor High Secure Forensic Hospital: Stratification of care pathways and moves to medium secure hospitals. *BJPsych Open*, *6*(4), e74. https://doi.org/10.1192/bjo.2020.56

McKenna, B., & Sweetman, L. (2021). *Models of care in forensic mental health services: A review of the international and national literature*. Ministry of Health. Retrieved from https://www.health.govt.nz/publications/models-of-care-in-forensic-mental-health-services-a-review-of-the-international-and-national

McLaughlin, P., Brady, P., Carabellese, F., Parente, L., Uhrskov Sørensen, L., et al. (2023). Excellence in forensic psychiatry services: International survey of qualities and correlates. *BJPsych Open*, *9*(6), e193. https://doi.org/10.1192/bjo.2023.e193

Mental Health Commission. (2010). *Rules governing the use of seclusion and mechanical means of bodily restraint*. Mental Health Commission. https://www.mhcirl.ie/for_H_Prof/Mental_Health_Commission_Rules/Seclusion_and_Mechanical_Restraint/Rules_Governing_the_use_of_Seclusion_and_Mechanical_Means_of_Bodily_Restraint1.html

Mental Health (Criminal Law) Review Board. (2024). *Mental Health Criminal Law Review Board*. Department of Justice, Ireland. https://www.mhclrb.ie/

Moynihan, G., O'Reilly, K., O'Connor, J., & Kennedy, H. G. (2018). An evaluation of functional mental capacity in forensic mental health practice: The Dundrum capacity ladders validation study. *BMC Psychiatry*, *18*(1), 78. https://doi.org/10.1186/s12888-018-1664-2

Naughton, M., Nulty, A., Abidin, Z., Davoren, M., O'Dwyer, S., & Kennedy, H. G. (2012). Effects of group metacognitive training (MCT) on mental capacity and functioning in patients with psychosis in a secure forensic psychiatric hospital: A prospective-cohort waiting list controlled study. *BMC Research Notes*, *5*, 302. https://doi.org/10.1186/1756-0500-5-302

O'Dwyer, S., Davoren, M., Abidin, Z., Doyle, E., McDonnell, K., & Kennedy, H. G. (2011). The DUNDRUM Quartet: Validation of structured professional judgement instruments DUNDRUM-3 assessment of programme completion and DUNDRUM-4 assessment of recovery in forensic mental health services. *BMC Research Notes*, *4*, 229. https://doi.org/10.1186/1756-0500-4-229

O'Keeffe, D., Kinsella, A., Waddington, J. L., & Clarke, M. (2022). 20-year prospective sequential follow-up study of heterogeneity in associations of duration of untreated psychosis with symptoms, functioning and quality of life following first-episode psychosis. *American Journal of Psychiatry*, *179*(4), 288–297. https://doi.org/10.1176/appi.ajp2021

O'Neill, A. M. (2005). *Irish mental health law*. First Law.

O'Reilly, K., Donohoe, G., O'Sullivan, D., Coyle, C., Corvin, A., O'Flynn, P., et al. (2019). A randomized controlled trial of cognitive remediation for a national cohort of forensic patients with schizophrenia or schizoaffective disorder. *BMC Psychiatry, 19*(1), 27. https://doi.org/10.1186/s12888-019-2022-0

O'Reilly, K., Donohoe, G., O'Sullivan, D., Coyle, C., Mullaney, R., O'Connell, P., et al. (2016). Study protocol: A randomised controlled trial of cognitive remediation for a national cohort of forensic mental health patients with schizophrenia or schizoaffective disorder. *BMC Psychiatry, 16*, 5. https://doi.org/10.1186/s12888-016-0716-7

O'Reilly, R., Allison, S., & Bastiampiallai, T. (2019). Observed outcomes: An approach to calculate the optimum number of psychiatric beds. *Administration and Policy in Mental Health and Mental Health Services Research, 46*(4), 507–517. https://doi.org/10.1007/s10488-019-00927-y

Parente, L., Carabellese, F., Felthous, A., La Tegola, D., Davoren, M., Kennedy, H. G., et al. (2023). Italian evaluation and excellence in REMS (ITAL-EE-REMS): Appropriate placement of forensic patients in REMS forensic facilities. *International Journal of Mental Health Systems, 18*, 33. https://doi.org/10.1186/s13033-024-00647-5

Pillay, S. M., Oliver, B., Butler, L., & Kennedy, H. G. (2008). Risk stratification and the care pathway. *Irish Journal of Psychological Medicine, 25*(4), 123–127.

Prior, P. M. (2003). Mad, not bad: Crime, mental disorder, and gender in nineteenth-century Ireland. In I. O'Donnell, & M. F. Gregory (Eds.), *Criminal justice history: Themes and controversies from pre-independence Ireland* (pp. 66–82). Four Courts Press.

Prior, P. M. (2008). *Madness and murder: Gender, crime, and mental disorder in nineteenth-century Ireland*. Irish Academic Press.

Prior, P. M. (Ed.). (2017). *Asylums, mental health care and the Irish: 1800–2010*. Irish Academic Press.

Quinlan, P. (2021). *Walls of containment: The architecture and landscapes of lunacy*. University College Dublin Press.

Richter, M. S., O'Reilly, K., O'Sullivan, D., O'Flynn, P., Corvin, A., Donohoe, G., et al. (2018). Prospective observational cohort study of 'treatment as usual' over four years for patients with schizophrenia in a national forensic hospital. *BMC Psychiatry, 18*(1), 289. https://doi.org/10.1186/s12888-018-1862-y

Schulmann, K., Bruen, C., Parker, S., Siersbaek, R., Conghail, L. M., & Burke, S. (2024). The role of governance in shaping health system reform: A case study of the design and implementation of new health regions in Ireland, 2018–2023. *BMC Health Services Research, 24*(1), 578. https://doi.org/10.1186/s12913-024-06678-2

Seppänen, A., Törmänen, I., Shaw, C., & Kennedy, H. G. (2018). Modern forensic psychiatric hospital design: Clinical, legal and structural aspects. *International Journal of Mental Health Systems, 12*, 58. https://doi.org/10.1186/s13033-018-0238-7

Sharma, A., Dunn, W., O'Toole, C., & Kennedy, H. G. (2015). The virtual institution: Cross-sectional length of stay in general adult and forensic psychiatry beds. *International Journal of Mental Health Systems, 9*, 25. https://doi.org/10.1186/s13033-015-0015-7

Tomlin, J., Lega, I., Braun, P., Kennedy, H. G., Herrando, V. T., Barroso, R., et al. (2020). Forensic mental health in Europe: Some key figures. *Social Psychiatry and Psychiatric Epidemiology*, 1–9. https://doi.org/10.1007/s00127-020-01936-8

Warburton, K. D., & Stahl, S. M. (2016). *Violence in psychiatry*. Cambridge University Press. https://doi.org/10.1017/CBO9781316275189

Wharewera-Mika, J., Cooper, E., Wiki, N., Prentice, K., Field, T., Cavney, J., et al. (2020). The appropriateness of DUNDRUM-3 and DUNDRUM-4 for Māori in forensic mental health services in New Zealand: Participatory action research. *BMC Psychiatry, 20*(1), 1–9. https://doi.org/10.1186/s12888-020-02521-8

Williams, H. K., Senanayke, M., Ross, C. C., Bates, R., & Davoren, M. (2020). Security needs among patients referred for high secure care in Broadmoor Hospital England. *BJPsych Open*, *6*(4), e55. https://doi.org/10.1192/bjo.2020.38

Wright, B., Duffy, D., Curtin, K., Linehan, S., Monks, S., & Kennedy, H. G. (2006). Psychiatric morbidity among women prisoners newly committed and amongst remanded and sentenced women in the Irish prison system. *Irish Journal of Psychological Medicine*, *23*(2), 47–53.

Zoghbi, A. W., Lieberman, J. A., & Girgis, R. R. (2023). The neurobiology of duration of untreated psychosis: A comprehensive review. *Molecular Psychiatry*, *28*(1), 168–190. https://doi.org/10.1038/s41380-022-01787-1

# 11 Lithuania

*Ilona Laurinaitytė, Vaiva Martinkienė, and Arūnas Germanavičius*

**Brief Description**

| | |
|---|---|
| **Location** | The Republic of Lithuania is a country located in the Baltic region of northeastern Europe. |
| **Size** | 65,300 km$^2$ |
| **Population** | 2.86 million |
| **Language** | Lithuanian is the official language and one of the official languages of the European Union. |
| **Political system** | Lithuania is a multiparty parliamentary democracy and a decentralised unitary state. The President and the Government (headed by the Prime Minister) exercise executive power. The Parliament (*Seimas*) is a single-chamber legislative body. The country is composed of 10 regions that are divided into 60 municipalities. |

*Source*: State Data Agency of Lithuania, 2024.

## Legal System

The legal system in Lithuania follows the civil law legal system and is primarily based on the legal traditions of Continental Europe, particularly those of France and Germany. Lithuania's judicial system consists of both general jurisdiction courts, such as the Supreme Court of Lithuania, the Court of Appeal of Lithuania, five regional courts, 12 district courts, special jurisdiction courts, including the Supreme Administrative Court of Lithuania, and two regional administrative courts (Lithuanian Courts Administration, 2023). Courts of general jurisdiction are responsible for hearing both civil and criminal cases.

Substantive branches of the law are codified in codes. In Lithuania, the grounds for conducting forensic psychiatric examinations and the procedures for prescribing such examinations are regulated by the Code of Criminal Procedure of the Republic of Lithuania (2002b) and the Code of Civil Procedure of the Republic of Lithuania (2002a) per the current legislation. The court determines

DOI: 10.4324/9781003376248-14

whether individuals with a mental illness who have committed dangerous acts and been identified as having reduced responsibility should be involuntarily hospitalised and treated. This decision is made in accordance with the Criminal Code of the Republic of Lithuania (2000) and the Law on the Forensic Examination of the Republic of Lithuania (2002c). Individuals deemed by a court to be legally incapacitated or of diminished legal capacity are admitted only to a specialised psychiatric hospital in Rokiškis or receive outpatient treatment at regional mental health centres. After six months—or sooner if necessary—the court must review the case of involuntary hospitalisation and treatment and extend it if required.

In Lithuania, the regulation of all types of forensic expertise is defined by the Law on the Forensic Examination of the Republic of Lithuania (2002c). Forensic experts are expected to adhere to the Ethics Code for Forensic Experts, which outlines the fundamental principles governing their work. The Coordination Council of Forensic Experts sets priorities and strategies for all forensic institutions in Lithuania under the Ministry of Justice's supervision. Only those on Lithuania's List of Forensic Experts can work in forensic science institutions as experts.

### *Mental Health Laws*

#### *Civil Capacity*

Civil capacity evaluation cases are made in civil processes when there is a question about a person's ability to perform their duties and to realise their rights independently. Each year, 1,100 forensic psychiatry assessments evaluate a person's civil capacity in civil cases. Between 2016 and 2022, 4% to 9% of the evaluated persons were found to have full civil capacity each year. Of the persons evaluated, approximately 15% had partial civil capacity, while approximately 77% were found to have complete civil incapacity. A person's level of civil capacity is re-evaluated every two years on a regular basis.

#### *Fitness to Stand Trial*

Article 38 of the Code of Civil Procedure of the Republic of Lithuania defines processual capability (or fitness to stand trial). Processual capability is detailed in other legal acts that implement the Code. The court determines a person's processual capability based on an evaluation by a forensic psychiatric expert. Processual capability is a subset of civil capacity, specifically relating to litigation and court procedures. According to the law, individuals who lack civil capacity or whose civil capacity is restricted shall participate in a hearing alongside their respective party or other participants in the proceedings.

*Criminal Responsibility*

According to Article 17 ('Criminal responsibility'[1]) of the Criminal Code of the Republic of Lithuania (2000),

> a person shall be considered legally not responsible (incapacitated) where, at the time of the commission of an act forbidden under this Code, he was unable to appreciate the dangerous nature of the act or to control his behaviour as a result of a mental disorder.

Diminished legal responsibility (Article 18 of the Code) is the lack of a capacity for a person to "fully appreciate the dangerous nature of the criminal act or to control [their] behaviour as a result of a mental disorder, even though the disorder is not a sufficient ground for finding [them] legally not responsible (incapacitated)". Between 2013 and 2022, approximately 28% of assessed individuals who committed criminal acts were deemed not responsible for their crimes due to serious mental illness or were found not guilty by reason of insanity under Article 17 of the Criminal Code of the Republic of Lithuania (2000). Each year, a small percentage of the assessed offenders, ranging from 1% to 5%, were found to have diminished responsibility. In the cases of persons with legal irresponsibility (incapacity), a forensic psychiatrist must recommend the level of compulsory medical measures that must be applied by the court to these persons.

## Structure and Function of the Forensic Psychiatric System

### *Role of National Forensic Psychiatry Service*

The National Forensic Psychiatry Service (NFPS, under the Ministry of Health; https://www.vtpt.lt), operating under the Ministry of Health of the Republic of Lithuania, is primarily responsible for providing pretrial consultations and conducting forensic psychiatric assessments for the courts. During the pretrial investigation, only the accused's medical records are reviewed to identify any signs of severe mental illness that may warrant a full forensic psychiatric examination. Approximately 2,500 consultations are carried out annually.

An accused person is deemed to have legally significant mental disturbances only if they have a severe mental illness such as psychosis, intellectual disability, or dementia. Individuals diagnosed with personality disorders, depression, anxiety, other neurotic conditions, or substance use disorders are not considered to have a legally significant mental illness requiring full expert evaluation.

Between 2013 and 2022, an average of 2,280 forensic psychiatric assessments were conducted annually, with approximately 50% relating to civil and criminal cases. After conducting an evaluation, the forensic psychiatrist prepares a 'statement of expertise' that meets the requirements outlined in the Law on the Forensic Examination (2002). The conclusions of this assessment are then presented to the court in writing. The forensic psychiatry expert may also be called to participate in a court hearing to confirm their findings verbally.

In criminal cases, the primary role of a forensic psychiatry expert is to:

(a) assess the mental health of the accused at the time the crime was committed,
(b) evaluate their ability to participate in legal proceedings (e.g., their fitness to stand trial or their capacity to undergo the legal process),
(c) recommend necessary medical interventions based on the individual's level of social risk.

The forensic psychiatrist also evaluates the mental health of the victim of the crime to:

(a) assess their ability to understand and resist criminal actions,
(b) evaluate their processual capability,
(c) determine the extent of any mental health disturbances.

In rare cases, the forensic psychiatry expert may be tasked with evaluating the mental state of a witness to determine their capacity to participate in court proceedings.

In civil cases, the forensic psychiatrist is responsible for:

(a) evaluating a person's mental health in civil capacity evaluations,
(b) assessing testamentary capacity in post-mortem forensic psychiatric assessments, where the individual's mental state at the time of creating a will is evaluated,
(c) evaluating the mental health of an individual before death by suicide,
(d) conducting assessments in child custody disputes in civil cases (in collaboration with forensic psychologists),
(e) evaluating a person's civil capacity to participate in legal proceedings.

The NFPS operates six outpatient forensic psychiatry departments across Lithuania, providing consultations and specialised expertise. In addition, it has an inpatient forensic psychiatry department offering expertise for periods typically ranging from 14 to 30 days or, in rare cases, up to 60 days. The Department for Children and Adolescents of the NFPS is focused on assessing the mental health of minors. The Central Forensic Psychiatry Department specialises in managing complex cases involving malingering and conducting repeat forensic psychiatric assessments, which are uncommon and account for only 1%–2% of all assessments annually.

Forensic psychiatric examinations are conducted by officially recognised experts (who are listed). These experts participate in all procedures until the court issues a decision on the case. If a person is found not legally responsible, they are sent to a specialised hospital, where a general psychiatrist treats them. Forensic psychiatry experts do not participate in the mandatory treatment of forensic psychiatric patients in Lithuania. Instead, all tasks related to compulsory treatment, whether in outpatient or inpatient settings, are managed by general psychiatrists without specialisation in forensic psychiatry.

#### *Training and Qualifications*

Lithuania has 22 forensic psychiatry experts and 15 forensic psychology experts. The NFPS is responsible for training these professionals through an apprenticeship programme. Only licensed psychiatrists who have completed their full training and psychologists who have studied clinical psychology are accepted.

During their time at the NFPS, apprentices work alongside experienced experts on various assignments. This usually lasts 6–12 months but can be extended upon request. At the end of the programme, apprentices take a forensic expert exam organised by the NFPS, which consists of two parts: specific methodological questions on forensic psychiatry or psychology and basic knowledge of the relevant laws. The apprentice is awarded a Forensic Expert Certificate upon completing the programme and exam. They then swear an oath, both orally and in writing, to the Minister of Justice, after which they are added to the official list of forensic experts.

The NFPS also ensures that forensic psychiatry and psychology experts maintain their qualifications. Experts must submit descriptions of their work results every five years and provide examples.

#### *National Networks and Collaborations*

There is no single organisation in Lithuania that unites experts in forensic psychiatry. Typically, forensic psychiatry experts are members of the Lithuanian Psychiatric Association, while forensic psychology experts are members of the Lithuanian Psychological Association.

### Provision of Care for Forensic Psychiatric Patients

In Lithuania, civilly committed patients are not classified as forensic psychiatric patients. Although a civil patient may still be subject to involuntary treatment ordered by a court, such treatment is typically administered in general psychiatric hospitals. Mandatory medical interventions for forensic psychiatric patients differ from involuntary treatments given to other civil patients. These interventions can be mandated by a court following forensic psychiatric evaluations of individuals who have been declared not guilty of a crime due to a severe mental illness or deemed unfit to stand trial due to a severe mental illness. The forensic psychiatrist is responsible for recommending the appropriate type of compulsory treatment, which may be either inpatient or outpatient care at a specialised psychiatric hospital.

The Rokiškis Psychiatric Hospital is the sole psychiatric facility in Lithuania that provides care for forensic patients. The hospital offers care to both voluntary and involuntary civil psychiatric patients and operates an occupation and rehabilitation centre that caters to both inpatients and outpatients. There are also 380 beds allocated for forensic psychiatric patients, with their distribution based on security levels: 15 in high-security, 55 in medium-security, and 310 in low-security wards.

A clinical psychologist and a treating psychiatrist conduct risk assessments for violent behaviour of the forensic patient once or twice a year. The attending treatment team must evaluate the mental health status of all forensic patients every six months. This requirement applies to all cases of compulsory inpatient and outpatient treatment. After the evaluation, the court is notified of the results and can recommend further compulsory treatment. These recommendations may include changing the level of treatment or even discontinuing the compulsory treatment for forensic patients altogether. Compulsory treatment measures are changed consecutively. A patient in compulsory treatment can progress to outpatient treatment only after receiving treatment in the general security ward. All changes to compulsory treatment measures are made solely by the court. The purpose of compulsory treatment of forensic psychiatric patients is to alleviate symptoms of mental illness and minimise the risk of violent behaviour. All patients are treated with individualised treatment plans, which may include medication, individual therapy, group therapy, and psychosocial rehabilitation.

### *Forensic Patient Characteristics*

According to the data from the Annual Report of the Rokiškis Psychiatry Hospital (2023), the age of forensic psychiatry patients ranges from 16 to 76 years, and about 80% of forensic psychiatry patients are men, 19% are women, and 1% are juveniles. Šileikaitė et al. (2016) found that most forensic psychiatry patients are diagnosed as psychotic (69.5 %). Substance abuse in the sample is also quite prevalent (41.2 %). The findings showed that violent crimes are the most prevalent among forensic patients (63.1 %).

### *Approaches to Treatment*

In Lithuania, the primary goal of treating forensic psychiatry patients is to provide medical intervention for alleviating psychiatric symptoms and minimising social risks. Rokiškis Psychiatric Hospital offers various rehabilitation programmes, such as psychosocial support and professional or vocational training. Psychosocial rehabilitation involves a range of therapeutic interventions, including psychological counselling, occupational therapy, physical therapy, bibliotherapy, recreational sports, and creative art therapies like floral design, ceramics, and other specialised crafts. In addition, professional rehabilitation comprises instruction in fundamental computer skills, construction and masonry training, and soap and candle making and cooking. Vocational training aims to help forensic psychiatry patients maintain their daily routines and take care of their living spaces.

#### *Length of Stay and Exiting the Forensic Psychiatric System*

In Lithuania, the length of treatment for forensic patients does not depend on the length of sentence for their crime. The average duration of treatment for forensic psychiatry patients at Rokiškis Psychiatric Hospital is approximately 800 days. Still, it can vary depending on treatment outcomes, lasting anywhere from two to five years or sometimes even longer. Additionally, the length of stay may differ depending on the required security level.

The European Committee for the Prevention of Torture and Inhuman or Degrading Treatment or Punishment (2018) stated that, in Lithuania, the average stay of such patients was 119 days in the maximum-security unit, 285 days in medium-security units, and 1,200 days in low-security units. Still, some patients had spent up to 16–20 years in the establishment (although usually with interruptions, patients have been meanwhile accommodated in general psychiatric hospitals, social care homes, or even at their homes).

### Strengths and Weaknesses

Lithuanian forensic psychiatry has several strengths, including the NFPS, which features a well-structured system of regional outpatient departments throughout the country. These departments offer expert services to the public in their respective regions and an inpatient expertise department. Moreover, the presence of a Forensic Expertise Law that formalises the role of experts across all domains, coupled with the Forensic Expert Activity Coordination Council that upholds the Code of Ethics of Experts (Forensic Expert Activity Coordination Council, 2014) and monitors the supervision of experts, serve as valuable strengths in Lithuanian forensic psychiatry. Another strength is that forensic psychiatry assessments are carried out only by certified forensic psychiatrists and psychologists with the necessary expertise. This helps to ensure that the quality of the assessments remains consistently high. Finally, a notable regional strength could be attributed to the robust global partnerships among forensic psychiatrists from the Baltic and Nordic regions and various international organisations, including the Forensic Psychiatry section of the World Psychiatric Association.

The system has several weaknesses, including lacking a robust statewide psychiatric continuum of care for forensic outpatients to meet their needs. Engaging challenging clients often falls on general psychiatrists, who may lack the specialised knowledge and skills required for this task. The Ministry of Health has had plans since 2024 to establish a few community treatment teams that are flexible and assertive. However, these teams are not yet specialised in forensic psychiatry.

The Lithuanian forensic psychiatry system's shortcomings contribute to a high rate of repeat offences among patients in forensic psychiatry and their readmission to Rokiškis Psychiatric Hospital (2021). Although there are individual treatment and rehabilitation plans for forensic patients that are reviewed regularly, and some aspects of multidisciplinary teamwork are present in specialised hospitals, these patients are not adequately engaged in psychosocial rehabilitation activities. In addition, clinical psychologists mainly focus on risk assessment and evaluation, with treatment being only an occasional focus.

## Note

1 Lithuanian legal documents often use different translations for 'criminal responsibility', such as 'criminal liability' or 'legal incapacity'. While English distinguishes between these terms—'criminal responsibility' referring to mental capacity and 'criminal liability' or 'legal incapacity' relating to legal accountability—many legal systems use them interchangeably in practice. To avoid ambiguity, we will use the term 'criminal responsibility' throughout this text.

## References

European Committee for the Prevention of Torture and Inhuman or Degrading Treatment or Punishment. (2018). *Report to the Lithuanian Government on the visit to Lithuania carried out by the European Committee for the Prevention of Torture and Inhuman or Degrading Treatment or Punishment (CPT) from 5 to 15 September 2016*. Strasbourg, France: Council of Europe. Retrieved from https://rm.coe.int/pdf/16807843ca

Forensic Expert Activity Coordination Council. (2014). *The Lithuanian Professional Ethics Code for Forensic Experts*. Retrieved from https://e-seimas.lrs.lt/portal/legalAct/lt/TAD/4f19a030a8c511e3840c893be7eb3526

Lithuanian Courts Administration. (2023). *Lithuanian Courts: Judicial System*. Retrieved from https://www.teismai.lt/en/courts/judicial-system/650

Republic of Lithuania. (2000). *The Criminal Code of the Republic of Lithuania*. Official Gazette *Valstybės žinios*, No. 89–2741.

Republic of Lithuania. (2002a). *The Code of Civil Procedure of the Republic of Lithuania*. Official Gazette *Valstybės žinios*, No. 36–1340.

Republic of Lithuania. (2002b). *The Code of Criminal Procedure of the Republic of Lithuania*. Official Gazette *Valstybės žinios*, No. 37–1341.

Republic of Lithuania. (2002c). *The Law on the Forensic Examination of the Republic of Lithuania*. Official Gazette *Valstybės žinios*, No. 112–4969

Rokiškis Psychiatry Hospital. (2021). *Annual report*. Retrieved from https://www.rpl.lt/veiklos-ataskaitos/

Rokiškis Psychiatry Hospital. (2023). *Annual report*. Retrieved from https://www.rpl.lt/uploads/2023%2520m-%2520veiklos%2520ataskaita.pdf

Šileikaitė, A., Germanavičius, A., & Česnienė, I. (2016). The relationships of clinical, socio-demographic and criminal factors in a sample of forensic psychiatric patients (Teismo psichiatrijos pacientų sociodemografinių ir klinikinių veiksnių bei nusikalstamo elgesio sąsajos). *Sveikatos mokslai / Health Sciences in Eastern Europe*, *26*(1), 47–51. https://doi.org/10.5200/sm-hs.2016.007

State Data Agency of Lithuania. (2024). *Official Statistics Portal*. Retrieved from https://osp.stat.gov.lt/

# 12 The Netherlands

*Vivienne de Vogel and Michiel van der Wolf*

## Brief Description

| | |
|---|---|
| **Location** | The Netherlands is located in Northwestern Europe. |
| **Size** | 41,865 km$^2$ |
| **Population** | 18 million |
| **Languages** | The official language of the Netherlands is Dutch (*Nederlands*). Frisian (*Frysk*) is an official language in the province of Friesland, where it is spoken alongside Dutch. |
| **Political system** | The Netherlands is a constitutional monarchy with a parliamentary system. The King is the head of state, and the prime minister is the head of government. The Dutch parliament comprises the House of Representatives (*Tweede Kamer*) and the Senate (*Eerste Kamer*). The judiciary is independent, with a supreme court as the highest legal institution. |

## Legal System

The legal system in the Netherlands comprises various legal branches, authoritative bodies, and distinct levels of court. The Dutch judicial system consists of 11 district courts, four courts of appeal, and the Supreme Court, which oversees national lawsuits and interprets the law in appeals. Each district court is made up of various sectors, such as those for civil, criminal, and administrative law. In the Netherlands, the judicial process for criminal cases is more inquisitorial than adversarial. This means that the courts take a leading role in investigating the trial and making the final verdict (van Koppen & Penrod, 2003; van der Wolf & Mevis, 2021).

The Netherlands is divided into geographically distinct areas, each with its own court system. These jurisdictions determine which court will handle a specific case and which higher court will hear an appeal if one or more parties disagree with the verdict or sentence. If the legal dispute remains unresolved, it is escalated to the Supreme Court, where the focus is not on the facts of the case but on the interpretation of the law. In the Netherlands, public prosecutors may

DOI: 10.4324/9781003376248-15

choose not to pursue criminal charges in certain cases, based on policy considerations and practical concerns. During such deliberations, the mental health of the suspect may be considered, and the prosecution may choose to seek mandated care through civil court as a means of diversion directed by the prosecution. The prosecution can impose non-custodial penalties for minor offences, such as treatment conditions. When an individual contests such a penalty, the judiciary will review the case (Crijns & van der Woude, 2022; van der Wolf & Mevis, 2021).

### *Dutch Criminal Justice System*

The Dutch criminal justice system has a dualistic or twin-track sanctioning system, whereby punishment is rendered when the defendant is found guilty and culpable. At the same time, a safety measure may still apply in the absence of culpability, for example, due to a mental illness (Jehle et al., 2021). Culpability is an important legal principle in Dutch criminal law. In legal practice, the conceptual area between total culpability and non-culpability, which is not explicitly defined, is referred to as 'diminished responsibility'. When conducting a forensic assessment and providing expert testimony for the court, it is generally accepted that the degree to which a mental disorder is linked to a criminal offence is directly proportional to the level of criminal responsibility. However, the exact number of distinguishable levels of responsibility is still debated (van der Wolf & van Marle, 2018). Judicial sentencing takes into strong consideration the degree to which individuals with a mental illness are found culpable. While a reduction in sentence may occur, courts are not required to match the level of culpability. However, the link between disorder and offence may increase the chance of a safety measure. A penalty cannot be imposed if a defendant is found non-culpable; however, a safety measure can be implemented instead (van der Wolf et al., 2022a).

In addition to the sentencing options available in the Dutch Criminal Code (*Wetboek van Strafrecht*), several mental health laws help determine the best placement and treatment for individuals with mental illness. Criminal courts can also use these laws as a court-led diversion for those who have committed a crime. In the Netherlands, it is the sole responsibility of a judge to issue a sentence, decide on mandatory confinement or treatment, and deliver a final verdict. However, forensic care can still be provided while a person serves their prison sentence, either at the Penitentiary Psychiatric Centre or by transferring them to a mental health facility. The Ministry of Justice and Security is the deciding authority in such cases. Forensic care is typically provided through conditional sentences or sanction modalities to which the justice-involved individual has consented (van der Wolf & Mevis, 2021). The Dutch criminal justice system has a distinct approach for individuals deemed to have diminished responsibility, offering a hybrid sentence that involves serving a detention order in a custodial institution and undergoing a mandated treatment order afterwards.

### *Dutch Forensic Care*

In the Netherlands, under the *Forensic Care Act (Wet forensische zorg)* of 2019, individuals who have consented or been compelled to receive forensic care are classified as forensic patients. The Act ensures that the Ministry of Justice and Security pays for their treatment. For the safety of society, forensic patients must receive appropriate treatment and the necessary security, with an adequate level of legal protection. Forensic care involves mental health, addiction, and intellectual disability care that may be included as a condition in a sentence, measure, or legal framework initiated by the prosecution during the criminal process. This may include conditional suspension of pretrial detention or mandated care as part of the penalties imposed by the prosecution. Forensic care moves at the intersection of criminal law and health care (van der Wolf & Mevis, 2021).

The main goal of forensic care is to prevent recidivism and promote a safe, gradual return to society. This may be accomplished by treating and supervising patients so that they can function again in society. In the Netherlands, there are currently 24 legal frameworks for forensic care, separate from the mentioned options to divert justice-involved individuals to mental health care.

#### *TBS Order*

In the Netherlands, a TBS, or *Terbeschikkingstelling van de staat* order, is the most widely recognised and intrusive criminal justice framework for forensic care involving the highest levels of security. The legal framework for TBS orders was introduced in 1928 and is primarily governed by Articles 37, 37a, and 37b of the Dutch Criminal Code (Criminal Code, 1928). The primary goal of a TBS order is to safeguard society from individuals with a mental illness who are considered high risk for recidivism by mandating their admission to secure hospitals and treating them until they can be gradually reintegrated into society.

A TBS order is legally considered a safety measure and constitutes a placement under a hospital order for high-risk forensic patients. There are two types of TBS orders: a hospital order that requires mandatory treatment and a conditional hospital order. Typically, the former is referred to most often. In cases of diminished responsibility, a TBS order enables the court to deliver a combined sentence of punishment, usually a prison term, and subsequent safety measures for individuals with a mental illness who have committed serious sexual or violent criminal offences. In such cases, the prison sentence is served before the start of the TBS order.

The mandated treatment period under a TBS order is, in principle, indefinite, except in some cases of non-violent offences where it is limited to a maximum of four years. The treatment period always begins with a two-year term. Following this, a criminal court comprising three judges may prolong or terminate a TBS order by one or two years, taking into account the advice from the patient's hospital and evaluating the appropriateness of the treatment duration concerning the offence committed. The hospital staff presents a comprehensive analysis of the patient's treatment to the court, encompassing the latest results of a structured risk assessment. The court can only decide to terminate or prolong a TBS order. The average length of a TBS order is currently eight to nine years (TBS Nederland, 2024).

In addition to the mandatory variant described earlier, there is also a conditional variant of a TBS order. While the criteria for the conditional variant are similar to those of the mandatory order, the risk factor is lower, and this means that society can be protected with fewer security measures. Patients must consent to the conditions, including placement in a medium-secure forensic hospital. When conditions are violated by the patient or the protection of society demands it, the court can convert a conditional variant into a mandatory one.

*Imposing a TBS Order*

There are three substantive prerequisites for imposing a TBS order: (1) the offence carries a maximum prison sentence of at least four years; (2) the defendant had a mental illness at the time of the offence, generally meaning they had diminished (or non-) responsibility for the offence; and (3) there is a risk of recidivism without mandated treatment. Next to these criteria, it is required that two mental health practitioners from different disciplines formally assess the individual to generate 'pro-Justitia' reports. Dutch 'pro-Justitia' reports examine the relation between a mental disorder and the offence and assess the chance that individuals will relapse into violent behaviours. While such an assessment was traditionally based on a clinical offence analysis, currently, guidelines stress the importance of incorporating validated risk assessment instruments being used in the Netherlands, like the Historical Clinical Risk Management-20 (HCR-20 v3; Douglas et al., 2013) or the Historical Clinical Future-Revised (HKT-R, a Dutch equivalent tool; Spreen et al., 2014). These reports must be completed before a TBS order can be issued, even though the court is not bound by the expert's conclusions.

In Dutch criminal legislation, the concept of criminal non-responsibility is defined as follows: "A person who commits an offence for which they cannot be held responsible due to a mental disorder, psychogeriatric condition or mental disability shall not be punishable" (Article 39, Criminal Code, 1928). Before 2023, no specific criteria existed to determine whether a person with a mental disorder was not responsible for their actions. However, such criteria were formulated in a recent landmark case (SC 17 October 2023, ECLI:NL:HR:2023:1295). Since then, courts have only reached a conclusion of non-responsibility when the defendant lacks insight into the wrongfulness of their actions or cannot control their behaviour. In the Netherlands, diminished responsibility has always been considered a gradation between responsibility and non-responsibility. Disciplinary guidelines differ in the number of gradations of the concept that can be established, as well as five or three levels of responsibility. As in classical criminal law theory, diminished responsibility meant a lesser sentence, while the causal relation with a mental disorder increased reoffending risk. The concept played a central role in the coming about of a TBS order, for example, in the possibility of combining the safety measure with a prison sentence (for the part that individuals are still held responsible). An example of diminished responsibility would be individuals diagnosed with a personality disorder or a mental disability who may have experienced impaired volitional control but not to the extent that they were not held criminally responsible at all.

#### *Gradual Return to Society*

It is important that the patient can safely and gradually return to society, and leave is considered an essential part of this process. During a TBS order, the Dutch Ministry of Justice and Security decides on leaves based on advice from the Dutch Advisory Board on Review of Leave. This Board was created in 2008 with the task of independent external evaluation of leave applications of forensic psychiatric patients with a TBS order. The Board consists of legal and mental health professionals with substantial experience in the forensic field. They independently review applications regarding new phases in forensic mental health treatment under a TBS order (first supervised leave, first unsupervised leave, transmural leave, and probationary leave) and advise the Ministry of Justice and Security. The Board has no legislative competence. Leave applications are written by mental health professionals from the forensic psychiatric setting where the patient is residing and always contain the results of a recent structured (sexual) violence risk assessment. The decision to conditionally or finally terminate a TBS order is a different process and can only be made by the court.

## Forensic Psychiatry System

### ***Structure and Function of the Forensic Psychiatric System***

The Dutch forensic system is elaborate and multitiered; specialised forensic mental hospitals have varying levels of security. Hospitals with the highest level of security are Forensic Psychiatric Centres (FPCs, often called TBS hospitals), which treat forensic patients who have received a TBS order. Currently, there are seven FPCs, two of which are government-operated and five of which are private institutions. There are forensic hospitals with lower security levels or wards in general psychiatry treating forensic patients. Several hospitals are part of a larger mainstream psychiatric hospital. Other hospitals have specialised in specific groups, such as patients who suffer from mental disabilities or individuals with severe addiction problems. A specialised Centre for Transcultural Psychiatry also provides care tailored to patients from various cultures and subcultures. Within the prison services, there are four Penitentiary Psychiatric Centres and other options for care.

Furthermore, several forensic hospitals also have outpatient facilities. Outpatient forensic psychiatry services are distinctly different from inpatient services in terms of the referral process, length of treatment, treatment type, forensic mental healthcare team, decision makers, and available treatments. Overall, there are a variety of inpatient and outpatient forensic facilities throughout the country (van der Wolf & Mevis, 2021; van der Wolf et al., 2022a).

### *Role of Forensic Psychiatrists and Psychologists in the Pretrial Phase*

In the pretrial phase, a forensic assessment can be requested from the courts and is usually conducted by psychologists and psychiatrists. In the Netherlands, the forensic assessment is undertaken through the mediation of a specialised centralised institute called the Netherlands Institute for Forensic Psychiatry and Psychology (NIFP). The Dutch government established this centralised NIFP to provide more unity in the quality of the assessments for the court. The Netherlands Register of Courts Experts (NRGD) independently evaluates and registers the professionals to further safeguard the quality of forensic assessment before the court.

Forensic mental health practitioners who conduct forensic assessments of individuals with mental illness generate reports for the court and are trained and appointed by the NIFP and evaluated by the NRGD. One chief responsibility of the NIFP is to mediate expert evaluations, which are carried out by a psychiatrist and/or psychologist ('pro-Justitia rapporteur'). The public prosecutor or the judge can instruct the NIFP to conduct such an evaluation. The registered forensic mental health specialist must determine whether the defendant had a mental disorder at the time of the crime and whether this influenced their behaviour when the crime was committed (either leading to a lower level of responsibility or not) as well as whether there is a risk of recidivism and a need for risk-reducing treatment in one of the possible legal frameworks (de Boer & Gerrits, 2007).

A part of the NIFP is the Pieter Baan Centrum, a specific forensic observation clinic operated by the Ministry of Justice and Security. In the clinic, the defendant undergoes a rigorous six-week evaluation by a team of forensic mental health professionals. Generally, individuals who undergo this rigorous and intensive testing are accused of serious offences. At the end of these evaluations, forensic experts will consult and write up a multidisciplinary evaluation report on the examinee for the courts. The courts will review these clinical recommendations to arrive at a final verdict for the placement and treatment of a forensic patient.

### *Forensic Psychiatry Profession*

#### *Qualifications and Specialised Training*

Mental health practitioners in forensic psychiatry involve multidisciplinary teams that span various occupational domains and disciplines. It is estimated that the Netherlands has approximately 25,000 practitioners working in the forensic field. The number of trained forensic psychologists and psychiatrists is much lower. For instance, current estimates suggest approximately 500 are registered in the NRGD in the Netherlands to conduct pro-Justitia reports.

Specialised training, education, and qualifications are required to become a certified forensic psychologist or psychiatrist. The Netherlands offers several specialised forensic psychology graduate (MSc) programmes, and successful candidates are prepared to practice as forensic psychologists. Postgraduate programmes are offered across various universities in the Netherlands; core forensic programmes are, for instance, offered at Maastricht University, University of Amsterdam, Erasmus University Rotterdam, and Tilburg University. These specialised graduate programmes take one to two years to complete. The NIFP offers specialised training programmes for psychologists and psychiatrists writing pro-Justitia reports. In the Netherlands, the universities of Applied Sciences offer minors and master's programmes and certifications to become forensic social work professionals; these students are educated to become social workers, psychiatric nurses (sociotherapists), nurses, or probation officers. In addition, various postgraduate programmes are offered to advance education for registered psychologists (clinical psychologists, mental health psychologists, and psychotherapists) focusing on forensic mental health. In the Netherlands, these forensic mental health practitioners offer treatment, conduct detailed assessments and evaluations on individuals with mental illness, track clinical progress, forecast trajectories based on anticipated risk, and provide expert opinions about recidivism risk.

### *National Networks and Collaborations to Improve the Quality of Forensic Care*

The Quality Framework Forensic Care is an umbrella under which all recent developments in the field of quality improvement have been placed in the Netherlands. It provides support and clarity within the forensic field for care providers, care professionals, clients and their relatives, and the Custodial Institutions Agency. Thus, clients know their expectations, and institutions and care professionals know what recovery-oriented and person-centred care is. All parties in the forensic sector cooperate in developing, practically elaborating, and implementing this framework. The sector intends to work entirely according to the framework by the end of 2028. To guide professionals in their daily work with this framework, in 2024, a forensic clinical mental healthcare standard was developed by a group of multidisciplinary experts. Mental healthcare standards in the Netherlands contain general recommendations for preventing, recognising, diagnosing, and treating psychological complaints and disorders. They are based on scientific knowledge and the experiences of patients and professionals. A general vision of care forms the starting point of all standards. Care standards, together with professional codes and legislation, form professional standards. They offer a solid basis for joint decision making and optimal care. Implementing this quality framework and standard is facilitated by the Dutch Expertise Centre Forensic Psychiatry (EFP) and the programme Quality Forensic Care (KFZ).

The EFP was established in 2002 to support the scientific foundation of care in forensic psychiatry, to promote cooperation among forensic institutions, and to establish more (knowledge) exchange with forensic (mental health) institutions, universities, and research institutes. The EFP's field of activity covers the entire field of forensic care. The mission of the EFP is to support the forensic care field in increasing the quality of care to promote societal safety.

In 2013, the KFZ programme was launched to increase the quality of forensic care through knowledge sharing, research, and collaboration. KFZ subsidises research projects in which organisations within forensic care work together to increase the quality and effectiveness of interventions, treatments, and methodologies, with the main goals of better care and a safer society. KFZ also stimulates the implementation of the KFZ products so the results can be widely used. The EFP facilitates the KFZ programme. The programme committee is responsible for substantive decisions within the KFZ programme. It consists of members working in the forensic care field, such as scientists, clinical professionals, and lived experience workers.

## Forensic Psychiatry Services (Provision of Care)

### *Forensic Patient Characteristics*

Most TBS patients are male (94%), and most settings in the Netherlands only admit male patients. There are a few forensic mental healthcare settings admitting women in gender-mixed wards, meaning that female and male patients reside together.[1] Most TBS patients (around 70%) were born in the Netherlands. The average age of a TBS patient is 44 years. Most patients have a personality and/or a psychotic disorder, and many also have an addiction problem. The percentage of TBS patients with a psychotic disorder is currently around 25%–30%; more than 60% have a history of substance abuse; and around 13% have an IQ below 80. Most patients in TBS hospitals have an Axis II personality disorder, either stand-alone or comorbid with other mental disorders.

### *Progression of Treatment*

In the Netherlands, on average, a TBS patient will spend approximately three to four years in a secure hospital facility (de Boer & Gerrits, 2007). Once the patient is no longer at high risk of absconding or reoffending, unsupervised leave and privileges are granted gradually. The aforementioned independent Advisory Board on Review of Leave is important in this gradual return to society. It makes a judgement for every new step based on a thorough assessment of risks and clinical progress. The leave modality after supervised and unsupervised leave is transmural leave. Generally, patients reside in the transmural phase for two to three years. After a proven track record of compliance and in the absence of aggressive or violent incidents, the next step is a conditional discharge of a TBS order, whereby patients are permitted to live in the community. At this phase of treatment, probation services and case managers take on the responsibility of supervising and monitoring the forensic patient.

#### *Facility for Long-Term Forensic Psychiatric Care*

In some cases, despite all clinical intervention and treatment plans, some TBS patients do not show progress or mental stability, or exhibit any reduction in recidivism risk. These forensic patients can be transferred to a facility for long-term forensic psychiatric care. Recent estimates indicate that approximately 7% of TBS patients are placed in one of these facilities. Still, the numbers are rising, since more than 22% of the total TBS population have already spent more than 15 years within the system (van der Wolf et al., 2022b). In the Netherlands, a TBS patient can only be transferred to such a facility when all other treatment possibilities have been tried, preferably in two TBS hospitals, without a significant reduction in reoffending risk (as shown by a validated risk assessment tool). Independent multidisciplinary 'pro-Justitia' reports and an assessment from a special advisory board are required in the placement procedure. An appeal against the placement can be made to the committee overseeing the legal protection of justice-involved individuals. The long-term forensic psychiatric care facility focuses on different clinical outcomes, as treatment focuses on improving the quality of life rather than intensive treatment programmes. In this facility, the courts and administration review a TBS order and the placement every two years. Also, many of the population will progress to less secure facilities, treatment clinics, and/or society. For some, lowering the 'treatment pressure' opens new opportunities for progression (Smeekens & Braun, 2019).

### ***Approaches to Assessment and Treatment***

Generally, the models of care in the Netherlands are eclectic. They differ based on the forensic settings and placement, whether they are an inpatient or outpatient, from proximal or distal sites (i.e., hospital, facilities, and residences), the phase of treatment, and the provisions of the treatment order. All Dutch psychiatric treatments and assessments are based on empirical research and evidence-based practices. Forensic mental health treatment utilises multi-methods and is implemented by multidisciplinary teams. Treatments are prioritised based on the dynamic risk factors that present a direct threat to recidivism.

*Risk Assessment*

Repeated structured risk assessments are crucial during forensic mental health care, and the results are used for multiple purposes, most notably for providing suggestions for treatment aimed at reducing risks. Since 2005, all inpatient forensic psychiatric institutions in the Netherlands have been mandated by the Ministry of Justice and Security to perform a structured risk assessment with the Dutch-language version of the HCR-20 v3 or the HKT-R plus, in the case of patients who have committed sexual offences, the STABLE-2007 (Fernandez et al., 2014), before deciding upon leaves for forensic patients with a TBS order. The risk assessment tools are routinely coded before every new leave application to the Advisory Board on Review of Leave and for the hospital's advice to the court to terminate or prolong a TBS order. In addition, the risk assessment is repeated at least once a year for all patients allowed outside the hospital. Usually, a researcher/diagnostician, a sociotherapist, and a treatment supervisor independently code the tool for each case. During a subsequent case conference, the three evaluators agree upon a consensus coding for all items, decide upon a final risk judgement, and discuss risk management strategies (de Vogel et al., 2014).

*Inpatient Services*

Most forensic mental health hospitals in the Netherlands provide individualised and group therapy. The fundamental theoretical models utilised in the Netherlands include the Risk-Need-Responsivity model and the Good Lives Model. There are a variety of tailored treatment programmes offered for forensic patients, which include addiction programmes, aggression management therapies, cognitive remediation programmes, recidivism prevention programmes for those who have engaged in violent sexual offences, and learning modules for personality and psychotic disorders. All treatment and professional programmes are geared towards gradual reintegration into society and avoiding hospitalisation. A psychologist and multidisciplinary teams generally lead Dutch forensic inpatient mental health teams to implement an individualised treatment plan for the patient. The Dutch forensic inpatient mental healthcare team consists primarily of psychologists, psychiatrists, sociotherapists, social workers, educational and vocational teachers, workshop supervisors, and recreational teachers. Secure forensic treatment in these settings is usually organised with approximately 10 to 12 patients living together in one ward, supported by sociotherapists. Sociotherapists support patients during daily routines, work and educational activities, individual and group therapy sessions, and leisure activities, in collaboration with psychologists, psychiatrists, and psychotherapists. Much of this clinical practice is learning coping strategies, avoiding high-risk situations, and utilising effective problem-solving skills.

*Transmuralisation*

The Dutch forensic system uses transmuralisation, equivalent to North American community health care (de Boer & Gerrits, 2007). Transmural treatment of forensic patients is provided to patients living outside of the hospital in rented flats or apartments supervised by clinical staff. A specialised team from the TBS hospital strictly monitors these patients in their residences, and they can be readmitted to the hospital if the conditions of leave or dispositional orders are breached or if they exhibit any warning signs of becoming a threat to public safety. Transmural treatment involves an intense resocialisation programme, whereby forensic patients are usually placed near the hospital once they are deemed stable and cease to display symptoms of a mental disorder. Forensic transmural teams follow and provide outpatient care to forensic patients in the community.

***Effectiveness of Forensic Inpatient Treatment***

Research by the Dutch Scientific Research and Data Centre has shown for many years that serious recidivism after discharge from forensic care, in particular a TBS order, is relatively low, significantly lower than after a prison sentence. However, the figures are difficult to compare because of important differences between the groups. Within two years after discharge, there is 19.2% general recidivism, 9.1% TBS order-worthy (a crime for which TBS can be imposed again), and 4.0% very serious recidivism (a crime with a maximum penalty of eight years or more). These figures are based on the outflow cohort 2011–2015.

Still, the effectiveness of treatment in inpatient forensic clinical care has not been convincingly proven, although society demands and expects it to be so. It is complicated to study treatment effectiveness properly, for instance, because of the lack of good control groups or outcome measures, and as treatment is comprehensive and is difficult to break down into separate elements. As part of the 'Learning project' (*de Lerende Praktijk*) of the Expertise Centre for Forensic Psychiatry, research on the effectiveness of Dutch forensic clinical care has been conducted in recent years (de Vogel et al., 2024). All forensic care facilities that provide clinical care were approached to provide effectiveness studies since 2005. In total, 55 studies were found, including six randomised clinical trials (RCTs) examining the effectiveness of several treatment programmes compared to a control group. It was concluded that recidivism rates after discharge are relatively favourable, and recidivism during leave is rare (0.15%). Several studies have also found significant reductions in risk factors and increases in protective factors. However, what exactly works, for whom and when is still unclear, and research on treatment effectiveness is complex. The six RCTs published between 2005 and 2023 found small or short-term effects for various treatments. Still, all RCTs had serious shortcomings, so no definitive conclusion about treatment effectiveness can be drawn. Interestingly, effects were also found for Treatment as

Usual (TAU). For future research, it is important to investigate TAU and conduct other research besides RCTs, including more qualitative research. Attention to context, patient characteristics, and the treatment relationship is essential here, as is collaboration between researchers from different institutions.

## Strengths and Weaknesses

Forensic patients in the Netherlands are assessed based on psychiatric diagnosis, level of criminal responsibility, risk, and treatment needs. Forensic mental health practitioners develop individualised treatment and risk management plans with the long-term goal of reintegration, rehabilitation, and reduction of recidivism. The most important strength of Dutch forensic mental health care is that it is elaborate and multitiered, allowing for a tailor-made approach for a large proportion of justice-involved individuals—not only those with major mental illness but also those with personality disorders. These individuals profit from care and treatment that the Ministry of Justice and Security is paying for, based on the expected cost-effectiveness ratio in terms of reducing reoffending. Another important strength is that, in high-security settings, treatment progress is tested through an extensive system of leave to allow for a gradual return to society. At the same time, legal protection is also strengthened to balance the dimensions of treatment and security. However, this is also costly in the short term, and the effectiveness of the overall forensic treatment has not yet been proven, as it is very complicated to disentangle the elements. Still, the recidivism rates are favourable in comparison to recidivism rates after a prison sentence without treatment. As care and treatment for these individuals are primarily administered within the criminal justice system and diversion to general mental health is rare, these patients remain prone to the double stigma. Moreover, as the numbers of forensic patients both in prison and mental health services are increasing, chances are that justice-involved individuals in need of forensic care are missed, while shortages in personnel and diminishing tolerance and support in society may eventually clog the system.

## Note

1 For more information about women and gender differences, see de Vogel, Stam et al. (2016), and for guidelines for gender-responsive working in gender-mixed forensic settings, see de Vogel et al. (2023).

## References

Crijns, J., & van der Woude, M. (2022). The justice system. In L. van den Herik, E. Hondius, & W. Voermans (Eds.), *Introduction to Dutch law* (pp. 501–534). Alphen aan den Rijn, Netherlands: Wolters Kluwer.

Criminal Code (*Wetboek van Strafrecht*), 1928.

de Boer, J., & Gerrits, J. (2007). Learning from Holland: The TBS system. *Psychiatry, 6*(11), 459–461. https://doi.org/10.1016/j.mppsy.2007.08.008

de Vogel, V., Bruijn, M., Klein Haneveld, E., Leong, J., Robbe, E., Steunenberg, D., Verhees, M. & Vissers, A. (2023). *Treating women in clinical forensic mental health care: A guide*. Kwaliteit Forensische Zorg (KFZ). Retrieved from https://kfz.nl/projecten/behandelen-van-vrouwen-in-forensische-klinische-zorg-een-vak-apart-het-ontwikkelen-van-richtlijnen-voor-de-behandeling-van-vrouwen-in-de-forensische-klinische-zorg

de Vogel, V., Keulen-de Vos, M., Bogaerts, S., Bulten, E., Delforterie, M., Schuringa, E., & Ter Horst, P. (2024). Werkt forensische behandeling? Een compilatie van onderzoek naar behandeleffectiviteit in de Nederlandse klinische forensische zorg. [Does forensic treatment work? A compilation of research on treatment effectiveness in Dutch clinical forensic care]. *Tijdschrift voor Forensische Psychiatrie & Psychologie, 2024*(01), 7–27.

de Vogel, V., Stam, J., Bouman, Y., Ter Horst, P., & Lancel, M. (2016). Violent women: A multicentre study into gender differences in forensic psychiatric patients. *The Journal of Forensic Psychiatry & Psychology, 27*, 145–168. https://doi.org/10.1080/14789949.2015.1102312

de Vogel, V., van den Broek, E., & de Vries Robbé, M. (2014). The value of the HCR-20V3 in Dutch forensic clinical practice. *International Journal of Forensic Mental Health, 13*(2), 109–121. https://doi.org/10.1080/14999013.2014.906518

Douglas, K. S., Hart, S. D., Webster, C. D., & Belfrage, H. (2013). *HCR-20V3: Assessing risk of violence—User guide*. Burnaby, British Columbia, Canada: Mental Health, Law, and Policy Institute, Simon Fraser University.

Fernandez, Y. M., Harris, A. J. R., Hanson, R. K., & Sparks, J. (2014). *STABLE-2007 coding manual—revised 2014 [Unpublished report]*. Ottawa, Ontario, Canada: Public Safety Canada.

Jehle, H. J., Lewis, C., Nagtegaal, M., Palmowski, N., Pyrcak-Górowska, M., van der Wolf, M. J. F., & Zila, J. (20). Dealing with Dangerous Offenders in Europe: A comparative study of provisions in England and Wales, Germany, the Netherlands, Poland and Sweden. *Criminal Law Forum 2021*. https://doi.org/10.1007/s10609-020-09411-z

Smeekens, M. V., & Braun, P. (2019). Long-term forensic psychiatric care: The Dutch Perspective. In B. Völlm, & P. Braun (Eds.), *Long-term forensic psychiatric care: Clinical, ethical and legal challenges* (pp. 235–250). Springer.

Spreen, M., Brand, E., Ter Horst, P., & Bogaerts, S. (2014). *Handleiding en Methodologische Verantwoording HKT-R, Historisch, Klinische en Toekomstige—Revisie [Guidelines and methodological research of the HKT-R, historical, clinical and future—revision]*. Groningen, The Netherlands: Dr. van Mesdag kliniek.

TBS Nederland. (2024, May 30). *Rapport 'Cijfers en Bijzonderheden 2023' gepubliceerd door TBS Nederland: stijging aantal tbs-patiënten zet door*. https://tbsnederland.nl/nieuws/rapport-cijfers-en-bijzonderheden-2023-gepubliceerd-door-tbs-nederland/

van der Wolf, M. J. F., & Mevis, P. A. M. (2021). Defendants and detainees with psychiatric disturbances in the criminal process and in the prison system in the Netherlands. In P. H. van Kempen, & M. Krabbe (Eds.), *Mental health and criminal justice: International and domestic perspectives on defendants and detainees with mental illness* (pp. 359–386). Den Haag, Netherlands: Eleven.

van der Wolf, M. J. F., Reef, J., Gunnink, L., Herzberger, J., & Doekhie, J. V. O. R. (2022b). *Binnen. Beeld. Buiten. Een evaluatie van zorgconferenties bij langverblijvers (15+) in de tbs* [Inside. Image. Outside. An evaluation of care conferences among long stayers (15+) in the TBS]. Den Haag, Netherlands: WODC.

van der Wolf, M. J. F., & van Marle, H. J. C. (2018). Legal approaches to criminal responsibility of mentally disordered offenders in Europe. In K. Goethals (Ed.), *Forensic psychiatry and psychology in Europe. A cross-border study guide* (pp. 31–44). Basel: Springer International Publishing.

van der Wolf, M. J. F., van Marle, H. J. C., & Roza, S. J. (2022a). A Dutch perspective. In M. J. F. van der Wolf (Ed.), *Safeguarding the quality of forensic assessment in sentencing: A review across western nations: International perspectives on forensic mental health* (pp. 200–229). London: Routledge.

van Koppen, P. J., & Penrod, S. D. (2003). Adversarial or inquisitorial: Comparing systems. In P. J. van Koppen, & S. D. Penrod (Eds.), *Adversarial versus inquisitorial justice: Psychological perspectives on criminal justice systems* (pp. 1–19). New York: Kluwer Academic.

# 13 Norway

*Terje Tørrissen*

## Brief Description

| | |
|---|---|
| **Location** | Norway is a country in Northern Europe, situated on the Scandinavian Peninsula. |
| **Size** | 385,207 km$^2$ |
| **Population** | 5.5 million |
| **Languages** | The official languages of Norway are Norwegian (*Norsk*) and Sami. Norwegian is the primary language, while Sami is mainly spoken by Indigenous populations in the northern regions of the country. |
| **Political system** | Norway is a unitary constitutional monarchy and a parliamentary democracy. The King of Norway serves as the head of state, while the prime minister is the head of government. Power is divided among the legislative branch (*Storting*—Parliament), the executive branch (*Regjering*—Government), and the judicial branch (*Rettsvesen*). |

## Legal System

### *Legislative Framework*

In Norway, the court system follows an adversarial (accusatorial) model. The judiciary consists of three levels of ordinary courts with general jurisdiction, handling both civil and criminal cases. These include 23 district courts (*Tingrett*), 6 courts of appeal (*Lagmannsrett*), and the Supreme Court (*Norges Høyesterett*) (Norges Domstoler, n.d.; Domstolsadministrasjonen, 2013). The Norwegian Courts Administration (NCA), an independent agency, manages and operates the country's ordinary courts of justice. Established in 2002, the NCA was created to ensure greater independence from the executive and legislative branches.

### *Mental Health Laws*

#### *Fitness to Stand Trial*

The Norwegian legal system has no specific rule for determining when a charged individual is unfit to stand trial. While the judge may consider a medical

DOI: 10.4324/9781003376248-16

certificate, this does not necessarily exempt the accused from appearing in court. In cases of acute medical conditions, such as infections or necessary treatment in hospitals, the court hearing will be postponed until it is possible to carry out the proceedings. However, if the accused, after a forensic evaluation, is diagnosed with an intellectual disability or a serious psychiatric disorder, such as schizophrenia or other psychotic disorders, the proceedings will not necessarily be postponed. The accused is expected to appear in court with their attorney and, if applicable, their legal guardian.

### *Criminal Responsibility*

In Norway, people who have a serious psychiatric disorder may be found not guilty by reason of insanity (NGRI). The country follows a 'medical model' to define criminal insanity and identifies insanity exclusively with serious psychiatric disorders, particularly psychosis, regardless of how the condition influenced the defendant's criminal actions.

A new amendment to the Norwegian Penal Code (2005) (*Straffeloven*) (Norwegian Penal Code, 2005) entered into force on October 1, 2020, introducing criteria allowing broader judicial discretion regarding NGRI findings. Section 20 of the Penal Code focuses on accountability (*tilregnelighet*) and outlines the conditions under which individuals may not be criminally responsible for their actions. To be considered not criminally responsible, one of the following must apply (Norges Domstoler, n.d.):

- Severely deviant state of mind, which includes people with a severe mental disorder, psychosis, or autism, as well as other mental states such as neurological illnesses that cause extensive impairment of cerebral functioning (Domstolsadministrasjonen, 2013).
- Severely impaired consciousness, which includes conditions such as hypoglycaemia, tumours, and epileptic seizures that impair consciousness (Norwegian Penal Code, 2005).
- Severe mental disability, defined as having an IQ below 60 and functioning accordingly. An IQ between 55 and 60 may be considered a 'mitigating circumstance' rather than insanity if adaptive functioning assessments (ABAS, Vineland III) indicate functioning at or close to an IQ of 60 (Norwegian Penal Code, 2005).

Section 80 of the Penal Code, titled 'Imposition of a penalty below the minimum penalty or a less severe type of penalty', addressed cases where a mental disorder may lead to a reduced penalty, even if the individual is not deemed accountable under Section 20. This provision allows for judicial discretion in cases where the accused's mental state significantly impacts their ability to understand or control their actions. To be considered for a reduced penalty, one of the following must apply (Norwegian Penal Code, 2005):

- At the time of the offence, the accused had a substantially impaired perception of reality due to a severely deviant state of mind (e.g., a delusional disorder of limited severity) (Domstolsadministrasjonen, 2013).
- The accused experienced impaired consciousness (e.g., severe dissociative disorder) (Norwegian Penal Code, 2005). The accused has a mental disability, defined as an IQ between 60 and 75, with corresponding functional limitations (Norwegian Penal Code, 2005, § 80 (5)).

Other laws that address mental health in Norway are included in Section 78 of the Penal Code. This section pertains to 'mitigating circumstances'. In connection with sentencing, mitigating factors consider situations where, at the time of the offence, individuals had an impaired perception of reality due to a deviant state of mind, a mild mental disability, impaired consciousness, or severe mental agitation. However, Section 78 is infrequently used in forensic psychiatry, as 'severe mental agitation' is not a recognised medical term (Norwegian Penal Code, 2005, § 78).

It is important to understand that, when assessing accountability (Section 20) or partial accountability (Section 80), emphasis shall be given to the degree of failure in the person's perception of reality and functional capacity, including social interactions, daily life activities, and cognitive functions. Before October 2020, the 'medical model' stated that if a person had a severe mental illness, such as psychosis, they should not be punished but receive treatment. However, after the amendments to the Penal Code, the 'medical model' was partly modified to create a 'modified mixed principle' that integrated both medical assessments and functional capacity evaluations to determine accountability. As a result, the system now considers not only the presence of a severe mental disorder but also the extent to which the condition impaired the individual's ability to understand or control their actions at the time of the offence. This shift has introduced a degree of legal ambiguity regarding the threshold for criminal insanity, leading to ongoing debates within forensic psychiatry and legal practice (Gröning, 2023).

The amendments to the Penal Code in October 2020 also shifted the responsibility for determining whether a condition leads to a verdict of not guilty by reason of insanity (NGRI) or a reduced sentence from forensic experts to the court. While forensic experts continue to provide medical evaluations, they serve only as advisers and do not make legal conclusions. The court now holds the primary authority to assess both medical findings and legal criteria when determining accountability, emphasising judicial discretion in insanity cases (Norwegian Penal Code, 2005, §20).

In 2023, the Norwegian Supreme Court issued a ruling (Norges Høyesterett, 2023) that redefined the interpretation of functional capacity in the context of criminal accountability. The Court specified that a significant impairment in functional capacity pertains to people with an intellectual disability, defined as an IQ below 75. Regarding Sections 20 and 80 of the Penal Code, the Supreme Court reaffirmed the pre-October 2020 'medical model', emphasising that the mere presence of a severe mental disorder, such as psychosis, could suffice for a verdict of NGRI. Additionally, the Court introduced 'planning of the crime' as an additional criterion in NGRI determinations. This means that people with schizophrenia who exhibit psychotic symptoms may receive different verdicts based on their capacity for premeditation. These legal interpretations have increased NGRI verdicts, partly due to the relaxation of penalty framework requirements. Consequently, there has also been a surge in forensic evaluations and a shortage of hospital beds in wards across Norway.

Norway's tort law (*Lov om Skadeerstatning*) (Justis-og beredskapsdepartementet, 1969) applies to both civil and criminal cases. Under the 'medical model', an NGRI verdict means the individual is not criminally responsible. However, according to tort law, they may still be liable for damages, including compensation to aggrieved parties or other financial claims. The compensation awarded is typically lower in cases where the defendant is not responsible, with adjustments based on their financial situation.

## Forensic Psychiatry System

### *Structure and Function of the Forensic Mental Health System*

In cases where a defendant is found NGRI, they are sentenced to compulsory mental health care under Sections 62–65 of the Norwegian Penal Code. This can be imposed as either a fixed-term (time-limited) or indefinite (time-unlimited) measure, depending on the severity of the offence and the risk of future violence. A 'time-limited' sentence is applied in cases involving less severe offences, typically with a single offence and a low risk of recurrence. These measures cannot extend beyond three years. A 'time-unlimited' sentence, on the other hand, is reserved for serious offences or repeated crimes, particularly those involving violence, sexual offences, or other acts posing a significant risk to public safety. These measures can be extended indefinitely in three-year increments based on periodic forensic evaluations and court assessments (Norwegian Penal Code, 2005, § 62, § 64, § 65).

All individuals under compulsory mental health care are initially hospitalised in an appropriate psychiatric facility (local or regional) for at least three weeks. However, many remain hospitalised for extended periods—sometimes years—until they are deemed safe for supervised living outside a hospital setting. Once discharged, an outpatient clinic takes over responsibility for their compulsory treatment until the measure expires or is extended. The initial duration of the measure is always three years; however, the individual may appeal after one year. Forensic experts are appointed to conduct evaluations at any time within three years and whenever the prosecution seeks an extension. Time-unlimited measures are typically extended only in cases where the individual is deemed as posing a continuous risk of committing serious criminal acts, such as murder, violent assault, rape, or other sexual violence.

People with intellectual disabilities (IQ less than 60) who are found NGRI are sentenced to mandatory care (*tvungen omsorg*) under Section 63 of the Penal Code. They are transferred to a national specialised ward for treatment and risk assessment after the verdict. After, they are transferred to a municipal or private institution specialising in caring for and treating this group. The sentence follows the same structure as the time-unlimited NGRI measures, with an initial duration of three years (Norwegian Penal Code, 2005, § 63).

Hospitals, municipalities, and private institutions must notify the public prosecutor of any significant changes, such as a patient's transition from hospital to outpatient care. If the prosecutor objects, the matter is reviewed by the hospital's Civil Control Commission (*Kontrollkommisjonen for psykisk helsevern*) (Helsedirektoratet, n.d.) rather than a criminal court. The Control Commission is responsible for safeguarding the patient's legal rights within the mental healthcare system in accordance with Norwegian mental health laws. It oversees compulsory treatment decisions, processes complaints, and conducts welfare checks. The Commission can revoke compulsory treatment orders in psychiatric specialist health services (hospitals or outpatient clinics) or transfer patients to voluntary care if they believe the statutory requirements are unmet. Each Commission is led by a lawyer, with a medical doctor and at least two lay members as additional representatives. Norway has 55 Control Commissions linked to hospitals and outpatient clinics. The Norwegian Directorate of Health (*Helsedirektoratet*), which operates under the Ministry of Health and Care Services (*Helse-og omsorgsdepartementet*), is responsible for mental health care in Norway (Helsedirektoratet, n.d.).

### *Role of Forensic Psychiatry*

Forensic experts are mandated under Sections 20 and 80 of the Norwegian Penal Code to assess the criminal responsibility of the accused. Forensic experts must also evaluate the prognosis of the disorder and the risk of recurrence in cases where there is uncertainty regarding criminal responsibility or when detention is being considered. The local police district provides forensic experts with case documents, which form the basis of their assessment. Their evaluation focuses on the accused's state of mind, psychiatric symptoms, medical history, substance use, and behaviour and functioning before, during, and after the crime.

Forensic experts must examine the accused at least twice, conducting a full anamnestic history and conducting structured interviews, psychological tests, and risk assessments. Norway still uses the ICD-10 classification system (World Health Organization, 1997), both in mental health care and forensic psychiatry. The transition to ICD-11 will occur once the official translation is ready.

Forensic experts can interview family members and attending physicians, with the accused's consent, to gather additional information. After completing a full assessment, the forensic experts send the report to the National Forensic Medical Board (*Den Rettsmedisinske Kommisjon* [DRK]) for peer review and approval. If DRK finds significant deficiencies in the report, it will ask for an additional report. Forensic psychiatric reports are conducted before the district court proceedings as part of the criminal investigation (Norwegian Board of Forensic Medicine, 2011).

The evaluation of the accused continues during the court proceedings. Forensic experts can question the accused, witnesses, and other relevant individuals. They formally present their report at the end of the hearing, after which the court, prosecutor, and defence may question them about their findings. If new information emerges during the trial significantly altering the forensic conclusions, an additional report must be written and submitted to DRK for peer review. In such cases, the court hearings may be postponed to accommodate the reassessment.

Under Section 168, Chapter 13 of the *Criminal Procedure Act* (Straffeprosessloven, Norwegian Ministry of Justice and Public Security, 1981; amended June 21, 2019), forensic experts were previously allowed to collect health information without consent. However, in 2024, the Supreme Court ruled that forensic experts cannot access health records without the accused's consent in cases where there is no doubt about accountability, even when the crime carries a sentencing frame of more than six years (e.g., detention cases). If the sentencing frame is less than six years, the accused must explicitly consent to collecting health information (Norwegian Ministry of Justice and Public Security, 1981/2019; Nasjonal Enhet for Rettspsykiatrisk Sakkyndighet [NERS], n.d.).

### *Reports by Forensic Experts for NGRI Verdicts*

Chapters 11 and 13 of the *Criminal Procedure Act* regulate the work of forensic experts. If an accused has a history of mental health issues, exhibits unusual behaviour during the investigation, or if there are other reasons to question their criminal responsibility, the prosecutor or defence attorney can request a preliminary forensic evaluation. In some cases, the court can appoint a forensic expert if there is doubt regarding Section 20 or 80 of the Penal Code during proceedings. The court will then adjourn until the preliminary or full evaluation has been completed and approved by DRK.

The preliminary report can be conducted by either an approved specialist in psychiatry or a specialist in psychology registered in the National Unit of Forensic Expertise (NERS). The report is a brief clinical assessment to determine whether there is doubt regarding Section 20 or 80. If doubt remains, a full forensic evaluation will be conducted by either two specialists in psychiatry or one specialist in psychiatry and one in psychology. The court always makes the decision, as forensic experts serve as advisers to the court rather than to the prosecutor or the defence. The full forensic evaluation results in a report detailing the defendant's mental state before, during, and after the crime. Based on this assessment, the court determines whether the defendant meets one or more of the criteria outlined in Section 20 or 80 and may subsequently issue a verdict of NGRI or a reduced sentence.

### *Forensic Psychiatry Profession*

#### *Qualifications or Specialised Training Required in Forensic Psychiatry*

Forensic psychiatry is not a formal subspecialty in Norway. However, forensic experts are normally registered in the National Unit of Forensic Expertise (*Nasjonal Enhet for Rettspsykiatrisk Sakkyndighet* [NERS]) (Nasjonal Enhet for Rettspsykiatrisk Sakkyndighet [NERS], n.d.). NERS maintains a registry of private practitioners, psychiatrists, and psychologists who conduct forensic assessments for the courts, working in hospitals and outpatient clinics. Forensic education is relatively brief, but specialists in psychiatry or psychology are eligible to participate in the courses. Additionally, forensic experts are expected to have clinical experience with relevant patient groups.

The first course (B-course) provides lectures on the legal system, forensic expert work, and how to present the assessments in court. This course is for all experts in forensic medicine. The second course (C-course) is specifically focused on forensic psychiatry and covers topics such as criminal responsibility, differential diagnoses, sexual offences, violence, and risk assessments. DRK oversees the B-courses and regularly publishes newsletters with interpretations and guidance on topics in forensic psychiatry.

The National Network of Research and Education in Forensic Psychiatry and Psychology (*Nasjonalt kompetansenettverk for sikkerhets-, fengsels-og rettspsykiatri* [SIFER]) consists of four centres (Regional Centre for Research and Education in Forensic Psychiatry and Psychology) located at the four university hospitals in Norway, which have primary goals in education and research. These centres organise the C-courses in forensic psychiatry (Nasjonalt kompetansesenternettverk for sikkerhets-, fengsels-og rettspsykiatri, SIFER, n.d.).

The NERS currently has 189 forensic experts in the register, although only 155 meet the formal competence requirements for conducting forensic evaluations (78 specialists in psychiatry and 77 specialists in psychology). Approximately 70 % of these experts have completed both B and C courses, while the remainder are in the process of completing them. Experts wishing to be included in the NERS registry must provide documentation proving they meet the necessary competence requirements and must inform NERS of any changes to their registered information. NERS classifies forensic experts into two groups: juniors (fewer than 25 forensic reports) and seniors (more experienced experts). Junior forensic experts are often paired with senior experts to ensure quality and mentorship. Currently, 40% of registered forensic experts are women. Of all forensic experts, 20%–25% work full-time in forensic evaluations (personal communication, NERS).

### *National Collaborations or Networks*

There is no national forensic psychiatry organisation in Norway. However, there is a forensic committee in Norway's psychiatric association (*Rettspsykiatriutvalget*) and psychological association (*Fagutvalg for rettspsykologi og sakkyndighet*). Norway's psychiatric association organises two meetings yearly with topics on forensic psychiatry.

## Forensic Psychiatry Service (Provision of Care)

### *Approaches to Assessment and Treatment*

As in many countries, the capacity of mental health services has been significantly reduced. Since 2000, the availability of hospital beds in Norway has seen a 60% reduction, making it more difficult to accommodate patients with schizophrenia who have a low criminal risk but still require follow-up care and rehabilitation. Community-based care is voluntary, meaning that once a patient transitions to housing or independent living, there is no legal mechanism to prevent them from discontinuing their medication. This lack of oversight can increase the risk of psychotic episodes and criminal behaviour. For outpatients under involuntary commitment, coercive medication is only permitted if their mental state deteriorates (e.g., becoming more psychotic). In such cases, they must be readmitted to a hospital, provided a bed is available (Helse-og omsorgsdepartementet, 2005).

## Strengths and Weaknesses

Norway's forensic system has three major strengths. First, all forensic experts operate independently from hospitals and outpatient clinics, ensuring objective assessments. Second, the courts, rather than healthcare institutions, appoint forensic experts, reinforcing impartiality. Third, people with severe psychiatric disorders are deemed not criminally responsible or NGRI and receive appropriate treatment instead of punishment.

However, there are notable weaknesses. Some forensic experts have limited experience, conducting only a small number of assessments per year, and may lack sufficient exposure to acute psychiatry, psychosis rehabilitation, forensic settings, and addiction treatment. The forensic assessment process is also relatively brief, lasting only two to four hours, which may not always capture the full extent of the accused mental state. As a result, some people may successfully conceal their symptoms, while others may exaggerate or simulate them. Additionally, few assessments are conducted under Section 167 of the *Criminal Procedure Act* (compulsory observation), and the capacity for forensic assessments in mental hospitals remains insufficient. Lastly, forensic psychiatric training in Norway could be more extensive and better to prepare experts for the complexities of criminal responsibility evaluations (Norwegian Ministry of Justice and Public Security, 1981/2019).

## References

Domstolsadministrasjonen. (2013, October). *Courts of Justice Act* (Unofficial translation) [PDF]. Retrieved February 2, 2025, from https://www.domstol.no/contentassets/ad9c-4449cbc14f93afed761c90360d5c/courts-of-justice-act−1915.pdf

Gröning, L. (2023). Has Norway abandoned its medical model? Thoughts about the criminal insanity reform post 22 July. *ResearchGate*. Retrieved from https://www.researchgate.net/publication/371918841_Has_Norway_abandoned_its_medical_model_Thoughts_about_the_criminal_insanity_reform_post_22_July

Helsedirektoratet. (n.d.). *Kontrollkommisjonen for psykisk helsevern* (The Control Commission) (in Norwegian). Retrieved February 2, 2025, from https://www.helsedirektoratet.no/tema/kontrollkommisjonen-for-psykisk-helsevern

Helsedirektoratet. (n.d.). *Norwegian Directorate of Health* (subordinate to the Ministry of Health and Care Services). Retrieved February 2, 2025, from https://www.helsedirektoratet.no/english

Helse-og omsorgsdepartementet. (2005, January). *Mental health legislation* (Chapter 5) [PDF]. Retrieved February 2, 2025, from https://www.regjeringen.no/globalassets/upload/kilde/hod/red/2005/0011/ddd/pdfv/233840-mentalhealthweb.pdf

Justis-og beredskapsdepartementet. (1969, June). *Lov om Skadeerstatning* (Tort law) (in Norwegian). Retrieved February 2, 2025, from https://lovdata.no/dokument/NL/lov/1969-06-13-26

Nasjonal Enhet for Rettspsykiatrisk Sakkyndighet (NERS). (n.d.). *National Unit of Forensic Expertise*, St. Olavs Hospital, NTNU (Norwegian University of Science and Technology) (In Norwegian). Retrieved February 2, 2025, from https://www.stolav.no/ners

Nasjonalt kompetansesenternettverk for sikkerhets-, fengsels-og rettspsykiatri, SIFER. (n.d.). *National network of research and education in forensic psychiatry and psychology*. Retrieved February 2, 2025, from https://sifer.no/about-sifer/

Norges Domstoler. (n.d.). *The courts of Norway*. Retrieved February 2, 2025, from https://www.domstol.no/en/about-the-legal-system/the-ordinary-courts/

Norges Høyesterett. (2023, June 29). *HR-2023–1243-A, sak nr. 23–036176STR-HRET* (in Norwegian) [PDF]. Retrieved February 2, 2025, from https://www.domstol.no/globalassets/upload/hret/avgjorelser/2023/juni/hr-2023–1243-a.pdf

Norwegian Board of Forensic Medicine. (2011). *DRK—The National Forensic Medical Board* (Wikipedia). Retrieved February 2, 2025, from https://en.wikipedia.org/wiki/Norwegian_Board_of_Forensic_Medicine

Norwegian Ministry of Justice and Public Security. (1981/2019). *Criminal Procedure Act* (Straffeprosessloven) [PDF] of 22 May 1981, No. 25, with amendments of 21 June 2019. Retrieved February 2, 2025, from https://app.uio.no/ub/ujur/oversatte-lover/data/lov-19810522–025-eng.pdf

Norwegian Penal Code. (2005). *The penal code*. Retrieved from https://lovdata.no/NLE/lov/2005-05-20-28

World Health Organization. (1997). *ICD-10* (in Norwegian). Retrieved February 2, 2025, from https://finnkode.helsedirektoratet.no/icd10/chapter/V/

# 14 Poland

*Inga Markiewicz*

## Brief Description

| | |
|---|---|
| **Location** | Poland is a country in Central Europe. |
| **Size** | 312,696 km$^2$ |
| **Population** | 37,490,000 |
| **Language** | The official language of Poland is Polish. |
| **Political system** | Poland is a unitary parliamentary republic, with a president as the head of state and a prime minister as the head of government. The legislature, or National Assembly (*Zgromadzenie Narodowe*), is made up of the lower house (*Sejm*) and the upper house (*Senat*). |

*Source*: Statistics Poland (GUS), 2024.

## Legal System

Poland's legal system is based on Roman codified law, meaning it does not follow the concept of precedent but instead relies on legal norms established by authorised legislative entities. The Constitution of the Republic of Poland, adopted on 2 April 1997 (as amended, 2009), is the country's most significant legal document. It upholds the principles of a democratic rule of law, including national sovereignty, the rule of law, the separation of powers, and pluralism.

The judiciary's authority in Poland is derived solely from the law and is independent of other branches of government. Poland operates a two-tiered system of jurisdiction, with lower courts handling initial cases and higher appellate courts reviewing those decisions to ensure fairness and consistency in the legal process. The judicial system comprises the Supreme Court, ordinary courts, and special courts, such as military and administrative courts, which issue judgements on behalf of the state.

### *Legislative Framework of Forensic Psychiatry*

Forensic psychiatry applies to civil and criminal cases, with various legal provisions outlining the specific roles of psychiatrists and psychologists in each area.

DOI: 10.4324/9781003376248-17

Their primary responsibility is to provide expert opinions on mental health. In civil law, for example, they can assess the mental state of a testator in will invalidation cases, evaluate an individual's awareness and freedom when making legal declarations (such as signing contracts), determine the nullity of marriage, and assess a person's ability to care for a child.

However, forensic psychiatry in Poland is primarily associated with criminal law. When examining its legal framework, it is essential to consider the criminal law provisions concerning individuals with mental disorders, the regulations governing proceedings when they commit a crime, the legal institutions that accommodate them, and the role of psychiatrists and psychologists in the criminal justice process.

### *Mental Health Laws*

#### *The Criminal Code and the Principle of Fault*

The current penal codes in Poland, including the Criminal Code, the Code of Criminal Procedure, and the Executive Penal Code, were adopted in 1997 and have since undergone several amendments. Earlier criminal codes from 1932 and 1969 already included provisions on the exclusion and limitation of criminal responsibility for individuals with mental illness, as well as measures to address the risks posed by those deemed not criminally responsible. However, the treatment of people with mental disorders has evolved significantly over the years, reflecting shifts in societal attitudes in Poland. Since the 1990s, as Poland transitioned from communist doctrine towards gradual democratisation, these broader systemic changes have also influenced legislative developments.

Polish criminal law is based on the principle of fault, which refers to an allegation against offenders who failed to meet a legal standard in a given situation despite being expected to do so (Zoll, 2016; Pyrcak-Górowska, 2021a). The attribution of fault is a prerequisite for criminal responsibility—if an offender cannot be deemed at fault, they cannot be punished under the Criminal Code (Article 1(3), Criminal Code). For fault to be attributed, the offender must be sufficiently mature, aware of their actions and consequences, and capable of refraining from behaviour they recognise as reprehensible (Indecki & Jurewicz, 2014).

#### *Fitness to Stand Trial*

Polish criminal law requires psychiatric experts to assess a defendant's mental health to determine their ability to stand trial and conduct a defence independently (Article 202 § 5, Code of Criminal Procedure). If a defendant is deemed incompetent due to mental illness or another serious condition, proceedings are suspended (Article 22 § 1, Code of Criminal Procedure). Additionally, pretrial detention should be avoided if it seriously threatens the defendant's life or health

(Article 259 § 1, Code of Criminal Procedure). However, Poland lacks clear criteria for determining when health conditions temporarily or permanently prevent trial participation, leaving the evaluation entirely to forensic psychiatrists and psychologists.

Mental illness can also justify the suspension or deferment of sentence execution under the Executive Penal Code. A severe or chronic illness may warrant postponing punishment if imprisonment would endanger the defendant's life or health (Article 150 § 2, Executive Penal Code). Psychiatric evaluations are crucial in determining whether a suspect, defendant, or convicted offender can endure detention or serve a sentence, or requires treatment outside the prison healthcare system. These assessments guide decisions on trial participation, custody, sentence deferment, and medical treatment needs.

### *Not Guilty by Reason of Insanity and Circumstances Excluding or Reducing the Degree of Fault*

In Poland, criminal responsibility can be classified as full, diminished, or absent. There is also specific consideration for individuals who commit offences while intoxicated. In forensic psychiatry, the most relevant legal provisions pertain to cases of lack of responsibility and diminished responsibility due to mental illness or disorders.

#### LACK OF CRIMINAL RESPONSIBILITY

The Criminal Code outlines that a person who, in a state of mental incapacity due to mental illness, impairment (intellectual disability), or another mental disturbance, was unable to recognise the significance of their actions or control their behaviour at the time of the offence is not criminally responsible (Article 31(1), Criminal Code). Under this provision, mental illness is defined narrowly and primarily associated with psychotic disorders such as schizophrenia or delusional disorders. The category of 'mental disturbance' is broader and may include sexual disorders, personality disorders, substance-induced disorders, and conditions resulting from somatic diseases (Cieślak et al., 1991).

For a state of mental incapacity to be recognised, it must be directly linked to a specific mental disorder. However, offenders diagnosed with such disorders are not automatically exempt from criminal responsibility. This designation only applies if the disorder results in an inability to recognise the significance of one's actions or to control them.

#### DIMINISHED CRIMINAL RESPONSIBILITY

In cases of diminished criminal responsibility, the prerequisites are the same as for mental incapacity but to a lesser degree. A person with limited mental capacity who commits a prohibited act is not exempt from criminal responsibility. However, if their ability to recognise the significance of their actions or control their conduct was significantly impaired at the time of the crime, the court may impose an extraordinarily mitigated penalty (Article 31(2), Criminal Code).

### CRIMINAL RESPONSIBILITY WHILE INTOXICATED

Establishing the principles of criminal responsibility becomes complex when an individual commits a prohibited act while in a state of intoxication (*stan nietrzeźwości*) or stupor. The Criminal Code states: "A person who voluntarily brings themselves into a state of intoxication or stupor, resulting in the exclusion or diminishment of their mental competence—where this was foreseen or could have been foreseen—remains criminally liable" (Article 28, Criminal Code).

Offenders are generally considered capable of recognising the significance of their actions and controlling their conduct if they voluntarily enter a state of intoxication or stupor (i.e., not under duress), provided they are not pathologically intoxicated or suffering from alcohol poisoning. Article 31(3) of the Criminal Code establishes objective criminal responsibility by introducing liability for committing a prohibited act while intoxicated. This provision aims to protect society from individuals who, while intoxicated, commit acts with serious consequences (Indecki & Jurewicz, 2014).

The Criminal Code strictly defines the conditions under which a person with mental disorders or incapacity may be deemed not criminally responsible at the time of the offence. Before reaching a decision, the court consults up to two forensic psychiatrists and a psychologist, who must provide an expert opinion addressing (1) whether the offender had a mental illness, mental impairment, or any other form of mental disturbance at the time of the act and (2) if so, whether the diagnosed mental disorder rendered them unable to recognise the significance of their actions or incapable of controlling their conduct.

The final issue, directly related to the presence of mental disorder symptoms in the offender and the determination of whether they committed the act in a state of mental incapacity, is the assessment of the risk of reoffending. How psychiatrists and psychologists evaluate this risk largely influences the court's decision on further measures, including whether to impose a penalty, such as a non-custodial sentence or deprivation of liberty, or apply protective measures, as outlined in the Criminal Code. The court could also order involuntary civil commitment to a mental health institution.

Risk assessment is conducted by a team of psychiatrists and psychologists at the sentencing stage and throughout the offender's stay in a forensic psychiatry unit. An expert opinion on the offender's mental state, progress in treatment or therapy, and overall condition is prepared at least every six months and submitted to the court. Based on the conclusions of this opinion, the criminal court determines whether to continue treatment in the current forensic facility, adjust the security level of the ward, or discharge the offender from the hospital.

The most widely used risk assessment method is based on intuition and experience (the clinical method). Although the Historical Clinical Risk Management (HCR)-20 v3 was translated into Polish a few years ago, it remains underutilised, as preparing risk assessments is not mandatory in Poland. Currently, tools such as Structured Assessment of Protective Factors (SAPROF) and Static-99 are available in Poland, and there are plans to gradually introduce tools like Sexual Violence Risk (SVR)-20, Structured Assessment of Violence Risk in Youth (SAVRY), DUNDRUM, and Sex Offender Treatment Intervention and Progress Scale (SOTIPS). Tools for structured professional risk assessment are gaining popularity; however, they are still not widespread, and there is a lack of specialised training.

### *Legal Regulations Concerning the Treatment of People With Mental Disorders*

In Poland, the treatment of people with mental disorders is regulated by provisions in both civil and criminal law, as well as various special legal acts. The criminal procedure only applies if a person with a mental disorder has committed a serious crime and continues to pose a threat to society.

#### *Act on Mental Health Protection*

As a rule, people with mental disorders are treated with their consent, provided they can express it consciously and freely, as stated in the *Act on Mental Health Protection* (*Ustawa o Ochronie Zdrowia Psychicznego*) of 19 August 1994 (1994, Article 22). The Act was the first Polish legislation that sanctioned the principles of treatment of a psychiatric patient in the spirit of respect for their dignity, subjectivity, and fundamental rights, at the same time strengthening the institutional protection of their rights (Heitzman & Markiewicz, 2012; Markiewicz et al., 2016). Under the Act, involuntary hospitalisation is permitted only in exceptional cases after specific statutory conditions have been met.

Polish law provides several procedures for involuntary commitment to a psychiatric hospital, with the choice of approach depending on factors such as the patient's current mental health status, clinical diagnosis, and the level of risk they pose. This includes whether their symptoms present an immediate threat to their own or others' life or health, whether their condition could lead them to commit a prohibited act, or if there is a risk of recidivism and a broader threat to society. In the latter case, the issues of involuntary treatment are regulated not by the Act but by criminal law provisions concerning the so-called protective measures in psychiatry.

Article 23 of the Act allows for the admission of a person with a mental illness to a psychiatric hospital without their consent if their previous behaviour indicates that, due to the illness, they pose a direct threat to their own life or the health of others. The article does not specify the length of mandatory hospitalisation. Instead, a person remains in the psychiatric hospital until the reason for their admission ceases to exist—specifically when they no longer pose a threat to their own life or the lives of others. The assessment of whether such a threat exists is always made by psychiatrists, who are responsible for deciding whether to detain or discharge the individual under Article 23 of the Act.

Additionally, if there is diagnostic uncertainty regarding the presence of a mental illness, a person exhibiting symptoms of mental disorders, whose previous behaviour indicates that, due to these disorders, they pose a direct threat to their own life or the health of others, may also be admitted to a psychiatric hospital without their consent. However, in this case, the admission is for observation, which lasts no longer than 10 days and is intended to establish a diagnosis and determine a treatment plan (Article 24). In both situations, admission to the hospital is decided by a doctor after a personal examination of the patient and consultation with a second psychiatrist or psychologist. The admission must then be approved by the doctor in charge of the ward, after which the hospital director notifies the court. This process initiates court proceedings to assess the validity of the involuntary hospitalisation. If the court finds the admission unjustified, it can immediately order the patient's release.

In addition to the procedures mentioned earlier, the Act (Article 29) provides another procedure for admitting a person with a mental illness to a psychiatric hospital without their consent—this time at the request of certain individuals, such as a spouse, relatives, or legal representative. In such cases, psychiatrists issue opinions on the legitimacy of hospital admission while the court makes the final decision on hospitalisation. In all the cases described, the court has the authority to order compulsory treatment.

#### *Treatment and Isolation of Offenders With Mental Illness Who Committed Serious Crimes*

One of the most important areas of forensic psychiatry in Poland is the treatment of individuals with mental disorders who have committed the most serious crimes and continue to pose a threat. The state has a duty to protect and safeguard its citizens from these individuals who may pose a risk to society while ensuring they receive appropriate treatment and rehabilitation. These objectives are achieved through protective measures outlined in the Criminal Code.

In Poland, protective measures serve not only a security function but also a therapeutic and rehabilitative role, enabling offenders to reintegrate into society once their mental state has improved. These measures may be imposed instead of a penalty or in conjunction with it. For offenders who are found not criminally responsible due to mental illness, protective measures replace a penalty. In contrast, protective measures can be applied alongside the penalty for those deemed mentally competent or who committed the crime while experiencing diminished capacity.

In principle, the Criminal Code provides four protective measures: electronic monitoring of a person's location, therapy, addiction therapy, and treatment in a psychiatric facility (Article 93(1), Criminal Code). The first three measures are non-custodial, whereas treatment in a psychiatric facility requires the individual to remain in a secure forensic psychiatry ward of a psychiatric hospital. Except for electronic monitoring, all protective measures involve various forms of psychiatric treatment. The choice and duration of the measure are determined by the court based on psychiatric and psychological opinions regarding the offender's mental health.

The Polish Criminal Code provides only one custodial protective measure: commitment to a psychiatric hospital. The court may impose this measure on an offender with a mental illness or intellectual disability if they have committed a criminal act of considerable social harm in a state of mental incapacity and if there is a high likelihood of reoffending (Criminal Code, Article 93 §1). A protective measure may also be imposed on an offender with an intellectual disability, sexual disorder, or personality disorder who has committed a serious crime in a state of significantly limited mental capacity (*stan znacznie ograniczonej poczytalności*) and has been sentenced to imprisonment.

The Criminal Code states that protective measures should only be imposed when strictly necessary and when the risk of reoffending cannot be reduced by other legal means (Criminal Code, Article 93b(1)). However, in some cases, this risk can be reduced through measures imposed by civil courts, such as involuntary psychiatric treatment under the *Act on Mental Health Protection* (1994, Article 23). If a protective measure under the Criminal Code is ultimately deemed necessary, a non-custodial measure should be prioritised. Only if this proves insufficient should commitment to a closed psychiatric facility be ordered. When protective measures accompany a prison sentence, they are applied after the sentence is served, as a post-penal protective measure. The decision to impose these measures is always made by the criminal court during criminal proceedings.

The duration of a protective measure is not determined in advance (Criminal Code, Article 93d(1)). Each decision to extend the measure is based on a current medical and psychological evaluation. To assess whether the measure should continue, the facility's psychiatrist and psychologist submit a written report on the offender's mental health and progress in treatment or therapy. At least every six months, the head of the psychiatric facility provides the court with an updated opinion, and the court determines whether to maintain the measure. The court must revoke the measure when continuation is no longer necessary. However, doctors alone cannot decide to terminate protective measures; a court ruling is required following proceedings that include consultations with psychiatrists and psychologists. If a measure is needed again within three years of its revocation—such as due to a deterioration in the offender's health—the court may reimpose any protective measure, even if no new criminal offence has been committed (Criminal Code, Article 93d(6)).

## Forensic Psychiatry System

### *Structure of the Forensic Psychiatry System*

Individuals subject to a protective measure are treated in healthcare facilities, hospitals, or outpatient systems.

#### *Inpatient System (Forensic Hospitals, Forensic Psychiatric Wards)*

Individuals ordered to be placed in a psychiatric hospital are housed in closed forensic psychiatry wards. The forensic psychiatry system consists of three security levels[1]: high (145 beds), medium (950 beds), and low (2,256 beds), totalling 3,351 beds.[2] However, the increasing number of individuals admitted to forensic wards is concerning, as the availability of beds has become insufficient. These units differ in several aspects, including the criteria for admission to a specific type of ward, the staff-to-patient ratio, the level of technical security to prevent escape, and the possibility of patient leave. Temporary releases are permitted only in basic-security units (Executive Penal Code, Article 204d).

Forensic psychiatric wards are typically part of local or regional general psychiatric hospitals. However, high-security wards, designated for individuals considered to be the most dangerous, are separate hospital units, with only two such facilities in the entire country. The criminal court determines the specific hospital and security level of the ward after reviewing the opinion of the National Psychiatric Board, the country's sole authority on the matter, which operates under the Ministry of Health. Qualification for a specific forensic ward is based on factors such as life-threatening behaviour, property destruction, the risk of unauthorised departure, and the feasibility of preventing such incidents.

During the execution of a protective measure, the security level may be adjusted—either increased or decreased—if justified by changes in the patient's health condition. Only the court can make any changes to the security level. Typically, patients are released from a basic-security unit of a psychiatric hospital. The criminal court oversees the application of the protective measure and is responsible for deciding on its repeal.

As of September 2024, the Polish Ministry of Health reported that forensic psychiatry wards housed 3,601 patients: 131 in high-security units, 1,122 in medium-security units, and 2,348 in low-security units. Due to the insufficient number of beds in low-security units, some patients are detained in general psychiatric hospitals; however, official data on this practice is not available.[3]

### *Outpatient System*

Outpatient treatment for offenders with mental illness was introduced in Poland in 2015 through an amendment to the Criminal Code. Upon discharge from a psychiatric hospital, courts may impose non-custodial protective measures, such as mandatory therapy, instead of continued psychiatric detention (Criminal Code, Article 93d(2)). This requires the offender to continue treatment in an outpatient setting. However, the court cannot mandate supervision, such as oversight by a court-appointed guardian, due to the absence of legal mechanisms to ensure compliance with treatment. If an offender discontinues treatment, leading to a deterioration in health and an increased risk of committing a serious criminal offence, the court may order them back to hospital (Criminal Code, Article 93d(6)).

The system functions in theory but encounters significant challenges in practice. There are no clear regulations governing the treatment of forensic patients in outpatient settings, a lack of cooperation between hospitals and outpatient services, and inadequate supervision and monitoring of outpatient therapy outcomes.

### *Funding of the Forensic Psychiatry System*

In Poland, the care of offenders with mental illness, both outpatient and inpatient, is funded exclusively by public resources from the State Treasury through the National Health Fund. Only hospitals with high-security wards receive separate, direct funding from the Ministry of Health. The Ministry of Justice does not participate in funding.

## ***Role and Qualifications of Forensic Psychiatrists and Psychologists***

### *Role and Tasks*

Forensic psychiatrists in the Polish system serve a dual role as both healthcare providers and experts for judicial authorities. They primarily administer pharmacological treatment to offenders in closed forensic psychiatry facilities and provide healthcare services in outpatient mental health clinics. Additionally, psychiatrists coordinate and develop therapeutic plans, assess treatment outcomes, and evaluate the risk of recidivism. In collaboration with psychologists, they issue opinions to the court regarding the necessity of continued treatment in a closed setting or the feasibility of outpatient care.

Another equally important role of forensic psychiatrists is issuing expert opinions to state authorities. In criminal law, the standard practice requires at least two forensic psychiatrists to prepare such an opinion. Expert witnesses, such as psychologists, sexologists, and neurologists, may be appointed to contribute to the evaluation. Experts provide their opinions in writing and may be summoned to court to present an oral opinion. Their assessments typically address questions posed by the procedural authority, including the individual's mental capacity at the time of the offence, risk of recidivism, competency to stand trial, and the necessity of imposing protective measures, whether inpatient or outpatient.

### *Education and Qualifications*

#### PSYCHIATRISTS

Poland has not yet established a separate specialisation or sub-specialisation in forensic psychiatry. However, forensic topics, including forensic psychiatric evaluation, have become integral to training for specialist psychiatrists and clinical psychologists. These subjects are covered in mandatory courses and seminars required for doctors and psychologists before obtaining the title 'specialist'. Institutions such as the Forensic Psychiatry Section of the Polish Psychiatric Association, the Polish Forensic Psychiatry Association, and the Forensic Psychiatry Clinic of the Institute of Psychiatry and Neurology in Warsaw play a significant role in postgraduate education. These organisations host or co-host numerous scientific conferences and provide training and postgraduate courses. The Forensic Psychiatry Clinic also conducts an annual seminar on implementing protective measures in psychiatry.

Despite the non-obligatory nature of forensic training, a doctor can become a forensic psychiatrist by obtaining a medical degree (following six years of medical studies) and completing a five-year specialisation in psychiatry, which combines theoretical and practical knowledge. The postgraduate internship takes place in a designated medical facility. However, this training remains general and does not include specific qualifications in forensic psychiatry.

#### PSYCHOLOGISTS

A forensic psychologist can work in a forensic psychiatry ward and begin issuing forensic opinions after obtaining a psychologist's diploma, which requires a five-year master's degree in psychology. Many higher education institutions offer a forensic specialisation in the final two years, including additional coursework in forensic psychology. However, graduates still receive the general title of Master of Psychology. There is no formal specialisation in forensic psychology, so psychologists must independently pursue courses, training, and conferences to develop expertise in this field.

### *National Forensic Psychiatry Organisations*

Poland has three national organisations dedicated to forensic psychiatry and psychology: the Polish Association of Forensic Psychiatry (PTPS), the Polish Psychiatric Association (PTP), Forensic Section, and the Association of Forensic Psychologists.

The PTPS, established in 2006, brings together psychiatrists, psychologists, and lawyers to advance forensic psychiatry, promote knowledge in the field, and facilitate the integration and exchange of expertise among professionals. It achieves these goals by organising conventions, congresses, conferences, and training sessions. Additionally, the PTPS sets standards for forensic opinions and provides expert recommendations to national authorities on key issues in forensic psychiatry.

The PTP, established in 1920, aims to advance the field of Polish psychiatry, improve psychiatric care, establish professional ethical standards, and oversee their observance. PTP promotes psychiatric knowledge by organising and co-organising congresses, meetings, sessions, courses, and exhibitions. It publishes scientific journals, collaborates with other publications, and provides expert opinions on psychiatric matters. Additionally, it works with health authorities to develop and enhance psychiatric care and cooperates with national and international scientific and social organisations. Within PTP, the Section of Forensic Psychiatry focuses specifically on forensic psychiatric issues.

The Association of Forensic Psychologists is a nationwide organisation that has been active since 1995. Its mission is to represent and advocate for forensic psychologists, uphold high ethical and professional standards, establish and monitor psychological opinion standards, and protect the interests of those in need of assistance and support. The association achieves these objectives through various initiatives, including submitting opinions, memoranda, plans, and studies to relevant authorities and institutions; organising symposia and conferences; conducting training sessions and courses; developing standards, norms, recommendations, and guidelines for diagnosis and intervention; assisting victims of crime, individuals with mental illness, children, and adolescents; and promoting mental health awareness.

## Forensic Psychiatry Service (Provision of Care)

### *Forensic Patient Characteristics*

In Poland, there is no comprehensive statistical data on the characteristics of all patients subjected to court-imposed protective measures. However, several studies conducted on smaller or larger samples provide insights that roughly reflect the profile of a typical forensic patient.

### *Psychiatric Diagnoses*

A study conducted on a group of 120 patients across 12 forensic psychiatry wards in Poland found that the majority were diagnosed with schizophrenia (77.5%), while a smaller proportion had mental impairment (5%). Additionally, nearly a quarter of the patients (23.33%) suffered from somatic diseases. Dependence on alcohol, drugs, or mixed substances was fairly evenly distributed (Markiewicz, 2023; see Table 14.1).

*Table 14.1* Distribution of individual mental disorders

| *Variable* | | *All patients (N = 120)* |
|---|---|---|
| Mental disorder type/diagnosis | Schizophrenia | 93 (77.5%) |
| | Affective disorders | 10 (8.33%) |
| | Delusional disorders | 12 (10%) |
| | Personality disorders | 20 (16.67%) |
| | Mental impairment | 6 (5%) |
| | Other | 1 (0.83%) |
| Somatic diseases | | 28 (23.33%) |
| Psychoactive substance dependence | Alcohol | 27 (22.5%) |
| | Drugs | 26 (21.67%) |
| | Mixed | 29 (24.17%) |

*Source:* Markiewicz (2023).

*Table 14.2* Socio-demographic data on patients in forensic psychiatry wards

| *Variable* | | *All patients (N = 120)* |
|---|---|---|
| Sex | Female | 16 (13%) |
| | Male | 104 (87%) |
| Age | | mean = 38.9<br>standard deviation = 12.3 |
| Marital status | Single | 89 (74%) |
| | Married | 8 (7%) |
| | Divorced | 18 (15%) |
| | Widow/Widower | 5 (4.17%) |
| Education | Basic | 42 (35%) |
| | Vocational | 24 (20%) |
| | Secondary | 39 (32.5%) |
| | Tertiary | 9 (7.5%) |
| Professional experience | Never worked | 20 (16.67%) |
| | Unskilled physical worker | 60 (50%) |
| | Skilled physical worker | 25 (20.83%) |
| | Office worker | 15 (12.5%) |

*Source:* Markiewicz (2023).

Table 14.1 shows that the majority of individuals with mental disorders who are placed in psychiatric hospitals by a criminal court ruling have psychosis. Those with personality disorders are only admitted if their condition is accompanied by a diagnosed mental illness or mental impairment. Additional socio-demographic characteristics of these patients are presented in Table 14.2 (Markiewicz, 2023).

### *Types of Crimes Committed by Persons With Mental Disorders*

Studies by Pyrcak-Górowska (2021b) identify the types of crimes committed by individuals with mental disorders who were placed in psychiatric hospitals under court-imposed protective measures. Based on the legal interests violated or threatened, these crimes include offences against family and care (approximately 27%–28%), freedom (around 20%–21%), life and health (about 18%–20%), property (roughly 16%–19%), and the functioning of state and local government institutions (about 5%–6%). While exact percentages vary yearly, the overall trend remains consistent (Barczak-Oplustil et al., 2021).

Since crimes against life and health constituted a significant majority, other studies have focused on analysing specific types of offences within this category of the Criminal Code.

Among all crimes against life and health, the most common were murder (31.8%) and attempted murder (14.5%). Serious bodily injury accounted for 20.9%, a percentage close to moderate and minor bodily injury (22.2%). Crimes related to fighting and assault made up 10%. Other offences in this category, such as infanticide and exposure to danger, were committed individually and infrequently (Markiewicz, 2023).

### *Length of Stay and Exiting the System*

In Poland, there are no official statistical data on the average length of stay or the total number of forensic patients in the forensic system. Research indicates that the average length of stay in forensic psychiatry facilities is about four years (Markiewicz, 2023). Another study suggests an average stay of approximately three years, although it was conducted only with patients from a single medium-security ward in one hospital (Gosek et al., 2020).

### *Therapeutic and Treatment Programmes Offered to Forensic Psychiatry Patients*

The therapeutic programme varies based on the nature of the centre, the security level of the ward, and the availability of specialists. It is tailored to the specific group of patients in each facility. All forensic psychiatry wards offer psychological care through individual sessions and therapeutic groups, as well as occupational therapy and support from social workers. Additionally, depending on patient needs, services may include addiction therapy, cognitive function training, social skills training, aggression replacement training, hygiene training, culinary classes, and therapy for offenders with mental illnesses related to sexual offences. Patients also have the opportunity to participate in religious practices in designated areas. Most centres are equipped with sports facilities and provide physical therapy.

Pharmacological treatment primarily involves antipsychotic drugs, mood stabilisers, antidepressants, and anti-anxiety medications registered in Poland. Many patients receive prolonged-release intramuscular preparations (depot form). For extremely rare electroconvulsive therapy procedures—used in cases of catatonia, intolerance to pharmacological treatment, or drug-resistant mood disorders—separate patient consent or additional forensic and internal medicine consultation is required (Heitzman et al., 2019).

## Strengths and Weaknesses

The Polish forensic psychiatry system has several strengths. One key advantage is the presence of detailed legal regulations governing forensic psychiatry, including provisions for psychiatric expert opinions, compulsory forensic treatment, and the clearly defined responsibilities of the National Psychiatric Board for Protective Measures. Additionally, specific ordinances issued by the Minister of Health regulate the organisation of forensic psychiatric facilities and the procedures for compulsory forensic treatment. Legal provisions also ensure the strict confidentiality of patient medical data and provide guidelines for using direct constraints. Beyond legal regulations, strengths also extend to the hospitals and their services.

The Polish forensic psychiatry system has several additional strengths. The National Psychiatric Board for Protective Measures, appointed by the Minister of Health, determines the appropriate forensic hospital and security level for each patient. Furthermore, compulsory forensic treatment is supervised by both the Penitentiary and Penal Court, with forensic expert opinions reviewed every six months. Patients also have unlimited access to the patient's ombudsman, ensuring their rights are protected. Scientific and academic bodies contribute to developing and implementing standards and guidelines. Lastly, the expanding activities of the Polish Association of Forensic Psychiatry serve as a valuable forum for experience exchange and professional development.

The Polish forensic psychiatry system also has several weaknesses. Financially, there is insufficient and unequal funding per patient, along with low staff salaries, despite the high risk of violence they face. This financial strain has led to staff shortages in key roles, including nurses, psychologists, occupational therapists, and social workers.

Within hospitals, challenges include the poor condition of many facilities and limited access to sports and therapeutic infrastructure, as most forensic units were adapted from general psychiatry wards. Additionally, forensic treatment in inpatient settings tends to be lengthy, with no structured mechanisms for a smooth, gradual transition between custodial and non-custodial care. There are no intermediate stages between closed psychiatric institutions and non-custodial therapy, making reintegration more difficult for patients.

Another significant weakness of the Polish forensic psychiatry system is the lack of a systemic approach to social rehabilitation and limited local community interest in forensic psychiatry. As a result, there are few community-based psychiatric services for ex-forensic patients, and no structured reintegration framework exists to support their transition back into society.

Despite these challenges, there are several opportunities for growth. Expanding the forensic research network in Poland and increasing international cooperation could enhance best practices and optimise forensic care procedures. European integration offers further opportunities for experience exchange and the refinement of forensic psychiatry standards. Additionally, ongoing discussions about forensic psychiatry within the broader mental health reform may help raise community awareness, strengthen financial support, and improve resources for facilities, patient care, research, and community-based forensic services.

The Polish forensic psychiatry system faces several challenges. One major issue is the difficulty in applying mental health laws to maintain a secure ward environment due to unclear or insufficient legal regulations. This lack of clarity complicates decision making and the enforcement of safety measures within forensic facilities. Additionally, the system is struggling with an ageing workforce and a lack of incentives for young professionals to enter the field, which could lead to long-term staffing shortages.

A particularly controversial challenge is the concept of 'psychiatric isolation'. Under current law, individuals deemed highly likely to commit further severe and harmful acts after imprisonment may be subjected to indefinite psychiatric confinement. This practice raises significant ethical and legal concerns, as prolonged isolation can contribute to mental health deterioration and may conflict with international human rights standards.

## Notes

1 The conditions for securing psychiatric facilities intended to implement a protective measure are laid down in the Regulation of the Minister of Health of 16 January 2017 on the psychiatric committee on protective measures and the execution of protective measures in psychiatric institutions (Journal of Laws of 2020, item 1780).
2 Data from the Ministry of Health, September 2024, unpublished.
3 Data from the Ministry of Health, September 2024, unpublished.

## References

*Act on Mental Health Protection* of 19 August 1994, Journal of Laws 2020, item 685, consolidated text

Cieślak, M., Spett, K., Szymusik, A., & Wolter, W. (1991). *Psychiatria w procesie karnym* [Psychiatry in criminal processes], Warsaw, Poland.

The Constitution of the Republic of Poland of 02 April 1997, Journal of Laws of 2009, No. 114, item 946.

Gosek, P., Kotowska, J., Rowińska-Garbień, E., Bartczak, D., & Heitzman, J. (2020). Factors influencing length of stay of forensic patients: Impact of clinical and psychosocial variables in medium secure setting. *Frontiers in Psychiatry, 11*. https://doi.org/10.3389/fpsyt.2020.00810.

Heitzman, H., & Markiewicz, I. (2012). Ustawa o ochronie zdrowia psychicznego—podstawowe zagadnienia [Act on mental health protection-basic issues]. In J. Wciórka, S. Pużyński, & J. Rybakowski (Eds.), *Psychiatria* (Rev., Vol. 3. *Metody leczenia, zagadnienia etyczne, prawne, publiczne, społeczne* [Methods of treatment; ethical, legal, public, social issues] pp. 475–489). Wroclaw, Poland: Elsevier Urban & Partner.

Heitzman, J., Markiewicz, I., & Gosek, P. (2019). Complementary model of long-term care in Poland as a result of the political transformation, law reform and service changes in forensic psychiatry. In B. Völlm, & P. Braun (Eds.). *Long-term forensic psychiatric care: Clinical, ethical and legal challenges* (pp. 287–300). Springer International Publishing.

Indecki, K., & Jurewicz, J. (2014). *The key issues of Polish penal law*, Łódź, Poland: Wydawnictwo Uniwersytetu Łódzkiego.

Markiewicz, I. (2023). *The needs and quality of life of forensic patients undergoing therapy in isolation as a protective measure*. Unpublished PhD dissertation, University of Gdansk, Gdansk, Poland.

Markiewicz, I., Gardyńska-Ziemba, E., & Heitzman, J. (2016), Przymusowa hospitalizacja psychiatryczna—struktura przyjęć bez zgody w trybie nagłym na przykładzie IPiN [Involuntary psychiatric hospitalisation—the structure of emergency admissions without consent on the example of the Institute of Psychiatry and Neurology], *Psychiatria Polska*, *50*(1), 7–18.

Pyrcak-Górowska, M. (2021a). How does Polish law respond to the threat posed by a person with mental disorders? *Journal of Criminal Law and Penal Studies*, *25*(2), 33–52.

Pyrcak-Górowska, M. (2021b). Założenia metodologiczne badań aktowych w sprawach środków zabezpieczających [Methodological assumptions of case files research on security measures]. In A. Barczak-Oplustil, M. Pyrcak-Górowska, & A. Zoll (Eds.), *Środki zabezpieczające. Ujęcie systemowe [Security measures. A systemic approach*]. Kraków.

Statistics Poland (GUS). (2024). *Ludność. Stan i struktura ludności oraz ruch naturalny w przekroju terytorialnym* [The population. The state and structure of the population and natural movement in the territorial section]. As of 31 December 2024, stat.gov.pl [accessed 2025-02-27] (Polish).

Zoll, A. (2016). Comment on Article 1, thesis 42. In W. Wróbel, & A. Zoll. (Eds.). *Kodeks karny. Część ogólna. Tom I. Cześć I. Komentarz do art. 1–52*, [Criminal Code. General part. Vol. 1. Commentary on Articles 1–52]. Wolters Kluwer Polska.

# 15 Portugal

*Márcia Mota, Maria João Peixoto, and Ricardo Barroso*

## Brief Description

| | |
|---|---|
| **Location** | Portugal is located on the Iberian Peninsula in southwestern Europe, sharing its only land border with Spain to the east and north. Portugal also includes the archipelagos of the Azores and Madeira, autonomous regions in the Atlantic Ocean. |
| **Size** | 92,212 km$^2$ |
| **Population** | 10,344,802 (2021) |
| **Language** | The official language of Portugal is Portuguese. |
| **Political system** | Portugal, or the Portuguese Republic, has a parliamentary republic system, with a president as the head of state and a prime minister as the head of government, leading the executive branch. The prime minister is appointed by the president from the majority party in the Parliament (*Assembleia da República*). The Parliament is unicameral and has 230 deputies elected every four years. Portugal's Constitution (*Constituição da República Portuguesa*) is the highest law of the country, which recognises the democratic and fundamental citizenship rights, the fundamental principles of the Portuguese state, the main political guidelines that all the government agencies must follow, and the organisation rules for the political establishment. The judiciary is independent and overseen by the Constitutional Court (*Tribunal Constitutional*). |

## Legal System

### *Legal Context*

The Portuguese legal system is grounded in several fundamental legal instruments, including the Constitution (*Constituição da República Portuguesa*) (Portugal, 1976, 2022), the Civil Code (*Código Civil*) (Portugal, 1966), and the Penal Code (*Código Penal*) (Portugal, 1982, 1995). The principles on which the judicial organisation in Portugal is based and the efficient functioning of all courts are enshrined in the Constitution, ensuring a clear separation between civil and

DOI: 10.4324/9781003376248-18

administrative jurisdictions (Portugal, 1976, Articles 205–214). Regarding civil jurisdiction, judicial courts handle both civil and criminal matters. They are divided into three instances, each having a distinct jurisdiction. From the highest level of hierarchy to the lowest, the judicial system includes the Supreme Court of Justice (*Supremo Tribunal de Justiça*), which has national jurisdiction; the Courts of Appeal (*Tribunais da Relação*), operating within judicial districts; and the Courts of First Instance (*Tribunais de Primeira Instância*), typically district courts (Coelho, 2024). The Supreme Court holds the highest position in the hierarchy of judicial courts, with the Constitutional Court having jurisdiction over certain civil, criminal, and social matters, as well as a section dedicated to hearing appeals related to the decisions of the Superior Council of Magistracy (*Conselho Superior da Magistratura*) (Cura, 2018). The Courts of Appeal are Courts of Second Instance, meaning they handle cases that are appealed from the lower courts or the Courts of First Instance, where civil and criminal cases are first heard. The Courts of Appeal handle both civil and criminal appeals from the lower courts. In Portugal, the Supreme Court is considered the final court of appeal in both civil and criminal matters.

Portugal also has Justices of the Peace, reintroduced into the legal system in 2001 (Ferreira, 2019). These are characterised by a different logic from the one used in traditional courts because they are oriented towards solving litigious issues and fostering social peace more than towards the strict application of the law, which is mandatory in the first stage of mediation (Coelho, 2003). The matters they handle must fall within the jurisdictional limits of the Courts of First Instance. Their proceedings typically involve civil property matters, but they may also consider civil claims for restitution arising from some criminal offences, including battery, defamation, bodily harm, and theft). With purely declarative competence, their decisions must be enforced by the Courts of First Instance.

The intersection of forensic psychiatry and psychology with the legal system is structured to ensure comprehensive evaluations and interventions for individuals involved in legal proceedings. The primary institution facilitating this integration is the National Institute of Legal and Forensic Medicine and Forensic Sciences (*Instituto Nacional de Medicina Legal e Ciências Forenses* [INMLCF]), a public institute with legal personality and administrative and financial autonomy, which operates under the Ministry of Justice, ensuring that mental health assessments are integral to the judicial process. This structure facilitates informed legal decisions that consider the psychiatric and psychological aspects of individuals involved in legal matters.

Forensic psychiatric expertise is requested whenever judicial or legal authorities require specialised assessment in criminal cases. In the context of penal law, forensic psychiatry plays a crucial role in evaluating defendants' mental health conditions, determining criminal responsibility, assessing dangerousness, and providing medico-legal insights into cases involving aggravated battery, homicide, or sexual offences. These evaluations assist courts in determining whether an individual was criminally responsible at the time of the offence and whether a psychiatric condition justifies alternative legal measures. Courts formally request these assessments from INMLCF's regional delegations, where specialised forensic psychiatrists (appointed through public tenders or hired for specific services) conduct diagnostic assessments, medico-legal examinations, and forensic psychiatric reports.

These evaluations are primarily conducted at INMLCF's delegations or medico-legal offices to ensure standardised procedures and adherence to ethical and legal guidelines. The resulting expert reports inform judicial decisions on criminal accountability, preventive detention, and security measures, particularly for individuals deemed dangerous due to psychiatric disorders. However, when an INMLCF delegation lacks sufficient specialists to meet demand, evaluations may be outsourced to specialised services within the National Healthcare System (*Serviço Nacional de Saúde*). These referrals consider service availability while ensuring that assessments occur within the subject's designated healthcare area. Some hospital psychiatric services have dedicated psychiatric and psychological forensic units, internally organised to provide timely evaluations when requested.

In forensic psychiatry, a coordinating expert psychiatrist oversees the distribution and supervision of forensic evaluations, ensuring adherence to the probative value of medico-legal psychiatric expertise as defined by law. In penal law, the scientific and technical judgement contained in expert reports is presumed independent of judicial discretion. If a judge disagrees with the expert's findings, they must justify their divergence with equally substantiated technical reasoning. In contrast, in civil law, the court determines the evidentiary value of expert reports.

### *Mental Health Laws*

Forensic psychiatry in Portugal is governed by several laws that cover lack of criminal responsibility, security measures, civil capacity assessments, and involuntary hospitalisation. Some of the most relevant are explained as follows.

#### *Mental Health Law*

Portugal's new *Mental Health Law* (*Lei de Saúde Mental*, Lei nº 35/2023, Portugal, 2023b) addresses the definition, foundations, and objectives of mental health policy; enshrines the rights and duties of individuals in need of mental health care; regulates the restrictions of their rights; and establishes guarantees to protect their freedom and autonomy. The regulation reflects the value framework through which all therapeutic approaches should be understood based on human dignity. This law is fundamental for psychiatric care practice. It replaces the former *Mental Health Law* of 1998 (Portugal, 1998), whose revision was justified after more than 20 years of enforcement, considering, on the one hand, the clinical advancements in this field and, on the other hand, the commitments made by Portugal in the framework of the World Health Organization, the Council of Europe, the European Union, and other international bodies (Vieira et al., 2023).

One of the key areas regulated by Portugal's *Mental Health Law* is the rights and duties of individuals in need of mental health care (Articles 7 and 9). It also outlines specific provisions (Article 10), including advance directives (*diretivas antecipadas da vontade*) and the healthcare proxy (*procurador de cuidados de saúde*). These allow individuals to document their treatment preferences and appoint a representative should they become unable to make healthcare decisions. In addition, the law regulates the application of coercive measures (Article 11). It sets clear guidelines for electroconvulsive therapy and transcranial magnetic stimulation (Article 12), ensuring these interventions are used safely and ethically.

An advanced directive, specifically in the form of a living will, is a unilateral document, freely revocable at any time by the individual, in which a person of legal age and capacity expresses their conscious, free, and informed will in advance regarding the health care they wish or do not wish to receive if, for any reason, they become incapable of autonomously expressing their personal will (Portugal, 2012, Article 2). In the case of a person in need of mental health care, they may clearly and unequivocally express in advance their preferences regarding mental health treatments, particularly concerning inpatient treatment, coercive measures (including isolation and chemical or physical restraints), electroconvulsive therapy, transcranial magnetic stimulation, and the use of psychotropic medication. Advanced directives apply when the person in need of mental health care is unable, at the time of consent, to express their conscious, free, and informed will. However, they are not followed if their observance would pose a risk to the legal rights, personal safety, or property of third parties.

A healthcare proxy is appointed by the person in need of mental health care, granting them representative powers to decide on the health care they should receive when they cannot autonomously express their personal will. People in need of mental health care also have the right to designate a trusted person to support them, particularly in exercising their rights to file complaints, make suggestions, and appeal or review the decision of involuntary treatment (Lei nº 35/2023, Portugal, 2023b, Article 9, nºs 4–5). The trusted person is an informally designated figure chosen by the individual in need of mental health care to provide support in exercising their rights, particularly regarding complaints, making suggestions, and appealing or reviewing the decision of involuntary hospitalisation. For this purpose, the trusted person may access health information and the involuntary hospitalisation process.

The *Mental Health Law* also regulates the involuntary treatment of individuals with mental illness. Involuntary treatment refers to treatment ordered or confirmed by judicial authority, either on an outpatient basis or through hospitalisation (Article 2), aimed at the full recovery of the individual through therapeutic intervention and psychosocial rehabilitation (Article 14). Under the law, the requirements for involuntary treatment are cumulative (Article 15, nº 1). These include the existence of a mental illness, the refusal of medically prescribed treatment necessary to prevent or eliminate an identified danger, and the presence of a threat to personal or property rights. This danger may be directed either towards third parties—arising from the individual's mental illness and refusal of treatment—or towards the individual themselves, in situations where the person lacks sufficient discernment to understand the nature and implications of giving or withholding consent. Additionally, involuntary treatment must promote the individual's full recovery through therapeutic intervention and psychosocial rehabilitation (*reabilitação psicossocial*) (Article 14).

In addition to the cumulative requirements, involuntary hospitalisation must adhere to several principles. Thus, involuntary hospitalisation can only occur if it is the only way to ensure the medically prescribed treatment, if it is appropriate to prevent or eliminate one of the dangerous situations anticipated, and if it is proportional to the severity of the mental illness, the level of danger, and the importance of the legal right involved (Article 15, nº 2).

Involuntary treatment occurs on an outpatient basis, facilitated by community mental health teams, except when hospitalisation is the only means to ensure the medically prescribed treatment. The individual is released from hospital as soon as the treatment can be resumed on an outpatient basis (Article 15, nº 3). The restrictions on the rights, will, and preferences of individuals in need of mental health care arising from involuntary treatment are strictly necessary and appropriate for the effectiveness of the treatment, safety, and proper functioning of the inpatient unit of the local or regional mental health service, in accordance with its internal regulations (Article 15, nº 4). Involuntary treatment, whether inpatient or outpatient, must also end when the conditions that initially justified it no longer exist. Discontinuation may occur either through a discharge issued by the clinical director of the health service, based on a clinical-psychiatric evaluation report and immediately communicated to the competent court, or by judicial decision (Article 26).

If the involuntary treatment is carried out on an inpatient basis, the individual remains hospitalised—subject to periodic reviews until one of three situations occurs: (1) the conditions for involuntary hospitalisation are no longer met, but the individual chooses to remain voluntarily hospitalised; (2) the conditions for involuntary hospitalisation are no longer met, and the patient is discharged for outpatient care (Article 26); or (3) the conditions for involuntary treatment persist, but hospitalisation is no longer the only means of ensuring the prescribed medical treatment. In this third case, the treatment transitions to involuntary outpatient care, and the court must be informed of this change (Article 27).

If the individual transitions from involuntary hospitalisation to involuntary outpatient treatment but subsequently no longer meets the conditions for outpatient care—or if hospitalisation once again becomes the only way to ensure the prescribed medical treatment—hospitalisation may resume. In such cases, the treating psychiatrist must notify the competent court of the change and request that the security forces execute a transport warrant if necessary (Article 27).

If the involuntary treatment is carried out on an outpatient basis, a review of the decision is mandatory after two months from the start of treatment or the decision that upheld it. The mental health service must submit a clinical-psychiatric evaluation report to the court 10 days before the review date to support this review. Two psychiatrists must prepare this report in collaboration with other professionals from the service. The review takes place with the participation of, among others, either one of the psychiatrists who signed the report or the psychiatrist responsible for the individual's treatment (Article 25).

### *Not Guilty by Reason of Insanity*

In Portugal, individuals found 'not guilty by reason of insanity' are referred to as *inimputáveis*, meaning not criminally responsible. Lack of criminal responsibility (*inimputabilidade*) is defined in the Penal Code (Portugal, 1995, Article 20) as the condition in which an individual is found not criminally responsible if, as a result of a mental disorder, they lack the capacity, at the time the offence is committed, to understand its illegality of their actions or to act in accordance with that understanding (Almeida, 2000). When discussing this concept in Portugal, we refer to criminal responsibility, which entails the objective incapacity to fulfil the obligation and the right to be held accountable for an act defined as a crime under Portuguese criminal law.

Therefore, for a person to be considered not criminally responsible, it is necessary not only to verify the presence of a mental disorder (biopsychological substrate) but also to prove that this disorder renders the individual incapable of determining the illicit nature of the act (normative substrate). The mere presence of a mental disorder is not sufficient to declare the absence of criminal responsibility (Cabral et al., 2009).

In Portugal, the absence of criminal responsibility is determined through a mixed approach, where the judge's decision is informed by an unbiased medical evaluation following the guidelines set in the Penal Code (Portugal, 1995). It is the responsibility of the forensic psychiatrist to confirm the presence of a psychiatric condition or mental disorder and to assess the connection between this condition and the unlawful act, as well as the individual's capacity for evaluation and discernment. The Penal Code also establishes diminished responsibility (*imputabilidade diminuída*) (Portugal, 1995, Article 20, nº 2), stating that a person may be declared not criminally responsible if, due to a severe, non-accidental mental disorder, their capacity to assess the unlawfulness of the act or to act according to that assessment is significantly reduced at the time of committing the act.

In cases where an individual is found to lack criminal responsibility due to a mental disorder, the expert must also assess their level of dangerousness (*perigosidade*), including the likelihood that the person may repeat similar unlawful acts as a result of their condition.

### *Fitness to Stand Trial*

In Portugal, the concept of fitness to stand trial is not defined in law. This concept refers to the definition of procedural capacity, which differs from the lack of criminal responsibility (*imputabilidade*). It consists of the defendant's ability to personally exercise their defence, regardless of whether they were capable of being judged guilty at the time of the offence (Albergaria, 2020). In this context, a person is procedurally incapable when they do not have the conditions to provide an intelligent and intelligible defence due to a psychological anomaly (Albergaria, 2020). According to Albergaria (2020), the Code of Criminal Procedure (Portugal, 1987) does not expressly provide for this issue in such a situation. Instead, it follows the model enshrined in it, which holds that the detection of a psychological anomaly with such effects has no consequence on the course of the process, which continues in its terms until judgement (if applicable).

In these circumstances, the safeguard for the defendant consists of the mandatory assistance of a defence attorney (Portugal, 1987, Article 64), the disregard for confessions (Portugal, 1987, Article 344), and the possibility that, in the case of an anomaly arising before or after the commission of the offence or after conviction, the defendant may be hospitalised in an institution for those found not criminally responsible due to a mental disorder (Portugal, 1995, Article 105), unless there is no evidence of dangerousness, in which case the sentence will be suspended until the condition that justified the suspension ceases (Portugal, 1995, Article 106).

### *Assisted Decision-Making Regime for Adults*

The assisted decision-making regime for adults (*Regime de Maior Acompanhado*) is a legal framework in Portugal that enables adults who, due to mental or physical conditions, have difficulty fully exercising their rights to receive support from a court-appointed representative (*acompanhante*). This regime replaced the former system of interdiction and incapacitation and was introduced through Law No. 49/2018. It aims to promote autonomy and uphold the dignity of the individual, aligning Portugal's legal system with the principles of the UN Convention on the Rights of Persons with Disabilities.

The assisted decision-making regime for adults is, therefore, intended for individuals who, for various reasons, are unable to exercise their rights, fulfil their duties, or manage their property consciously and autonomously without the support or intervention of another person. The purpose of this regime is to safeguard their wellbeing, promote recovery, and enable the full exercise of all their rights and responsibilities, except where legal exceptions apply or where otherwise determined by judicial decision. The measure does not apply where its objective can already be achieved through general duties of cooperation and assistance under existing legal obligations (Portugal, 2018, Article 140).

Therefore, the objective of the regime is to preserve the autonomy that the person still has and, where possible, to enhance it. In this context, after reviewing all the relevant information and psychiatric expertise, the court determines which actions the person can and should continue to practice independently and which actions, for their protection, must be carried out by, or with the support of, another person or court-appointed representative. However, certain actions, such as hospitalisation, may only be performed by the representative with prior permission from the court (Portugal, 2018, Article 148).

This law also provides that the person subject to this regime may participate in the choice of a court-appointed representative and that more than one representative may be appointed as necessary (Portugal, 2018, Article 143). However, this role is limited to acting on behalf of the individual only to the extent necessary (Portugal, 2018, Article 145). Likewise, the law requires a personal and direct hearing of the person subject to the regime by the judge to ascertain their situation and determine the most appropriate accompanying measures.

As part of the judicial proceedings under the assisted decision-making regime for adults, the court conducts a formal hearing where the judge asks questions to determine the scope and nature of the support measures required. When the judge deems it appropriate, the expert or experts prepare a clinical-psychiatric evaluation report that outlines, whenever possible, the disease or condition of the person, its consequences, the likely date of onset, and recommended support and treatment options for that condition. The court may review or lift the accompanying measures if the individual's progress warrants it. The court reviews these measures based on the schedule specified in the ruling, with reviews occurring at least every five years (Portugal, 2018, Article 155).

## Forensic Psychiatry System

### *Structure and Function of the Forensic Psychiatric System*

Decree-Law No. 70/2019 (Decreto-Lei nº 70/2019; Portugal, 2019a) amended paragraph 2 of Article 126 of the Code of Execution of Sentences and Measures Depriving Liberty (*Código de Execução de Penas e Medidas Privativas de Liberdade*; Portugal, 2009). According to this amendment, measures involving deprivation of liberty, including preventive detention, should preferably be carried out in mental health units outside the prison system. This applies specifically to individuals placed in institutions intended for persons found not criminally responsible, regardless of whether or not they have been deemed criminally responsible.

In Portugal, there are three forensic psychiatry inpatient units integrated into the following healthcare facilities: Magalhães Lemos Hospital, integrated into the Unidade Local de Saúde de Santo António in Porto; Sobral Cid Hospital, integrated into the Unidade Local de Saúde de Coimbra, in Coimbra; and Júlio de Matos Hospital, Unidade Local de Saúde de São José, in Lisbon.

There is a shared responsibility between the Ministries of Justice and Health, with the director of each forensic unit holding responsibilities similar to those of a prison facility director. These units are staffed by a multidisciplinary clinical team that includes doctors, nurses, and professionals from psychology, occupational therapy, and social work. Social reintegration services play a key role in implementing inpatient measures in accordance with legal provisions, working closely with the multidisciplinary clinical team.

There are two units for the detention of individuals found not criminally responsible due to a mental disorder within the prison system: the first is located at the Santa Cruz do Bispo Prison Establishment in Porto, and the second is at the Hospital Prisional de S. João de Deus in Lisbon. This is a prison hospital that provides specialised healthcare services to the incarcerated population. It also has a psychiatric clinic with 19 beds for men and eight beds for women, specifically for acute treatment. The unit accepts inmates from across the country and receives patients sent directly from the criminal court following the initial hearing.

### *Role of Forensic Psychiatry*

Forensic psychiatry aims to assist the legal system in evaluating the mental health and integrity of individuals, particularly in determining the presence or absence of a mental disorder and the implications of having or not having a psychiatric diagnosis. In Portugal, forensic psychiatry plays a significant role in various legal contexts, engaging in expert activities across areas such as criminal, civil, labour, and administrative law. In addition to expert practice, forensic psychiatry also encompasses penitentiary practice and addresses questions regarding medical error, assessment, and prevention.

### *Forensic Psychiatry Profession*

Forensic psychologists and psychiatrists have a shared foundation in their field, with many overlapping training requirements (Anciães & Agulhas, 2020). In 2016, the Portuguese Psychological Association (*Ordem dos Psicólogos Portugueses*) established a subspecialty in justice psychology to enhance the practice of forensic psychologists, strengthen their training, and promote research in this field. As of March 2025, there were 595 certified forensic psychology specialists registered with the association. Before 2015, although many psychiatrists worked in forensic psychiatry within hospital settings, no specialised degree or training was required for practice in this field.

In 2015, the Portuguese Medical Association (*Ordem dos Médicos*) established a subspecialty in forensic psychiatry to enhance expert practice and improve training and research in this area. To support this objective, the specific training programme for psychiatry internships was revised in 2016, making forensic psychiatry a mandatory component for all future psychiatrists. This change is expected to ensure that experts play an essential supportive role within psychiatry.

These internships last three months and must be completed at reputable psychiatry services focusing on training in forensic psychiatry. Nine hospital services accredited by the Portuguese Medical Association offer these internships in Portugal. While there are no official statistics on the number of psychiatrists specialising in forensic psychiatry, the authors of this chapter learned from the Portuguese Medical Association that, as of 2022, there were 46 psychiatrists in this subspecialty.

To gain admission to the subspecialty in forensic psychiatry of the Portuguese Medical Association, applicants must meet several criteria: they must be registered with the College of Psychiatry of the Portuguese Medical Association, engage in regular expert practice in forensic psychiatry across various Portuguese jurisdictions, complete a theoretical and practical training programme with a minimum duration of 180 hours, and have practical experience in damage evaluation or welfare clinical activities in a non-prison setting, such as through an internship or clinical work, or by conducting a research project in forensic psychiatry. The required theoretical and practical training programme specifically covers technical and scientific areas pertinent to forensic psychiatry, as recognised by the subspecialty section of forensic psychiatry. However, the specific institutions authorised to offer these training courses are not listed.

### *National Networks and Collaborations*

An essential aspect of forensic psychiatry is the presence of national networks and collaborative initiatives that foster interdisciplinary cooperation, knowledge sharing, and the development of best practices. These networks play a pivotal role in advancing forensic mental health by facilitating dialogue among professionals from various fields, including psychiatry, psychology, and law.

In Portugal, the Portuguese Society of Psychology and Psychiatry of Justice (*Sociedade Portuguesa de Psicologia e Psiquiatria da Justiça*) exemplifies such collaboration. This organisation unites a multidisciplinary group of members, primarily psychiatrists and psychologists, who operate at the intersection of mental health and the justice system. Through conferences, training sessions, and academic publications, the society seeks to enhance understanding of forensic mental health and promote evidence-based practices within judicial contexts.

Like many professional associations in specialised fields, the Portuguese Society of Psychology and Psychiatry of Justice has faced typical sustainability challenges that limit its potential impact. Financial constraints and inconsistent institutional support have created ongoing difficulties, restricting the society's ability to develop larger scale, long-term initiatives. Additionally, membership engagement has varied as professionals attempt to balance these voluntary activities with their primary clinical and academic responsibilities. The reliance on voluntary contributions and the lack of stable funding mechanisms have made it challenging to maintain consistent programming and expand society's reach.

Despite these challenges, these networks are a significant asset, offering crucial platforms for professional development, interdisciplinary collaboration, and the sharing of best practices. Addressing these weaknesses requires innovative funding approaches, greater institutional support, and the establishment of strategic partnerships. Strengthening these networks is crucial not only for advancing forensic psychiatry but also for ensuring that legal systems have access to the most up-to-date, scientifically informed mental health expertise.

## Forensic Psychiatry Service (Provision of Care)

### *Forensic Patient Characteristics*

In Portugal, forensic patients are individuals who have committed a criminal offence but were found not criminally responsible due to a mental disorder and are still considered a danger to society. In such cases, instead of receiving a prison sentence, the court may impose a preventative security measure, resulting in hospitalisation in designated inpatient facilities governed by the Ministries of Justice and Health. In addition to these cases, the legal system also accounts for individuals who are found criminally responsible but are considered particularly vulnerable. These individuals may be placed in specialised facilities—rather than the general prison system—if the judge determines that incarceration in a standard prison would be detrimental to their wellbeing.

It is important to distinguish involuntary hospitalisation as a preventative security measure from involuntary treatment under the *Mental Health Law* (Lei nº 35/2023; Portugal, 2023b). The former is a judicial measure intended to address criminal dangerousness (*perigosidade*), while the latter is an administrative measure aimed at providing medical assistance (Albergaria, 2003), with the goal of supporting the individual's full recovery through therapeutic intervention and psychosocial rehabilitation.

In practice, when a finding of non-criminal responsibility due to a mental disorder is confirmed, the forensic psychiatrist must also assess and provide an opinion on the individual's level of dangerousness. Legally, dangerousness refers to the likelihood of repeating similar unlawful acts. In forensic psychiatry, it denotes the probability that an individual, as a result of a mental disorder, will commit further criminal offences. In Portugal, a finding of non-criminal responsibility alone is not a sufficient legal basis for imposing a security measure.

It must also be established that there is a high risk of recidivism. When this is the case, the individual is classified as a dangerous offender. Consequently, the court imposes a security measure, which is served in a treatment, rehabilitation, or secure facility, in accordance with Article 91 of the Portuguese Penal Code (Portugal, 1995).

Security measures and preventive detention are preferably enforced in non-custodial mental health units and, when necessary, in prisons or specialised units as prescribed by law. The decision to assign an individual to a specially designated prison facility or unit falls under the authority of the Director-General of Prison Services. It is then communicated to the Sentence Enforcement Court.

Initially, the individual is placed in a facility or unit within the prison system and undergoes an initial evaluation, including a direct hearing and a forensic psychiatric assessment. This process is conducted in accordance with Article 19 of the Portuguese Penal Code (Portugal, 1995) and Articles 19 and 67 of Decree-Law No. 51/2011, of April 11 (Portugal, 2011) to determine appropriate future placement. The following facilities are designated for the initial assessment of individuals subject to security measures or preventive detention to determine their placement in either a mental health unit or a prison facility: the Psychiatry and Mental Health Clinic of Santa Cruz do Bispo Prison serves northern and central Portugal and the Psychiatry Service of S. João de Deus Prison Hospital serves greater Lisbon, and the southern, and island regions of Portugal (Despacho n.º 1564/2023, Portugal, 2023a).

The placement decision is based on an assessment of the individual's risks and needs, with special consideration given to their clinical, rehabilitation, security, and social reintegration requirements. If the evaluation determines that the individual poses a significant threat to public safety or a risk of escape, they are assigned to a facility or unit within the prison system. This evaluation is communicated to the Public Prosecutor's Office and the Sentencing Execution Court.

In cases where a security measure is imposed or an individual found not criminally responsible is placed in a designated facility, the development of a therapeutic and rehabilitation plan is mandatory. This plan must be tailored to the individual's needs, capabilities, and risk assessment profile. It must be created with the involvement of mental health professionals and submitted to the Sentencing Execution Court for approval. Efforts must be made to obtain consent from the individual involved unless their health condition makes such participation impractical or ineffective. The therapeutic and rehabilitation plan is periodically evaluated and revised based on the individual's changing treatment needs and their family and social reintegration circumstances, in accordance with Article 128 of the Code for the Execution of Sentences and Measures Involving Deprivation of Liberty (Portugal, 2009).

The primary objectives of this inpatient treatment are to rehabilitate the individual and help them reintegrate into their family and social environment. This approach aims to prevent further criminal behaviour while also ensuring the safety of society, especially that of the victim.

If it is determined that a defendant held in pretrial detention has a mental disorder, the judge may order—after consulting the defence attorney and, whenever possible, a family member—that, instead of detention, the defendant be placed in a psychiatric hospital or another appropriate facility, for as long as the disorder persists. In such cases, appropriate measures must be implemented to prevent the risk of escape and the commission of further offences (Portugal, 1987, Article 202(2)).

The Portuguese Penal Code (Portugal, 1995) provides that any incarcerated individual suffering from a mental disorder whose condition prevents them from serving their sentence in a standard correctional facility may be placed in a facility designated for individuals found not criminally responsible for treatment, care, and security, and for as long as the mental disorder persists. This is outlined in Articles 104 and 105 of the Penal Code.

According to the National Institute of Statistics (2023), 347 individuals deemed not criminally responsible were subject to security measures. Of these, 166 were admitted to S. João de Deus Prison Hospital in Caxias and the Psychiatry and Mental Health Clinic attached to the Santa Cruz do Bispo Prison Facility, while 181 were placed in non-prison mental health institutions.

### *Exiting the System*

For individuals under the joint responsibility of the Ministries of Justice and Health, the duration of the security measure is subject to a maximum limit, which cannot exceed the maximum prison sentence applicable to the type of offence committed (Portugal, 1995, Article 91). However, if the offence qualifies as a crime against persons or a crime of common danger punishable by a prison sentence exceeding five years, the security measure must last a minimum of three years unless an earlier release is deemed compatible with the defence of the legal order and social peace (Article 91).

Unlike prison sentences, security measures may end when the court determines that the individual no longer poses a risk of dangerousness (Portugal, 1995, Article 92). The risk assessment is mandatory one year after the start of the measure or after the decision that upheld it—except for the minimum detention period in the situation described earlier (Article 93). If, following this review, the court concludes that the objectives of the security measure can reasonably be achieved in a less restrictive environment, the individual may be released on probation (Portugal, 1995, Article 94).

### *Approaches to Treatment*

For individuals under a security measure, the intervention model prioritises clinical and forensic aspects, focusing on clinical recovery and social and forensic rehabilitation. According to Article 11 of Decree-law no 70/2019 (Decreto-Lei nº 70/2019, 2019a), a therapeutic and rehabilitation plan must be developed for each individual. This plan is designed to address risk factors associated with mental illness and its treatment, individual risk factors linked to maladaptive personality traits, and contextual risk factors. It includes targeted treatment for the primary psychiatric disorder, as well as the management of other psychiatric comorbidities and medical-surgical diseases.

Rehabilitation promotes the acquisition and development of individual and social skills. These aspects include self-care and health behaviour management, psychoeducation on the illness, therapeutic adherence, communication skills, shared responsibilities, problem-solving and conflict resolution skills, activities that foster social interaction, occupational and professional engagement, education on the illegality of specific behaviours, increased awareness of unlawful acts in the context of mental disorder, and the development of strategies to minimise and prevent unlawful behaviour, as established in Article 128 of the Portuguese Code for the Execution of Sentences and Measures Involving Deprivation of Liberty (Portugal, 2009). Rehabilitation equips individuals under security measures for reintegration through clinical monitoring, personal responsibility, and skill development to enable a lawful and self-sufficient life.

Following the release of the individual—particularly during the probationary period and after the termination of the security measure—the continuation of care within the National Health Service becomes essential. This requires coordination with the local mental health services in the individual's area of residence. Under Article 20 of Decree-Law No. 70/2019 (Decreto-Lei n° 70/2019, 2019a), appropriate public, private, or social sector measures shall be implemented to provide residential accommodation or facilitate the individual's reintegration into the community, where necessary.

During the probationary period, the originating unit, in coordination with local mental health services and social reintegration services, monitors the individual's compliance with obligations imposed by the probation decision, including undergoing treatment and attending medical examinations and evaluations. If the individual fails to attend scheduled consultations, treatments, or examinations, as mandated, local mental health services must report this non-compliance to the Sentence Enforcement Court (Article 20).

## Strengths and Weaknesses

One of the most positive developments is the recent reform of the *Mental Health Law,* which represented a significant shift in the legal and clinical approach to individuals with mental disorders who have committed criminal acts in Portugal. The reform eliminated the automatic extension of the security measure of individuals found not criminally responsible and introduced a framework for involuntary treatment. The reform redefined the approach to individuals requiring mental health care by establishing that once they have served the imposed security measure, they must be released. It also abolished the successive renewal of security measures, which had previously been subject to renewal every two years, potentially resulting in indefinite hospitalisation.

Another innovative aspect of the *Mental Health Law* reform was the revision and modernisation of the rights and duties of individuals needing mental health care. These updates reflect advances in medical sciences and pharmacology and align with international, European, and Portuguese legal frameworks, namely the *Basic Health Law* (*Lei de Bases da Saúde*, Lei nº 95/2019b), the assisted decision-making regime for adults (*Regime de Maior Acompanhado*, Portugal, 2018), and the law governing advance directives (*Diretivas Antecipadas da Vontade*, Portugal, 2012).

However, several areas still require improvement, despite the provisions outlined in Decree-Law No. 70/2019 (Decreto-Lei nº 70/2019, 2019a), which require that adequate residential accommodation or community-based support be provided by the public, private, or social sector during the probation period and following the termination of the security measure, such resources remain insufficient and inadequate in scale. Many individuals affected by severe mental disorders experience significant impairments in functionality and autonomy. They would particularly benefit from residential facilities offering continuous (24-hour) support—currently limited or inadequate services in many regions.

Furthermore, although the law mandates the development of specialised programmes tailored to the individual characteristics of those under security measures—taking into consideration factors such as age, gender, mental disorder, the nature of the unlawful act committed, criminogenic factors, and specific social reintegration needs—these programmes have not consistently available. In practice, they are often implemented on a limited or experimental basis by voluntary teams or researchers whose involvement is not formally integrated into the system, resulting in a lack of continuity and sustainability.

Another concerning issue is the absence of legal provisions addressing deviant behaviours that fall outside of formal psychiatric diagnoses but still warrant intervention. These behaviours should be recognised as areas for forensic psychiatry and psychology intervention.

## References

Albergaria, P. (2003). *A Lei de Saúde Mental Anotada*. Coimbra: Almedina.

Albergaria, P. (2020). Incapacidade do Arguido Para, Em Razão de Anomalia Psíquica, Providenciar Pela Sua Defesa. In M. J. Antunes (Ed.), *Anomalia Psíquica e Direito. Colóquio Comemorativo dos 20 Anos da Entrada em Vigor da Lei de Saúde Mental* (pp. 31–52). Instituto Jurídico. Faculdade de Direito da Universidade de Coimbra. https://doi.org/10.47907/livro/2020/anomalia_psiquica/livro

Almeida, C. P. (2000). *Modelos de inimputabilidade: Da teoria à prática*. Almedina.

Anciães, A., & Agulhas, R. (2020). Interligação da psicologia da justiça com a psiquiatria forense. In R. Barroso, & D. Neto (Eds.), *A prática profissional da psicologia na justiça* (pp. 25–36). Ordem dos Psicólogos Portugueses.

Cabral, A., Macedo, A., & Vieira, D. N. (2009). Da psiquiatria ao direito. *Julgar, 7*, 185–196.

Coelho, J. M. G. (2003). *Julgados de paz e mediação de conflitos*. Lisboa: Âncora Editora.

Coelho, N. (2024). *Organização do sistema judicial e jurisdição: Para uma sistemática alargada da realização do direito pelo juiz*. Almedina.

Cura, A. A. V. (2018). *Organização judiciária portuguesa*. Coimbra: GestLegal.

Ferreira, J. O. C. (2019). *Julgados de paz: Legislação anotada* (4ª ed.). Coimbra: Almedina.

National Institute of Statistics. (2023). *Directorate-General for Justice Policy 2023*. Retrieved from https://www.ine.pt/xportal/xmain?xpid=INE&xpgid=ine_indicadores&indOcorrCod=0000852&contexto=bd&selTab=tab2&xlang=pt

Portugal. (1966). *Código Civil* [Civil code]. *Diário da República, 1*(274). Retrieved from https://dre.pt

Portugal. (1976). *Constituição da República Portuguesa* [Constitution of the Portuguese Republic]. *Diário da República, 1*(86). Retrieved from https://dre.pt

Portugal. (1982). *Código Penal* [Penal Code]. *Diário da República, 1*(100). Retrieved from https://dre.pt

Portugal. (1987). Código do Processo Penal [Code of criminal procedure]. *Diário da República, 1*(40). Retrieved from https://dre.pt

Portugal. (1995). Código Penal [Penal code] (Decreto-Lei n.º 48/95, de 15 de março [Decree-Law No. 48/95]). *Diário da República, 1A*(63), 1350–1416. Retrieved from https://dre.pt

Portugal. (1998). Lei nº 36/98[Law nº 36/98], de 24 de julho. *Diário da República, 1A* (169), 3544–3550. Retrieved from https://dre.pt

Portugal. (2009). Código da Execução das Penas e das Medidas Privativas da Liberdade Lei n.º 115/2009 [Law No. 115/2009)], de 12 de outubro. *Diário da República, 1*(197), 7422–7464. Retrieved from https://dre.pt

Portugal. (2011). Decreto-Lei n.º 51/2011[Decree-Law nº 51/2011], de 11 de abril. *Diário da República, 1*(71), 2180–2225. Retrieved from https://dre.pt

Portugal. (2012). Lei nº 25/2012 [Law nº 25/2012], de 16 de julho. *Diário da República, 1*(136), 3728–3730. Retrieved from https://dre.pt

Portugal. (2018). Lei nº 49/2018 [Law nº 49/2018] de 14 de agosto. *Diário da República, 1*(156), 4072–4086. Retrieved from https://dre.pt

Portugal. (2019a). Decreto-Lei nº 70/2019 [Decree-Law nº 70/2019], de 24 de maio. *Diário da República, 1*(100), 2599–2608. Retrieved from https://dre.pt

Portugal. (2019b). Lei nº 95/2019 [Law nº 95/2019], de 4 de setembro. *Diário da República, 1*(169), 55–66. Retrieved from https://dre.pt

Portugal. (2022). *Constituição da República Portuguesa* (8ª ed.). Lisboa: Assembleia da República.

Portugal. (2023a). Despacho n.º 1564/2023, de 31 de janeiro. *Diário da República, 2*(22), 147–147. Retrieved from https://dre.pt;

Portugal. (2023b). Lei nº 35/2023 [Law nº 35/2023], de 21 de julho. *Diário da República, 1*(141), 2–23. Retrieved from https://dre.pt

Vieira, F., Cabral, A., Trancas, B., Almeida, F., Barreto, H., Robalo, I., Pimentel, J., Castelão, J., & Ramos da Fonseca, M. J. (2023). Novos Tempos, Novas Realidades, Novas Leis: A Continuidade, a Mudança e os Novos-Velhos Desafios em Psiquiatria e Saúde Mental em Portugal. *Acta Médica Portuguesa, 36*(12), 773–775. https://doi.org/10.20344/amp.20746

# 16 Scotland

*Lindsay Thomson and Caroline Kelly*

## Brief Description

| | |
|---|---|
| **Location** | Scotland is part of the United Kingdom, in Europe. |
| **Size** | 78,720 km$^2$ |
| **Population** | As of 2021, Scotland has a population of approximately 5.51 million, accounting for 9.5% of the UK population. |
| **Languages** | Scotland's main language by custom and usage is English, with Gaelic, Scots, British Sign Language, and minority languages making up the country's other main language groups. Scotland's 2011 census found that more than 150 languages other than English are used in Scottish homes. |
| **Political system** | Scotland is a democracy, represented in both the Scottish Parliament and the Parliament of the United Kingdom (Westminster) since the *Scotland Act 1998*. In a 1997 referendum, nearly three-fourths of the Scottish electorate favoured the establishment of a Scottish Parliament, which formally began sitting in 1999. |

## Legal System

Scotland has a distinct legal and judicial system based on Roman law. The country is divided into six sheriffdoms, each containing 49 sheriff courts. The High Court of Justiciary has jurisdiction over the most serious criminal offences, which are tried by jury. It also serves as the highest court for criminal cases. The judges in this court also sit in Scotland's highest civil court, the Court of Session. In civil disputes, parties can appeal to the Supreme Court of the United Kingdom. Scots law governs the legal framework for the care and treatment of people with mental disorders, intersecting with both UK law and European Union regulations.

DOI: 10.4324/9781003376248-19

### *The Legal Context: the United Kingdom*

The *Human Rights Act 1998* incorporates most of the European Convention on Human Rights and Fundamental Freedoms (ECHR) into the United Kingdom's legal systems. It ensures that the rights set out in the Convention are effective for UK citizens by allowing individuals to bring human rights cases before domestic courts without needing to go to the European Court of Human Rights (the Strasbourg Court). The Act prohibits public bodies from acting in a manner inconsistent with the ECHR unless an Act of Parliament explicitly mandates otherwise. It also requires UK judges to consider Strasbourg Court rulings and interpret legislation as far as possible in a way that aligns with the ECHR. While designed to uphold the principle of parliamentary sovereignty, the Act still allows individuals to take their cases to the Strasbourg Court as a final recourse if necessary.

### *The Legal Context: Scotland*

Scotland has a separate legal system from the rest of the United Kingdom in both civil and criminal law. It is a mixed legal system, incorporating elements of both civil (Roman) law and common law. Scots law derives its authority from past court decisions, the writings of legal scholars, and Acts of Parliament. It is not codified. The *Scotland Act 1998* ensures that laws passed by the Scottish Parliament can be challenged and overturned by the courts if they are found to be incompatible with rights protected under the ECHR. Additionally, every Government Bill introduced to the Scottish Parliament must be certified by a Scottish Government Minister as compliant with the ECHR.

In Scotland, arrangements for the detention, care, and treatment of people who have a mental disorder fall under the *Mental Health (Care and Treatment) (Scotland) Act 2003b*. The Act established the Mental Health Tribunal for Scotland as the principal forum for approving and reviewing compulsory measures related to detention, care, and treatment of people with mental disorders. It also set out the roles and functions of the Mental Welfare Commission for Scotland, which is responsible for safeguarding the rights of people with mental disorders, conducting inspections, and issuing reports on psychiatric services. This framework serves as a crucial protective mechanism for patients.

### *Mental Health Laws*

#### *Mental Health Act*

In Scotland, most individuals receiving care in forensic mental health services are detained under the *Mental Health (Care and Treatment) (Scotland) Act 2003b,* with many referred through provisions in the *Criminal Procedure (Scotland) Act 1995*. The policy on Health, Social Work and Related Services for Mentally Disordered Offenders in Scotland defines offenders with mental disorders as those who are

> considered to suffer from a mental disorder as defined in the *Mental Health (Care and Treatment) (Scotland) Act 2003b*, whether or not they are, or may be, managed under its provisions and come to the attention of the criminal justice system, or whose behaviour poses a risk of such contact.
>
> (The Scottish Office, 1999, updated for the Act of 2003)

This policy set out principles for the care of offenders with mental disorders and others requiring similar services. These principles include the following: people should receive high-quality care tailored to their needs; where possible, they should be supported in the community rather than in institutions; security measures should be no greater than necessary, based on the level of risk they pose to others and public safety; rehabilitation should be actively promoted to help people sustain an independent life; and care should be provided as close to their homes and families as possible.

The 1999 Mentally Disordered Offenders Policy outlined the range of services that should be available across Scotland and emphasised the importance of partnership between health services, local authorities, and the criminal justice system, including housing agencies and the police.

### *Fitness to Plead*

It is a well-established legal principle that it is unfair to try accused people whose mental disorder prevents them from mounting a proper defence. In Scots law, such individuals are referred to as 'unfit to plead' or 'insane in bar of trial' (*Criminal Procedure (Scotland) Act 1995,* Section 53F). Historically, the criteria for fitness to plead were vague, medical evidence was rarely questioned, and psychosis was often assumed to meet the threshold. Additionally, fitness to plead was frequently confused with aspects of criminal responsibility. Until the 1970s, most people with mental disorders in the forensic system were formally detained in Scotland under the insanity in bar of trial provision. Until the 1980s, Scotland recorded a higher frequency of findings of unfitness to plead compared to England and Wales. Although fresh proceedings could be initiated against individuals who later regained fitness to plead, such cases were rare.

Dissatisfaction with the mandatory hospital disposal and the possibility of indefinite detention for an offence that an accused person had not been found guilty of led to changes in the procedures for handling cases of insanity in bar of trial. The *Criminal Justice (Scotland) Act 1995*, which amended relevant provisions of the *Criminal Procedure (Scotland) Act 1975*, introduced the Examination of Facts (EOF) procedure and greater flexibility in disposal.

Following a 2004 recommendation by the Scottish Law Commission, the *Criminal Justice and Licensing (Scotland) Act 2010* introduced the statutory plea of 'unfitness for trial'. This replaced the term 'insanity', which was considered outdated and stigmatising, and which had caused confusion with the psychiatric defence of 'insanity at the time of the offence'.

The statutory criteria for fitness to plead are set out in Section 53F of the *Criminal Procedure (Scotland) Act 1995*, as amended by Subsection 170(1) of the *Criminal Justice and Licensing (Scotland) Act 2010*. The Act states the following regarding fitness to plead:

1) A person is unfit for trial if it is established on the balance of probabilities that the person is incapable, by reason of a mental or physical condition, of participating effectively in a trial.
2) In determining whether a person is unfit for trial, the court is to have regard to:
    a. The ability of the person to
        i. understand the nature of the charge
        ii. understand the requirement to tender a plea to the charge and the effect of such a plea
        iii. understand the purpose of, and follow the course of, the trial
        iv. understand the evidence that may be given against the person
        v. instruct and otherwise communicate with the person's legal representative
3) The court is not to find that a person is unfit for trial by reason only of the person being unable to recall whether the event which forms the basis of the charge occurred in the manner described in the charge.

The Crown, defence, or court may raise the issue of fitness to plead, which will be unchanged with respect to unfitness for trial. At present, the trial judge determines the defendant's fitness to plead based on written or oral evidence from two doctors during a preliminary hearing on the balance of probabilities. The amendment in 2010 repealed the requirement for written or oral evidence from two doctors to determine unfitness for trial. Statutory criteria still must be supported by medical or psychological evidence.

When a person is deemed unfit for trial, the court records the finding, discharges the trial diet, and orders an Examination of Facts (EOF). While awaiting the EOF, the accused may be remanded on bail, held in custody, or committed to hospital. At the EOF, the court must determine beyond reasonable doubt whether the accused committed the act charged and, on the balance of probabilities, whether there are grounds for acquittal. The accused is not required to attend the EOF. If the court does not find the facts proven, the accused is acquitted, and no further proceedings take place.

Section 57 of the *Criminal Procedure (Scotland) Act 1995* sets out the available disposals, which include a compulsion order, a compulsion order with a restriction order, an interim compulsion order, a guardianship order, a supervision and treatment order, and a discharge with no order. Therefore, mental health professionals may tailor a flexible set of disposals to the person's mental health and risk. Previously, the mandatory disposal for a murder charge was a hospital order and a restriction order, but this is no longer the case. Under Section 57 (3) of the *Criminal Procedure (Scotland) Act 1995*, a mandatory compulsion order with a restriction order is available where, although the person has a mental illness, following assessment on an interim compulsion order, the court determines the person poses a high risk according to the criteria set out in Section 210E of the Act.

The compulsion and restriction orders are identical to analogous disposals for convicted people with mental disorders. The interim compulsion order is available primarily for the assessment of potentially high-risk cases (Part 1 of the *Criminal Justice (Scotland) Act 2003a*) and, unlike the interim compulsion order after conviction, cannot be followed by a penal disposal.

The supervision and treatment order is unique to procedures related to unfitness for trial and is similar to a community payback order with a condition of psychiatric treatment following conviction. It is a mechanism "to secure access to supervision and assistance in the community, including medical treatment" (*Mental Health Care and Treatment (Scotland) Act 2003b).* It requires medical evidence from two approved doctors and requires the person to submit to treatment, comply with instructions, maintain contact with a supervising officer, and comply with residential requirements. Nevertheless, it is important to note that none of these measures can be legally enforced, and there are no significant consequences for breaching the conditions of the order.

The accused may appeal to the High Court against a finding or refusal to make a finding of unfitness for trial, against an EOF finding, and against any imposed disposal. The Crown can appeal in cases of unfitness for trial only on a point of law.

### *Criminal Responsibility*

The age of criminal responsibility in Scotland is 12 years. This means a child under 12 cannot be arrested, charged, or prosecuted for a crime and, therefore, cannot be criminally convicted. The *Age of Criminal Responsibility (Scotland) Act 2019* came into effect in December 2021 and introduced changes for children under 12 to protect them from the harmful effects of early criminalisation. The Scottish Government subsequently published guidance to support police, local authorities, and others when interviewing children under 12. The guidance seeks to ensure that the child and their family receive the necessary support and that their rights are protected according to the United Nations Convention on the Rights of the Child. The Act provides for a Child Interview Rights Practitioner to support a child involved in an investigative interview, a solicitor who will provide any advice, further support, and assistance to the child and their family should they be involved in an investigative interview.

Children between 12 and 16 can be tried in adult courts if approved by the Lord Advocate, but only for serious crimes or if a co-accused over 16 is involved.

### *Decision Makers in Forensic Psychiatry*

#### *Tribunal System*

The Mental Health Tribunal for Scotland makes decisions regarding people with mental disorders, including those who have been convicted of an offence. The Tribunal grants civil orders and renews various compulsory measures for the detention, care, and treatment of people in Scotland who have a mental disorder. The Tribunal reviews cases of individuals who are involuntarily placed in the mental health system, whether they enter through psychiatric services or the criminal justice system. The Tribunal holds the authority to review, modify, or revoke the appropriate order determined by the criminal courts in the case of offenders with mental disorders. A tribunal panel consists of three members: a legally qualified convener, a medical expert, and a general member.

The guiding principles of the Act mandate the following:

1. The patient's current and past wishes are taken into account.
2. The viewpoints of the patient's named person, carer, guardian, or welfare attorney are considered.
3. The patient is encouraged to participate as fully as possible, with access to the necessary information and support.
4. A range of options for the patient, prioritising maximum benefit and minimal security, must be explored.
5. Reciprocity is ensured, meaning that patients subjected to compulsion can also access required services, including accommodation, education, activities, and social interaction.

Tribunal hearings take place in over 70 locations throughout Scotland. The hearings occur when the patient is detained in hospital or the community if subject to community-based measures. Proceedings before the Tribunal are generally private, but a patient can make an application for a hearing to be held in public. After each hearing, the Tribunal must write and issue a decision that includes a complete statement of the facts found by the Tribunal and the reasons for its decision. Any decision by the Tribunal is a decision by all three members. When Tribunal members hold a dissenting view, it is considered best practice to record the reasons for the decision and document the dissenting view separately.

## Forensic Psychiatry System

### *Structure and Function of the Forensic Psychiatric System*

Forensic mental health services offer specialised care and treatment rather than penal punishment, and a large majority of people in these services are detained under the *Criminal Procedure (Scotland) Act 1995*, as amended by the *Mental Health (Care and Treatment) (Scotland) Act 2003b*. The two Acts work in partnership to safeguard both patients and the public. People with mental disorders can be transferred to forensic mental health services at the time of arrest, during court proceedings, when on remand, awaiting trial, or after trial from prison. The Act of 1995 gives Scottish courts the power to ensure that a person receives care and treatment under the Act of 2003 while they are involved in legal or court proceedings. National Health Service (NHS) Health Boards, Scotland, provide and govern forensic psychiatric services.

If police, prosecutors, court staff, or legal representatives are concerned about a person's mental health, they will request a mental health assessment. This helps the court to decide whether treatment is necessary and how best to deal with the case. Many types of orders can be imposed. A full list of types of orders and their description are outlined in Table 16.1.

Scotland's forensic mental health services operate across three levels of security: high, medium, and low. The State Hospital, Carstairs, provides high secure care for patients from Scotland and Northern Ireland. Medium secure services are regionally distributed across the country, with dedicated facilities including the Orchard Clinic in NHS Lothian (South East Region), Rohallion Clinic in NHS Tayside (North Region), and Rowanbank Clinic in NHS Greater Glasgow and Clyde (West). There are 12 low-secure units nationwide, varying from purpose-built facilities to adapted wards. These units accommodate patients whose mental health conditions and offending behaviour necessitate a lower level of security, as well as those transitioning from higher security settings as part of their rehabilitation process. Although many of the forensic mental health services are run by NHS Health Boards, Scotland also has two privately run low secure forensic mental health services.

*Table 16.1* Types of orders and their descriptions

| *Order type* | *Description* |
|---|---|
| Assessment Order | An order imposed by a criminal court which authorises hospital detention for up to 28 days in the first instance so that the patient's mental condition may be assessed. Medical treatment may be given in certain circumstances under this order. |
| Treatment Order | An order imposed by a criminal court which authorises hospital detention for mental illness. |
| Interim Compulsion Order | An order imposed by a criminal court that authorises hospital detention for assessment and treatment for up to 12 months. |
| Compulsion Order | A final disposal imposed by a criminal court which authorises hospital detention or compulsory powers in the community for six months. A compulsion order can be renewed for six months and then annually. |
| Restriction Order | When added to a compulsion order, it allows restrictions to be implied to limit the potential risk of serious harm to others while the person progresses through rehabilitation. A compulsion order with a restriction order authorises the detention of a person in hospital. |
| Hospital Direction | This allows a person to receive appropriate medical treatment in hospital and then be transferred to prison to complete any prison sentence that has been imposed. Time in hospital counts towards the overall time served of the prison sentence. This may be used when the link between any mental disorder and offending is weak. |
| Transfer for Treatment Direction | An order made by Scottish ministers that allows the transfer of a sentenced prisoner to hospital for treatment of a mental disorder. |
| Emergency Detention Certificate | This is a civil procedure authorising the removal of a person to hospital within 72 hours and the detention of that person in hospital for a further 72 hours. This is granted by a fully registered medical practitioner who has (where practical) sought the consent of a mental health officer. |
| Short-term Detention Certificate | A civil procedure that authorises a person to be transferred to hospital within 3 days of being granted, and then the detention of that person in hospital for up to 28 days. The Certificate is granted by an approved medical practitioner with the consent of a mental health officer. This period can be extended through an Extension Certificate for three working days. |
| Compulsory Treatment Order | An order granted by the Tribunal which authorises compulsory measures for six months. A compulsory treatment order can be renewed for six months and then annually. |

### *Forensic Patients in Scotland*

There are approximately 504 patients currently receiving inpatient forensic care in Scotland (Forensic Mental Health Services Managed Care Network, 2022). There are various levels of secure psychiatric care available, ranging from open wards to locked wards, intensive psychiatric care units, and low-, medium-, and high-secure facilities. Forensic mental health oversees the latter facilities. Sometimes, mental health staff in different areas, like general adult psychiatry or learning disability, look after patients who have a forensic history. The reasons for this include deteriorating mental health, police use of a 'place of safety', less serious offences not requiring a specialist service, rehabilitation, and geographical area of origin. The security level depends on clinical risk assessment or the crime committed. It is important that patients are correctly placed to meet their health care and security needs.

### *Role of Forensic Psychiatry*

Forensic psychiatry is a speciality of medicine based on detailed knowledge of relevant law, the working interface between criminal and civil justice systems and mental health systems, and the relationship between mental disorders, antisocial behaviour, and offending. Forensic psychiatrists in Scotland lead the care and treatment of forensic patients and others who require similar services, including risk assessment, management, and the prevention of serious harm. They also contribute to designing treatment facilities and programmes and provide expert advice to other health and social care professionals.

Forensic psychiatry comprises two areas: clinical and legal psychiatry. The first involves clinical work similar to that found in general psychiatry but is often related to serious offences and requires the additional task of negotiating legal matters. Legal psychiatry involves the relationship between law and mental disorders. This is perhaps more commonly observed in civil and criminal legal cases.

Forensic psychiatrists work closely with criminal justice agencies and courts, which requires them to thoroughly understand pertinent legislation and various forms of law, including criminal and civil law. Forensic psychiatrists also provide specialist advice to the courts, criminal justice services, the prison service, and other psychiatric colleagues, and they are responsible for preparing reports for tribunals and criminal justice agencies.

Traditionally, forensic psychiatry trainees in Scotland have taken a central role in participating in and leading various teaching activities. The School of Forensic Mental Health (SoFMH) and teaching centres across the country offer a wealth of opportunities for developing skills related to teaching undergraduate and postgraduate doctors and other professionals.

### *Forensic Psychiatry Profession*

#### *Qualifications and Specialised Training*

After medical school, all doctors spend two foundation years working in hospitals. They then enter a speciality training scheme in psychiatry and, after three years, can choose to specialise in forensic psychiatry. Three years of specialist training is required before applying for a consultant position.

The Scottish Forensic Psychiatry Training Programme prides itself on providing exceptionally high-quality training. Specialty trainees primarily work within one of the four regional hubs (Aberdeen, Edinburgh, Glasgow, and Perth), although the programme operates nationally. This allows speciality trainees to settle in a specific area while having easy access to nationwide training opportunities.

Each of the regional hubs has a Local Programme Lead/Educational Supervisor. On appointment to the programme, speciality trainees will meet with this supervisor and plan a training programme tailored to their needs, career goals, and personal circumstances.

The programme lasts three years, and the majority of placements are in secure units and community mental health teams within the regional hub. Scotland offers excellent access to high secure placements at the State Hospital in Carstairs, where most speciality trainees opt to spend six months as part of the programme. Speciality trainees are offered opportunities to develop expertise in prison psychiatry and can acquire essential skills in multi-agency working through participating in court and police liaison work. Access to opportunities to prepare court reports is particularly good. For example, speciality trainees will typically prepare 30–40 reports each year, which exceeds that generally possible in other areas of the United Kingdom. According to the Royal College of Psychiatrists Workforce Census 2021, 37 full-time consultant forensic psychiatrists are currently employed in Scotland (Royal College of Psychiatrists, 2021).

#### *Training in Forensic Psychology*

To become a forensic psychologist, people must take a postgraduate training route and undertake a British Psychology Society (BPS) accredited degree. Graduates who complete this degree receive the Graduate Basis for Chartered Membership (GBC) of the BPS and qualify for membership. They can also gain membership by completing an accredited conversion course if they do not have a BPS-accredited degree. After gaining GBC membership, graduates would commence employment and undertake postgraduate training. This includes a BPS-accredited Master of Science in Forensic Mental Health and a BPS qualification in Forensic Psychology Stage 2. This involves two years of supervised practice. Some universities offer a doctorate (Scottish Credit and Qualifications Framework Level 12), which combines a master's degree and the Stage 2 qualification.

Completing postgraduate training qualifies practitioners to become Chartered Members of the BPS. Practitioners must register with the Health and Care Professionals Council to start working as a forensic psychologist. According to the National Career Service, there are approximately 2,900 forensic psychologists employed in Scotland, working in various settings such as the NHS, the Scottish Prison Service, and private providers.

*National Networks and Collaborations*

The Scottish Government established the Forensic Mental Health Services Managed Care Network (Forensic Network) in 2003, which oversees the development and organisation of forensic mental health services in Scotland. While it has no direct managerial control over services or purchasing power, its role is to encourage and coordinate service development and promote consistency throughout the country.

The Forensic Network achieves its goals through the Forensic Network Advisory Board, a national oversight group of stakeholders (see Figure 16.1). Since its inception, the Forensic Network has strongly committed to using a multi-agency approach, facilitating information sharing, and supporting effective working relationships with partners in the third and independent sectors. These relationships have supported continuous improvement in planning services to improve the patient journey across forensic mental health services.

The Forensic Network has played a central role in developing Scotland's forensic mental health estate by bringing together practitioners, supporting policy and guidance development, and covering topics such as monitoring patient flow, security levels, conflict resolution, and services for women and those with intellectual disability.

Practitioners across the Forensic Network can access the SoFMH to meet their teaching, training, and research needs. It also runs a short course programme for practitioners across Scotland's forensic mental health estate. The SoFMH has received commissions from the Risk Management Authority, NHS Education for Scotland, the Scottish Government, and the Scottish Social Services Council and regularly develops and delivers training. This includes a suite of 'New to Forensic' programmes and risk assessment and management training. The SoFMH is also involved in developing and delivering three academic courses in partnership with the University of the West of Scotland, including a Master of Science in Forensic Mental Health. The SoFMH also has a strong research focus and supports the dissemination and commissioning of research to establish an evidence base for future service development.

The Royal College of Psychiatrists (RCPsych) in Scotland is the professional medical body for psychiatry in Scotland. It sets standards and promotes excellence in psychiatry and mental health care by leading, representing, and supporting psychiatrists nationally. It aims to improve the outcomes of people with

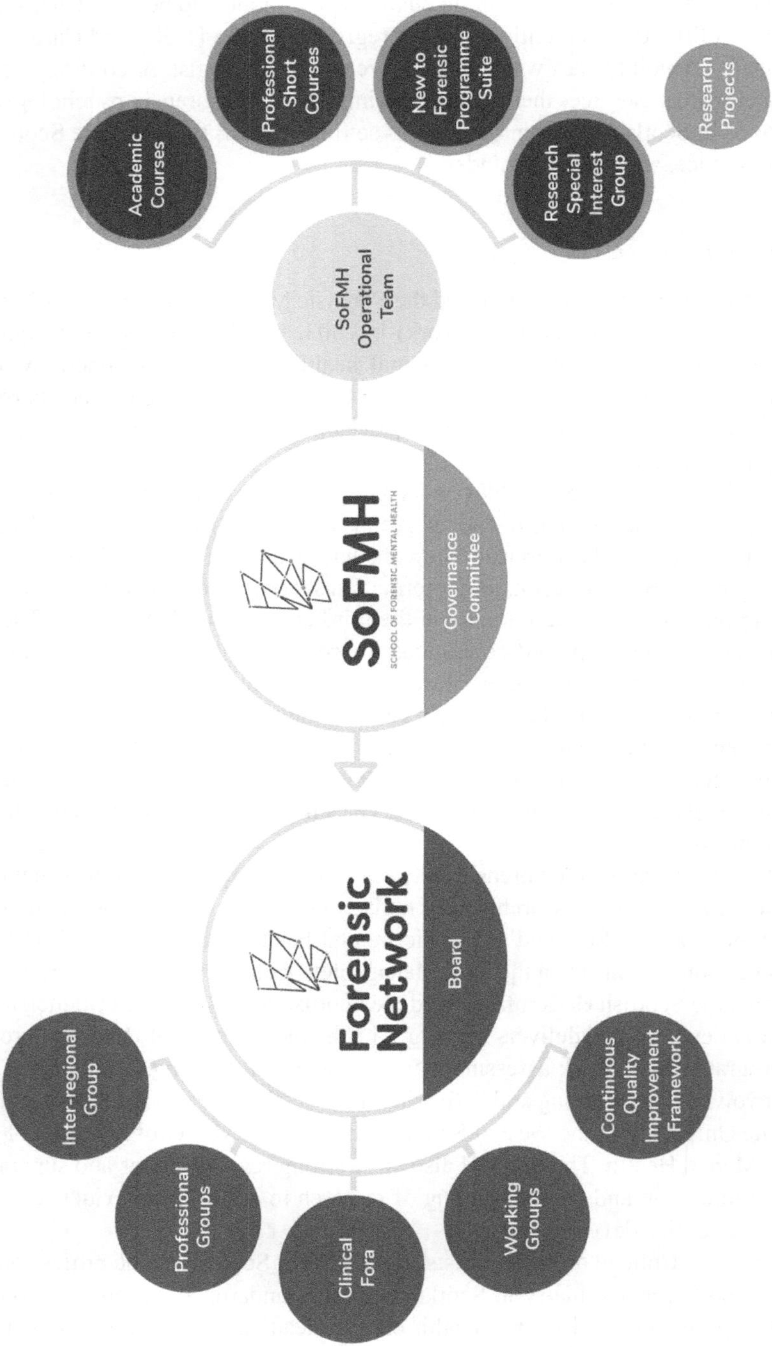


*Figure 16.1* Structure of the Forensic Network and School of Forensic Mental Health.

mental disorders and the mental health of people, their families, and communities. The RCPsych in Scotland is a devolved nation and council of the Royal College of Psychiatrists (UK) with over 1,300 members, fellows, affiliates, and pre-membership trainees. The RCPsych in Scotland has several faculties dedicated to the specialities of psychiatry, including the faculties of forensics and intellectual disability.

## Forensic Psychiatry Service (Provision of Care)

### *Forensic Patient Characteristics*

The Forensic Network conducts an annual census. In November 2022, there were 504 patients (92.4% male and 7.6% female) under the care of forensic mental health services in Scotland (Forensic Mental Health Services Managed Care Network, 2022). Inpatients range in age from 17 to 84 years, with an average age of 42.9 years. Male patients currently stay an average of 1,656 days, which is equivalent to approximately 4.5 years. This period is slightly shorter for female patients, at 1,534 days (around 4.2 years).

The Forensic Network census also provides data on patient diagnosis or diagnostic categories. This is limited to the patient being categorised as having a mental illness, intellectual disability, or personality disorder. Out of the 504 patients, 421 (83.5%) had a mental illness, 69 (13.7%) had an intellectual disability, and 14 (2.8%) had a personality disorder.

### *Exiting the System*

Forensic mental health services in Scotland embrace an ethos of recovery, rehabilitation, and reciprocity. Decisions to move down the security pyramid and into the community are made based on risks to others and the ability to manage these risks. In theory, patients should be able to progress through levels of secure care and return to their communities in a timely manner. In reality, services at low- and medium security have waiting lists, and transitions from secure services to the community often face delays. As a result, there is a risk that patients will be held in conditions of excessive security, which may breach their human rights. While patients being held in conditions of excessive security at high- and medium-secure levels have access to an appeal process, patients in low secure services do not currently have this option. The Scottish Mental Health Law Review (Scottish Government, 2022a) has recently proposed introducing an appeal process for low-secure patients. A comprehensive follow-up over 20 years of forensic patients in special security in Scotland (high and medium security) found that 56% of patients reached the community (Thomson & Rees, 2023).

The successful rehabilitation of patients through forensic inpatient services relies on the availability of support for them to return to the community. Section 25 of the *Mental Health (Care and Treatment) (Scotland) Act 2003b* specifies that local authorities shall provide the necessary care and support services (including residential accommodation) for people with a mental illness who are not in hospital. However, for people in hospital, the requirements are less stringent, and local authorities may provide these services. This can lead to patients commencing on a discharge-planning pathway where no specific agency assumes responsibility for ensuring that the necessary arrangements are put in place to support their successful discharge to the community. These issues are particularly likely to affect patients with more complex needs, such as intellectual disabilities.

### *Approaches to Assessment and Treatment*

At all stages and settings of the criminal justice process, a range of services must provide people with mental disorders in the forensic system access to psychiatric assessment and treatment. According to Section 329 of the *Mental Health (Care and Treatment) (Scotland) Act 2003b*, 'treatment' for mental disorders encompasses nursing, psychological interventions, habilitation, and rehabilitation. When discussing medical treatment in relation to compulsion orders, it includes not only psychiatric medication and electroconvulsive therapy but also interventions by nursing staff, psychologists, and other disciplines. The core purpose of mental health legislation is to secure the right to treatment for people who are unwell, even if they have lost sight of their own need for treatment.

The care and treatment options offered to people receiving forensic mental health services vary between providers but typically include pharmacological interventions and therapy-based approaches. Medication is often the first line of treatment. The care team may prescribe a combination of medications, which may include antipsychotic medication, antidepressants, mood stabilisers, and anti-anxiety medication. Psychological-based therapies generally fall into one of the four categories: behavioural therapies, which focus on thoughts and behaviours; psychoanalytical and psychodynamic therapies, which focus on unconscious relationship patterns that evolved from childhood; humanistic therapies, which focus on self-development; and arts therapies, which use creative arts within the therapeutic process.

In Scotland, psychological therapies in forensic services are delivered in line with the Forensic Mental Health Matrix (Forensic Mental Health Services Managed Care Network, 2011). This guide helps providers of NHS mental health services deliver evidence-based psychological therapy for patients who pose a risk of harming others. It is intended to apply to both community and inpatient services. It was written as an addition to the *Guide to Delivering Evidence Based Psychological Therapies in Scotland*, also known as the Matrix (NHS Education for Scotland, 2023). The principles in that document are endorsed, and a model of matched stepped care for forensic patients is proposed (see Figure 16.2).

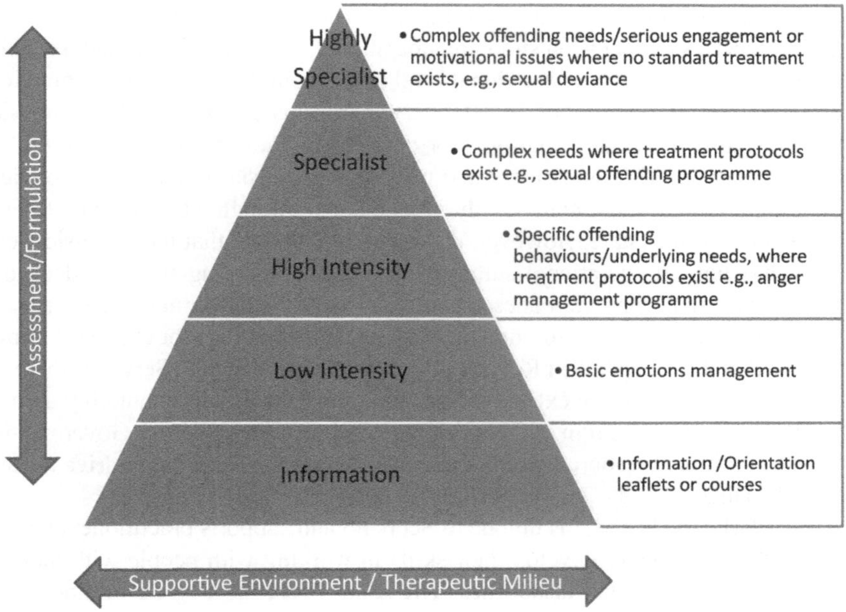


*Figure 16.2* Stepped care model for forensic mental health services with examples of offending behaviour interventions.

Scottish forensic psychiatry programmes provide occupational therapy to assist people in achieving maximum functioning and independence in daily life through practical and purposeful activities such as cooking, self-care, and budgeting. These programmes also utilise arts therapies such as drama, art, and music.

## Strengths and Weaknesses

Since its introduction into practice, the *Mental Health (Care and Treatment) (Scotland) Act 2003b* has proven to be a legislative and clinical success. In Scotland, forensic psychiatry has undergone significant developments in recent years, and further changes are expected due to national independent reviews on forensic mental health services and a review of mental health law in Scotland.

Scotland provides forensic mental health services for people with mental illness or intellectual disability, including community care and high-, medium-, and low secure care. Services are based on policy and legislation and are carefully reviewed by the Mental Welfare Commission. The Mental Health Tribunal system also has effective review mechanisms in place to oversee the use of compulsory measures for the detention, care, and treatment of people with mental disorders.

Scotland is unique in that it has a national Forensic Network that brings together services to decide on strategic, operational, and educational matters. This coordination of services at a national level helps promote consistency in practice and facilitates the sharing of knowledge, expertise, and resources. The Forensic Network also serves as a platform for developing national policies and guidelines concerning risk assessment and management, ensuring that these policies are evidence-based and consistently implemented throughout Scotland's forensic mental health estate. However, it is important to note that the Forensic Network has limited operational authority, especially regarding strategic decision making and management. It does not currently have the power to require services to follow its guidelines or to implement its recommendations for change. As emphasised in the Independent Review of Forensic Mental Health Services, there is a pressing need for more extensive strategic oversight and accountability across Scotland's entire spectrum of forensic psychiatry services (Scottish Government, 2021). Additional resources and increased authority are essential to drive meaningful change.

Similarly, the SoFMH is unique to Scotland and supports practitioners working within services to develop their skills in working with people with mental disorders or intellectual disabilities. The result is a cohort of well-trained and highly committed staff working across services. The broad range of academic and short course opportunities offered by the SoFMH is valued by staff and was highly praised within the Independent Review into Forensic Mental Health Services. The SoFMH also plays a key role in ensuring that practice within Scottish services is current, evidence-based, and research-focused.

One area for future development within Scottish forensic psychiatry is to ensure that mental health services in prison are equivalent to those available in the community or NHS care, particularly in terms of accessibility, quality, and the range of available interventions. A mental health needs assessment of Scotland's prison population (Scottish Government, 2022b) showed that current mental health services in prisons do not adequately address the high levels of need within the population. It also found a wide variation in the interventions available to support mental health needs across prisons. The report concluded that a change in the approach to prison care and prison mental health services must adequately address the mental health needs of people in prison in Scotland.

## References

Forensic Mental Health Services Managed Care Network. (2011). *The Forensic Mental Health Matrix: A guide to delivering evidence based psychological therapies in forensic mental health services in Scotland.* Retrieved from www.forensicnetwork.scot.nhs.uk

Forensic Mental Health Services Managed Care Network. (2022). *Annual report 2021–2022.* Retrieved from https://forensicnetwork.scot.nhs.uk/publications/?type%5B%5D=7

NHS Education for Scotland. (2023). *Matrix—A guide to delivering evidence-based psychological therapies and interventions in Scotland.* Retrieved from https://www.nes.scot.nhs.uk/our-work/matrix-a-guide-to-delivering-evidence-based-psychological-therapies-in-scotland/

Royal College of Psychiatrists. (2021). *Workforce census 2021.* Retrieved from https://www.rcpsych.ac.uk/docs/default-source/improving-care/workforce/census-2021-completed-draft.pdf?sfvrsn=191319cb_2

Scottish Government. (2021). *Independent review into the delivery of forensic mental health services: Final report.* Retrieved from https://www.gov.scot/publications/independent-forensic-mental-health-review-final-report/

Scottish Government. (2022a). *Scottish Mental Health Law Review: Final report.* Retrieved from https://webarchive.nrscotland.gov.uk/20230327160310/https://cms.mentalhealthlawreview.scot/wp-content/uploads/2022/09/SMHLR-FINAL-Report-.pdf

Scottish Government. (2022b). *Understanding the mental health needs of Scotland's prison population.* Retrieved from https://www.gov.scot/binaries/content/documents/govscot/publications/research-and-analysis/2022/09/understanding-mental-health-needs-scotlands-prison-population/documents/understanding-mental-health-needs-scotlands-prison-population-research-summary/understanding-mental-health-needs-scotlands-prison-population-research-summary/govscot%3Adocument/understanding-mental-health-needs-scotlands-prison-population-research-summary.pdf

The Scottish Office. (1999). *Health, social work and related services for mentally disordered offenders in Scotland, NHS MEL(1999)5.* Edinburgh, Scotland: Department of Health. Retrieved from https://www.publications.scot.nhs.uk/files/1999-05.pdf

Thomson, L., & Rees, C. (2023). Long-term outcomes of the recovery approach in a high-security mental health setting: A 20 year follow-up study. *Frontiers in Psychiatry, 23.* https://doi.org/10.3389/fpsyt.2023.1111377/full

United Kingdom. (1975). *Criminal Procedure (Scotland) Act 1975, c. 21.* Retrieved from https://www.legislation.gov.uk/ukpga/1975/21/contents

United Kingdom. (1995). *Criminal Justice (Scotland) Act 1995, c. 20.* Retrieved from https://www.legislation.gov.uk/ukpga/1995/20/contents

United Kingdom. (1998). *Human Rights Act 1998, c. 42.* Requested from https://www.legislation.gov.uk/ukpga/1998/42/contents

United Kingdom, Acts of the Scottish Parliament. (2003a). *Criminal Justice (Scotland) Act 2003.* Retrieved from https://www.legislation.gov.uk/asp/2003/7/contents

United Kingdom, Acts of the Scottish Parliament. (2003b). *Mental Health (Care and Treatment) (Scotland) Act 2003.* Retrieved from https://www.legislation.gov.uk/asp/2003/13/contents

United Kingdom, Acts of the Scottish Parliament. (2010). *Criminal Justice and Licensing (Scotland) Act 2010.* Retrieved from https://www.legislation.gov.uk/asp/2010/13/contents

United Kingdom, Acts of the Scottish Parliament. (2019). *Age of Criminal Responsibility (Scotland) Act 2019.* Retrieved from https://www.legislation.gov.uk/asp/2019/7/contents

# 17 Spain

*Vicenç Tort-Herrando and Carles Martín-Fumadó*

## Brief Description

| | |
|---|---|
| **Location** | Spain is located in southwestern Europe on the Iberian Peninsula. |
| **Size** | 505,990 km$^2$ |
| **Population** | 47.4 million |
| **Languages** | Spain is a multilingual state. Spanish (Castilian) is the official national language, spoken natively by 74% of the population. Additionally, Catalan (17%), Galician (7%), and Basque (2%) are co-official languages in their respective regions. |
| **Political system** | Spain is a parliamentary monarchy, combining a secular parliamentary democracy led by the Prime Minister (Head of Government) with a hereditary monarchy, where the King serves as Head of State. The Spanish Constitution of 1978 establishes the separation of powers into the executive, legislative, and judicial branches. |

## Legal System

The Spanish Constitution of 1978 provides the legal framework for Spain. The Spanish judicial system primarily follows an inquisitorial model, and ordinary jurisdiction is categorised into four areas of law: civil, criminal (penal), administrative, and labour courts. The legal system includes various courts, such as civil courts, commercial courts, and family law courts for civil cases; and examining courts, criminal courts, gender-based violence courts, prison supervision courts, and juvenile courts for criminal cases. The Spanish judicial system follows a hierarchical structure with the Supreme Court at the top, followed by the National High Court, High Courts of Justice, provincial courts, and various lower courts.

The issue of criminal responsibility for offenses is addressed in the criminal courts. Experts are qualified to advise the judicial authority on the medical, biological, or psychological conditions that may have affected a person at the time of the alleged commission of a crime. In Spain, this expert assessment is known as *valoración de la imputabilidad* (assessment of imputability). This evaluation is one of the factors—arguably the most important from a psychiatric

DOI: 10.4324/9781003376248-20

perspective—that judges consider when determining criminal responsibility. Additionally, judicial proceedings in Spain follow a system of double instance, meaning that any judgement can be appealed to a higher court within the same jurisdiction, allowing for the re-evaluation of aspects disputed by either party.

### *Mental Health Laws*

Spain does not have legislation specific to mental health. Instead, mental health regulations are incorporated into different health laws, most notably, the General Health Law (*Ley General de Sanidad*) 14/1986 of 25 April 1986. This law establishes the principles of health care, including mental health services. Article 18 of this law assigns the responsibility for promoting and improving mental health to public administrations through their health services and other competent bodies. However, the key provision ensuring the full integration of mental health services within the general healthcare system—guaranteeing equal treatment for individuals with mental illness in outpatient, inpatient, and home care settings—is found in Article 20, Chapter III of the same law.

Article 20 establishes several key principles for mental health care. Mental health services should be provided at the community level, prioritising outpatient care, partial hospitalisation, and home care systems to reduce the need for full hospitalisation whenever possible. Special attention is given to child psychiatry and psychogeriatrics to address the specific needs of these populations. When hospitalisation is necessary, it should take place in psychiatric units within general hospitals rather than in separate psychiatric institutions.

Additionally, the law emphasises the development of rehabilitation and social reintegration services to ensure comprehensive care for individuals with mental illness. These services should be closely coordinated with social services to provide the necessary support for reintegration into society. Mental health and psychiatric care services within the general health system must also, in collaboration with social services, address primary prevention and the psychosocial challenges that arise from general health issues.

### *Criminal Responsibility*

In Spain, experts in forensic psychiatry are often consulted on various legal matters, with the most common being the assessment of *imputabilidad*—a defendant's criminal responsibility. Additionally, under the Criminal Procedure Law (*Ley de Enjuiciamiento Criminal*, 1882), they may evaluate a defendant's competence to stand trial (*capacidad para ser juzgado*), which involves assessing their ability to understand the proceedings, the charges against them, and the potential consequences. The Criminal Procedure Law establishes the procedural rules and guidelines for these assessments, while the Penal Code (*Código Penal,* 1995) outlines the specific circumstances under which mental illness may modify criminal responsibility. It also defines the conditions that must be met for these legal considerations to apply in each case.

Expert opinions and advice on the medical, biological, or psychological conditions that may have affected an individual during an alleged criminal offence are governed in Spanish law by the Penal Code. Articles 20 and 21 outline medical circumstances that can modify criminal responsibility. Article 20 lists conditions that, when all specified criteria are met, result in an exemption from criminal responsibility. These include mental abnormalities or disorders, temporary mental disturbances, severe intoxication or withdrawal states, perceptual disturbances (currently considered in cases of autism spectrum disorder), and rarer conditions such as what is known as 'insurmountable fear' (*miedo insuperable*). Additionally, Spanish courts assess these circumstances through expert reports from forensic doctors and psychologists, who evaluate how the condition impaired the defendant's ability to understand or control their actions. Applying these provisions is subject to judicial interpretation, ensuring each case is analysed based on its specific medical and legal context. Article 21, on the other hand, includes circumstances such as those outlined in Article 20 when not all the requirements for full exemption from criminal responsibility are met. It also covers cases where the offender acted due to a severe addiction to substances or was driven by causes or stimuli so intense that they resulted in a state of rapture, obsession, or another comparable passionate state (*arrebato, obcecación u otro estado pasional*). Additionally, Article 21 allows for considering any other circumstances of similar significance that may justify a mitigation of criminal responsibility.

## Forensic Psychiatric System

### *Structure and Function of the Forensic Psychiatric System*

In Europe, two main legal systems form the basis of most national legal frameworks: Roman and common law. Roman law serves as the foundation for most legal systems in Continental Europe, including Spain. It emphasises the psychological element of an offence, especially the concept of criminal responsibility. When an offender has a mental disorder or limited mental capacity at the time of the crime, their criminal responsibility may be considered diminished or absent.

During the 1990s, most European countries introduced legal reforms in response to changes in European and international laws concerning human rights, prison mental health, and related issues. These reforms led to a review of penal codes and mental health legislation, particularly regarding criminal responsibility, and the placement of offenders with mental illness (Tort-Herrando et al., 2018).

Spain does not have a formal forensic psychiatry system. Instead, following the legal tradition inherited from Roman law, Latin forensic medicine has shaped a system in which doctors play a key role in providing expertise in judicial proceedings—not only in forensic pathology but also in other biological aspects relevant to the legal process, including psychiatry.

These specialised doctors, who obtain their posts as civil servants through a competitive examination, are called forensic doctors (*médicos forenses*). Their expertise includes, among other areas, conducting psychiatric assessments across all judicial proceedings. However, the Spanish legal system does not exclude other medical professionals from providing expert advice to the courts. In cases involving psychiatric patients, some psychiatrists with forensic training may advise the court, typically after conducting an assessment. Consequently, psychiatrists responsible for treating psychiatric patients in prison or those subject to security measures (*medida de seguridad*)—when they have been deemed not criminally responsible due to psychiatric reasons—are considered forensic psychiatrists.

Depending on the severity of the offence, a sentence must be served in either a mental health facility or a hospital. These services range from community mental health services for minor offences to prison psychiatric hospitals for more violent crimes. These psychiatric hospitals are located in various places. For example, some are in prisons, and others are in the community. Security measures have variable lengths of stay determined by the severity of the offence. Unfortunately, official sources do not report the average length of stay for forensic psychiatry patients in Spain. As a result, there is a lack of substantial research and data on the demographic, psychosocial, and criminological characteristics of forensic psychiatric patients in Spain.

Spain's legal framework for civil jurisdiction, established by the Civil Code (*Código Civil,* 1889) and the Civil Procedure Law (*Ley de Enjuiciamiento Civil,* 2000), safeguards the rights of patients admitted to psychiatric hospitals through a regulated legal process. Depending on their mental capacity to provide informed consent, individuals may be admitted to psychiatric hospitals either voluntarily or compulsorily. In cases of compulsory admission, a forensic doctor must conduct an assessment, and the court must be notified within 24 hours. Importantly, individuals admitted to psychiatric hospitals for reasons unrelated to criminal behaviour are not considered forensic patients within Spain's criminal justice system.

### *Role of Forensic Psychiatry*

In Spain, forensic mental health experts primarily serve as medical advisers to the courts, providing expert assessments on the accused's mental state and its connection to the alleged offence in criminal proceedings. Their role includes evaluating both the accused and victims involved in the case. Forensic psychiatry patients receive treatment from psychiatrists specialising in forensics, particularly those in the prison system. Treatment options may include hospitalisation in outpatient penitentiary clinics or civil healthcare facilities. Civil treatment is typically reserved for minor offences, whereas individuals convicted of more serious crimes, such as homicide or sexual offences, are subject to imprisonment and treatment. In cases of severe offences, imprisonment may be required unless the individual demonstrates sustained mental health improvement, in which case they may transition from hospitalisation to community-based mental health services, including general psychiatric hospitals, day centres, or mental health community teams. Prisoners released from incarceration continue to receive psychiatric care from general psychiatrists under the supervision of the penal system until their sentence is fully served.

Risk assessment is not highly developed within Spain's psychiatric system, with a stronger focus on evaluating suicide risk than potential violence in patients. These assessments are often conducted informally. In forensic psychiatry, offenders with a mental illness undergo risk assessments before trial, which include standard tools such as the Psychopathy Checklist-Revised (PCL-R) and the Historical, Clinical, and Risk Management-20 (HCR-20). Additionally, more specialised tools are used for assessing the risk of sexual or gender-based violence, such as the Sexual Violence Risk-20 (SVR-20) and the Spousal Assault Risk Assessment (SARA).

Catalonia has developed a specific risk assessment tool called RisCanvi for the prison population (Departament de Justícia i Qualitat Democràtica, 2024). This tool assesses and manages risk across the entire Catalan prison system, including ordinary and open-regime prisons and conditional release centres. RisCanvi evaluates multiple types of risk, including self-directed violence, intra-institutional violence, violent recidivism, and sentence breaches. It is also applied to offenders with mental illnesses to guide their risk management and rehabilitation within the penitentiary system.

### *Qualifications or Specialised Training Required in Forensic Psychiatry*

Spain currently lacks a nationally recognised training programme for forensic psychiatry (Gómez-Durán & García-Largo, 2012). Instead, two distinct groups play a role in forensic mental health assessments: forensic doctors and psychiatrists. Forensic doctors are medical professionals specialising in legal and forensic medicine. The role of forensic doctors was formally established in 1855, leading to the creation of the Corps of Forensic Doctors (*Cuerpo de Médicos Forenses*) in 1862. To join, candidates must pass a competitive examination administered by the Ministry of Justice. Currently, the only academic requirement is a medical degree, although a specialist degree in Forensic and Legal Medicine will soon become mandatory.

As of the latest available data from 2022, there are 920 forensic doctors in Spain, with 72 of them currently on leave. These forensic doctors in Spain serve as expert court witnesses, assessing various topics, including pathology, toxicology, and psychiatry. However, they are not necessarily trained in clinical psychiatry or psychiatric treatment, although some receive specific training. Their primary role is to evaluate offenders, victims, and other relevant individuals in legal cases and submit forensic reports to the judiciary. Forensic doctors obtain their positions as civil servants through a competitive examination and work directly within the justice system.

In Spain, psychiatrists are medical doctors specialising in mental health. While there is no formal speciality training in forensic psychiatry within the country, some psychiatrists develop expertise by working in prisons or court-mandated evaluations. In other words, these professions gain experience through practice or seek additional training, sometimes abroad, to specialise in forensic psychiatry.

Psychiatrists working in prisons are responsible for providing treatment to individuals who have mental disorders and making recommendations to the courts regarding their progression to different levels of freedom. These recommendations are included in reports sent to the magistrate court, especially in cases involving security measures. Forensic doctors often collaborate with psychiatrists trained in clinical management and treatment. While forensic doctors can conduct pretrial assessments, magistrates' courts may also mandate them.

Forensic doctors in Spain follow a structured four-year residency programme in Legal and Forensic Medicine, which includes two years of training in health teaching centres and two years in various services of the Institutes of Legal Medicine and Forensic Sciences (*Institutos de Medicina Legal y Ciências Forenses*) (Arimany-Manso et al., 2020). This residency, updated by the National Commission of the Specialty of Legal and Forensic Medicine following Royal Decree 704/2020, was extended from three to four years to align with European standards set by the European Council of Legal Medicine and the European Union of Medical Specialists. The curriculum covers forensic pathology, toxicology, and legal medicine, equipping forensic doctors with the expertise required as court-appointed experts (Orden PCM/997/2022).

The general psychiatry training programme covers basic legal and forensic concepts (Orden PCM/205/2023). Although not compulsory, general psychiatry trainees can spend several months training in forensic psychiatry during their final year. Trainees interested in forensic psychiatry can enhance their training by undertaking postgraduate qualifications. Universities such as the Universitat Internacional de Catalunya, the Universidad de Barcelona, the Universidad Complutense de Madrid, and the Universidad Nacional de Educación a Distancia offer postgraduate courses specialising in forensic psychiatry and psychology. This complementary training is often delivered through a multidisciplinary approach, with psychologists, criminologists, and lawyers contributing as trainers. Such programmes help psychiatry professionals develop expertise in forensic assessments, legal procedures, and the intersection between mental health and the justice system, thereby bridging the gap left by the absence of a formal forensic psychiatry speciality in Spain.

## Forensic Psychiatry Service (Provision of Care)

### *Approaches to Forensic Psychiatric Assessment and Treatment*

Rehabilitation and treatment programmes for psychiatric patients primarily focus on managing psychiatric symptoms, with less emphasis on addressing criminogenic factors. There are no standardised assessment and treatment procedures, and clinical judgement remains the most commonly used risk assessment in daily practice. Although some assessment tools are used locally—such as the HCR-20, Structured Assessment of Protective Factors (SAPROF), and PCL-R—their application is not uniform across Spain. In Catalonia, however, all inmates undergo risk assessment using RisCanvi, as described earlier. The treatment of prisoners with severe mental disorders is mainly carried out in penitentiary psychiatric hospitals (*hospitales psiquiátricos penitenciarios*), some of which are separate institutions close to the prison centres. In the case of Catalonia, the hospital is located on the prison premises.

According to Article 25.2 of the Spanish Constitution (*Constitución Española*, 1978), sentences involving deprivation of liberty and security measures must be aimed at rehabilitation and social reintegration and not consist of forced labour. In forensic and penitentiary settings, rehabilitation programmes are based on the recovery model. The recovery model is a framework for addressing mental disorders or substance dependence that emphasises a person's potential for recovery. Rather than focusing solely on symptom management, this model views recovery as a personal journey that fosters hope and establishes a stable sense of self, supportive relationships, empowerment, social inclusion, coping skills, and meaning (Anthony, 1993). In Spain, the recovery model is crucial in forensic psychiatry, particularly in prison settings. Beyond managing psychiatric symptoms and reducing reoffending, a key objective of prison and forensic services is the social reintegration of offenders with mental illnesses.

#### *National Collaborations or Networks*

In Spain, two prominent national organisations play pivotal roles in the field of forensic psychiatry: the Spanish Society of Legal Psychiatry (*Sociedad Española de Psiquiatría Legal*) and the Spanish Society of Forensic Psychiatry (*Sociedad Española de Psiquiatría Forense*). These organisations are dedicated to advancing forensic psychiatry by organising scientific events and disseminating research findings (Sociedad Española de Psiquiatría Legal & Sociedad Española de Sanidad Penitenciaria, 2023). Additionally, sectors within the Spanish Society of Psychiatry and Mental Health (*Sociedad Española de Psiquiatría y Salud Mental*) have expressed growing interest in forensic psychiatry, particularly concerning mental health care in prisons.

## Strengths and Weaknesses

One of the key strengths of forensic psychiatry in Spain is the uniformity of legal provisions nationwide. However, significant challenges remain, including the limited availability of community mental health resources and the absence of dedicated forensic psychiatric services. Additionally, the lack of a structured, tiered system of forensic units—from high-security to low-security facilities—makes it challenging to ensure a gradual and secure transition from institutional care to community-based treatment. Stigma remains a significant barrier to rehabilitation within professional settings and the broader community. Addressing these issues is crucial to improving outcomes for forensic psychiatric patients and fostering their successful reintegration into society.

## References

Anthony, W. A. (1993). Recovery from mental illness: The guiding vision of the mental health service system in the 1990s. *Psychosocial Rehabilitation Journal*, *16*(4), 11–23. https://doi.org/10.1037/h0095655

Arimany-Manso, J., Grijalba-Mazo, M., Garrido-Lestache, E., Perea-Pérez, B., Galtés, I., Baena-Pinilla, S., et al. (2020). Legal and forensic medicine specialty in Spain: The consolidation by the medical residency system. *Spanish Journal of Legal Medicine*, *46*, 159–161. https://doi.org/10.1016/j.remle.2020.09.001

Departament de Justícia i Qualitat Democràtica. (2024). *Protocol de valoració del risc (RisCanvi)*. Retrieved from https://justicia.gencat.cat/ca/ambits/reinsercio_i_serveis_penitenciaris/serveis_penitenciaris/RisCanvi/

Gómez-Durán, E. L., & García-Largo, L. M. (2012). Training in forensic psychiatry when no nationally recognised scheme exists. *Criminal Behaviour and Mental Health*, *22*, 257–260. https://doi.org/10.1002/cbm.1840

Sociedad Española de Psiquiatría Legal, & Sociedad Española de Sanidad Penitenciaria. (2023). *Libro Blanco sobre la atención sanitaria a las personas con trastornos mentales graves en los centros penitenciarios de España*. Retrieved from https://www.psiquiatrialegal.org/libroblanco2023

Spain. (1995). *Penal Code (Código Penal)*. BOE-A-1995–25444 Ley Orgánica 10/1995, de 23 de noviembre, del Código Penal. Retrieved from https://www.boe.es/buscar/act.php?id=BOE-A-1995–25444

Spain. (1882). *Criminal Procedure Law (Ley de Enjuiciamiento Criminal)*. BOE-A-1882–6036 Real Decreto de 14 de septiembre de 1882 por el que se aprueba la Ley de Enjuiciamiento Criminal. Retrieved from https://www.boe.es/buscar/act.php?id=BOE-A-1882–6036

Spain. (1978). *Constitución Española*. Retrieved from https://www.boe.es/eli/es/c/1978/12/27/(1)/con

Spain. (1986). *General Health Law (Ley General de Sanidad)*. 14/1986 of 25 April 1986, Article 20. Retrieved from https://www.boe.es/eli/es/l/1986/04/25/14/con

Spain. (2022). *Orden PCM/997/2022, de 18 de octubre, por la que se aprueba y publica el programa formativo de la especialidad de Medicina Legal y Forense, los criterios de evaluación de los especialistas en formación y los requisitos de acreditación de las unidades docentes*. Retrieved from https://www.boe.es/boe/dias/2022/10/22/pdfs/BOE-A-2022–17310.pdf

Spain. (2023). *Orden PCM/205/2023, de 2 de marzo, por la que se aprueban y publican los programas formativos de las especialidades de Psiquiatría y Psiquiatría Infantil y de la Adolescencia, los criterios de evaluación de los especialistas en formación y los requisitos de acreditación de las Unidades Docentes Multiprofesionales de salud mental. BOE-A-2023–5700.* Retrieved from https://www.boe.es/eli/es/o/2023/03/02/pcm205

Tort-Herrando, V., Tataru, N., & Barrios-Flores, F. L. (2018). National laws and their history. In K. Goethals (Eds.), *Forensic psychiatry and psychology in Europe*. Springer. https://doi.org/10.1007/978-3-319-74664-7_2

# Part IV

# Middle East

# 18 Israel

*Assaf Shelef, Shmuel Hess, Nathan Kaspi, Michal Shayit, and Naama Barkai*

## Brief Description

| | |
|---|---|
| **Location** | Israel is in Western Asia, between the Eastern Mediterranean and the Red Sea. |
| **Size** | 21,937 km$^2$ |
| **Population** | 9.6 million |
| **Languages** | Hebrew (official) and Arabic (recognized) |
| **Political system** | Israel is a parliamentary democracy. The prime minister is the head of the government and leader of a multiparty coalition in the Parliament (Knesset). Executive power is held by the government. Legislative power is in the Parliament. The judiciary is independent of the executive and the legislature. The political system and the state principles are set out in the Basic Laws. |

## Legal System

### *Legislative Framework*

The Israeli legal system is adversarial. It is based on common law (judicial precedent) and reflects the country's history under Ottoman and British regimes before its independence. The Declaration of Israel's Independence 1948 claims a constitution will be written for Israel, although that has yet to happen. Instead, the declaration outlines the Basic Laws of Israel, which function as constitutional laws.

The judiciary system consists of three levels of courts. At the top is the Supreme Court, followed by the district and the magistrate courts. In Israel, the Supreme Court serves two distinct functions. As the Highest Appellate Court, it hears appeals from lower courts (district courts). As the High Court of Justice, it functions as a court of first instance for petitions against state authorities, public officials, and government bodies. The High Court also handles administrative and constitutional law cases, such as human rights violations, government

DOI: 10.4324/9781003376248-22

decisions, and policy disputes. Decisions made by the Supreme Court are binding on all lower courts. The district courts function as appellate courts for decisions made by the magistrate courts and serve as trial courts for significant civil and criminal cases. The magistrate courts handle civil and criminal cases at the first instance, as well as matters related to local governance, family disputes, small claims, and tenancy issues.

### *Mental Health Laws*

#### *Fitness (Competency) to Stand Trial*

A trial's outcome is determined by the defendant's ability to defend themselves with the assistance of a lawyer, comprehend their charges, grasp the roles of lawyers and judges in the court, and effectively communicate with their legal counsel. The relevant law and section is Israel's *Penal Law*, Section 34 (1977).

#### *Criminal Responsibility*

Under Section 34, an individual is not criminally responsible for the act he did, if, at the time of the act, due to an illness that harmed his spirit or to a defect in his mental capacity, he was entirely incapacitated in terms of (1) understanding what he was doing or the wrongness of his act or (2) avoiding doing the act.

It should be noted that there is an amendment to this law stating that, if the incapacitated state was induced by drugs, the defendant is held responsible for his act under the influence even if one or two of the conditions above are met.

### *Decision Makers in Forensic Psychiatry*

A judge may order a psychiatric evaluation for a defendant during the trial. After this evaluation, the patients with mental disorders may be admitted to a hospital through a court order that deems them unfit to stand trial or not responsible for their actions at the time of the crime. The courts are responsible for making decisions regarding changes in an individual's situation, such as discharges, extensions of stay, or transfers. The district psychiatrist committee has the authority to determine the hospitalization location, as mandated by the court. An appeal of the court order can be submitted to the court. The district psychiatric committee, comprising a lawyer and two psychiatrists, can discharge the patient by court order. If the defendant is released, the attorney can file charges again and request another order for hospitalization from the court. The district psychiatric committee oversees all decisions related to forensic patients, including discharges. A special psychiatric committee holds the same responsibilities for individuals accused of murder, attempted murder, and serious sex crimes.

As for civil admissions not by court order, the Israel *Treatment of Mental Patients Law, 1991,* allows compulsory hospitalization orders by the district psychiatrist. In contrast, appeals are considered by the district psychiatric committee. The order is initially restricted to one week. It may be extended for up to 14 days upon written request from the hospital's treating psychiatrist, subject to approval by the district psychiatrist. The committee can extend the order for an additional period of up to six months.

## Forensic Psychiatry System

### *Structure and Function of the Forensic Psychiatric System*

The Israeli forensic system is not formal or specific. Throughout the legal process, the judge determines whether a psychiatric evaluation is necessary to evaluate the defendant's competency or responsibility. If so, the defendant either is admitted to a hospital based on a court order or undergoes evaluation later, on an outpatient basis. The decision to admit or evaluate a patient outside of a hospital is based on factors such as the urgency of the case, the mental state and background of the defendant, their legal status, and the seriousness of the offense (*Treatment of Mental Patients Law*, 1991).

There are no dedicated hospitals or tribunals for forensic patients. However, a comprehensive network of psychiatric hospitals and outpatient clinics is available to serve psychiatric patients. Until 1997, mentally disordered offenders (MDOs) found not criminally responsible were admitted to a private psychiatric hospital, while convicted prisoners who had mental illness were transferred to the hospital wing of Ramla Prison (now called Ayalon Prison). In 1997, a new forensic psychiatry unit was established at Sha'ar Menashe Psychiatric Hospital near Hadera. This unit, equipped with 128 beds, operates at a security level ranging from medium to maximum, and serves male patients exclusively. This unit was designed for MDOs requiring an exceptionally high level of security due to a significant risk of escape. Conversely, MDOs with lower security needs can be accommodated in closed wards at psychiatric hospitals nationwide. One additional facility available for forensic patients is the secured psychiatric unit at Magen Prison near Ramla. This unit comprises 35 psychiatric beds and provides both forensic evaluations for prisoners with mental illness (defendants posttrial and during incarceration) and ongoing psychiatric care.

### *Role of Forensic Psychiatry*

Forensic psychiatry acts as a connection between psychiatry and law. Upon the judge's request, forensic psychiatrists will evaluate defendants who have committed a felony to determine their criminal responsibility and competency to stand trial. The forensic assessment involves conducting repetitive semi-structured interviews and psychodiagnostic assessments, and using specific diagnostic tools to evaluate violence, sexual violence, and malingering. Furthermore, data can be gathered from various sources, including psychiatric institutions, medical documents, forensic records, and diagnostic reports. Forensic psychiatrists are responsible for treating psychiatric patients undergoing court-ordered hospitalization. They also evaluate whether to mandate medical treatment for forensic patients after discharge. Upon deciding to discharge a patient, the psychiatric committee determines whether to change a court-issued hospitalization order to an order for outpatient treatment.

### *Forensic Psychiatry Profession*

#### *Qualifications or Specialized Training Required in Forensic Psychiatry*

In Israel, there is no subspecialization for forensic psychiatry or psychology. Child psychiatry is the only subspecialty recognized by the Israel Medical Association. In 1995, the Israel Forensic Psychiatry Association requested that forensic psychiatry be recognized as a specialty. However, the request was declined due to a lack of secure facilities and established training programs. The field of forensic psychiatry is growing in Israel, with established postgraduate programs available. There are a few courses in various universities across the country teaching forensic psychiatry and forensic psychology—for example, the Annual Forensic Psychiatry Course at the Israel Institute of Technology (Technion). The course is designed for psychiatrists (including trainees before Stage A) and mental health professionals, including social workers, psychologists, criminologists, legal advisers, psychiatric nursing managers, and other specialist physicians.

No formal specific training is required to practice forensic psychiatry or psychology.

Nevertheless, many doctors and staff members with extensive experience in the field have acquired knowledge. They now impart their expertise by training and teaching others in postgraduate programs and hospitals while on duty. In forensic psychology, the situation is similar; while there is no specific specialty, it is a growing field. In 2004, Professor Amnon Karmi established the Department of Psychology, Law, and Ethics at Haifa University. This department conducts seminars and training courses for psychologists, legal professionals, and judges in forensic psychology.

#### *National Collaborations or Networks*

There is an association for forensic psychiatry (founded in 1987). However, there is no subspecialty in forensic psychiatry for medical specialists in psychiatry.

## Forensic Psychiatry Service (Provision of Care)

### *Patient Demographics*

According to the 2021 Statistical Abstract on Mental Health in Israel (the latest available data; Ministry of Health, 2023), there were 8,073 involuntary hospital admissions, representing 34% of all psychiatric admissions that year. Specifically, 27% were civilian admissions mandated by the district psychiatrist, while 6% were court-ordered. By 2021, the rate of court-ordered psychiatric admissions in Israel stood at 0.18 per 1,000 people (Ministry of Health, 2023).

Numerous forensic patients have backgrounds marked by challenging circumstances, including low socioeconomic status, poverty, drug abuse, and violence. Only a small number of individuals face serious charges, including assault, sex crimes, weapon possession, murder, and attempted murder.

Most of the individuals are charged with minor offenses such as threats, theft, and low-grade violence. Civilly committed patients are not considered forensic patients. Only patients committed by a court order during a criminal procedure found not criminally responsible or not guilty by reason of insanity are considered forensic patients.

### *Exiting the System*

The district psychiatric committee approval is required for a patient to be discharged from the forensic system. While hospitalized, the attending doctor may propose discharge to the committee, which will then determine whether to approve or deny the request and potentially extend the stay. The doctor's decision is based on psychiatric clinical evaluation, risk assessment, follow-up by nursing staff, and input from the patient's family and multidisciplinary team. If the committee approves discharge, the patient will promptly leave the hospital and be referred for mandatory medical treatment at an outpatient clinic (*Treatment of Mental Patients Law*, 1991).

In terms of the length of stay, the judge establishes a maximum hospitalization period through a court order, which coincides with the duration the defendant would have spent in prison if convicted. However, in reality, the judge's set time frame is not obligatory and does not affect the typical length of stay, which is generally much shorter than the judge's imposed maximum period. Individuals convicted of crimes with a maximum punishment of three years typically spend approximately six months in the hospital for treatment. Those guilty of more severe offenses, like murder or attempted murder, are likely to serve half the maximum sentence determined by the judge.

For example, when the judge establishes a maximum hospitalization duration of 20 years, the typical length of stay would be around 10 years. It is crucial to understand that the hospital stay is intended for therapy, not punishment. The decision to discharge is made based on medical assessments of the patient's mental state and the potential risk they pose to society. The severity of the offense is not the only factor taken into account. Other factors related to the severity of the individual's current mental condition are also considered.

### *Approaches to Assessment and Treatment*

While hospitalized under a court order, the MDO receives medical treatment similar to that given to any other patient in a psychiatric hospital in Israel. A psychiatrist provides treatment, prescribes medication, conducts physical examinations, refers the individual to a psychologist for therapy sessions, and offers assistance from a social worker or occupational therapist. The MDO participates in therapy groups like art, music, and sports. In general, in psychiatric hospitals, there are no clinical criminologists. Some clinical criminologists provide legal assessment and therapy for patients in the forensic unit at Sha'ar Menashe Hospital, Abarbanel Mental Hospital, and Magen Prison Psychiatric Ward. Clinical criminologists evaluate and provide treatment in forensic and clinical settings. They specialize in evaluating and treating specific elements of the forensic population, such as violence and sexual violence assessments.

'Rehabilitation Basket' is a set of services provided to eligible individuals under the *Rehabilitation of the Mentally Disabled in the Community Law* (Lerner et al., 2012). Its purpose is to help individuals coping with mental illness integrate into the community and improve their quality of life.

The Rehabilitation Basket includes a wide range of services across different areas:

- Housing—Supported living arrangements such as hostels, supervised housing, and independent apartments
- Employment—Vocational rehabilitation programs, professional training, job placement assistance, and employment support
- Education—Support for academic, vocational, or secondary education
- Social and leisure activities—Social groups, recreational programs, and adapted leisure activities
- Additional services—Personal guidance, family support, psychosocial assistance, and more

Eligibility for Rehabilitation Basket services is determined by a professional committee within the Ministry of Health based on medical and functional criteria.

To get these rehabilitation benefits, the patient has to apply and provide a recommendation from the treating psychiatrist. This procedure is done mainly when the hospitalization is consensual. That means that, after the district psychiatric committee approves the discharge of the patient admitted by court order, they must agree to stay, willingly, in the hospital to attain rehabilitation, which, unfortunately, rarely happens. In rare cases, individuals admitted by court order are also eligible for these rehabilitation benefits (Lerner et al., 2012).

There are also options for rehabilitation in outpatient clinics, under a forced medical treatment basis recommended by the treating psychiatrist in the hospital, in which there is some enforcement of the patient's arrival or regular follow-ups (Lerner et al., 2012).

With that in mind, the Rehabilitation Basket focuses on improving the criminogenic risk factors such as housing solutions for the patient, assisted jobs, and meetings with a social worker. This guide helps with day-to-day tasks as well as social occupations (Lerner et al., 2012).

## Strengths and Weaknesses

An effective treatment system is in place for forensic patients who are hospitalized. While not perfect, the team includes qualified psychiatrists, psychologists, criminologists, nursing staff, social workers, and other professionals. The management of forensic patients in Israel reflects years of experience in forensic psychiatry.

The primary weakness of the system in Israel is the absence of specialized facilities designated for forensic patients. Forensic patients are often transferred to general psychiatric hospitals, which may not always be equipped to meet their specific needs. For example, patients might be discharged sooner without considering their safety conditions and requirements. Moreover, they may quickly stabilize medically and not require hospitalization from a general psychiatric standpoint. Due to the limited number of beds in a general psychiatric hospital, forensic patients may be discharged early once they have stabilized, as there is a high demand for hospital beds. Moreover, the idea that a general psychiatric hospital may not be the most suitable environment for them can lead to early discharge. In these cases, the patients will likely return to their familiar environment and may reoffend.

Another disadvantage of placing forensic patients in general psychiatric hospitals is that they are often mixed with other psychiatric patients who are not considered 'forensic' within the same ward. Placing MDOs, who pose a very high risk for violence, alongside patients with low risk could expose the low-risk patients to significant risks of physical, verbal, sexual, and financial abuse due to antisocial behaviors by the high-risk patients. It is imperative to establish dedicated long-term facilities for forensic patients specializing in forensic psychiatry to address recidivism effectively.

Another weakness lies in how the system is perceived by the public. When an individual considered fit to stand trial commits a crime, they are sent to a correctional facility for a designated period as mandated by a judge. When an individual unfit to stand trial commits a crime, their duration in the hospital may not accurately indicate the gravity or nature of the offense. This aspect can also be seen as a strength of our system, highlighting its compassion. There are situations where individuals with severe mental illness should not be subject to the same penalties as those without mental illness.

## References

Israel. (1977). *Penal Law*, §34/H, p. 12.

Israel. (1991). *Treatment of Mental Patients Law*.

Lerner, Y., Hornik-Lurie, T., & Zilber, N. (2012). The effect of the implementation of the Rehabilitation of the Mentally Disabled in the Community Law in Israel on the pattern of psychiatric hospitalizations: A national case register study. *International Journal of Mental Health, 41*(3), 45–59.

Ministry of Health. (2023). *Mental health in Israel: Statistical abstract 2021* (p. 114). Ministry of Health.

# 19 Kuwait

*Abdulmohsen Al-Humoud*

## Brief Description

| | |
|---|---|
| **Location** | Kuwait is a country in West Asia, on the northern edge of the Arabian Peninsula, at the head of the Persian Gulf. |
| **Size** | 17,818 km$^2$ |
| **Population** | Just over 4 million, with almost 3 million being non-Kuwaitis. |
| **Languages** | Arabic is the official language, and at least 13 other languages are commonly used. |
| **Political system** | Kuwait is a constitutional monarchy where the Emir is the head of state and the executive power. The head of government is the Prime Minister, appointed by the Emir. |

## Legal System

### *Legal Context*

Kuwait's government consists of three key branches: the Executive Branch, the Legislative Branch, and the Judicial Branch. The Legislative Branch is represented by the National Assembly (*Majlis Al-Umma*), which comprises 50 members elected by the people. It is responsible for enacting laws, overseeing the government, approving budgets, and questioning ministers. The Judicial Branch includes courts of first instance, courts of appeal, the Supreme Court, and the Constitutional Court (Constitute Project, n.d.).

Kuwait follows a civil law system modelled on the French legal system, which is primarily secular. Sharia law applies only to family law for Muslim residents, while non-Muslims in Kuwait are governed by secular family law. The legal system of Kuwait, like that of most Gulf Cooperation Council countries, is a hybrid system primarily derived from Egyptian law and influenced by British common law, French civil law, and Islamic legal principles (Induragi, 2017).

DOI: 10.4324/9781003376248-23

***Mental Health Law***

Historically, Kuwait operated without a dedicated mental health law. Although mental health professionals and legislators made multiple attempts to draft such a law, repeated parliamentary dissolutions hindered the finalisation of previous drafts (Al-Humoud et al., 2018). However, in 2018, the Ministry of Health appointed a new team to draft a mental health law. This team included consultant psychiatrists and legal experts from both the Ministry of Health and Parliament. In developing the draft, the team examined several international mental health laws, including Ontario's *Mental Health Act, 1990* (Ontario, 1990) and *Health Care Consent Act, 1996* (Ontario, 1996); British Columbia's *Mental Health Act, 1996* (Government of British Columbia, 1996); the *Criminal Code of Canada, 1985* (Government of Canada, 1985); Egypt's *Law No. 71 of 2009 for the Care of Mentally Ill Patients* (Egypt, 2009); Qatar's *Law No. 16 of 2016 on Rights of Patients with Mental Illness* (Qatar, 2016); and the Kingdom of Saudi Arabia's *Mental Health Care Law, 2014* (Kingdom of Saudi Arabia, 2014). These laws served as references, ensuring that Kuwait's new mental health law would be uniquely shaped to provide the right balance between public safety and the protection of the rights of patients with mental illness.

The finalised law, Law No. 14 of 2019 (*Kuwait Mental Health Law*), was officially enacted in February 2019, making it Kuwait's first comprehensive legal framework governing mental health (*Kuwait Mental Health Law*, 2019). The law comprises 40 sections and aligns with international best practices.

Law No. 14 established a Supreme Council of Mental Health, modelled on Egypt's system, to oversee all mental health-related affairs, including the Review and Assessment Board (RAB). Inspired by Canada's Consent and Capacity Board and Review Board, the RAB plays a central role in reviewing involuntary admissions, treatment decisions, and forensic psychiatric cases. The law sets a 72-hour assessment period, following Ontario's *Mental Health Act*, and allows involuntary admission for up to two weeks with RAB approval. Further extensions can be granted for one, three, and six months, all requiring RAB approval. However, admissions beyond six months need approval from the Supreme Council, a system influenced by Saudi Arabia (*Kuwait Mental Health Law*, 2019).

Kuwait's forensic psychiatry provisions are unique, incorporating elements from Canada's *Criminal Code*. The law defines procedures for forensic detention, conditional discharge, and final discharge. At the same time, treatment decisions follow Ontario's *Health Care Consent Act*, ensuring that no psychiatric treatment is administered without consent except in emergencies. Legal protections include an appeal process for RAB decisions, with cases escalating to a legal board and, if necessary, the courts. The burden of proving incapacity rests on the party raising the issue, safeguarding patient autonomy. Additionally, the law introduces community treatment orders and mandates the establishment of residential care homes for individuals with mental illnesses without housing (*Kuwait Mental Health Law*, 2019).

*Review and Capacity Board*

Before the enactment of Law No. 14, the admission and discharge processes to and from psychiatric facilities in Kuwait, such as the Kuwait Centre for Mental Health (KCMH), largely depended on a family member's consent, which raised serious ethical concerns. Without legal backing, psychiatrists could not admit patients without a relative's consent (Al-Humoud et al., 2018). In many instances, families refused to authorise the admission of individuals who posed a significant risk to themselves or others, leaving mental health professionals powerless to intervene effectively. Furthermore, families could refuse to discharge their relatives even after medical clearance, resulting in unnecessary delays in patient release (Al-Humoud et al., 2018). The absence of comprehensive mental health legislation left healthcare providers unable to address such critical situations, often exposing them to public scrutiny and legal liability, particularly in cases where adverse events, such as crimes committed by untreated individuals, occurred.

On the other hand, another ethical dilemma arose when families refused to discharge patients who no longer met the criteria for hospitalisation. This scenario posed a moral dilemma for healthcare professionals: either discharge patients without the consent of their families, potentially exposing them to risks in the community, or continue to keep them hospitalised unnecessarily, thereby infringing on their autonomy and personal freedoms. Both scenarios highlighted the urgent need for a legal framework that balances the rights of patients with the responsibilities of healthcare providers.

In response to these challenges, KCMH established the Review and Capacity Board (RCB) in 2017. This innovative model was inspired by two Canadian tribunal systems: the Consent and Capacity Board, which oversees matters related to involuntary treatment and admission in Ontario, Canada, and the Review Board, a nationally established system that adjudicates issues concerning individuals with mental disorders detained under the *Criminal Code of Canada* in forensic settings, operating at both the provincial and territorial levels across Canada (Consent and Capacity Board, n.d.; Canadian Association of Mental Health and Law, n.d.; Government of Canada, 1985, s. 672.38). The RCB was created to address both civil and forensic psychiatric issues, filling a crucial gap in Kuwait's mental health management. Comprising three consultant psychiatrists, the RCB reviews cases involving involuntary admissions, assesses patients' capacity to consent to treatment, and conducts annual reviews of forensic psychiatric patients. The board's dual mandate ensures the protection of patients' rights while also safeguarding the clinical and legal interests of healthcare professionals.

The RCB served as the conceptual foundation for developing the Review and Appeals Board (RAB), which was later formalised within Law No. 14. The RAB now operates with jurisdiction over both civil psychiatric patients and individuals admitted to the forensic unit. This legal evolution reflects the pivotal role of the RCB in shaping Kuwait's contemporary mental health framework.

### *Mental Health in Kuwait*

Globally, one in seven people (15%) experience one or more mental or substance use disorders (Whiteford et al., 2013), and Kuwait falls within that range at 14% (Ritchie et al., 2018). The stigma surrounding mental illness in the Middle East remains undeniably prevalent. It is estimated that over 90% of individuals in the region who experience mental illness do not receive the necessary treatment despite their need (Saraceno et al., 2015). Government spending on mental health worldwide has been disappointing, with the average annual expenditure on mental health being less than USD2 per person. Furthermore, most allocated funds are directed towards mental health institutions, despite the World Health Organization's recommendation to reallocate resources to community-based mental health services to improve health outcomes (World Health Organization, 2021). The number of mental health professionals globally is insufficient, with Kuwait having an estimated 3.3 psychiatrists per 100,000 people, compared to 14.6 in the United Kingdom and 12.4 in the United States (World Health Organization, 2014).

The recent directive from the World Health Organization urges all member countries to establish comprehensive mental healthcare policies and regulations, including legislative frameworks and community-based mental health services to ensure universal access (World Health Organization, 2021). It is crucial for Kuwait to implement these recommendations and update its current mental healthcare system by allocating more funding for mental health services. This would enhance training and education for both healthcare professionals and the public in the country.

#### *The Kuwait Centre for Mental Health*

The KCMH is the only publicly operated psychiatric institution in Kuwait. The Kuwaiti government continues to impose restrictions on establishing private forensic psychiatric hospitals or centres due to concerns about potential misuse by private entities, so the KCMH remains the primary provider of mental health services in the country. The Hospital for Mental and Neurological Diseases was founded in 1954, then renamed the Psychological Medicine Hospital in 1980, and the KCMH in 2013 (Eid, 2010; Zahid & Al-Zayed, 2009). With over 600 inpatient beds spread across multiple buildings, KCMH accommodates more than 7,000 patients monthly from all six provinces of Kuwait. Its psychiatric services are organised into 13 specialised units, including six adult psychiatry units serving various regions, as well as dedicated units for forensic psychiatry, geriatric psychiatry, child and adolescent psychiatry, consultation-liaison psychiatry, daycare and outreach services, rehabilitation, neurophysiology, and emergency psychiatry (Eid, 2010).

*Kuwait Addiction Treatment Centre*

The Kuwait Addiction Treatment Centre was established in the mid-1980s through an Amiri Decree (Law No. 74), initially operating with a 60-bed capacity (Zahid & Al-Zayed, 2009). Over the years, the Centre has experienced significant growth, now offering 350 beds, 180 designated for rehabilitation and 170 for acute treatment and stabilisation. The Centre provides a broad range of services, including both outpatient care and inpatient treatment, with specialised units for patients diagnosed with dual conditions—both mental illness and substance use disorders.

The Centre works closely with the Forensic Mental Health Services (FMHS) at KCMH, particularly in managing forensic patients with co-occurring mental health and substance use disorders. This collaboration ensures a comprehensive approach to care, addressing the psychiatric and legal complexities of this population. In response to the growing need for community reintegration services, the Centre established a halfway house in 2010. This facility focuses on assisting individuals in their recovery and supporting their transition back into society.

## Forensic Psychiatry System in Kuwait

### *Forensic Mental Health Services*

Established in 1981, the FMHS operates within the KCMH. It includes a dedicated hospital ward with 36 inpatient beds designated for assessment and detention purposes (Al-Humoud et al., 2024).

*Forensic Services*

The FMHS is operated by a multidisciplinary team of professionals, including two consultant psychiatrists, a senior psychiatrist, three staff psychiatrists, three psychologists, a clinical psychologist, and a social worker. In addition, a specialised clinic within the prison—an extension of the FMHS—is staffed by two psychiatrists and three psychologists. This set-up ensures comprehensive mental health support within the correctional system.

The FMHS provides a comprehensive range of services for both inpatient and outpatient care. Inpatient care primarily focuses on court-ordered forensic assessments, including evaluations of criminal responsibility, fitness to stand trial, and risk assessments requested by the authorities. It also offers treatment for detained forensic patients and manages complex cases in prisons that exceed the scope of standard prison health care. Outpatient services include follow-up care for discharged forensic patients or those on conditional leave, court-ordered competency assessments, consultations with other psychiatric services, and rehabilitation programmes to reintegrate forensic patients into society through therapy, risk management, and medical treatment.

The FMHS plays a crucial role in rehabilitation by offering both individual and group therapy, vocational support, and social reintegration strategies. These services are designed to reduce recidivism and support recovery. Additionally, the FMHS serves as an educational centre, providing forensic psychiatry training for medical students, psychiatry residents, and healthcare professionals. This includes workshops focused on risk assessment and violence management.

*Referral Categories*

Cases referred to the FMHS are primarily categorised as criminal or civil. In criminal cases, the majority involve evaluations of criminal responsibility and violence risk assessments, with only a small proportion addressing fitness to stand trial. In civil cases, the focus is mainly on court-ordered assessments of financial capacity, evaluating the ability of individuals diagnosed with severe mental illness to manage their finances. Families often request these assessments to appoint a guardian to manage the individual's finances. Additional civil referrals may include evaluations for fitness for duty, contractual competency, child custody and parenting abilities, as well as assessments related to impairment or disability resulting from mental illness.

*Assessment Procedures*

Unlike practices in many Western countries, where a single psychiatrist typically conducts forensic assessments, Kuwait mandates that a committee of three psychiatrists conduct all forensic psychiatric evaluations. This structure reflects the preferences of legal authorities, who generally request assessments be handled by expert panels (Al-Humoud et al., 2024).

*Referral Sources*

Criminal cases involving felonies are usually brought to court by prosecutors, while the Department for General Investigation, under the Ministry of Interior, handles referrals related to infractions and misdemeanours. When individuals with mental illness are found not criminally responsible due to their disorder, courts typically issue detention orders. Public prosecutors also have the authority to order detention if an individual with a documented mental illness is deemed a threat to public safety (Al-Humoud et al., 2024).

*Assessment and Detention Process*

When a court requests an assessment of an individual's criminal responsibility, the forensic psychiatry team conducts a thorough evaluation. Depending on the case's complexity, the individual may be admitted to the FMHS for a period ranging from several days to a few weeks. If the court agrees with the forensic team's opinion that the individual is not criminally responsible due to a mental disorder, it can order their detention at the FMHS within KCMH. The individual remains detained until the court, following recommendations from the forensic psychiatric team, determines they are fit for discharge (Al-Humoud et al., 2024).

### *Kuwait Criminal Act and Forensic Psychiatry*

The *Kuwait Criminal Act* (Kuwait, 1960a) establishes the legal framework governing criminal responsibility in Kuwait, specifically in Sections 22 and 23.

#### *Section 22: Criminal Responsibility and Mental Disorders*

This section stipulates that an individual is not criminally responsible for actions committed if, at the time of the offence, they were incapable of understanding the nature and quality of their actions or lacked the capacity for rational decision making due to a mental disorder, cognitive impairment, or other abnormal mental conditions. In such cases, if the individual poses a risk to public safety, the court may mandate admission to a treatment facility until the underlying issue is resolved (Kuwait, 1960a).

#### *Section 23: Substance-Induced Disorders*

This section addresses criminal responsibility concerning substance-induced states. It absolves individuals of criminal responsibility if their impairment resulted from involuntary ingestion of substances, unawareness of the substance's presence, or if the substance caused a mental disorder. In the latter case, the provisions of Section 22 apply. In other words, Kuwaiti criminal law does not absolve responsibility for crimes resulting from the voluntary ingestion of alcohol or illicit substances (Kuwait, 1960a).

### *Fitness to Stand Trial*

The assessment of fitness to stand trial is governed by Section 118 of the Procedures and Penal Trials Law. This provision mandates the suspension of legal proceedings if the accused is found, through forensic evaluation, to be mentally ill, cognitively impaired, or otherwise incapable of adequately defending themselves. Proceedings may resume once the individual regains the capacity to participate in their defence (Kuwait, 1960b).

#### Kuwait Mental Health Law *of 2019: Reforming the Forensic System*

After extensive deliberations and multiple drafts, Kuwait enacted the *Mental Health Law* in 2019, marking a significant milestone in developing forensic mental health services (*Kuwait Mental Health Law*, 2019). Recognising the challenges of amending the existing *Criminal Act*, policymakers included specific provisions addressing forensic mental health within this new legislation. These reforms were made possible through collaborations between the Ministry of Health, the Kuwaiti Parliament, and the Public Prosecutor's office.

### ***Key Additions and Reforms***

#### *Definition of Mental Illness*

Before the enactment of Law No. 14, no legal definition of mental illness existed in Kuwaiti legislation. Section 1 defines mental illness as "a mental or psychological condition caused by an imbalance in mental or psychological functioning that impairs the person from functioning within society, excluding substance use and addiction". Notably, the exclusion of substance use disorders was influenced by political considerations, a practice also observed in other Arab countries, such as Saudi Arabia (*Kingdom of Saudi Arabia Mental Health Care Law*, 2014).

#### *Establishment of the Review and Assessment Board*

Sections 20 and 21 of the law explicitly address forensic mental health. Section 20 mandates the formation of a committee of mental health experts appointed by the Ministry of Health to conduct assessments upon request from the courts or the Public Prosecutor's Office. Section 21 stipulates that when courts order the detention of individuals with mental illness, they must be treated in a forensic mental health facility under the Ministry of Health. Furthermore, the Review and Assessment Board must be notified within two weeks of detention, and detention decisions must be reviewed at least annually.

#### *Conditional Discharge and Annual Review*

Law No. 14 introduces provisions for conditional leave and discharge, contingent on the individual no longer posing a significant threat to public safety. Both RAB and the detaining court must approve such decisions. The inclusion of conditional discharge mechanisms aligns Kuwait's legal framework with international best practices in forensic mental health.

#### *Clarification of Detention and Discharge Criteria*

Law No. 14 explicitly states that detention is for treatment purposes, including pharmacological interventions, psychotherapy, and other therapeutic modalities. The criteria for discharge are now clearly defined as the absence of a significant threat to public safety. This shift moves the final decision-making authority from the treating team to an independent tribunal, enhancing procedural fairness.

*Appeal Process*

Section 7 of Law No. 14 introduces an appeal mechanism, enabling individuals detained to contest decisions made by the RAB. Appeals are reviewed by a legal board, providing an additional layer of oversight and safeguarding the rights of individuals subject to involuntary treatment. Furthermore, patients have the option to appeal the decision to the court.

## Strengths and Weaknesses

Kuwait's forensic psychiatry system has made significant progress with enacting *Kuwait Mental Health Law* No. 14 of 2019, which established a clear legal framework, strengthened patient rights, and introduced independent oversight through the RAB. The system benefits from structured forensic assessments, multidisciplinary services, and alignment with international legal models, ensuring fairness and accountability in patient management.

However, critical challenges persist. Limited infrastructure—represented by the existence of only one forensic psychiatric facility—combined with the absence of private forensic psychiatric centres and a shortage of forensic psychiatrists strain the system's capacity. Moreover, the lack of community-based rehabilitation programmes, such as halfway houses and employment support, hampers effective patient reintegration. Legal delays and ongoing stigma further complicate access to care and prolong forensic detentions.

While Kuwait has established a strong foundation for forensic mental health, addressing resource shortages, expanding community support, and improving coordination between the judiciary and mental health services will be crucial for creating a more effective and sustainable system.

## References


Al-Humoud, A., Al-Zayed, A., & Al-Hasan, F. (2024). Forensic mental health in Kuwait: Filling the gaps. *Psychiatry, Psychology and Law, 0*, 1–13. https://doi.org/10.1080/13218719.2023.2272913

Al-Humoud, A., Zahid, M., Ibrahim, S., Syed, T., & Naguy, A. (2018). Forensic psychiatry in Kuwait: Characterization of forensic psychiatry patients evaluated over a year in the only available forensic psychiatry unit. *International Journal of Law and Psychiatry, 60*, 12–16. https://doi.org/10.1016/j.ijlp.2018.06.010

Canadian Association of Mental Health and Law. (n.d.). *Review boards in Canada: A comprehensive guide*. Retrieved from https://www.camhl.org/review-boards-canada

Consent and Capacity Board. (n.d.). *About the consent and capacity board*. Retrieved from https://www.ccboard.on.ca/scripts/english/aboutus/index.asp

Constitute Project. (n.d.). *Kuwait's Constitution of 1962 with amendments through 1992*. Retrieved from https://www.constituteproject.org/constitution/Kuwait_1992

Egypt. (2009). *Egypt Mental Health Act*. Retrieved from https://www.mindbank.info/item/3713

Eid, S. (2010). P02–55—Forensic psychiatric services in Kuwait and the need for mental health legislation. *European Psychiatry*, *25*(S1), 675. https://doi.org/10.1016/s0924-9338(10)70669-6

Government of British Columbia. (1996). *British Columbia Mental Health Act, RSBC 1996, c. 288*. Retrieved from https://www.bclaws.gov.bc.ca/civix/document/id/complete/statreg/00_96288_01

Government of Canada. (1985). *Criminal Code (RSC, 1985, c. C-46), s. 672.38*. Retrieved from https://laws-lois.justice.gc.ca/eng/acts/c-46/

Induragi, D. (2017). *The legal system of Kuwait: An evaluation of its applicability*. Academia. Retrieved from https://www.academia.edu/27337551

Kingdom of Saudi Arabia. (2014). *Mental Health Care Law, 2014*. https://www.mindbank.info/item/5921

Kuwait. (1960a). *Criminal Act*. Retrieved from https://www.e.gov.kw/sites/kgoenglish/Pages/Business/InfoSubPages/LawsAndRegulations.asx & http://www.helplinelaw.com/article/kuwait/73

Kuwait. (1960b). *Law No 16 Penal Code 1960 and Law No 17 Penal Proceedings and Trials Code 1960*.

Kuwait. (2019). *Mental Health Law*. Retrieved from http://site.eastlaws.com/GeneralSearch/Home/ArticlesTDetails?MasterID=1935295

Ontario. (1990). *Ontario Mental Health Act*, R.S.O. 1990, c. M.7. Retrieved from https://www.ontario.ca/laws/statute/90m07

Ontario. (1996). *Ontario Health Care Consent Act*, 1996, S.O. 1996, c. 2, Sched. A. Retrieved from https://www.ontario.ca/laws/statute/96h02

Qatar. *Law No. 16 of 2016 on Rights of Patients with Mental Illness*. Retrieved from http://www.ilo.org/dyn/natlex/natlex4.detail?p_lang=en&p_isn=105416&p_country=QAT

Ritchie, H., Roser, M., & Dattani, S. (2018, April). *Mental health*. Our World in Data. https://ourworldindata.org/mental-health

Saraceno, B., Gater, R., Rahman, A., Saeed, K., Eaton, J., Ivbijaro, G., Kidd, M., Dowrick, C., Servili, C., Funk, M. K., & Underhill, C. (2015). Reorganization of mental health services: From institutional to community-based models of care. *Eastern Mediterranean Health Journal*, *12*(7), 477–485. https://doi.org/10.26719/2015.21.7.477

Whiteford, H. A., Degenhardt, L., Rehm, J., Baxter, A. J., Ferrari, A. J., Erskine, H. E., Charlson, F. J., Norman, R. E., Flaxman, A. D., Johns, N., Burstein, R., Murray, C. J. L., & Vos, T. (2013). Global burden of disease attributable to mental and substance use disorders: Findings from the Global Burden of Disease Study 2010. *The Lancet*, *382*(9904), 1575–1586. https://doi.org/10.1016/S0140-6736(13)61611-6

World Health Organization. (2014). *Mental health atlas 2014*. Retrieved from https://www.who.int/publications/i/item/mental-health-atlas-2014

World Health Organization. (2021). *Mental health*. Retrieved from https://www.who.int/health-topics/mental-health#tab=tab_2

Zahid, M. A., & Al-Zayed, A. (2009). Psychiatry in Kuwait. *International Psychiatry*, *6*(2), 34–36.

# 20 Oman

*Badar Al Habsi and Lara Al Harthi*

## Brief Description

| | |
|---|---|
| **Location** | Oman (the Sultanate of Oman) is a country on the southeast coast of the Arabian Peninsula. |
| **Size** | 309,500 km$^2$ |
| **Population** | Approximately 5 million |
| **Languages** | Arabic is the main language, but other languages are used by some people: Belushi, originally from Iran and Pakistan; Zanzibari, originally from Zanzibar, Africa; and Al Mahri, originally from Yemen. |
| **Political system** | Oman is a monarchy ruled by a hereditary Sultan, who is the head of state and head of the government. The Sultan is a direct descendant of Said Bin Sultan, appointed in 1804. |

## Legal System

Oman's legal system is adversarial and is based on two primary legal codes: the *Penal Law* (Royal Decree No. 7/2018) and the *Civil Code* (Royal Decree No. 29/2013). The judicial system in Oman is divided into civilian and military branches. The civilian court system is structured in multiple levels, starting with courts of first instance, then courts of appeal, and, finally, the Supreme Court. The lower courts of first instance deal with the initial stages of cases, including civil, criminal, and commercial matters. The appellate courts handle appeals, with the Supreme Court serving as the highest judicial authority for civilians in Oman. The military has its own courts that handle offences committed exclusively by military personnel.

## Forensic Psychiatry System

Al-Masarra Hospital (AMH) is the only psychiatric hospital in Oman that offers services for assessing and managing forensic psychiatric patients. Forensic cases at AMH are managed in two male wards, which have a combined capacity

DOI: 10.4324/9781003376248-24

of 42 beds, and one female ward. All of these wards are classified as minimum security. The bed capacity is deemed insufficient, with 21 beds in each male ward and a limited number of beds in the female ward. These wards are designed for assessment and short-term management, as AMH lacks long-term rehabilitation services. The assessments conducted at AMH include evaluations of criminal responsibility, capacity assessments, and risk assessments. Despite this, many court orders exist to detain high-risk offenders indefinitely. In this context, judges serve as the final decision makers in forensic psychiatric cases, and their rulings have largely aligned with the expert opinions provided.

Forensic psychiatry has been significant in the Western world for many years, but it has only recently begun to gain momentum in Oman. Several factors contribute to this delay, the most notable being a lack of resources. Only one forensic psychiatrist in Oman has completed a two-year clinical fellowship in forensic psychiatry at McMaster University in Ontario, Canada.

The forensic psychiatrist is dedicated to conducting court-ordered assessments in accordance with both the *Penal Law* and the *Civil Code* of Oman. Assessments performed under the *Penal Law* generally include evaluations of criminal responsibility, mental capacity assessments, risk assessments, and comprehensive psychiatric evaluations. In contrast, assessments conducted under the *Civil Code* typically involve evaluations of capacity, fitness-to-work assessments, and assessments related to significant mental disabilities. The *Criminal Code of Oman* was recently revised, with the new version approved by His Majesty the Sultan in 2018. Article 50 of the Penal Law of Oman states,

> Whoever, at the time of the commission of the crime, is in a state of loss of perception or volition due to insanity, mental handicap or coma arising from narcotic or intoxicating drugs or substances of any kind given to him against his will or without his knowledge, or for any other reason science determines that it causes loss of perception or volition, shall not be criminally responsible.
> (Royal Decree No. 7/2018, 2018, Article 50)

However, it is important to note that the concept of 'fitness to stand trial' is not explicitly addressed in the *Penal Law*.

In Oman, all forensic psychiatry assessments are conducted in a hospital setting, unlike in the Western world, where forensic psychiatry teams are typically situated in prisons. After receiving the offender's court orders from the unit coordinators at the hospital, the forensic psychiatrist conducts an initial assessment in the outpatient department at AMH. Based on this assessment, a decision will be made about whether the individual will be admitted for further observation or whether an outpatient assessment will be sufficient. During the assessment period, whether the patient is admitted or seen in the outpatient department, a forensic psychologist will conduct essential psychometric tests, including cognitive and IQ assessments, personality evaluations, and assessments for malingering or feigned symptoms, as well as risk assessments for violence. Additionally, family history may be gathered through interviews with the patient's family. Concurrently, interviews with witnesses and victims can also take place, and further imaging tests, such as CT scans, may be performed based on clinical judgement. Collaboration with the general psychiatry department is essential to the assessment process. Once the assessment is completed, a final medical board is convened, with the forensic psychiatrist leading the meeting to provide recommendations and opinions. A report is then issued and sent to the court via Oman's Public Prosecution.

Once individuals are found not criminally responsible due to a mental disorder, a court order is issued for their detention in protective custody at AMH. They will undergo annual reassessments, and, if it is determined that they no longer pose a risk of reoffending, a report will be submitted to the court seeking approval for their community reintegration.

Until the end of 2023, dangerous offenders were held at the central jail, after which they were all transferred to the AMH. This reflects the growth of forensic psychiatry in a developing country like Oman and highlights the increasing awareness of the importance of providing appropriate care and treatment for psychiatric patients. Moreover, research has shown that, due to the differing objectives of the general prison system and therapeutic interventions, it is almost impossible to treat offenders with mental disorders effectively within a prison environment. This is because the primary aim of the prison system is to maintain security and order, whereas therapeutic interventions focus on rehabilitation and mental health treatment. As such, segregating psychiatric patients from the general prison population reduces the risks for vulnerable individuals, such as those with mental disorders (Konrad, 2024).

For patients who were previously incarcerated, risk assessments are conducted at AMH either annually or every two years, depending on the court's order. This assessment incorporates both clinical judgement and structured risk assessment tools such as the Psychopathy Checklist-Revised (PCL-R), the Historical Clinical Risk Management-20 (HCR-20), and the Structured Assessment of Protective Factors for violence risk (SAPROF). If the final risk assessment indicates that the patient poses a significant risk with low protective factors, the patient will be returned to the central jail and reassessed after two years. Conversely, if the patient is deemed to pose a low risk, the judge will issue a final decision for community reintegration.

## Mental Health Laws

The legislative process in Oman involves several key steps, with His Majesty the Sultan of Oman playing a central role in the country's legal system. As both head of state and government, the Sultan holds supreme authority and has the exclusive power to issue and ratify laws. Consequently, all legislation must receive the

Sultan's approval to become legally binding, giving him ultimate control over the country's legal and political framework.

The Sultan plays a crucial role in the approval and issuance of royal decrees, which officially enact laws. The legislative process starts with the Council of Ministers, which reviews and approves proposed laws before submitting them to higher legislative bodies, such as the Council of Oman. This council consists of two chambers: the State Council (*Majlis Al-Dawla*) and the Shura Council (*Majlis Al-Shura*). After these councils review and deliberate on the proposed law, it is sent to the Sultan for final approval, at which point it becomes legally binding (Wigley, 2020).

Oman currently lacks specific mental health legislation, which presents significant challenges in the sector. However, key government entities have finalised and approved a proposed *Mental Health Act*, including the Ministry of Justice and Legal Affairs, the Ministry of Social Development, the Ministry of Education, and the Royal Oman Police, among others. This development follows the Ministerial Circular outlining the *Mental Health Act* framework (Ministry of Health, 2023). The proposed legislation is now in the legal review process under the Higher Council before it can move forward to enactment.

After a patient is discharged from the forensic system, reconnecting them with professional forensic psychiatric services can be very challenging, especially if they have not followed their medication regimen or have declined follow-up appointments with their psychiatrist. Unfortunately, in many instances, the only way for these individuals to re-enter treatment is by reoffending, which leads to court-mandated intervention. This lack of structured community integration results in longer stays within the forensic system, as conditional release into the community is not allowed, even for individuals assessed as low risk.

In 2014, a proposal was introduced to establish an extended forensic psychiatry rehabilitation centre, but it did not progress due to governance challenges arising from the involvement of multiple government sectors. However, a new proposal is currently being considered for a long-term detention facility, which the Ministry of Social Development will manage in collaboration with other sectors, including the Ministry of Health and the Royal Oman Police.

## Forensic Psychiatry Service (Provision of Care)

Oman currently lacks evidence-based rehabilitation programmes specifically designed for offenders. However, psychologists in forensic psychiatry units apply evidence-based methods to address individual patient issues, such as anxiety disorders, depression, trauma, social skills, cognitive restructuring, and anger management. A crucial component of rehabilitation is psychoeducation, which enables patients to comprehend their psychiatric diagnoses, appreciate the importance of adhering to their medication regimens, and gain confidence in their treatment plans. These initiatives are vital for reducing criminogenic risk factors and promoting long-term stability.

In Oman, social workers play a vital role by collaborating with patients' families and the Ministry of Social Development to provide essential support services. They help establish stable living environments and, when appropriate, facilitate a monthly stipend. These interventions strengthen protective factors for patients and reduce the risk of recidivism. By attending regular follow-up appointments in the outpatient department with their psychiatrist and adhering to prescribed medications, individuals released after serving their sentences can work towards leading fulfilling and enriching lives.

## Strengths and Weaknesses

In Oman, forensic psychiatry has several strengths and weaknesses. One of its key strengths is the presence of Al-Massara Hospital, a dedicated facility that offers comprehensive services for assessing, managing, and treating offenders with mental disorders. The expertise of the psychiatrists and psychologists in the forensic psychiatry unit is essential for conducting accurate assessments and evaluations, formulating expert opinions, and making decisions about managing forensic psychiatry patients. Additionally, Oman's legal framework, which includes royal decrees and provisions for patients deemed not responsible for criminal acts, significantly enhances the integration of forensic psychiatry within the legal system.

However, there are also significant weaknesses. There is a clear lack of resources to address the increasing number of forensic cases in Oman, and the limited bed capacity at Al-Massara Hospital is considered inadequate. Furthermore, there are considerable challenges in providing follow-up care after a patient is discharged from the forensic system, making it difficult to reconnect them with professional services. This often results in extended stays in the forensic system or a higher risk of reoffending. Additionally, the absence of a mental health act in Oman prevents the conditional release of patients with mental disorders, leading to longer stays in both the forensic system and the hospital. Consequently, this results in gaps in the effectiveness of treatment and rehabilitation efforts.

## References

Konrad, A. O.-W. (2024). Ethical approaches in prison psychiatry. In E. Abdalla-Filho (Ed.), *Forensic psychiatry: Clinical and ethical approach* (pp. 150–157). Newcastle upon Tyne: Cambridge Scholars Publishing.

Ministry of Health. (2023). *Ministerial circular number 255/2023.*

Royal Decree 7/2018. (2018). *The penal law.* Royal Court of Oman. Retrieved from https://oman.om/docs/default-source/default-document-library/omani-penal-law.pdf

Royal Decree No. 29/2013. (2013). *Civil code of Oman.* Royal Court of Oman. Retrieved from https://www.lexismiddleeast.com/law/Oman/SultaniDecree_29_2013

Wigley, T. (2020, March). *GlobaLex.* Retrieved from https://www.nyulawglobal.org/globalex/oman1.html#:~:text=The%20Sultan's%20powers%20include%20the,Peace%20and%20War%2C%20issuing%20and

# 21 Türkiye

*Yasin Hasan Balcıoğlu and Fatih Öncü*

Reproduced, with modifications, from Balcıoğlu, Y. H., Öncü, F., and Kennedy, H. G. (2023). Forensic psychiatry in Turkiye. *International Review of Psychiatry*, *36*(7), 739–755. https://doi.org/10.1080/09540261.2023.2255255, with the permission of Taylor & Francis.

**Brief Description**

| | |
|---|---|
| **Location** | Türkiye (Republic of Türkiye) is a transcontinental country in Eastern Europe and Western Asia. |
| **Size** | 783,562 km$^2$ |
| **Population** | 85.3 million |
| **Language** | The official language of Türkiye is Turkish. |
| **Political system** | Türkiye is a secular state under a presidential representative democracy and a constitutional republic within a pluriform multiparty system. The President (the head of state and head of government), parliament, and judiciary share powers reserved to the national government. The political system is based on a separation of powers. Executive power is exercised by the Council of Ministers, appointed and headed by the President. Legislative power is vested in the Grand National Assembly. The judiciary is independent of the executive and the legislature. |

## Legal System

### *Legislative Framework*

The Turkish legal system is based on the Continental European legal tradition, sharing its fundamental characteristics. It operates under a unified legal framework, emphasising written laws. Jurisprudence, or case law, is primarily derived from high or supreme courts in the country. The system distinguishes between public and private law and maintains a separation of judicial functions. As a unitary state, Türkiye does not have administrative regions with distinct legal

DOI: 10.4324/9781003376248-25

systems; as such, there are no 'federal' legal structures. The legislative authority of the Turkish Grand National Assembly covers the entire country, ensuring the uniform application of laws. On certain occasions, presidential decrees may have the force of law; however, they cannot contradict existing laws regulating fundamental rights and freedoms or political rights.

The Turkish legal system follows an inquisitorial system but incorporates some adversarial elements. Lawyers (i.e., solicitors) can directly question witnesses, and the use of unlawful evidence is prohibited. The judiciary operates hierarchically and consists of courts of first instance, regional courts of appeal, and the Court of Cassation (*Yargıtay*), the highest appellate authority for criminal and civil cases. The administrative system follows a similar organisational model. It includes courts of first instance, regional courts of appeal, and the Council of State (*Danıştay*), the highest appellate authority of administrative cases. The Constitutional Court (*Anayasa Mahkemesi*) oversees constitutional matters and human rights violations, and the Court of Jurisdictional Disputes (*Uyuşmazlık Mahkemesi*) resolves conflicts regarding verdicts and competencies between the judicial and administrative courts.

The Constitution states that international treaties and conventions to which Türkiye is a signatory apply directly to the national legislative, executive, and judicial authorities. Additionally, as a founding member of the Council of Europe and a party to the European Convention on Human Rights, Türkiye is subject to the jurisdiction of the European Court of Human Rights.

### *Mental Health Legislation: Current Framework in Criminal Law*

The Turkish Penal Code of 1926, which replaced the 19th-century Ottoman code partly modelled on the Napoleonic Penal Code, drew partly from the Zanardelli Code, then in effect in Italy (Sen, 2014). The current Turkish Penal Code (Law no. 5237) was enacted in 2004 and has been in force since 2005. It aligns with the core principles of criminal legislation in mainland European countries (Turkish Penal Code, Law No. 5237, 2004).

#### *Fitness to Plead*

Turkish criminal law does not explicitly recognise the concept of 'fitness to plead' or 'competence to stand trial'. Even when a defendant has a severe mental illness and lacks the capacity to understand the charges, follow proceedings, or assist in their defence, they may still be brought before the court. In some cases, if expert opinion suggests the defendant's statements are unreliable, and the court agrees, a trial of the facts may be held to ensure due process. This can lead to a finding of diminished or no criminal responsibility and diversion to mental health services for treatment.

*Criminal Responsibility*

Article 32 of the Turkish Penal Code outlines the principles governing the insanity defence and the criminal responsibility of offenders. Forensic psychiatric evaluations to assess criminal responsibility are typically carried out by a medical board (Turkish Penal Code, Law no. 5237, 2004, Article 32). Although the law does not explicitly require an opinion from a medical board or a psychiatrist, established jurisprudence gives greater weight to board opinions than to those of individual experts when criminal responsibility is at issue. This practice, however, does not require the board to be composed solely of psychiatrists. In practice, many institutions that provide expert testimony to courts or prosecutors have boards primarily—but not exclusively—made up of psychiatrists. However, mental health hospitals and high-secure forensic psychiatry units often conduct such assessments exclusively through psychiatrists.

According to Article 32/1, a person who commits an offence and is unable "to perceive the legal meaning and consequences of the offence, or [has] considerably lost the capacity to control his actions due to mental illness may not be subject to any punishment". Article 32/1 states that while punishment may not be imposed, security measures can be enforced in such cases (Turkish Penal Code, Law no. 5237, 2004, Article 32/1).

The absence of a clear legal definition of mental illness (*akıl hastalığı*) in Turkish law has created challenges in determining which mental disorders qualify for legal insanity under Article 32 of the Penal Code. This ambiguity can lead to confusion among experts regarding the criteria for mental illness as it relates to criminal responsibility. In cases involving crimes committed under the influence of severe mental disorders—such as psychotic disorders, full-blown mood episodes, moderate to severe intellectual disability, or dementia—expert assessments tend to be more consistent, as these conditions more clearly align with the timing of the offence. By contrast, in cases involving severe personality disorders, substance-induced conditions, or mild intellectual disability, experts may disagree on whether the disorder meets the threshold for legal insanity, leading to inconsistent court rulings. Nonetheless, the prevailing view among Turkish psychiatrists is that personality disorders alone do not typically affect criminal responsibility. These disorders are generally not seen as sufficient grounds for reduced legal accountability, except when they coexist with other severe mental illnesses, such as psychotic disorders.

Experts—psychiatrists in particular—in Türkiye commonly adopt a case-based approach to assessing criminal responsibility. This approach may be advantageous, as it allows for personalised evaluations rather than relying solely on predefined diagnoses. The relationship between certain mental disorders and criminal behaviour can vary widely depending on factors such as the nature of the offence, how it was committed, and the underlying motivation.

The law requires that, due to mental illness, either an individual's capacity to understand the legal meaning and consequences of their actions or their ability to control their behaviour in relation to the act must be significantly impaired. Although not explicitly stated, it is generally understood that establishing non-responsibility or diminished responsibility due to mental illness requires a demonstrable connection and temporal overlap between the disorder and the offence. In other words, the illness must substantially impair specific cognitive or volitional capacities at the time of the act. This requirement is consistent with legal standards in many countries, where non-responsibility is defined as the absence of at least one of these two elements (Tsimploulis et al., 2018).

Article 32/2 of the Penal Code provides for reduced sentences in cases where a defendant's mental capacity is significantly impaired, although not entirely absent, at the time of the offence. This applies when a mental illness or disorder substantially limits the individual's ability to control their behaviour in relation to the offence but does not meet the threshold for full non-responsibility as defined in the first paragraph. For example, this provision may apply to psychotic or mood disorders that are not in acute relapse but still affect behavioural control. In practice, it may also be invoked in cases of mild intellectual disability, particularly when accompanied by difficulties in behavioural regulation or impulse control disorders that impair volitional capacity.

For offences carrying an aggravated life sentence, the penalty may be commuted to 25 years' imprisonment. In other cases, the sentence may be reduced by up to one-sixth. The law also allows the court to impose the sentence as a security measure specific to individuals with mental illness, either fully or partially, based on the criminal responsibility opinion. This is at the court's discretion, provided that the total duration of the sentence remains unchanged (Turkish Penal Code, Law no. 5237, 2004, Article 32/2).

If a mental disorder is suspected to be related to the offence, the court may order an inpatient psychiatric evaluation (observation) for up to three weeks under Article 74 of the Turkish Penal Procedure Code (Law No. 5271). According to this article, if there are strong indications that a suspect or defendant may have a mental illness affecting their actions, the Justice of the Peace during the investigation phase or the trial court during the trial phase may order inpatient observation based on expert recommendation. This period may be extended to a maximum of three months by further order of the authorised court (Turkish Penal Procedure Code, Law no. 5271, 2004, Article 74).

Such observation is almost always considered part of the forensic psychiatric assessment for determining criminal responsibility under Article 32 of the Penal Code. Involuntary treatment during this period is not permitted unless the individual poses a risk due to a mental disorder. In these cases, a civil commitment order must be issued by a civil court under Article 432 of the Turkish Civil Code (Law No. 4721) based on an official request from the medical board (Turkish Civil Code, Law no. 4721, 2001, Article 432).

*A Comparative Legal Perspective on the Insanity Defence*

The legal framework in Türkiye differs significantly from Anglo-American criminal jurisdictions that follow the common law system. In these systems, when a mental illness negates *mens rea* required for criminal responsibility, the defendant can be found 'not guilty by reason of insanity', even if *actus reus* is established. In contrast, in the Turkish criminal law system, which aligns with mainland European legal traditions, a defendant who commits an offence under the influence of severe mental illness and is found not responsible is still subjected to a compulsory treatment order as a security measure, following a guilty verdict. However, in Türkiye, this verdict is not classified as 'not guilty by reason of insanity', 'acquittal', or 'guilty but mentally ill' and results in a 'decision not to impose a sentence'.

*Other Exemptions From Criminal Responsibility Under the Turkish Penal Code*

In addition to individuals found not criminally responsible due to mental illness, the Turkish Penal Code also provides exemptions based on age and other specific conditions. Under the 2004 Code, criminal responsibility begins at the age of 15 (Turkish Penal Code, Law no. 5237, 2004, Article 31). Offenders under the age of 12 at the time of the offence are exempt from punishment (Turkish Penal Code, Law no. 5237, 2004, Article 31/1). Those between the ages of 12 and 15 may also be exempt if a psychiatric evaluation determines they lack sufficient capacity for discernment or behavioural control (Turkish Penal Code, Law no. 5237, 2004, Article 31/2). In such cases, minors may instead be subject to security measures specifically designed for children. Juvenile offenders between 12 and 15 who are found to possess sufficient capacity and those aged 15–18 are subject to reduced sentences (Turkish Penal Code, Law no. 5237, 2004, Article 31/2–3).

The provisions outlined earlier for minors also apply to individuals who are deaf and mute, with an adjustment of three additional years to each age threshold (Turkish Penal Code, Law no. 5237, 2004, Article 33). Accordingly, no sentence is imposed on individuals under the age of 15. Those aged between 15 and 18 may receive a reduced sentence or no sentence, depending on an assessment of their capacity for discernment and behavioural control. Individuals aged between 18 and 21 at the time of the offence may be eligible for a reduced sentence.

Any person who, due to a transient condition such as diabetic ketoacidosis, an epileptic seizure, hepatic encephalopathy, or the involuntary consumption of alcohol or drugs—for example, by accident or under coercion—is unable to comprehend the legal meaning and consequences of an act they have committed, or whose ability to control their behaviour is significantly impaired, is exempt from punishment (Turkish Penal Code, Law no. 5237, 2004, Article 34/1). However,

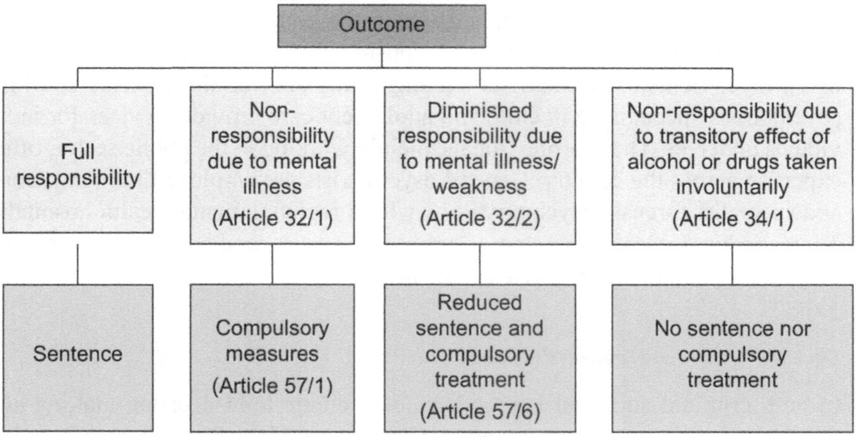


*Figure 21.1* Criminal responsibility outcomes of adults in forensic psychiatric practice according to Turkish Penal Code, 2004.

(Reproduced from Balcıoğlu, Y. H., Öncü, F., & Kennedy, H. G. (2023). Forensic psychiatry in Turkiye. *International Review of Psychiatry*, *36*(7), 739–755. https://doi.org/10.1080/09540261.2023.2255255, with the permission of Taylor & Francis.)

this exemption does not apply to individuals who commit an offence under the influence of alcohol or drugs taken voluntarily (Figure 21.1).

### *The Ongoing Efforts for a Mental Health Law in Türkiye*

Türkiye is one of several developed and developing countries that do not have any well-established mental health laws. The major professional association of psychiatrists, the Psychiatric Association of Türkiye, paved the way for the resumption of discussions on mental health laws in 1995. Since then, the association has intensively campaigned to pass a mental health law. Although the association has proposed many drafts of mental health laws in collaboration with governmental bodies, including the Ministry of Health, non-governmental organisations, and associations of other mental health professionals, the issue has remained inconclusive due to various obstacles such as upcoming elections and changes in the government (Artvinli & Uslu, 2023; Öncü, 2020). The latest draft of the mental health law was primed in 2023; however, its enactment remains pending.

### *Forensic Psychiatry in Legal Contexts: Scope and Decision Making*

#### *Role of Forensic Psychiatry*

Forensic psychiatry is not officially recognised as a medical specialisation or a higher subspecialty of psychiatry in Türkiye. As a result, the title 'forensic psychiatrist' is not formally defined within the country's medical framework. However, forensic psychiatry forms a considerable part of psychiatric practice in Türkiye. General psychiatrists treating adults provide these services, while psychiatrists specialising in child and adolescent care provide services for individuals under 18. These professionals, mainly working in the public sector, offer expertise across the country. General psychiatrists are employed in high-secure and specialist forensic psychiatry units within regional mental health hospitals. They conduct forensic assessments, provide expertise, and handle court-ordered compulsory treatments of forensic patients.

### *Decision Makers in Forensic Psychiatry*

In both criminal and civil law, independent courts hold decision-making authority in Türkiye. Public prosecutors (Prosecutor of the Republic) are a major component of criminal law, representing the public interest. They can initiate and conduct investigations on behalf of the public. They are also responsible for executing court orders and managing legal correspondence between judicial authorities. Law enforcement agencies act only under judicial instruction, playing a role in criminal investigations, particularly in the evidence-collection phase, under the supervision and direction of the public prosecutor. Notably, neither public prosecutors nor law enforcement officials are considered decision makers in the Turkish legal system, as this authority remains solely with the courts.

### *Expert Evaluation*

The roles, responsibilities, limitations, and powers of expert witnesses are defined in both the Turkish Penal Procedure Code and the Turkish Civil Procedure Code. Expert opinions are used in the adjudication and decision-making processes of independent courts. Courts or public prosecutors may appoint expert witnesses from a list maintained by the judicial commission, which includes individuals who have voluntarily applied to serve in this capacity. Institutions may also be appointed to provide expert opinions through their staff specialists or internal medical boards. These institutions—mainly public bodies such as the Council of Forensic Medicine, universities, hospitals, and other specialised scientific or technical institutions—are recognised as official sources of forensic expert opinion.

Individuals listed by the judicial commission must have at least five years of experience in their field and are required to complete brief training on the general procedures for providing expert testimony, as outlined in the Law on Experts. These requirements do not apply to experts or board members appointed through institutions. In rare cases, courts or prosecutors may appoint individuals who are not on the official list or affiliated with an institution.

While many expert witnesses work in the public sector, private expert opinions are also permitted under Turkish law. Upon request, parties may obtain their own expert reports to submit during court proceedings or appeals. In Türkiye, expert opinions are typically submitted in writing, although experts may also provide oral testimony before the court or prosecutor when requested.

### FORENSIC PSYCHIATRIC EXPERTISE

In Türkiye, the vast majority of forensic psychiatric expertise is provided by public institutions, particularly through medical boards operating within state bodies such as the Council of Forensic Medicine, universities, and public hospitals. Although not all members of these boards are psychiatrists, there is typically at least one psychiatrist responsible for conducting the primary assessment. In contrast, evaluations carried out in specialist mental health institutions—such as regional mental health hospitals or high-secure forensic units—are performed by boards composed entirely of psychiatrists.

The Council of Forensic Medicine, an official expert institution affiliated with the Ministry of Justice and governed by its own legislation, plays a central role in this area. Its medical boards usually include psychiatrists, forensic medicine specialists, and neurologists, and they may also involve experts from other medical fields when needed. Criminal responsibility assessments are a core function of forensic psychiatry in Türkiye, and public prosecutors may make requests for such evaluations during the investigation phase or by criminal courts during trial.

The psychiatric interview remains the gold standard in assessing criminal responsibility and other areas of forensic psychiatric evaluation. When a stationary examination is ordered under Article 74 of the Turkish Penal Procedure Code, additional tools such as staff observation reports, laboratory screenings, electrophysiological tests, and brain imaging studies may be used. Psychological testing and psychometric scales can assist in complex diagnostic cases and help detect malingering. Social worker reports may be included to further support the evaluation, and interviews with family members or caregivers are conducted with their consent when appropriate.

The assessment process also involves reviewing various sources of information, including investigation files, court records, police reports, witness and party statements, and—crucially—medical records, particularly those dated near the time of the alleged offence. A medical board typically issues a final opinion on criminal responsibility through a written report, which is then submitted to the public prosecutor or the criminal court.

These reports adhere to the *sine qua non* elements of forensic expertise reporting. This includes a clear statement of the evaluation's purpose, the specific questions the judicial authority poses, a detailed list of information sources, a description and date of the alleged offence, findings from the mental status examination and any relevant testing, and a set of final medico-legal conclusions.

These conclusions must be well-reasoned and sufficiently detailed to inform the court's decision making (Norko & Buchanan, 2015).

However, due to the high demand for forensic psychiatric evaluations and the limited availability of time and resources, reports often include only the most basic information—such as reviewed documents, procedures conducted, the psychiatric opinion, and the conclusion. This constraint can limit the ability to present detailed, explanatory, and discussion-oriented expert testimony in written form. In such cases, the court or, at times, the public prosecutor may request additional evaluations from other experts or institutions until they are satisfied with the level of expertise and can proceed with adjudication.

The Turkish Penal Code includes provisions for aggravated sentencing in cases where the victim is mentally unable to defend themselves in all offences against the person, including physical, verbal, sexual, and socially harmful offences (Turkish Penal Code, Law no. 5237, 2004). Forensic psychiatric expertise is utilised to assess the victim's mental state at the time of the offence, their ability to resist, and their capacity to discern the wrongfulness of the act. This approach is especially crucial for victims with mental illness, considering various factors and psychopathology involved in the incident (Uygur, 2022).

Psychiatric opinions provided by medical boards of psychiatrists are used in civil law cases to assess decision-making capacity and determine whether restrictions on legal rights are warranted for individuals with mental illness. These evaluations are crucial, including the appointment of guardians or advisers. Psychiatric expertise is also provided in other civil and family law matters, such as cases of nullity of marriage due to mental illness.

## Forensic Mental Health System

### *Structure and Function of the Forensic Mental Healthcare System*

In Türkiye, security measures, including compulsory treatment, can be applied to offenders found to have no or diminished responsibility due to mental illness at the time of their offence in place of incarceration. Under Article 57/1 of the Penal Code, such compulsory measures are carried out in high-secure forensic psychiatry units, where individuals receive appropriate treatment and rehabilitation for an indeterminate period (Turkish Penal Code, Law no. 5237, 2004, Article 57/1). For offenders with diminished responsibility, a reduced sentence may be partially or completely replaced by a security measure specific to individuals with mental disorders to be served in a high-secure forensic psychiatry unit, provided the length of the sentence remains the same (Turkish Penal Code, Law no. 5237, 2004, Article 57/6). In practice, specialist forensic psychiatry units also carry out court-ordered forensic inpatient treatment due to a lack of adequate capacity of high-secure units (Figure 21.2).

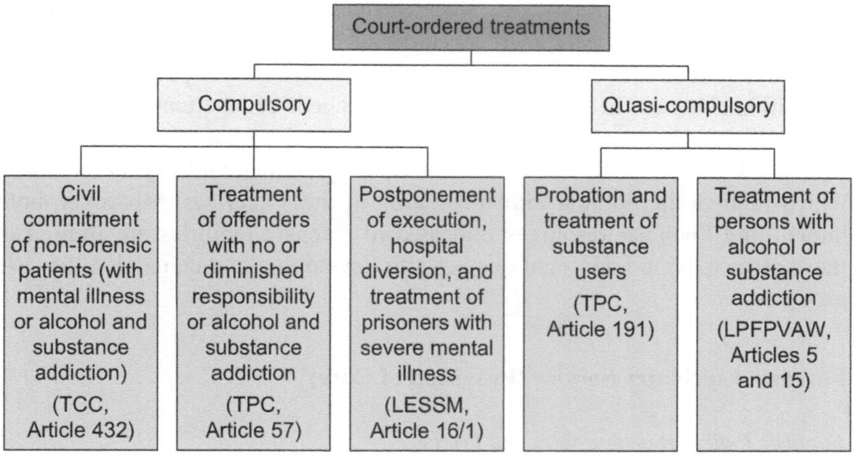


*Figure 21.2* Court-ordered treatments in Türkiye.

(Reproduced from Balcıoğlu, Y. H., Öncü, F., & Kennedy, H. G. (2023). Forensic psychiatry in Turkiye. *International Review of Psychiatry*, *36*(7), 739–755. https://doi.org/10.1080/09540261.2023.2255255, with the permission of Taylor & Francis.)

Abbreviations: TCC = Turkish Civil Code, TPC = Turkish Penal Code, LESSM = Law on Execution of Sentences and Security Measures, LPFPVAW = Law to Protect Family and Prevent Violence Against Women

The primary objective of forensic psychiatric care is to minimise the likelihood of reoffending by addressing the intricate biopsychosocial needs of people with mental disorders who have committed offences. In a contemporary forensic psychiatric treatment setting, the emphasis is on ensuring maximum safety while maintaining the least restrictive conditions feasible. The ultimate aims for the patients encompass the restoration of psychosocial functioning and successful reintegration into society (Seppänen et al., 2018). Hence, the care model must establish a benchmark for the secure and proficient delivery of treatments to achieve these objectives. Additionally, it necessitates ongoing assessment of performance on a population level and improving individual health outcomes (Glancy et al., 2021; Kennedy, 2022, 2002).

In Türkiye, despite facing challenges, such as high patient turnover and a shortage of qualified staff, the specialised forensic units within regional mental health hospitals prioritise providing excellent therapeutic care and a conducive environment. In particular, the newly established high-secure units offer a more modern and superior standard of forensic psychiatric treatment, with a strong emphasis on creating a therapeutic setting. While psychopharmacological interventions remain crucial for achieving symptomatic recovery, both high-secure units and regional mental health hospitals also offer individual and group psychotherapy interventions, psychosocial rehabilitation programmes, occupational therapies, and general medical care.

Although there may be a lack of structured protocols and policies, the clinical staff endeavours to meet the psychosocial needs of inpatients to the best of their abilities. However, the main challenge lies in the insufficient employment of trained professionals for rehabilitation programmes and psychotherapies, which hinders the optimal implementation of these services. Moreover, both human and financial resources allocated to forensic facilities are limited in these areas, posing additional obstacles to developing and enhancing the care provided.

## Forensic Psychiatry Service (Provision of Care)

### *Forensic Patient Demographics and Profile*

In Türkiye, individuals are considered forensic patients if they have committed a crime, entered the criminal justice system with a medical opinion of treatment needs, and been referred by the judicial authorities for mental health care. The demographic, psychosocial, and criminological profiles of forensic psychiatric patients resemble those of Eastern countries more than those of Western Europe (Mundt et al., 2012; Tomlin et al., 2021). Social or family support is relatively strong in Türkiye compared to Western societies. In Türkiye, forensic psychiatric patients with psychotic disorders generally were not living alone or were experiencing homelessness at the time of the offence; fewer than 20% are homeless or living alone (Balcıoğlu et al., 2023; Öncü et al., 2007), appears lower than the patient population in Western countries (Baird et al., 2020; Carabellese et al., 2021).

Comorbid substance use is a significant problem among forensic psychiatric patients. The incidence of intoxication at the time of the offence in Türkiye ranges from 10% to 20% (Balcıoğlu et al., 2023; Batmaz & Öncü, 2023; Belli et al., 2010; Öncü et al., 2002; Ural et al., 2013), lower than reported in European countries and the United States (Novak et al., 2007; Seppänen et al., 2020). Among patients with schizophrenia, reoffenders tend to have an earlier onset of illness than first-time offenders (Balcıoğlu et al., 2021), whereas those who commit homicide have a later onset compared to non-violent patients (Balcıoğlu et al., 2022; Karabekiroğlu et al., 2016). Among patients with schizophrenia who are violent, stranger victims are uncommon, ranging from 4% to 11% (Balcıoğlu et al., 2023; Belli et al., 2010; Inan et al., 2018; Ural et al., 2012). Adherence to antipsychotic medication at the time of the offence is poor, with studies reporting non-adherence rates exceeding 70% (Balcıoğlu et al., 2022; Gümüş et al., 2022). Finally, individuals receiving forensic psychiatric care have high readmission and recidivism rates due to insufficient community-based mental health care.

*Facilities*

Throughout modern history, Türkiye has developed a national model of care for treating people with severe mental illness within the public sector. In the first years of the Republic, the Toptaşı Lunatic Asylum was moved to Bakırköy by Dr. Mazhar Osman, the widely acknowledged 'father' of modern Turkish psychiatry. Since then, the Bakırköy Psychiatric Hospital has remained the first and largest regional mental health hospital serving general and forensic psychiatric patients. As part of health reforms addressing the needs of individuals requiring specialised mental health care, psychiatric hospitals were established in Elazığ and Manisa during the early years of the modern Republic. These became Türkiye's first specialist psychiatric hospitals after Bakırköy, Istanbul. Along with later-established facilities across the country, these hospitals served as regional mental health centres, providing acute and long-term specialist care for both general and forensic psychiatric patients.

Although the Turkish Penal Code (2004) mandated compulsory admission to high-secure forensic psychiatry units for offenders found to have no or diminished criminal responsibility due to a mental illness at the time of the offence, the first high-secure unit did not become operational until 2018 in Adana. Until then, all court-ordered treatments for forensic psychiatry cases were conducted exclusively at regional mental health hospitals. As of April 2025, Türkiye's forensic psychiatric care model includes nine high-secure units across various cities (Adana, Kayseri, Elazığ, Eskişehir, Bursa, Ankara, İzmir, Gaziantep, and Kocaeli), with a total capacity of 652 inpatient beds catering to both male and female patients. Plans are underway to construct additional high-secure units. However, despite these efforts, the existing facilities remain insufficient to meet the growing demand for inpatient care. A significant number of forensic patients are still being admitted to regional mental health hospitals due to the insufficient capacity of high-secure units.

The waiting list for each high-secure unit includes approximately 100 patients, with wait times ranging from 6 to 12 months. Those in need of acute care are often redirected to acute or closed psychiatric wards in regional mental health hospitals or other medical facilities. Unlike in the United Kingdom, Türkiye lacks designated medium- or low-secure forensic units, leaving no structured pathways for transitioning from higher to lower secure units in regional mental health hospitals (Table 21.1).

It is important to note that the term 'high-secure' used in the Turkish Penal Code (2004) is not explicitly defined concerning security levels in forensic or prison settings. Moreover, the law does not establish a formal legal distinction between high- and medium-secure forensic hospitals. In contrast, other jurisdictions differentiate these facilities based on architectural structures, risk management procedures, and relational characteristics, including staffing levels and skills (Kennedy, 2002). Alternatively, classification often depends on the level

*Table 21.1* Forensic psychiatry services in specialist units in Türkiye (as of April 2025)

| | *Total forensic psychiatry inpatient beds* | *Male* | *Female* | *Adolescent* | *CT* | *SME*[*] |
|---|---|---|---|---|---|---|
| *High-secure units* | | | | | | |
| Adana | 100 | 90 | - | 10 | ⊕ | ⊕ |
| Ankara | 70 | 50 | 20 | - | ⊕ | ⊕ |
| Bursa | 100 | 85 | 10 | 5 | ⊕ | ⊕ |
| İzmir | 20 | 20 | - | −(5) | ⊕ | ⊕ |
| Elazığ | 100 | 80 | 10 | 10 | ⊕ | ⊕ |
| Eskişehir | 100 | 90 | 10 | - | ⊕ | ⊕ |
| Gaziantep | 30 | 20 | 10 | - | ⊕ | ⊕ |
| Kayseri | 72 | 56 | 16 | - | ⊕ | ⊕ |
| Kocaeli | 60 | 50 | 10 | - | ⊕ | ⊕ |
| *Regional mental health hospitals* | | | | | | |
| Adana | No specialist forensic unit[**] | | | | ⊖ | ⊕ |
| Bolu | No specialist forensic unit[**] | | | | ⊕ | ⊕ |
| Elazığ | No specialist forensic unit[**] | | | | ⊖ | ⊖ |
| İstanbul Bakırköy[***] | 271 | 241 | 30 | - | ⊕ | ⊕ |
| İstanbul Erenköy | No specialist forensic unit[**] | | | | ⊖ | ⊕ |
| Manisa[***] | 84 | 50 | 34 | - | ⊕ | ⊕ |
| Samsun | 52 | 52 | - | - | ⊕ | ⊕ |
| Tokat | No specialist forensic unit[**] | | | | ⊕ | ⊕ |
| Trabzon Ataköy | No specialist forensic unit[**] | | | | ⊕ | ⊕ |
| *Units as specialist psychiatric hospitals affiliated with general hospitals* | | | | | | |
| Bursa Dörtçelik | No specialist forensic unit[**] | | | | ⊖ | ⊕ |
| Konya Beyhekim | 26 | 26 | - | - | ⊕ | ⊕ |
| *Convict units* | | | | | | |
| Ankara[†] | 20 | 20 | - | - | ⊕ | ⊕ |
| Adana[‡] | 30 | 24 | 6 | - | ⊕ | ⊕ |
| Elazığ[†] | 50 | 40 | 4 | 6 | ⊕ | ⊕ |
| İstanbul Bakırköy[‡] | 50 | 42 | 8 | - | ⊕ | ⊕ |
| İstanbul Erenköy[‡] | 3 | 3 | - | - | ⊖ | ⊖ |
| İzmir | 16 | 12 | 4 | - | ⊕ | ⊕ |
| Kayseri[†] | 28 | 22 | 6 | 6[a] | ⊕ | ⊕ |
| Manisa[‡] | 17 | 15 | 2 | - | ⊕ | ⊕ |
| Samsun[‡] | 5 | 5 | - | - | ⊕ | ⊕ |

(*Continued*)

*Table 21.1* (Continued)

| | *Total forensic psychiatry inpatient beds* | *Male* | *Female* | *Adolescent* | *CT* | *SME** |
|---|---|---|---|---|---|---|
| *Council of Forensic Medicine (stationary unit)* | | | | | | |
| İstanbul | 57 | 54 | 3 | - | ⊖ | ⊕ |

*Notes*: *Stationary mental examinations are also performed in general psychiatry inpatient units in general hospitals across the country. Criminal responsibility assessments are occasionally performed in outpatient units of these institutions without a stationary period due to the heavy amount of requests by the courts.

**CTs or SMEs may be performed in general psychiatry inpatient units in hospitals without specialist forensic units.

***Compulsory treatment according to Turkish Penal Code Art. 57 is also performed in general psychiatry inpatient units due to the limited space in the forensic psychiatry unit and the high patient turnover.

†Affiliated with the high-secure unit,

‡Affiliated with the regional mental health hospital,

[a]Depending on the presence

Abbreviations: CT: Compulsory treatment according to the Turkish Penal Code 57/1, SME: Stationary mental examination according to the Turkish Penal Procedure Code 74 (for criminal responsibility assessment), HSUs: High-secure units, RMHHs: Regional mental health hospitals

of risk patients pose to the public, other patients, and staff, as well as the corresponding need for higher or moderate levels of therapeutic security (Adams et al., 2018; Freestone et al., 2015; Williams et al., 2020).

*Length of Stay*

No national statistics are available on the length of stay in forensic psychiatry care in Türkiye. The duration of inpatient treatment varies significantly throughout the country and between hospitals, influenced by patient characteristics and turnover rates. At Bakırköy Psychiatric Hospital, the average length of stay for current inpatients is approximately four years, while for discharged patients, it averages less than one year. In many high-secure units, the minimum stay is typically around three months. After discharge, conditional psychiatric follow-up generally lasts between 5 and 10 years.

*Exiting the System*

According to Article 57 of the Turkish Penal Code, discharge from a secure forensic hospital is permitted only when the treating institution's medical board concludes that the individual is no longer dangerous to society due to their mental illness or that their level of dangerousness has significantly diminished. As it is neither scientifically nor clinically feasible to determine the complete elimination of dangerousness in real-world psychiatric practice, the criterion of significantly diminished risk functions as a safeguard for clinicians making discharge decisions. This determination is based on unstructured but comprehensive and regular risk assessments conducted by the treating team. These assessments typically consider the individual's clinical history, criminal background, social support, socio-economic status, and comorbidities.

Despite the growing international use of structured professional judgement tools—such as the HCR-20 or the DUNDRUM Toolkit—for evaluating dangerousness (Davoren et al., 2013, 2015; Douglas et al., 2003; Gray et al., 2008; Kennedy, O'Reilly, et al., 2019; Lam et al., 2022; McCullough et al., 2020; Seppänen et al., 2020), such instruments have not yet been translated, validated, or implemented in forensic psychiatric settings in Türkiye.

Once inpatient forensic treatment is completed, the medical board submits a report to the court stating that the individual's dangerousness due to mental illness has significantly diminished and recommending conditional discharge. The authorised court must then issue an additional order for the individual's release from the hospital.

The release order prescribes conditional discharge, requiring ongoing medical care, assessment, and supervision for a specified period (e.g., five years) at specific intervals (e.g., every three months) based on the medical board's recommendations. Following discharge, individuals enter a psychiatric follow-up system similar to community treatment orders in many countries, such as Australia, Canada, the United Kingdom, and the United States (Maughan et al., 2014). Those who attend regular follow-ups, maintain treatment compliance, do not reoffend during the follow-up period, and whose clinical condition remains stable and in remission are cleared from the system once the follow-up period ends. However, in cases of relapse or non-adherence to treatment, the court may issue an additional order for compulsory inpatient treatment based on a psychiatrist's report from the most recent follow-up (Figure 21.3).

### *Mental Health Services in Correctional Processes*

The need for mental health care in prisons is growing, and improving access to qualified services is essential to address mental health issues among inmates, maintain security and peace in correctional settings, and support rehabilitation to reduce reoffending upon release. As of 2021, Türkiye has had the second-highest incarceration rate in Europe (after Russia), with 325.4 prisoners per 100,000 inhabitants (Aebi et al., 2022). High inmate density in Turkish correctional facilities limits access to health services, rehabilitation, and progressive penal processes. The challenge is even greater in managing mental disorders, affecting

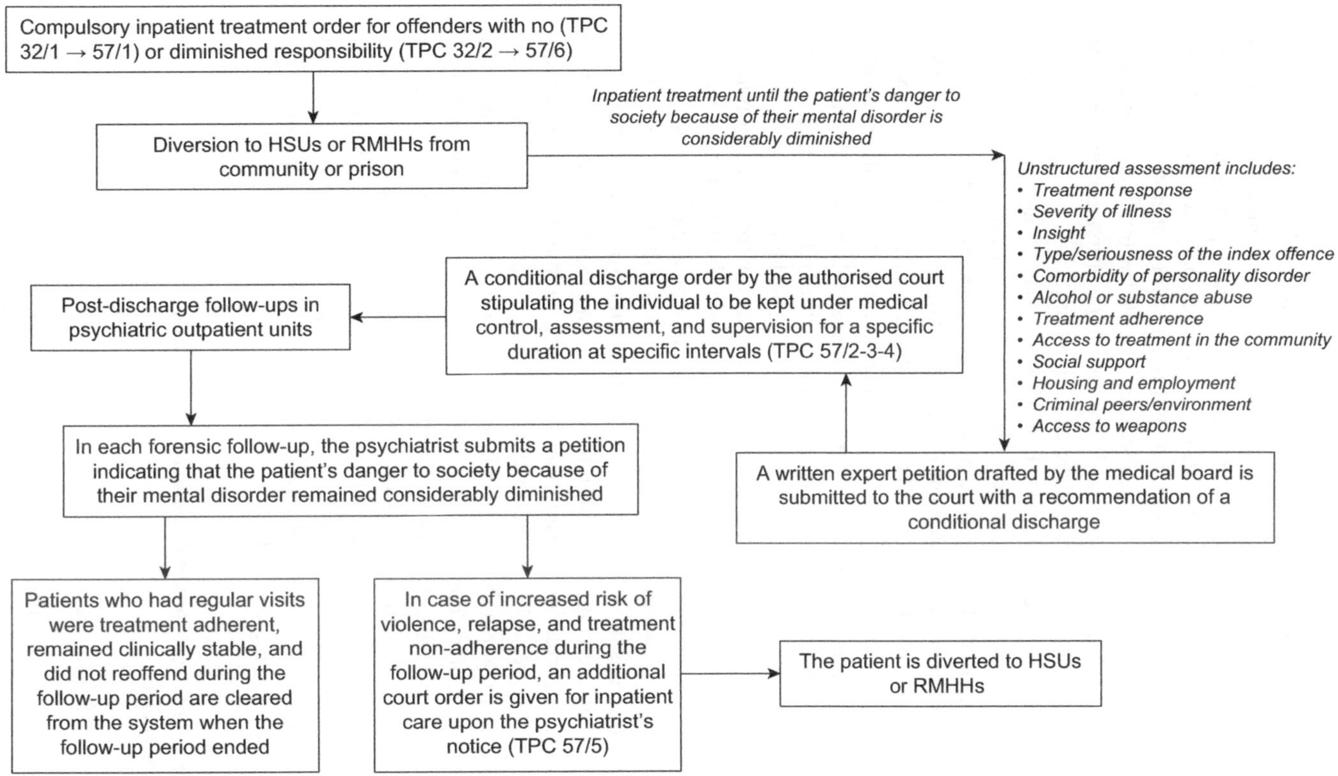


*Figure 21.3* Visualisation of the pathway for individuals not criminally responsible due to mental illness according to the Turkish Penal Code.

(Reproduced from Balcıoğlu, Y. H., Öncü, F., & Kennedy, H. G. (2023). Forensic psychiatry in Turkiye. *International Review of Psychiatry*, *36*(7), 739–755. https://doi.org/10.1080/09540261.2023.2255255, with the permission of Taylor & Francis.)

Abbreviations: TPC = Turkish Penal Code (2004), HSU = high-secure unit, RMHH = regional mental health hospital

institutional stability and security. Typically, staff psychologists conduct initial psychological assessments and follow-ups for inmates.

Despite recent improvements, the number of mental health professionals providing psychosocial monitoring and support in Turkish prisons remains insufficient. Direct interaction between inmates and mental health professionals is also limited in effectiveness (Amil et al., 2021). Türkiye has only two rehabilitation-focused correctional institutions, Istanbul and Izmir, which operate as auxiliary units within designated prisons. These facilities provide treatment and rehabilitation for inmates with physical disabilities or mental disorders during their sentences, with eligible inmates being directed to these units.

According to Article 16 of the Law on Execution of Sentences and Security Measures (Law No. 5275, 2004), the sentence of an offender diagnosed with a mental illness shall be postponed. They shall be placed under protection and treatment at a mental health institution (high-secure unit) specified in Article 57 of the Turkish Penal Code until rehabilitation is complete. They should be officially released from prison for an indeterminate treatment period during this period. Such individuals are diverted to either high-secure units or regional mental health hospitals for compulsory treatment. After completing inpatient treatment, the convict must return to prison to serve the remaining sentence, with the time spent at the mental health institution

Türkiye has established designated psychiatric units for convicted individuals within lower security prisons. These facilities provide short-term treatment or inpatient forensic psychiatric evaluations for incarcerated individuals who require psychiatric care while serving their sentence or awaiting trial without being released from custody. These units are distributed across various regions of the country. They are equipped with infrastructure and security features similar to those found in correctional institutions, including perimeter fencing, surveillance systems, secure walls, and security personnel.

This model is comparable to psychiatric treatment facilities integrated into prison systems in other countries. Similar approaches can be seen in Japan's prison hospitals or medical prisons and several European and North American jurisdictions. Examples include federal prison hospitals in Canada, penitentiary hospitals in the Netherlands and Switzerland, social defence units in Belgium, psychiatric prison wards in Finland, and special support units for the voluntary treatment of inmates with mental illness in the United Kingdom, Ireland, Italy, and other countries (Figure 21.4).

### ***The Academic and Organisational Landscape of Forensic Psychiatry in Türkiye***

#### *Qualifications or Specialised Training*

Forensic psychiatry is not defined as a specialisation or higher specialisation in Türkiye, so the country has no officially defined designation of 'forensic psychiatrist'.

*Figure 21.4* Forensic psychiatric service structure in Türkiye.

(Reproduced from Balcıoğlu, Y. H., Öncü, F., & Kennedy, H. G. (2023). Forensic psychiatry in Turkiye. *International Review of Psychiatry*, *36*(7), 739–755. https://doi.org/10.1080/09540261.2023.2255255, with the permission of Taylor & Francis.)

However, some regional mental health hospitals, in addition to high-secure units, have specialist forensic psychiatry units and adult psychiatry specialists.

Some universities in Türkiye offer postgraduate programmes in 'forensic psychology'; however, graduates of these programmes do not qualify as 'forensic psychologists', do not receive a diploma conferring this title, and cannot be appointed to positions designated for forensic psychologists in either the public or private sector. Psychology graduates may work in courts, correctional facilities, probation services, forensic psychiatry clinics, and the Council of Forensic Medicine. However, the absence of formally recognised forensic psychologists and the limited number of adequately trained psychologists in the forensic field restrict access to qualified mental health expertise and care—particularly in correctional settings.

To practice forensic psychiatry in Türkiye, individuals must complete six years of medical education. After this, graduates must pass the Medical Specialty Exam to begin residency. Psychiatry training lasts four years and is obligatory for becoming a consultant psychiatrist. Although not obligatory, the national core training curriculum recommends at least one month of forensic psychiatry rotation. Forensic psychiatric evaluation and report preparation are among the required competencies. Some psychiatry training institutions follow this recommendation and ensure residents complete forensic psychiatry rotations. In Bakırköy, home to the country's largest forensic psychiatry unit, residents undergo four-month forensic psychiatry rotations, and psychiatry residents from other institutions, such as universities, training and research hospitals, are sent there for forensic psychiatry training.

### *Academic Contributions*

The first book on forensic psychiatry in Türkiye was *Tababet-i Adliye-i Mecanin* (Forensic Medicine of the Insane), written by Dr. Mustafa Hayrullah Diker in 1915, before the founding of the Republic. It addressed mental illness, criminal and legal responsibility, and forensic expertise (Biçer et al., 2009). Following the establishment of the Republic in 1923, the Council of Forensic Medicine and regional mental health hospitals played important roles in developing forensic psychiatry practice and expertise in forensic treatment. However, their academic contributions remained limited. The first comprehensive book on forensic psychiatry in the Republican era was not published until 1966, when Dr. Zati Dokuz authored *Forensic Psychiatry: Mental Illnesses and Our Toxicomania Legislation* (*Adli Psikiyatri: Akıl Hastalıkları ve Toksikomani Mevzuatımız*) in Bakırköy (Dokuz, 1966). In 2007, the Psychiatric Association of Türkiye released the *Forensic Psychiatry Practice Guideline*, a contemporary and comprehensive textbook. Its fourth edition, published in 2022, incorporates recent legislative amendments (Uygur, 2022).

Since the early 2000s, Turkish psychiatrists have made increasingly significant contributions to the scientific literature on forensic psychiatry. These studies have explored diverse topics, including the profiles of individuals deemed not criminally responsible (Kilic-Demir et al., 2024; Batmaz & Öncü, 2023; Gurkan et al., 2021), forensic psychiatric patients undergoing compulsory treatment (Öncü et al., 2007), the association between psychotic disorders and violent behaviour (Gümüş et al., 2022; Ural et al., 2012, 2013), and homicide (Balcıoğlu et al., 2022, 2023; Belli et al., 2010; Inan et al., 2018; Karabekiroğlu et al., 2016). Further areas of focus include recidivism among forensic psychiatric patients (Balcıoğlu et al., 2021; Öncü et al., 2002) and the reliability and validity of malingering inventories in forensic samples (Ardic et al., 2019; Keyvan et al., 2015). More recently, comparative studies examining forensic psychiatric populations in Türkiye and other countries have also been published (Balcıoğlu, Golenkov et al., 2024; Balcıoğlu, Margari et al., 2024).

The strategy for clinical research and development in forensic psychiatry in Türkiye includes implementing structured professional judgement instruments, evaluating patient characteristics, and comparing secure forensic hospitals to other countries. All specialist medical services, including forensic psychiatry, should strive for excellence through continuous improvement in patient outcomes via research, service development, teaching, and training (Kennedy, Simpson et al., 2019). This should begin with strengthening university ties with forensic psychiatric institutions.

### *National Collaborations or Networks*

There is no official institution dedicated solely to forensic psychiatry in Türkiye. In high-secure units and regional mental health hospitals (affiliated with the Ministry of Health), both forensic psychiatric expertise and treatment services are provided. State and university hospitals (also under the Ministry of Health) conduct forensic psychiatric assessments and provide expertise. The Council of Forensic Medicine has specialised units for forensic psychiatric expert evaluations.

The Psychiatric Association of Türkiye has a section dedicated to forensic psychiatry that serves as a professional and academic task force. As of June 2023, it had 200 members and led several initiatives, including publishing the first forensic psychiatry textbook in Turkish, organising scientific sessions in national and international congresses, and hosting periodical seminars and webinars. The organisation also works actively on assignments from the Association's Executive Committee, such as drafting position statements and comments on newly enacted legislation through task forces for using international associations, such as the World Psychiatric Association, governmental bodies, or other professional initiatives.

## Strengths, Weaknesses, and Future Implications

Forensic psychiatry in Türkiye presents a promising area for research, partly due to the high number of patients entering the system. However, this high admission rate also leads to challenges, including premature discharge from inpatient care. While criminal legislation regarding offenders with mental illnesses has a well-established tradition in Türkiye, the absence of specific mental health legislation and limited consideration of civil rights hinder the advancement of forensic mental health care.

Despite recent improvements, legal oversight, supervision mechanisms, and community-based mental health services remain inadequate, contributing to high rates of readmission and reoffending among forensic psychiatric patients. Additionally, the mental healthcare system lacks interconnectivity in many regions of the country.

Establishing modern, high-secure units has significantly improved forensic psychiatric treatment and care standards. Additionally, the clinical staff in specialist forensic units within regional mental health hospitals have extensive experience providing the best possible therapeutic care and environment. However, further improvements are needed. Implementing a standardised model of care that integrates physical, relational, and procedural security, along with structured psychosocial rehabilitation and therapeutic programmes, can enhance the quality of patient care.

Türkiye's strategic location as a junction for international drug trafficking directly contributes to the onset and exacerbation of mental disorders. Despite recent legislative amendments, substance abuse remains a significant challenge for both forensic and general psychiatric patients. Addressing this issue through governmental initiatives is essential to mitigating its adverse impact on mental health in the country.

Enhancing prison mental health services is essential to address the complex psychosocial needs of people within the forensic system. Timely and effective referral and diversion of individuals entering the judicial system to mental healthcare services have been commendable, allowing many to receive their initial diagnosis and begin effective treatment within the forensic psychiatric system.

In Türkiye, forensic psychiatric evaluations of criminal responsibility are now conducted more frequently and often based on less stringent psychiatric criteria than in the past. This shift is largely attributed to the lowered referral threshold adopted by criminal courts. For instance, defendants who have merely been prescribed antidepressants in the past, or who are described by their solicitors as having 'psychological issues', may be referred for a criminal responsibility assessment. While this practice has expedited the referral process, it has also increased the workload for psychiatrists and, in turn, reduced the overall quality and depth of expert evaluations across the system.

While forensic psychiatry in Türkiye holds significant potential for research and development, several challenges remain. These include the need for specific mental health legislation, stronger protections for civil rights, improved legal oversight, and enhanced community-based mental health services. Strengthening interconnectivity within the mental healthcare system and implementing a standardised model of care can further improve treatment outcomes for forensic patients in prison settings. Additionally, addressing substance abuse and prioritising prison mental health services are essential to meeting the complex psychosocial needs of forensic populations, promoting effective rehabilitation, and supporting reintegration into society.

## References


Adams, J., Thomas, S. D. M., Mackinnon, T., & Eggleton, D. (2018). The risks, needs and stages of recovery of a complete forensic patient cohort in an Australian state. *BMC Psychiatry*, *18*(1), 1–13. https://doi.org/10.1186/s12888-017-1584-8

Aebi, M. F., Cocco, E., Molnar, L., & Tiago, M. M. (2022). *Council of Europe annual penal statistics SPACE I-2021*.

Amil, B., Balcıoğlu, Y. H., & Öncü, F. (2021). Mental health practices and roadmap in prison population with world examples. *Current Research and Reviews in Psychology and Psychiatry*, *1*(1), 46–76.

Ardic, F. C., Kose, S., Solmaz, M., Kulacaoglu, F., & Balcıoğlu, Y. H. (2019). Reliability, validity, and factorial structure of the Turkish version of the Structured Inventory of Malingered Symptomatology (Turkish SIMS). *Psychiatry and Clinical Psychopharmacology*, *29*(2), 182–188. https://doi.org/10.1080/24750573.2019.1599237

Artvinli, F., & Uslu, M. K. B. (2023). On a long, narrow road: The mental health law in Turkey. *International Journal of Law and Psychiatry*, *86*(December 2022), 101845. https://doi.org/10.1016/j.ijlp.2022.101845

Baird, A., Webb, R. T., Hunt, I. M., Appleby, L., & Shaw, J. (2020). Homicide by men diagnosed with schizophrenia: National case-control study. *BJPsych Open*, *6*(6), 1–8. https://doi.org/10.1192/bjo.2020.129

Balcıoğlu, Y. H., Golenkov, A. V., Yıldız, A., Uzlar, R. D., & Öncü, F. (2024). Homicide perpetrators with psychotic illness found not criminally responsible in Türkiye and Russia: An international comparison. *International Journal of Law and Psychiatry*, *93*, (March–April), 101962. https://doi.org/10.1016/j.ijlp.2024.101962

Balcıoğlu, Y. H., Kırlıoğlu Balcıoğlu, S. S., Öncü, F., & Türkcan, A. (2021). Psychopathy, temperament, and character dimensions of personality as risk determinants of criminal recidivism in schizophrenia patients. *Journal of Forensic Sciences*, *66*(6), 2340–2353. https://doi.org/10.1111/1556-4029.14834

Balcıoğlu, Y. H., Kırlıoğlu Balcıoğlu, S. S., Öncü, F., & Türkcan, A. (2023). Profiling homicides based on impulsive or proactive natures in male schizophrenia patients. *Journal of the American Academy of Psychiatry and the Law*, *51*(2), 215–226. https://doi.org/10.29158/JAAPL.220064–22

Balcıoğlu, Y. H., Kırlıoğlu Balcıoğlu, S. S., Öncü, F., Türkcan, A., & Yorulmaz, A. C. (2022). Impulsive and aggressive traits and increased peripheral inflammatory status as psychobiological substrates of homicide behavior in schizophrenia. *European Journal of Psychiatry*, *36*(3), 207–214. https://doi.org/10.1016/j.ejpsy.2022.01.004

Balcıoğlu, Y. H., Margari, A., Yıldız, A., Mandarelli, G., Parente, L., Carabellese, F., Uzlar, R. D., Catanesi, R., & Öncü, F. (2024). Homicides by offenders with psychotic illness in Italy and Türkiye: A comparison of offender and crime-scene profiles. *International Journal of Law and Psychiatry*, *97*(November–December), 102041. https://doi.org/10.1016/j.ijlp.2024.102041

Batmaz, M., & Öncü, F. (2023). Clinical and offense-related characteristics of male patients with schizophrenia and schizophrenia-like psychotic disorders found not criminally responsible: A sample from Türkiye. *Dusunen Adam: The Journal of Psychiatry and Neurological Sciences*, *36*(1), 22–32. https://doi.org/10.14744/dajpns.2022.00203

Belli, H., Ozcetin, A., Ertem, U., Tuyluoglu, E., Namli, M., Bayik, Y., & Simsek, D. (2010). Perpetrators of homicide with schizophrenia: Sociodemographic characteristics and clinical factors in the eastern region of Turkey. *Comprehensive Psychiatry*, *51*(2), 135–141. https://doi.org/10.1016/j.comppsych.2009.03.006

Biçer, Ü., Tırtıl, L., Kurtaş, Ö., & Aker, T. (2009). Adli psikiyatri. *Klinik Gelişim Dergisi (Adli Tıp Özel Sayı)*, *22*, 126–132.

Carabellese, F., Mandarelli, G., Felthous, A. R., & Catanesi, R. (2021). Forensic psychiatric evaluation of 187 homicidal assailants with and without a schizophrenia spectrum disorder: Clinical, criminological and behavioral characteristics. *Behavioral Sciences and the Law*, *39*(2), 190–204. https://doi.org/10.1002/bsl.2515

Davoren, M., Abidin, Z., Naughton, L., Gibbons, O., Nulty, A., Wright, B., & Kennedy, H. G. (2013). Prospective study of factors influencing conditional discharge from a forensic hospital: The DUNDRUM-3 programme completion and DUNDRUM-4 recovery structured professional judgement instruments and risk. *BMC Psychiatry*, *13*(1), 1–16. https://doi.org/10.1186/1471-244X-13-185

Davoren, M., Hennessy, S., Conway, C., Marrinan, S., Gill, P., & Kennedy, H. G. (2015). Recovery and concordance in a secure forensic psychiatry hospital—the self-rated DUNDRUM-3 programme completion and DUNDRUM-4 recovery scales. *BMC Psychiatry*, *15*(1), 1–12. https://doi.org/10.1186/s12888-015-0433-x

Dokuz, Z. (1966). *Adli Psikiyatri: Akıl hastalıkları ve toksikomani mevzuatımız* [*Forensic psychiatry: Mental illnesses and our legislation on toxicomania*]. Istanbul: Istanbul Matbaası.

Douglas, K. S., Ogloff, J. R. P., & Hart, S. D. (2003). Evaluation of a model of violence risk assessment among forensic psychiatric patients. *Psychiatric Services*, *54*(10), 1372–1379. https://doi.org/10.1176/appi.ps.54.10.1372

Freestone, M., Bull, D., Brown, R., Boast, N., Blazey, F., & Gilluley, P. (2015). Triage, decision-making and follow-up of patients referred to a UK forensic service: Validation of the DUNDRUM toolkit. *BMC Psychiatry*, *15*(1), 1–11. https://doi.org/10.1186/s12888-015-0620-9

Glancy, G., Choptiany, M., Jones, R., & Chatterjee, S. (2021). Measurement-based care in forensic psychiatry. *International Journal of Law and Psychiatry*, *74*, 101650. https://doi.org/10.1016/j.ijlp.2020.101650

Gray, N. S., Taylor, J., & Snowden, R. J. (2008). Predicting violent reconvictions using the HCR−20. *British Journal of Psychiatry*, *192*(5), 384–387. https://doi.org/10.1192/bjp.bp.107.044065

Gümüş, T., Cesur, E., Keyvan, A., & Türkcan, A. (2022). Comparison of the sociodemographic, clinical and offense-related data of delusional disorder patients with and without a criminal history. *Psychiatry, Psychology and Law*, *29*(4), 631–643. https://doi.org/10.1080/13218719.2021.1956386

Gurkan, S., Can, K. C., Kaya, H., Nazik Yuksel, R., & Goka, E. (2021). Retrospective evaluation of cases examined to determine criminal responsibilities. *Noropsikiyatri Arsivi*, *58*(4), 321–326. https://doi.org/10.29399/npa.27548

Inan, S., Yıldızhan, E., & Öncü, F. (2018). The disease history, sociodemographics, and criminal features of the homicidal forensic psychiatric patients. *Turk Psikiyatri Dergisi*, *29*(4), 1–10. https://doi.org/10.5080/u22822

Karabekiroğlu, A., Pazvantoğlu, O., Karabekiroğlu, K., Böke, Ö., & Korkmaz, I. Z. (2016). Associations with violent and homicidal behaviour among men with schizophrenia. *Nordic Journal of Psychiatry*, *70*(4), 303–308. https://doi.org/10.3109/08039488.2015.1109139

Kennedy, H. G. (2002). Therapeutic uses of security: Mapping forensic mental health services by stratifying risk. *Advances in Psychiatric Treatment*, *8*(6), 433–443. https://doi.org/10.1192/apt.8.6.433

Kennedy, H. G. (2022). Models of care in forensic psychiatry. *BJPsych Advances*, *28*(1), 46–59. https://doi.org/10.1192/bja.2021.34

Kennedy, H. G., O'Reilly, K., Davoren, M., O'Flynn, P., & O'Sullivan, O. P. (2019). How to measure progress in forensic care. *Long-Term Forensic Psychiatric Care*, 103–121. https://doi.org/10.1007/978-3-030-12594-3_8

Kennedy, H. G., Simpson, A., & Haque, Q. (2019). Perspective on excellence in forensic mental health services: What we can learn from oncology and other medical services. *Frontiers in Psychiatry*, *10*, 733. https://doi.org/10.3389/FPSYT.2019.00733

Keyvan, A., Ger, M. C., Ertürk, S. G., & Türkcan, A. (2015). The validity and reliability of the Turkish version of miller forensic assessment of symptoms test (M-FAST). *Noropsikiyatri Arsivi*, *52*(3), 296–302. https://doi.org/10.5152/npa.2015.7587

Kilic-Demir, B., Kizilpinar, S. C., & Polat, S. (2024). The violence profile of male mentally disordered offenders in a high secure unit in Türkiye. *International Journal of Law and Psychiatry*, *94*(May–June), 101983. https://doi.org/10.1016/j.ijlp.2024.101983

Lam, A. A., Penney, S. R., & Simpson, A. I. F. (2022). Construct validity and concordance of clinician-and patient-rated DUNDRUM programme completion and recovery scales. *International Journal of Forensic Mental Health*, 1–10. https://doi.org/10.1080/14999013.2022.2151671

Maughan, D., Molodynski, A., Rugkåsa, J., & Burns, T. (2014). A systematic review of the effect of community treatment orders on service use. *Social Psychiatry and Psychiatric Epidemiology*, *49*(4), 651–663. https://doi.org/10.1007/s00127-013-0781-0

McCullough, S., Stanley, C., Smith, H., Scott, M., Karia, M., Ndubuisi, B., Ross, C. C., Bates, R., & Davoren, M. (2020). Outcome measures of risk and recovery in Broadmoor High Secure Forensic Hospital: Stratification of care pathways and moves to medium secure hospitals. *BJPsych Open*, *6*(4), e74. https://doi.org/10.1192/bjo.2020.61

Mundt, A. P., Frančišković, T., Gurovich, I., Heinz, A., Ignatyev, Y., Ismayilov, F., Kalapos, M. P., Krasnov, V., Mihai, A., Mir, J., Padruchny, D., Potočan, M., Raboch, J., Taube, M., Welbel, M., & Priebe, S. (2012). Changes in the provision of institutionalized mental health care in post-communist countries. *PLoS ONE*, *7*(6), e38490. https://doi.org/10.1371/journal.pone.0038490

Norko, M. A., & Buchanan, M. A. (2015). The forensic psychiatric report. *Journal of Psychiatric Practice*, *21*(1), 67–71. https://doi.org/10.1097/01.pra.0000460623.40923.47

Novak, B., McDermott, B. E., Scott, C. L., & Guillory, S. (2007). Sex offenders and insanity: An examination of 42 individuals found not guilty by reason of insanity. *Journal of the American Academy of Psychiatry and the Law*, *35*(4), 444–450.

Öncü, F. (2020). Türkiye'nin Ruh Sağlığı Yasasıyla İmtihanı [Turkey's examination with a mental health act]. *Toplum ve Hekim*, *35*(4), 316–320.

Öncü, F., Sercan, M., Ger, C., Bilici, R., Ural, C., & Uygur, N. (2007). The impact of socioeconomic and sociodemographic factors on the criminal behavior of patients with a psychotic disorder. *Turk Psikiyatri Dergisi*, *18*(1), 1–8.

Öncü, F., Soysal, H., Uygur, N., Özdemir, F., Türkcan, S., Yeşilbursa, D., & Alataş, G. (2002). Evaluation of forensic psychiatry cases who committed recurrent crimes after compulsory clinical treatment in terms of diagnosis and crime characteristics. *Düşünen Adam: The Journal of Psychiatry and Neurological Sciences*, *15*(3), 132–148.

Sen, M. (2014). The historical development of Turkish law. *HUFS Global Law Review*, *6*(2), 65–76.

Seppänen, A., Joelsson, P., Ahlgren-Rimpiläinen, A., & Repo-Tiihonen, E. (2020). Forensic psychiatry in Finland: An overview of past, present and future. *International Journal of Mental Health Systems*, *14*(1), 1–8. https://doi.org/10.1186/s13033-020-00362-x

Seppänen, A., Törmänen, I., Shaw, C., & Kennedy, H. (2018). Modern forensic psychiatric hospital design: Clinical, legal and structural aspects. *International Journal of Mental Health Systems*, *12*(1), 1–12. https://doi.org/10.1186/s13033-018-0238-7

Tomlin, J., Lega, I., Braun, P., Kennedy, H. G., Herrando, V. T., Barroso, R., Castelletti, L., Mirabella, F., Scarpa, F., Völlm, B., Pham, T., Müller-Isberner, R., Taube, M., Rivellini, G., Calevro, V., Liardo, R., Pennino, M., Markiewicz, I., Barbosa, F., . . . Čėsnienė, I. (2021). Forensic mental health in Europe: Some key figures. *Social Psychiatry and Psychiatric Epidemiology*, *56*(1), 109–117. https://doi.org/10.1007/s00127-020-01909-6

Tsimploulis, G., Niveau, G., Eytan, A., Giannakopoulos, P., & Sentissi, O. (2018). Schizophrenia and criminal responsibility: A systematic review. *Journal of Nervous and Mental Disease*, *206*(5), 370–377. https://doi.org/10.1097/NMD.0000000000000805

*Turkish Civil Code (Law no. 4721)*. (2001). Retrieved from https://rm.coe.int/turkish-civil-code-familylaw-book/1680a3bcd4

*Turkish Penal Code (Law no. 5237)*. (2004). Retrieved from https://www.venice.coe.int/webforms/documents/default.aspx?pdffile=CDL-REF(2016)011-e

*Turkish Penal Procedure Code (Law no. 5271)*. (2004). Retrieved from https://sherloc.unodc.org/cld/uploads/res/document/tur/2005/turkish_criminal_procedure_code_html/2014_Criminal_Procedure_Code.pdf

Ural, C., Belli, H., Öncü, F., & Soysal, H. (2012). Profile of population targeted by violent behavior of psychotic patients. *Turk Psikiyatri Dergisi*, *23*(1), 26–32.

Ural, C., Öncü, F., Belli, H., & Soysal, H. (2013). Violent behavior variables among patients with schizophrenia under forensic psychiatric process: A case-control study. *Turk Psikiyatri Dergisi*, *24*(1), 15–21.

Uygur, N. (2022). *Adli psikiyatri uygulama kılavuzu* [Forensic psychiatry practice guideline] (4th ed.). Ankara: Türkiye Psikiyatri Derneği.

Williams, H. K., Senanayke, M., Ross, C. C., Bates, R., & Davoren, M. (2020). Security needs among patients referred for high secure care in Broadmoor Hospital England. *BJPsych Open*, *6*(4), e55. https://doi.org/10.1192/bjo.2020.35

# Part V

# Asia

# 22 China

*Xiaoping Wang*

## Brief Description

| | |
|---|---|
| **Location** | China is a country in East Asia. |
| **Size** | 9.6 million km$^2$, the third largest country in the world by geography. |
| **Population** | More than 1.4 billion. |
| **Language** | The official language is Mandarin, spoken by 70% of the population. |
| **Political system** | The political system of China is composed of the Chinese Communist Party, state agencies, and the People's Political Consultative Conference. |

## Legal System

### *Legislative Framework*

The Chinese legal system is a criminal litigation system centered around trial. The laws of China largely adhere to the characteristics of a statute law system rather than those of common law.

The courts in China consist of four levels according to the descending order of powers, from top to bottom: the Supreme People's Court (the SPC), high people's courts, intermediate people's courts, and primary people's courts. Courts at the latter three levels are collectively referred to the local courts. The Chinese authorities range from the central government to the local governments, including governments at provincial, municipal, county (district), and township levels. The courts are established corresponding to the highest four levels of government.

Each court has jurisdiction over cases within the territorial scope of the authority at the same level, which includes cases at first instance under its jurisdiction and appeal cases against the judgments or rulings at first instance made by the lower court under its jurisdiction. In addition, China also has specialized courts, including military courts and nonmilitary courts, but there is no dedicated forensic tribunal.

As mentioned, the Chinese criminal procedure is a court-centered litigation system, led by the trial judge. During the trial, the prosecution and defense can fully

DOI: 10.4324/9781003376248-27

debate and cross-examine evidence. The system emphasizes the implementation of the trial-centered concept, the implementation of the pretrial conference system, the advancement of the substantive trial, the implementation of evidence judgment rules and illegal evidence exclusion rules, the elimination of suspected crimes, and the protection of the litigation rights of the parties and defenders according to the law.

### *Legal Capacity Assessment*

#### *Capacity to Stand Trial*

In China, capacity to stand trial, or competency to stand trial, refers to the ability of defendants to participate in the court process, understand the consequences of proceedings, and accept trials. Incompetency to stand trial means that criminal defendants with mental illness or other serious illnesses unable to accept interrogation, cannot understand their position and the meaning of their actions in the proceedings, and cannot defend themselves. Article 206 of the *Criminal Procedure Law of the People's Republic of China* (amended in 2018) stipulates that, during the trial of a case, if the defendant is unable to appear before court because they are suffering a serious illness, which makes the trial impossible for a relatively long period of time, the trial may be suspended. There is no clear provision in the law regarding permanent inability to stand trial. After the court makes a decision to suspend the trial, some defendants will be sent to a forensic psychiatric hospital (Ankang Hospital) or general psychiatric hospital for treatment, and some will be released on bail pending trial. During the suspension period, the defendant needs to undergo regular assessment on their capacity to stand trial. In China, re-evaluation is generally conducted every six months, but there is no explicit deadline for treatment recovery. Resumption of the trial does not necessarily require complete recovery from the condition. Even if there are still some mental symptoms, as long as it does not affect the proceedings, the trial can resume. The trial of the case will continue upon restoration of competency to stand trial. In addition, Article 296 of the *Criminal Procedure Law* also stipulates that

> where the defendant is unable to appear before court for suffering a serious illness, and trial is suspended for more than six months, if the defendant is still unable to appear before court, and the defendant or his or her legal representative or close relative applies for or agrees to the resumption of the trial, the people's court may try the case in absentia without the defendant's presence in court, and render a judgment in accordance with the law.

#### *Criminal Responsibility*

Criminal responsibility refers to the ability of an individual to identify the nature, significance, and consequences of their behavior in the criminal law sense, and to consciously control their behavior. In China, when patients with mental disorders engage in harmful behavior toward others, the assessment of criminal responsibility is mainly based on Article 18 of the *Criminal Law*, which states,

> If a mental patient causes harmful consequences at a time when he is unable to recognize or control his own conduct, upon verification and confirmation through legal procedure, he shall not bear criminal responsibility, but his family members or guardian shall be ordered to keep him under strict watch and control and arrange for his medical treatment. When necessary, the government may compel him to receive medical treatment. Any person whose mental illness is of an intermittent nature shall bear criminal responsibility if he commits a crime when he is in a normal mental state. If a mental patient who has not completely lost the ability of recognizing or controlling his own conduct commits a crime, he shall bear criminal responsibility; however, he may be given a lighter or mitigated punishment. Any intoxicated person who commits a crime shall bear criminal responsibility.

According to this regulation, there are two requirements for assessing the state of responsibility of persons with mental illness when they perform harmful acts. The first is a medical element, which requires the person to be diagnosed with a mental illness; the other is a legal element, which means that the person's mental state has an impact or damage on his ability to recognize and control. After completing the appraisal and evaluation of the person, the appraiser only needs to submit recommendations on diagnosis and criminal responsibility to the judicial institution initiating forensic psychiatric assessment (public security, procuratorate, or the court).

For those mental patients legally exempted from criminal liability, Chapter V of the *Criminal Procedure Law* (Articles 302 and 303) stipulates that

> a mental patient who has committed any violent behavior compromising public security or seriously endangering the personal safety of citizens who is legally exempted from criminal responsibility after identification under statutory procedures shall be subject to involuntary medical treatment if the mental patient may continue to endanger the society. Whether a mental patient is subject to involuntary medical treatment under this Chapter shall be decided by a people's court.

### *Forensic Psychiatry Decision Makers*

The Chinese criminal justice system and forensic psychiatry healthcare system have a number of key decision makers involved in the treatment and placement of forensic patients (Hu et al., 2011). The police, prosecutor, and judge all have the right to initiate forensic psychiatric assessment. For the victim and defendant, only their legal representatives and close relatives have the right to apply for assessment. After completing the appraisal and evaluation of the appraised person, the expert opinion about the diagnosis and criminal responsibility is submitted to the judicial institution initiating forensic psychiatric assessment (the public security, procuratorate, or the court). The police, prosecutor, and judge should review the expert opinion and inform both parties of the result. Either party can apply for reassessment, when there is evidence of skepticism regarding the expert opinion. In addition, in China, almost all forensic psychiatric assessments were done in an outpatient setting. Usually, the police, prosecutor, or judge will transport the examinee to the site of the forensic organization to do the assessment. In a few cases, the experts will come to the examinee, if it is inconvenient for the examinee to go to the forensic organization. The police, prosecutor, or judge will pay for the assessment (Li et al., 2016).

## Forensic Psychiatry System

China has a formal forensic psychiatry system with forensic psychiatric hospitals, also called 'Ankang' hospitals, which are medical institutions reserved for patients with 'no criminal responsibility on account of mental disorder' (NCR-MD) who pose a threat to public safety (Hu et al., 2011). Offenders with mental illnesses, such as those with diminished responsibility, received medical treatments in general psychiatric hospitals. These hospitals provide a full range of clinical assessments and treatments. However, before 2013, many offenders with NCR-MD were discharged to their families and received no treatment due to lack of resources and information (Wang et al., 2007), although this is no longer the case. The majority of 'Ankang' hospitals are run by the public security system. According to statistics, there are 25 'Ankang' hospitals with over 7,000 forensic psychiatric beds established in 21 different provinces, autonomous regions, and municipalities, among which, 23 of them are run by the public security system, and two of them are run by health system. Among them, taking Hunan Province as an example, data from 2019 showed that there were five wards and admitted more than 460 patients in Hunan Ankang Hospital (Guo et al., 2021).

'Ankang' hospitals are structurally similar to maximum-security hospitals in North America and moderate-to-high-security facilities in the United Kingdom; patients are admitted in a similar fashion (Hu et al., 2011). Involuntary admission to the Ankang Hospital requires the completion of a forensic psychiatric assessment and obtaining a court order. A public security authority which discovers that a mental patient meets the conditions for involuntary medical treatment shall prepare a written opinion on involuntary medical treatment and transfer it to the people's procuratorate. For a written opinion on involuntary medical treatment transferred by a public security authority or after discovering that a mental patient meets the conditions for involuntary medical treatment in the process of examination and prosecution, a people's procuratorate shall file an application for involuntary medical treatment with a people's court. A people's court which discovers that a defendant meets the conditions for involuntary medical treatment in the process of trial of a case may make an involuntary medical treatment decision.

Persons subject to involuntary medical treatment and their close relatives shall have the right to apply for termination of involuntary medical treatment. Article 306 of the Criminal Procedure Law of the PRC (amended in 2018) states that Involuntary medical treatment institutions shall regularly diagnose and assess persons subject to involuntary medical treatment. For those who are no longer dangerous to personal safety and no longer need involuntary medical treatment, involuntary medical treatment institutions shall prepare opinions on termination of involuntary medical treatment in a timely manner and report such opinions to the people's courts which made the involuntary medical treatment decisions for approval. Article 542, Paragraph 1 of the Forensic Interpretation of the Criminal Procedure Law of the PRC stipulates that for those subject to involuntary medical treatment who are no longer to personal safety and no longer need involuntary medical treatment, the court shall make the decision to terminate the involuntary medical treatment and order the family members of them to strictly supervise and treat the patient. Once the court agrees to terminate involuntary medical treatment, the patient will be released back into the community. However, there is currently no clear regulation on the identity of patients who are terminated from involuntary medical treatment in China, and they can be regarded as general patients with mental disorders. In addition, there are currently no relevant regulations on the maximum period of involuntary medical treatment. There are research reports about 38.2%–80% of forensic psychiatric patients were treated in hospitals for long periods of time (some for more than 10 years) (Fang et al., 2006; Wang et al., 2006; Gu et al., 2023). At present, most of the patients defined as NCR-MD in China are receiving involuntary medical treatment for an indefinite period of time.

### *Role of Forensic Psychiatrists*

Chinese forensic psychiatrists are contacted primarily to provide expert opinions, assessments, and consultations for public security authorities, courts, or tribunals for criminal cases (Hu et al., 2011). Forensic psychiatrists mainly serve to study and solve the status and legal responsibilities of patients with mental disorders in criminal and civil proceedings. A forensic psychiatrist in China is required to give an expert opinion regarding the criminal responsibility of the suspects, competency to stand trial and to serve a sentence, civil competency in different forms of civil litigation, and disability, based on psychological and medical criteria.

The medical criterion primarily used in forensic psychiatric evaluations is ICD–10. The Chinese criminal justice system heavily weighs the importance of scientific evidence and expert medical opinions in litigation procedures for both civil and criminal cases (Hu et al., 2011). Because of the significance of scientific evidence in litigation activities, expert opinions play an important role in the investigation and trial processes of criminal and civil cases, and also protecting the human rights of the patients in the judicial process.

### *Training for Forensic Mental Health Practitioners*

In China, there is no fellowship program for forensic psychiatry right now. Any individual who applies to become a forensic psychiatrist must be reviewed and registered, if eligible. Then a formal announcement will be made by the administration at the provincial level of justice. However, there are still no uniform standards for how to become a forensic psychiatrist in China. It is generally recognized that, if a clinical psychiatrist has the medical rank of attending doctor or above with more than five years of clinical practice and has passed the examination set by the administration at provincial level, they can obtain a license as a forensic psychiatrist. In addition, they must obtain a practicing certificate by registering with an organization (or hospital), which must have a legal basis. It is estimated that there are approximately 2,800 forensic psychiatrists in China.

## Forensic Psychiatry Service (Provision of Care)

### *Forensic Patient Characteristics*

Civilly committed patients in China refer to those who meet the criteria of involuntary admission according to the *Chinese Mental Health Act*, but they are not considered forensic patients. Only patients who committed criminal acts and are found NCR-MD, as well as some patients with diminished responsibility, are considered forensic patients. There is still a lack of comprehensive research on the profile of patients in forensic mental health hospitals in China (Gu et al., 2023). In one hospital, Hunan Provincial Forensic Psychiatric Hospital (Hunan Ankang Hospital), most patients were male and unmarried, and had a low level of education; most of them were diagnosed with schizophrenia and hospitalized for a lengthy period. The main types of crimes were homicide and intentional injury, with family members accounting for over half of the victims. However, these results reflect the profile of patients at only one particular hospital, and it is unknown whether these results are generalizable to other areas of China (Gu et al., 2023).

### *Approaches to Assessment and Treatment*

The main aim of the forensic psychiatric services is to improve the patients' psychiatric symptoms and reduce the risk of violence. At present, the treatment of forensic psychiatric patients focuses on drug therapy (including antipsychotic drugs, mood stabilizers, and antidepressants), supplemented by psychotherapy, physical therapy, and rehabilitation training.

Involuntary medical institutions will conduct regular diagnostic assessments on patients. Article 5 of the Measures for the Diagnosis and Evaluation of Involuntary Medical Treatment (Trial Implementation) 2022 stipulates that the items of the diagnosis and evaluation of involuntary medical treatment include the evaluation of the effectiveness of treatment of mental disorders, dangerous behaviors, dangerous cognition, and the social support of these patients. The evaluation of the effectiveness of treatment of mental disorders refers to the evaluation of the clinical treatment effect of patients, and the results are divided into 'cured,' 'significantly effective,' 'improved,' and 'ineffective.' The evaluation of dangerous behaviors refers to the evaluation of whether the patient has dangerous behaviors that threaten his or her own and social security over a period of time. The evaluation of dangerous cognition refers to the evaluation of the patient's awareness of the nature, consequences, responsibilities of his or her own violent behavior, and his or her own mental disorders and the risk of recidivism, which is divided into three dimensions: complete, partial, and none. The evaluation of social support refers to the evaluation of the patient's residence, source of economic income, guardian, and medical resources, which is divided into three levels: good, general, and poor.

## Strengths and Weaknesses

In terms of strengths, the Chinese forensic psychiatry system has played an important role in safeguarding and balancing public security and the rights of the forensic psychiatric patients.

As for the weaknesses of the forensic system, first, although the situation of forensic psychiatry in China is improving and relevant laws are being refined, problems such as broad and ambiguous definition of 'patients with psychiatric disorder' or violence risk assessments on offenders are far beyond solved, which become the main tasks for forensic psychiatrists in the future. Second, in forensic psychiatric services, received long-term hospitalization or even lifelong treatment in Ankang Hospital is relatively common. Although long-term treatment is beneficial to social security, it may damage the patient's right to personal freedom, and resulting in a waste of limited medical resources and a heavy burden to the society. Third, there is still no clear regulation on the identity of patients who are terminated from involuntary medical treatment in China, and they can be regarded as general patients with mental disorders. In fact, most of them are diagnosed with schizophrenia, have poor treatment compliance with higher violent risk. There are also no clear regulations on their management after returning to the community, which may easily lead to relapse of the disease and recidivism of violence.

## References

Fang, X. L., Qi, Y. H., Feng, Z. Q. (2006). Follow-up of disposal of 90 psychiatric cases with irresponsibility after forensic assessment [in Chinese]. *Shanghai Archives of Psychiatry, 18*(5), 273e5.

Gu, Y., Guo, H., Zhou, J., et al. (2023). Socio-demographic, clinical and offense-related characteristics of forensic psychiatric inpatients in Hunan, China: A cross-sectional survey. *BMC Psychiatry, 23*(1), 48. https://doi.org/10.1186/s12888-022-04508-8

Guo, H., Zhong, S., Yue, Y., Gou, N., Sun, Q., Liang, X., Wang, F., Lu, J., Li, Q., Zhou, J., & Wang, X. (2021). Self-harm history, anxiety-depression, severity of disease, and insight are significantly associated with suicide risk in forensic psychiatric inpatients of China. *Frontiers in Psychiatry, 12*, 706416. https://doi.org/10.3389/fpsyt.2021.706416

Hu, J., Yang, M., Huang, X., & Coid, J. (2011). Forensic psychiatry in China. *International Journal of Law and Psychiatry, 34*(1), 7–12. https://doi.org/10.1016/j.ijlp.2010.11.002

Li, G., Gutheil, T. G., & Hu, Z. (2016). Comparative study of forensic psychiatric system between China and America. *International Journal of Law and Psychiatry, 47*, 164–170. https://doi.org/10.1016/j.ijlp.2016.04.002

Wang, X. P., Livingston, J. D., Brink, J., & Murphy, E. (2006). Persons found 'Not criminally responsible on account of mental disorder': A comparison of British Columbia, Canada and Hunan, China. *Forensic Science International, 164*(2e3), 93e7.

Wang, X. P., Zhang, D., Jiang, S., Bai, Y., Cucolo, H. E., & Perlin, M. L. (2007). Reassessing the aftercare treatment of individuals found not guilty due to a mental disability in Hunan, China: Supplemental study into the disposition of mentally ill offenders after forensic psychiatric assessment. *Australian & New Zealand Journal of Psychiatry, 41*(4), 337–342. https://doi.org/10.1080/00048670701213252

# 23 India

*Rakesh K. Chadda and Sanjiv Gulati*

## Brief Description

| | |
|---|---|
| **Location** | India is located in South Asia. |
| **Size** | 3.3 million $km^2$ |
| **Population** | 1.45 billion |
| **Languages** | The Constitution of India identifies 22 languages as the official languages of various states. English and Hindi remain the most prominent official languages. Others include Urdu, Telugu, Bengali, Tamil, Assamese, Odia, Gujarati, Malayalam, Kannada, Marathi, Punjabi, Manipuri, Konkani, and Dogri. |
| **Political system** | India has a parliamentary democratic republic with a federal structure, where power is divided between the central government and 28 states and eight union territories. Each state and certain union territories have their own elected governments for local governance. The President of India is the head of state, while the Prime Minister is the head of government and the executive authority in the country. India has a bicameral Parliament consisting of the House of the People (*Lok Shaba*) and the Council of States (*Rajya Sabha*). The judiciary is independent and is headed by the Supreme Court, the highest judicial authority in India. |

## Legal System

The judicial system in India is generally divided into civil and criminal courts, along with a third category of consumer courts that address consumer-related grievances. Civil courts handle disputes between individuals or organisations, whereas criminal courts manage cases related to criminal offences. Criminal courts in India are categorised into the Supreme Court of India, the country's highest judicial authority; High Courts in each state, which hear appeals from lower courts; Sessions Courts in all districts responsible for serious offences; and Magistrates' Courts, which handle minor offences. Both the Supreme Court and the High Courts hear criminal and civil cases (Jiloha et al., 2019). The Indian Government has also established Fast-track Courts, specialised courts

DOI: 10.4324/9781003376248-28

designed to speed up trials for certain criminal cases, particularly those involving sensitive issues such as sexual offences, murder, terrorism, or corruption (*Criminal Law (Amendment) Act, 2013*; Ministry of Law and Justice, 2000).

The Supreme Court, located in Delhi, the capital of India, serves as the highest court of appeal and is responsible for interpreting the country's laws. While it primarily hears appeals from the High Courts, certain cases can also be filed directly (Sharma, n.d.). The Supreme Court's decisions are final and cannot be further appealed. High Courts are the highest judicial tribunals at the state level, usually based in the state capital. They also function as courts of appeal within their respective states. Both the Supreme Court and the High Courts have the authority to impose any sentence prescribed by law, including the death penalty.

Sessions Courts serve as the highest judicial authority within a district and are located at the district headquarters. Each Sessions Court is presided over by a judge, hears criminal cases referred by Magistrates' Courts, and is authorised to impose any sentence prescribed by law. However, any death sentence passed by a Sessions Court must be confirmed by the High Court. Magistrates' Courts are lower courts in each district that handle cases involving cognisable offences. These courts are authorised to issue arrest warrants in cases such as homicide, rape, and other offences causing serious bodily harm.

The Indian legal system is primarily based on British law, a legacy of British colonial rule. Many aspects of India's legal framework, including the application of British common law principles, the judicial structure, and criminal procedures, were established during colonial rule and continue to function in India today. The *Indian Penal Code* (IPC) was first enacted in 1860, establishing a framework for defining various offences and their corresponding punishments. Over the next 160 years, it underwent multiple amendments before being repealed and replaced by the *Bharatiya Nyaya Sanhita* (BNS), 2023, which came into effect on July 1, 2024.

Similarly, the *Code of Criminal Procedure* (CrPC), 1973, which governed the procedural aspects of the IPC, 1860, remained in use until recently. The CrPC, 1973 has now been repealed and replaced by the *Bharatiya Nagarik Suraksha Sanhita* (BNSS), 2023, which also came into effect on July 1, 2024 (*Bharatiya Nagarik Suraksha Sanhita*, 2023; *Bharatiya Nyaya Sanhita*, 2023; *Code of Criminal Procedure*, 1973; *Indian Penal Code*, 1860).

India has 1,319 prisons, categorised into different types based on their functions and the inmates they house. There are 148 Central Jails, high-security prisons housing inmates convicted of serious offences, often serving long-term or life sentences. India has 88 Open Jails, low-security facilities for inmates who have demonstrated good behaviour and are granted more liberties, such as supervised work opportunities outside the prison, as part of rehabilitation efforts. There are 424 District Jails, which are local prison facilities accommodating inmates awaiting trial or serving short-term sentences for minor offences. The 564 Sub-Jails are smaller facilities located in rural areas, designed to house fewer inmates. Similar to District Jails, these prisons are used for short-term sentences related to minor offences.

India also has 41 Special Jails, which house inmates requiring specialised treatment or protection, such as those facing political charges. Additionally, 32 Women's Jails accommodate female inmates, and 19 Borstal Schools are reformation centres for juvenile offenders focused on rehabilitation, education, skills training, and reform (Prison Statistics in India, 2024).

### *Mental Health Laws*

Laws governing mental health in India were first introduced by the British during colonial rule. The *Indian Lunatic Asylums Act 1858* was the first law regulating asylums. It was amended in 1886 and 1889 before being replaced by the *Indian Lunacy Act, 1912.* Following significant advocacy from the Indian Psychiatric Society, this Act was later replaced by the *Mental Health Act 1987*, which introduced several reforms. One of its key changes was the removal of outdated, stigmatising terminology related to mental illness and psychiatric hospitals. It sought to recognise mental illness as a health condition like any other (Chadda, 2020). The *Mental Healthcare Act, 2017*, India's most recent mental health legislation, officially replaced the Act of 1987.

#### *Mental Healthcare Act, 2017*

The *Mental Healthcare Act, 2017* was enacted "to provide for mental health care and services for persons with mental illness and to protect, promote and fulfil the rights of such persons during delivery of mental health care and services and for matters connected therewith or incidental thereto" (*Mental Healthcare Act, 2017*). The Government of India enacted the Act on May 29, 2018, officially replacing the *Mental Health Act 1987*, which was considered inadequate in safeguarding the rights of individuals with mental illness and ensuring their access to mental health care in the country. The Act adopts a rights-based approach, aligning mental health care with international human rights standards (*Mental Healthcare Act, 2017*).

The Act has been widely regarded as ambitious legislation, particularly given the limited mental health resources available in the country. It was designed to protect and promote the rights of individuals with mental illness during the delivery of health care in both institutions and the community while also ensuring care, treatment, and rehabilitation in the least restrictive and burdensome environment possible.

The Act, comprising 16 chapters and 126 sections, outlines the creation of the Central Mental Health Authority at the national level and the State Mental Health Authorities (SMHA) in each state. Additionally, it provides for establishing Mental Health Review Boards at the district level, incorporating input from patients, family members, mental health professionals, and the voluntary sector. All mental health treatment facilities, including hospitals, psychiatric nursing homes, rehabilitation centres, and other institutions providing mental health care in India, are designated as Mental Health Establishments (MHEs). MHEs must be registered with the SMHA.

The Act establishes minimum standards for mental health facilities and outlines procedures for the admission, discharge, and leave of individuals with mental illness, including emergency treatment. Additionally, the Act introduced the concept of advance directives and designated representatives for individuals with mental illness. Chapter 5 of the Act outlines the safeguards for the rights of individuals with mental illness. It provides detailed provisions on their entitlements to mental health care, support for living in the community, protections against mistreatment, confidentiality, and access to legal assistance.

Following its enactment, the Government of India introduced additional rules for its implementation, including the Mental Health Care (Central Mental Health Authority and Mental Health Review Boards) Rules 2018, the Mental Health Care (State Mental Health Authority) Rules 2018, and the Mental Health Care (Rights of Persons with Mental Illness) Rules 2018 (*Mental Healthcare Act, 2017*).

Certain other laws enacted in India pertain to mental health, such as the *Rights of Persons with Disability Act, 2016*, the *Narcotic Drugs and Psychotropic Substances Act, 1985*, and the *Protection of Children from Sexual Offences Act, 2012*.

The *Rights of Persons with Disabilities Act, 2016* guarantees equal rights and privileges to individuals with disabilities, ensuring they are not discriminated against due to their disability. The Government of India enacted it in accordance with the United Nations Convention on the Rights of Persons with Disabilities of 2006. The Act expanded the number of recognised disabilities from 7, as defined in the previous *Disability Act, 1996*, to 21. The Act now covers mental illnesses, intellectual disability, cerebral palsy, dwarfism, muscular dystrophy, acid attack victims, hard of hearing, speech and language disability, specific learning disabilities, autism spectrum disorders, and chronic neurological disorders like multiple sclerosis and Parkinson's disease, among others.

The *Narcotic Drugs and Psychotropic Substances Act, 1985,* is a comprehensive legislation on narcotic drugs and psychotropic substances, enforcing effective control over psychotropic substances and implementing international conventions concerning narcotic drugs and psychotropic substances. The Act has been amended periodically in the last 40 years, with the latest amendment made in 2021.

The *Protection of Children from Sexual Offences Act, 2012,* was enacted to protect children from sexual offences, harassment, and pornography. The Act includes administrative mechanisms for reporting and recording evidence. It has provisions for establishing special courts and appointments of special public prosecutors. It also provides for speedy trials to ensure ease of legal functioning and establish special courts to trial such offences.

***Process of Trial in Courts in India***

Criminal law in India is governed by the BNS, 2023, which defines criminal offences and their punishments. The BNSS, 2023 governs criminal procedure, including investigations, arrests, trials, and sentencing, replacing the CrPC, 1973. Trials in Indian courts follow a structured legal procedure, as outlined in the BNSS (Hegde et al., 2024).

Broadly, trials in India fall into two categories: civil and criminal. A civil trial involves a dispute between individuals or organisations where no crime has been committed against the state. The rules governing civil trials are outlined in the BNSS. The process begins when a court issues a summons to the defendant following a complaint. The defendant must appear in court and submit a statement, after which the plaintiff may submit a rejoinder, and the defendant can provide further admission or denial. Civil trials typically involve a series of hearings where both parties present evidence and arguments before the court. The process concludes with a judgement issued by the court.

A criminal trial is conducted when a crime has been committed against the state or society. In these cases, the government files charges against the accused. The principle of 'not guilty unless and until proved otherwise' applies, ensuring that the burden of proof lies with the state to establish guilt beyond a reasonable doubt. The accused is granted full opportunity to defend themselves in accordance with due process.

***Role of Psychiatrist in Different Phases of Trial***

A psychiatrist is expected to assist the legal process at various trial stages. In the pretrial phase, they may be asked to assess the accused for mental illness, determine the need for treatment, and evaluate their fitness for interrogation (Chadda, 2013). During the trial phase, a psychiatrist may be required to assess the accused's fitness to stand trial, provide an evaluation for an insanity defence or criminal responsibility, or screen for mental illness and offer treatment in prison. In the post-trial phase, they may be involved in providing treatment for ongoing mental health conditions and assessing the accused's fitness for execution.

***Mental Illness and Criminal Responsibility***

Criminal responsibility refers to whether a person with a mental illness is legally responsible for a criminal act they have committed or can be exempted from charges on the grounds of having a mental illness. In Indian law, the definition of criminal responsibility has been adapted from the M'Naghten Rules, 1843 and is outlined in Section 22 of the BNS, 2023: "Nothing is an offence which is done by a person who, at the time of doing it, is incapable of knowing the nature of the act, or that he/she is doing any wrong or anything contrary to law" (*Bharatiya Nagarik Suraksha Sanhita*, 2023).

A defendant typically invokes an insanity defence to avoid facing the death penalty in cases involving a murder charge. If the defence succeeds, the court deems the accused 'not guilty'. However, there are provisions for hospital diversion, where the individual is not released but is instead sent to a mental hospital for treatment.

For an insanity defence to be valid, the unsoundness of mind must have been present when committing the offence. Lack of mental capacity after committing an act is not generally accepted as a defence, although it can impact trial proceedings. Unless proven otherwise, every individual is presumed to be of sound mind and responsible for their actions. The burden of proving insanity lies with the accused.

A person who was under the influence of a substance at the time of the offence is not exempt from charges if they willingly consumed the substance (known as voluntary intoxication) and understood the consequences. However, according to Section 23 of the BNS, it is not considered an offence if the person was unable to comprehend the nature of the act due to involuntary intoxication, provided the substance that caused the intoxication was administered without their consent or knowledge (*Bharatiya Nyaya Sanhita*, 2023).

### *Fitness to Stand Trial*

Mental illness may affect an individual's ability to comprehend legal proceedings and adequately prepare a defence. Under Indian law, Sections 367–378 of the BNSS provide guidelines for the trial of a person suspected to have a mental illness and outline the procedures to be followed if an individual appears to be of unsound mind during their trial.

If evidence of mental illness is presented during court proceedings and contested by the opposing party, the judge will refer the individual for further evaluation by the relevant mental health review board. If the court determines that the accused is of unsound mind and unable to defend themselves, further proceedings will be suspended. The accused may then be detained in safe custody under the *Mental Healthcare Act, 2017* or be released pending investigation or trial if bail is granted, provided a relative offers sufficient security for their treatment and care (Section 378 of the BNSS). The trial may resume if the accused is no longer deemed to be of unsound mind (Chadda, 2013; Hegde et al., 2024).

## Forensic Psychiatry System

### *Structure and Function of the Forensic Psychiatry System*

India, home to nearly one-sixth of the world's population, has significantly fewer mental healthcare facilities and professionals when compared to Western countries. Formal forensic psychiatry services are scarce, with most forensic mental health care provided by general psychiatrists, who themselves are already overburdened with general mental health care. There is currently very little infrastructure and organised training in forensic psychiatry in India. Only the National Institute of Mental Health and Neuro-Sciences in Bengaluru has a dedicated forensic psychiatric unit. Many psychiatric units lack a specialised forensic psychiatry ward, requiring general psychiatrists to assume forensic psychiatry responsibilities as needed.

When directed by local courts, general psychiatrists working in state-run general hospitals or mental hospitals are often required to provide forensic psychiatry-related assessments. However, many prisons in India lack adequate mental health professionals, resulting in insufficient psychiatric care for inmates. Despite high occupancy rates and a significant number of incarcerated individuals with mental disorders, full-time psychiatrists are employed in limited numbers within the prison system (Ayirolimeethal et al., 2014).

As a result, most forensic evaluations in India are conducted by psychiatrists with little or no formal training in forensic psychiatry. Nonetheless, some Indian psychiatrists have shown a growing interest in the field. The first handbook on forensic psychiatry in India, written by J. C. Marfatia, was published in 1972. More recently, two additional books on forensic psychiatry by R. C. Jiloha et al. and S. Nambi, along with a monograph from the National Institute of Mental Health and Neuro-Sciences, have contributed to the academic development of the field in India (Jiloha et al., 2019; Marfatia, 1972; Naik et al., 2021; Nambi, 2013).

### *Specialist Training and Qualifications*

Postgraduate training in psychiatry includes a three-year residency after completing a Bachelor of Medicine, Bachelor of Surgery (MBBS) degree. During this period, trainees spend approximately one month in a mental hospital, gaining exposure to forensic psychiatry. Additionally, they participate in teaching sessions such as seminars and case discussions focused on the subspecialty as part of their postgraduate training.

Notably, the National Institute of Mental Health and Neuro-Sciences introduced a one-year postdoctoral fellowship in forensic psychiatry, which remains the only formal training programme in this field in India (National Institute of Mental Health & Neuro-Sciences, n.d.). The programme was established in 2015 and is designed to equip psychiatrists with the expertise required to assist individuals with mental health disorders who are involved in the justice system. The fellowship combines clinical practice, research, and forensic evaluations, addressing criminal responsibility, competency, and risk assessments.

### *Training in Forensic Psychology*

Forensic psychology is an emerging discipline in India. Rashtriya Raksha University and the National Forensic Sciences University in Gandhinagar offer a master's programme in forensic psychology and further research opportunities. The Directorate of Forensic Science Services in India was established in 2002 by the Ministry of Home Affairs, Government of India. The two universities offering training programmes in forensic psychology also operate under the Ministry of Home Affairs. The Ministry runs six Central Forensic Science Laboratories (CFSLs) in Chandigarh, Kolkata, Hyderabad, Pune, Guwahati, and Bhopal. The CFSLs provide scientific assistance to the justice delivery system in forensic science and conduct specialised training programmes for forensic scientists, police, and the judiciary. CFSLs also provide forensic laboratory services to the local investigation teams.

## Strengths and Weaknesses

Forensic psychiatry in India is still in its infancy, although J.C. Marfatia's 1972 handbook on forensic psychiatry was an early contribution to the field. With just one psychiatrist per nearly 200,000 people, forensic psychiatry has not yet developed as a formal discipline in the country. General psychiatrists typically manage forensic psychiatry services. Due to the limited number of psychiatrists in India, formal risk assessment is lacking in most settings. It is generally restricted to cases involving self-harm or suicide attempts presenting as emergencies in general hospitals with psychiatric facilities.

Most treatment in forensic services is currently pharmacological. However, change is expected in the near future, as a new generation of forensic psychologists is likely to contribute to forensic mental health services in India.

## References

Ayirolimeethal, A., Ragesh, G., Ramanujam, J. M., & George, B. (2014). Psychiatric morbidity among prisoners. *Indian Journal of Psychiatry*, *56*(2), 150–153. https://doi.org/10.4103/0019-5545.130581

Chadda, R. K. (2013). Forensic evaluations in psychiatry. *Indian Journal of Psychiatry*, *55*, 393–399. https://doi.org/10.4103/0019-5545.115593

Chadda, R. K. (2020). Influence of the new mental health legislation in India. *BJPsych International*, *17*, 20–22. https://doi.org/10.1192/bji.2020.16

*Code of Criminal Procedure, 1973*. (2025). Retrieved from https://www.indiacode.nic.in/bitstream/123456789/1501764528-Criminal-Procedure-Code-CrPC-1973

*Criminal Law (Amendment) Act, 2013*. (2013). Government of India.

*Bharatiya Nagarik Suraksha Sanhita (BNSS), 2023*. (2025). Government of India. https://www.indiacode.nic.in/bitstream/123456789/20099/3/aa2023–46.pdf

*Bharatiya Nyaya Sanhita, 2023*. (2023). Government of India. https://www.mha.gov.in/sites/default/files/2024-04/250883_english_01042024.pdf

Hegde, P. R., Malik, Y., Kumar, C. N., & Math, S. B. (2024). The Bharatiya Nyaya Sanhita Act (BNSA) 2023: Implications for forensic psychiatry in India. *Indian Journal of Psychological Medicine*. https://doi.org/10.1177/02537176241281465

*Indian Penal Code, 1860*. (2025, March 9). Retrieved from https://www.indiacode.nic.in/bitstream/123456789/15289/1/ipc_act.pdf

Jiloha, R. C., Kataria, D., & Kukreti, P. (2019). *Forensic psychiatry: An Indian perspective*. New Delhi: Jaypee Brothers Medical Publishers.

Marfatia, J. C. (1972). *Psychiatry and law*. Popular Prakashan.

*Mental Healthcare Act, 2017. (2017). Government of India.*

Ministry of Law and Justice, Government of India. (2000). *Fast-track court scheme*.

Naik, S. S., Damodharan, D., Kumar, C. N., & Math, S. B. (Eds.). (2021). *Forensic psychiatry in India—Interface between Indian law and mental health*. NIMHANS Publication No. 196. Bengaluru, India: National Institute of Mental Health and Neuro-Sciences.

Nambi, S. (2013). *Forensic psychiatry (psychiatry and law): Indian perspective*. New Delhi: Jaypee Brothers Medical Publishers.

*Narcotic Drugs and Psychotropic Substances Act, 1985*. (1985). Government of India.

National Institute of Mental Health and Neuro-Sciences. (n.d.). *Forensic psychiatry*. Retrieved February 17, 2025, from https://nimhans.co.in/forensic-psychiatry/

Prison Statistics in India. (2024, February 29). Retrieved from https://data.gov.in/catalog/prison-statistics-india-psi-2021

*Protection of children from sexual offences act, 2012*. (2012). Government of India.

*Rights of Persons with Disabilities Act, 2016*. (2016). Government of India.

Sharma, S. M. (n.d.). *Can a case be directly filed in Supreme Court of India or High Courts without approaching subordinate courts?* Retrieved from https://www.hg.org/legal-articles/can-a-case-be-directly-filed-in-supreme-court-of-india-or-high-courts-without-approaching-subordinate-courts-55472

# 24 Japan

*Akiko Kikuchi, Junko Koike, Miki Hirano, and Chiyo Fujii*

## Brief Description

| | |
|---|---|
| **Location** | Japan is an island country in East Asia. |
| **Size** | 378,000 km$^2$ |
| **Population** | 123,802,000 (October 1, 2024, final estimate) (Statistics Bureau of Japan, 2025) |
| **Language** | Japanese |
| **Political system** | The Emperor is the symbol of the state, with power limited to a ceremonial role. Japan adopted a system of separation of powers (*Sanken Bunritsu*) based on its post-World War II Constitution, which was enacted in 1947. This system divides the state power into three independent branches: Legislative power rests with the National Diet (*Kokkai*), which consists of the House of Representatives (*Shūgi-in*) and the House of Councillors (*Sangi-in*). The Cabinet (*Naikaku*) is the executive branch headed by the Prime Minister, who has the authority to appoint and dismiss Ministers of State. The judiciary *(Saibansho*) is the third independent branch.<br>Japan comprises 47 administrative prefectures, each with its own governance and regional administration. |

## Judicial System

In the Japanese judiciary (*Saibansho*), the Supreme Court is the highest judicial authority, overseeing constitutional matters and the rule of law. Lower, High, District, Family, and Summary Courts handle civil, criminal, and administrative cases. The High Court is the most senior among the lower courts. If a person is dissatisfied with the court's decision, they can appeal to the higher court twice.

## Legislation Related to Forensic Psychiatry

Forensic psychiatry in Japan is the medical specialty at the intersection of mental health and the law, focusing on the assessment, treatment, and legal management of individuals with mental disorders who have committed crimes or are involved

DOI: 10.4324/9781003376248-29

in legal proceedings (referred to in Japan as 'mentally disordered offenders' [MDOs]). Three major pieces of legislation shape the practice.

### *Penal Code (*Keiho*)*

The Penal Code is the primary source of criminal law in Japan, defining crimes and their corresponding punishments. It was enacted in 1907 and was influenced by European (mainly German and French) legal traditions. It has been revised over time, especially after World War II.

Article 39 is crucial for determining criminal responsibility based on mental state. It states that "(1) Actions due to insanity is not subject to punishment and (2) An act of diminished capacity leads to the punishment being reduced" (Ministry of Justice, 2020). Insanity (*Shin Sōshitsu*) refers to a condition where the offender completely lacks the capacity to understand the nature of their actions or to control their behavior at the time of the offense. Diminished capacity (*Shin Shin Kōjaku*), or diminished responsibility, refers to a mental state where a person's ability to understand the nature of their actions or to form the intent necessary to commit a crime is reduced.

If mental illness is suspected, the court may order a psychiatric evaluation by psychiatrists to determine whether Article 39 applies. When the court determines that the offender was in a state of insanity at the time, the person may be found not guilty by reason of insanity. Offenders found to have had diminished capacity at the time of the offense may be found guilty but with a reduced sentence. The final decision lies with the court. If found not guilty by reason of insanity, or when the sentence is reduced by reason of diminished capacity and the offender is not imprisoned, the individual may be indicted by the prosecutor to the *Medical Treatment and Supervision Act* system.

### *Mental Health and Welfare Act*

The *Mental Health and Welfare Act* (MHWA, *Seishin Hoken Fukushi Hō*) provides the legal framework for mental health care and the welfare of individuals with mental disorders. Enacted in 1950, the MHWA has been revised multiple times to incorporate modern psychiatric practices, protect human rights, and promote social inclusion (Ministry of Justice, 2019).

The law regulates different types of psychiatric hospitalization. The three main types are as follows: voluntary admission (*Nin'i Nyūin)*; medical protection admission (*Iryō Hogo Nyūin*), which is involuntary admission that requires the consent of a family member or equivalent as defined by law; and involuntary admission (*Sochi Nyūin*) by the prefectural governor if the person poses a danger to themselves or others. While this law primarily governs general psychiatric care, it overlaps with forensic psychiatry in cases of involuntary hospitalization for individuals who may be a danger to others.

*Act on Medical Care and Treatment for Persons Who Have Caused Serious Harm Due to Mental Disorders*

The *Act on Medical Care and Treatment for Persons Who Have Caused Serious Cases Under the Condition of Insanity* (*Shinshin Sōshitsu-tō no Jōtai de Jūdai na Tagai Kōi o Okonatta Mono no Iryō oyobi Kansatsu-tō ni Kansuru Hōritsu*), better known as the *Medical Treatment and Supervision Act* (MTSA; *Iryō Kansatsu Hō*), is a Japanese law enacted in 2005 to address how society responds to individuals with mental disorders who have committed serious offenses while in a state of insanity or diminished capacity. This law provides a legal and medical framework for such individuals' treatment, supervision, and social reintegration. It is Japan's central legislation in forensic psychiatry and is jointly administered by the health and justice ministries. As of April 1, 2025, no formal English translation of the act has been published by the Ministry of Justice. The full legal text of the MTSA in Japanese can be referenced at e-Gov Developer (2025).

***Eligibility***

The person must have committed a 'serious harmful act' *(jūdai na tagai kōi)*—homicide, arson, bodily harm (only when serious), robbery, penetrative sexual assault (formerly called rape until the amendment of the Penal Code came into effect on July 13, 2023), or indecent assault—while in a state of insanity or diminished capacity. When the above conditions are met, the prosecutor files a motion for an MTSA hearing to the district court. Therefore, there are three referral routes to the MTSA system:

1. The prosecutor determines the case eligible for MTSA and decides not to prosecute. The decision is usually made with input from psychiatrists.
2. Those found not guilty by reason of insanity in court, and the offense is one of the aforementioned 'serious harmful acts.'
3. The court sentence is reduced because of diminished capacity, the offender is not imprisoned, and the offense was a 'serious harmful act.'

***Judicial Process and the Decision Makers***

After the prosecutor files a petition for an MTSA hearing with the District Court, a mental health examination is ordered, in which a psychiatrist evaluates whether the person was legally insane (*shin shin sōshitsu*) or had diminished capacity (*shin shin kōjaku*) at the time of the offense. A mental health examination report is submitted within three months.

The Probation Office prepares and submits a 'Living Environment Investigation Report' (*Seikatsu Kankyō Chōsa*). This report includes interviews with family members, an evaluation of housing, social support, and access to local mental health services.

A panel of one judge and one Mental Health Judge (*Seishin Hoken Shinpan'in,* a psychiatrist) is formed. The Panel reviews the mental health examination report, Living Environment Investigation Report, and recommendations by the Mental Health Counselor (*Seishin Hoken San'yo'in,* usually a psychiatric social worker) and makes the final decision.

For the Panel to issue a treatment order under the MTSA, the following three conditions must be met during the judicial hearing:

(a) Presence of mental disorder: the mental disorder that caused insanity or diminished capacity at the time of the offense is still present.
(b) Treatability: The individual with the mental disorder is expected to respond to medical treatment.
(c) Factors impeding the person's reintegration into society: There are factors that would impede the person's rehabilitation if the recurrence of similar acts is not prevented by treatment.

The decision is one of the following:

1. Inpatient treatment order (hospitalization in a designated inpatient facility).
2. Outpatient treatment order (community-based treatment under mental health probation). The length can be no longer than three years, although it can be extended to five years in cases where the risk of reoffending is high.
3. Dismissal of petition (no treatment order is issued).

## Forensic Psychiatry in Japan

As explained, there are three main laws related to forensic psychiatry in Japan. In response, three main facilities provide forensic psychiatric treatment to MDOs: medical prisons, psychiatric hospitals, and designated inpatient medical institutions under the MTSA.

Medical prisons (*Iryō Keimusho*) are specialized correctional facilities designed to house inmates who require ongoing medical care due to physical or mental illness. These institutions are part of the Japanese penal system and serve a dual function: providing appropriate medical treatment while enforcing the custodial sentence. Medical prisons are intended for:

1. Inmates with chronic or severe physical illnesses.
2. Inmates with serious mental disorders who cannot be adequately treated in general correctional facilities. The onset of mental disorders can be either before or after imprisonment.

3. Elderly inmates requiring long-term care.
4. Prisoners needing rehabilitation from severe injuries.

As of April 2025, there are four main medical prisons in Japan for adults: Medical Correction Center in East Japan, Osaka Medical Prison, Kita Kyushu Medical Prison, and Okazaki Medical Prison. While medical prisons aim to provide individualized care, time and resource constraints often lead to medication-centered approaches and minimal psycho-social interventions.

General psychiatric hospitals play an important role in forensic psychiatry in Japan. The three main roles are the following:

1. Not all individuals with mental illness who commit offenses fall under the purview of the MTSA. Offenders who are deemed fully responsible or who have committed minor infractions may be hospitalized under the MHWA.
2. Upon completion of the court-mandated treatment under the MTSA, many patients require continued psychiatric care, often at a less intensive level. General psychiatric hospitals frequently assume this role.
3. The limitation of the MTSA is that it only applies to individuals who have already committed a criminal act and are found to meet specific legal criteria. As a result, the MTSA cannot be used preemptively to detain or treat individuals who are considered high risk for future violent behavior but have not yet committed a crime. Because of this limitation, the role of involuntary hospitalization for public safety (*Sochi Nyūin,*) under the MHWA becomes crucial. *Sochi Nyūin* allows for the involuntary hospitalization of individuals who are deemed to pose a serious risk of harming themselves or others due to a mental disorder, based on the judgment of two designated psychiatrists. This measure can be taken before any criminal offense occurs and thus functions as a preventive mechanism for protecting public safety.

MTSA facilities form the central axis of Japan's forensic psychiatric system, discussed in detail in the next section.

## Forensic Psychiatry System Under the MTSA

### *Designated Medical Institutions*

Designated inpatient medical institutions (*Shitei Nyūin Iryō Kikan*)[1] are specialized psychiatric hospitals officially designated by the Ministry of Health, Labour, and Welfare to provide inpatient care under the MTSA (Ministry of Health, Labour and Welfare, 2025a). Only national or prefectural psychiatric hospitals can be designated to provide MTSA inpatient care. These hospitals have specialized medium-secure wards with enhanced staffing and security measures to manage potentially violent or high-risk patients. The bed number in each forensic unit is between 5 and 33. As of April 1, 2023, there are 35 designated inpatient medical institutions throughout Japan, with 856 beds (Ministry of Health, Labour and Welfare, 2023). Each Designated Inpatient Medical Institution has a multidisciplinary team trained in forensic psychiatry and must meet standards set by the government. Treatment in these hospitals occurs in a structured environment separated from general psychiatric wards, and the patients cannot leave the hospital without authorization while under the inpatient order.

Designated outpatient medical institutions (*Shitei Tsūin Iryō Kikan*) are specialized psychiatric hospitals officially designated by the Ministry of Health, Labour, and Welfare to provide outpatient care under the MTSA. Any qualified psychiatric hospital or clinic can apply for the designation. As of April 2023, there were 718 designated outpatient medical institutions in Japan (622 general hospitals and 96 clinics) authorized to treat MTSA patients. In addition to these primary treatment sites, the MTSA outpatient system includes affiliated services such as designated pharmacies (2,686 nationwide) and home-visit nursing stations (770 nationwide) to support medication management and in-home care, bringing the total number of outpatient-related designated service sites to 4,174 (Ministry of Health, Labour and Welfare, 2025b).

The designated outpatient medical institutions must coordinate closely with probation offices and local authorities, effectively acting as the clinical arm of the forensic system. The availability of many designated outpatient medical institutions across Japan makes it feasible for patients to receive the required treatment in their community without relocating far from home. This community-based approach aligns with the MTSA's goal of reintegration—treatment happens in real-world settings rather than exclusively behind hospital walls.

### *Approaches to Treatment and Assessment Under the MTSA*

#### *Multidisciplinary Team and Multiagency Collaboration*

Psychiatric care under MTSA is delivered by a multidisciplinary team (MDT) at inpatient and outpatient designated medical institutions, typically including psychiatrists, psychiatric nurses, clinical psychologists, and psychiatric social workers experienced in forensic psychiatry. The probation office's Rehabilitation Coordinator (*Shakai Fukki Chōsei-kan*) begins coordinating community multiagency care while the patient is still hospitalized. The coordination will continue into outpatient treatment and to the end of care under MTSA.

#### *Phased Approach to Treatment*

Inpatient care has three phases: acute, recovery, and rehabilitation phase (Fujii et al., 2014). The acute phase generally lasts three months, and psychiatric treatment focuses on improving mental health symptoms, physical recovery, achieving mental stability, increasing motivation for treatment, and building trust and relationships. The recovery phase lasts around nine months. The goal is to gain awareness of the mental illness, master self-control, learn daily living skills, and increase privileges and responsibilities over time. The final rehabilitation phase occurs over six months, and patients are permitted escorted leave at increasing lengths of time as their condition improves and stabilizes. Other components of the rehabilitation phase are the acceptance of disability, recovery of social life skills (i.e., medication management, financial management), preparation for social reintegration, and community involvement. Inpatient orders have no absolute time limit in the law, but guidelines suggest roughly 18 months as a typical course for hospitalization (Ministry of Health, Labour and Welfare, 2023).

Inpatient treatment programs offer group interventions such as psychoeducation, relapse prevention, social skills training, metacognitive training, substance abuse treatment programs, index offense introspection groups, and cognitive remediation programs. Some designated inpatient medical institutions provide family intervention groups. Once a forensic patient has completed inpatient treatment and the district court determines an outpatient treatment order, the patient is discharged and begins treatment in a designated outpatient institution.

Outpatient treatment has three stages—early, middle, and late—each with specific goals and levels of support. An Individualized Outpatient Treatment Plan (*Kobetsus Shogu Keikaku*) is developed by the rehabilitation coordinators at the probation office in collaboration with the MDT to coordinate interventions in each phase, putting patients' wishes and personal goals at the center. In the early stage, contact and care coordination meetings are usually frequent because patients tend to destabilize during the transition due to environmental changes. By the middle stage, the frequency of contact usually decreases as community activities increase. The late stage prepares for the end of the order, with reduced supervision and planning and preparing for the transition to routine mental health services.

During the outpatient treatment order, if and when the individual's psychiatric illness worsens, they are admitted to a general psychiatric unit under the MHWA. Hospitalization is not necessarily involuntary. However, if the patient shows signs of significant mental health deterioration or engages in behaviors that raise concern about the risk of harming themselves or others, the patient can be rehospitalized in the designated inpatient medical institution under the MTSA (Article 61).

### *Approaches to Assessment*

The MTSA emphasizes comprehensive, multidisciplinary assessment. The goal is to determine appropriate treatment, assess the risk of recidivism, and facilitate safe reintegration into society. Assessments are carried out by psychiatrists, clinical psychologists, psychiatric social workers, nurses, occupational therapists, and probation officers. A Common Assessment Items (*Kyōtsū Hyōka Kōmoku)* framework ensures that all professionals involved in the case use a common language, promoting smooth transitions from hospital to community settings and continuity of care. This framework plays important role in case conferences, discharge planning, and follow-up under the MTSA. Other widely used violence risk assessment and complementary tools such as HCR-20 V2 (Webster et al., 1997; Arai et al., 2016), START (Short-Term Assessment of Risk and Treatability; Webster et al., 2009; Kikuchi et al., 2021), SAPROF (Structured Assessment of Protective Factors; de Vogel et al., 2007; Kashiwagi et al., 2018) are validated in Japanese and used on a needs-based basis.

### *Exiting the MTSA System*

#### *Discharge From Designated Inpatient Institutions*

There are several routes to exit the MTSA system. In most cases, when the patient is no longer in need of forensic psychiatric care at a designated inpatient institution, a discharge petition will be prepared by the MDT and filed by the designated inpatient institution. A discharge petition occurs when the patient achieves the following state:

1. a stable psychiatric condition,
2. the ability to seek necessary medical care autonomously, and
3. an appropriate support system in place (Ministry of Health, Labour and Welfare, 2025a).

During the first two weeks after the ruling, patients or prosecutors can submit an appeal to the High Court through the district court about their treatment order. Also, hospitalized patients, guardians, or attendants may petition the district court for permission to leave or terminate medical treatment under this law (MTSA Article 50). Upon receiving such a petition, the district court conducts a hearing by a panel of one judge and one mental health judge, hearing the opinions of mental health counselors as necessary. The panel makes one of the following decisions:

1. continued hospitalization decision,
2. outpatient treatment decision,
3. decision not to provide medical treatment under the MTSA, or
4. dismissal of the petition.

### *Final Exit From the MTSA System*

The standard outpatient treatment order lasts three years, but it can be shorter or extended for up to two more years (maximum of five years). If the person has maintained stable mental health, complied with treatment, and is judged to no longer pose a significant risk to society, the probation office can recommend early termination of supervision. If the court agrees that further MTSA-based supervision is unnecessary, the treatment order can be lifted early. In most cases, exit from the MTSA system occurs at the end of the third year, and the individual is then formally discharged from MTSA supervision and becomes a regular member of society. Often, the person continues psychiatric treatment voluntarily through general mental health services.

## Key Statistics and Facts Related to the MTSA

**Cumulative caseload:** From the start of the MTSA on July 15, 2005, to December 30, 2020, 3,761 individuals were admitted to the designated inpatient medical institutions under the MTSA. Approximately 250 new cases have been added each year in recent years, showing a steady flow of MDOs being diverted to treatment (Committee for the Establishment of Standardized Treatments for Severe Mental Illness, 2022).

**Diagnostic profile:** In terms of psychiatric diagnosis (ICD-10), schizophrenia or related psychoses (F2) accounted for 80% of psychiatric diagnoses, followed by mood disorders (F3) and substance use disorders (F1). There have been no significant changes in the composition of psychiatric diagnoses over the years (Committee for the Establishment of Standardized Treatments for Severe Mental Illness, 2022).

**Offense profile**: By definition, all MTSA cases involve serious harm. In that same sample, the most common offense was homicide (32.7%), followed by injury (36.3%), arson (23.4%), and a small number of sex crimes (3.6%) and robbery (4.0%). Homicide, injury, and arson comprise over 90% of index offenses (Committee for the Establishment of Standardized Treatments for Severe Mental Illness, 2022).

**Duration of orders:** Many patients who start treatment as inpatients will subsequently complete three years as outpatients—a complete course through both phases can thus span around four and a half to five years of supervision. However, recent statistics show that the average length of stay in designated inpatient medical institutions was 1,022 days and the median was 827 days (Committee for the Establishment of Standardized Treatments for Severe Mental Illness, 2022).

Designated outpatient medical institutions have up to three years to provide forensic psychiatric treatment from the date of the court decision. The period can be extended to five years (Nakatani, 2012). When the patient no longer needs forensic mental health care, according to the MTSA, the head of the probation office consults the administrator of the designated outpatient medical institution and files a petition for termination of care under the MTSA with the district court (MTSA Article 54). Recent statistics, show that the average length of MTSA outpatient treatment was 951 days, and the median was 1,094 days (Committee for the Establishment of Standardized Treatments for Severe Mental Illness, 2022).

**Recidivism outcomes**: The MTSA system has achieved low reoffense rates. A 2019 study followed forensic patients discharged from designated forensic treatment facilities and found that the reoffending rate was 0.4% after one year and 2.0% after three years (Nagata et al., 2019). The authors discuss that one reason for this low reoffense rate may be that the MTSA patients rarely include those with the primary diagnosis of personality disorder.

**Incidents during treatment:** While under treatment, a significant portion of patients exhibit problematic behaviors, the majority of which fall short of reoffence. In one report, about 46.2% of MTSA outpatients showed some problematic behavior during the treatment period—such as refusal to take medication, verbal or minor physical aggression, self-harm ideation, or absconding from appointments—and 6.0% had suicidal behaviors (Ando et al., 2016).

One study found that, compared to the general population, the all-cause mortality and completed suicide rates were higher in forensic participants than observed in the general population (Takeda et al., 2019). The suicide standardized mortality ratios of MTSA patients were 17.9 overall. Women had a higher risk of completed suicide than men.

## Forensic Psychiatry Profession

### *Training for Psychiatrists/Psychologists*

Japan has no national accreditation program or specific qualifications for becoming a forensic psychiatrist. Eligible medical school candidates complete a medicine degree and finalize residency training. Psychiatrists are required to gain experience in the forensic mental health field over time. Although there is no specific forensic psychiatry certification program, the Japanese Society of Forensic Mental Health oversees and qualifies psychiatrists as experts in conducting mental health examinations.

According to the Japanese Society of Forensic Mental Health, 54 certified mental health examination specialists are available as of September 11, 2023. The association provides training in forensic psychiatric evaluations (*seishin kantei*).

For other professions, such as nurses, clinical psychologists, psychiatric social workers, and occupational therapists, no certification body exists to certify subspecialties in forensic mental health.

### *National Organizations and Collaborations*

There is no national forensic psychiatry organization in Japan. However, the Japanese Society of Forensic Mental Health and the MTSA-Related Multi-Disciplinary Training Program are collaborations strongly related to MTSA.

The Japanese Society of Forensic Mental Health (*Shihō Seishin Igakkai*) was founded in 2005 when the MTSA was enacted and has been instrumental in the communication and collaboration of a wide range of disciplines in law and psychiatry.

The MTSA-Related Multi-Disciplinary Training Program (*Iryō Kansatsuhō Kanren Shokushu Kenshūkai*) is a training initiative designed for professionals implementing MTSA. This training ensures that professionals from various disciplines develop a shared understanding, acquire practical skills, and strengthen collaborative practices in forensic mental health care.

Another important nationwide collaboration is the MTSA Database Project (Koike et al., 2024). This project collects monthly data on 'basic information,' 'orders and hospitalizations under the MTSA,' 'treatment process,' 'criminal and medical treatment history,' and 'problematic behavior in the unit' via an online system from designated inpatient medical facilities throughout Japan. The database is expected to disseminate a wide range of knowledge that will contribute to the future development of forensic care in Japan.

## Strengths and Weaknesses of the MTSA System

The MTSA system aims to ensure both public safety and the recovery and reintegration of MDOs. Over 20 years have passed since its implementation, and its strengths and challenges have become increasingly evident.

### *Strengths*

1. Structured legal and medical integration: The MTSA provides a specialized legal process for individuals found not guilty by reason of insanity or with diminished capacity.
2. Individualized and multidisciplinary treatment as models of psychiatric care in Japan: The MTSA emphasizes individualized treatment plans based on clinical needs and risk assessments and involves MDTs. When the MTSA was enacted in 2003, the MDT approach was uncommon in psychiatric care. Article 3 of the Supplementary Provisions of the Act clearly states that "it is the responsibility of the government to strive for the improvement of the overall standards of psychiatric care and mental health and welfare services."
3. Use of risk assessment tools: Not only Common Assessment Items (*Kyōtsū Hyōka Kōmoku*) but also structured professional judgment tools (e.g., HCR-20, START, SAPROF) are used to assess violence risk and guide treatment. Risk assessment is rarely utilized outside of the MTSA system.

4. Focus on community reintegration: This approach supports the gradual transition from hospitalization to community life, with systems for supervised outpatient care and social rehabilitation.
5. Continuity and consistency of care: In the MTSA system, the same Rehabilitation Coordinator of the Probation Office oversees the patients through different stages of forensic treatment (i.e., during mental health examination, inpatient phase, and outpatient phase). Such an arrangement reinforces the continuity and consistency of psychiatric care and coordination of multiagency intervention. This may be one of the factors supporting the low reoffense rate.

### *Weaknesses and Challenges*

1. Limited scope: The MTSA applies only to individuals who committed certain serious offenses while in a state of insanity or diminished responsibility. Thus, it excludes those who have a mental illness but are found fully responsible or who have not committed a serious crime, although they are at a high risk of doing so.
2. Long hospitalization periods: Some patients are hospitalized for extended periods, sometimes longer than prison sentences for the same offense. The long hospitalization periods may be due to risk aversion and a lack of community resources.
3. Uneven regional implementation: Availability and quality of services vary depending on the region.
4. Lack of specialized training: Forensic psychiatry does not have a formal national certification, leading to variation in evaluation and treatment quality. More structured training is needed.
5. Lack of a diversion system between the MTSA and criminal justice system: Because there is no diversion system, MDOs serving sentences in prison cannot benefit from the specialized forensic treatment provided in the designated inpatient medical facilities, even when their mental illness is severe.

## Note

1 'Designated Inpatient Medical Institutions' is the direct translation of the Japanese term '*Shitei Nyūin Iryō Kikan.*' Past articles have frequently used 'Designated Inpatient Facilities' instead (Fujii et al., 2014; Koike et al., 2024; Takeda et al., 2019).

## References

Ando, K., Soshi, T., Nakazawa, K., Noda, T., & Okada, T. (2016). Risk factors for problematic behaviors among forensic outpatients under the Medical Treatment and Supervision Act in Japan. *Frontiers in Psychiatry*, *7*, 144. https://doi.org/10.3389/fpsyt.2016.00144

Arai, K., Takano, A., Nagata, T., & Hirabayashi, N. (2016). Predictive accuracy of the Historical-Clinical-Risk Management-20 for violence in forensic psychiatric wards in Japan. *Criminal Behaviour and Mental Health, 27*(5), 451–461. https://doi.org/10.1002/cbm.2007

Committee for the Establishment of Standardized Treatments for Severe Mental Illness (Jūdo Seishin Shikkan Hyōjun Chiryō Kakuritsu Iinkai). (2022). *Medical treatment and supervision act statistical data, 2020 edition (Iryo Kansatsu Hou Tokei Shiryou 2020 nen ban)*. https://www.ncnp.go.jp/common/cms/docs/toukeishiryou20221226.pdf

de Vogel, V., de Ruiter, C., Bouman, Y., & de Vries Robbé, M. (2007). *SAPROF: Structured assessment of protective factors for violence risk*. Forum Educatief.

e-Gov Developer. (2025, March 31). *Shinshin Sōshitsu-tō no Jōtai de Jūdai na Tagai kōi o Okonatta Mono no Iryō oyobi Kansatsu-tō ni Kansuru Hōritsu*. https://laws.e-gov.go.jp/law/416CO0000000310

Fujii, C., Fukuda, Y., Ando, K., Kikuchi, A., & Okada, T. (2014). Development of forensic mental health services in Japan: Working towards the reintegration of offenders with mental disorders. *International Journal of Mental Health Systems, 8*, 21. https://doi.org/10.1186/1752-4458-8-21

Kashiwagi, H., Kikuchi, A., Koyama, M., Saito, D., & Hirabayashi, N. (2018). Strength-based assessment for future violence risk: A retrospective validation study of the Structured Assessment of Protective Factors for violence risk (SAPROF) Japanese version in forensic psychiatric inpatients. *Annals of General Psychiatry, 17*(1), 5. https://doi.org/10.1186/s12991-018-0175-5

Kikuchi, A., Soshi, T., Kono, T., Koyama, M., & Fujii, C. (2021). Validity of short-term assessment of risk and treatability in the Japanese Forensic Probation Service. *Frontiers in Psychiatry, 12*, 645927. https://doi.org/10.3389/fpsyt.2021.645927

Koike, J., Kono, T., Takeda, K., Yamada, Y., Fujii, C., & Hirabayashi, N. (2024). Data resource profile of an online database system for forensic mental health services. *BMC Medical Informatics and Decision Making, 24*(1), 47. https://doi.org/10.1186/s12911-024-02433-2

Ministry of Health, Labour and Welfare. (2025a, March 31). *Shitei Nyūin Iryō Kikan no Seibi Jōkyō (Status of designated inpatient medical facilities)*. https://www.mhlw.go.jp/stf/seisakunitsuite/bunya/hukushi_kaigo/shougaishahukushi/sinsin/iryokikan_seibi.html

Ministry of Health, Labour and Welfare. (2025b, March 31). *Shitei Tsūin Iryō Kikan no Shitei Jōkyō (Designation status of designated outpatient medical institutions)*. https://www.mhlw.go.jp/stf/seisakunitsuite/bunya/hukushi_kaigo/shougaishahukushi/sinsin/iryokikan_sitei.html

Ministry of Health, Labour and Welfare. (2023). *Iryō kansatsu-hō nyūin shogu gaidorain [Guidelines for inpatient treatment under the Medical Treatment and Supervision Act]*.

Ministry of Justice, Japan. (2019). *Act on Mental Health and Welfare for Persons with Mental Disorders (Act No. 123 of 1950)*. https://www.japaneselawtranslation.go.jp/en/laws/view/4235/en

Ministry of Justice, Japan. (2020). *Penal Code (Act No. 45 of 1907)*. https://www.japaneselawtranslation.go.jp/en/laws/view/3581/en

Nagata, T., Tachimori, H., Nishinaka, H., Takeda, K., Matsuda, T., & Hirabayashi, N. (2019). Mentally disordered offenders discharged from designated hospital facilities under the medical treatment and supervision act in Japan: Reoffending and readmission. *Criminal Behaviour and Mental Health, 29*(3), 157–167. https://doi.org/10.1002/cbm.2117

Nakatani, Y. (2012). Challenges in interfacing between forensic and general mental health: A Japanese perspective. *International Journal of Law and Psychiatry*, *35*(5–6), 406–411. https://doi.org/10.1016/j.ijlp.2012.09.021

Statistics Bureau of Japan. (2025, March 31). *Ministry of internal affairs and communications website*. https://www.stat.go.jp/english/data/jinsui/tsuki/index.html

Takeda, K., Sugawara, N., Matsuda, T., Shimada, A., Nagata, T., Kashiwagi, H., Hirabayashi, N., & Okada, T. (2019). Mortality and suicide rates in patients discharged from forensic psychiatric wards in Japan. *Comprehensive Psychiatry*, *95*, 152131. https://doi.org/10.1016/j.comppsych.2019.152131

Webster, C. D., Douglas, K. S., Eaves, D., & Hart, S. D. (1997). *HCR-20: Assessing risk for violence (Version 2)*. Mental Health, Law, and Policy Institute, Simon Fraser University.

Webster, C. D., Martin, M. L., Brink, J., Nicholls, T. L., & Desmarais, S. L. (2009). *Manual for the short-term assessment of risk and treatability*. British Columbia Mental Health and Addiction Services.

# 25 Pakistan

*Tariq Hassan*

### Brief Description

| | |
|---|---|
| **Location** | Pakistan is a country in South Asia. |
| **Size** | 881,913 km$^2$ |
| **Population** | 241.4 million |
| **Languages** | Urdu and English are the official languages of Pakistan. More than 60 languages are spoken in Pakistan, many of which are provincial (dialects). While Urdu is understood by most of the population, it is not the primary language of Pakistanis. Punjabi is the most common language. |
| **Political system** | Pakistan is a democratic federal republic with a parliamentary system in which the President is the head of state, and the Prime Minister wields executive power. The country features a bicameral legislature comprising the National Assembly (lower house) and the Senate (upper house). The judiciary is independent, with the Supreme Court as the highest judicial authority. Pakistan follows a multiparty system, holding elections every five years. Provincial governments have autonomy, with each province having its own legislature and chief minister. |

### Legal System

The criminal justice system in Pakistan is based on codified laws that outline provisions and guidelines for each criminal offence or act. The *Pakistan Penal Code* (Pakistan, 1860) serves as a legislative framework and a guide for all punishments relating to criminal offences. Most of Pakistan's laws are derived from the *Indian Penal Code* and Anglo-Saxon law. These legal foundations stem from Indian laws established under the authority of the British government during colonial rule, when the Indian subcontinent was known as British India, which lasted from the mid-18th century until 1947. Following the end of British colonial rule in 1947, the partition of British India created Pakistan and India as two sovereign states. As a result, many of Pakistan's laws and legal practices remain rooted in the legal structures introduced under British rule.

DOI: 10.4324/9781003376248-30

Today, Pakistan's judicial system is essentially a combination of British common law and Shariah law, forming a legal framework that governs the citizens of Pakistan in accordance with Islamic principles of justice. Another key legal instrument in Pakistan's criminal justice system is the *Code of Criminal Procedure* (Pakistan, Ministry of Law and Justice 1898/1997), which sets out the rules that govern the criminal procedure in Pakistani courts and provides specific guidelines for the legal consequences of criminal offences. Additionally, the *Qanun-e-Shahadat Order* (Pakistan, Ministry of Law and Justice, 1984) is crucial in ensuring that Islamic values and ethics are upheld regarding evidence in the legal system. The purpose of the *Qanun-e-Shahadat Order* is to align Islamic legal principles and provisions, specifically those derived from the Quran and the Hadith.

In Pakistan, the judiciary is divided into superior and subordinate courts. The superior courts consist of the Supreme Court, the five High Courts, and the Federal Shariat Court. The five High Courts are responsible for hearing cases related to various crimes and criminal offences. Each of the four provinces of Pakistan has one High Court, with an additional High Court located in the country's capital, Islamabad. Subordinate courts include civil and criminal courts, which are situated at the district level (Hussain, 2015). The Federal Shariat Court, as an Islamic court, is responsible for ensuring the inclusion of traditional Islamic laws and practices into the federal system of courts and national laws.

Additionally, tort law exists in Pakistan, which is applied when a civil wrong is committed against an individual, resulting in legal liability and punishment. Pakistan's tort law is administered in accordance with the principles of justice, equality, and good conscience.

### *Mental Health Laws*

In Pakistan, forensic mental health laws within the criminal justice system are not well established, particularly in addressing the role of mental health and criminal responsibility, such as cases of not guilty by reason of insanity or due to a mental disorder. The forensic psychiatry system in Pakistan is still in its early stages. When people who have mental illness commit a crime, they are processed in the same way as those without mental illness. In Pakistan, there is generally no legal distinction between these two populations, nor any difference in treatment or placement, except for a limited number of specialised facilities across the country. Pakistan has laws defining 'not criminally responsible', rather than the commonly known 'not guilty by reason of insanity'.

#### *Lunacy Act of 1912*

The *Lunacy Act* of 1912 was a significant piece of legislation in British India that was used in the colonial administration of mental health laws. The Act aimed to reform and modernise the legal framework surrounding mental health in British India, replacing earlier laws related to the treatment and institutionalisation of people with mental illness, and introduced key administrative reforms, including clearer regulations for the management of mental asylums and legal procedures for detaining people deemed to have a mental illness. It was influenced by developments in the United Kingdom's mental health policies, including the role of the Board of Control for Lunacy and Mental Deficiency, which was established under the *Mental Deficiency Act* of 1913. The Board's policies and administrative framework influenced colonial mental health governance, including in British India.

The *Lunacy Act* remained largely custodial, focusing on institutional care rather than patient rights. Unlike later mental health legislation, it did not introduce voluntary admissions or outpatient care. The Act remained in effect in Pakistan until it was replaced by the *Mental Health Ordinance* of 2001. Following this, the 18th Amendment to the Constitution of Pakistan (2010) devolved health responsibilities from the federal government to the provinces, including mental health legislation. This allowed each provincial assembly to formulate its own mental health laws. Sindh became the first province to enact its own legislation, passing the *Sindh Mental Health Act* of 2013.

### *Capacity to Defend (Fitness to Stand Trial)*

In Pakistan, fitness to stand trial is referred to as 'capacity to defend', which is essential for the criminal justice system to determine whether individuals who have committed a crime can defend themselves in court. Interestingly, unlike many Western and European countries, the test to determine the capacity to defend is not explicitly outlined in the *Code of Criminal Procedure* (Hassan et al., 2015). This absence of a clear standard makes determining the capacity to stand trial somewhat ambiguous and subjective, with no clear protocol assessment.

In stark contrast, Chapter 14 of the *Code of Criminal Procedure*, which carries the outdated title 'Lunatics', clearly outlines conditions and legal procedures for determining whether the accused person is a 'lunatic'. If the individual involved in the case is suspected of having a mental illness, the magistrate can order a mental status examination by a physician (Pakistan, Ministry of Law and Justice, 1898/1997, Chapter 14).

Section 465 of the *Code of Criminal Procedure* states that, if the criminally charged individual is of unsound mind and incapable of a defence, the legal proceedings are postponed until the individual's mental health is restored. Section 466 outlines the procedure of release of forensic patients with mental illness, ensuring the person is placed in a safe environment to prevent harm to themselves or others (Pakistan, Ministry of Law and Justice, 1898/1997, Chapter 14, Sections 465–466).

In Pakistan, when a justice-involved individual must be detained in a safe, monitored environment, a family member or friend can apply to the provincial government to request that their relative or friend with a mental illness be taken under their care. The family member then takes on the critical responsibility to ensure the individual complies with conditions set by the provincial government or the court. However, a key shortcoming of this seemingly inclusive and flexible approach to forensic patient care is the lack of mechanisms to ensure the patient receives adequate care and that all conditions of their release are strictly followed. In Pakistan, there is no follow-up process to monitor whether patients are receiving quality care or whether their family members are fulfilling their responsibilities.

#### *Criminal Responsibility*

In Pakistan, under Section 470 of the *Code of Criminal Procedure*, the law stipulates that the accused can be acquitted on the grounds of lunacy. The court's findings must specifically address whether the accused's mental condition influenced their behaviour in committing the criminal act. According to Section 471, the law ensures that the justice-involved individual who is confirmed to have a mental illness must be detained in a safe institution so they cannot harm themselves or others (Pakistan, Ministry of Law and Justice, 1898/1997, Section 471).

### ***Decision Makers in Forensic Psychiatry***

When individuals with mental illness commit a crime, they are generally processed in the same manner as the general population. This is largely due to a lack of training within the police force on how to manage and process individuals with mental illness. A police officer takes a statement and completes a 'First Information Report' detailing the incident and applying the various charges applicable in the form of a challan, which refers to the police report submitted to a court after completing an investigation. This document presents the investigation findings and forms the basis for the court's proceedings. The accused is held in custody or released on bail, depending on whether the charges are bailable.

As a result, forensic psychiatry in Pakistan exists in a very rudimentary way. If there are suspicions that the accused may have a mental illness, the court will direct the relevant general hospital superintendent to have the psychiatry department assess the accused. The resulting report only confirms or denies the existence of a mental disorder. Unfortunately, this process does not adequately serve the justice system, which requires an interpretation of whether the accused, in their altered mental state at the time of the offence, is capable of pleading or is criminally responsible for the charges.

These legal interpretations of an accused's *mens rea* are not commonly addressed by general psychiatrists due to their lack of training and trained specialist forensic psychiatrists. As a result, people with mental illness are typically sentenced to prison or, in some cases, sent to hospital under the provincial mental health legislation. During their detention, psychiatrists are responsible for making decisions related to treatment. Discharge decisions are part of a multidisciplinary process involving professionals from various fields, such as psychology, social work, and non-government organisations—depending on the resources available in the specific city.

## Forensic Psychiatry System

### *Structure and Function of the Forensic Psychiatric System*

Pakistan lacks a formal forensic psychiatry system. Instead, general psychiatry manages such cases, as forensic patients in Pakistan are treated as civilly committed patients under a detention order. If a person with mental illness is acquitted on the grounds of their condition, the relevant provincial mental health legislation is applied where they continue to pose a risk to public safety or themselves. In such instances, the patient is transferred to a general psychiatry ward. However, there are no tribunals to independently review detention or treatment decisions. Moreover, no data is available on the demographics of these individuals.

### *Role of Forensic Psychiatry*

Pakistan's population is estimated at over 241 million (Pakistan Bureau of Statistics, 2023). According to a 2009 report by the World Health Organization, there were only 342 psychiatrists in the country, equating to 0.20 psychiatrists per 100,000 people (World Health Organization, 2009). Most experienced psychiatrists live in metropolitan areas, while rural areas remain severely underserved. Pakistan lacks specialist forensic psychiatrists; general psychiatrists interested in forensic psychiatry are rare. Recent estimates suggest that fewer than 20 general psychiatrists in Pakistan are currently engaged in medico-legal work and providing expert opinions to the courts (Malik et al., 2021).

Pakistan has some of the poorest mental health indicators in the world, with nearly 90% of people who have mental disorders without treatment due to limited access to psychiatrists and other mental health professionals (Bashir, 2018). Rural areas of Pakistan are particularly underserved, with little to no professional support for mental health. There is a profound treatment gap in Pakistan for forensic medicine for individuals living in rural areas, impoverished areas, or simply inability to see a forensic psychiatrist because of the high demand and limited supply.

Forensic psychiatrists and forensic mental health practitioners play a critical role in healthcare systems, particularly when individuals with serious mental illnesses are diverted from the general justice system to hospitals to receive treatment. Forensic psychiatrists conduct specialised assessments for the courts, providing expert opinions on an accused individual's capacity to plead or their criminal responsibility. Forensic mental health practitioners specialise in violence mitigation through a bio-psycho-social approach, focusing on the treatment and rehabilitation of sentenced offenders with mental illnesses.

In Pakistan, it is relatively uncommon for a forensic psychiatrist to evaluate a justice-involved individual suspected of having a mental illness, and such evaluations typically occur only in specific cases or circumstances. This represents a significant shortcoming in forensic mental health care, as assessments by a forensic psychiatrist should be a basic right for all citizens of Pakistan.

Additionally, the *Juvenile Justice System Act, 2018* outlines the legal procedures for handling juvenile offenders with mental illnesses in the criminal justice system. The Act applies to individuals under 18 and provides diversion, rehabilitation, and treatment guidelines instead of traditional punitive measures (Pakistan, Ministry of Law and Justice, 2018).

In Pakistan, forensic psychiatry plays a crucial role by ensuring that citizens with mental health conditions receive appropriate medication while incarcerated. This treatment aims to support their rehabilitation and guide them towards reintegration as productive members of society once they begin reintegrating into the community.

### *Forensic Psychiatry Profession*

#### *Qualifications and Specialised Training*

Formal forensic psychiatry training in Pakistan has been minimal to non-existent until recent decades, when institutions began to recognise the importance of this specialisation within psychiatry. As a result, its inclusion in educational curricula has grown. Undergraduate medical education in Pakistan is regulated by the Pakistan Medical and Dental Council, which initially offered only didactic lectures on forensic psychiatry without incorporating these topics into examinations. Before the late 1990s, forensic psychiatry was not emphasised in undergraduate studies and was not even included as a topic in examinations. However, after the late 1990s, its relevance began to be recognised, leading to the incorporation of clinical residency for three to six weeks and an exam in the final year as part of the General Medicine Paper (Naeem & Ayub, 2004).

In Pakistan, postgraduate studies in psychiatry are regulated by the College of Physicians and Surgeons Pakistan (CPSP), which has increasingly adapted its psychiatric training programmes to meet the population's needs. In 1965, Jinnah Postgraduate Medica Centre became the country's first institution to offer psychiatry residency training. Over time, psychiatric training has grown steadily, with a notable surge in recent years. Between 2007 and 2012, 25 institutions introduced psychiatric residency programmes, bridging the total to around 41 institutions offering such programmes today (Hassan et al., 2015; College of Physicians & Surgeons in Pakistan, 2012c, 2012d).

The first part of the Fellowship of the College of Physicians and Surgeons (FCPS) exam, which the CPSP administers, assesses the clinical application of basic scientific knowledge relevant to psychiatry. To be eligible to sit the first part of the FCPS exam, a trainee must graduate and complete one year of internship. Afterwards, a four-year residency at a CPSP-accredited institution must be completed before the second part of the FCPS exam.

The four-year residency training programme in Pakistan is structured into two main phases, with the first phase known as the intermediate module. This spans two years, during which trainees participate in rotations that last three months each. The rotations cover clinical psychology, medicine, and neurology to ensure a broad-based foundation in medicine and psychiatric practice. The programme uses the entrustable professional activity (EPA) model to assess competency in these areas. The EPA levels range from one to five. Level one represents 'observer status', and level five represents the 'ability to teach others and critically evaluate' (Ten Cate & Scheele, 2007). During the first two years, psychiatric residents must achieve an EPA level of 3–4 to progress to the next stage of their residency programme. By the end of the fourth year, residents must achieve an EPA level of five for most learning objectives (Rana et al., 2010).

At the end of the residency programme, trainees are required to pass a formal examination administered by the CPSP. This exam consists of multiple-choice and short-answer questions and internal assessments that include a portfolio, feedback sessions, and evaluations of both written and clinical encounters (College of Physicians and Surgeons in Pakistan, 2012a, 2012b, 2012c, 2012d).

Forensic psychiatry education is integrated into the overall syllabus for psychiatric residency training in Pakistan. Residents are required to assess 10 forensic patients under supervision as part of their training. They are also expected to fully understand six key components of forensic psychiatry: mental health legislation, administrative management of psychiatric cases; forensic psychiatric syndromes; the role of psychiatrists in court; management of violence and risk assessment; and the preparation of psychiatric reports. Forensic psychiatry training is considered complete after successful patient assessments and a solid understanding of the above-listed concepts (College of Physicians and Surgeons in Pakistan, 2012b).

In 2022, the Division of Forensic Psychiatry at Queen's University and I launched a fully online certificate course in forensic mental health. This course was developed in collaboration with Prof. Mowaddat Hussein Rana, former Dean of Psychiatry at the College of Physicians and Surgeons of Pakistan, and Prof. Ali Burhan Mustafa, Head of the Department of Psychiatry at Sheikh Zayed Medical College in Rahim Yar Khan, Pakistan. The certificate course aims to raise awareness among professionals about forensic mental health. In the future, we plan to create additional educational opportunities for graduates to refine their skills according to their specific fields. Participants come from diverse backgrounds, including police, prison staff, lawyers, psychiatrists, and psychologists. For psychiatrists, this initiative will eventually lead to establishing a second accredited residency programme in forensic psychiatry once there are enough trained professionals in the field.

The course consists of 12 weekly modules that combine synchronous teaching and discussion with asynchronous assignments. The first six modules aim to establish a foundation in the basics of law, psychiatry, and psychology. The final six modules delve into more specialised forensic topics, including the capacity to plead, criminal responsibility, mental disorders and their presentation in the criminal justice system, court report writing, paraphilias, and risk assessment and management.

#### *National Networks and Collaborations*

In 2019, I delivered the first seminar on forensic psychiatry to the Islamabad High Court Bar Association, which was attended by legal experts and three High Court judges. This initiative paved the way for developing mental health training programmes for lawyers and judges. In December 2020, the then-president of the Pakistan Psychiatric Society, Prof. Iqbal Afridi, inaugurated several new sections, including forensic psychiatry, under the Pakistan Psychiatric Society (Pakistan Psychiatric Society, 2020). The objectives include building networks and enhancing capacity with relevant institutions and affiliated organisations. The focus also includes promoting research, preventative strategies, workshops, and advocacy outreach initiatives. In 2022, Queen's University in Canada, Islamia University, and the Department of Psychiatry at Sheikh Zayed Medical College in Pakistan developed a certificate course on forensic mental health, which they plan to offer annually.

## Forensic Psychiatry Service (Provision of Care)

### *Forensic Patient Characteristics*

Forensic psychiatric patients in Pakistan often exhibit a range of social and clinical characteristics indicative of the fundamental problems within the mental health and criminal justice systems. Many come from lower socioeconomic backgrounds, are less educated, and are thus less likely to access healthcare services. This population experiences severe mental illnesses, with high prevalence rates of schizophrenia and other psychotic disorders, frequently coupled with substance use disorders, particularly involving cannabis and heroin. Forensic patients typically have a history of violent crimes, such as homicide and assault, often without prior psychiatric intervention or recognition of their mental health issues. The inadequacies of poorly organised forensic psychiatric services reflect the limited representation and underexplored mental health legislation within the judicial system. Addressing these gaps will necessitate a shift in perspective towards a public health approach, enabling the implementation of appropriate measures for assessment, treatment, and rehabilitation.

### *Exiting the System*

Forensic patients will transition into the civil system under the relevant provincial mental health legislation, where it will be determined whether they qualify for a detention order or compulsory treatment. These patients must undergo assessment and remain under the authority of the custodial institution. Patients are discharged from a detention order when they are no longer deemed a risk to themselves or others; however, there is currently no formal forensic system in place, resulting in the absence of a structured exit process. At present, Pakistan lacks both an average length of stay and any estimates regarding the duration that forensic patients remain under a detention order.

### *Approaches to Assessment and Treatment*

In most central prisons, a separate block is designated for patients with comorbid psychiatric or behavioural issues. Depending on available resources, all patients in this block are seen every two weeks for assessment and management by a postgraduate trainee who works under the supervision of a consultant psychiatrist from a tertiary-care facility. Alternatively, in consultation with senior staff, the postgraduate trainee may transfer the patient to the tertiary-care facility, where a team of three senior consultants will evaluate the patient. After their review, the case is presented to the medical board for their opinion and recommendations to the court. These recommendations are then forwarded to the courts by the hospital's medical superintendent, where the psychiatrists are based. There are no psychiatrists employed by the prison authority. In Pakistan, there have been rare cases where individuals with mental illnesses have been sentenced to death while still in a state of mental illness. In February 2021, the country saw a significant advancement in forensic psychiatry when Ms. Safia Bano and others presented a case before the Supreme Court of Pakistan. This case highlighted the improper adherence to legal procedures in trials involving individuals with mental health issues. It raised concerns about the execution of death penalties for convicts with mental illnesses (*Safia Bano v. Home Department, Punjab & Others, 2021 SCMR 361*). The landmark ruling in this case made several important decisions. The judgement began by highlighting the significance of mental health, asserting that it holds equal weight to physical health. The first issue addressed was the definition of mental illness, with a shift towards broader definitions in line with the World Health Organization's International Classification of Diseases (ICD-10).

Furthermore, the Supreme Court ordered the replacement of outdated terminology, including 'unsound mind' and 'lunatics', with 'mental disorder' or 'mental illness' in legal texts. The Court emphasised the importance of a person's ability to defend themselves, ensuring adherence to constitutional and legal due process. The Court mandated the establishment of a medical board when the accused is prima facie incapable of mounting a defence and ruled that court reports should not merely provide a diagnosis but must include a comprehensive account of the individual's condition, particularly concerning their psychopathology.

The 2021 ruling established a new legal standard regarding the execution of convicted individuals with mental illnesses. The Court stated that if a condemned prisoner is unable to comprehend the reasons for their punishment due to mental illness, carrying out the death sentence would not be in the interest of justice. However, the Court clarified that not all mental illnesses automatically exempt a person from the death penalty. A medical board will evaluate whether the condemned prisoner lacks the cognitive ability to understand the reasons for their sentence.

The psychiatric community in Pakistan is increasingly acknowledging the necessity for specialised forensic psychiatry services, which have thus far developed on an 'as-needed' basis. In April 2016, Pakistan hosted its inaugural international conference on forensic psychiatry, titled 'Healing the Held', in Lahore. Additionally, I initiated the country's first certificate course in forensic psychiatry in 2022. Policymakers in Pakistan need to ensure the effective implementation of the relevant provincial mental health acts. The complex social, cultural, and religious landscape poses significant risks in the field of forensic psychiatry, endangering not only the patients but also the psychiatrists who are conducting the assessments.

A study conducted in 2016 by Bhutta and Wormith demonstrated the effectiveness of the Level of Service/Case Management Inventory (LS/CMI) risk assessment tool within the context of a deeply religious Islamic culture (Bhutta & Wormith, 2016). The research produced three key findings with real-world implications that remain relevant for further theory development.

The first finding showed that the tool successfully validated its risk assessment claim but did so within an Islamic cultural setting, which differs significantly from the contexts in which the tool was traditionally applied. The second finding highlighted the resources available to low-risk pretrial offenders, often overlooked compared to high-risk offenders, demonstrating a wider application of the risk assessment claim. Lastly, the third finding reintroduced religiosity into the discourse, albeit with different implications. The study found that religiosity had a negative impact on recidivism and risk assessments. However, when the LS/CMI was used, religiosity did not contribute additional predictive value in determining recidivism.

The findings on religiosity's incremental validity are bounded by the context of secular nations, where religion and state remain separate. However, the study raises the possibility that the LS/CMI's application in a highly religious paradigm may yield different implications.

## Strengths and Weaknesses

It is a crucial time for Pakistan to enhance its forensic psychiatry services. Both federal and provincial governments must recognise that effectively addressing the needs of offenders with mental illness will help reduce overcrowding in prisons. To achieve this, Pakistan's prison staff and psychiatric professionals must collaborate to develop a comprehensive system for assessing and rehabilitating these offenders. This includes establishing psychiatric services within prisons and ensuring adequate care for inmates who develop mental health issues while in custody.

## References

Bashir, A. (2018). The state of mental health care in Pakistan. *Lancet*, *5*(6), 471. https://doi.org/10.1016/S2215-0366(18)30191-3

Bhutta, M. H., & Wormith, J. S. (2016). An examination of a risk/needs assessment instrument and its relation to religiosity and recidivism among probationers in a Muslim culture. *Criminal Justice and Behavior*, *43*(2), 204–229. https://doi.org/10.1177/0093854815604011

College of Physicians and Surgeons in Pakistan (CPSP). (2012a). *About CPSP*. Karachi, Pakistan: CPSP. Retrieved from http://www.cpsp.edu.pk/index.php?code=dGhlX2NvbGxlZ2V8Y29sbGVnZS5waHB8MHwwfDA=#

College of Physicians and Surgeons in Pakistan (CPSP). (2012b). *Examination guidelines*. Karachi, Pakistan: CPSP.

College of Physicians and Surgeons in Pakistan (CPSP). (2012c). *Structured training programme for FCPS psychiatry, intermediate module*. Karachi, Pakistan: CPSP.

College of Physicians and Surgeons in Pakistan (CPSP). (2012d). *Structured training programme, FCPS Part II (3rd and 4th year) psychiatry*. Karachi, Pakistan: CPSP. Retrieved from http://www.cpsp.edu.pk/index.php?code=ZXhhbWluYXRpb258Z3VpZGVsaW5lLnBocHwwfEZDUFMtSXww.

Hassan, T., Hirji, S., & Nizami, A. (2015). Forensic psychiatry in Pakistan. *International Journal of Law and Psychiatry*, *41*, 95–104. https://doi.org/10.1016/j.ijlp.2015.05.001

Hussain, F. (2015). *The judicial system of Pakistan* (4th ed.). Islamabad, Pakistan: Federal Judicial Academy. Retrieved from https://www.supremecourt.gov.pk/downloads_judgements/all_downloads/Judicial_System_of_Pakistan/thejudicialsystemofPakistan.pdf

Malik, W. A., Arnold, C., Vithiananthan, A., & Hassan, T. (2021). Forensic psychiatry in Pakistan: An update. *International Journal of Risk and Recovery*, *4*(2), 42–50. https://doi.org/10.15173/ijrr.v4i2.4622

Naeem, F., & Ayub, M. (2004). Psychiatric training in Pakistan. *Medical Education Online*, *9*(19), 1–4.

Pakistan Bureau of Statistics. (2023). *The population of Pakistan reaches 241.49 million as the digital census concludes* [press release]. Retrieved from https://www.pbs.gov.pk/sites/default/files/population/2023/Press%20Release.pdf

Pakistan, Ministry of Law and Justice. (1860). *Pakistan penal code*. Retrieved from https://pakistancode.gov.pk/english/UY2FqaJw1-apaUY2Fqa-apaUY2Npa5lo-sg-jjjjjjjjjjjj

Pakistan, Ministry of Law and Justice. (1898). *The code of criminal procedure*. Retrieved from https://pakistancode.gov.pk/english/UY2FqaJw1-apaUY2Fqa-apaUY2Npa5lp-sg-jjjjjjjjjjjj

Pakistan, Ministry of Law and Justice. (1984). *Qanun-e-Shahadat order, 1984*. Retrieved from https://pakistancode.gov.pk/english/UY2FqaJw1-apaUY2Fqa-apaUY2Npa5plaw%3D%3D-sg-jjjjjjjjjjjjj

Pakistan, Ministry of Law and Justice. (2018). *Juvenile justice system act, 2018*. Retrieved from https://pakistancode.gov.pk/english/UY2FqaJw1-apaUY2Fqa-ap%2BVZA%3D%3D-sg-jjjjjjjjjjjjj

Pakistan Psychiatric Society. (2020). *Notification regarding PPS sections / Special interest groups (SIG)*. Retrieved from https://ppspk.com/wp-content/uploads/2021/09/Special-Interests-Group.pdf

Rana, M. H., Farooq, S., & Afridi, M. I. (2010). An outline of structured training programme (STP) for FCPS in psychiatry (3rd and 4th year of training). *Journal of Pakistan Psychiatric Society*, *7*(1), 6–12.

Ten Cate, O., & Scheele, F. (2007). Competency-based postgraduate training: Can we bridge the gap between theory and clinical practice? *Academic Medicine*, *82*(6), 542–547.

World Health Organization. (2009). *WHO-AIMS report on mental health system in Pakistan*. WHO.

# Part VI

# Africa

# 26 South Africa

*Nyameka Dyakalashe*

### Brief Description

| | |
|---|---|
| **Location** | South Africa is located at the southernmost tip of Africa. |
| **Size** | 1,221,037 km$^2$ |
| **Population** | 60,867,000 |
| **Languages** | The South African Constitution recognises 11 official languages. The most commonly spoken are isiZulu (23%), isiXhosa (16%), Afrikaans (14%), and English (9.6%). |
| **Political system** | South Africa is a parliamentary representative democratic republic. The President serves as both the head of state and head of government and is elected by the National Assembly. The executive branch, led by the President and the Cabinet, enforces laws and policies. The legislative branch, made up of Parliament (the National Assembly and National Council of Provinces), creates laws. The judicial branch is independent, with courts like the Constitutional Court ensuring laws comply with the Constitution. |

### Legal System

South Africa's Constitution includes a Bill of Rights, which is upheld by the Constitutional Court and determines whether court decisions, legislation, or regulations comply with constitutional requirements. The Constitutional Court, comparable to the Supreme Courts in several countries, including the United States, is the highest in South Africa.

The district magistrate's courts are located below the Constitutional Court and handle criminal and civil matters that are not considered serious. The regional magistrate courts deal with criminal and civil cases as well. However, they are only empowered to impose sentences under 15 years or hear civil claims involving amounts below R300,000 (South African Rand or ZAR). The High Courts have jurisdiction over many cases, including those that may lead to lengthy sentences or substantial civil claims. In addition, the High Courts can adjudicate on constitutional matters, which are typically subject to appeal. Appeals progress

DOI: 10.4324/9781003376248-32

from lower to higher courts, with the Supreme Court of Appeal in Bloemfontein handling appeals from the various high courts. If appellants are unsatisfied with the rulings, they can request their case to be heard in the Constitutional Court, but only if they believe the decision violates the directives laid out in the Constitution.

There are several specialised courts, such as those dealing with sexual offences, family matters, inquests, competition appeals, labour and labour appeals, small claims, electoral disputes, land disputes, and Indigenous populations. Despite the majority of the South African population being Indigenous, legal matters that pertain to Indigenous populations are still marginalised and are heard, in part, within the existing common law courts. Legal issues concerning Indigenous populations are usually referred to as customary law. Customary law consists of legislation that addresses legal matters concerning Indigenous populations. It includes customary marriages, the rights of children, the law of succession, and inheritance, among others (Maimela & NLMC, 2021)). However, these laws have not been fully developed or interpreted to be wholly applied. Therefore, in each case, before customary law can be applied in judicial courts, the relevant parties must first convince the courts that there is a connection between the litigants and an applicable Indigenous law or custom. Despite calls to establish mental health courts or tribunals, there are currently no indications that such courts will be established in the near future.

South Africa has adopted an adversarial system inherited from the United Kingdom. However, in some cases, such as in family court proceedings, both parties may be ordered to work collaboratively towards reaching a consensus. Plea bargaining was formalised more than 20 years ago when the *Criminal Procedure Second Amendment Act 62 of 2001*, was passed and serves as an example of how inquisitorial methods are sometimes utilised. This Act states that the prosecutor may negotiate with the accused and their legal representative (defence attorney) before the case is brought to court for a plea. The accused would then have to agree to plead guilty to the charges brought against them. Should the court convict the accused of the offence to which they pleaded guilty, the plea bargain negotiations could result in one of four outcomes.

First, the accused may receive a lenient sentence, considering their personal circumstances and the community's interests. Alternatively, the court may postpone sentencing for a period not exceeding five years, subject to certain conditions. These conditions may include community service, correctional supervision, compulsory treatment, or financial compensation. The third possible outcome is a lenient sentence that is wholly or partially suspended for less than five years, with conditions similar to those outlined in the second outcome. Finally, the court may order compensation if it is proven that the offence has caused damage to or loss of property. There has been an increased use of mediation accordingly.

In 1917, during the apartheid era, South Africa used a uniform jury system; however, jurors were exclusively white males, with all other racial groups excluded from participation (except in one area of the country, the former Cape Province). In South Africa, as a racially diverse country, the jury system began losing relevance and popularity, and it was gradually phased out in the late 1960s (Seligon, 2001). In 1969, the jury system that presided over serious offences was formally abolished. Since the end of apartheid, the previous jury system was clearly in conflict with the Constitution adopted with the birth of a democratic judicial system. It was, therefore, officially abolished in 1990. To date, South Africa does not use juries; instead, decisions are made by magistrates and judges (*Abolition of Juries Act 34 of 1969*).

### *Mental Health Laws*

In line with the rest of the world, mental illness in South Africa was not widely recognised as a distinct medical condition until the early 1800s. In 1818, the first psychiatric ward was built within a hospital in Cape Town. Between 1876 and 1922, nine specialised psychiatric hospitals were established across the country, including Fort England Hospital in Makhanda (formerly Grahamstown) in 1876, Valkenberg Hospital in Cape Town in 1891, and Weskoppies Hospital in Pretoria in 1892 (Kleintjes & Lund, 2023).

The first comprehensive mental health legislation, the *Mental Disorders Act*, was enacted in 1916. This was later replaced by the *Mental Health Act 18 of 1973*, which aimed to provide for the reception, detention, and treatment of individuals with mental illnesses. The current governing law, the *Mental Health Care Act 17 of 2002*, came into effect in 2004, strengthening protections for people with mental illnesses and emphasising human rights-based care (Department of Justice, 2004).

The *Mental Health Care Act* was established to govern the treatment, care, and psychosocial rehabilitation of persons with mental illness or intellectual disability. The Act refers to psychiatric patients as mental healthcare users rather than patients. It also provides for the care and administration of their property. The Act makes clear distinctions between the general population with mental illness, sentenced prisoners with mental illness, and those who have been declared state patients by the courts (Department of Justice, 2004).

South African mental health laws are also outlined in the *Child Justice Act 75 of 2008* and the *Criminal Procedure Act 51 of 1977*. The *Child Justice Act* governs legislation pertaining to children under the age of 14 who are in conflict with the law. This Act states that any child who commits an offence under 12 lacks criminal capacity and, therefore, cannot be prosecuted. Instead, the matter must be addressed through alternative provisions outlined in the Act under the supervision of a probation officer (a professionally trained social worker who assists the courts).

A child who is 12 years old but younger than 14 when committing an offence is also presumed to lack criminal capacity unless the state can prove otherwise.

However, the burden of proof lies with the prosecution, which must demonstrate that the child had criminal capacity at the time of the offence. The state must prove beyond a reasonable doubt that the accused child could appreciate the wrongfulness of their actions at the time of the alleged offence. Additionally, it must be established that the child has attained the expected cognitive, emotional, psychological, moral, and social development required to understand the implications of their actions.

The *Criminal Procedure Act* governs criminal matters involving accused persons above the age of 14 and presumed to possess criminal capacity. Chapter 13 of this Act addresses an accused person's capacity to follow court proceedings and their mental capacity to appreciate the wrongfulness of their actions at the time of the alleged offence (*Criminal Procedure Act 51 of 1977*).

### *Fitness to Stand Trial*

Since 1977, Sections 77–79 of the *Criminal Procedure Act* have outlined laws regarding fitness to stand trial and criminal capacity. This legislation applies to all defendants aged 14 or older who may be referred for a fitness assessment at any stage of the court proceedings before sentencing. Section 77 of the Act specifically addresses fitness to stand trial (*Criminal Procedure Act 51 of 1977*). If, at any point during criminal proceedings, the court determines that the accused may be unable to understand the proceedings or defend themselves adequately due to mental illness or intellectual disability, it must request an inquiry into the matter and obtain a report as outlined in Section 79.

This section of the Act empowers the court to issue an order directing either the head of a designated psychiatric hospital or a psychiatrist appointed by the hospital to conduct an inquiry. The psychiatrist must provide a written report on the accused's mental condition, diagnosis, and ability to understand court proceedings and mount an adequate defence. The report is submitted to the court, and the final ruling is based on the findings of the appointed psychiatrists. The accused or the prosecutor can dispute the report's findings, and the psychiatrists who conducted the assessment may be called to provide expert testimony in court.

The court must be convinced by the findings of the appointed psychiatrists, confirming that the accused has a mental illness or intellectual disability. Furthermore, if the accused cannot adequately comprehend the court proceedings or participate in their defence due to their condition, they will be deemed unfit to stand trial. In cases involving serious violent offences, the court may order the accused to be indefinitely admitted to a psychiatric hospital for treatment as a 'state patient'. For minor offences, the accused may be admitted to the hospital as an 'involuntary user', similar to general psychiatric admissions. Defendants deemed unfit to stand trial due to mental illness or intellectual disability may be prosecuted at a later stage if they receive treatment and are subsequently found fit to stand trial. However, this is rare in practice.

### *Criminal Responsibility in Children*

In South Africa, for an accused person to be convicted of a crime, the state prosecutor must prove all elements of the offence beyond a reasonable doubt. Criminal liability is a legal concept that holds an accused person criminally responsible for their act or omission. Anyone aged 14 or older can be prosecuted when brought before a court, as they are presumed to have criminal capacity when committing the alleged offence(s). If found guilty, they can be held criminally responsible for the crimes of which they have been accused.

The *Child Justice Act* states that all children under the age of 12 lack criminal capacity and, therefore, cannot be held criminally responsible for any alleged offence. The police cannot arrest these children, and such matters are referred to the Children's Court, which handles cases involving the care and protection of minors rather than criminal prosecution (*Child Justice Act 75 of 2008*).

This section addresses criminal matters involving children aged 12 to 14. While the law presumes that children under 12 lack criminal capacity, those between 12 and 14 may be assessed if the state believes they possess it. The prosecution bears the burden of proving beyond a reasonable doubt that the child had criminal capacity at the time of the offence. In South Africa, criminal capacity is defined as the ability to appreciate the wrongfulness of one's actions and act accordingly. If proven, the court proceeds with the trial, and the child is held criminally responsible if found guilty.

Children in this age group who are suspected of possessing criminal capacity must be assessed by a qualified practitioner, such as a child psychiatrist, general psychiatrist, or clinical psychologist. This assessment, usually conducted on an outpatient basis, does not necessarily require a forensic psychiatrist. If the assessment confirms criminal capacity, the case continues in the Child Justice Court. In serious violent offences, Chapter 6 of the *Child Justice Act* allows the court to order the child's participation in a diversion programme. If the assessment determines that the child lacks criminal capacity, the case is handled similarly to that of a child under 12 deemed not criminally responsible (*Child Justice Act 75 of 2008*). A probation officer evaluates the child and makes appropriate recommendations in such cases.

### *Criminal Responsibility of Adolescents Above 14 Years and Adults*

If the mental status of the accused is raised at any point during court proceedings, an inquiry into their mental capacity must be conducted before sentencing. This inquiry should include an assessment similar to the one described earlier to determine their criminal capacity at the time of the alleged offence(s). Section 78 of the *Criminal Procedure Act* outlines the laws governing criminal responsibility (*Criminal Procedure Act 51 of 1977*).

Following the criminal capacity assessment, the appointed clinicians must submit a report to the court, which will make a final ruling based on their findings. If the prosecution or defence disputes the report, the psychiatrists who conducted the assessment may be summoned to provide expert testimony in court. However, if there is consensus that the accused lacks criminal capacity, the court will find them not guilty by reason of mental illness or intellectual disability. Those who lack criminal capacity cannot be held criminally responsible for any offences they have committed.

Individuals who have committed serious violent offences are ordered to be admitted as state patients, while those who have committed minor offences are admitted involuntarily to general psychiatry. Such admissions occur at designated psychiatric hospitals (forensic psychiatry units/hospitals) under the *Mental Health Care Act* (Department of Justice, 2004). State patients are admitted for care, treatment, and psychosocial rehabilitation for an indeterminate period. In practice, state patients are accused persons who cannot be held criminally responsible for their actions due to a lack of criminal capacity and are regarded as not guilty by reason of mental illness or intellectual disability, or both. 'Not guilty by reason of insanity' is an outdated term that is no longer used in South African legislation.

Due to limited human, infrastructure, and financial resources, defendants may have to wait up to two years before being admitted to a designated psychiatric hospital for criminal capacity assessments. In some parts of the country, even after this process is completed, defendants who have been found not criminally responsible and declared state patients may still have to wait in prison for a bed to become available at a designated forensic unit. When a defendant is suspected of lacking the mental capacity to stand trial or lacking criminal responsibility, the courts typically require both evaluations to be conducted simultaneously. The treatment, psychosocial rehabilitation, and discharge procedures for state patients remain consistent, regardless of whether they were declared as such due to a lack of criminal capacity or being unfit to stand trial.

## FORENSIC PSYCHIATRY DECISION MAKERS

Numerous decision makers are involved in a person's entering and exiting the forensic system. The six major entities include members of the public; the South African Police Service; the National Prosecuting Authority (NPA), which is headed by the Director of Public Prosecutions (DPP); the Department of Justice, which governs the criminal courts; and the Department of Health, which employs forensic clinical examiners, forensic psychiatrists, and other health professionals working in forensic psychiatry. The Mental Health Review Board is a statutory body that makes decisions regarding involuntary mental health care and treatment, among other duties (Department of Justice, 2004).

The police usually arrest accused persons after complainants lay charges. In some cases, they may be arrested later if they have evaded law enforcement. The police assign an investigating officer (detective), who has the discretion not to bring the charge before a presiding officer of the court. The investigating officer may instead facilitate the accused person's civil admission to a district hospital for a 72-hour psychiatric observation, after which the individual may be transferred to a specialised psychiatric hospital.

The investigating officer refers the case to a state prosecutor, who may consult with the NPA, specifically the DPP's office, in preparing formal charges. If an accused person's mental health prevents them from participating in court proceedings, it can be raised as a concern at any stage of the trial to ensure they can make a proper defence. Mental health concerns are typically identified through testimony from family members, police officers, probation officers, or the defence attorney during consultation and through observations made by the presiding magistrate or judge. The court will refer the accused for a brief outpatient mental health screening interview and assessment by a medical practitioner at a district hospital.

Clinical forensic examiners are medical practitioners designated to conduct non-specialised forensic examinations, such as assessing rape victims, victims of other crimes, and drunken drivers. They work at district hospitals, examining and collecting evidence from individuals they assess, and are increasingly assigned to conduct brief preliminary mental health assessments of defendants. This was previously the function of the district surgeon, who also conducted post-mortem examinations, but this is now a specialised role performed only by forensic pathologists. The report from the initial screening assessment, conducted by a medical practitioner or clinical forensic examiner, along with other evidence, such as the accused's psychiatric history, serves as the basis for a formal forensic psychiatry assessment referral.

The presiding officer (judge or magistrate) makes a ruling ordering the accused to undergo a 30-day evaluation, specifying whether this must be conducted by a single psychiatrist or a panel of psychiatrists (which may include a psychologist) at a specialised forensic unit requiring admission. The order for a 30-day evaluation is also sent to the office of the DPP, who advises on the referral. The distinction between individual and panel cases depends on whether the charge involves serious violence or if there are other factors, such as being a repeat offender, that necessitate evaluation by a panel. Unfortunately, the forensic system in South Africa has limited resources, resulting in long waiting lists for admission. As a result, most non-violent cases requiring assessment by a single psychiatrist are now conducted as forensic outpatient evaluations.

Based on the report submitted and expert testimony, the ultimate disposal of an observation referral rests with the court. The lead author of the report usually provides expert testimony. However, in some cases, the court or the defence may insist on hearing from other panel members or contributors to the assessment, such as a social worker. If a report states that the accused has a serious mental illness that affects their ability to stand trial or criminal capacity, the court has several options for proceeding. It may decide to discharge the accused, continue with the case, certify the defendant as a state forensic patient with admission to a forensic unit for an indefinite period, or refer the defendant as an involuntary mental healthcare user to a general or acute psychiatric hospital.

Once an individual has been deemed not criminally responsible by reason of mental illness or intellectual disability, they are ordered to be a state patient under the *Criminal Procedure Act (Criminal Procedure Act 51 of 1977)*. They are then admitted as a state patient under the *Mental Health Care Act* (Department of Justice, 2004). Once they are admitted, the multidisciplinary clinical team assumes responsibility for their care, treatment, and psychosocial rehabilitation.

There are no forensic tribunals in South Africa; however, oversight is administered by the Mental Health Review Board and the DPP, who also acts as the curator ad litem for all state patients. The DPP serves as the prosecution authority within the jurisdiction of that court. The Department of Health and the DPP receive annual reports, called periodicals, which outline the progress and treatment plans for all forensic patients. In addition to clinical decisions, the team determines permissions for access to hospital grounds, town parole, and, ultimately, long leave in the community.

An application for discharge may be submitted by the state patient, a family member, a treating clinician, or any individual with a vested interest in the state patient's case. This application must be submitted to both the Registrar of the High Court and the DPP. The DPP may choose to reject the petition. At the same time, a High Court judge in chambers has the authority to call witnesses and issue an order either denying the application or granting the release of the state patient with specific conditions for a defined period, typically two to five years. Alternatively, the state patient may be reclassified as an involuntary mental healthcare user. General psychiatrists, not forensic psychiatrists, manage involuntary mental healthcare users.

## Forensic Psychiatry System

### *Structure and Function of the Forensic Psychiatric System*

In South Africa, formal forensic mental health services are provided through specialised psychiatric hospitals equipped with forensic units. Across the country, approximately 10 to 12 designated forensic units conduct forensic evaluations, each varying in resources and capacities.

In the Western Cape, forensic services are offered at three psychiatric hospitals. Valkenberg Hospital has one maximum-security ward for high-risk patients and those undergoing court evaluations, two medium-secure wards, and one low-secure ward. Lentegeur Hospital has four medium-secure wards and one dedicated female ward. Alexandra Hospital provides two wards for state patients with intellectual disabilities.

Forensic units in South Africa operate with multidisciplinary teams, including psychiatrists, psychologists, occupational therapists, social workers, and professional nurses. Other healthcare professionals, such as speech therapists and physiotherapists, are also involved when needed to ensure comprehensive treatment for state patients. These teams collaborate to provide care, share information, and implement treatment plans.

### *The Role of Forensic Psychiatry*

In South Africa, forensic psychiatrists perform various tasks, including clinical assessments, to determine fitness to stand trial and criminal responsibility. These assessments are conducted in a clinical environment by professionals with diverse specialities, including psychiatric nurses, clinical psychologists, occupational therapists, social workers, and a forensic psychiatrist. Structured clinical interviews are conducted to obtain a comprehensive history and mental status examination using the Maudsley clinical interview guidelines (Owen et al., 2014).

Physical examinations, bedside tests, laboratory investigations, and specialised tests—including neuro-radiological scans and electroencephalograms (EEG)—are also conducted. Neurocognitive tests administered include the Mini-Mental Status Examination, Montreal Cognitive Assessment (MoCA), Brief Neuropsychological Cognitive Examination, and the Rey Auditory Verbal Learning Test (RAVLT). Functional assessments cover basic and instrumental activities of daily living. Psychometric tests used include the Wechsler Adult Intelligence Scale IV (WAIS-IV), Raven's Coloured Progressive Matrices, and Raven's Standard Progressive Matrices (SPM).

Structured professional judgement and risk assessment instruments used include the Psychopathy Checklist-Revised (PCL-R), the youth version of the Psychopathy Checklist (PCL:YV), Historical, Clinical, and Risk Management (HCR-20), Sexual Violence Risk-20 (SVR-20), as well as the Violence Risk Appraisal Guide (VRAG) and the Sex Offender Risk Appraisal Guide (SORAG). Malingering tests, such as the forced-choice, dot-counting, and Test of Memory Malingering (TOMM), are also utilised. Personality assessments include the Minnesota Multiphasic Personality Inventory (MMPI). These instruments are not administered to every referred defendant but are used only when clinically relevant.

In addition to conducting criminal assessments, forensic psychiatrists provide expert testimony in court. They also assess convicted criminals for dangerousness, as outlined in Section 286A of the *Criminal Procedure Act*, to determine whether they should be declared dangerous criminals and subjected to a harsher or indefinite sentence (Hamman & ACaNWPP, 2019).

### *Declaration of Certain Persons as Dangerous Criminals*

In South Africa, the death penalty was abolished in 1995, as it was deemed unconstitutional for violating the rights to life, dignity, and freedom from torture and cruel punishment (Magobotiti, 2022). In response, Section 286 of the

*Criminal Procedure Act* was introduced to address the declaration of dangerous criminals. A dangerous criminal is defined as a person who poses a threat to the physical or mental wellbeing of others. The law further states that such individuals should be declared dangerous criminals to protect the community (Hamman & ACaNWPP, 2019).

Dangerous criminals are individuals who have already been convicted of their crimes and are not considered to have a mental illness. Before sentencing, they undergo a 30-day forensic evaluation to determine whether they present an ongoing danger to others (Kaliski, 2006). Psychiatrists are responsible for conducting a risk assessment of the convicted criminal and providing the referring court with an evaluation of their future risk to others. A maximum prison sentence will be imposed if the assessing psychiatrist and the court agree that the convicted criminal is dangerous. The court will also set a date, usually 20 years later, for the offender to return for a follow-up forensic psychiatric assessment to determine whether the sentence should be reimposed.

Forensic psychiatrists are also responsible for the care, treatment, and psychosocial rehabilitation of state patients, as outlined in Chapter 6, Sections 41–48 of the *Mental Health Care Act* (Department of Justice, 2004). These are those who have been found not guilty by reason of mental illness or intellectual disability.

Forensic psychiatrists may also participate in civil litigation, typically including third-party insurance claims, child custody disputes, curatorship and testamentary capacity assessments, and impaired professional assessments. Private practitioners often handle these matters. While forensic psychiatrists can conduct witness assessments, many choose not to. However, a small number provide clinical psychiatric assessments for both convicted prisoners and those awaiting trial. These psychiatrists do not conduct criminal assessments on the same prisoners, as doing so may be considered unethical and a conflict of interest.

South Africa currently has approximately 30 registered forensic psychiatrists. While clinical psychologists are present in all forensic mental health facilities, forensic psychology has yet to be recognised as a subspecialty despite ongoing lobbying efforts (Pillay et al., 2019; Laher & Cockcroft, 2014). The Health Professions Council of South Africa (HPCSA) has no registration category for specialist forensic psychologists. One of the main obstacles is the lack of uniformity in training across the country.

### ***Forensic Psychiatry Profession***

#### *Training and Specialised Qualifications*

In South Africa, forensic psychiatry is recognised as a specialised field and requires a postgraduate qualification for psychiatrists. To work as a forensic psychiatrist, a registered psychiatrist with the HPCSA must undergo training under the supervision of a forensic psychiatrist in an HPCSA-accredited forensic mental health hospital or unit for a minimum of 18 months. During this period, they must be enrolled in a Master of Philosophy (MPhil) in Forensic Psychiatry degree.

To enrol in an MPhil programme, a candidate must select a university accredited by the HPCSA that provides the necessary training. The university assigns the candidate an HPCSA training number, indicating their status as a sub-specialist trainee. Candidates must be employed full-time or part-time in the public sector as trainees. Training sites conduct formative assessments at 6, 12, and 18 months to evaluate progress.

During training, trainees are expected to complete specific outputs, which are formally recorded in a portfolio of learning (logbook) (College of Psychiatrists of South Africa). These include conducting court assessments, treating forensic patients, performing civil assessments, and providing expert court testimony for adults and children. Academic requirements include reviewing and presenting forensic journal articles, participating in academic meetings, workshops, seminars, symposia, and congresses, and engaging in journal club presentations, conference presentations, and research activities. While a minor master's thesis or dissertation is recommended, it is not a requirement for registering as a sub-specialist forensic psychiatrist.

The Colleges of Medicine of South Africa (CMSA) is the only authorised entity recognised for conducting specialist and sub-specialist examinations in South Africa. Within the CMSA, the College of Psychiatrists administers a single exit examination for trainees specialising in subspecialty forensic psychiatry. Trainees must submit their application at least three months before the exam date. Applications are only considered if the trainee has completed a minimum of 18 months of training, as verified through a portfolio of learning records signed by their supervisors and the head of the academic department at the university.

The examination, known as the Subspecialty Certificate in Forensic Psychiatry, consists of both written and clinical components, which may be case-based or oral (College of Psychiatrists of South Africa). The coursework assessed in this examination is based on the expected learning outcomes outlined in the CMSA regulations. It includes questions on various forensic topics, which are openly published on the CMSA website and accessible to examination candidates at any time. The curriculum covers relevant South African legislation, civil litigation, forensic assessments, riskassessment tools, dangerous offenders, capacity assessments, neuropsychiatry, ethics, and special interest groups such as individuals with intellectual disabilities, children, and the elderly.

The examiners are qualified forensic professionals from various training centres across the country who centrally set and moderate the examinations. The CMSA executive council monitors and audits the examination process. The MPhil degree in Forensic Psychiatry is awarded when the trainee completes a research dissertation in a forensic psychiatry-related field. Upon successfully passing the examination's written and clinical components, candidates become eligible for graduation as sub-specialist forensic psychiatrists.

*National Networks and Collaborations*

There are no national forensic psychiatry organisations in South Africa. However, a professional society for psychiatrists is the South African Society of Psychiatrists (SASOP). Within SASOP, there is a special interest subgroup for forensic psychiatrists. Membership in SASOP is not compulsory for psychiatrists practising in South Africa. All forensic psychiatrists are registered with the HPCSA, the statutory body responsible for regulating the clinical practice of all medical practitioners. South Africa does not currently have any international forensic agreements or collaborations.

## Forensic Psychiatry Service (Provision of Care)

### *Demographic, Psychosocial, and Criminological Profiles*

The *Criminal Procedure Act* states that individuals who have committed violent offences but are found not guilty by reason of mental illness or intellectual disability must be ordered to be state patients (*Criminal Procedure Act 51 of 1977*). It is, therefore, not surprising that the majority (over 80%) of state patients have been charged with serious violent offences. However, some non-violent offenders are also state patients (Pienaar et al., 2011). These individuals repeatedly reoffend, receive treatment, relapse, and commit minor crimes, requiring long-term care. Almost all come from impoverished backgrounds where crime, gangsterism, and substance abuse are prevalent. Some are homeless, while many have been charged with offences against family members, including domestic violence.

An increasing number of individuals with learning disabilities are being arrested for sexual offences, primarily against minors. Patients with psychotic illnesses typically have a long history of previous admissions, polysubstance abuse, and poor social support. Patterns of substance abuse vary across the country, reflecting broader trends in state patient populations. According to a report released in July 2023 by the South African Community Epidemiology Network of Drug Use (SACENDU), crystal methamphetamine was identified as the most prevalent substance of abuse (34.8%) in the Western Cape (Watt et al., 2014; Hornsby et al., 2023). In other parts of the country, cannabis, alcohol, and heroin were the predominant substances.

State patients are predominantly male (over 90%), with an average age of 31 years. Most are single, unemployed, have low levels of education, a previous psychiatric diagnosis, and a history of substance abuse upon admission. These demographic trends were consistent across studies conducted in different provinces, except race, which reflected the population composition of each region (Houidi et al., 2018; Mogase et al., 2022; Marais & Subramaney, 2015; Morgan & Del Fabbro, 2018). However, there is a growing trend of women and adolescents being certified as state patients, although research on these groups remains limited. A multi-site national study revealed that female offenders were referred primarily for serious violent crimes, most often murder, and had histories of severe mental illness, poor socio-economic conditions, alcohol abuse, and victimisation (Nagdee et al., 2018). Defendants from privileged backgrounds represent a significant minority.

Only individuals diagnosed with significant severe mental illnesses, such as psychotic disorders, bipolar disorder, neurocognitive disorders, neurodevelopmental disorders, and intellectual disabilities—conditions that diminish capacity and impair reality testing—are considered forensic patients. Those whose primary diagnoses are personality disorders, depression, anxiety, or similar conditions are not certified as forensic patients. Additionally, civilly committed patients are not classified as forensic patients. Forensic psychiatrists typically manage most cases in the civil system in private practice or general psychiatrists in the state sector.

### *Exiting the Forensic System*

Very few patients in the forensic system achieve a full discharge. The discharge procedure is complex, as a judge in chambers and the DPP must be satisfied that the patient no longer poses a danger to others, will abstain from substance abuse, will remain compliant with medication, and will attend outpatient (ambulatory) services under the supervision of a responsible person.

Once declared a state patient, individuals are admitted to maximum or high-security units before transitioning to medium-security units for a minimum of 6–12 months of intensive treatment. Only after this period may they be granted graded leave of absence (LOA) to their families. This may take longer in some cases, depending on their response to treatment, social circumstances, and risk profile.

From an inpatient perspective, there is no standard length of stay. However, at the earliest opportunity—typically between six months and two years—most state patients are granted an LOA for a specified period, with conditions set out. They then return to the hospital as inpatients and are granted additional LOA increments if they adhere to the conditions. If a state patient remains mentally stable and is assessed as low risk for reoffending, they will continue to be treated as an outpatient. On average, state patients remain in the forensic system for more than 10 years, often spending their lifetime within it. However, many individuals in the forensic system live in the community and are managed by community-based general mental health practitioners or attend specialist forensic outpatient services. The average length of stay as an outpatient is between 10 and 15 years.

The prolonged stay in the forensic system is due to multiple factors, including the stark contrast between hospital resources and the limited support available in the community. South Africa has a high prevalence of substance abuse. A study conducted in the Eastern Cape found a lifetime prevalence of 64.4% for alcohol use and 39.7% for other psychoactive substances among individuals with mental illness. Cannabis was the most widely used substance (37.7%) (Tindimwebwa et al., 2021).

When state patients are granted LOA, they often return to communities where access to substances is easy and exposure to violence—whether through family conflict, gangsterism, or crime—is high. Many of these communities are impoverished, with low levels of education and high unemployment, leading to inadequate supervision by family members. As a result, some state patients fail to adhere to their release conditions, including compliance with prescribed treatment and abstinence from substances. This often leads to relapse, readmission, and eventual release once they are stabilised and reassessed as low risk. When a state patient relapses and exhibits difficult or violent behaviour in the community, the police are notified, as they are the only agents permitted to forcibly remove individuals for readmission under Sections 44–45 of the *Mental Health Care A*ct (Department of Justice, 2004).

### *Approaches to Assessment and Treatment*

All new patients are admitted to a high-security ward for stabilisation, comprehensive treatment, and psychosocial rehabilitation. This is stipulated in Section 42 of the *Mental Health Care Act*, which outlines the provision of medication, psychological interventions (including group therapy), and family interventions facilitated by social workers. Most patients remain in the high-security ward for at least one year. The assessments conducted upon admission of state patients are not standardised but are similar to those performed during observation assessments, as described earlier. Additional investigations and assessments are conducted if clinically indicated. The state imposes no mandatory treatment regimens; the clinical team determines treatment plans based on their assessments. As patients progress to medium- and low-security care, elements of a recovery model are introduced, allowing them increasing periods in the community—either under the supervision of family members or in community facilities—while being monitored by the multidisciplinary team at forensic outpatient services. Patients' primary needs are assessed from admission, and efforts are made to align their care with the recovery model, although this can often be challenging.

## Strengths and Weaknesses

There are three primary strengths of the South African forensic system. The first is the ease of entry into the system. The second is the availability of long-term care, which is not provided in general or acute psychiatric services. Lastly, when patients relapse in the community, the police are legally required to return them, a safeguard that does not necessarily apply to other psychiatric patients in the community.

However, the system also has several weaknesses. One major issue is the complex discharge process. Discharging patients, many of whom feel stranded after spending years in the forensic system, is extremely difficult. Numerous attempts have been made to amend legislation to simplify the discharge process or introduce a specified duration of incarceration for forensic patients.

Another significant weakness is the limited human resources in forensic psychiatry. There are very few mental health practitioners with expertise in this field, and forensic psychiatry units, hospitals, and facilities are insufficiently equipped to admit and assess patients adequately. This is particularly evident in prison hospitals, where staffing is inadequate, and mental healthcare services—including screening, assessment, and treatment—are poorly delivered. These challenges have major implications for the forensic system. The waiting list for forensic assessments has grown significantly, and the number of beds for forensic patients must be increased periodically. As a result, some forensic wards are overcrowded. In other provinces, the shortage of beds has led to forensic patients being housed in prisons while awaiting admission to forensic units.

A further weakness is the limited community resources, which complicate efforts to permanently place patients on extended leave or reintegrate them into the community. Additionally, despite existing plans and previously allocated funds, there is a lack of political will and commitment to rebuild and expand forensic psychiatry services. Finally, forensic patients face significant challenges when attempting to appeal against their commitment, limiting their ability to challenge their placement within the system.

## References

Department of Justice. (2004). *Mental Health Care Act 17 of 2002*. Government Gazette, 25–30.

Hamman, A., & ACaNWPP. (2019). "Deciphering dangerousness": A critical analysis of section 286A and B of the *criminal procedure act 51 of 1977. Potchefstroom Electronic Law Journal*, *47*, 1–26.

Hornsby, N., Burnhams, N. H., Erasmus, J., Pretorius, C., & SANCA Research Workgroup. (2023). *Monitoring alcohol, tobacco and other drug abuse treatment admissions in South Africa* (Report No. 1). South African Community Epidemiology Network on Drug Use.

Houidi, A., Paruk, S., & Sartorius, B. (2018). Forensic psychiatric assessment process and outcome in state patients in KwaZulu-Natal, South Africa. *South African Journal of Psychiatry*, *24*, 1142. https://doi.org/10.4102/sajpsychiatry.v24i0.1142

Kaliski, S. (2006). The dangerous offender and risk assessment. In S. Kaliski (Ed.), *Psycholegal assessment in South Africa* (pp. 111–125). Oxford University Press.

Kleintjes, S., & Lund, C. (2023). History and politics of mental health policy and care in South Africa. *SSM—Mental Health*, *3*.

Laher, S., & Cockcroft, K. (2014). Psychological assessment in post-apartheid South Africa: The way forward. *South African Journal of Psychology*, *44*(3), 303–314.

Magobotiti, C. D. (2022). Historical reflections on the deterrent effect of the death penalty on capital crimes in South Africa: Lessons from 1917–1995. *Scientia Militaria: South African Journal of Military Studies*, *50*(3). https://doi.org/10.5787/50-3-1393

Maimela, I., & NLMC. (2021). The indigenisation of customary law: Creating an indigenous legal pluralism within the South African dispensation: Possible or not? *De Jure Law Journal*, *54*.

Marais, B., & Subramaney, U. (2015). Forensic state patients at Sterkfontein Hospital: A 3-year follow-up study. *South African Journal of Psychiatry*, *21*(3), 86–92. https://doi.org/10.4102/sajpsychiatry.v21i3.708

Mogase, K., Moeketsi, T., & Sokudela, B. F. (2022). Social determinants of health in male forensic patients admitted at a tertiary psychiatric hospital in South Africa. *International Journal of Social Psychiatry*, *68*(8), 1806–1814. https://doi.org/10.1177/00207640211060261

Morgan, N., & Del Fabbro, G. (2018). Factors associated with recidivism at a South African forensic psychiatric hospital. *South African Journal of Psychiatry*, *24*, 1125. https://doi.org/10.4102/sajpsychiatry.v24i0.1125

Nagdee, M., Artz, L., Corral-Bulnes, C., Heath, A., Subramaney, U., de Clercq, H. G., Erlacher, H., Kotze, C., Lippi, G., Naidoo, S., & Sokudela, F. (2018). From victim to perpetrator to survivor: The psychosocial context of South African women offenders. *South African Journal of Psychiatry*, *24*, a1160. https://doi.org/10.4102/sajpsychiatry.v24i0.1160

Owen, G., Sarkar, S., & Murray, R. (2014). *The Maudsley handbook of practical psychiatry* (6th ed.). Oxford University Press.

Pienaar, C., Dreyer, A., van der Merwe, L., van Rensburg, B. J., Calitz, F. J. W., van der Merwe, L. M., & Joubert, G. (2011). Profile of forensic psychiatric inpatients referred to the free state psychiatric complex, 2004–2008. *South African Journal of Psychiatry*, *17*(2), 40–43. https://doi.org/10.4102/sajpsychiatry.v17i2.274

Pillay, A. L., Gowensmith, W. N., & Banks, J. M. (2019). Towards the development of a forensic psychology training curriculum in South Africa. *South African Journal of Psychology*, *49*(4), 536–549. https://doi.org/10.1177/0081246319879291

Seligon, M. (2001). Lay participation in South Africa from apartheid to majority rule. *International Review of Penal Law*, *72*, 273–284.

South Africa. (1973). *Mental Health Act 18 of 1973.*

South Africa. (1977). *Criminal Procedure Act 51 of 1977.*

South Africa. (1979). *Abolition of Juries Act 34 of 1969.*

South Africa. (2001). *Criminal Procedure Second Amendment Act 62 of 2001.*

South Africa. (2002). *Mental Health Care Act 17 of 2002.*

South Africa. (2008). *Child Justice Act 75 of 2008.* (2008).

Tindimwebwa, L., Ajayi, A. I., & Adeniyi, O. V. (2021). Prevalence and demographic correlates of substance use among adults with mental illness in Eastern Cape, South Africa. *International Journal of Environmental Research and Public Health*, *18*(10), 5428. https://doi.org/10.3390/ijerph18105428

Watt, M. H., Meade, C. S., Kimani, S., MacFarlane, J. C., Choi, K. W., Skinner, D., Pieterse, D., Kalichman, S. C., & Sikkema, K. J. (2014). The impact of methamphetamine ("tik") on a peri-urban community in Cape Town, South Africa. *International Journal of Drug Policy*, *25*(2), 219–225. https://doi.org/10.1016/j.drugpo.2013.10.007

# 27 Tanzania

*Enock Eteregho Changarawe*

## Brief Description

| | |
|---|---|
| **Location** | Tanzania is a country in East Africa and is made up of the Tanzania mainland and the semi-autonomous archipelago of Zanzibar. |
| **Size** | 945,087 km$^2$ |
| **Population** | The 2022 census puts the population of Tanzania at 62 million, an increase of 37% from 2012 (approximately 60 million in Mainland and 1.9 million in Zanzibar). |
| **Languages** | Tanzania, a multilingual country, with 126 spoken languages. Swahili and English, the latter adopted from colonial times, are prevalent, with Swahili designated as the official national language, although not spoken natively by a significant portion of the population. |
| **Political system** | Tanzania is a unitary presidential democratic republic, where the President of Tanzania serves as both head of state and head of government within a multiparty system. The government exercises executive power, while legislative power is shared between the government and parliament. Chama Cha Mapinduzi (CCM), the Revolutionary Party, dominates the party system. The judiciary operates independently from the executive and the legislature. |

## Legal System

The legal system in Tanzania is primarily based on common law but also incorporates Islamic and customary laws, with the latter being applied to personal or family matters. The judiciary consists of various courts of judicature and operates independently from the government. Tanzania upholds and respects the constitutional principles of the separation of powers. The *Constitution of Tanzania, 1977* provides for establishing an independent judiciary and respects the principles of the rule of law, human rights, and good governance (United Republic of Tanzania, 2005).

DOI: 10.4324/9781003376248-33

The judiciary in Tanzania consists of four tiers: the Primary Courts, which are at the lowest level of the hierarchy; the Magistrate Courts, comprising the Resident Magistrate Courts and the District Court, both with concurrent jurisdiction at different levels; the High Court of Mainland Tanzania, which serves as the superior court at the national level; and, at the apex of the judicial hierarchy, the Court of Appeal of the United Republic of Tanzania.

The High Court of Zanzibar holds exclusive original jurisdiction over all matters within Zanzibar, similar to the jurisdiction of the High Court on the mainland of Tanzania. The Zanzibar court system closely mirrors the Tanzania mainland system, with the distinction that Zanzibar maintains Islamic courts. These courts specifically handle legal matters pertaining to Muslim families, including divorce, child custody, and inheritance cases, based on Islamic (Sharia) law.

Tanzania's *Criminal Procedure Act* outlines the laws governing the procedure in the case of insanity (refers to mental illness at the time of committing an alleged offence) or incapacity (refers to inability to make decisions) of an accused person (United Republic of Tanzania, 2022a).

### *Insanity of Accused*

Section 216 of Tanzania's *Criminal Procedure Act* Revised Edition of 2022, outlines the procedure when the accused is believed to be of unsound mind. In such instances, during a trial, the court will request that the prosecution provide or present evidence to support the charges. If there is sufficient evidence, the court shall proceed to inquire about the unsoundness of mind of the accused and, for this purpose, may order them to be detained in a mental health hospital for medical examination or, in the case where bail may be granted, may place them on bail on sufficient security and on the condition that they submit themselves to a medication examination or observation by a medical officer.

In this case, it means that, during the trial, when the accused is observed to show some abnormal behaviours, the court will see that they probably have a mentally ill. So, to be sure of the assumption, the court will order the accused to be examined by a medical doctor/psychiatrist, to prove their mental illness.

Within 42 days of detention, the medical officer is required to provide a report on the mental state of the accused. This report should clearly state the opinion that the accused is deemed to be of unsound mind and therefore unable to participate in their defence. Upon review of the report and other pertinent evidence concerning the mental state of the accused, if the court determines that the accused is unfit to stand trial due to being of unsound mind, it will officially note this finding, delay further court proceedings, and direct that the accused be held in a mental health facility or appropriate custodial setting until either deemed fit to stand trial or released. Upon restoration of mental competence, the trial will continue.

### *Defence of Insanity*

In Tanzania, the Penal Code outlines reasons that a defendant may be not criminally responsible, also referred to as the 'defence of insanity' (United Republic of Tanzania, 2022b). Where any act or omission is charged against any person as an offence, and the accused intends to raise the defence of insanity, that defence shall be raised when the person is called to plead. The defence excuses an accused from criminal responsibility if it appears to the court that the accused committed the act but was insane, so as not to be responsible for their actions. In this case, the court shall make a finding that the accused did commit the act or made the omission charged but is not guilty of the offence by reason of insanity.

If the accused is charged with an offence under the Penal Code involving physical violence or damage to property that would, on conviction, be liable to a prison sentence of seven years or more, or death, but is deemed insane (not criminally responsible), the court will order the person to be detained in a mental health hospital, prison, or other suitable place of custody as a 'mentally disordered offender'. In any other case, it is at the discretion of the court to send the individual to a mental health hospital, discharge them, or otherwise sentence them (subject to conditions ensuring the safety and welfare of the individual and the public).

When the offender is detained under a court order, the superintendent of a mental health hospital, prison, or other place of custody shall report to the Minister on the individual's condition, history, and circumstances. The first report shall be written three years after the court order, and the following reports will be written every two years. Any person authorised by the Minister may also report to the minister on the individual's condition, history, and circumstances. After considering any report, the Minister may order the individual to be discharged or dealt with in some other way. At any time, the court may also order that the individual be transferred from a mental health hospital to a prison, or from any place where they are detained to a prison or mental health hospital.

## Forensic Psychiatry System

### *Structure and Function of the Forensic Mental Health System*

Before trial, if an accused person is found to be insane or incapable of standing trial, they are considered a 'mentally disordered offender' (wording in the law) and taken to the Isanga Institution (the only institution dealing with mentally disordered offenders in the country), part of Mirembe National Mental Health Hospital in Dodoma region, Tanzania. They undergo three years of treatment and rehabilitation before being discharged by the Minister of Constitutional and Legal Affairs. Those found incapable of standing trial by the court are treated, and once they are mentally stable and able to stand trial, they are sent back to court to resume their cases. There is no set length of stay for these individuals; the time spent at the Isanga Institution depends on the time it takes for their symptoms to improve so they may stand trial.

After assessments, the medical reports are usually sent to courts which referred the accused people for assessment. The magistrates/judges decide whether the accused people are guilty or not guilty due to mental illness. If they are found not guilty due to mental illness, they are said to be 'insane'. When they are found insane, the courts order them back to the hospital, for treatment and rehabilitation, for three years, under the *Criminal Procedure Act*.

## Forensic Psychiatry Profession

### *The Role of Forensic Psychiatry and Training*

There is no training programme in Tanzania in forensic psychiatry. As a result, there are no specialised forensic psychiatrists or psychologists in Tanzania. For court-ordered assessments of defendants or offenders (discussed earlier), assessments are completed by a psychiatrist or one of the two medical officers, with help from other staff, such as nurses, who may report any observed abnormal behaviour during the patient's stay in hospital. Most of the time, a psychiatrist (the author) conducts the assessments. But other psychiatrists (four) may do so as needed. For Tanzania's mainland; the courts are the decision makers, and the Minister of Legal Affairs also makes some decisions regarding the defence of insanity. In Zanzibar, there is a lack of forensic health services and no special centre to accommodate mentally disordered offenders, who are not recognised as such and may be detained in prisons like other prisoners.

### *National Collaborations or Networks*

There is no national forensic psychiatry organisation in Tanzania.

## Forensic Psychiatry Service (Provision of Care)

### *Forensic Patient Characteristics*

All mentally disordered offenders are considered to be forensic psychiatric patients. Civilly committed patients are not considered to be forensic patients.

### *Approaches to Assessment and Treatment*

Three years of treatment is mandatory for all individuals who are found to be mentally ill. Treatment programmes target psychiatric symptoms; no programme in the Isanga Institution focuses on criminogenic risk factors. Rehabilitation programmes offered to forensic psychiatry patients are mainly occupational therapies, where patients participate in activities such as agricultural activities, animal husbandry, carpentry, sewing, and various trades such as plumbing.

## Strengths and Weaknesses

Strengths of Tanzania's forensic system include the courts' recognition of patients with mental illness who commit crimes. Additionally, through the Ministry of Constitution and Legal Affairs, the government also respects mentally disordered offenders.

One major weakness is that there are no specialised forensic psychiatrists or psychologists in the country. Furthermore, the Isanga Institution is the only facility dealing with mentally disordered offenders in the country. Most of the time, it is overwhelmed with patients, making caring for patients who are mentally ill. Similarly, because of the large number of patients from all over the country, they may take a very long time to reach the institution, causing delays in examinations and reports, which delays the courts and hence justice for the accused. There is also limited funding from the government, especially for medication and the general welfare of the mentally disordered offenders when they are at the Isanga Institution. Last, some parts of the legal system do not acknowledge offenders with mental illnesses; hence, they are usually sentenced in the same way as other criminals.

## References

United Republic of Tanzania. (2005). *The Constitution of the United Republic of Tanzania of 1977* [PDF]. Retrieved from https://www.nao.go.tz/uploads/Constitution_of_the_United_Republic_of_Tanzania_en.pdf

United Republic of Tanzania. (2022a). *The Criminal Procedure Act Rev.* [PDF], CAP. 20 R.E. 2022. Retrieved from http://parliament.go.tz/polis/uploads/bills/acts/1662103298-CHAPTER%2020-THE%20CRIMINAL%20PROCEDURE%20ACT.pdf

United Republic of Tanzania. (2022b). *The Penal Code Rev.* [PDF], CAP. 16 R.E. 2022. Retrieved from https://www.parliament.go.tz/polis/uploads/bills/acts/1662102362-CHAPTER%2016-THE%20PENAL%20CODE.pdf

# 28 Uganda

*Irene Apio Wengi, Mark Mohan Kaggwa, and Julius Muron*

## Brief Description

| | |
|---|---|
| **Location** | Uganda is a landlocked country in East Africa. |
| **Size** | 241,038 km² |
| **Population** | 48 million |
| **Languages** | In Uganda, the official languages are English and Swahili. English is used in government, education, and business, while Swahili serves as the national language and is widely spoken for communication across the country. Uganda is home to over 60 tribes, all with their own Indigenous languages. Many Ugandans are multilingual, reflecting the country's rich linguistic diversity. |
| **Political system** | Uganda operates as a presidential republic with three distinct branches of government: the executive branch, headed by the president who serves as both the Head of State and the Head of Government; the legislative branch, consisting of a parliament responsible for creating laws and comprising elected members and special representatives; and the judiciary, which functions independently to interpret and enforce the law. Elections are conducted every five years within a multiparty system. |

## Legal System

The court system in Uganda was established under the *Constitution of the Republic of Uganda in 1995*, as amended (Parliament of Uganda, 1995). Chapter 8 provides for the judiciary, with Article 129 outlining the structure of the Supreme Court, the Court of Appeal, and the High Court of Uganda. These courts are arranged in a hierarchy according to their respective powers.

The *Judicature Act*, Chapter 13, and the *Local Council Courts Act*, Chapter 13, establish local council courts which deal with matters of a minor nature (Parliament of Uganda, 1996, 2006). The *Public Health Act*, Chapter 281, and the *Mental Health Act*, Chapter 280, provide Uganda's legal framework for health and mental health services, including the establishment of psychiatric facilities—although these have not been fully developed or utilised (Parliament of Uganda,

DOI: 10.4324/9781003376248-34

2018). The *Trial on Indictments Act*, Chapter 23, governs the prosecution and trial of serious criminal offences (Parliament of Uganda, 1971). It addresses issues such as court jurisdiction and committal procedures, whereby cases originating from lower courts that require High Court attention must be formally transferred. The Act also outlines guidelines, criteria for sentencing, and appeals provisions.

Uganda is a common-law country that follows a common law legal system. In this system, the prosecution and defence competitively present their cases, while the judge serves as a presiding officer to ensure that procedural rules are upheld. The judge assesses the evidence presented in court and issues a sentence in criminal cases or a ruling in civil matters.

The court system in Uganda is hierarchical, starting with the Magistrates' Courts. These courts are structured from lowest to highest: Magistrate Grade 2, Magistrate Grade 1, and the Chief Magistrate. The Chief Magistrate is responsible for hearing appeals from decisions made by a Magistrate Grade 2. Above the Magistrates' Courts is the High Court of Uganda, which includes the Principal Judge and approximately 80 judges, a number determined by Parliament. Next in the hierarchy is the Court of Appeal, which consists of the Deputy Chief Justice and 14 Justices of Appeal. At the top of the hierarchy is the Supreme Court, which comprises the Chief Justice and 10 Justices of the Supreme Court.

In addition to these four main courts, the Industrial Court was established in 2006 to handle labour and employment issues. Parliament may also establish subordinate courts, such as the Qadhis' Courts, which deal with matters of Islamic personal law, including marriage, divorce, inheritance, and guardianship for Muslim communities.

## Mental Health Laws

### *Fitness to Stand Trial*

In Uganda, the issue of fitness to stand trial is legally referred to as an "inquiry by the court regarding the insanity of the accused" under the *Magistrates Courts Act*, Part 8, Section 113 (Parliament of Uganda, 2020). The question of fitness arises when the court has reason to believe that the accused is of unsound mind. This may occur either before proceedings commence or during the trial.

If the court determines that the accused is of unsound mind and is incapable of making a defence, it must postpone further proceedings. In cases where bail may be granted, the court may release the accused on the condition that sufficient security is provided. The accused must also be properly cared for and prevented from causing harm to themselves or others and must appear before the court or an appointed officer as required.

If the offence is one for which bail may not be granted, or if sufficient security is not available, the court shall order the accused to be detained in safe custody as appropriate. The court must then transmit the court record or a certified copy to the Minister. Upon reviewing the record, the Minister may, by warrant, order that the accused be confined as a 'criminal lunatic' in a mental hospital or other suitable place of custody. The court is responsible for issuing any further directions necessary to implement the Minister's order, which serves as sufficient authority for detention. The Minister or court may later direct that the accused be brought back before the court under Section 114 (certified as capable of making a defence) or Section 115 (resumption of trial or investigation) (Parliament of Uganda, 2020).

*Certified as Capable of Making a Defence (Section 114)*

If any person confined in a mental hospital or another place of custody under Section 113 is found by the medical officer in charge to be capable of making a defence, the medical officer must immediately forward a certificate to that effect to the Director of Public Prosecutions (Parliament of Uganda, 2020). The medical officer responsible for this determination is not necessarily a forensic psychiatrist.

Upon receiving the certificate, the Director of Public Prosecutions must inform the court whether the state intends to proceed with the case. If the proceedings are to continue, the court will order that the accused be removed from custody and brought before the court in accordance with Section 115. If the state decides not to continue the proceedings, the court must immediately order to release the person from custody (Parliament of Uganda, 2020).

*Resumption of Trial or Investigation (Section 115)*

Whenever any preliminary proceeding or trial is postponed under Section 113, the court may, at any time and subject to Section 114, resume the proceeding and require the accused to appear or be brought before the court. The preliminary investigation or trial shall proceed if the court considers the accused capable of defending themselves (Parliament of Uganda, 2020).

Any certificate issued to the Director of Public Prosecutions under Section 114 may be admitted as evidence in proceedings under this section without further proof, unless it is shown that the medical officer who purportedly signed the certificate did not do so. There is no requirement for further defence of the accused's fitness to stand trial once the court accepts the certificate (Parliament of Uganda, 2020).

If the court considers the accused incapable of making a defence, it shall proceed as though the accused were being brought before it for the first time. The defence of insanity remains admissible where the person was in an insane state at the time the offence was committed. However, it does not apply in cases where the individual, though generally suffering from a mental disorder, committed the offence during a period of sanity or mental clarity.

*Not Criminally Responsible: Defence of Insanity (Section 116)*

In Uganda, the legal concept of being not criminally responsible due to a mental illness is referred to as the 'defence of insanity'. It is based on the M'Naghten rules outlined in the *Magistrates Courts Act*, Part 8, Section 116 (Parliament of Uganda, 2020). Under this defence, an accused person may be excused from criminal responsibility if it is found that their mental illness prevented them from forming the intent required to commit a criminal offence. In such cases, the court must make a special finding that the accused is not guilty of the act or omission charged by reason of insanity. Once this finding is made, the court must report the case to the Minister, who holds significant authority over subsequent decisions.

While awaiting the Minister's order, the accused is held in custody as a 'criminal lunatic' in a place and manner directed by the court. The Minister may order that the individual be confined in a mental hospital, prison, or other suitable place of custody. If the accused is detained, the facility's superintendent must submit a report on the individual's condition, history, and circumstances. The first report must be submitted three years after the Minister's order, with subsequent reports every two years. Reports may also be submitted by the Commissioner of Prisons or the Chief Medical Officer. Upon reviewing any report, the Minister may order the individual's discharge. At any time, the Minister may also order the person's transfer between a mental hospital and a prison or to any other appropriate place of custody.

***Decision Makers in Forensic Psychiatry***

In Uganda, various individuals administer justice in criminal and civil matters. The *Mental Health Act* (Parliament of Uganda, 2018) outlines the decision-making processes and the roles of those involved in matters relating to forensic psychiatry.

*Local Council Authorities (Part 6, Section 73)*

When a forensic patient is released from prison or a mental health unit, the local council executive monitors the individual to ensure they do not pose a risk to community members. If the person is found to present a risk, the local council executive shall arrange for their admission to a mental health unit as an involuntary patient.

*The Police (Part 6, Section 66)*

When an arresting officer believes that an individual has a mental illness, the police officer shall not arrest or detain the person. Instead, the police officer shall take the individual for a mental health assessment by a qualified mental health practitioner. The police officer shall act in accordance with the results of the assessment. Where it is determined that the individual requires treatment for a mental illness, the police officer shall take the person to an appropriate health unit.

*The Prison and Prison Officers (Part 6, Section 67)*

When it appears to the officer in charge of a prison, whether through personal observation or based on information received, that a prisoner or a child in a remand home may have a mental illness, the officer shall order that an examination of the individual's mental health status be carried out. Where a psychiatrist is not readily available, the examination shall be conducted by a medical practitioner or a mental healthcare practitioner. The examiner shall submit a report to the officer in charge of the prison. The report shall specify the mental health status of the prisoner or child in the remand home and, where necessary, include a proposed treatment plan. Details of treatment are outlined later in this chapter.

*The Court*

The court meets with individuals who have already been seen by the police and have cases. The court will deal with these individuals in accordance with the *Magistrate Court Act*, Part 8; the *Trial on Indictments Act*, Part 4; and the *Mental Health Act* (Parliament of Uganda, 1971, 2018, and 2020). Details relating to fitness, criminal responsibility, and civil laws are outlined later in this chapter.

*Government*

The Minister of Justice shall make most final decisions concerning forensic patients, as outlined in the *Mental Health Act*, Part 6, Section 76 (Parliament of Uganda, 2018). In consultation with the board, the Minister shall make regulations concerning the care, treatment, and rehabilitation of persons with mental illness; the designation and appointment of mental health units and hospitals; the control and management of mental health units; the prescribing of standards to be maintained by mental health units in Uganda; the content of the Act; the procedure for the treatment of persons with mental illness; and the procedure for the integration of community mental health services and psychosocial support in the care and treatment of persons with mental illness.

*Experts/Senior Mental Health Practitioners*

Experts write certificates to inform the court or the Minister about the status of forensic patients. These certificates are prepared by the same experts who are currently managing, have managed, or are responsible for managing the mental health conditions of the individuals in question.

## Forensic Psychiatry System

### *Structure and Function of the Forensic Mental Health System*

Uganda has a formal forensic psychiatry system. The main psychiatric hospital, Butabika National Referral Hospital, has two wards and 116 beds designated for forensic patients held under the Minister's order. However, due to the high prevalence of mental illness in Uganda, many of these beds are occupied by non-forensic patients; only around 10% are currently used by forensic patients. The unit is operated by two forensic psychiatrists who received their training in the United Kingdom.

In addition to Butabika, there are wards within prisons that provide care for various illnesses. Psychiatric clinical officers are based at Luzira Prison, the country's main correctional facility, while most other prisons rely on psychiatric nurses as the primary providers of mental health care. Outside of the national referral hospital, it is rare for individuals with mental health conditions to receive services from psychiatrists.

There are three main pathways by which a person may exit Uganda's forensic system: by order of the Minister, sometimes following a report from the Chief Medical Officer; by being found fit, returned to court, and subsequently found guilty and sentenced; or by being found not guilty and released.

### *The Role of Forensic Psychiatry in Uganda*

In Uganda, the role of a forensic psychiatrist is closely associated with the role of the Chief Medical Officer. According to the *Mental Health Act* (Parliament of Uganda, 2018), no special qualifications beyond a medical degree are required to practise as a forensic psychiatrist. However, in some cases, a senior mental health practitioner, such as a general psychiatrist, senior psychiatry clinical officer, senior psychiatric nursing officer, senior mental health social worker, or senior clinical psychologist, may be required to perform forensic psychiatric functions. Two of Uganda's forensic psychiatrists (one now retired) completed specialised training placements in forensic psychiatry in the United Kingdom.

Forensic psychiatrists in Uganda carry out a range of responsibilities. Within the forensic context, they contribute to the administration of justice in both criminal and civil matters by assessing and treating forensic patients, providing expert testimony in court, and conducting evaluations of individuals' fitness to make a police statement, stand trial, or plead insanity as a defence. They may also assess for mitigation, manage placement and community resettlement issues, and provide opinions concerning wills, estate management, and guardianship. In addition to these duties, forensic psychiatrists are responsible for treating prisoners, diverting cases, and rehabilitating and reintegrating individuals into the community.

### Forensic Psychiatry Profession

#### *Qualifications and Specialised Training*

There are no formal forensic psychiatry training programmes in Uganda. However, the only practising forensic psychiatrist in the country received specialised training through an apprenticeship in the United Kingdom.

#### *National Collaborations or Networks*

There are no national forensic psychiatry organisations in Uganda.

## Forensic Psychiatry Service (Provision of Care)

### Forensic Patient Characteristics

About one in nine Ugandans were reported to be affected by mental health challenges in 2022 (Kaggwa et al., 2022). Despite this high burden, the country has fewer than 70 practising psychiatrists, one main psychiatric hospital—Butabika National Referral Mental Hospital—and psychiatric units within each regional referral hospital. Uganda had operated under legislation since the 1960s, but in 2022, it enacted updated legislation: the *Mental Health Act, 2018*.

Uganda does not have a clearly defined legal category for a forensic psychiatry patient. However, under the *Mental Health Act* (Parliament of Uganda, 2018), a forensic patient is generally understood to include anyone receiving treatment in a mental health facility under the order of the Minister. Civilly committed patients are also regarded as forensic patients, and there are few significant differences in the demographics of those who are criminally versus civilly committed. However, on average, criminally committed forensic patients tend to come from lower socioeconomic backgrounds and typically have less formal education than civilly committed patients.

### Exiting the System

There are three primary routes by which a patient may exit Uganda's forensic system. First, the individual may be discharged by order of the Minister, which may or may not be based on a report from the Chief Medical Officer. Second, if the patient is found fit, they may be returned to court, where they are either found guilty and sentenced accordingly or found not guilty and released.

### Approaches to Assessment and Treatment

In Uganda, there is no formally prescribed model of care for forensic psychiatry patients. The type and quality of care provided largely depend on the availability of services, the level of funding, and the patient's specific condition.

## Strengths and Weaknesses

Like any other system, Uganda's forensic psychiatry system has both strengths and weaknesses. One of its key strengths is the widespread presence of medical and psychiatric clinical officers in hospitals and prisons across the country. These professionals help to fill the gap left by the limited number of psychiatrists, which is critical given that Uganda has only 48 psychiatrists to serve a large and growing population. Another strength is the strong social cohesion among individuals working within the forensic system, which supports collaboration and continuity of care.

However, several weaknesses remain. Forensic patients, also referred to as mentally disordered offenders, are housed together with non-criminal patients at the national referral mental hospital, making it impossible to distinguish between them by observation alone. Security measures at the national and regional referral hospital mental health units are inadequate, resulting in frequent escapes of mentally disordered offenders back into the community. There are significant delays in the delivery of justice for remanded prisoners, with many lacking legal representation due to their low socioeconomic status. Furthermore, the field suffers from a severe shortage of trained forensic psychiatry professionals. Only two psychiatrists in Uganda received specialised training abroad and are expected to train others, placing a disproportionate burden on them. The country also lacks sufficient infrastructure, structured procedures, and training environments conducive to high-quality education and supervision in forensic psychiatry.

## References

Kaggwa, M. M., Harms, S., & Mamun, M. A. (2022). Mental health care in Uganda. *Lancet Psychiatry*, *9*(10), 766–767. https://doi.org/10.1016/S2215-0366(22)00305-4

Parliament of Uganda. (1971). *Trial on Indictments Act* [as amended]. Retrieved from https://ulii.org/akn/ug/act/decree/1971/26/eng@2020-02-14

Parliament of Uganda. (1995). *Constitution of the Republic of Uganda* [as amended]. Retrieved from https://ulii.org/akn/ug/act/statute/1995/constitution/eng@2018-01-05

Parliament of Uganda. (1996). *Judicature Act* [as amended]. Retrieved from https://ulii.org/akn/ug/act/statute/1996/13/eng@2020-06-19

Parliament of Uganda. (2006). *Local Council Courts Act, 2006*. Retrieved from https://mlhud.go.ug/wp-content/uploads/2019/03/Local-Council-Courts-Act-2006.pdf

Parliament of Uganda. (2018). *Mental Health Act 2018*. Retrieved from https://bills.parliament.ug/attachments/Mental%20Health%20Act%202018.pdf

Parliament of Uganda. (2020). *Magistrates Courts Act* [as amended], Part 8 (VIII), Section 113. Retrieved from https://ulii.org/akn/ug/act/1998/10/eng@2020-02-14

# Part VII

# Oceania

# 29 Aotearoa New Zealand

*Jacqueline Short and Jennifer Falce*

Of note is the use of Te Reo Māori with English throughout this document, reflecting the partnership with the Māori people in keeping with the principles of Te Tiriti o Waitangi.

## Brief Description

| | |
|---|---|
| **Location** | Aotearoa New Zealand comprises a number of islands in the middle of the Pacific Ocean. North and South Island are the two largest islands, followed by the considerably smaller Stewart Island. |
| **Size** | 268,021 km$^2$ |
| **Population** | 5.2 million. The population mainly live on North Island, with about a third living in the Auckland region. |
| **Languages** | The two official languages are Te Reo Māori and NZ Sign Language. However, English is spoken by the majority of the population, followed by Te Reo Māori (4%), Samoan (2.2%), northern Chinese (including Mandarin) (2%), and Hindi (1.5%). |
| **Political system** | Aotearoa New Zealand is a constitutional monarchy with a unitary parliamentary democracy. The British monarch is the head of state, represented in the country by the Governor-General, and the Prime Minister is the head of government. The legislature is a unicameral parliament (House of Representatives), and the judiciary is an independent branch. |

## Legal System

Aotearoa New Zealand's legal system is based on Anglo-Saxon/English common law. The current legal framework primarily comprises the *Constitution Act, 1986*, the principles of the Treaty of Waitangi 1840, the *New Zealand Bill of Rights Act 1990*, and the *Human Rights Act 1993* (*Constitution Act, 1986*; Treaty of Waitangi, 1840; *New Zealand Bill of Rights Act 1990*; *Human Rights Act 1993*). Based on an adversarial model, the court system comprises the Supreme Court (highest authority), the Court of Appeal, the High Court, and the District Court. Specialist

DOI: 10.4324/9781003376248-36

courts within the District Court include the New Beginnings Court and the Special Circumstances Court for homeless individuals, the Alcohol and Other Drug Treatment Court, and the Youth Court. Since 2020, the District Court in Auckland has held dedicated hearings for defendants with potential mental health issues, improving justice access for vulnerable individuals. However, specialist courts are not universally available, limiting access for some defendants.

### *Mental Health Laws*

In Aotearoa New Zealand, the *Mental Health (Compulsory Assessment and Treatment) Act 1992* provides the legal framework for people experiencing a mental illness who require compulsory psychiatric assessment and treatment (*Mental Health (Compulsory Assessment and Treatment) Act 1992*). The Act also sets out the protection of rights for detained patients. A responsible clinician makes the application, usually a treating psychiatrist, supported by a second health professional (usually a nurse), to a judge in the Family Court. Before the hearing of the application for the compulsory treatment order to be made, the patient is seen by a District Inspector, who is an independent lawyer appointed under the Act, to ensure patient rights are upheld. The patient is legally represented at the hearing. They may choose their own lawyer or use a lawyer appointed by the Family Court.

The criminal courts in Aotearoa New Zealand rely on expert health and cultural reports to inform their decisions. Under Section 38 of the *Criminal Procedure (Mentally Impaired Persons) Act 2003*, courts can order assessments by a health professional to determine whether a defendant is unfit to stand trial as defined in Section 4 of the Act or insane under Section 23 of the *Crimes Act 1961* (*Criminal Procedure (Mentally Impaired Persons) Act 2003* Section 38; Section 4 *Unfit to stand trial*; *Crimes Act 1961* Section 23 *Insanity*). These assessments, conducted by psychiatrists or psychologists acting as expert witnesses, assist the court in making determinations. For inquiries regarding disposition, at least one psychiatrist's opinion is required.

A defendant is assessed as unfit to stand trial if they have a 'mental impairment' (a legal construct) that renders them unable to plead to a criminal charge or comprehend the proceedings to mount a defence, as defined by Section 4 of the *Criminal Procedure (Mentally Impaired Persons) Act 2003* (*Criminal Procedure (Mentally Impaired Persons) Act 2003* Section 4 *Unfit to stand trial)*. If a finding of unfitness is made, the accused cannot be lawfully convicted, but a special hearing is held to evaluate the evidence on the balance of probabilities. A defendant is assessed as having a defence of insanity if, as defined in Section 23 of the *Crimes Act 1961*, they have a 'natural imbecility' or a 'disease of the mind' that prevents them from understanding their actions or recognising their moral wrongfulness (*Crimes Act 1961* Section 23 *Insanity)*.

A finding of insanity requires the defendant to raise an insanity defence, the prosecution to agree that insanity is the only reasonable verdict, and the judge to be satisfied that the defendant meets the legal criteria for insanity. These legal requirements ensure that mental health considerations are properly accounted for in criminal proceedings where relevant.

## Forensic Mental Health System

Aotearoa New Zealand's forensic mental health system is integrated into the publicly funded health framework, which was recently restructured under the *Pae Ora (Healthy Futures) Act 2022* (*Pae Ora (Healthy Futures) Act 2022*). This reform replaced 20 district health boards with a single national health entity, Te Whatu Ora | Health New Zealand, supported by the Public Health Agency within the Ministry of Health.

There are five regional forensic psychiatry services across the country: Northern, Midland, Central on the North Island, Canterbury, and Southern on the South Island. Together, they provide assessment, treatment, and rehabilitation for offenders with mental disorders. These services include the following:

1. Inpatient care in medium- and minimum-security units is divided into acute and rehabilitative areas. Some units have a specific Māori focus.
2. Community forensic services offer rehabilitation and risk management for individuals in the community, in forensic step-down supported accommodation (some with a specific Māori focus), and independent living. This includes outpatient clinics, support to access community-based treatment programmes such as alcohol and drug programmes, and assistance with community reintegration.
3. Court liaison nurses assist with mental health assessments for the judicial system. Court liaisons mainly involve communication between the courts and general and forensic mental health services, alcohol and drug services, and other community providers.
4. Prison in-reach teams provide specialist forensic mental health support to the most seriously unwell prisoners within correctional facilities. Aotearoa New Zealand has 19 prisons, primarily managed by the Department of Corrections. Prison healthcare services manage mild to moderate mental illness, while the most acutely unwell prisoners are transferred from prison and treated in forensic facilities or general mental health units. Compulsory treatment is not allowed in prison. Although legislative provisions exist, voluntary transfers for treatment from prison to hospital are infrequent due to bed shortages.
5. Youth forensic services are available for justice-involved youth aged 13–18, with specialised inpatient facilities for youth with severe mental health or intellectual disabilities. Forensic programmes offer age-appropriate care and community reintegration through recovery-focused rehabilitation that addresses mental health, addiction, and offending behaviours.

There are specialised national and regional inpatient and community services for adults and youth with intellectual disabilities who are involved in the justice system. While some regional forensic psychiatry services provide spaces for women, no national strategy for securing female-specific care exists. Public consultation on a Women's Health Strategy began in 2023.

The Fixated Threat Assessment Centre New Zealand is a prevention-focused collaboration between health, police, and the Parliamentary service to share appropriate information, conduct assessments, and facilitate mental health, law enforcement, or other interventions to address the risks posed by fixated individuals to themselves and others (usually members of Parliament and their staff). A small, dedicated team of forensic mental health clinicians works with police to assess the level of concern a person poses to themselves or others. A 'health-first' approach with supportive interventions aims to prevent escalating situations where harm or a criminal conviction may result.

### *Role of Forensic Psychiatry*

Regional forensic psychiatry services operate at the intersection of mental health and criminal justice, providing specialised services for serious mental health conditions in various settings: prisons, courts, communities, and secure inpatient units. They offer secure, culturally responsive care focused on assessment, treatment, rehabilitation, and safe community reintegration. Services are responsible for balancing the recovery and rehabilitation needs of offenders with a mental disorder detained within the national legislative framework, alongside the management of risk and the maintenance of therapeutic security and safety for both patients and the public.

### *Workforce*

Approximately 30–50 forensic psychiatrists in Aotearoa New Zealand practice primarily in public health, with some in private practice. Training as a forensic psychiatrist takes up to 12 years, including basic medical training, vocational training in psychiatry (involving examinations, research requirements, and competence in psychotherapy), and sub-specialisation to obtain a Certificate of Advanced Training in Forensic Psychiatry. In addition to the academic component, the certificate includes 24 months in accredited forensic psychiatry training posts. Some forensic psychiatrists are dual-trained, for example, in general adult psychiatry, child and adolescent psychiatry, or addictions psychiatry. The Royal Australian and New Zealand College of Psychiatrists has a Faculty of Forensic Psychiatry, and continued professional development activities are required to maintain medical registration with the Medical Council of New Zealand.

Training as a clinical psychologist in Aotearoa New Zealand takes about six or seven years, including completing at least a bachelor's degree in psychology and a postgraduate diploma in clinical psychology. Additional training in forensic psychology is available through a Postgraduate Certificate in Science in Forensic Psychology and a Master's programme in Forensic Psychology. However, there is no dedicated forensic psychology scope of practice in Aotearoa New Zealand. A small number (approximately 170) of psychologists trained in the United Kingdom in a specialist forensic psychology programme identify themselves as forensic psychologists (Personal communication: Analytics and Intelligence I People and Culture. Te Whatu Ora |Health New Zealand.). About a third are employed in the public health system, a quarter in the criminal justice sector, and another quarter in private practice—the remainder work across non-governmental organisations, academic institutions, and the Accident Compensation Corporation.[1] However, forensic psychologists are not eligible for the clinical scope of practice in Aotearoa New Zealand, as the UK programme lacks the broader mental health/psychopathology content. There is another group whose scope of practice is clinical psychology, which works mainly in the public health (forensic) and criminal justice (prisons) sectors and identifies as forensic psychologists.

### *National Collaborations and Networks in Forensic Mental Health*

Two organisations have separate but complementary roles: the New Zealand Forensic Psychiatry Advisory Group and the Bi-national Faculty of Forensic Psychiatry of the Royal Australian and New Zealand College of Psychiatrists. The Advisory Group comprises service leads from each of the five regional forensic psychiatry services and meets quarterly. This is the main national leadership forum for forensic services. Representatives from the Ministry of Health, including the Director of Mental Health, and representatives from Ara Poutama/Department of Corrections, including the Director of Mental Health and Addiction Services, as well as the executive leads for Te Whatu Ora | Health New Zealand, are invited to attend for part of the meeting. Members report this as a useful forum for engagement on high-level strategic and national issues and for providing strong collegial support.

The Bi-national Faculty of Forensic Psychiatry of the Royal Australian and New Zealand College of Psychiatrists promotes the highest standards in professional practice, training, and research pertaining to forensic psychiatry. The faculty aims to promote the College's objectives relating to forensic psychiatry, advise on training in forensic psychiatry through the subcommittee of advanced training, advance and disseminate research in forensic psychiatry, and contribute to and promote the highest standards of professional practice (Royal Australian and New Zealand College of Psychiatrists, n.d.).

### *Entering Regional Forensic Psychiatry Services: the Decision Makers in Forensic Psychiatry*

In Aotearoa, New Zealand, access to forensic psychiatry services is governed by criminal and civil legislation, as interpreted by the courts, prisons, and forensic services. The *Mental Health (Compulsory Assessment and Treatment) Act 1992* regulates the treatment of non-forensic, civilly detained patients and forensic 'special patients' and 'restricted patients', as defined in Section 2 of the Act. 'Special patients' are persons with a mental impairment whose actions have resulted in the involvement of the criminal justice system, as defined by the *Criminal Procedure (Mentally Impaired Persons) Act* (Section 24), and 'restricted patients' are civilly committed patients who are assessed as posing a significant danger to others (*Mental Health (Compulsory Assessment and Treatment) Act 1992* Section 2 *special patient, restricted patient* and *Criminal Procedure (Mentally Impaired Persons) Act 2003* Section 24 *Detention of defendant found unfit to stand trial or insane as special patient or special care recipient*). The *Mental Health Act* is undergoing reform following a 2018 national inquiry into mental health and addiction services (*Mental Health (Compulsory Assessment and Treatment) Act 1992*; Government Inquiry into Mental Health and Addiction, 2018). Future legislation will adopt a more human rights-based approach, promote supported decision making, and align with recovery-focused mental health models while minimising coercive treatments.

All patients admitted to forensic services are compulsorily detained under relevant legislation. The Act makes provisions for five categories of special patients (*Mental Health (Compulsory Assessment and Treatment) Act 1992*). These include people found unfit to stand trial; those acquitted on account of their insanity; those sentenced to a combination of imprisonment and treatment; remanded or sentenced prisoners who require treatment in a psychiatric hospital, usually in a forensic inpatient unit; and those remanded for a court-ordered health assessor report pending trial or sentencing (Soosay & Kydd, 2016).

Defendants found unfit to stand trial or acquitted by reason of insanity undergo court-ordered psychiatric assessments under the *Criminal Procedure (Mentally Impaired Persons) Act 2003* Section 23, to determine disposition (*Criminal Procedure (Mentally Impaired Persons) Act 2003* Section 23 *Insanity)*. Disposition options include detention as a 'special patient' under the *Mental Health Act*, for the most serious offending by those with a serious mental illness; as a 'special care recipient' for the most serious offending by those with an intellectual disability under the *Intellectual Disability (Compulsory Care and Rehabilitation) Act 2003* Section 6; compulsory treatment orders under the *Mental Health Act*; or release (*Intellectual Disability (Compulsory Care and Treatment) Act 2003* Section 6 *Meaning of care recipient and related terms*; *Mental Health (Compulsory Assessment and Treatment) Act 1992*). Public safety is a key consideration for special patients whose treatment pathway is subject to oversight by the Director of Mental Health and the Ministry of Health.

Defendants with a mental disorder who are fit to plead and stand trial and who do not have a defence of insanity may also be ordered to receive treatment upon conviction. Disposition options under the *Criminal Procedure (Mentally Impaired Persons) Act* Section 34, include the making of a hybrid order under

Section 34(1)(a)(i) of the Act, detaining an offender as a special patient in hospital (usually a forensic unit) for treatment under the *Mental Health Act*, or under Section 34(1)(a)(ii) of the Act, detaining an offender with an intellectual disability as a special care recipient in a secure unit under the *Intellectual Disability (Compulsory Care and Treatment) Act* while also sentencing them to imprisonment. Once treated, the person is transferred to prison, and the treatment order ends (*Criminal Procedure (Mentally Impaired Persons) Act 2003* Section 34 (1)(a)(i); *Mental Health (Compulsory Assessment and Treatment) Act 1992*; *Criminal Procedure (Mentally Impaired Persons) Act 2003* Section 34 (1)(a)(ii); *Intellectual Disability (Compulsory Care and Treatment) Act 2003*).

Hybrid orders are used for the most serious convictions to treat major mental illnesses. They are used sparingly due to ethical and clinical concerns about combining treatment for mental illness with criminal punishment.

For less serious offending, instead of passing a sentence, the court can order the offender to be treated as a patient subject to compulsory treatment under the *Mental Health Act* or to be cared for as a care recipient under the *Intellectual Disability (Compulsory Care and Rehabilitation) Act* (*Mental Health (Compulsory Assessment and Treatment) Act 1992*; *Intellectual Disability (Compulsory Care and Treatment) Act 2003* Section 6 *Meaning of care recipient & related terms*). The compulsory treatment order may be as an inpatient or in the community, under the care of general adult mental health services. Some patients are treated within the forensic system if their assessed risks require a forensic pathway of care.

Prisoners requiring psychiatric care unavailable in prison can be transferred to hospital, with their consent and that of the prison manager. However, they cannot receive compulsory treatment unless assessed and detained under the *Mental Health Act* (*Mental Health (Compulsory Assessment and Treatment) Act 1992* Section 45). Prisoners can be compulsorily transferred to hospital if the prison manager initiates an application for an examination under the Act (*Mental Health (Compulsory Assessment and Treatment) Act 1992* Section 46). If detention criteria are met, prisoners receive short-term care in hospital and return to prison when they no longer require compulsory care. A few prisoners remain in the forensic system, where they are managed as special patients, with their treatment and eventual release overseen by the Parole Board and the Ministry of Health. Wait-`lists have grown in recent years as the demand for forensic beds outstrips available resources, with many prisoners facing lengthy delays in accessing inpatient treatment. Services are improving patient flow and facilitating earlier community transition where possible (Ministry of Health, 2010).

### *Exiting Regional Forensic Psychiatry Services*

Exiting the forensic system depends on the patient's legal status. Each exit pathway balances public safety, patient recovery, and legal requirements, with varying degrees of oversight by health and justice authorities. Special patients who have been deemed unfit to stand trial or acquitted on account of insanity can remain in hospital and community care for extended periods, sometimes up to 20 years for those with high-risk and complex needs. Prolonged hospitalisation raises issues such as institutionalisation, loss of social and vocational skills, and challenges with community reintegration.

Regaining fitness to stand trial is the focus of care for special patients who are found unfit to stand trial. Competency assessments are conducted regularly and reported to the Director of Mental Health at the Ministry of Health. When fitness is regained, the responsible clinician informs the Director of Mental Health and the Attorney-General, who decides whether to bring the defendant back to court to stand trial or end their detention as a special patient, as provided by the *Criminal Procedure (Mentally Impaired Persons) Act* Section 31(2) (*Criminal Procedure (Mentally Impaired Persons) Act 2003*). Those patients not remitted for trial continue compulsory treatment under the *Mental Health Act* as patients (*Mental Health (Compulsory Assessment and Treatment) Act 1992*). If fitness is not regained, the defendant remains a special patient until half of the maximum sentence they would have been eligible to receive on conviction has elapsed (or 10 years for life sentences), after which they cease being a special patient. The *Criminal Procedure (Mentally Impaired Persons) Act* Section 31(3), enables compulsory treatment to continue as a patient under the *Mental Health Act*, in either the community or hospital (*Criminal Procedure (Mentally Impaired Persons) Act 2003*; *Mental Health (Compulsory Assessment and Treatment) Act 1992*). Care typically remains with forensic services until a safe transfer to general mental health services is feasible.

Special patients acquitted on account of insanity receive acute inpatient and rehabilitative care focused on stabilising their illness, addressing the offending behaviour, and managing criminogenic risks. Incremental leave progression to the community is overseen by the Ministry of Health, with longer periods of leave requiring the approval of the Minister of Health.

Approval is subject to conditions such as place of residence, regular reviews with the responsible clinician, and abstinence from substance use. When the public risk is sufficiently mitigated, and the special patient has been successfully reintegrated into the community, approval is required from the Minister of Health under the *Criminal Procedure (Mentally Impaired Persons) Act* Section 33, for a change of legal status from special patient to patient under the *Mental Health Act*, or discharge (*Criminal Procedure (Mentally Impaired Persons) Act 2003*; *Mental Health (Compulsory Assessment and Treatment) Act 1992*). Care typically remains with forensic services until a safe transfer to general mental health services is feasible.

A change of legal status from special patient to patient indicates that the person is no longer considered a significant risk to the public. As a result, there are fewer restrictions on their treatment and discharge. The responsible clinician can approve a leave from hospital, transfer the inpatient compulsory treatment order to a community treatment order, and discharge the order. The person cannot be directed to live at a particular address. Additionally, the Mental Health Review Tribunal can end the order if it determines the person is fit to be released from compulsory status. In contrast, other considerations apply to special and restricted patients (*Mental Health (Compulsory Assessment and Treatment) Act 1992*).

The Mental Health Review Tribunal operates within the *Mental Health Act* (*Mental Health (Compulsory Assessment and Treatment) Act 1992* Sections 101–108A). It is an independent body appointed by the Minister of Health. The tribunal panel comprises a lawyer, a psychiatrist, and a community member. A fourth member, with specific expertise, cultural insight, or gender representation, joins the panel when needed. Detained patients can apply to the tribunal for release from their compulsory status, and the tribunal can make recommendations regarding forensic patients with special and restricted status. Additional responsibilities include investigating breaches of patient rights, appointing psychiatrists to provide second opinions on treatment, and deciding whether proposed electroconvulsive therapy is in the patient's best interest. There is no separate tribunal for forensic cases; the tribunal handles all relevant matters.

## Forensic Psychiatry Service (Provision of Care)

### *Population Demographics*

#### *Prison*

Incarceration rates in Aotearoa New Zealand have been rising since the 1990s, particularly for women, despite a relatively stable serious crime rate. A 2017 initiative aimed at reducing the prison population led to a drop in the imprisonment rate over five years, from the eighth highest in the Organisation for Economic Co-operation and Development to sixteenth, aligning more closely with Australia and the average (Justice Sector Public Consultation, 2022; Foulds et al., 2022). Consistent with international trends, youth crime has declined in recent decades, and this, coupled with a 2019 law change that extended the age of admission to Youth Justice Residences to 18 years, has resulted in fewer young people being imprisoned.

Although Māori represent 16.5% of the general population, they comprise just over half of the prison population. They are significantly over-represented at every stage in the criminal justice process and in forensic mental health services (Hōkai Rangi, 2019; Geheran et al., 2022). The other half of the prison population comprises Pacific Island Peoples who are also over-represented (15%, compared to 8% of the male general population), Europeans (30%) and other ethnicities, including Asian (5%) (Geheran et al., 2022). Notably, while women constitute 6% of the total prison population, about two-thirds of them are Māori women, whereas Pacific Island women are generally under-represented (Justice Sector Public Consultation, 2022). Of particular concern is that young wāhine

Māori make up to 90% of the incarcerated female population of 16–22 years old (McKenna & Sweetman, 2020). While the numbers of Māori and Pacific Island Peoples in prison have fallen over recent years, consistent with the fall in the general prison population, their rate of fall has been lower, resulting in Māori and Pacific Island Peoples still making up a larger proportion of the prison population (Justice Sector Public Consultation, 2022).

To understand the disproportionate over-representation of Māori in the criminal justice system, it is essential to appreciate that Aotearoa New Zealand is a settler colonial state, meaning it was established through the displacement and subjugation of Indigenous Peoples by settlers from a foreign country. Colonisation by British imperialists in the 17th century fundamentally changed the Māori traditional way of life, leading to land dispossession, cultural disconnection, urbanisation, and enduring intergenerational inequity and trauma. The Western patriarchal ideology particularly impacted Māori women, who found themselves at 'the bottom of the heap' behind Māori men and the colonisers, exposing them to racism, sexism, and misogyny (Quince, 2010). It is posited by Māori legal academics that the combination of these factors is manifest in the over-criminalisation of Māori women (Quince, 2010).

The majority of people in prison are charged with or sentenced for serious sexual or violent offending, with drug-related offences (particularly methamphetamine) accounting for about 8% of the population (Justice Sector Public Consultation, 2022). Women commit less serious crimes and pose a lower risk to the community than men, with most having committed persistent non-violent offences, such as theft, breaches of community sentences, burglary, intent to injure, and drug offences (Ara Poutama Aotearoa | Department of Corrections, 2021; Issues Paper, n.d.). However, charges for violent offending have increased, and in 2022, just under half of convictions for women were related to violent crimes (Justice Sector Public Consultation, 2022). Psychiatric morbidity is high, with a 2016 survey revealing that nearly two-thirds of male prisoners and three-quarters of female prisoners had experienced some form of mental health or addiction disorder in the past year, a rate three times higher than the general population (Indig et al., 2016). A substantial majority of prisoners (87%) had a lifetime diagnosis of a substance use disorder, and just under half (47%) had a 12-month diagnosis. One in three prisoners were found to have a clinically significant personality disorder, with a slightly higher prevalence among men. Psychotic symptoms were present in 13% of prisoners over their lifetime and 7% in the past year.

A 2016 naturalistic study of women in the country's largest women's prison found that forensic psychiatrists diagnosed more than one-third of the referred female prisoners with psychotic disorders (Collier & Hatters Friedman, 2016). Over two-thirds of women in prison report a history of personal victimisation due to family violence, and just over half have suffered from post-traumatic stress disorder throughout their lifetime, compared to one in five male prisoners (Indig et al., 2016).

*Forensic Mental Health Services*

Most users of forensic mental health services have been found unfit to stand trial, acquitted on account of insanity, disposed of in the criminal court through a 'hybrid' order, or are prisoners requiring compulsory mental health treatment in a hospital setting. Occasionally, a civilly committed patient who does not meet these criteria may be admitted if their illness and behaviours necessitate the security and specialised care a forensic unit can provide. There are also a small number of civilly committed 'restricted patients' who have not gone through the criminal justice system but are assessed as posing a significant danger to others.

The rise in the prison population has not been accompanied by a substantial increase in forensic inpatient or community management capacity (Ministry of Health, 2007). As a result, forensic services have had to prioritise specific populations and illness profiles. Psychosis is the most common reason for treatment (80%–90%), with schizophrenia being the most common diagnosis, averaging 72% across services (McKenna & Sweetman, 2020). The demographic of forensic mental health service users largely reflects that of the prison population (Geheran et al., 2022). They are primarily men in their mid-30s, often presenting with violent and sexual offending. Māori men are significantly over-represented, and most have a major psychotic disorder, such as schizophrenia. Women make up a small but growing proportion of forensic service users, typically with significant histories of victimisation and complex needs (McKenna & Sweetman, 2020). Despite the high proportion of young Māori females in incarceration, two-thirds of admissions to the national mixed-gender secure inpatient facility for youth are Māori males aged 16–17.

### *Approaches to Assessment and Treatment*

While there is no nationwide overarching model of care, the goals of care are consistent across regional forensic psychiatry services: to reduce symptom burden, enhance quality of life, manage risk, and reduce reoffending. These goals are achieved through evidence-based, recovery-oriented, trauma-informed, and culturally responsive approaches (the latter being constitutionally obligated). Care is holistic and multidisciplinary, considering biological, psychological, social, cultural, and spiritual factors.

### *Cultural and Holistic Models*

Regional forensic psychiatry services recognise the centrality of Te Ao Māori (a Māori world-view) in service delivery, placing tāngata whaiora (service users) and their whānau (family) at the centre of care provision. A Māori health model, Te Whare Tapa Whā (literal translation being 'the house with four walls'), is widely incorporated into forensic practice. The model describes health and wellbeing as a wharenui/meeting house with four walls. These walls represent taha wairua/spiritual wellbeing, taha hinengaro/mental and emotional wellbeing, taha tinana/physical wellbeing, and taha whānau/family and social wellbeing. The foundation of the house is our connection with the whenua/land. When all these things are in balance, we thrive. Our wellbeing is impacted when one or more of these is out of balance.

Some regional forensic psychiatry services have dedicated Kaupapa Māori inpatient services, which blend mental health rehabilitation with Māori cultural concepts. The National Secure Youth Forensic Inpatient Mental Health Service follows a bicultural model of care, integrating both traditional and contemporary Western and Māori frameworks to treat severe mental health and substance use disorders.

Similar to Te Whare Tapa Whā, the Fonofale model also uses the analogy of a fale (a traditional Samoan house), using the walls, foundation, and ceiling to represent the different constructs of health. Some regional forensic psychiatry services have incorporated this into service delivery when working with Pacific Island patients. It is worth noting that the Pacific Island population is a young and growing population in Aotearoa New Zealand. Pacific Island men are overrepresented in the prison population, and their population in forensic mental health services is projected to increase. They are a priority population for forensic service development and intervention.

### *Specialised Services Models*

Forensic intellectual disability services provide a comprehensive approach to care and rehabilitation for offenders with intellectual disabilities and complex behavioural needs, from admission to secure inpatient services through to community transition. Guided by the Good Lives model of care, this approach incorporates positive behaviour support principles, focusing on the strengths of the individual and all staff disciplines while remaining responsive to the risks associated with working with this population.

In the community, forensic assertive community teams and case management models are used variably across regional forensic psychiatry services. The primary focus is on maintaining mental health stability, managing criminogenic risk factors, and supporting rehabilitation and recovery. Community services may be integrated with or parallel to general mental health services, which provide consultation and liaison. Each regional forensic psychiatry service develops relationships with local health services, non-governmental organisations providing mental health, addiction, and disability services, commissioning bodies, regional and nationwide health services, local police, iwi (Māori community), and community cultural organisations. Many regional forensic psychiatry services adopt a risk-need responsivity model for patient care alongside a nationwide trend towards recovery-oriented practice. While most special patients are eventually discharged to general mental health services, some continue to require specialist care from a forensic community team.

Most regional forensic psychiatry service users are transferred from and return to prison. In recent years, significant investment has been made in mental health and addiction services for prisoners with mild to moderate mental health issues, delivered by mental health teams employed by Ara Poutama/Department of Corrections. Those with severe mental illness are managed by forensic in-reach teams using an evidence-based in-reach model of care developed in New Zealand called STAIR (Screening, Triage, Assessment, Intervention, and Reintegration) (Simpson et al., 2022). Forensic in-reach teams aim to provide a standard of care comparable to that available in the general community. However, this goal is sometimes hindered by the inaccessibility of multidisciplinary services like occupational therapy and psychology.

***Treatment Programmes***

Aotearoa New Zealand's Forensic Mental Health Services prioritise the treatment of mental disorders and the reduction of offending, with the main objective of ensuring safe reintegration into the community. A person's care is coordinated by a multidisciplinary team led by a responsible clinician tasked with providing psychiatric treatment, risk assessment, and long-term pathway planning. Responsible clinicians are typically senior mental health professionals, either psychiatrists or registered health professionals, such as psychologists, senior nurses, or nurse practitioners. They must have undergone training and be deemed competent in assessing, treating, and caring for people with mental disorders, as determined by the Director of Area Mental Health Services. The psychiatrist is responsible for managing the person's mental illness and physical health, usually with the assistance of a psychiatric registrar. Forensic services also offer placements for allied health interns, medical student interns, and nursing students as part of the multidisciplinary team.

All forensic patients undergo a comprehensive risk assessment using standard tools such as the Historical Clinical Risk Management-20 Version 3 (HCR-20 V3), the HCR-20 Female Additional Manual, and the Structured Assessment of Violence Risk in Youth (SAVRY). Additional tools, including the Risk for Sexual Violence Protocol and Static-99 for sexual reoffending, are used depending on the type of offending risk presented. The DUNDRUM Toolkit helps inform assessments of acuity, the need for secure hospital care, and readiness for rehabilitation and community discharge. Cultural assessments are conducted, and both individual and group cultural interventions are offered. The Meihana model is a clinical assessment framework that integrates Māori beliefs, values, and experiences to guide assessment and intervention with Māori clients and whānau.

Treatment programmes are individually tailored to stabilise and optimise mental health and wellbeing. Typically, patients complete a personal Wellness

Recovery Action Plan or a similar dynamic document, which they update as they progress through the treatment pathway. Occupational therapists assess daily living skills using the Assessment of Motor and Process Skills. Various psychological interventions are available to target specific symptoms and optimise wellbeing, including individual and group-based approaches like dialectical behaviour therapy, cognitive behaviour therapy, acceptance commitment therapy, eye movement desensitisation and reprocessing, and supportive psychotherapy. Psychological interventions also address offending and criminogenic risk factors. Offending-related programmes focus on violence prevention, sexual offending, and drug and alcohol use. Patients are encouraged to join established community groups, such as Alcoholics Anonymous, once appropriate community leave is granted.

As the person moves from medium security to an open rehabilitation setting in the forensic hospital, they assume greater responsibility for their wellbeing. Movement to the community typically involves supported forensic step-down accommodation before moving to independent housing. This process can span several years, depending on individual progress and oversight from the Special Patient Review process and the Ministry of Health.

Structured community support is essential for reducing the risk of relapse and reoffending. Occupational therapists and social workers play key roles in ensuring appropriate community support. Many people are assisted in finding employment, initially within the forensic campus or in sheltered employment settings, with some moving into open employment. Support is also provided to pursue vocational or educational opportunities, from improving literacy and numeracy skills to taking higher level educational courses through online or distance learning and in-person classes as leave status permits. Quality-of-life programmes are also available, such as fitness and walking groups, music groups, and escorted community outings. These programmes are especially important for those with enduring high and complex needs, for whom a structured environment remains necessary to manage ongoing risk.

## Strengths and Weaknesses

### *Strengths*

In Aotearoa New Zealand, strengths lie in the legislation and governance within the forensic mental health system, particularly the presence of an independent judiciary and a comprehensive legal framework that supports the assessment and treatment of offenders with mental disorders within a high-quality, publicly funded forensic system while balancing public safety interests. Legislative reforms are underway to enhance human rights compliance within the *Mental Health Act*, improve equitable healthcare access and outcomes—especially for Māori and women—through the *Pae Ora (Healthy Futures) Act*, and strengthen the rights of victims of offenders deemed insane through amendments to the

*Victims' Rights Act 2002* (*Mental Health (Compulsory Assessment and Treatment) Act 1992*; *Pae Ora (Healthy Futures) Act 2022*; *Victims' Rights Act 2002*).

In Aotearoa New Zealand, the forensic mental health system benefits from a highly skilled and dedicated workforce. In contrast to comparable health systems, the country's relatively small size enables effective communication between regional forensic psychiatry services, the Ministry of Justice, the Department of Corrections, and the National Director of Mental Health and Addiction within the Ministry of Health. This streamlined communication supports decision making at both the strategic level and for individual special patients, such as when the Ministry of Health considers leave applications and pathway progressions.

Although geographically distant, Aotearoa New Zealand is well-connected through global technology. While maintaining its unique context, forensic service development is informed by international research and developments, supported by a thriving academic research community that publishes leading studies in the field. The country is undergoing major national health reforms aimed at creating equitable, accessible, and people-centred services. Clinical networks are proposed to improve access and outcomes across regions, and forensic mental health services could be more effectively delivered through these networks.

However, challenges remain. The country's size and population distribution mean that regional forensic psychiatry services cover vast geographic areas, and admission to inpatient services, particularly at national units, often requires long journeys by road or air, making it difficult for some whānau (families) to maintain contact. Additionally, some patients lack access to the technology needed to stay in touch, and certain areas are too remote for regional forensic community teams to provide a direct service. In such cases, joint work with local services is explored to determine whether a safe and adequate service for forensic community patients can be provided.

### *Weaknesses*

Chronic underinvestment, particularly in mental health services over the last two decades, in the face of increased demand, has placed enormous pressure on both forensic and general mental health services. These services now operate at, and often above, capacity. The growth in the prison population, particularly the remand population, has not been matched by an expansion in forensic service capacity. Prisoners with mental disorders can wait several weeks for a forensic bed to become available, often untreated, only to have their transfer further delayed by a court-ordered admission for health assessment reports.

There is also limited capacity for planned transfers from prison to hospital to optimise treatment before release. This lack of capacity particularly impacts women, for whom few dedicated secure forensic facilities address their unique needs. Additionally, regional forensic psychiatry services struggle to manage patients with traumatic brain injuries or those with communication and language barriers. These challenges highlight significant gaps in service provision and underscore the need for better resourcing and planning.

The demand for health reports ordered by the criminal courts and, to a lesser extent, the Parole Board has grown rapidly in recent years, far outstripping the forensic health resources available in the public health system. Workforce challenges have made some regional forensic psychiatry services increasingly unable to provide court-ordered reports, requiring them to concentrate their available resources on the inpatient population. This has resulted in significant delays in the provision of health assessments to the courts, prolonging the justice process for this very vulnerable group and victims.

Chronic underinvestment in forensic mental health facilities has left many services in a poor state of repair. Many facilities are old and not suitable for contemporary specialist forensic practice. Auckland Regional Forensic Psychiatry Services, the largest forensic service in the country, faces major infrastructure issues and requires significant new buildings. Furthermore, uneven service development across regions exacerbates inequities in access and outcomes, particularly for Māori, Pacific Island People, and women.

There has been underinvestment in the mental health workforce in general, and the global post-pandemic health workforce shortages present a significant challenge for a country that has relied heavily on overseas clinicians in mental health. Many forensic psychiatrists and psychologists are from overseas and require upskilling and support to practice in a culturally safe way. Training the workforce from within Aotearoa New Zealand is a priority, particularly Māori and Pacific Island clinicians, who are under-represented across the health system. Given the over-representation of these populations in forensic services, this is especially important within the forensic mental health workforce.

As the largest workforce, nurses face challenges due to an ageing demographic and a shortage of appropriately experienced nurses. Initiatives to improve forensic sub-specialisation, particularly for nursing and allied health clinicians, are essential to equip staff to work safely and therapeutically in secure settings. This is equally important for support workers, the growing peer workforce, and non-government organisation sector providers who work in partnership with regional forensic psychiatry services.

Aotearoa New Zealand has a well-established forensic system that is evolving towards recovery-oriented, trauma-and violence-informed services that are culturally and gender-responsive. These services place the detained person and their whānau at the centre of care while maintaining public safety. With the repeal and reform of the *Mental Health Act* and a major transformation of the health system underway, these changes will impact the forensic system. However, the exact nature and extent of those impacts remain uncertain.

*The authors would like to acknowledge the assistance of Rebecca Shenton, Personal Assistant to the principal author, and forensic colleagues across the country for their contribution and support of this research.*

## Note

1 The Accident Compensation Corporation is a public health and no-fault accident compensation system, unique to Aotearoa New Zealand.

## References

Ara Poutama Aotearoa | Department of Corrections. (2019). *Hōkai Rangi: Ara Poutama Aotearoa strategy 2019–2024*. Wellington, New Zealand: Department of Corrections.

Ara Poutama Aotearoa | Department of Corrections. (2021). *Wāhine—E rere ana ki te pae hou. Women rising above a new horizon: Women's strategy 2021–2025*. Wellington, New Zealand: Department of Corrections.

Collier, S., & Hatters Friedman, S. (2016). Mental illness among women referred for psychiatric services in a New Zealand women's prison. *Behavioural Sciences and the Law*, *34*(4), 539–550. https://doi.org/10.1002/bsl.2246

*Constitution Act, 1986* (NZ). (1986). Public Act—New Zealand Legislation. No. 114.

*Crimes Act 1961* (NZ). (1961). Public Act—New Zealand Legislation. No. 43.

*Criminal Procedure (Mentally Impaired Persons) Act 2003* (NZ). (2003). Public Act—New Zealand Legislation. No. 115.

Foulds, J. A., Monasterio, E., & Young, J. T. (2022). Return from the precipice: New Zealand's rapid prison population decrease and its implications. *Australian & New Zealand Journal of Psychiatry*, *56*(9), 1057–1059. https://doi.org/10.1177/00048674221108312

Geheran, B., Kumar, S., & Ma'u, E. (2022). Care pathways in forensic mental health services in New Zealand. *Psychiatry, Psychology and Law*, *30*(4), 553–564. https://doi.org/10.1080/13218719.2022.2059030

Government Inquiry into Mental Health and Addiction. (2018). *He Ara Oranga | Pathways to Wellness: Report of the government inquiry into mental health and addiction*. New Zealand.

*Human Rights Act 1993* (NZ). (1993). Public Act—New Zealand Legislation. No. 82.

Indig, D., Gear, C., & Wilhelm, K. (2016). *Comorbid substance use disorders and mental health disorders among New Zealand prisoners*. Wellington, New Zealand: Department of Corrections.

*Intellectual Disability (Compulsory Care and Treatment) Act 2003* (NZ). (2003). Public Act—New Zealand Legislation. No. 116.

*Issues Paper: Women's Prisons in the Spotlight*. (n.d.).

Justice Sector Public Consultation. (2022). *Long term insights briefing: Focus on imprisonment in Aotearoa 2022*.

McKenna, B., & Sweetman, L. E. (2020). *Models of care in forensic mental health services: A review of the international and national literature*. Wellington, New Zealand: Ministry of Health.

*Mental Health (Compulsory Assessment and Treatment) Act 1992* (NZ). (1992). Public Act—New Zealand Legislation. No. 46.

Ministry of Health. (2007). *Census of forensic mental health services 2005*. Wellington, New Zealand: Ministry of Health.

Ministry of Health. (2010). *Review of forensic mental health services: Future directions*. Wellington, New Zealand: Ministry of Health.

*New Zealand Bill of Rights Act 1990* (NZ). (1990). Public Act—New Zealand Legislation. No. 109.

*Pae Ora (Healthy Futures) Act 2022* (NZ). (2022). Public Act—New Zealand Legislation. No. 30.

Quince, K. (2010). The bottom of the heap? Why Māori women are over-criminalised in New Zealand. *Te Tai Haruru Journal*, *8*(3), 99–111.

Royal Australian and New Zealand College of Psychiatrists. (n.d.). *Forensic Psychiatry*. Retrieved from https://www.ranzcp.org/membership/faculties-sections-and-networks/forensic-psychiatry

Simpson, A. I. F., Gerritsen, C., Maheandiran, M., Adamo, V., Vogel, T., Fulham, L., Kitt, T., Forrester, A., & Jones, R. M. (2022). A systematic review of reviews of correctional mental health services using the STAIR framework. *Frontiers in Psychiatry*, *12*, 747202. https://doi.org/10.3389/fpsyt.2021.747202

Soosay, I., & Kydd, R. (2016). Mental health law in New Zealand. *BJPsych International*, *13*(2), 43–45.

*Treaty of Waitangi* (*Te Tiriti o Waitangi*). (February 6, 1840). Retrieved from https://waitangitribunal.govt.nz/treaty-of-waitangi/te-reo-maori-version

*Victims' Rights Act 2002* (NZ). (2002). Public Act—New Zealand Legislation. No. 39.

# Part VIII

# Analysis

# 30 The Future of Research in Forensic Psychiatry

*Harry G. Kennedy and Mary Davoren*

## Introduction

Forensic psychiatry is the area of psychiatry that treats the most severely ill people with the most treatment-resistant mental illnesses. Neurodegenerative diseases with perceptual and processing disturbances, such as schizophrenia and bipolar affective disorder, are life-shortening illnesses, leading on average to 16 years of lost life expectancy from all causes, not just suicide (Crump et al., 2013; Laursen, 2019; Lomholt et al., 2019; Uhrskov Sørensen et al., 2020). There is, therefore, an urgent agenda for forensic psychiatrists to increase clinical and translational research that rapidly improves the physical health and mental health of our patients (Schizophrenia Commission, 2012) while doing so safely for all patients, their families, the healthcare workers who treat and care for them, and the communities where they live (Kennedy, 2021; Simpson et al., 2022). This is also likely the best way to prevent violent recidivism.

This chapter will endeavour to avoid the enthusiasms of the peak of hype cycles and the pessimism of disillusionment when peak expectations prove less than promised (Oosterhoff & Doornberg, 2020). Philosophers of science enable us to reflect on how we think about our subject and think about it innovatively. More often, the shift from one mode of analysis to a better one, leading from one scientific model to another, takes a scientific development from incremental change through a period of paradigm 'strain' to a paradigm shift and change of model. Paradigm shifts are urgently needed in several areas of forensic psychiatry now. Popper (Birner, 2018; Popper, 2014) and Kuhn (Kuhn & Hacking, 2012) are familiar, but Kenny (Kenny, 1984, 1985, 1992, 2011), Hacking (Hacking, 1984, 1986, 2001a, 2002; Hacking & Hacking, 1990), Deutsch (Deutsch, 2011), and Noble (Noble, 2008a, 2008b, 2017) should be taken as guides to our imminent future.

## Evolution of Research in Forensic Psychiatry

In the 19th century, psychiatric psychopathology and the classification of mental illnesses often evolved by way of legal argument in the courts (Walker, 1985;

DOI: 10.4324/9781003376248-38

Walker & McCabe, 1968). A separate strand in the development of psychopathology evolved from philosophy of mind into phenomenology. However, the courts required acceptable and scientifically conventional definitions of what was and was not a disease of the mind (Kenny, 1985, 1992, 2011). The language of 'insanity', and debates about whether to accept continental concepts of 'partial insanity' into the common law of the English-speaking world developed from dialogues between the leading forensic psychiatrists of the day and the leading jurists of the day (Walker & McCabe, 1968; West & Walk, 1977). In criminal law, free will must be accepted as a ground rule that is a necessary precondition for responsibility before the law. In so far as this position is capable of evolution, it had already evolved when mental disorders were recognised as causes for diminished or absent responsibility. The logic model here is that mental disorders impair free will and thereby diminish responsibility. It is a long way from this process to complete absence of responsibility (legal 'insanity'); therefore, a moral test has been added for insanity. The legal concept of mind as a collection of mental capacities crystallised the separation of forensic psychopathology from philosophical phenomenology (Kenny, 1985, 1992, 2011), and there has been no paradigm shift since then (Parmigiani et al., 2019; Scarpazza et al., 2021), although there may be some attempt at legal imposition through non-scientific legislative change (Slobogin, 2015).

Forensic psychiatry in the 20th century developed from medical legal descriptive psychopathology, epidemiology, criminology, and systems research. In the first part of this chapter, the development of these key topics over time will be considered, setting the stage for a discussion of future research needs.

## Descriptive Psychopathology and the Natural History of Appetitive Mental States

### *Appetitive Mental States*

Descriptive psychopathology in forensic psychiatry has focused on the relationship between psychopathology (abnormal mental states) and violence (violent behaviour) (Shepherd, 1961). Some forms of violent behaviour appear to be predatory, and predatory behaviour in some species is seen as appetitive (a biological urge to satisfy a bodily need). It is not clear that this biological mechanism is represented in humans. Substance misuse and addiction, however, can be understood as altered appetites (Klausen et al., 2022; Orford, 2001).

### *Sexual Offending as an Appetitive State*

Early work on the psychopathology of sexual behaviour and sexual offending had barely evolved from handbooks of witchcraft (Krafft-Ebing & Klaf, 1998; Kramer et al., 2007) to early 20th-century psychodynamic theories, then late 20th-century biopsychosocial descriptions and classifications when the boundaries of social norms were radically changed. This led to a widespread withdrawal from the medicalisation of rape and paedophilia. There is no 'psychiatry' of burglary or theft, so why should there be a psychiatry of sex offending? (Grubin & Kennedy, 1991). Nevertheless, the evidence that antiandrogen treatment is effective for preventing recidivist sexual offending has been reconsidered recently. It is generally accepted in Western cultures that antiandrogen treatment to prevent sexual recidivism can only be given with consent (Davoren, 2021; Thibaut et al., 2020).

> *Research ethics: Would antiandrogen treatment without consent be sanctioned in constitutional and legal systems which place a higher value on community rights rather than individual rights? If so, the consequences of research in one legal system being used differently in another might bear thought in the future.*

The psychiatric understanding of the sexual murderer was described by Brittain (1970) and further developed by MacCulloch and Snowden into the syndrome of fantasy, rehearsal, and escalation (MacCulloch et al., 1983). Efforts to apply classification algorithms dominated the 1990s, to little effect (Knight & Prentky, 1990). While most experienced clinicians will recognise this pattern in patients or defendants they have assessed, they will also recognise that this pattern of behaviour over time is not necessarily related to mental illness or any diminution of responsibility (Grubin & Kennedy, 1991). Nor is there any evidence of any treatment that is effective other than antiandrogens. Antiandrogens reduce libido, sexual fantasy, and sexual preoccupation. This is a rare example of a biological intervention that directly affects a specific mental state in a straightforward way. Finding alternatives to antiandrogens is a likely field for research in the near future.

> *Research and service development: The more recent introduction of glucagon-like peptide-1 (GLP-1) agonists such as semaglutide and terzepatide to directly alter appetite and body weight is another very similar example of a biological intervention that directly affects a specific mental state, specifically an appetite for food. How specific is an appetite? The prospect for similar biological interventions that may alter appetites for intoxicants such as alcohol, opiates, or cocaine, should they appear (Klausen et al., 2022; Leggio et al., 2023), will be enormously useful in forensic psychiatry patients and in the majority of prisoners, where substance misuse and addiction is present in 40% to 60% of prisoners and forensic patients, or more.*

#### ***Development of the Psychopathology of Substance Misuse***

The psychopathology of substance misuse has evolved without attracting sufficient attention. This is particularly important in forensic psychiatry, where there is a common overlap between mental illnesses and disorders of all varieties and substance misuse and dependence of all varieties, and between both mental disorders, substance misuse disorders, suicide, and violence. Patients with schizophrenia, and forensic patients particularly, appear to be vulnerable to substance misuse. The combination of psychosis and substance misuse is established as relevant to violence (Coid et al., 2021; Fleischman et al., 2014; Swanson et al., 2000; Witt et al., 2013).

Kraepelin described 'intoxication psychoses' (Kraepelin, 1915, p.150), including features of withdrawal, delirium, and forms of psychosis that occurred particularly with what he called 'combined morphinism and cocainism' (Kraepelin, 1904, pp.180–189, 1915, p.212), a common cause of intoxication psychoses in Germany in the early 20th century. Kraepelin described this as a syndrome where confusion (disorientation in time, place, person) and clouding of the sensorium occurred (Kraepelin, 1904, p.187), with fleeting or fixed false beliefs, often with partially preserved insight, hallucinations in multiple modalities, again often with partially preserved insight, excitement or obtundation, and a fluctuating course where delusions could last for weeks or even months (Kraepelin, 1915, p.212). Kraepelin was clear in his recommendation that the only successful method of treatment was complete abstinence. However, recurrence or persistence of symptoms due to relapse of using intoxicants was common. In modern times, Hill (Hill, 1947) and later Connell (Connell, 1957, 1958) described a very pure 'schizophreniform' psychosis due to the use of pharmaceutical amphetamine in the 1950s and 1960s. This resolved much more quickly than Kraepelin's intoxication psychoses, which Connell appeared not to be aware of initially (Connell, 1957, 1958; Hill, 1947). In later papers, however, Connell also described longer lasting and non-schizophreniform psychoses due to polysubstance misuse (Connell, 1968).

The World Health Organization's International Classification of Diseases, Mental and Behavioural chapter (WHO ICD) (WHO, 2018) and the American Psychiatric Association's Diagnostic and Statistical Manual of Mental Disorders (APA DSM) (American Psychiatric Association, 2022) now describe operational criteria for acute intoxication, harmful use, dependence syndrome, withdrawal state, delirium and substance-induced psychosis, amnesic syndrome, and residual and late-onset psychotic disorder. Each of these syndromes is described for alcohol, opioids, cannabinoids, sedatives and hypnotics, cocaine, other stimulants, hallucinogens, tobacco, volatile solvents, and multiple drug use and use of other psychoactive substances. Multiple substance misuse is much more common in offender populations—and probably in substance-misusing populations generally. It is common to see patients on reception in prison, in emergency departments of general hospitals, admission units in psychiatric hospitals, and secure forensic hospitals who test positive for multiple substances, who confirm this by history and who show Kraepelin's signs and symptoms of intoxication psychosis. These are entirely unlike a 'schizophreniform' psychosis, which occurs in clear consciousness and has certain narrowly defined forms of delusion and hallucination. Even more characteristic of these substance-induced states is that the patient may be acutely intoxicated with one or more substances (e.g., long-acting tranquillisers and opiates); at the same time, they may be withdrawing from others (e.g., cocaine, and alcohol) and suffering from the fleeting and atypical abnormal beliefs and experiences arising from any intoxicant but most often stimulants, hallucinogens such as LSD and ecstasy, and synthetic cannabinoids. Simultaneously, they may be delirious due to impaired consciousness because of all of these together. States of prolonged anger and arousal commonly occur, particularly with the use of cocaine and other stimulants and during the rebound withdrawal states of alcohol and benzodiazepines. Kraepelin was clear that these states could last for weeks or months (Kraepelin, 1915, p.212), and this is in keeping with the known effects of substance-induced tolerance arising from modulation of numbers and sensitivity of receptors in multiple neurological pathways during the development of tolerance and dependence.

The wider availability of legally sold cannabis is already having an impact on the incidence and prevalence of psychosis (Fischer et al., 2024) and has increased the risk of harm to others, including violence, driving-related injuries, and teratogenic effects, and harm due to passive smoking (Fischer et al., 2023).

*Research: The highly variable clinical presentations of polysubstance misuse and the unstudied effects of novel psychoactive substances where the neurotoxic, pharmacological, and neurocognitive effects are not yet fully elucidated adds complexity and should make the need for observational, descriptive, and outcome studies a priority.*

*Research: Testing for substances consumed acutely (in breath, urine, and plasma) and over longer periods of time (in hair and other body tissues and body fluid compartments) and observational studies of the development and resolution of symptoms over time are urgently needed, given the links between substance misuse, violence towards others, self-harm, and suicide in this highly vulnerable population.*

Remarkably, substance-induced abnormal mental states have received so little attention, if only because they are generally recognised as very dangerous, causing cardiac irritability, arrhythmias, and cardiac arrest, particularly when combined with psychoactive medications, causing or contributing to suicide during prolonged intense dysphoria of withdrawal and to violence throughout all phases of intoxication and withdrawal (Fazel et al., 2017; Gore, 1999; Kamali et al., 2000; Pratt et al., 2006; Shaw et al., 2017). Prison suicides are particularly linked to substance misuse (Iqtidar et al., 2018).

Duff has provided a new approach to prospective responsibility for the foreseeable effects of self-intoxication (Duff, 2007, 2008). Duff also offers an ethical limit to the responsibility a psychiatrist might have for the acts of a patient, based on the limits to the duty of care—to whom is a duty owed, and for what? This was of considerable interest during the 1990s in the United Kingdom, where non-judicial inquiries subjected psychiatrists to trial by media following crimes by their patients or former patients (Peay, 1996). This remains of interest in other countries where psychiatrists are sometimes charged with criminal offences because of the behaviour of their patients (Carabellese et al., 2017; Gualtieri et al., 2020). As the legalisation of cannabis proceeds across many countries, the consequences for psychiatry and forensic psychiatry will become increasingly pressing for resources, psychiatric intensive care services, and surprising areas of medico-legal interest.

*Ethics and law: A closer consideration of prospective responsibility for the consequences of relapse, where discontinuation of medicine and return to use of intoxicants occurs when in remission and when having full decision-making capacities, offers a new approach to motivational and cycle of change therapies.*

Substance-induced abnormal mental states carry an excellent prognosis for remission and long-term good outcomes if correctly diagnosed and treated. Misdiagnosis by lumping all as 'psychosis' and treating all as 'schizophreniform psychosis' misses the opportunity for better outcomes in substance-induced states and probably alienates the misdiagnosed.

*Service development: There is clear evidence that substance misuse is closely associated with deaths in custody (Iqtidar et al., 2018), so missing or minimising the importance of testing for and eliciting histories of substance misuse will adversely impact patient outcomes.*

The ICD-10 Diagnostic Criteria for Research point out that a psychoactive substance-induced psychosis can last up to six months (WHO, 1993, p.62, F1x.5). Nevertheless, it has a much better prognosis than schizophrenia and is easier to treat. Conversely, misdiagnosing psychoactive substance-induced psychosis as schizophrenia misses the opportunity to advise about the need for abstinence, leads to serious stigma with potential deprivation of insurance, exclusion from certain forms of employment, and mistaken treatment for schizophrenia or, in some cases, misdiagnosis as treatment-resistant schizophrenia.

*Research: Future forensic psychiatry research on substance misuse should focus on better diagnostic practice and more appropriate tailoring of treatment plans, treatment resources, and research on treatment effectiveness for substance misuse and addiction, whether as a single disorder or a comorbid disorder over longer-term follow-up.*

All those arrested on suspicion of driving offences are obliged to submit to testing for alcohol and other intoxicants. However, the same is not the case when arrested for suspected crimes of violence. Pathologists' reports regarding the *victims* of murder almost always include a toxicology report, which is read into the court record. This area requires better scientific knowledge and legal reform in the interests of fairness.

*Service development: Good clinical practice and good clinical research and service evaluation should require that all patients seen with psychiatric presentations in emergency departments should have an alcohol and drug screen.*

*Service development: Good clinical practice and harm prevention should require all those arrested for violence and all those received in jails and prisons to have alcohol and drug screens.*

*Research: In Germany, criminal courts may detain defendants for addiction treatment. It would be helpful to see how patients are selected for such treatment, what the treatment is, and what the outcomes are.*

## Physiological Systems, Dynamic Equilibria, and Syndemics

Appetites tend to maintain some dynamic equilibrium, for example, the constancy of substance dependence over time, with rapid reinstatement when relapsing from abstinence. Noble, a computational physiologist and systems biologist, has recently asserted the primacy of physiological mechanisms over the fashion for genetic determinism and genetic reductionism. Noble points out that the servo-feedback control mechanisms that maintain inner equilibrium in all bodily systems are always bi-directional in the flow of information (top-down as well as bottom-up), and genetic factors are never simply deterministic due to epigenetic feedback (Noble, 2008a, 2008b, 2017). Noble's biological systems theory has yet to appear fully in the neuropathology and neuropsychiatry of schizophrenia. In the looser application of biological systems theory to social and disease phenomena, the modelling of syndemics may be a version of this approach (Coid et al., 2020). A syndemic arises when there is a confluence of social and environmental factors, including structural violence, that is associated with multiple health conditions and health disparities in a local population or community, often with a dynamic equilibrium that is difficult to change.

*Research and service development: In forensic psychiatry, our approach to models of care is becoming progressively more systems-oriented (Kennedy, 2021) and more aware of the necessity of excellence in highly specialised services—research-driven teaching and training, evaluating the effectiveness of models of care as means of achieving progressively better outcomes for patients (Kennedy et al., 2019, 2020a; McLaughlin et al., 2023; Sørensen et al., 2020).*

## Descriptive Psychopathology and Statistical Method

Medically recognised and diagnosed mental disorders are set by law as a precondition for evidence of diminished mental capacity that can diminish responsibility. The great descriptive psychopathology of the early 20th century distinguished between dementia praecox (schizophrenia, non-affective psychosis, a process illness where there is progression over time from relapses and remissions to an enduring state with residual or continuous symptoms, and, most characteristically, enduring loss of functional ability) and bipolar affective disorder (manic depression, a cyclical biological alternation between elation and biological depression with remission of symptoms and less severely impaired functional capacities between episodes) (Kraepelin, 1904). This raises many questions about the overlap or otherwise between these two. Epidemiology suggests a clear distinction between the two (Tsuang et al., 1980), whereas genetics suggests a large overlap (Carroll & Owen, 2009; Smeland et al., 2020).

> *Research: The importance for forensic psychiatry lies in the long-term, enduring impairment of functional mental capacities in the advanced stages of 'process' illnesses. The staging of the progression of schizophrenia as a neurodegenerative disease with perceptual and processing disturbances as a future research topic will be discussed later in this chapter.*

Anxiety disorders are closely related to rage, while depressive disorders may be related to more pervasive forms of anger and resentment (Kennedy et al., 1992). These are relevant to psychiatric causes of violence (Davoren et al., 2017; Kennedy et al., 1992; Ullrich et al., 2014). In the 1980s, a purely statistical scientific debate raged about the distinction between depression and anxiety. This debate is instructive for future research because it turned on using the normal distribution and the psychometric properties of rating scales (Eysenck & Fajkowska, 2018; Möller et al., 2016), some of which were self-reported checklists. Others were based on more objective structured or semi-structured interview rating scales. Much interest was focused on the validity of self-reported checklist scores and the validity of structured or semi-structured interview rating scales in research, as well as in diagnosis and classification. Little interest was focused on the uncritical acceptance of normal distributions, sometimes trimming outliers and transforming skewed or oddly distributed data for statistical convenience in various ways. In other areas of medical research, various forms of log-normal, logistic, and exponential functions, Poisson distributions, and Bayesian functions are just beginning to enter into clinical research methodology in psychiatry.

> *Research method: It is always necessary to keep in mind that a new approach to the mathematical structure of data (normal, log-normal, Poisson) may improve the understanding of a biological process; the use of transformations and exclusions*

*in order to make biological data 'fit' or approximate a convenient distribution, such as the normal curve, may introduce bias or invalidate the analysis entirely.*

*Research methods: Further problems arise from the inherent assumptions when social data is analysed as if it were biological in its properties.*

Factor analysis was commonly used in survey and social data analysis but is now recognised as problematic. Factor analysis will yield as many or as few 'factors' as one wishes when setting the parameters of an algorithm or program. There is little reason to believe that these 'factors' reflect some 'real' underlying biological or social process unless they have face validity. However, face validity depends on the expertise of the researcher, who recognises some patterns based on their clinical experience and expertise. For diagnostic analysis, or the classification of groups, using factor analysis long since gave way first to cluster analysis, then to latent class analysis, in a field that has become increasingly complex and reliant on pragmatic interpretive approaches to descriptive data, provided the descriptive parameters bear some real relation to underlying biological processes.

*Research method: Many studies of the length of stay in secure forensic hospitals and time to reoffending or time to readmission still measure and report mean time and still use normally distributed statistics tests (means, standard deviations) when survival curve analysis is the correct metric and mode of analysis, citing half-lives or, as an approximation, medians (Davoren et al., 2015; McClean & Millard, 1996; Priest et al., 1995; Sharma et al., 2015).*

In the future, machine learning systems and artificial intelligence currently promise great advances from using real-world data (Cao & Reilly, 2019; Passos et al., 2019a; Torous et al., 2019) and 'a priori free' findings (Cao et al., 2018; Chen et al., 2022; Koppe et al., 2021; Passos et al., 2019b, 2016). There are early suggestions of advances in the assessment of suicide risk (Kessler et al., 2019). However, there are problems in accepting that this is truly 'a priori free' data. The use of medical records to train the machine learning system is biased by existing presentations to primary care, referral to specialist services, clinical assessment, and note writing. The greatest advantage of these new 'big data' methods may be improving the consistency and reliability of pattern recognition based on the human expertise used for training the large language model. A future research question is whether the increasing use of structured professional judgement to train clinicians and to improve consistency and reliability in clinical judgements will add to the consistency and reliability of large-data artificial intelligence approaches or limit it.

*Research method: Since the old rule 'garbage in, garbage out' is currently the limiting factor for machine learning and artificial intelligence systems, improving clinical input and clinical expertise by greater use of structured professional judgement (Collins, 2010; Galanter & Patel, 2005; Patel et al., 1996, 1999, 2005; Patel, Cytryn, et al., 2000; Patel, Glaser, et al., 2000; Patel & Ramoni, 1997) is likely to be beneficial.*

## Screening Studies and Populist Interpretation

The need for large-scale screening instruments to study large samples or entire populations gave rise to highly simplistic approximations, such as the General Health Questionnaire (GHQ) (Boardman, 1987). These rough screening questionnaires are seldom used in the two-step process originally intended, in which a positive screen by self-report checklist or researcher using a very simplified and brief interview should be followed by a rigorous diagnostic assessment by an expert clinician (McKinnon & Grubin, 2013; Shaw et al., 1999).

Larger epidemiological studies should always include, at the very least, a validation sample using rigorous diagnostic assessment by expert clinicians to measure the sensitivity and specificity of the screening process in the sample studied, including the false positive and false negative rates. There are a few examples of rigorous practice (Birmingham et al., 2000; McKinnon & Grubin, 2013). This is particularly relevant to studies of psychiatric morbidity in criminal justice populations.

## Diagnosis and Diagnostic Criteria

In more rigorous research methodology, semi-structured interviews were used to apply research diagnostic criteria, which have evolved into operationalised diagnostic criteria. This has greatly improved inter-rater reliability. The proliferation of diagnostic categories in successive editions of the WHO ICD has led to criticism (Hacking, 1986, 2013). The use of committees and the inclusion of unscientific early 20th-century psychodynamic categories continue to cause difficulty in the courts, where multiple personality, fugue states, and dissociative disorders, as well as a range of other similar non-biological categories, continue to generate confusion. Of greater concern has been the variability in operational criteria for the same disorders between one revision and the next. The evidence relied on for these changes is never cited, and the authors of the documents prefer to rely on the authority of the publishing body instead. Classification systems change in methodology over time, progressing from hierarchies that give precedence to biological over non-biological categories through multiaxial systems and increasingly fragmented collections of symptoms and syndromes. The most recent revisions of the WHO ICD and APA DSM have avoided introducing the staging of schizophrenia and other major mental illnesses.

*Research: The staging of severe mental illnesses is likely to be one of the most productive areas of research in psychiatry generally (Kapczinski et al., 2009;*

*Lavoie et al., 2019; McGorry et al., 2018) and in forensic psychiatry in the near future.*

An alternative approach to symptom classification in research has been to pursue individual symptoms rather than syndromes or diseases, notably by the National Institutes of Mental Health Research Domain Criteria (NIMH RDoC) (Insel et al., 2010; Insel, 2014). This approach is sometimes seen as part of personalised medicine. The symptomatic approach to diagnosis has been unproductive so far, from the perspective of forensic psychiatry, since the NIMH RDoC system lacks a clear approach to anger.

## Staging of Schizophrenia and Future Research in Forensic Psychiatry

Bipolar affective disorder (Kapczinski et al., 2009) and schizophrenia are observed to develop in stages, by analogy with the staging of cancers (Lavoie et al., 2019; McGorry et al., 2018).

Stage 0 is an 'at-risk mental state' in which unusual beliefs and experiences occur, along with a marked decline in family and social function and occupational or school function; actual delusions or hallucinations can occur but are fleeting and not sufficiently prolonged to meet diagnostic criteria for an episode of schizophrenia or mania. At-risk mental states may go on to evolve into any of the major mental illnesses or none. Comorbid substance misuse does not exclude a diagnosis of Stage 0 using the Comprehensive Assessment of At-Risk Mental States (CAARMS) criteria (Yung et al., 2008, 2007, 2005), although substance-induced psychoses exclude a diagnosis of a schizophreniform psychosis or manic episode in the WHO ICD-10 Diagnostic Criteria for Research (WHO, 1993). In a study of newly committed young male offenders aged 16 to 20 inclusive, the at-risk mental state was found in 23%. This was strongly associated with substance misuse, and the prevalence of at-risk mental state increased with the number of substances misused and with age. No one substance appeared to have a larger effect than others (Flynn et al., 2012). Since cannabis is often the most common intoxicant used in prisons and the community among younger people, it is of particular concern (D'Souza et al., 2022; Wainberg et al., 2021). An alternative approach to the assessment of 'at-risk' mental states is the assessment of 'basic symptoms', subtle disturbances in mental processes including stress tolerance, drive, affect, thinking, speech, bodily perception, motor action, and central vegetative functions, self-perceived with full insight. These are considered antecedents to the development of delusions and hallucinations (Huber & Gross, 1989; Ruhrmann et al., 2003; Schultze-Lutter et al., 2015, 2016).

*Research: The research agenda arising from the high incidence or prevalence of at-risk mental states in young offenders should focus on prospective studies of the subsequent mental health outcomes of young offenders found to have at-risk mental states.*

*Service development: Preventive interventions should focus on psychoeducation, particularly emphasising the need for abstinence from all intoxicants—not just harm reduction.*

*Research and service development: Research concerning prison reform should examine means to make prisons drug free and violence free, since (subject to evaluation) this is the most likely way to prevent progression from at-risk mental states to first-episode psychosis, at least while in the care and custody of the state.*

## Epidemiology: Social Risks and Biological Causes

The close ecological relationship between urban violence and homicide, on the one hand, and suicide rates, on the other, is notable (Kennedy et al., 1999). Durkheim sought explanations for variations in suicide rates by looking at age, sex, and religion (Durkheim, 2005; Hacking, 2006; Hacking & Hacking, 1990). The Chicago school extended this methodology, for example, relating urban crime and mental illness rates to other demographic and economic characteristics (Faris & Dunham, 1939; Kennedy et al., 1999). There is a close correlation, following an exponential function, between population density, urban economic deprivation, and urban lack of social cohesion, on the one hand, and arrest rates for violence, coroner's recorded suicide rates, and homicide rates, on the other hand (Kennedy et al., 1999). These correlate with population-based rates for secure forensic bed use (Pierzchniak et al., 1999).

When urban and rural areas are considered together, social cohesion has a protective effect, which appears to offset the effect of economic deprivation on forensic admission rates (O'Neill et al., 2005). It is unlikely that specialist mental health or primary care services can have much impact on violence, homicide, or suicide at a societal, whole population level. Employment, housing, social solidarity, social cohesion, and policing to regulate substance misuse are more likely to be effective levers of change or prevention. However, these are all observations of ecological associations, mixing social and biological phenomena. None can be taken as evidence of cause.

*Ethics: The occasional legal move to hold psychiatrists responsible for the crimes of their patients in the community (Dyer, 2012; Terranova & Rocca, 2016) may need rebuttal on these grounds from time to time (Peay, 1996).*

### *Epidemiology and Causal Inference*

Koch's four postulates for microbial pathogenesis set out criteria for proof that an infectious agent causes a particular disease (Segre, 2013). In epidemiology, where naturalistic data is gathered in ways that are not precise and where data mixes biological and social factors, a much more diffident assertion about causation is required. Doll and Hill were able to relate smoking habits to deaths certified as caused by lung cancer and ischaemic heart disease (Doll & Hill, 1950, 1954, 1964; Doll et al., 2004). In one of the great contributions to medical research in epidemiology, Bradford Hill set out nine criteria for distinguishing mere associations from causal relationships (Hill, 1965; Hill & Hill, 1991). Bradford Hill concluded that "clearly none of these nine viewpoints can bring indisputable evidence for or against a cause and effect hypothesis, and equally none can be required as a *sine qua non*."

*Research method: Compared to the causal certainties of Koch's postulates, Hacking pointed out that for modern theories, such as childhood trauma leading to dissociation and multiple personality disorder, the claimed causal certainties were often constructed from poorly cited scholarship (Hacking, 1995). Bebbington pointed out that, for remote and social causes of depression, the most that one can say is that only a weak implication may be drawn 'in some cases, of X, some cases of Y may follow' (Bebbington, 1980; Hacking, 1963, 1995, 2001b, 2016).*

#### *Risk Assessment*

Despite Bradford Hill's caution and Hacking's analysis of weak inference or implication about remote risk factors, risk assessment has come to dominate research in forensic psychiatry. Practitioners often assume that risk assessment is more powerful and reliable than science claims. The evolution of this paradigm, from unstructured clinical judgement to actuarial 'prediction' and on to structured clinical judgement, has been extensively reviewed elsewhere.

Attempts to perfect risk assessment started by adding simplistically scored numbers of risk factors present and avoiding the more informative weighting factors for each factor because weighting factors heavily depend on the characteristics of the specific population studied (Dawes, 1979). Weighting factors cannot be reliably generalised to other populations. Further refinement was achieved by minimising the effect of base rates by using receiver operating characteristic area under the curve (ROC AUC) statistics (Mossman, 1994, 2006). However, a wealth of useful information has been ignored by not studying interactive effects between risk factors (Coid et al., 2015, 2016, 2018). The recent introduction of protective factors in violence risk assessment has not always proceeded on the necessary basis that a true protective factor must be shown to have an interactive (protective, offsetting) effect with risk factors (Abidin et al., 2013; Penney et al., 2023; Rutter, 1985, 1990; Ullrich et al., 2018).

It is worth considering how the study of epidemiological associations about risk has developed and how inferences about causes are developing in other fields of medicine and psychiatry.

*Social Psychiatry and Social Causes of Psychiatric Illness*

The field of social psychiatry involves the careful study of the associations between recalled adverse life events and difficulties and the development of mental illness (Dohrenwend & Dohrenwend, 1974). Brown and his associates conducted large-scale prospective studies in inner city London at the Institute of Psychiatry in South London (Birley & Brown, 1970). The demonstration that recall for adverse life events, when assisted in a structured way, could be reliable only for up to six months was an example of methodological rigour, originating in Columbia, New York (Dohrenwend, 2006). The necessity to distinguish objectively between independent and non-independent life events was a further methodological advance. Brown and colleagues claimed that independent life events, combined with difficulties such as childhood loss of a parent or lack of a confiding relationship in adult life, were associated with the development of depression in young mothers (Brown & Harris, 1978, 1989). Bebbington, also at London's Institute of Psychiatry, used an early form of regression analysis, in effect, a multidimensional association matrix to overcome simple confounding by combining multiple factors into one test of association with an outcome. Bebbington showed that the apparent association between antecedent life events and difficulties and subsequent depression was due to confounding, disguised by Brown's reliance on a simplistic statistical model of association (using multiple two-dimensional association matrices in parallel). There was no evidence of additivity or interactive effects (Bebbington, 1980; Tennant & Bebbington, 1978). This new advance is a statistical methodology that debunked the early research on life events and difficulties and required a greater integration of biological factors with social factors (Bebbington, 1986).

Years later, textbooks continue to quote Brown's work and seldom quote Bebbington's correction (Brown & Harris, 1989), although regression analysis has taken on an almost sacrosanct status. Despite this, the civil courts continue to be exercised by psychiatric opinions regarding the claimed social causes of depressive illnesses. This is not surprising, however, when Bradford Hill's test of biological coherence and biological plausibility is so easily defeated by diagnostic criteria for the milder forms of depression and anxiety that require no biological signs or symptoms. If the 'illness' has no biological or pathological reality (scoring two or more on the GHQ, having a purely cognitive bias towards negative thoughts without any biological symptoms such as early morning wakening or loss of appetite and anhedonia), then it is not surprising that weak inferences about the causative role of adverse social events will be difficult to study when the outcome ('depression') is a set of non-biological beliefs and negative habits of thought. It is important to note that there is no evidence that treating these mild forms of distress in primary care prevents the development of severe mental illness, such as bipolar affective disorder or schizophrenia. However, there is increasing evidence for ways of making progress with disease-modifying treatments for biological mental illnesses. Longer durations of untreated psychosis have long-term adverse consequences (O'Keeffe et al., 2022).

*Service and policy development: Despite the lack of evidence for prevention of severe mental illnesses in primary care, policy documents continue to advocate shifting resources from specialist services for severe mental illness, including forensic psychiatry, to primary care and community services offering non-biological treatments for non-biological problems, on the specious grounds that this is a part of prevention.*

## New Statistical Methods: Better Scientific Models

The emergence of new statistical methods commonly leads to new scientific findings, such as the use of regression analysis by Bebbington. In violence risk assessment, the most notable finding has been the emergence of short-term risk assessment instruments (Dynamic Appraisal of Situational Aggression, DASA; and Brøset Violence Checklist, BVC). These generate much stronger associations with violent acts over the next 24 hours in the closely observed 'laboratory-like' conditions of inpatient intensive care and high-dependency wards in secure hospitals. The enormous amount of repeated measurements in the same patients should generate serious confounding due to autoregression, and so the new statistical method correcting for this—General Estimating Equations (GEE)—allows increasingly sophisticated analysis of the predisposing and precipitating factors and events on the pathway to violence for inpatients under conditions of high incidence (Lockertsen et al., 2021; Maguire et al., 2017, 2019). GEE has also been applied to demonstrate in a secure forensic admission ward that using a range of interventions to prevent and manage violence, including de-escalation and restrictive practices, is proportionate to the measured short-term risk and actual behaviour (Kennedy et al., 2020b).

*Research and service development: This approach (short-term risk assessment and quantitative description of behaviours and interventions in psychiatric intensive care units) should form the basis for future research on preventing and managing violence in hospitals.*

## Epidemiology and Prison Psychiatric Morbidity

A series of increasingly rigorous surveys of psychiatric morbidity in prison populations in the United Kingdom established a reliable methodology for estimating the prevalence of severe mental illness in prisoners (Gunn et al., 1991a, 1991b; Maden et al., 1995). The purpose was to estimate the need for secure forensic hospital beds in the community, given the policy of diverting those with severe mental illness from prison to secure forensic hospitals in the United Kingdom.

Accordingly, the focus of these surveys was on identifying those with severe mental illness, particularly schizophrenia and bipolar affective psychosis. Rigorous diagnostic instruments were used by post-membership psychiatrists (equivalent to 'fellows' in the United States). Depression and anxiety also emerged as unmet needs for treatment, and substance misuse and addiction were present in the majority of prisoners. Over time, it was realised that preventing suicide in prisons required a different approach because of the very high prevalence of substance misuse in prisons (Boys et al., 2002; Brugha et al., 2005; Farrell et al., 2002; Maden et al., 1995; Melzer et al., 2002; Singleton et al., 1998, 2003). Focusing all policy and resources on diverting those with psychosis out of prison did little to reduce suicide, address substance misuse and addiction, prevent violence in prison, or improve the mental health of the majority of prisoners.

Because the policy consensus has been that all those with severe mental illnesses should be diverted from prisons to hospitals in the community, the studies of prison psychiatric morbidity have generated services for prison screening on committal to prison to divert to community mental health teams and hospitals for treatment. This has led to studies of severe mental illness at or close to the point of reception in prison.

Large-scale international meta-analyses (starting with a review of 62 studies of 23,000 prisoners from 12 countries) demonstrated that the prevalence of psychosis in prison surveys around the world was remarkably constant, as was the prevalence of depressive illness and substance misuse (Fazel et al., 2006; Fazel & Danesh, 2002; Fazel, Doll, et al., 2008; Fazel, Xenitidis, et al., 2008). What little information there was concerning newly arrested, remanded or newly committed prisoners (Birmingham et al., 1996, 2000; Curtin et al., 2009; Gavin et al., 2003; Kennedy et al., 2005; McKinnon & Grubin, 2013; Parsons et al., 2001) also showed a surprising degree of consistency between countries and over time.

### *Modelling the Prevalence of Psychosis in Prisoners*

Young offenders on reception to a young offenders' institution had a high rate of 'at-risk mental states' (Stage 0), and there was a biological gradient—the more substances misused, the greater the likelihood of an at-risk mental state (Flynn et al., 2012). This finding indicates that psychosis in prisoners, including adult prisoners, is developing in a population with a high level of vulnerability to psychosis. Meta-analysis shows that the prevalence of psychosis in prisoners is remarkably constant across countries and over successive decades (for example, 33,588 prisoners in 109 samples from 24 countries between 1966 and 2010) (Fazel & Danesh, 2002; Fazel, Hayes, et al., 2016; Fazel & Seewald, 2012). The relatively few studies of psychosis on reception to prison also show remarkably constant rates (Birmingham et al., 2000; Curtin et al., 2009).

Policy in most developed countries is to divert prisoners with psychosis from prison to mental health services outside prison. However, there has been no systematic test of the assumption underlying this policy. It is assumed that those with 'psychosis' are more likely to be imprisoned. Surveys of prisoners on reception support this (Birmingham et al., 2000; Brooke et al., 1996; Curtin et al., 2009; Parsons et al., 2001). However, formal surveys of prison psychiatric morbidity generally use representative sampling methods, research diagnostic criteria and structured or semi-structured diagnostic interviews (Gunn et al., 1991a; Maden et al., 1995). Studies of the effectiveness of diversion, on the other hand, seldom use systematic sampling, seldom report sensitivity and specificity, rarely use reliable diagnostic criteria or research standard interviews or drug screening, or report the substantial overlap between psychoses and substance misuse. An unknown but likely large proportion of those diverted from the criminal justice system to mental health services have substance-induced abnormal mental states. Some substance-induced states occur in those with pre-existing schizophrenia. However, others are likely to have only substance-induced psychoses or mixed states of intoxication, withdrawal, delirium, and psychosis due to polysubstance misuse.

The finding of an epidemiological constant—that almost all prison populations almost everywhere have a prevalence of psychosis of between 3% and 5% and a prevalence of depression of between 5% and 10% (Fazel & Seewald, 2012) ought to prompt attempts at modelling the nature of this phenomenon. Diversion has not succeeded in reducing the incidence or prevalence of psychosis in prisoners despite being widely implemented across many jurisdictions by many different clinical teams over decades.

*Research: An explanation for why the rate of psychosis in prisons remains so constant is required.*

The likely elements of an explanatory model are fairly obvious. About 23% of newly detained young offenders test positive for the 'at-risk mental state' for psychosis and are biologically vulnerable (Cooper et al., 2018; Flynn et al., 2012; Jarrett et al., 2012), while in one comprehensive national survey using research diagnostic criteria and systematic sampling, 2% have an active psychosis, approximately 4% have a six-month prevalence of psychosis on reception, with 8% having a lifetime prevalence of psychosis (Kennedy et al., 2005), where psychosis is broadly defined. Many cases are likely to be complicated by substance misuse or to be substance-induced. The prevalence of substance misuse in the prison population (assessed by the number testing positive and cross-checked by anonymous self-reports) is another factor in the model, since there is a known gradient relationship between polysubstance misuse and the at-risk mental state. Finally, other stressors are most likely to arise from the prevalence and incidence of violence by prisoners on prisoners (a rate that is almost impossible to find in published data or research) since the pervasive danger of violent victimisation is a likely factor also in the onset and maintenance of psychosis in prisoners. There are obvious interactive (reinforcing) relationships between prison drug trafficking, drug debt, threats and violence, all magnified by gang culture, conflict, and stress, although these will be less easily measured. An interactive effect between the prevalence of substance misuse, violent incidents, and at-risk mental states and psychosis should be taken as objective evidence for these qualitative factors. Diversion of those who become psychotic in prison can also be factored into an equation describing the constant prevalence of psychosis, but this model constructed around a constant prevalence of psychosis addresses the failure of diversion to reduce the amount of psychosis in prisons. As soon as one vulnerable prisoner with polysubstance misuse and violent victimisation becomes psychotic (relapses or first episodes) and is diverted, other vulnerable prisoners will take his place in the drug culture and violent milieu.

*Research: This explanatory model, if developed to account for the constant level of psychosis, will generate testable hypotheses.*

*Research hypothesis: High or low diversion rates will make no difference to the prevalence of psychosis in prisoners.*

*Research hypothesis: Reducing the prevalence of drug misuse (fewer testing positive in random screening) will reduce the incidence and prevalence of psychosis. Random drug testing will not, in itself, reduce drug use (Nguyen et al., 2021). Some preventive interventions are needed, and their success should be monitored by random testing.*

*Research hypothesis: Reducing the prevalence of drug misuse will reduce the incidence of violence.*

*Research hypothesis: Lower rates of violence will also reduce the incidence and prevalence of psychosis in prisons.*

### *Screening at Reception in Prisons*

There have been very few studies of the outcomes of prison reception screening for mental illness and diversion. The sensitivity and specificity of such committal screening have seldom been studied and less often replicated. Studies reporting combined screening and diversion do not report the use of research diagnostic interviews, only diagnostic categories such as combined ICD categories, so the broad term psychosis is used while testing for substance misuse and using diagnostic criteria to distinguish between schizophrenia, schizophreniform psychosis, and substance-induced states are never reported and probably not applied with much rigour.

### *Modelling the Effectiveness of Diversion at or Before Trial*

Studies of the effects of diversion at the pretrial stage—in remand prisons or courts—tend to emphasise the operational parameters, such as delay time before achieving diversion and the numbers who attend for treatment subsequently

(Walsh et al., 2024). These outcomes are much more disappointing than might be expected. While lack of community resources may be a factor (James, 1999; Joseph & Potter, 1993b), much of the reported lack of engagement may be explained by a lack of diagnostic precision, the alienation of the misdiagnosed, and the alienation also of the services for individuals who have a severe mental illness and who receive the misdirected substance misusers. This is a lost opportunity to both reduce the duration of untreated psychosis due to delayed transfers to hospital (McInerney et al., 2013; O'Neill et al., 2016; Pierzchniak et al., 1997, 1999) and a lost opportunity to engage with specialist substance misuse services.

There is some recognition that diversion services are generating a new version of the painful circular pathways of homeless, drug-misusing individuals who have a mental illness and who are shunted from streets to prisons to psychiatric hospitals to temporary hostels to the streets and around again (Rollin, 1969). This group of 'frequent returns' in diversion schemes can be characterised as 'Pareto' patients. A Pareto function emerging from descriptive data on the admission and readmission of prisoners who have a mental illness is a model of the underlying process.

*Research: The numbers circling through streets, prisons, and psychiatric hospitals could be estimated by applying the estimating methods of tag, release, and 're-capture'.*

*Research: The parameters of the Pareto function could also be used to estimate changes over time due to diversion schemes and treatment—or the lack of effect.*

The presence of this group of 'Pareto patients' who are repeatedly diverted from the criminal justice system to mental health services and treatment, only to relapse, reoffend, and return to the criminal justice system and diversion services should prompt a research-driven search for better solutions for this vulnerable group. All treatment programmes or parts of a model of care should be constantly evaluated for efficacy and whether the resources devoted could be deployed to better effect (more health gains) in some other approach.

Community treatment orders (Carabellese & Felthous, 2016; Dawson et al., 2016; Fazel, Fimińska, et al., 2016; Gupta et al., 2018; Quinn et al., 2018; Swanson et al., 2000), combined with a 'housing first' approach, offer a way of maintaining stability and optimum levels of global function and quality of life. However, these can only take effect if there is a useful period of intensive hospital treatment to achieve remission or as near remission as possible; for example, directly providing legally sanctioned treatment in legally approved hospitals as soon as a prisoner is identified as a case, rather than later in an idealised place that may not be available except through harmful delays.

*Service development: Diversion alone may not reduce the amount of psychosis in prisons in future years. Two additions to diversion need evaluation—reforming prisons to make them drug free and violence free, and ending the system of prolonged duration of untreated psychosis while waiting for diversion to a hospital outside prison by providing legally approved psychiatric hospitals inside prisons, as in the Netherlands (World Health Organization, 2024), Finland (Health Care Services for Prisoners VTH, 2025), and Spain (Arnau-Peiró et al., 2012).*

***Prison to Community Mental Health Service Diversion***

A large proportion of those diverted from the criminal justice system to community mental health teams or psychiatric admission wards either fail to attend community services even with enhanced aftercare (Leonard et al., 2020) or have only fleeting contact with the admission ward (James, 1999; James & Hamilton, 1992; Joseph, 1994; Joseph & Potter, 1993a, 1993b; Walsh et al., 2024). Diverting those in need of recovery-and abstinence-oriented treatment for substance misuse and addiction to the wrong service—that is, to community mental health services for patients with severe and enduring mental illnesses—may explain this lack of engagement. Patients will either fail to engage (feeling they have been misdiagnosed), which may lead to alienation of the community mental health teams and scepticism when patients who do not have severe mental illnesses are referred. Implementation research for such services is badly needed.

In countries where there are no legally designated psychiatric hospitals inside prisons, studies of prison screening and court diversion consistently show very long delays before inmates are diverted and begin treatment. The higher the level of therapeutic security required, the longer the delay (McInerney et al., 2013; Pierzchniak et al., 1997). This is in contrast to community patients. Anyone in the community who has completed orders for admission and treatment under civil mental health law will be admitted and treated at once. Prisoners find themselves discriminated against by this delay. The evidence that the duration of untreated psychosis has an adverse effect on long-term neurocognitive function and functional outcomes has recently firmed up (Howes et al., 2021; Scully et al., 2004). It has always been possible that the number of men passing through prisons with psychosis or developing psychosis in prison was a driver for the incidence and prevalence of psychosis in men generally (Duffy et al., 2003; Flynn et al., 2014) or accounted for the more severe forms of psychosis and later-stage, harder-to-treat illnesses in forensic populations.

*Service development: After several decades of diversion as a policy and well-resourced services to achieve this, it is unlikely that further development of diversion services will successfully reduce the duration of untreated psychosis in prisoners to the same level as in the community. An additional service model is now required.*

***Psychosis as Part of a Prison Syndemic***

Vulnerability to psychosis in youths committed to a young offenders institution, measured by the at-risk mental state, is related to polysubstance misuse (Flynn et al., 2012), childhood adversity (Zhang & Coid, 2024) but also to the co-occurrence or syndemic of psychotic experiences and anxiety, substance dependence, high-risk sexual behaviour, and violence and criminality, that interact with cultures and areas (Coid et al., 2020). Hodgins has observed that psychosis in young offenders and adults with delinquency or antisocial personality disorder, substance misuse, violence, and poor physical health and developmental disorders, including attention deficit hyperactivity disorder, specific learning disabilities and autism spectrum disorders, has a better prognosis, with less cognitive and functional impairment, than non-delinquent, non-drug-related schizophrenia (Hodgins, 2008; Hodgins et al., 2013). The drug-fuelled, violent, and gang-maintained culture of prisons is toxic (Coid, Ullrich, Keers, et al., 2013; Wood et al., 2017). Prison regime and design features leading to high spatial density, social density, and the experience of crowding (Baum & Paulus, 1987; Canter, 1987) are likely also toxic factors (Cox et al., 1982; Sommer, 1979).

*Research: Modelling the relationship between numbers testing positive for drugs, the number of violent incidents, and numbers found to have psychosis, and testing the effects of changes to prison regimes in a controlled and measured way are long overdue.*

*Service development: The Dutch example of new legally sanctioned psychiatric hospitals inside prisons to minimise the duration of untreated psychosis is also notable (Goethals, 2012; World Health Organization, 2024).*

*Research hypothesis: An outcome to evaluate would be a fall in the duration of untreated psychosis on reception in prison or on diagnosis in prison.*

*Research hypothesis: The incidence and prevalence of schizophrenia in prisoners or at least a fall in the more severe forms due to reduced duration of untreated psychosis should also be evaluated.*

## Epidemiological Method and the Relationship Between Mental Illness and Violence

There has been a long and chequered exploration of the relationship between psychopathology and violence (Appelbaum et al., 2000; Link et al., 1999; Steadman et al., 1998; Swanson et al., 1990, 1996, 1997; Swanson, 1994; Teasdale et al., 2006). Observational studies and case series demonstrated that delusions led to violent behaviour, particularly when associated with fear and anger (Kennedy, 1992; Kennedy et al., 1992).

### *Population Studies of Association*

Mental illness was first reliably related to violence by the epidemiological catchment area study in the United States, using unbiased, population-based sampling and research diagnostic criteria (Swanson et al., 1990, 1996, 1997; Swanson, 1994). This demonstrated the stronger relationship between substance misuse (not just addiction) and violence, and not just for alcohol, but for all intoxicants, including cannabis. Since severe mental illness was associated with substance misuse, a series of further epidemiological studies of statistical association and confounding between mental illness, substance misuse, and violence continued inconclusively for some time (Appelbaum et al., 2000; Steadman et al., 1998).

Initial efforts to relate delusions and hallucinations to violence at an epidemiological risk or causal level were remarkable for the repeated negative findings. At several points, meta-analyses of selected negative studies yielded negative results, demonstrating the limitations of meta-analysis.

### *Causal Modelling*

Coid and his group brought a fresh approach, pointing out that causal modelling was entirely different from the use of mere statistical association studies. As is often the case in the evolution of psychiatric research, new statistical methods and novel approaches to modelling complex systems have enabled a more rigorous study of causes and effects—particularly in cases where multiple factors interact, as seen in syndemics. In this case, the new method was the use of mediation analysis of existing data sets for pathways from one presumed cause via a mediating factor to a presumed effect. Coid and his group re-analysed the data sets for the MacArthur study. They found that when they considered only short time intervals between the measurement of symptoms and the occurrence of violent acts, a significant association between delusions and violence emerged, but only when mediated by anger (Coid, Ullrich, Kallis, et al., 2013; Keers et al., 2014; Ullrich et al., 2014). Anger had long been thought relevant to violence (Kennedy, 1992; Kennedy et al., 1992) and had been studied using earlier analytical models and meta-analysis (Reagu et al., 2013). Mediation analysis showed that a delusion that was associated with anger was followed by violence within a short time period, but not if the delusion was not associated with anger, nor could this effect be found over longer time periods between the measurement of the symptoms and the violent outcome, plausibly explained by the attenuation over time of delusions or anger or both.

Coid and colleagues illustrated the weakness of studies and meta-analyses that used baseline measures of symptoms (delusions or hallucinations) to examine the link with violence over subsequent periods of six months or more, usually using regression models. The unexamined assumption here is that symptoms present at baseline will also be present at all times up to six months later and specifically at the time of the violent act. Not surprisingly, studies based on this model usually showed no association between symptoms and violence or an association that was confounded by substance misuse, where substance misuse was also measured at baseline and also assumed to apply at all time points up to six months later (Appelbaum et al., 2000). It is more likely that substance misuse will persist at all time points over a prolonged period of follow-up than that a symptom will persist over the same follow-up. Coid et al. used the same databases but applied a different explanatory model.

In Coid's model, only symptoms measured a short time before the violent act were analysed, so the assumption that they were present at the time of the act was more likely to be correct. Using mediation analysis instead of simple regression analysis, Coid could show that only delusions associated with anger could be significantly associated with violence (Coid et al., 2018; Ullrich et al., 2014). This presents a 'good' explanation because it complies with most or all of Bradford Hill's criteria and also with Deutsch's characteristics (Deutsch, 2011) of a 'good' explanation—hard to vary and in keeping with a known natural (or biological) mechanism—a delusion gives rise to anger, anger gives rise to violence.

> *Research method: A new mode of analysis allows for a better model and yields a better explanation of data in accordance with real-world outcomes, clinical experience, and expertise.*

***Delusions of Moral Imperatives***

The reframing of delusions—from persecutory, religious, grandiose, or other forms to moral delusions—in accordance with a psychopathological analysis of moral dispositions or cognitions by Haidt led to a relationship between strong moral dispositions and more severe violence in schizophrenia (O'Reilly et al., 2017), and moral delusions at the time of a violent act with more severe violence (O'Reilly et al., 2019b). Since moral beliefs are considered universal, actionable, and punishable, violence may also be strongly related to moral delusions that provoke anger. Strong moral convictions and commitments may also be relevant to acts of terrorism that are not related to mental illness, for example, in the Middle East (Atran, 2016; Atran et al., 2014; Gill et al., 2021; Gómez et al., 2017, 2022).

> *Research: Other mediating effects between symptoms and violence, and between symptoms and suicide, remain to be studied. The mediating or moderating role of substance misuse requires a similar approach. The relationship between delusions, moral dispositions, moral beliefs, anger (rage and resentment), and the role of amoral dispositions await further research.*

## Treatment: Paradigms and Models, Theories and Experiments

Research on treatment in psychiatry has stalled. While intense progress happens in the laboratory sciences, the gap between genetics, epigenetics, proteomics, anatomy, neurophysiology, and neuropharmacology, on the one hand, and neuropsychology and philosophy of mind, on the other hand, shows no sign of converging. Connecting the biophysical and the mentalistic domains or generating answers of a strictly scientific nature to the questions posed by courts concerning functional mental capacities to make decisions or the functional mental capacity to form specific criminal intentions also remain elusive. For example, no expert would introduce even the most progressive forms of functional brain imaging in a murder trial, since the lack of connection between what can be imaged and measured and what a court would regard as relevant to responsibility or even mental illness is still at the level of internal phrenology. It is instructive to see where progress is likely to emerge. Friston (Friston et al., 2021), with collaborators including Frith (Schultz & Frith, 2022) and Dolan (Eldar et al., 2016; Hauser et al., 2019; Kurth-Nelson et al., 2023), has developed a mathematical model of how the brain works, drawing heavily on Bayesian approaches. For Friston, consciousness arises because the brain constantly performs 'sophisticated inferences' based on sensory inputs and pattern recognition to avoid dangerous surprises. In related work, Dolan considers moods part of consciousness, specifically concerning attention or motivation (Eldar et al., 2016). This seems compatible with a phenomenological understanding of anger and fear. For example, anger can be defined as the affective experience of the motivation to act in ways that warn, intimidate, or attack those perceived as challenging or threatening, associated with sensitivity to the perception of challenges and heightened awareness of threats. Fear has the same sensitivity and awareness of threats but motivates to escape, appease, or avoid (Kennedy, 1992).

*Research method: Dolan's 'mood as representation of momentum' is a possible connection to definitions of anger and fear. Whether these Bayesian approaches to modelling neuronal and imaging findings can provide a laboratory method for studying such mental states remains to be seen.*

*Research: Friston's concept of 'sophisticated inference' approximates insight or reflectiveness. The potential for the study of abnormal beliefs and experiences is promising.*

### *Treating Risks, Conjectures, and Explanations*

Treating a risk factor associated with a disease outcome with no causal role will have no benefit. The so-called risk factors may have no causal relation to the things they are associated with. Some risk factors may have contributory or moderating effects on the outcome but may be neither necessary nor sufficient as causes. Causal factors are antecedent, proximate, and explanatory. A 'good' explanation (Deutsch, 2011) must account for what exists and why. It should be falsifiable, difficult to modify arbitrarily, and consistent with other knowledge and other 'good' explanations. Good explanations often have 'reach'—they extend to explain other things as well. They are not necessarily reductionist or minimalist. When better explanations emerge, they often introduce improved modes of explanation.

> *Research: The future of research in forensic psychiatry is unlikely to devote more resources to risk assessment when it would be inherently more productive to research the causes of violence in individuals with mental disorders, the difference between serious and less serious violence, and the related causes of mental disorders.*

### *Scientific Models as a Guide to Causes*

Most clinical scientists working in medicine were educated to understand that science progresses by making falsifiable hypotheses and then finding experimental ways to test them. We forget that scientific, falsifiable hypotheses can arise only from scientific models. McLaren (McLaren, 1998, 2023) reviewed the predominant position of the biopsychosocial model (Engel, 1980), which he criticised because it is not a 'model' in any scientific or identifiable sense. The biopsychosocial 'model' is more correctly described as an ethos or point of view and has little purchase outside psychiatry. Many other concepts seek scientific status by appending 'model' to their title but are not scientific models.

A scientific model should have all the characteristics of a good explanation in science. Scientific models are reductive in that they should be grounded in the mechanisms of natural functions, although they are not necessarily simplistic. Models of natural functions describe underlying laws of nature. Often, these are expressed in mathematical terms. Social functions may arise from natural functions, but an entirely social phenomenon may closely approximate some natural mathematical function if that social function arises from some underlying biological process—suicide rates as described by Durkheim, homicide rates as described by the Chicago school (Kennedy et al., 1999).

### *Models of Care as a Guide to Improving Health Gains*

A model of care is a written account of how an open or closed healthcare social institution fulfils its defined goals—to achieve health gains for patients, including preventing violence (Kennedy, 2021). Measurement-based care is an essential element of a modern model of care in forensic psychiatry or any area of medical clinical practice (Glancy et al., 2021). Measurement and evaluation are essential for excellence in the continuous improvement of outcomes for patients through the virtuous cycle of research, development, teaching, and training (Kennedy et al., 2019; McLaughlin et al., 2023). The model of care itself must be subject to continuous evaluation (Davoren et al., 2022) and assessment of service strain (Jeandarme et al., 2021; R. O'Reilly et al., 2019) or unmet need (Jewell et al., 2023; Parente et al., 2024).

***Future Research on Treatment for Forensic Psychiatry Patients***

Secure forensic hospitals offer a unique setting to treat the most severe and treatment-resistant mental illnesses in conditions where the environment, the milieu, and levels of relational and procedural care and safety are closely monitored and controlled. Case mix can now be measured and compared between hospitals, and community groups of patients within and across national boundaries (Kennedy et al., 2019; McLaughlin et al., 2023; Tomlin et al., 2020), for example, in Australia (Adams et al., 2018), Belgium (Jeandarme et al., 2019), Canada (Jones et al., 2019; Penney et al., 2023), Ireland (Davoren et al., 2015), Italy (Parente et al., 2024), New Zealand (Jewell et al., 2023), the Netherlands (Eckert et al., 2017), and the United Kingdom (Freestone et al., 2015; McCullough et al., 2020; Williams et al., 2020). Models of care designed to provide standardised non-pharmacological treatments can now be continuously assessed for outcomes and compared across services. For example, McLaughlin and colleagues (2023) compared 48 forensic psychiatry services in five jurisdictions: Belgium, Canada, Denmark, Ireland, and Italy. Measurement-based care is being recognised after many decades as an essential part of the treatment of the most severe and life-shortening mental illnesses (Glancy et al., 2021).

The most effective treatments for schizophrenia and bipolar disorder and the most effective approaches to preventing suicide and violence now available are not psychosocial interventions but pharmacological treatments (Fazel et al., 2014; Sariaslan et al., 2021). Various medications can be characterised as 'downstream' from treatments that address underlying pathological processes. If drugs acting at dopamine receptors and other small molecules acting at neuroreceptors have beneficial effects, they are probably acting to correct the consequences of other more fundamental disorders in the brain. Analogies are helpful here. In the same way, diuretics can act to palliate the pathophysiology of congestive cardiac failure, but only a disease-modifying treatment can address the underlying causes (cardiac valve replacement, cardiac transplant), and vasodilators such as glyceryl trinitrate can compensate for ischaemic heart disease. However, coronary stents or coronary artery bypass grafts address the underlying cause. There are as yet no disease-modifying treatments for schizophrenia.

Nevertheless, new disease-modifying treatments in closely analogous diseases are appearing now. GLP-1 agonists can change some brain-level homeostatic mechanisms for appetite control and weight maintenance, including patients with schizophrenia (Trott et al., 2024), enabling many patients to discontinue oral hypoglycaemics, cholesterol-lowering drugs, and other 'palliative' treatments. Disease-modifying drugs for Alzheimer's disease and multiple sclerosis are being licensed. It is possible that mRNA vaccines against common viruses such as varicella will also prove to be disease-modifying in some forms of dementing or neuro-inflammatory diseases.

If disease-modifying treatments appear for schizophrenia, they are likely to be effective at the earliest stages before neural pruning, intoxicants, or inflammation has done permanent damage. There may be preventive treatments—although avoiding cannabis is already likely to be preventive at the population level.

*Ethics: Forensic psychiatry will first have to consider the legal and ethical processes for offering disease-modifying treatments to patients who already have impaired functional mental capacities to give or withhold consent. Should the threshold for intervention and treatment without consent be lower for a disease-modifying drug than for a palliative drug? Should the threshold for treatment without consent to prevent violence to others (for example, long-lasting injections of medication to prevent relapse of psychosis) be different than for treatment to prevent a life-shortening illness such as schizophrenia?*

#### *Meta-Analysis of Causes and Treatments, or Better Scientific Models*

A problem in forensic psychiatry is that we have accumulated a lot of data from large-scale epidemiology studies of causes and treatment outcomes. However, unlike meta-analyses of randomised controlled trials, we have been limited to using observational case register data and observational data in atheoretical meta-analyses. These cannot exceed the explanatory power of the models of the studies that generated the data. Indeed, the 'model' used for meta-analysis may reinforce the limitations of weak models by excluding outliers or studies using different methodology or models. Repeated surveys or trials using a poor but standard model will only lend false weight to that model.

*Research: All routine clinical and social data should be available for linked anonymised clinical research to evaluate models of care and ensure that outcomes, particularly health gains, are continuously improving for patients. This should include the legal process of linking databases across the life cycle, primary care, pharmacy, specialist medical and psychiatric services, biobanks, criminal justice, and coroner's data in forensic practice. Linking databases makes it possible to study limited causal models.*

*Ethics: The public's right to better health services and better health outcomes should outweigh supposed data privacy rights in an anonymised system built on unique identifiers and encryption (Ludvigsson et al., 2015).*

## Ethics as a Subject for Research

Deutsch (2011), in a surprising claim, says that aesthetics and ethics can be treated as capable of continuous improvement through seeking better causal explanations for how these decision-making processes work in the real world.

> *Ethics: Deutsch's extension of the use of good scientific explanation should allow a scientific modelling approach to testing and improving such practical ethics as using structured professional judgement instruments within judgement support frameworks (e.g., admissions panels and review boards) to enhance teaching, training, inter-rater reliability, and consistent decision making (Daniels & Sabin, 2008; Davoren et al., 2013; Davoren et al., 2012; Flynn, O'Neill, & Kennedy, 2011; Flynn, O'Neill, McInerney, et al., 2011; Habets et al., 2019; Jeandarme et al., 2019; McCullough et al., 2020; Williams et al., 2020) as well as research ethics committees.*

### *Disease Staging, Functional Mental Capacity, and Ethics of Treatment Without Consent*

Staging of a disease represents a model of the disease. Progression (Allott et al., 2019; Kapczinski et al., 2009; Peralta et al., 2023; Yung et al., 2005) from Stage 0, the 'at-risk mental state', to Stage 1: 'first-episode' psychosis; Stage 2: relapsing and remitting psychosis with full remission of symptoms between episodes; Stage 3: relapses and remissions with decline in global function between episodes; and Stage 4: continuous symptoms with varying degrees of treatment resistance and enduring impairments of global function. This understanding of how severe mental illnesses work is no longer new. Perhaps what is surprising is that even bipolar affective disorder can be staged.

This has implications for research and practice. Progression to enduring cognitive impairment leads to a medical view that decision-making capacity is largely determined by impairments of global function (Ganzini et al., 2004; McCleery et al., 2014; Smeland et al., 2020). Impaired real-world global function can be related to impaired cognitive function through measures weighted by the weakest subscale of a composite test, the MATRICS Consensus Cognitive Battery (MCCB) (McCleery et al., 2014). The MCCB relates to global function and clinical outcomes (O'Reilly et al., 2015; O'Reilly et al., 2020; Richter et al., 2018).

> *Ethics: Effective psychological treatment strategies have small effects on cognition but may have larger effects on capacity and competence (Naughton et al., 2012; O'Reilly et al., 2019a, 2016; Rutledge et al., 2008). This should lead to a re-examination of how the functional mental capacity to give or withhold consent is assessed, particularly to set the threshold for intervention.*

At present, only a very severe impairment of functional mental capacity is taken as sufficient to intervene with substituted judgement and, where necessary, detention and restrictive practices to prevent violence and initiate treatment. Evidence that functional impairments of global ability and specific functional mental capacities are impaired early in the course of a process illness and persist between episodes of obvious delusions and hallucinations ought to lead to a change of the direction of law reform. However, this is likely more successful when treatment is qualitatively more successful.

*Service development (legal reform): Law reform should set a lower threshold of cognitive impairment for intervention at earlier stages of illness and for more continuous periods, not just during brief acute relapses of delusions and hallucinations.*

### *Dropping the Diagnostic First Step in the Justification of Detention and Treatment Without Consent*

The proposal that an approach to legally sanctioned preventive detention should be possible, regardless of diagnosis and impaired capacity, as a response to an interpretation of a human rights convention, involves the adoption of an 'integrationist defence' in the criminal context. This would include an 'undeterrability requirement' when the state seeks preventive detention outside the criminal process and a 'basic rationality and self-regard test' for incompetency determinations. None of these proposals requires proof of a mental disorder as a predicate condition (Slobogin, 2015). However, the 'basic rationality and self-regard test' would inevitably become a capacity test. At the same time, psychiatric evidence regarding 'undeterrability' in a criminal justice context, on the one hand, would carry all the uncertainties of current risk assessments while also using psychiatric evidence for social hygiene at best and political control at worst.

*Ethics: All such proposals that lead to any separation between detention without consent and treatment without consent are inherently forms of imprisonment in the public interest, not psychiatric treatment in the patient's best interests. Deutsch's 'good' explanations for better ethics can assist here (Deutsch, 2011). Psychiatry cannot be used as an instrument of state control (Kosenko & Steger, 2023).*

## Future Research and Development

Forensic psychiatry is a medical scientific field bound by medical ethics. Research in forensic psychiatry, as with all medical scientific fields, must be ethical, accurate, and honest. We must evaluate the programmes and treatments we use and be willing to change those models of care or parts of care that do not show measurable health benefits for patients. We must accept the challenge that this brings to develop new, effective, and modern services and treatments.

It is part of the role of forensic psychiatrists in the clinic or the court to respond rationally and persuasively to populist criticism of science, medicine, or expertise. While politicians, journalists, and sometimes lawyers addressing juries may say that 'the public has had enough of experts' (Ross, 2018), forensic psychiatrists should stay within the boundaries of medical expertise and medical ethics while being sceptical of our biases and prejudices. Hacking's and Bebbington's advice should be a guide for many of the questions regarding the social causation of biological illnesses. The most that an offer is a weak implication: 'in some cases of X, some cases of Y many follow'. We are on stronger ground the closer we adhere to biological and clinical evidence of causes rather than associations and to biological illnesses rather than social discontents and fashionable forms of unhappiness. We should be willing to diagnose medical illnesses, offer reliable prognoses, and recommend effective treatments. However, we should also be cautious about offering conjectures and projections about the future outside the scientific forum of discourse between experts. Occasionally, as experts, forensic psychiatrists must go to court to advocate for treatment for individuals with severe mental illness and advise the courts in the interests of justice against the more unreliable forms of non-scientific evidence regarding socially deviant behaviour and its consequences.

> *Ethics: Politically generated policies that purport to shape or form clinical practice in psychiatry should be guided by the expert advice of contributory experts (Collins & Evans, 2008), research practitioners capable of innovation and communication. Expert advice should be grounded in the operation and evaluation of models of care, where the model of care is itself a quantitative description of pathways, processes, and expected health gains (Harrison & Millard, 1991; Kennedy, 2021; Millard & McClean, 1994; Tansella & Thornicroft, 1998).*

### *The Medical Model Is the Application of Causal Explanation and Ethical Practice*

Researchers and clinical leaders in forensic psychiatry have a duty to make our patients less diffident when confronted with criticism of the 'medical model' of psychiatry. Most criticism of the medical model comes from those who are not themselves medical practitioners and cannot explain what they mean by the medical model they criticise. In psychiatry, the medical model requires quantitative models of diagnosis, prognosis, and treatment (models of care) that can be evaluated for health gains. The medical model upholds ethical obligations in accordance with the law to provide active treatment in the best interests of patients, ensuring the avoidance of harm and respecting patient autonomy, dignity, and confidentiality while responsibly using data for research and service evaluation. It also requires teaching effective and ethical practices to students and demonstrating these practices through professional conduct. Confidentiality should be maintained while using data responsibly for research and service evaluation, in compliance with applicable laws allowing such use. There is a social obligation to prevent harm to others, including harm to clinicians treating severely unwell and violent patients, and to prevent harm by clinicians or managers who may be straying from best practices. There is also an obligation within the medical model and medical ethics to assist the courts in exercising justice by giving unprejudiced, truthful, and expert advice. These duties are universal, not local.

This review of future research in forensic psychiatry has emphasised the biological and scientific aspects of forensic psychiatric practice and services. This is not a denial of the importance of humanities in forensic psychiatry—the prominence given to philosophers of science should be evidence of this. Much of the criticism of psychiatry and even scientific medicine has roots in postmodern literary criticism, an argument based on categorical error (Barish, 2014). Bronowski emphasised the importance of resolving debates within and about science by referencing some real thing (Bronowski, 1956). Vaccine scepticism, the denial of the organic, embodied basis of consciousness and severe mental illnesses, libertarian assertions of strict liability and the rejection of diminished responsibility, and the refusal to recognise a shared public duty to provide social protection and dignity for individuals who have severe mental illnesses, all stem from a broader denial of the validity and reality of science itself (Sokal & Bricmont, 1998). Forensic psychiatrists have an obligation to defend core medical ethical values such as the primacy of acting in the best interests of our patients and advocating for the right to health as a priority, including the public duty to preserve human dignity and to restore embodied consciousness and decision-making capacity (Carrara, 2018). Deutsch's concept of achieving better ethics and aesthetics through seeking 'good explanations' should guide the development of forensic psychiatric practice, ethics, and law (Slobogin, 2015).

## References

Abidin, Z., Davoren, M., Naughton, L., Gibbons, O., Nulty, A., & Kennedy, H. G. (2013). Susceptibility (risk and protective) factors for in-patient violence and self-harm: Prospective study of structured professional judgement instruments START and SAPROF, DUNDRUM-3 and DUNDRUM-4 in forensic mental health services. *BMC Psychiatry*, *13*, 197. https://doi.org/10.1186/1471-244X-13-197

Adams, J., Thomas, S. D., Mackinnon, T., & Eggleton, D. (2018). The risks, needs and stages of recovery of a complete forensic patient cohort in an Australian state. *BMC Psychiatry*, *18*(1), 35.

Allott, K., Wood, S. J., Yuen, H. P., Yung, A. R., Nelson, B., Brewer, W. J., Spiliotacopoulos, D., Bruxner, A., Simmons, M., Broussard, C., Mallawaarachchi, S., Pantelis, C., McGorry, P. D., & Lin, A. (2019). Longitudinal cognitive performance in individuals at ultrahigh risk for psychosis: A 10-year follow-up. *Schizophrenia Bulletin*, *45*(5), 1101–1111. https://doi.org/10.1093/schbul/sby143

American Psychiatric Association. (2022). *Diagnostic and statistical manual of mental disorders: DSM-5-TR*. American Psychiatric Association Publishing. Retrieved from https://books.google.co.uk/books?id=PIGizgEACAAJ

Appelbaum, P. S., Robbins, P. C., & Monahan, J. (2000). Violence and delusions: Data from the MacArthur violence risk assessment study. *American Journal of Psychiatry*, *157*(4), 566–572. https://doi.org/10.1176/appi.ajp.157.4.566

Arnau-Peiró, F., García-Guerrero, J., Herrero-Matías, A., Castellano-Cervera, J., Vera-Remartínez, E., Jorge-Vidal, V., & Iranzo-Tatay, C. (2012). Description of the psychiatric unit in prisons in the autonomous community of Valencia. *Revista Española de Sanidad Penitenciaria*, *14*, 50–60.

Atran, S. (2016). The devoted actor: Unconditional commitment and intractable conflict across cultures. *Current Anthropology*, *57*(S13), S192–S203. https://doi.org/10.1086/685495

Atran, S., Sheikh, H., & Gomez, A. (2014). Devoted actors sacrifice for close comrades and sacred cause. *Proceedings of the National Academy of Sciences of the United States of America*, *111*(50), 17702–17703. https://doi.org/10.1073/pnas.1420474111

Barish, E. (2014). *The double life of paul de man*. WW Norton & Company.

Baum, A., & Paulus, P. B. (1987). Crowding. In *Handbook of environmental psychology* (Vol. 1, pp. 533–570). Wiley.

Bebbington, P. (1980). Causal models and logical inference in epidemiological psychiatry. *British Journal of Psychiatry*, *136*, 317–325. https://doi.org/10.1192/bjp.136.4.317

Bebbington, P. (1986). Establishing causal links—recent controversies. In H. Katschnig (Ed.), *Life events and psychiatric disorders: Controversial issues* (pp. 188–200). Cambridge University Press.

Birley, J., & Brown, G. W. (1970). Crises and life changes preceding the onset or relapse of acute schizophrenia: Clinical aspects. *The British Journal of Psychiatry*, *116*(532), 327–333.

Birmingham, L., Gray, J., Mason, D., & Grubin, D. (2000). Mental illness at reception into prison. *Criminal Behaviour and Mental Health*, *10*(2), 77–87.

Birmingham, L., Mason, D., & Grubin, D. (1996). Prevalence of mental disorder in remand prisoners: Consecutive case study. *BMJ*, *313*(7071), 1521–1524.

Birner, J. (2018). Karl Popper's the poverty of historicism after 60 years. *Metascience*, *27*(2), 183–193. https://doi.org/10.1007/s11016-018-0303-5

Boardman, A. (1987). The general health questionnaire and the detection of emotional disorder by general practitioners: A replicated study. *British Journal of Psychiatry*, *151*(3), 373–381.

Boys, A., Farrell, M., Bebbington, P. E., Brugha, T., Coid, J. W., Jenkins, R. A., Lewis, G., Marsden, J., Meltzer, H., Singleton, N., & Taylor, C. (2002). Drug use and initiation in prison: Results from a national prison survey in England and Wales. *Addiction*, *97*(12), 1551–1560.

Brittain, R. P. (1970). The sadistic murderer. *Medicine, Science and the Law*, *10*(4), 198–207. https://doi.org/10.1177/002580247001000402

Bronowski, J. (1956). The educated man in 1984. *Science*, *123*(3200), 710–712.

Brooke, D., Taylor, C., Gunn, J., & Maden, A. (1996). Point prevalence of mental disorder in unconvicted male prisoners in England and Wales. *BMJ*, *313*(7071), 1524–1527.

Brown, G. W., & Harris, T. O. (1978). *Social origins of depression: A study of psychiatric disorder in women*. Free Press. Retrieved from https://books.google.ie/books?id=X3jvq8NJZ6YC

Brown, G. W., & Harris, T. O. (1989). *Life events and illness*. Guilford Publications. Retrieved from https://books.google.ie/books?id=emXzjtZmULEC

Brugha, T., Singleton, N., Meltzer, H., Bebbington, P., Farrell, M., Jenkins, R., Coid, J., Fryers, T., Melzer, D., & Lewis, G. (2005). Psychosis in the community and in prisons: A report from the British National Survey of psychiatric morbidity. *American Journal of Psychiatry*, *162*(4), 774–780.

Canter, D. (1987). Implications for "new generation" prisons of existing psychological research into prison design and use. In A. Bottoms, & R. Light (Eds.), *Problems of long-term imprisonment*. Aldershot: Gower.

Cao, B., & Reilly, J. (2019). Major challenges and limitations of big data analytics. In I. C. Passos, B. Mwangi, & F. Kapczinski (Eds.), *Personalized psychiatry: Big data analytics in mental health* (pp. 15–36). Springer International Publishing. https://doi.org/10.1007/978-3-030-03553-2_2

Cao, H., Meyer-Lindenberg, A., & Schwarz, E. (2018). Comparative evaluation of machine learning strategies for analyzing big data in psychiatry. *International Journal of Molecular Sciences*, *19*(11), 3387.

Carabellese, F., & Felthous, A. R. (2016). Closing Italian forensic psychiatry hospitals in favor of treating insanity acquittees in the community. *Behavioral Sciences & the Law*, *34*(2–3), 444–459. https://doi.org/10.1002/bsl.2234

Carabellese, F., Urbano, M., Coluccia, A., & Gualtieri, G. (2017). Workers safety in public psychiatric services: Problems, laws and protections. *Clinical Therapeutics*, *168*(6), e406–e414. https://doi.org/10.7417/t.2017.2043

Carrara, A. (2018). Updating the philosophical concept of form (morphé) as the embodied structural and teleological informational program in human beings. *HUMANA.MENTE Journal of Philosophical Studies*, *11*(34), 1–15.

Carroll, L. S., & Owen, M. J. (2009). Genetic overlap between autism, schizophrenia and bipolar disorder. *Genome Medicine*, *1*, 1–7.

Chen, Z. S., Kulkarni, P., Galatzer-Levy, I. R., Bigio, B., Nasca, C., & Zhang, Y. (2022). Modern views of machine learning for precision psychiatry. *Patterns*, *3*(11), 100602. https://doi.org/10.1016/j.patter.2022.100602

Coid, J. W., Gonzalez Rodriguez, R., Kallis, C., Zhang, Y., Bhui, K., De Stavola, B., Bebbington, P., & Ullrich, S. (2020). Ethnic disparities in psychotic experiences explained by area-level syndemic effects. *British Journal of Psychiatry*, *217*(4), 555–561. https://doi.org/10.1192/bjp.2019.203

Coid, J. W., Kallis, C., Doyle, M., Shaw, J., & Ullrich, S. (2015). Identifying causal risk factors for violence among discharged patients. *PloS One*, *10*(11), e0142493. https://doi.org/10.1371/journal.pone.0142493

Coid, J. W., Kallis, C., Doyle, M., Shaw, J., & Ullrich, S. (2018). Shifts in positive and negative psychotic symptoms and anger: Effects on violence. *Psychological Medicine*, *48*(14), 2428–2438. https://doi.org/10.1017/S0033291718000077

Coid, J. W., Ullrich, S., Kallis, C., Freestone, M., Gonzalez, R., Bui, L., Igoumenou, A., Constantinou, A., Fenton, N., Marsh, W., Yang, M., DeStavola, B., Hu, J., Shaw, J., Doyle, M., Archer-Power, L., Davoren, M., Osumili, B., McCrone, P., Barrett, K., Hindle, D., & Bebbington, P. (2016). Improving risk management for violence in mental health services: A multimethods approach. *Programme Grants in Applied Research*, *4*(16). https://doi.org/10.3310/pgfar04160

Coid, J. W., Ullrich, S., Kallis, C., Keers, R., Barker, D., Cowden, F., & Stamps, R. (2013). The relationship between delusions and violence: Findings from the East London first episode psychosis study. *JAMA Psychiatry, 70*(5), 465–471. https://doi.org/10.1001/jamapsychiatry.2013.12

Coid, J. W., Ullrich, S., Keers, R., Bebbington, P., Destavola, B. L., Kallis, C., Yang, M., Reiss, D., Jenkins, R., & Donnelly, P. (2013). Gang membership, violence, and psychiatric morbidity. *American Journal of Psychiatry, 170*(9), 985–993. https://doi.org/10.1176/appi.ajp.2013.12091188

Coid, J. W., Zhang, Y., Bebbington, P., Ullrich, S., de Stavola, B., Bhui, K., & Tsai, A. C. (2021). A syndemic of psychiatric morbidity, substance misuse, violence, and poor physical health among young Scottish men with reduced life expectancy. *SSM Population Health, 15*, 100858. https://doi.org/10.1016/j.ssmph.2021.100858

Collins, H. (2010). *Tacit and explicit knowledge*. University of Chicago Press. Retrieved from https://books.google.ie/books?id=ONzRalXOtEMC

Collins, H., & Evans, R. (2008). *Rethinking expertise*. University of Chicago Press.

Connell, P. H. (1957). Amphetamine psychosis. *British Medical Journal, 1*(5018), 582. Retrieved from https://www.ncbi.nlm.nih.gov/pmc/articles/PMC1974659/

Connell, P. H. (1958). *Amphetamine psychosis*. Oxford University Press.

Connell, P. H. (1968). Drug addiction [abridged]: Amphetamine dependence. *Proceedings of the Royal Society of Medicine, 61*(2), 178–181. https://doi.org/10.1177/003591576806100228

Cooper, J., Jarrett, M., Forrester, A., di Forti, M., Murray, R. M., Huddy, V., Roberts, A., Phillip, P., Campbell, C., Byrne, M., McGuire, P., Craig, T., & Valmaggia, L. (2018). Substance use and at-risk mental state for psychosis in 2102 prisoners: The case for early detection and early intervention in prison. *Early Intervention in Psychiatry, 12*(3), 400–409. https://doi.org/10.1111/eip.12343

Cox, V. C., Paulus, P. B., McCain, G., & Karlovac, M. (1982). The relationship between crowding and health. *Advances in Environmental Psychology, 4*, 271–294.

Crump, C., Winkleby, M. A., Sundquist, K., & Sundquist, J. (2013). Comorbidities and mortality in persons with schizophrenia: A Swedish national cohort study. *American Journal of Psychiatry, 170*(3), 324–333. https://doi.org/10.1176/appi.ajp.2012.12050599

Curtin, K., Monks, S., Wright, B., Duffy, D., Linehan, S., & Kennedy, H. G. (2009). Psychiatric morbidity in male remanded and sentenced committals to Irish prisons. *Irish Journal of Psychological Medicine, 26*(4), 169–173. https://doi.org/10.1017/S079096670000063X

Daniels, N., & Sabin, J. E. (2008). *Setting limits fairly: Learning to share resources for health*. Oxford University Press.

Davoren, M. (2021). Anti-androgens in forensic psychiatric settings. In A. M. Doherty, A. M. Egan, & S. Dinneen (Eds.), *Mental health, diabetes and endocrinology* (pp. 127–136). Cambridge University Press. https://doi.org/10.1017/9781911623625.013

Davoren, M., Abidin, Z., Naughton, L., Gibbons, O., Nulty, A., Wright, B., & Kennedy, H. G. (2013). Prospective study of factors influencing conditional discharge from a forensic hospital: The DUNDRUM-3 programme completion and DUNDRUM-4 recovery structured professional judgement instruments and risk. *BMC Psychiatry, 13*, 185. https://doi.org/10.1186/1471-244X-13-185

Davoren, M., Byrne, O., O'Connell, P., O'Neill, H., O'Reilly, K., & Kennedy, H. G. (2015). Factors affecting length of stay in forensic hospital setting: Need for therapeutic security and course of admission. *BMC Psychiatry, 15*, 301. https://doi.org/10.1186/s12888-015-0686-4

Davoren, M., Kallis, C., González, R. A., Freestone, M., & Coid, J. W. (2017). Anxiety disorders and intimate partner violence: Can the association be explained by coexisting conditions or borderline personality traits? *Journal of Forensic Psychiatry & Psychology, 28*(5), 639–658. https://doi.org/10.1080/14789949.2016.1172659

Davoren, M., O'Dwyer, S., Abidin, Z., Naughton, L., Gibbons, O., Doyle, E., McDonnell, K., Monks, S., & Kennedy, H. G. (2012). Prospective in-patient cohort study of moves between levels of therapeutic security: The DUNDRUM-1 triage security, DUNDRUM-3 programme completion and DUNDRUM-4 recovery scales and the HCR-20. *BMC Psychiatry, 12*, 80. https://doi.org/10.1186/1471-244X-1280

Davoren, M., O'Reilly, K., Mohan, D., & Kennedy, H. G. (2022). Prospective cohort study of the evaluation of patient benefit from the redevelopment of a complete national forensic mental health service: The Dundrum Forensic Redevelopment Evaluation Study (D-FOREST) protocol. *BMJ Open, 12*(7), e058581.

Dawes, R. M. (1979). The robust beauty of improper linear models in decision making. *American Psychologist, 34*(7), 571.

Dawson, S., Lawn, S., Simpson, A., & Muir-Cochrane, E. (2016). Care planning for consumers on community treatment orders: An integrative literature review. *BMC Psychiatry, 16*(1), 394. https://doi.org/10.1186/s12888-016-1107-z

Deutsch, D. (2011). *The beginning of infinity: Explanations that transform the world.* Penguin UK.

Dohrenwend, B. P. (2006). Inventorying stressful life events as risk factors for psychopathology: Toward resolution of the problem of intracategory variability. *Psychological Bulletin, 132*(3), 477–495. https://doi.org/10.1037/0033-2909.132.3.477

Dohrenwend, B. S., & Dohrenwend, B. P. (Eds.). (1974). *Stressful life events: Their nature and effects*. John Wiley and Sons, Inc.

Doll, R., & Hill, A. B. (1950). Smoking and carcinoma of the lung. *British Medical Journal, 2*(4682), 739.

Doll, R., & Hill, A. B. (1954). The mortality of doctors in relation to their smoking habits. *British Medical Journal, 1*(4877), 1451.

Doll, R., & Hill, A. B. (1964). Mortality in relation to smoking: Ten years' observations of British doctors. *British Medical Journal, 1*(5395), 1399.

Doll, R., Peto, R., Boreham, J., & Sutherland, I. (2004). Mortality in relation to smoking: 50 years' observations on male British doctors. *BMJ, 328*(7455), 1519.

D'Souza, D. C., DiForti, M., Ganesh, S., George, T. P., Hall, W., Hjorthøj, C., Howes, O., Keshavan, M., Murray, R. M., Nguyen, T. B., Pearlson, G. D., Ranganathan, M., Selloni, A., Solowij, N., & Spinazzola, E. (2022). Consensus paper of the WFSBP task force on cannabis, cannabinoids and psychosis. *World Journal of Biological Psychiatry*, 1–24. https://doi.org/10.1080/15622975.2022.2038797

Duff, R. A. (2007). *Answering for crime: Responsibility and liability in the criminal law.* Bloomsbury Publishing.

Duff, R. A. (2008). Responsibility and liability. In M. H. Kramer, C. Grant, B. Colburn, & A. Hatzistavrou (Eds.), *The legacy of H.L.A. Hart: Legal, political, and moral philosophy.* Oxford University Press. https://doi.org/10.1093/acprof:oso/9780199542895.003.0006

Duffy, D., Lenihan, S., & Kennedy, H. (2003). Screening prisoners for mental disorders. *Psychiatric Bulletin, 27*(7), 241–242.

Durkheim, E. (2005). *Suicide: A study in sociology*. Routledge.

Dyer, C. (2012). French psychiatrist is convicted of manslaughter after her patient kills an elderly man. *BMJ, 345*, e8693. https://doi.org/10.1136/bmj.e8693

Eckert, M., Schel, S. H., Kennedy, H. G., & Bulten, B. H. (2017). Patient characteristics related to length of stay in Dutch forensic psychiatric care. *Journal of Forensic Psychiatry & Psychology, 28*(6), 863–880.

Eldar, E., Rutledge, R. B., Dolan, R. J., & Niv, Y. (2016). Mood as representation of momentum. *Trends in Cognitive Sciences, 20*(1), 15–24. https://doi.org/10.1016/j.tics.2015.07.010

Engel, G. L. (1980). The clinical application of the biopsychosocial model. *American Journal of Psychiatry, 137*(5), 535–544. https://doi.org/10.1176/ajp.137.5.535

Eysenck, M. W., & Fajkowska, M. (2018). Anxiety and depression: Toward overlapping and distinctive features. *Cognition and Emotion*, *32*(7), 1391–1400. https://doi.org/10.1080/02699931.2017.1330255

Faris, R. E. L., & Dunham, H. W. (1939). *Mental disorders in urban areas: An ecological study of schizophrenia and other psychoses*. University of Chicago Press.

Farrell, M., Boys, A., Bebbington, P. E., Brugha, T., Coid, J. W., Jenkins, R. A., Lewis, G., Meltzer, H., Marsden, J., Singleton, N., & Taylor, C. (2002). Psychosis and drug dependence: Results from a national survey of prisoners. *British Journal of Psychiatry*, *181*, 393–398.

Fazel, S., & Danesh, J. (2002). Serious mental disorder in 23 000 prisoners: A systematic review of 62 surveys. *Lancet*, *359*(9306), 545–550.

Fazel, S., & Seewald, K. (2012). Severe mental illness in 33 588 prisoners worldwide: Systematic review and meta-regression analysis. *British Journal of Psychiatry*, *200*(5), 364–373.

Fazel, S., Bains, P., & Doll, H. (2006). Substance abuse and dependence in prisoners: A systematic review. *Addiction*, *101*(2), 181–191.

Fazel, S., Doll, H., & Långström, N. (2008). Mental disorders among adolescents in juvenile detention and correctional facilities: A systematic review and metaregression analysis of 25 surveys. *Journal of the American Academy of Child & Adolescent Psychiatry*, *47*(9), 1010–1019.

Fazel, S., Fimińska, Z., Cocks, C., & Coid, J. (2016). Patient outcomes following discharge from secure psychiatric hospitals: Systematic review and meta-analysis. *British Journal of Psychiatry*, *208*(1), 17–25.

Fazel, S., Hayes, A. J., Bartellas, K., Clerici, M., & Trestman, R. (2016). Mental health of prisoners: Prevalence, adverse outcomes, and interventions. *Lancet Psychiatry*, *3*(9), 871–881.

Fazel, S., Ramesh, T., & Hawton, K. (2017). Suicide in prisons: An international study of prevalence and contributory factors. *Lancet Psychiatry*, *4*(12), 946–952.

Fazel, S., Xenitidis, K., & Powell, J. (2008). The prevalence of intellectual disabilities among 12 000 prisoners—a systematic review. *International Journal of Law and Psychiatry*, *31*(4), 369–373.

Fazel, S., Zetterqvist, J., Larsson, H., Långström, N., & Lichtenstein, P. (2014). Antipsychotics, mood stabilisers, and risk of violent crime. *Lancet*, *384*(9949), 1206–1214. https://doi.org/10.1016/s0140-6736(14)60379-2

Fischer, B., Jutras-Aswad, D., & Robinson, T. (2024). How has non-medical cannabis legalization served the health and welfare of under-age (adolescent) youth in Canada? *Lancet Regional Health-Americas*, *35*.

Fischer, B., Lindner, S. R., Jutras-Aswad, D., & Hall, W. (2023). Cannabis use and health-related "harm to others": Toward a conceptual framework and evidence base for public health. *Journal of Studies on Alcohol and Drugs*, *84*(4), 636–643.

Fleischman, A., Werbeloff, N., Yoffe, R., Davidson, M., & Weiser, M. (2014). Schizophrenia and violent crime: A population-based study. *Psychological Medicine*, *44*(14), 3051–3057. https://doi.org/10.1017/S0033291714000695

Flynn, D., Smith, D., Quirke, L., Monks, S., & Kennedy, H. G. (2012). Ultra high risk of psychosis on committal to a young offender prison: An unrecognised opportunity for early intervention. *BMC Psychiatry*, *12*, 100. https://doi.org/10.1186/1471-244X-12-100

Flynn, G., O'Neill, C., & Kennedy, H. G. (2011). DUNDRUM-2: Prospective validation of a structured professional judgment instrument assessing priority for admission from the waiting list for a forensic mental health hospital. *BMC Research Notes*, *4*, 230. https://doi.org/10.1186/1756-0500-4-230

Flynn, G., O'Neill, C., McInerney, C., & Kennedy, H. G. (2011). The DUNDRUM-1 structured professional judgment for triage to appropriate levels of therapeutic security: Retrospective-cohort validation study. *BMC Psychiatry*, *11*, 43. https://doi.org/10.1186/1471-244X-11-43

Flynn, S., Rodway, C., Appleby, L., & Shaw, J. (2014). Serious violence by people with mental illness: National clinical survey. *Journal of Interpersonal Violence*, *29*(8), 1438–1458. https://doi.org/10.1177/0886260513507133

Freestone, M., Bull, D., Brown, R., Boast, N., Blazey, F., & Gilluley, P. (2015). Triage, decision-making and follow-up of patients referred to a UK forensic service: Validation of the DUNDRUM toolkit. *BMC Psychiatry*, *15*, 239. https://doi.org/10.1186/s12888-015-0620-9

Friston, K., Da Costa, L., Hafner, D., Hesp, C., & Parr, T. (2021). Sophisticated inference. *Neural Computation*, *33*(3), 713–763. https://doi.org/10.1162/neco_a_01351

Galanter, C. A., & Patel, V. L. (2005). Medical decision making: A selective review for child psychiatrists and psychologists. *Journal of Child Psychology and Psychiatry, and Allied Disciplines*, *46*(7), 675–689.

Ganzini, L., Volicer, L., Nelson, W. A., Fox, E., & Derse, A. R. (2004). Ten myths about decision-making capacity. *Journal of the American Medical Directors Association*, *5*(4), 263–267. https://doi.org/10.1097/01.Jam.0000129821.34622.A2

Gavin, N., Parsons, S., & Grubin, D. (2003). Reception screening and mental health needs assessment in a male remand prison. *Psychiatric Bulletin*, *27*(7), 251–253.

Gill, P., Corner, E., Farnham, F., Wilson, S., Marchment, Z., Taylor, A., Taylor, R., & James, D. (2021). Predictors of varying levels of risks posed by fixated individuals to British public figures. *Journal of Forensic Sciences*, *66*(4), 1364–1376. https://doi.org/10.1111/1556-4029.14708

Glancy, G., Choptiany, M., Jones, R., & Chatterjee, S. (2021). Measurement-based care in forensic psychiatry. *International Journal of Law and Psychiatry*, *74*, 101650. https://doi.org/10.1016/j.ijlp.2020.101650

Goethals, K. (2012). AS03-02—reactions and consequences following ECHR judgements in the Netherlands. *European Psychiatry*, *27*, 1. https://doi.org/10.1016/S0924-9338(12)73959-7

Gómez, A., Atran, S., Chinchilla, J., Vázquez, A., López-Rodríguez, L., Paredes, B., Martínez, M., Blanco, L., Alba, B., & Bautista, H. (2022). Willingness to sacrifice among convicted Islamist terrorists versus violent gang members and other criminals. *Scientific Reports*, *12*(1), 1–15.

Gómez, Á., López-Rodríguez, L., Sheikh, H., Ginges, J., Wilson, L., Waziri, H., Vázquez, A., Davis, R., & Atran, S. (2017). The devoted actor's will to fight and the spiritual dimension of human conflict. *Nature Human Behaviour*, *1*(9), 673–679.

Gore, S. M. (1999). Suicide in prisons. *British Journal of Psychiatry*, *175*(1), 50–55.

Grubin, D., & Kennedy, H. (1991). The classification of sexual offenders. *Criminal Behaviour & Mental Health*, *1*, 123.

Gualtieri, G., Traverso, S., Pozza, A., Ferretti, F., Carabellese, F., Gusinu, R., & Coluccia, A. (2020). Clinical risk management in high-security forensic psychiatry residences. Protecting patients and health professionals: Perspectives and critical issues of the Law 81/2014. *Clinical Therapeutics*, *171*(2), e97–e100. https://doi.org/10.7417/ct.2020.2196

Gunn, J. C., Maden, T., & Swinton, M. (1991b). *Mentally disordered prisoners*. Home Office London.

Gunn, J. C., Maden, A., & Swinton, M. (1991a). Treatment needs of prisoners with psychiatric disorders. *British Medical Journal*, *303*(6798), 338–341.

Gupta, S., Akyuz, E. U., Baldwin, T., & Curtis, D. (2018). Community treatment orders in England: Review of usage from national data. *BJPsych Bulletin*, *42*(3), 119–122. https://doi.org/10.1192/bjb.2017.33

Habets, P., Jeandarme, I., & Kennedy, H. G. (2019). Applicability of the DUNDRUM-1 in a forensic Belgium setting. *Journal of Forensic Practice*, *21*(1), 85–94.
Hacking, I. (1963). What is strict implication? *Journal of Symbolic Logic*, *28*(1), 51–71.
Hacking, I. (1984). Experimentation and scientific realism. In *Science and the quest for reality* (pp. 162–181). Springer.
Hacking, I. (1986). Making up people. *London Review of Books*, *28*(16).
Hacking, I. (1995). Rewriting the soul. In *Rewriting the soul: Multiple personality and the sciences of memory*. Princeton University Press. https://doi.org/10.1515/9781400821686
Hacking, I. (2001a). Degeneracy, criminal behavior, and looping. *Genetics and Criminal Behavior*, 141–168.
Hacking, I. (2001b). *An introduction to probability and inductive logic*. Cambridge University Press.
Hacking, I. (2002). *Mad travelers: Reflections on the reality of transient mental illnesses*. Harvard University Press.
Hacking, I. (2006). *The emergence of probability: A philosophical study of early ideas about probability, induction and statistical inference*. Cambridge University Press.
Hacking, I. (2013). Lost in the forest. *London Review of Books*, *35*(15), 7–8.
Hacking, I. (2016). *Logic of statistical inference*. Cambridge University Press.
Hacking, I., & Hacking, T. (1990). *The taming of chance*. Cambridge University Press.
Harrison, G. W., & Millard, P. H. (1991). Balancing acute and long-term care: The mathematics of throughput in departments of geriatric medicine. *Methods of Information in Medicie*, *30*(3), 221–228.
Hauser, T. U., Will, G. J., Dubois, M., & Dolan, R. J. (2019). Annual research review: Developmental computational psychiatry. *Journal of Child Psychology and Psychiatry*, *60*(4), 412–426. https://doi.org/10.1111/jcpp.12964
Health Care Services for Prisoners VTH. (2025). *Psychiatric hospital for prisoners*. VTH. Retrieved February 4, 2025 from https://vth.fi/en/psychiatric-prison-hospital/
Hill, A. B. (1965). The environment and disease: Association or causation? *Proceedings of the Royal Society of Medicine*, *58*(5), 295–300. Retrieved from https://www.ncbi.nlm.nih.gov/pmc/articles/PMC1898525/
Hill, A. B., & Hill, I. D. (1991). *Bradford Hill's principles of medical statistics*. Edward Arnold. Retrieved from https://books.google.ie/books?id=r0ViQgAACAAJ
Hill, D. (1947). Amphetamine in psychopathic states. *British Journal of Addiction to Alcohol & Other Drugs*, *44*(2), 50–54.
Hodgins, S. (2008). Violent behaviour among people with schizophrenia: A framework for investigations of causes, and effective treatment, and prevention. *Philosophical Transactions of the Royal Society B: Biological Sciences*, *363*(1503), 2505–2518.
Hodgins, S., Piatosa, M. J., & Schiffer, B. (2013). Violence among people with schizophrenia: Phenotypes and neurobiology. *Neuroscience of Aggression*, 329–368.
Howes, O. D., Whitehurst, T., Shatalina, E., Townsend, L., Onwordi, E. C., Mak, T. L. A., Arumuham, A., O'Brien, O., Lobo, M., Vano, L., Zahid, U., Butler, E., & Osugo, M. (2021). The clinical significance of duration of untreated psychosis: An umbrella review and random-effects meta-analysis. *World Psychiatry*, *20*(1), 75–95. https://doi.org/10.1002/wps.20822
Huber, G., & Gross, G. (1989). The concept of basic symptoms in schizophrenic and schizoaffective psychoses. *Recenti Progressi in Medicina*, *80*(12), 646–652.
Insel, T. R. (2014). The NIMH research domain criteria (RDoC) project: Precision medicine for psychiatry. *American Journal of Psychiatry*, *171*(4), 395–397.
Insel, T. R., Cuthbert, B., Garvey, M., Heinssen, R., Pine, D. S., Quinn, K., Sanislow, C., & Wang, P. (2010). Research domain criteria (RDoC): Toward a new classification framework for research on mental disorders. *American Journal of Psychiatry*, *167*(7), 748–751. https://doi.org/10.1176/appi.ajp.2010.09091379

Iqtidar, M., Sharma, K., Mullaney, R., Kelly, E., Keevans, M., Cullinane, M., Kennedy, H., & Mohan, D. (2018). Deaths in custody in the Irish prison service: 5-year retrospective study of drug toxicology and unnatural deaths. *BJPsych Open*, *4*(5), 401–403.

James, D. (1999). Court diversion at 10 years: Can it work, does it work and has it a future? *Journal of Forensic Psychiatry*, *10*(3), 507–524. https://doi.org/10.1080/09585189908402156

James, D., & Hamilton, L. (1992). Setting up psychiatric liaison schemes to magistrates' courts: Problems and practicalities. *Medicine, Science and the Law*, *32*(2), 167–176.

Jarrett, M., Craig, T., Parrott, J., Forrester, A., Winton-Brown, T., Maguire, H., McGuire, P., & Valmaggia, L. (2012). Identifying men at ultra high risk of psychosis in a prison population. *Schizophrenia Research*, *136*(1–3), 1–6.

Jeandarme, I., Habets, P., & Kennedy, H. (2019). Structured versus unstructured judgment: DUNDRUM-1 compared to court decisions. *International Journal of Law and Psychiatry*, *64*, 205–210. https://doi.org/10.1016/j.ijlp.2019.04.006

Jeandarme, I., Habets, P., O'Reilly, K., & Kennedy, H. G. (2021). Is non-completion of treatment related to security need? *Criminal Behaviour and Mental Health*, *31*(5), 321–330. https://doi.org/10.1002/cbm.2213

Jewell, M., Pillai, K., Cavney, J., Garrett, N., & McKenna, B. (2023). Examining the need for a high level of therapeutic security at a regional forensic mental health service in Aotearoa New Zealand. *Psychiatry, Psychology and Law*, 1–18. https://doi.org/10.1080/13218719.2023.2192261

Jones, R. M., Patel, K., & Simpson, A. I. F. (2019). Assessment of need for inpatient treatment for mental disorder among female prisoners: A cross-sectional study of provincially detained women in Ontario. *BMC Psychiatry*, *19*(1), 98. https://doi.org/10.1186/s12888-019-2083-x

Joseph, P. L. (1994). Psychiatric assessment at the magistrates' court: Early intervention is needed in the remand process. *British Journal of Psychiatry*, *164*(6), 722–724.

Joseph, P. L., & Potter, M. (1993a). Diversion from custody. I: Psychiatric assessment at the magistrates' court. *British Journal of Psychiatry*, *162*(3), 325–330.

Joseph, P. L., & Potter, M. (1993b). Diversion from custody. II: Effect on hospital and prison resources. *British Journal of Psychiatry*, *162*(3), 330–334.

Kamali, M., Kelly, L., Gervin, M., Browne, S., Larkin, C., & O'Callaghan, E. (2000). The prevalence of comorbid substance misuse and its influence on suicidal ideation among in-patients with schizophrenia. *Acta Psychiatrica Scandinavica*, *101*(6), 452–456.

Kapczinski, F., Dias, V. V., Kauer-Sant'Anna, M., Frey, B. N., Grassi-Oliveira, R., Colom, F., & Berk, M. (2009). Clinical implications of a staging model for bipolar disorders. *Expert Review of Neurotherapeutics*, *9*(7), 957–966.

Keers, R., Ullrich, S., Destavola, B. L., & Coid, J. W. (2014). Association of violence with emergence of persecutory delusions in untreated schizophrenia. *American Journal of Psychiatry*, *171*(3), 332–339. https://doi.org/10.1176/appi.ajp.2013.13010134

Kennedy, H. G. (1992). Anger and irritability. *British Journal of Psychiatry*, *161*, 145–153. https://doi.org/10.1192/bjp.161.2.145

Kennedy, H. G. (2021). Models of care in forensic psychiatry. *BJPsych Advances*, 1–14. https://doi.org/10.1192/bja.2021.34

Kennedy, H. G., Iveson, R. C., & Hill, O. (1999). Violence, homicide and suicide: Strong correlation and wide variation across districts. *British Journal of Psychiatry*, *175*, 462–466. https://doi.org/10.1192/bjp.175.5.462

Kennedy, H. G., Kemp, L. I., & Dyer, D. E. (1992). Fear and anger in delusional (paranoid) disorder: The association with violence. *British Journal of Psychiatry*, *160*, 488–492. https://doi.org/10.1192/bjp.160.4.488

Kennedy, H. G., Mohan, D., & Davoren, M. (2020a). Forensic psychiatry and Covid-19: Accelerating transformation in forensic psychiatry. *Irish Journal of Psychological Medicine*, 1–26. https://doi.org/10.1017/IPM.2020.58

Kennedy, H. G., Monks, S., Curtin, K., Wright, B., Linehan, S., Duffy, D., Teljeur, C., Kelly, A. (2005). *Mental illness in irish prisoners: Psychiatric morbidity in sentenced, remanded and newly committed prisoners*. Dublin, Ireland: National Forensic Mental Health Service.

Kennedy, H. G., Mullaney, R., McKenna, P., Thompson, J., Timmons, D., Gill, P., O'Sullivan, O. P., Braham, P., Duffy, D., Kearns, A., Linehan, S., Mohan, D., Monks, S., McLoughlin, L., O'Connell, P., O'Neill, C., Wright, B., O'Reilly, K., & Davoren, M. (2020b). A tool to evaluate proportionality and necessity in the use of restrictive practices in forensic mental health settings: The DRILL tool (Dundrum restriction, intrusion and liberty ladders). *BMC Psychiatry*, *20*(1), 515. https://doi.org/10.1186/s12888-020-02912-6

Kennedy, H. G., Simpson, A., & Haque, Q. (2019). Perspective on excellence in forensic mental health services: What we can learn from oncology and other medical services. *Frontiers in Psychiatry*, *10*, 733. https://doi.org/10.3389/fpsyt.2019.00733

Kenny, A. (1984). The psychiatric expert in court. *Psychological Medicine*, *14*(2), 291–302.

Kenny, A. (1985). *The ivory tower: Essays in philosophy and public policy*. Blackwell.

Kenny, A. (1992). *The metaphysics of mind*. Oxford University Press. https://books.google.ie/books?id=FihyQgAACAAJ

Kenny, A. (2011). *Freewill and responsibility (Routledge revivals)*. Routledge. Retrieved from https://books.google.ie/books?id=dPCsAgAAQBAJ

Kessler, R. C., Bernecker, S. L., Bossarte, R. M., Luedtke, A. R., McCarthy, J. F., Nock, M. K., Pigeon, W. R., Petukhova, M. V., Sadikova, E., VanderWeele, T. J., Zuromski, K. L., & Zaslavsky, A. M. (2019). The role of big data analytics in predicting suicide. In I. C. Passos, B. Mwangi, & F. Kapczinski (Eds.), *Personalized psychiatry: Big data analytics in mental health* (pp. 77–98). Springer International Publishing. https://doi.org/10.1007/978-3-030-03553-2_5

Klausen, M. K., Thomsen, M., Wortwein, G., & Fink-Jensen, A. (2022). The role of glucagon-like peptide 1 (GLP-1) in addictive disorders. *British Journal of Pharmacology*, *179*(4), 625–641. https://doi.org/10.1111/bph.15677

Knight, R. A., & Prentky, R. A. (1990). Classifying sexual offenders: The development and corroboration of taxonomic models. In *Handbook of sexual assault: Issues, theories, and treatment of the offender* (pp. 23–52). Springer.

Koppe, G., Meyer-Lindenberg, A., & Durstewitz, D. (2021). Deep learning for small and big data in psychiatry. *Neuropsychopharmacology*, *46*(1), 176–190. https://doi.org/10.1038/s41386-020-0767-z

Kosenko, O., & Steger, F. (2023). Politicization of psychiatry and the improvement of ethical standards in the 1970s. *Frontiers in Psychiatry*, *14*, 1151048. https://doi.org/10.3389/fpsyt.2023.1151048

Kraepelin, E. (1904). *Lectures on clinical psychiatry* (T. Johnstone, Trans.; authorised translation from the German ed.). William Wood and Company.

Kraepelin, E. (1915). *Clinical psychiatry: A text book for students and physicians* (A. R. Dieffendorf, Trans.; abstracted and adapted from the seventh Gernan edition of Kraepelin's "LehrbuchDer Psychiatrie" 1902 ed.). The Macmillan Company.

Krafft-Ebing, R., & Klaf, F. S. (1998). *Psychopathia sexualis: With especial reference to the antipathic sexual instinct: A medico-forensic study*. Arcade Pub. Retrieved from https://books.google.ie/books?id=nzr8Tw7xcsUC

Kramer, H., Sprenger, J., & Summers, M. (2007). *The malleus maleficarum*. Cosimo. Retrieved from https://books.google.ie/books?id=bbLe57H2GcUC

Kuhn, T. S., & Hacking, I. (2012). *The structure of scientific revolutions*. University of Chicago Press. Retrieved from https://books.google.ie/books?id=3eP5Y_OOuzwC

Kurth-Nelson, Z., Behrens, T., Wayne, G., Miller, K., Luettgau, L., Dolan, R., Liu, Y., & Schwartenbeck, P. (2023). Replay and compositional computation. *Neuron, 111*(4), 454–469. https://doi.org/10.1016/j.neuron.2022.12.028

Laursen, T. M. (2019). Causes of premature mortality in schizophrenia: A review of literature published in 2018. *Current Opinion in Psychiatry*, *32*(5), 388–393. https://doi.org/10.1097/yco.0000000000000530

Lavoie, S., Polari, A. R., Goldstone, S., Nelson, B., & McGorry, P. D. (2019). Staging model in psychiatry: Review of the evolution of electroencephalography abnormalities in major psychiatric disorders. *Early Intervention in Psychiatry*, *13*(6), 1319–1328. https://doi.org/10.1111/eip.12792

Leggio, L., Hendershot, C. S., Farokhnia, M., Fink-Jensen, A., Klausen, M. K., Schacht, J. P., & Simmons, W. K. (2023). GLP-1 receptor agonists are promising but unproven treatments for alcohol and substance use disorders. *Nature Medicine*, *29*(12), 2993–2995.

Leonard, S. J., Webb, R. T., & Shaw, J. J. (2020). Service transitions, interventions and care pathways following remittal to prison from medium secure psychiatric services in England and Wales: National cohort study. *BJPsych Open*, *6*(5), e80. https://doi.org/10.1192/bjo.2020.62

Link, B. G., Monahan, J., Stueve, A., & Cullen, F. T. (1999). Real in their consequences: A sociological approach to understanding the association between psychotic symptoms and violence. *American Sociological Review*, 316–332.

Lockertsen, Ø., Varvin, S., Færden, A., & Vatnar, S. K. B. (2021). Short-term risk assessments in an acute psychiatric inpatient setting: A re-examination of the Brøset Violence Checklist using repeated measurements—differentiating violence characteristics and gender. *Archives of Psychiatric Nursing*, *35*(1), 17–26. https://doi.org/10.1016/j.apnu.2020.11.003

Lomholt, L. H., Andersen, D. V., Sejrsgaard-Jacobsen, C., Øzdemir, C. M., Graff, C., Schjerning, O., Jensen, S. E., Straszek, S. P. V., Licht, R. W., Grøntved, S., & Nielsen, R. E. (2019). Mortality rate trends in patients diagnosed with schizophrenia or bipolar disorder: A nationwide study with 20 years of follow-up. *International Journal of Bipolar Disorders*, *7*(1), 6. https://doi.org/10.1186/s40345-018-0140-x

Ludvigsson, J. F., Håberg, S. E., Knudsen, G. P., Lafolie, P., Zoega, H., Sarkkola, C., von Kraemer, S., Weiderpass, E., & Nørgaard, M. (2015). Ethical aspects of registry-based research in the Nordic countries. *Clinical Epidemiology*, 491–508.

MacCulloch, M. J., Snowden, P. R., Wood, P. J., & Mills, H. E. (1983). Sadistic fantasy, sadistic behaviour and offending. *British Journal of Psychiatry*, *143*, 20–29. https://doi.org/10.1192/bjp.143.1.20

Maden, A., Taylor, C. J., Brooke, D., & Gunn, J. (1995). *Mental disorder in remand prisoners*. Great Britain, Home Office, Research and Planning Unit.

Maguire, T., Daffern, M., Bowe, S. J., & McKenna, B. (2017). Predicting aggressive behaviour in acute forensic mental health units: A re-examination of the dynamic appraisal of situational aggression's predictive validity. *International Journal of Mental Health Nursing*, *26*(5), 472–481. https://doi.org/10.1111/inm.12377

Maguire, T., Daffern, M., Bowe, S. J., & McKenna, B. (2019). Evaluating the impact of an electronic application of the dynamic appraisal of situational aggression with an embedded aggression prevention protocol on aggression and restrictive interventions on a forensic mental health unit. *International Journal of Mental Health Nursing*, *28*(5), 1186–1197. https://doi.org/10.1111/inm.12630

McClean, S. I., & Millard, P. H. (1996). *Go with the flow: A systems approach to healthcare planning*. London: Royal Society of Medicine Press.

McCleery, A., Ventura, J., Kern, R., Subotnik, K., Gretchen-Doorly, D., Green, M., Hellemann, G., & Nuechterlein, K. (2014). Cognitive functioning in first-episode schizophrenia: MATRICS Consensus Cognitive Battery (MCCB) profile of impairment. *Schizophrenia Research*, *157*(1–3), 33–39. https://doi.org/10.1016/j.schres.2014.04.039

McCullough, S., Stanley, C., Smith, H., Scott, M., Karia, M., Ndubuisi, B., Ross, C. C., Bates, R., & Davoren, M. (2020). Outcome measures of risk and recovery in Broadmoor High Secure Forensic Hospital: Stratification of care pathways and moves to medium secure hospitals. *BJPsych Open*, *6*(4), e74. https://doi.org/10.1192/bjo.2020.61

McGorry, P. D., Hartmann, J. A., Spooner, R., & Nelson, B. (2018). Beyond the "at risk mental state" concept: Transitioning to transdiagnostic psychiatry. *World Psychiatry*, *17*(2), 133–142. https://doi.org/10.1002/wps.20514

McInerney, C., Davoren, M., Flynn, G., Mullins, D., Fitzpatrick, M., Caddow, M., Caddow, F., Quigley, S., Black, F., Kennedy, H. G., & O'Neill, C. (2013). Implementing a court diversion and liaison scheme in a remand prison by systematic screening of new receptions: A 6 year participatory action research study of 20,084 consecutive male remands. *International Journal of Mental Health Systems*, *7*, 18. https://doi.org/10.1186/1752-4458-7-18

McKinnon, I. G., & Grubin, D. (2013). Health screening of people in police custody—evaluation of current police screening procedures in London, UK. *European Journal of Public Health*, *23*(3), 399–405.

McLaren, N. (1998). A critical review of the biopsychosocial model. *Australian & New Zealand Journal of Psychiatry*, *32*(1), 86–92. https://doi.org/10.3109/00048679809062712

McLaren, N. (2023). The biopsychosocial model and scientific deception. *Ethical Human Psychology and Psychiatry*, *25*(2). https://doi.org/10.1891/EHPP-2023-0008

McLaughlin, P., Brady, P., Carabellese, F., Carabellese, F., Parente, L., Uhrskov Sorensen, L., Jeandarme, I., Habets, P., Simpson, A. I. F., Davoren, M., & Kennedy, H. G. (2023). Excellence in forensic psychiatry services: International survey of qualities and correlates. *BJPsych Open*, *9*(6), e193. https://doi.org/10.1192/bjo.2023.578

Melzer, D., Tom, B., Brugha, T., Fryers, T., Grounds, A., Johnson, T., Meltzer, H., & Singleton, N. (2002). Prisoners with psychosis in England and Wales: A one-year national follow-up study. *Howard Journal of Criminal Justice*, *41*, 1–13. https://doi.org/10.1111/1468-2311.00221

Millard, P. H., & McClean, S. I. (1994). *Modelling hospital resource use: A different approach to the planning and control of health care systems*. Royal Society of Medicine Press.

Möller, H.-J., Bandelow, B., Volz, H.-P., Barnikol, U. B., Seifritz, E., & Kasper, S. (2016). The relevance of "mixed anxiety and depression" as a diagnostic category in clinical practice. *European Archives of Psychiatry and Clinical Neuroscience*, *266*(8), 725–736. https://doi.org/10.1007/s00406-016-0684-7

Mossman, D. (1994). Assessing predictions of violence: Being accurate about accuracy. *Journal of Consulting and Clinical Psychology*, *62*(4), 783.

Mossman, D. (2006). Critique of pure risk assessment or, Kant meets Tarasoff. *University of Cincinnati Law Review*, *75*, 523.

Naughton, M., Nulty, A., Abidin, Z., Davoren, M., O'Dwyer, S., & Kennedy, H. G. (2012). Effects of group metacognitive training (MCT) on mental capacity and functioning in patients with psychosis in a secure forensic psychiatric hospital: A prospective-cohort waiting list controlled study. *BMC Research Notes*, *5*, 302. https://doi.org/10.1186/1756-0500-5-302

Nguyen, H., Midgette, G., Loughran, T., & Zhang, Y. (2021). Random drug testing in prisons: Does a little testing go a long way? *Criminology & Public Policy*, *20*(2), 329–349. https://doi.org/10.1111/1745-9133.12543

Noble, D. (2008a). Claude Bernard, the first systems biologist, and the future of physiology. *Experimental Physiology*, *93*(1), 16–26. https://doi.org/10.1113/expphysiol.2007.038695

Noble, D. (2008b). *The music of life: Biology beyond the Genome*. Oxford University Press. Retrieved from https://books.google.ie/books?id=Z9QaCmsSGf8C

Noble, D. (2017). *Dance to the tune of life: Biological relativity*. Cambridge University Press. Retrieved from https://books.google.ie/books?id=INlsDQAAQBAJ

O'Keeffe, D., Kinsella, A., Waddington, J. L., & Clarke, M. (2022). 20-year prospective, sequential follow-up study of heterogeneity in associations of duration of untreated psychosis with symptoms, functioning, and quality of life following first-episode psychosis. *American Journal of Psychiatry*, *179*(4), 288–297. https://doi.org/10.1176/appi.ajp.2021.20111658

O'Neill, C., Kelly, A., Sinclair, H., & Kennedy, H. (2005). Deprivation: Different implications for forensic psychiatric need in urban and rural areas. *Social Psychiatry and Psychiatric Epidemiology*, *40*(7), 551–556. https://doi.org/10.1007/s00127-005-0919-9

O'Neill, C., Smith, D., Caddow, M., Duffy, F., Hickey, P., Fitzpatrick, M., Caddow, F., Cronin, T., Joynt, M., Azvee, Z., Gallagher, B., Kehoe, C., Maddock, C., O'Keeffe, B., Brennan, L., Davoren, M., Owens, E., Mullaney, R., Keevans, L., Maher, R., & Kennedy, H. G. (2016). STRESS-testing clinical activity and outcomes for a combined prison in-reach and court liaison service: A 3-year observational study of 6177 consecutive male remands. *International Journal of Mental Health Systems*, *10*, 67. https://doi.org/10.1186/s13033-016-0097-z

Oosterhoff, J. H. F., & Doornberg, J. N. (2020). Artificial intelligence in orthopaedics: False hope or not? A narrative review along the line of Gartner's hype cycle. *EFORT Open Reviews*, *5*(10), 593–603. https://doi.org/10.1302/2058-5241.5.190092

O'Reilly, K., Donohoe, G., Coyle, C., O'Sullivan, D., Rowe, A., Losty, M., McDonagh, T., McGuinness, L., Ennis, Y., Watts, E., Brennan, L., Owens, E., Davoren, M., Mullaney, R., Abidin, Z., & Kennedy, H. G. (2015). Prospective cohort study of the relationship between neuro-cognition, social cognition and violence in forensic patients with schizophrenia and schizoaffective disorder. *BMC Psychiatry*, *15*, 155. https://doi.org/10.1186/s12888-015-0548-0

O'Reilly, K., Donohoe, G., O'Sullivan, D., Coyle, C., Corvin, A., O'Flynn, P., O'Donnell, M., Galligan, T., O'Connell, P., & Kennedy, H. G. (2019a). A randomized controlled trial of cognitive remediation for a national cohort of forensic patients with schizophrenia or schizoaffective disorder. *BMC Psychiatry*, *19*(1). https://doi.org/10.1186/S12888-019-2018-6

O'Reilly, K., O'Connell, P., Corvin, A., O'Sullivan, D., Coyle, C., Mullaney, R., O'Flynn, P., Grogan, K., Richter, M., & Kennedy, H. (2017). Moral cognition and homicide amongst forensic patients with schizophrenia and schizoaffective disorder: A cross-sectional cohort study. *Schizophrenia Research*, *193*, 468–469. https://doi.org/10.1016/J.SCHRES.2017.07.026

O'Reilly, K., O'Connell, P., Donohoe, G., Coyle, C., O'Sullivan, D., Azvee, Z., Maddock, C., Sharma, K., Sadi, H., McMahon, M., & Kennedy, H. G. (2016). Anticholinergic burden in schizophrenia and ability to benefit from psychosocial treatment programmes: A 3-year prospective cohort study. *Psychological Medicine*, *46*(15), 3199–3211. https://doi.org/10.1017/S0033291716002154

O'Reilly, K., O'Connell, P., O'Sullivan, D., Corvin, A., Sheerin, J., O'Flynn, P., Donohoe, G., McCarthy, H., Ambrosh, D., O'Donnell, M., Ryan, A., & Kennedy, H. G. (2019b). Moral cognition, the missing link between psychotic symptoms and acts of violence: A cross-sectional national forensic cohort study. *BMC Psychiatry*, *19*(1), 408. https://doi.org/10.1186/s12888-019-2372-4

O'Reilly, K., O'Connell, P., Ryan, A., Ambrosch, D., Walshe, E., Davoren, M., Corvin, A., & Kennedy, H. G. (2020). Deficit not bias: A quantifiable neuropsychological model of delusions. *Schizophrenia Research*, *222*, 496–498. https://doi.org/10.1016/j.schres.2020.05.055

O'Reilly, R., Allison, S., & Bastiampiallai, T. (2019). Observed outcomes: An approach to calculate the optimum number of psychiatric beds. *Administration and Policy in Mental Health*, *46*(4), 507–517. https://doi.org/10.1007/s10488-018-00917-8

Orford, J. (2001). *Excessive appetites: A psychological view of addictions* (2nd ed.). John Wiley & Sons Ltd.

Parente, L., Carabellese, F., Felthous, A., La Tegola, D., Davoren, M., Kennedy, H. G., & Carabellese, F. F. (2024). Italian Evaluation and Excellence in REMS (ITAL-EE-REMS): Appropriate placement of forensic patients in REMS forensic facilities. *International Journal of Mental Health Systems*, *18*(1), 33.

Parmigiani, G., Mandarelli, G., Meynen, G., Carabellese, F., & Ferracuti, S. (2019). Translating clinical findings to the legal norm: The Defendant's Insanity Assessment Support Scale (DIASS). *Translational Psychiatry*, *9*(1), 278. https://doi.org/10.1038/s41398-019-0628-x

Parsons, S., Walker, L., & Grubin, D. (2001). Prevalence of mental disorder in female remand prisons. *Journal of Forensic Psychiatry*, *12*(1), 194–202.

Passos, I. C., Ballester, P. L., Barros, R. C., Librenza-Garcia, D., Mwangi, B., Birmaher, B., Brietzke, E., Hajek, T., Lopez Jaramillo, C., Mansur, R. B., Alda, M., Haarman, B. C. M., Isometsa, E., Lam, R. W., McIntyre, R. S., Minuzzi, L., Kessing, L. V., Yatham, L. N., Duffy, A., & Kapczinski, F. (2019b). Machine learning and big data analytics in bipolar disorder: A position paper from the international society for bipolar disorders big data task force. *Bipolar Disorders*, *21*(7), 582–594. https://doi.org/10.1111/bdi.12828

Passos, I. C., Ballester, P. L., Pinto, J. V., Mwangi, B., & Kapczinski, F. (2019a). Big data and machine learning meet the health sciences. In I. C. Passos, B. Mwangi, & F. Kapczinski (Eds.), *Personalized psychiatry: Big data analytics in mental health* (pp. 1–13). Springer International Publishing. https://doi.org/10.1007/978-3-030-03553-2_1

Passos, I. C., Mwangi, B., & Kapczinski, F. (2016). Big data analytics and machine learning: 2015 and beyond. *Lancet Psychiatry*, *3*(1), 13–15.

Patel, V. L., Arocha, J. F., & Kaufman, D. R. (1999). Expertise and tacit knowledge in medicine. In R. J. S. J. A. Horvath (Ed.), *Tacit knowledge in professional practice: Researcher and practitioner perspectives* (pp. 75–99). Lawrence Erlbaum Associates Publishers.

Patel, V. L., Cytryn, K. N., Shortliffe, E. H., & Safran, C. (2000). The collaborative health care team: The role of individual and group expertise. *Teaching and Learning in Medicine*, *12*, 117–132.

Patel, V. L., Glaser, R. E., & Arocha, J. F. (2000). Cognition and expertise: Acquisition of medical competence. *Clinical and Investigative Medicine. Medecine clinique et experimentale*, *23*(4), 256–260.

Patel, V. L., Kaufman, D. R., & Magder, S. A. (1996). The acquisition of medical expertise in complex dynamic environments. In *The road to excellence: The acquisition of expert performance in the arts and sciences, sports and games* (pp. 127–165). Lawrence Erlbaum Associates.

Patel, V. L., Patel, N., Arocha, J. F., & Zhang, J. (2005). Thinking and reasoning in medicine. In K. Holyoak (Ed.), *Cambridge handbook of thinking and reasoning*. Cambridge, UK: Cambridge University Press.

Patel, V. L., & Ramoni, M. (1997). Cognitive models of directional inference in expert medical reasoning. In P. J. Feltovich, K. M. Ford, & R. R. Hoffman (Eds.), *Expertise in context: Human and machine* (pp. 67–99). American Association for Artificial Intelligence; The MIT Press.

Peay, J. (1996). *Inquiries after homicide*. Duckworth. Retrieved from https://books.google.ie/books?id=JH_aAAAAMAAJ

Penney, S. R., Faziluddin, S., Simpson, A. I. F., Socha, P., & Wilkie, T. (2023). Risk, resilience, and recovery in forensic mental health: An integrated conceptual model. *Behavioral Sciences & the Law*, *41*(5), 280–291. https://doi.org/10.1002/bsl.2615

Peralta, V., de Jalón, E. G., Moreno-Izco, L., Peralta, D., Janda, L., Sánchez-Torres, A. M., Cuesta, M. J., Ballesteros, A., Fañanás, L., Gil-Berrozpe, G., Hernández, R., Lorente, R., Papiol, S., Ribeiro, M., Rosero, A., & Zandio, M. (2023). A clinical staging model of psychotic disorders based on a long-term follow-up of first-admission psychosis: A validation study. *Psychiatry Research, 322*, 115109. https://doi.org/10.1016/j.psychres.2023.115109

Pierzchniak, P., Farnham, F., Taranto, N. D., Bull, D., Gill, H., Bester, P., McCallum, A., & Kennedy, H. (1999). Assessing the needs of patients in secure settings: A multidisciplinary approach. *Journal of Forensic Psychiatry, 10*(2), 343–354.

Pierzchniak, P., Purchase, N., & Kennedy, H. (1997). Liaison between prison, court and psychiatric services. *Health Trends, 29*(1), 26–29.

Popper, K. (2014). *Conjectures and refutations: The growth of scientific knowledge*. Routledge.

Pratt, D., Piper, M., Appleby, L., Webb, R., & Shaw, J. (2006). Suicide in recently released prisoners: A population-based cohort study. *Lancet, 368*(9530), 119–123.

Priest, R. G., Fineberg, N., Merson, S., & Kurian, T. (1995). Length of stay of acute psychiatric inpatients: An exponential model. *Acta Psychiatrica Scandinavica, 92*(4), 315–317. https://doi.org/10.1111/j.1600-0447.1995.tb09589.x

Quinn, C., Byng, R., Shenton, D., Smart, C., Michie, S., Stewart, A., Taylor, R., Maguire, M., Harris, T., & Shaw, J. (2018). The feasibility of following up prisoners, with mental health problems, after release: A pilot trial employing an innovative system, for engagement and retention in research, with a harder-to-engage population. *Trials, 19*(1), 530. https://doi.org/10.1186/s13063-018-2911-1

Reagu, S., Jones, R., Kumari, V., & Taylor, P. J. (2013). Angry affect and violence in the context of a psychotic illness: A systematic review and meta-analysis of the literature. *Schizophrenia Research, 146*(1–3), 46–52. https://doi.org/10.1016/j.schres.2013.01.024

Richter, M. S., O'Reilly, K., O'Sullivan, D., O'Flynn, P., Corvin, A., Donohoe, G., Coyle, C., Davoren, M., Higgins, C., Byrne, O., Nutley, T., Nulty, A., Sharma, K., O'Connell, P., & Kennedy, H. G. (2018). Prospective observational cohort study of "treatment as usual" over four years for patients with schizophrenia in a national forensic hospital. *BMC Psychiatry, 18*(1), 289. https://doi.org/10.1186/s12888-018-1862-0

Rollin, H. R. (1969). *The mentally abnormal offender and the law: An inquiry into the working of the relevant parts of the mental health act, 1959*. Pergamon Press. Retrieved from https://books.google.ie/books?id=GYFqAAAAMAAJ

Ross, N. (2018). "We've had enough of experts": The enduring charm of quackery. *British Journal of Psychiatry, 212*(5), 265–268. https://doi.org/10.1192/bjp.2018.64

Ruhrmann, S., Schultze-Lutter, F., & Klosterkötter, J. (2003). Early detection and intervention in the initial prodromal phase of schizophrenia. *Pharmacopsychiatry, 36*(S3), 162–167.

Rutledge, E., Kennedy, M., O'Neill, H., & Kennedy, H. G. (2008). Functional mental capacity is not independent of the severity of psychosis. *International Journal of Law and Psychiatry, 31*(1), 9–18. https://doi.org/10.1016/j.ijlp.2007.11.002

Rutter, M. (1985). Resilience in the face of adversity: Protective factors and resistance to psychiatric disorder. *British Journal of Psychiatry, 147*(6), 598–611.

Rutter, M. (1990). Psychosocial resilience and protective mechanisms. In J. Rolf, A. S. Masten, D. Cicchetti, K. H. Nuechterlein, & S. Weintraub (Eds.), *Risk and protective factors in the development of psychopathology*. Cambridge, UK: Cambridge Unversity Press.

Sariaslan, A., Leucht, S., Zetterqvist, J., Lichtenstein, P., & Fazel, S. (2021). Associations between individual antipsychotics and the risk of arrests and convictions of violent and other crime: A nationwide within-individual study of 74,925 persons. *Psychological Medicine*, 1–9. https://doi.org/10.1017/s0033291721000556

Scarpazza, C., Miolla, A., Zampieri, I., Melis, G., Sartori, G., Ferracuti, S., & Pietrini, P. (2021). Translational application of a neuro-scientific multi-modal approach into forensic psychiatric evaluation: Why and how? *Frontiers in Psychiatry*, *12*, 597918. https://doi.org/10.3389/fpsyt.2021.597918

Schizophrenia Commission. (2012). *The abandoned illness: A report by the schizophrenia commission*. London: Rethink Mental Illness.

Schultz, J., & Frith, C. D. (2022). Animacy and the prediction of behaviour. *Neuroscience and Biobehavioral Reviews*, *140*, 104766. https://doi.org/10.1016/j.neubiorev.2022.104766

Schultze-Lutter, F., Debbané, M., Theodoridou, A., Wood, S. J., Raballo, A., Michel, C., Schmidt, S. J., Kindler, J., Ruhrmann, S., & Uhlhaas, P. J. (2016). Revisiting the basic symptom concept: Toward translating risk symptoms for psychosis into neurobiological targets [Perspective]. *Frontiers in Psychiatry*, *7*. https://doi.org/10.3389/fpsyt.2016.00009

Schultze-Lutter, F., Michel, C., Schmidt, S. J., Schimmelmann, B., Maric, N., Salokangas, R., Riecher-Rössler, A., Van der Gaag, M., Nordentoft, M., & Raballo, A. (2015). EPA guidance on the early detection of clinical high risk states of psychoses. *European Psychiatry*, *30*(3), 405–416.

Scully, P. J., Owens, J. M., Kinsella, A., & Waddington, J. L. (2004). Schizophrenia, schizoaffective and bipolar disorder within an epidemiologically complete, homogeneous population in rural Ireland: Small area variation in rate. *Schizophrenia Research*, *67*(2–3), 143–155.

Segre, J. A. (2013). What does it take to satisfy Koch's postulates two centuries later? Microbial genomics and Propionibacteria acnes. *Journal of Investigative Dermatology*, *133*(9), 2141–2142. https://doi.org/10.1038/jid.2013.260

Sharma, A., Dunn, W., O'Toole, C., & Kennedy, H. G. (2015). The virtual institution: Cross-sectional length of stay in general adult and forensic psychiatry beds. *International Journal of Mental Health Systems*, *9*, 25. https://doi.org/10.1186/s13033-015-0017-7

Shaw, J., Conover, S., Herman, D., Jarrett, M., Leese, M., McCrone, P., Murphy, C., Senior, J., Susser, E., Thornicroft, G., Wright, N., Edge, D., Emsley, R., Lennox, C., Williams, A., Cust, H., Hopkin, G., & Stevenson, C. (2017). Health services and delivery research. In *Critical time intervention for severely mentally ill prisoners (CrISP): A randomised controlled trial*. NIHR Journals Library.

Shaw, J., Creed, F., Price, J., Huxley, P., & Tomenson, B. (1999). Prevalence and detection of serious psychiatric disorder in defendants attending court. *Lancet*, *353*(9158), 1053–1056. https://doi.org/10.1016/s0140-6736(98)08094-5

Shepherd, M. (1961). Morbid jealousy: Some clinical and social aspects of a psychiatric symptom. *Journal of Mental Science*, *107*(449), 687–753. https://doi.org/10.1192/bjp.107.449.687

Simpson, A. I. F., Gerritsen, C., Maheandiran, M., Adamo, V., Vogel, T., Fulham, L., Kitt, T., Forrester, A., & Jones, R. M. (2022). A systematic review of reviews of correctional mental health services using the STAIR framework [systematic review]. *Frontiers in Psychiatry*, *12*. https://doi.org/10.3389/fpsyt.2021.747202

Singleton, N., Farrell, M., & Meltzer, H. (2003). Substance misuse among prisoners in England and Wales. *International Review of Psychiatry*, *15*(1–2), 150–152.

Singleton, N., Gatward, R., & Meltzer, H. (1998). *Psychiatric morbidity among prisoners in England and Wales*. Stationery Office London.

Slobogin, C. (2015). Eliminating mental disability as a legal criterion in deprivation of liberty cases: The impact of the convention on the rights of persons with disabilities on the insanity defense, civil commitment, and competency law. *International Journal of Law and Psychiatry*, *40*, 36–42. https://doi.org/10.1016/j.ijlp.2015.04.011

Smeland, O. B., Bahrami, S., Frei, O., Shadrin, A., O'Connell, K., Savage, J., Watanabe, K., Krull, F., Bettella, F., Steen, N. E., Ueland, T., Posthuma, D., Djurovic, S., Dale, A. M., & Andreassen, O. A. (2020). Genome-wide analysis reveals extensive genetic overlap between schizophrenia, bipolar disorder, and intelligence. *Molecular Psychiatry*, *25*(4), 844–853. https://doi.org/10.1038/s41380-018-0332-x

Sokal, A. D., & Bricmont, J. (1998). *Intellectual impostures: Postmodern philosophers' abuse of science*. London, UK: Profile Books.

Sommer, R. (1979). Are crowded jails harmful? *American Journal of Forensic Psychiatry*, *1*, 7–21.

Sørensen, L. U., Pedersen, M. L., Brandt-Christensen, M., & Kennedy, H. G. (2020). *Excellence networks in Denmark*. Abstract from 20th Annual International Association of Forensic Mental Health Services Conference, Krakow, Poland.

Steadman, H. J., Mulvey, E. P., Monahan, J., Robbins, P. C., Appelbaum, P. S., Grisso, T., Roth, L. H., & Silver, E. (1998). Violence by people discharged from acute psychiatric inpatient facilities and by others in the same neighborhoods. *Archives of General Psychiatry*, *55*(5), 393–401.

Swanson, J. W. (1994). Mental disorder, substance abuse, and community violence: An epidemiological approach. In J. Monahan, & H. J. Steadman (Eds.), *Violence and mental disorder: Developments in risk assessment* (pp. 101–136). The University of Chicago Press.

Swanson, J. W., Borum, R., Swartz, M. S., & Monahan, J. (1996). Psychotic symptoms and disorders and the risk of violent behaviour in the community. *Criminal Behaviour and Mental Health*, *6*(4), 309–329.

Swanson, J. W., Holzer, C. E., 3rd, Ganju, V. K., & Jono, R. T. (1990). Violence and psychiatric disorder in the community: Evidence from the epidemiologic catchment area surveys. *Hospital and Community Psychiatry*, *41*(7), 761–770. https://doi.org/10.1176/ps.41.7.761

Swanson, J. W., Swartz, M. S., Borum, R., Hiday, V. A., Wagner, H. R., & Burns, B. J. (2000). Involuntary out-patient commitment and reduction of violent behaviour in persons with severe mental illness. *British Journal of Psychiatry*, *176*, 324–331. https://doi.org/10.1192/bjp.176.4.324

Swanson, J., Estroff, S., Swartz, M., Borum, R., Lachicotte, W., Zimmer, C., & Wagner, R. (1997). Violence and severe mental disorder in clinical and community populations: The effects of psychotic symptoms, comorbidity, and lack of treatment. *Psychiatry*, *60*(1), 1–22. https://doi.org/10.1080/00332747.1997.11024781

Tansella, M., & Thornicroft, G. (1998). A conceptual framework for mental health services: The matrix model. *Psychological Medicine*, *28*(3), 503–508. https://doi.org/10.1017/s0033291796005880

Teasdale, B., Silver, E., & Monahan, J. (2006). Gender, threat/control-override delusions and violence. *Law and Human Behavior*, *30*(6), 649–658. https://doi.org/10.1007/s10979-006-9044-x

Tennant, C., & Bebbington, P. (1978). The social causation of depression: A critique of the work of Brown and his colleagues. *Psychological Medicine*, *8*(4), 565–575.

Terranova, C., & Rocca, G. (2016). Homicide committed by psychiatric patients: Psychiatrists' liability in Italian law cases. *Medicine, Science and the Law*, *56*(1), 58–64. https://doi.org/10.1177/0025802415588120

Thibaut, F., Cosyns, P., Fedoroff, J. P., Briken, P., Goethals, K., & Bradford, J. M. W. (2020). The World Federation of Societies of Biological Psychiatry (WFSBP) 2020 guidelines for the pharmacological treatment of paraphilic disorders. *World Journal*

*of Biological Psychiatry*, *21*(6), 412–490. https://doi.org/10.1080/15622975.2020.1744723
Tomlin, J., Lega, I., Braun, P., Kennedy, H. G., Herrando, V. T., Barroso, R., Castelletti, L., Mirabella, F., Scarpa, F., & Völlm, B. (2020). Forensic mental health in Europe: Some key figures. *Social Psychiatry and Psychiatric Epidemiology*, 1–9. https://doi.org/10.1007/S00127-020-01909-6
Torous, J., Namiri, N., & Keshavan, M. (2019). A clinical perspective on big data in mental health. In I. C. Passos, B. Mwangi, & F. Kapczinski (Eds.), *Personalized psychiatry: Big data analytics in mental health* (pp. 37–51). Springer International Publishing. https://doi.org/10.1007/978-3-030-03553-2_3
Trott, M., Arnautovska, U., & Siskind, D. (2024). GLP-1 receptor agonists and weight loss in schizophrenia—past, present, and future. *Current Opinion in Psychiatry*, *37*(5), 363–369. https://doi.org/10.1097/yco.0000000000000952
Tsuang, M. T., Winokur, G., & Crowe, R. R. (1980). Morbidity risks of schizophrenia and affective disorders among first degree relatives of patients with schizophrenia, mania, depression and surgical conditions. *British Journal of Psychiatry*, *137*(6), 497–504. https://doi.org/10.1192/bjp.137.6.497
Uhrskov Sørensen, L., Bengtson, S., Lund, J., Ibsen, M., & Långström, N. (2020). Mortality among male forensic and non-forensic psychiatric patients: Matched cohort study of rates, predictors and causes-of-death. *Nordic Journal of Psychiatry*, 1–8.
Ullrich, S., Keers, R., & Coid, J. W. (2014). Delusions, anger, and serious violence: New findings from the MacArthur violence risk assessment study. *Schizophrenia Bulletin*, *40*(5), 1174–1181. https://doi.org/10.1093/schbul/sbt126
Ullrich, S., Keers, R., Shaw, J., Doyle, M., & Coid, J. W. (2018). Acting on delusions: The role of negative affect in the pathway towards serious violence. *The Journal of Forensic Psychiatry & Psychology*, *29*(5), 691–704. https://doi.org/10.1080/14789949.2018.1434227
Wainberg, M., Jacobs, G. R., di Forti, M., & Tripathy, S. J. (2021). Cannabis, schizophrenia genetic risk, and psychotic experiences: A cross-sectional study of 109,308 participants from the UK Biobank. *Translational Psychiatry*, *11*(1), 211. https://doi.org/10.1038/s41398-021-01330-w
Walker, N. (1985). Psychiatric explanations as excuses. *Psychiatry, Human Rights and Law*, 96–113.
Walker, N., & McCabe, S. (1968). *Crime and insanity in England: The historical perspective*. Edinburgh University Press. Retrieved from https://books.google.ie/books?id=4gBXAAAAYAAJ
Walsh, J., Smith, D., Byrne, F., Hickey, P., Taylor, E., Caddow, M., Reynolds, O., & O'Neill, C. (2024). Transfer to community and prison mental health care from Ireland's main remand prison over three years: 2015–2017. *Frontiers in Psychiatry*, *15*, 1392072.
West, D. J., & Walk, A. (1977). *Daniel McNaughton: His trial and the aftermath*. Headley for the British Journal of Psychiatry. Retrieved from https://books.google.ie/books?id=jNgsrjZxBh4C
Williams, H. K., Senanayke, M., Ross, C. C., Bates, R., & Davoren, M. (2020). Security needs among patients referred for high secure care in Broadmoor Hospital England. *BJPsych Open*, *6*(4), e55. https://doi.org/10.1192/bjo.2020.35
Witt, K., van Dorn, R., & Fazel, S. (2013). Risk factors for violence in psychosis: Systematic review and meta-regression analysis of 110 studies. *PLoS One*, *8*(2), e55942. https://doi.org/10.1371/journal.pone.0055942
Wood, J. L., Kallis, C., & Coid, J. W. (2017). Differentiating gang members, gang affiliates, and violent men on their psychiatric morbidity and traumatic experiences. *Psychiatry*, *80*(3), 221–235. https://doi.org/10.1080/00332747.2016.1256144

World Health Organization. (1993). *The ICD-10 classification of mental and behavioural disorders: Diagnostic criteria for research*. World Health Organization.

World Health Organization. (2018). *International Classification of Diseases (ICD): 11—mortality and morbidity statistics*. World Health Organization.

World Health Organization. (2024). *The Netherlands paves the way for improved prison health policies*. World Health Organization. Retrieved February 4, 2025 from https://www.who.int/europe/news-room/15-04-2024-the-netherlands-paves-the-way-for-improved-prison-health-policies

Yung, A. R., Nelson, B., Stanford, C., Simmons, M. B., Cosgrave, E. M., Killackey, E., Phillips, L. J., Bechdolf, A., Buckby, J., & McGorry, P. D. (2008). Validation of "prodromal" criteria to detect individuals at ultra high risk of psychosis: 2 year follow-up. *Schizophrenia Research*, *105*(1–3), 10–17.

Yung, A. R., Yuen, H. P., Berger, G., Francey, S., Hung, T.-C., Nelson, B., Phillips, L., & McGorry, P. (2007). Declining transition rate in ultra high risk (prodromal) services: Dilution or reduction of risk? *Schizophrenia Bulletin*, *33*(3), 673–681.

Yung, A. R., Yung, A. R., Pan Yuen, H., Mcgorry, P. D., Phillips, L. J., Kelly, D., Dell'olio, M., Francey, S. M., Cosgrave, E. M., & Killackey, E. (2005). Mapping the onset of psychosis: The comprehensive assessment of at-risk mental states. *Australian & New Zealand Journal of Psychiatry*, *39*(11–12), 964–971.

Zhang, Y., & Coid, J. (2024). Childhood adversity determines the syndemic effects of violence, substance misuse, and sexual behavior on psychotic spectrum disorder among men. *Schizophrenia Bulletin*, *50*(3), 684–694. https://doi.org/10.1093/schbul/sbad165

# Index